University Textbook Series

April, 1977

Especially Designed for Collateral Reading

HARRY W. JONES
Directing Editor
Professor of Law, Columbia University

ADMIRALTY, Second Edition (1975)
Grant Gilmore, Professor of Law, Yale University.
Charles L. Black, Jr., Professor of Law, Yale University.

ADMIRALTY AND FEDERALISM (1970)
David W. Robertson, Professor of Law, University of Texas.

AGENCY (1975)
W. Edward Sell, Dean of the School of Law, University of Pittsburgh.

CIVIL PROCEDURE, BASIC (1972)
Milton D. Green, Professor of Law, University of California, Hastings College of the Law.

COMMERCIAL TRANSACTIONS—Selected Statutes, Fourth Edition (1968)
Robert Braucher, Professor of Law, Harvard University.
Arthur E. Sutherland, Jr., Professor of Law, Harvard University.

COMMERCIAL TRANSACTIONS, INTRODUCTION TO (1977)
Hon. Robert Braucher, Associate Justice, Supreme Judicial Court of Massachusetts.
Robert A. Riegert, Professor of Law, Cumberland School of Law.

CONFLICT OF LAWS, COMMENTARY ON THE (1971)
Russell J. Weintraub, Professor of Law, University of Texas.

CORPORATIONS, Second Edition (1971)
Norman D. Lattin, Professor of Law, University of California, Hastings College of the Law.

CORPORATIONS IN PERSPECTIVE (1976)
Alfred F. Conard, Professor of Law, University of Michigan.

CRIMINAL LAW, Second Edition (1969)
Rollin M. Perkins, Professor of Law, University of California, Hastings College of the Law.

ESTATES IN LAND & FUTURE INTERESTS, PREFACE TO (1966)
Thomas F. Bergin, Professor of Law, University of Virginia.
Paul G. Haskell, Professor of Law, Case Western Reserve University.

EVIDENCE: COMMON SENSE AND COMMON LAW (1947)
John M. Maguire, Professor of Law, Harvard University.

EVIDENCE, STUDENTS' TEXT ON THE LAW OF (1935)
John Henry Wigmore.

FUNDAMENTALS

OF

LEGAL RESEARCH

By

J. MYRON JACOBSTEIN

Professor of Law and Law Librarian
Stanford University

and

ROY M. MERSKY

Professor of Law and Director of Research
University of Texas, Austin

Successor Volume
to
Pollack's Fundamentals of Legal Research, Fourth
Edition by Jacobstein and Mersky

Mineola, N. Y.
THE FOUNDATION PRESS, INC.
1977

Jacobstein & Mersky, Legal Research, F.P.
1st Reprint—1977

To our Families

Belle, Ellen, and Bennett
Deena, Lisa, Deborah, and Ruth

He Who Cites His Source, Brings Deliverance to the World.
Mishnah, Avot. VI

PREFACE

This book is the successor to our Fourth Edition of *Pollack's Fundamentals of Legal Research*, published in 1973. The first three editions were authored by Ervin H. Pollack, late Professor of Law and Director of Research Services at Ohio State University. His work has been acclaimed as a major contribution to the teaching of legal bibliography. The changing nature of legal materials, however, dictated continuing revision of the work were it to retain its utility. Thus, after Professor Pollack's untimely death, we assumed the authorship of a Fourth Edition. Numerous changes in both content and organization of this revision were necessary to keep pace with trends in legal research and bibliography. Still, sufficient material remained from Professor Pollack's work to merit the retention of his name on the new volume. In retaining his name on our revision of the Fourth Edition, we followed a tradition established by scholars like Professor Williston in his preparation of Parsons' Eighth Edition on *Contracts* and Justice Oliver Wendell Holmes in his preparation of the Twelfth Edition of Kent's *Commentaries*.

The current edition, however, represents a work so substantially altered that it would be unfair for us to do less than assume full responsibility for it. We have strived, however, to carry on the inspiration and scholarship so admirably pioneered in the first three editions. The influence of Professor Pollack will continue.

Authors of books on legal research have always faced the dilemma of reconciling their desire for completeness with the realization that their work is intended primarily for students beginning the study of law. We have consciously kept in mind that this book is not intended to be the definitive source for legal bibliography, but is rather an aid to students who are learning to do legal research. A careful study of the text should enable law students, lawyers, and others to sufficiently understand the use of law books to find the required legal sources for the problem under research. We are aware, however, that there will be instances when sources beyond those covered in this book will need to be consulted. For this purpose we have included in the footnotes references to sources where legal research may be pursued in greater depth.

It is intended that the text and the illustrations in each chapter be studied together for a proper understanding of the format and use of the legal materials described. Only the summary and citation sections of the chapters are intended primarily for reference purposes.

PREFACE

As most law students begin the study of law with the reading of court decisions, it is our belief that it is easier to begin the study of legal research with case law. The organization of the chapters, however, is such that instruction may conveniently begin with any part of the book.

Published concurrently with this book is a separate pamphlet of problem assignments to be used by instructors. Periodically a revised assignment problem book will be prepared with a supplement noting changes in law books described in this book and will bring to the reader's attention any new sets that have appeared.

J. MYRON JACOBSTEIN
ROY M. MERSKY

April, 1977

ACKNOWLEDGMENTS

We wish to express our deep appreciation to the many instructors who have adopted Fundamentals of Legal Research for classroom use. Their kind suggestions concerning possible additions to the text, and thoughts on revisions of it, have been invaluable aids in writing the new edition. For their help we are most grateful.

We would also like to take this opportunity to express our gratitude to the persons who have helped in the preparation of the manuscript for this new edition:

Robert C. Berring, Jr., John E. Christensen, Barbara C. Marquardt of the Tarlton Law Library, and Stella Win-Shin Chiang, formerly of the Tarlton Law Library now Law Librarian at Loyola University School of Law in New Orleans, who have helped us immeasurably with their review and suggestions for improvements in early drafts of certain chapters.

Jenni Parrish, Research Assistant at the University of Texas School of Law, who assisted in the preparation of the "Glossary of Terms" and who with Thomas M. Whiteside, also a University of Texas Research Assistant, checked innumerable footnotes and citations.

Ronald E. Day, formerly of the Tarlton Law Library now at the Biddle Law Library, University of Pennsylvania, for his assistance in preparing the "Appendix on Selective Legal Materials and their Abbreviations," the "Table of Abbreviations," and for his other contributions.

Rosalee Long, Iris Wildman, Joan Howland, and Howard Sugarman of the Stanford Law Library staff whose constructive criticism has been reflected throughout this work.

Signe M. Larson, U. S. Department of the Interior, Natural Resources Library, Law Branch, for her important work incorporated as a major part of the chapter "Computers and Microforms in Legal Research."

Charles W. (Tim) McCoy, Jr., of the Sheppard, Mullin, Richter & Hampton Law Firm in Los Angeles, for his contribution to the chapter "A General Summary of Research Procedure."

F. Diane Teeple, librarian at the York University Law Library of Osgoode Hall Law School, who contributed to the chapter "Canadian Law" and to Appendix A. III. "Canadian Citations."

ACKNOWLEDGMENTS

The University of Texas Legal Research Board under the direction of Thomas Ray Guy, Jr., now law clerk to Judge Thomas G. Gee, United States Court of Appeals for the Fifth Circuit, and Josh R. Morriss for their assistance in the preparation of Appendix A. I. "United States Citations."

Karen Kretschman, formerly of the Tarlton Law Library staff now with the State of Texas Comptroller of Public Accounts staff, who typed the manuscript and assisted in the preparation of the early drafts of the manuscript.

Susan Parker of the Tarlton Law Library staff, who assisted in the final typing of the manuscript and Susan Plante for her help in final proofing.

Sally Little of the Stanford Law Library staff who assisted in more detail than can be recorded here.

The entire staff of the Stanford and Tarlton Law Library to whom we owe a debt of gratitude for their generosity in giving their advice and help in the preparation of this book.

Finally, a special note of thanks to our secretaries, Gwyn Anderson of the Tarlton Law Library and Ann Vogel of the Stanford Law Library who perhaps are more thankful than we that this book is now completed.

J.M.J.
R.M.M.

SUMMARY OF CONTENTS

TABLE OF CONTENTS

TABLE OF CONTENTS

*

GLOSSARY OF TERMS USED IN LEGAL RESEARCH

This glossary of terms is limited in scope and the definitions of words are restricted in meaning to their legal or legal research context. Words whose meanings conform to general usage and are obvious are omitted from the list, e. g., Index.

ACQUITTAL—

the verdict in a criminal trial in which the defendant is found not guilty.

ACT—

an alternative name for statutory law. When introduced into the first house of the legislature, a piece of proposed legislation is known as a bill. When passed to the next house, it may then be referred to as an act. After enactment the terms "law" and "act" may be used interchangeably. An act has the same legislative force as a joint resolution but is technically distinguishable, being of a different form and introduced with the words "Be it enacted" instead of "Be it resolved."

ACTION—

the formal legal demand of one's rights from another person brought in court.

ADJUDICATION—

the formal pronouncing or recording of a judgment or decree by a court.

ADVANCE SHEETS—

current pamphlets containing the most recently reported opinions of a court or the courts of several jurisdictions. The volume and page numbers usually are the same as in the subsequently bound volumes of the series, which cover several numbers of the advance sheets.

ADVISORY OPINION—

may be rendered by a court at the request of the government or an interested party indicating how the court would rule on a matter should adversary litigation develop. An advisory opinion is thus an interpretation of the law without binding effect. The International Court of Justice and some state courts will render advisory opinions; the Supreme Court of the United States will not.

AFFIDAVIT—

a written statement or declaration of facts sworn to by the maker, taken before a person officially permitted by law to administer oaths.

AMICUS CURIAE—

means, literally, friend of the court. A party with strong interest in or views on the subject matter of the dispute will petition the court for permission to file a brief, ostensibly on behalf of a party but actually to suggest a rationale consistent with its own views.

ANALYSIS—

generally follows the scopenote in an ALR Annotation, giving a conceptual breakdown of the topic into main and subordinate categories.

ANNOTATIONS—

(1) Statutory: brief summaries of the law and facts of cases interpreting statutes passed by Congress or state legislatures which are included in codes, or (2) Textual: expository essays of varying length on significant legal topics chosen from selected cases published with the essays.

ANSWER—

the pleading filed by the defendant in response to plaintiff's complaint.

APPEAL PAPERS—

the briefs and transcripts of records on appeal filed by attorneys with courts in connection with litigation. A brief consists of a summary of the facts and circumstances or legal propositions as presented by a party to a pending action.

APPELLANT—

the party who requests that a higher court review the actions of a lower court. Compare with APPELLEE.

APPELLEE—

the party against whom an appeal is taken (usually, but not always the winner in the lower court). It should be noted that a party's status as appellant or appellee bears no relation to his status as plaintiff or defendant in the lower court.

ARBITRATION—

the hearing and settlement of a dispute between opposing parties by a third party. This decision is often binding by prior agreement of the parties.

ASSAULT—

an unlawful, intentional show of force or an attempt to do physical harm to another person. Assault can constitute the basis of a civil or criminal action. See also BATTERY.

ASSAULT AND BATTERY—

See BATTERY.

GLOSSARY OF TERMS USED IN LEGAL RESEARCH

ATTORNEY GENERAL OPINIONS—

are issued by the government's chief counsel at the request of some governmental body and interpret the law for the requesting agency in the same manner as a private attorney would for his client. The opinions are not binding on the courts but are usually accorded some degree of persuasive authority.

AUTHORITY—

refers to the precedential value to be accorded an opinion of a judicial or administrative body. A court's opinion is binding authority on other courts directly below it in the judicial hierarchy. Opinions of lower courts or of courts outside the hierarchy are governed by the degree to which it adheres to the doctrine of stare decisis. See: **Stare decisis.**

Authority may also be either primary or secondary. Statute law, administrative regulations issued pursuant to enabling legislation, and case law are primary authority and if applicable will usually determine the outcome of a case. Other statements of or about law are considered secondary authority, and thus not binding.

BAIL—

security given, in the form of a bail bond or cash as a guarantee that a released prisoner will present him/herself for trial. This security may be lost if the released person does not appear in court at the appointed time.

BATTERY—

an unlawful use of force against another person resulting in physical contact (a tort); it is commonly used in the phrase "assault and battery," assault being the threat of force, and battery the actual use of force. See also ASSAULT.

BILL—

refers to a legislative proposal introduced in the legislature. The term distinguishes unfinished legislation from directly enacted law.

BLACK LETTER LAW—

an informal term indicating the basic principles of law generally accepted by the courts and/or embodied in the statutes of a particular' jurisdiction.

BLUE BOOK—

a popular name for *A Uniform System of Citation*, which is published and distributed by the Harvard Law Review Association, and is bound in a blue cover. See also WHITE BOOK.

BREACH OF CONTRACT—

the failure to perform any of the terms of an agreement.

BRIEF—

(1) in American law practice, a written statement prepared by the counsel arguing a case in court. It contains a summary of the facts of the case, the pertinent laws, and an argument of how the law applies to the facts supporting counsel's position; or (2) a summary of a published opinion of a case prepared for studying the opinion in law school.

BRIEFS AND RECORDS—

See APPEAL PAPERS.

CALENDAR—

can mean the order in which cases are to be heard during a term of court. *Martindale-Hubbel Law Directory* contains calendars for state and federal courts, and includes the name of the court, the name of the judge, and the date of the term's beginning.

CASEBOOK—

a textbook used to instruct law students in a particular area of substantive law. The text consists of a collection of court opinions, usually from appellate courts, and notes by the author(s).

CAUSE OF ACTION—

a claim in law and in fact sufficient to bring the case to court; the grounds of an action. (Example: breach of contract.)

CERTIORARI—

a writ issued by a superior to an inferior court requiring the latter to produce the records of a particular case tried therein. It is most commonly used to refer to the Supreme Court of the United States, which uses the writ of certiorari as a discretionary device to choose the cases it wishes to hear. The term's origin is Latin, meaning "to be informed of."

CHARTER—

a document issued by a governmental entity which gives a corporation legal existence.

CHATTEL—

any article of personal property, as opposed to real property. It may refer to animate as well as inanimate property.

CHOSE—

any article of personal property. See PROPERTY.

CITATION—

the reference to authority necessary to substantiate the validity of one's argument or position. Citation to authority and supporting references is both important and extensive in any form of legal writing. Citation form is also given emphasis in legal writing, and early familiarity with *A Uniform System of Citation* will stand the law student in good stead.

GLOSSARY OF TERMS USED IN LEGAL RESEARCH

CITATORS—

a set of books which provide, through letter-form abbreviations or words, the subsequent judicial history and interpretation of reported decisions, and lists of cases and legislative enactments construing, applying or affecting statutes. In America, the most widely used set of citators is *Shepard's Citations*.

CITED CASE—

a case which is treated by other cases.

CITING CASE—

the case which operates on the cited case.

CIVIL LAW—

(1) Roman law embodied in the Code of Justinian which presently prevails in most countries of Western Europe other than Great Britain and which is the foundation of Louisiana law; (2) the law concerning non-criminal matters in a common law jurisdiction.

CLAIM—

(1) the assertion of a right, as to money or property; (2) the accumulation of facts which give rise to a right enforceable in court.

CLASS ACTION—

a lawsuit brought by a representative party on behalf of a group, all of whose members have the same or a similar grievance against the defendant.

CODE—

by popular usage a compilation or a revised statute. Technically, the laws in force are rewritten and arranged in classified order, with the addition of material having the force of law taken from judicial decrees. The repealed and temporary acts are eliminated and the revision is re-enacted.

CODIFICATION—

the process of collecting and arranging systematically, usually by subject, the laws of a state or country. The end product may be called a code, revised code or revised statutes.

COMMON LAW—

is the origin of the Anglo-American legal systems. English common law was largely customary law and unwritten, until discovered, applied, and reported by the courts of law. In theory, the common law courts did not create law but rather discovered it in the customs and habits of the English people. The strength of the judicial system in pre-parliamentary days is one reason for the continued emphasis in common law systems on case law. In a narrow sense, common law is the phrase still used to distinguish case law from statutory law.

xxv

COMPILED STATUTES—

by popular usage means a code. Technically, however, it prints acts verbatim as originally enacted but in a new classified order. The text is not modified; however, the repealed and temporary acts are omitted.

COMPLAINT—

the plaintiff's initial pleading and, according to the Federal Rules of Civil Procedure, is no longer full of the technicalities demanded by the common law. A complaint need only contain a short and plain statement of the claim upon which relief is sought, an indication of the type of relief requested, and an indication that the court has jurisdiction to hear the case.

CONGRESSIONAL DOCUMENTS—

are important sources for legislative histories, which are often necessary for proper interpretation of statutory law. Congressional documents are most accessible through specialized indexes and include hearings before Congressional committees, reports by or to House or Senate committees, and special studies conducted under Congressional authority.

CONSIDERATION—

something to be done or abstained from, by one party to a contract in order to induce another party to enter into a contract.

CONSOLIDATED STATUTES—

by popular usage means a code. Technically, however, in it the text of the acts are rewritten, arranged in classified order and re-enacted. The repealed and temporary acts are eliminated.

CONSTITUTION—

contains the fundamental law of any organization possessing one. Most national constitutions are written; the English and Israeli constitutions are unwritten.

CONVERSION—

the wrongful appropriation to oneself of the personal property of another.

CONVEYANCE—

the transfer of title to property from one person to another.

COUNT—

a separate and independent claim. A civil petition or a criminal indictment may contain several counts.

COUNTERCLAIM—

a claim made by the defendant against the plaintiff in a civil lawsuit; it constitutes a separate cause of action.

COURT DECISION—

the disposition of the case by the court. See OPINION.

DAMAGES—

monetary compensation awarded by a court for an injury caused by the act of another. Damages may be *actual* or *compensatory* (equal to the amount of loss shown), *exemplary* or *punitive* (in excess of the actual loss and which is given to punish the person for the malicious conduct which caused the injury), or *nominal* (less than the actual loss—often a trivial amount) which is given because the injury is slight or because the exact amount of injury has not been determined satisfactorily.

DECISION—

See COURT DECISION.

DECREE—

is a special type of court order, most often used in divorce actions where the court sets out the details of alimony, custody, support and visitation rights. Before certain administrative agencies, consent decrees are awarded where a corporation agrees to act in a certain matter and thus ends litigation against it.

DEFENDANT—

the person against whom a civil or criminal action is brought.

DEMURRER—

a means of objecting to the sufficiency in law of a pleading by admitting the actual allegations made, but disputing that they frame an adequate legal claim.

DICTUM—

See OBITER DICTUM.

DIGEST—

is an index to reported cases, providing brief, unconnected statements of court holdings or facts of cases, which is arranged by subject and subdivided by jurisdiction and courts.

DUE CARE—

the legal duty one owes to another according to the circumstances of a particular case.

DUE PROCESS OF LAW—

a term found in the Fifth and Fourteenth Amendments of the Constitution and also in the constitutions of many states. Its exact meaning varies from one situation to another and from one era to the next, but basically it is concerned with the guarantee of every person's enjoyment of his rights (e.g., the right to a fair hearing in any legal dispute).

EN BANC—

refers to a session where the entire bench of the court will participate in the decision rather than the regular quorum. In other countries, it is common for a court to have more members than are
usually necessary to hear an appeal. In the United States, the Circuit Courts of Appeal usually sit in groups of three judges but for
important cases may expand the bench to nine members, when they
are said to be sitting *en banc.*

ENCYCLOPEDIA—

contains expository statements on principles of law, topically arranged, with supporting footnote references to cases in point.

EQUITY—

justice administered according to fairness as contrasted with the
strictly formulated rules of common law. It is based on a system of
rules and principles which originated in England as an alternative
to the harsh rules of common law and which were based on what
was fair in a particular situation. One sought relief under this
system in courts of equity rather than in courts of law.

ESTATE—

(1) the interest or right one has in real or personal property;
(2) the property itself in which one has an interest or right.

EXECUTIVE AGREEMENT—

is an international agreement, not a treaty, concluded by the President without senatorial consent on his authority as Commander-in-
Chief and director of foreign relations. The distinction between
treaty and executive agreement is complicated and often of ques-
tionable constitutionality, but the import of such agreements as
that of Yalta or Potsdam is unquestionably great.

EXECUTIVE ORDERS—

are issued by the President under specific authority granted to him
by Congress. There is no precise distinction between presidential
proclamations and executive orders; however, proclamations generally cover matters of widespread interest, and executive orders often
relate to the conduct of government business or to organization of
the executive departments. Every act of the President authorizing
or directing the performance of an act, in its general context, is
an executive order. See: Presidential Proclamations.

FORMS OF ACTION—

governed common law pleading and were the procedural devices used
to give expression to the theories of liability recognized by the common law. Failure to analyze the cause of action properly, to select
the proper theory of liability and to choose the appropriate procedural
mechanism or forms of action could easily result in being thrown
out of court. A plaintiff had to elect his remedy in advance and
could not subsequently amend his pleadings to conform to his proof

FORMS OF ACTION—Continued

or to the court's choice of another theory of liability. According to the relief sought, actions have been divided into three categories: real actions were brought for the recovery of real property; mixed actions were brought to recover real property and damages for injury to it; personal actions were brought to recover debts or personal property, or for injuries to personal, property, or contractual rights. The common law actions are usually considered to be eleven in number: trespass, trespass on the case, trover, ejectment, detinue, replevin, debt, covenant, account, special assumpsit, and general assumpsit.

FORM-BOOKS—

include sample instruments which are helpful in drafting legal documents.

FRAUD—

a deception which causes a person to part with his property or a legal right.

GRAND JURY—

a jury of six to twenty-three persons that hears criminal accusations and evidence, and then determines whether indictments should be made. Compare with PETIT JURY.

HEADNOTE—

is a brief summary of a legal rule or significant facts in a case, which, among other headnotes applicable to the case, precedes the printed opinion in reports.

HEARINGS—

are extensively employed by both legislative and administrative agencies and can be adjudicative or merely investigatory. Adjudicative hearings can be appealed in a court of law. Congressional committees often hold hearings prior to enactment of legislation; these hearings are then important sources of legislative history.

HOLDING—

is the declaration of the conclusion of law reached by the court as to the legal effect of the facts of the case.

HOLOGRAPH (olograph)—

a will, deed, or other legal document that is entirely in the handwriting of the signer.

HORNBOOK—

is the popular reference to a series of textbooks published by West Publishing Company which reviews a certain field of law in summary, textual form, as opposed to a casebook which is designed as a teaching tool and includes many reprints of court opinions.

INDEMNITY—

a contractual arrangement whereby one party agrees to reimburse another for losses of a particular type.

INDICTMENT—

a formal accusation of a crime made by a grand jury at the request of a prosecuting attorney.

INFORMATION

an accusation based not on the action of a grand jury but rather on the affirmation of a public official.

INJUNCTION—

a judge's order that a person do or, more commonly, refrain from doing a certain act. An injunction may be preliminary or temporary pending trial of the issue presented, or it may be final if the issue has already been decided in court.

INTESTATE—

the condition of dying without having made a valid will.

JURISDICTION—

the power given to a court by a Constitution or a legislative body to make legally binding decisions over certain persons or property.

JURISPRUDENCE—

(1) the science or philosophy of law;
(2) a collective term for case law, as opposed to legislation.

KEY NUMBER—

part of the major indexing system devised for American case law, developed by West Publishing Company. The key number is a permanent number given to a specific point of this case law. (For examples, see pages 66–67.)

LEGISLATIVE HISTORY—

provides the meanings and interpretations (intent) of a statute as embodied in legislative documents. Also, citations and dates to legislative enactments, amendments and repeals of statutes are sometimes imprecisely identified as legislative histories. More accurate designations of these citations of legislative changes, as included in codes, are historical notes or amendatory histories.

LIABILITY—

the condition of being responsible either for damages resulting from an injurious act or for discharging an obligation or debt.

LIBEL—

(1) written defamation of a person's character. Compare with SLANDER.
(2) in an admiralty court, the plaintiff's statement of his cause of action and the relief sought.

LIEN—

a claim against property as security for a debt, under which the property may be seized and sold to satisfy the debt.

GLOSSARY OF TERMS USED IN LEGAL RESEARCH

LITIGATE—
to bring a civil action in court.

LOOSELEAF SERVICES AND REPORTERS—
contain federal and state administrative regulations and decisions or subject treatment of a legal topic. They consist of separate, perforated leaves in special binders, simplifying frequent substitution and insertion of new leaves.

MALPRACTICE—
professional misconduct or unreasonable lack of skill. This term is usually applied to such conduct by doctors and lawyers.

MEMORANDUM—
(1) an informal record.
(2) a written document which may be used to prove that a contract exists.
(3) (referred to as a MEMORANDUM OF LAW.) an exposition of all the points of law pertaining to a particular case.
(4) an informal written discussion of the merits of a matter pending in a lawyer's office, usually written by a law clerk or junior associate for a senior associate or partner. (Referred to as OFFICE MEMORANDUM).

MODEL CODES—
are formulated by various groups or institutions to serve as model laws for legislatures, and may be intended as improvements over existing laws or as sources of unification of diverse state legislation.

MOOT—
points are no longer subjects of contention and are raised only for purposes of discussion or hypothesis. Many law schools have moot courts where students gain practice by arguing hypothetical or moot cases.

MOTION—
a formal request made to a judge pertaining to any issue arising during the pendency of a lawsuit.

NEGLIGENCE—
the failure to exercise due care.

NISI PRIUS—
generally refers to a court where a case is first tried, as distinguished from an appellate court.

NOTER-UP—
is the term used in the British Commonwealth countries for a citator.

OBITER DICTUM—
is an official, incidental comment, not necessary to the formulation of the decision, made by the judge in his opinion which is not binding as precedent.

OFFICIAL REPORTS—
are court reports directed by statute.

OLOGRAPH—
See HOLOGRAPH.

OPINION—
an expression of the reasons why a certain decision (the judgment) was reached in a case. A *majority* opinion is usually written by one judge and represents the principles of law which a majority of his colleagues on the court deem operative in a given decision; it has more precedential value than any of the following. A *separate opinion* may be written by one or more judges in which he or they concur in or dissent from the majority opinion. A *concurring opinion* agrees with the result reached by the majority, but disagrees with the precise reasoning leading to that result. A *dissenting opinion* disagrees with the result reached by the majority and thus disagrees with the reasoning and/or the principles of law used by the majority in deciding the case. A *plurality opinion* (called a "judgment" by the Supreme Court) is agreed to by less than a majority as to the reasoning of the decision, but is agreed to by a majority as to the result. A *per curiam opinion* is an opinion "by the court" which expresses its decision in the case but whose author is not identified. A *memorandum opinion* is a holding of the whole court in which the opinion is very concise.

ORDINANCE—
is the equivalent of a municipal statute, passed by the city council and governing matters not already covered by federal or state law.

PARALLEL CITATION—
is a citation reference to the same case printed in two or more different reports.

PERMANENT LAW—
is an act which continues in force for an indefinite time.

PERSONAL PROPERTY—
See PROPERTY.

PETIT JURY—
a group of six, nine, or twelve persons that decides questions of fact in civil and criminal trials. Compare with GRAND JURY.

PETITION—
a formal, written application to a court requesting judicial action on a certain matter.

PETITIONER—
the person presenting a petition to a court, officer, or legislative body; the one who starts an equity proceeding or the one who takes an appeal from a judgment.

PLAINTIFF—
the person who brings a lawsuit against another.

PLEA BARGAINING—
the process whereby the accused and the prosecutor in a criminal case work out a mutually satisfactory disposition of the case. It usually involves the defendant's pleading guilty to a lesser offense or to only one or some of the counts of a multi-count indictment in return for a lighter sentence than that possible for the graver charge.

PLEADINGS—
are the technical means by which parties to a dispute frame the issue for the court. The plaintiff's complaint or declaration is all followed by the defendant's answer; subsequent papers may be filed as needed.

POCKET SUPPLEMENT—
is a paper-back supplement to a book, inserted in the book through a slit in its back cover. Depending on the type of publication, it may have textual, case or statutory references keyed to the original publication.

POWER OF ATTORNEY—
a document authorizing a person to act as another's agent.

PRECEDENT—
See STARE DECISIS.

PRESENTMENT—
in criminal law, a written accusation made by the grand jury without the consent or participation of a prosecutor.

PRESIDENTIAL PROCLAMATIONS—
are issued under specific authority granted to the President by Congress. Generally, they relate to matters of widespread interest. Some proclamations have no legal effect but merely are appeals to the public, e.g., the observance of American Education Week. See: Executive Orders.

PRIMARY AUTHORITY—
judicial precedent or legislative enactment which is cited as first or mandatory authority.

PRIVATE LAW—
is an act which relates to a specific person.

PROPERTY—
ownership or that which is owned. Real property refers to land; personal property refers to moveable things or chattel; chose in action refers to a right to personal property of which the owner does not presently have possession but instead has a right to sue to gain possession (e.g., a right to recover a debt, demand, or damages in a contractual action or for a tort or omission of a duty).

PUBLIC LAW—

is an act which relates to the public as a whole. It may be (1) general (applies to all persons within the jurisdiction), (2) local (applies to a geographical area), or (3) special (relates to an organization which is charged with a public interest).

RATIO DECIDENDI—

is the point in a case which determines the result—the basis of the decision.

REAL PROPERTY—

See PROPERTY.

RECORDS AND BRIEFS—

See APPEAL PAPERS.

REGULATIONS—

are issued by various governmental departments to carry out the intent of the law. Agencies issue regulations to guide the activity of their employees and to ensure uniform application of the law. Regulations are not the work of the legislature and do not have the effect of law in theory. In practice, however, because of the intricacies of judicial review of administrative action, regulations can have an important effect in determining the outcome of cases involving regulatory activity. United States Government regulations appear first in the *Federal Register,* published five days a week, and are subsequently arranged by subject in the *Code of Federal Regulations.*

REMAND—

to send back for further proceedings, as when a higher court sends back to a lower court.

REPORTS—

are (1) (court reports) published judicial cases arranged according to some grouping, such as jurisdiction, court, period of time, subject matter or case significance, (2) (administrative reports or decisions) published decisions of an administrative agency, (3) annual statements of progress, activities or policy issued by an administrative agency or an association.

RESOLUTION—

a formal expression of the opinion of a rule-making body adopted by the vote of that body.

RESPONDENT—

the party who makes an answer to a bill in an equity proceeding or who contends against an appeal.

RESTATEMENTS OF THE LAW—

an attempt to restate in systematic form the existing common law in certain areas as developed by the Courts. This project, directed by the American Law Institute since 1923, provides a valuable secondary research source, but lacks the legislative sanction to make it binding.

GLOSSARY OF TERMS USED IN LEGAL RESEARCH

REVISED STATUTES—

by popular usage means a code. Technically, however, it identifies a compilation of statutes in the identical order as originally passed by the legislature with the temporary and repealed acts eliminated.

RULES OF COURT—

regulate practice and procedure before the various courts. In most jurisdictions, these rules are issued by the court itself, or by the highest court in that jurisdiction.

SANCTION—

(1) to assent to another's actions;
(2) a penalty for violating a law.

SCOPE NOTE—

delimits and identifies the content of a topic and appears below the topic's heading in a publication.

SECONDARY AUTHORITY—

are sources of the law which have only persuasive and no mandatory authority, e.g., encyclopedia.

SECTION LINE—

is preceded by the key number, indicating the subject of the key number.

SESSION LAWS—

are published laws of a state enacted by each assembly and separately bound for the session and for extra sessions. The session laws are published in bound or pamphlet volumes after adjournment of the legislatures for the regular or special sessions.

SHEPARDIZING—

is a term which is the trade-mark property of Shepard's Citations, Inc. and is descriptive of the general use of its publications.

SLANDER—

oral defamation of a person's character. Compare with LIBEL.

"SLIP" LAW—

is a legislative enactment which is separately and promptly published in pamphlet or in single sheet format after its passage.

"SLIP" OPINION—

is an individual court decision published separately soon after it is rendered.

STAR PAGINATION—

is a scheme in reprint editions of Court reports, showing on its pages where the text of the pages of the official edition begins and ends.

STARE DECISIS—

is the doctrine of English and American law which states that when a court has formulated a principle of law as applicable to a given set of facts, it will follow that principle and apply it in future cases where the facts are substantially the same. It connotes the decision of present cases on the basis of past precedent.

STATUS TABLE—

gives the current status of a bill or court decision.

STATUTES—

are acts of a legislature. Depending upon its context in usage, a statute may mean a single act of a legislature or a body of acts which are collected and arranged according to a scheme or for a session of a legislature or parliament.

STATUTES AT LARGE—

the official compilation of acts passed by the Congress. The arrangement is currently by Public Law number, and by chapter number in pre-1951 volumes. This is the official print of the law for citation purposes where titles of the United States Code have not been enacted into positive law.

STATUTES OF LIMITATIONS—

laws setting time periods during which disputes may be taken to court.

STATUTORY INSTRUMENTS—

are English administrative regulations and orders. The term applies especially to the administrative rules published since 1939, supplementing the English administrative code, Statutory Rules and Orders . . . .

STATUTORY RULES AND ORDERS—

are English administrative regulations and orders.

SUBPOENA—

a court order compelling a witness to appear and testify in a certain proceeding.

SUMMONS—

a notice delivered by a sheriff or other authorized person informing a person that he/she is the defendant in a civil action and telling him/her when and where to appear in court to present his/her side.

SUPERSEDE—

to displace or to supplant one publication or its segment with another.

SUPREME COURT—

(1) the court of last resort in the federal judicial system. (It also has original jurisdiction in some cases.)

(2) in most states, the highest appellate court or court of last resort (but not in New York or Massachusetts).

GLOSSARY OF TERMS USED IN LEGAL RESEARCH

SYLLABUS—
   See HEADNOTE.

TABLE OF CASES—
   is a list of cases, arranged alphabetically by case names, with citations and references to the body of the publication where the cases are treated.

TEMPORARY LAW—
   an act which continues in force for a specific period of time.

TERM OF COURT—
   signifies the space of time prescribed by law during which a court holds session. The court's session may actually extend beyond the term. The October Term of the Supreme Court of the United States is now the only term during which the Court sits, and lasts from October to June.

TORT—
   a civil wrong which does not involve a contractual relationship. The elements of a tort are a duty owed, a breach of that duty, and the resultant harm to the one to whom the duty was owed.

TRANSCRIPT OF RECORD—
   refers to the printed record as made up in each case of the proceedings and pleadings necessary for the appellate court to review the history of the case.

TREATISE—
   is an exposition, which may be critical, evaluative, interpretative, or informative, on case law or legislation. Usually it is more exhaustive than an encyclopedia but less detailed or critical than a periodical article.

TREATY—
   is an agreement between two or more sovereign nations.

TRESPASS—
   an unlawful interference with one's person, property, or rights. At common law, trespass was a form of action brought to recover damages for any injury to one's person or property or relationship with another.

UNIFORM LAWS—
   on various subjects have been drafted. A considerable number have been approved by the National Conference of Commissioners on Uniform State Laws, and may have been adopted in one or more jurisdictions in the United States and its possessions. The Uniform Commercial Code is now the law in forty-nine states.

UNOFFICIAL REPORTS—
   are court reports published without statutory direction. They are not distinguished from official reports on grounds of varying quality or accuracy of reporting.

VENUE—

the particular geographical area where a court with jurisdiction may try a case.

WAIVER—

the voluntary relinquishment of a known right.

WHITE BOOK—

a popular name for *A Uniform System of Citation* which is published and distributed by the Harvard Law Review Association, and which was formerly bound in a white cover. See also BLUE BOOK.

WRIT—

of which there are many types, is a written order, issued by a court and directed to an official or party, commanding the performance of some act.

WRONGFUL DEATH —

a type of lawsuit brought on behalf of a deceased person's beneficiaries that alleges that death was attributable to the willful or negligent act of another.

†

FUNDAMENTALS OF LEGAL RESEARCH

Chapter 1

THE LEGAL PROCESS

SECTION A. SOURCES OF THE LAW

1. Introduction

The American legal system, as that of most English-speaking countries, is part of the common law tradition. The term "common law" is used here in the sense that distinguishes it from Roman law, modern civil law, canon law, and other systems of law. The common law has been defined as:

> " * * * [T]hat body of law and juristic theory which was originated, developed, and formulated and is administered in England, and has obtained among most of the states and peoples of Anglo-American stock." [1]

In the early history of English law, the custom developed of considering the decision of the courts as precedents. This was interpreted as "furnishing an example or authority for an identical or similar case afterwards arising or for a similar question of law." [2] This, in turn, led to the development of the doctrine of *stare decisis* which has been defined as:

> " * * * [T]hat when [a] court has once laid down a principle of law as applicable to a certain state of facts, it will adhere to that principle, and apply it to all future cases where facts are substantially the same." [3]

[1] BLACK'S LAW DICTIONARY 345 (4th ed. 1968). [Hereinafter cited as BLACK'S.]

[2] *Id.* at 1340. For a succinct and scholarly treatment of the development of case law, *see* J. DAWSON, THE ORACLES OF THE LAW 1–80 (1968).

[3] Moore v. City of Albany, 98 N.Y. 396, 410 (1895). *See also* West, *The Doctrine of Stare Decisis*, 21 WAYNE L.REV. 1043 (1975).

Under the doctrine of *stare decisis* the law became embodied in the written decisions of the English courts and was to be found in the decisions of the courts rather than in a codified body of law as in other countries of Europe with legal systems based on the Roman law. It is in this sense that the common law became known as the "unwritten" law. The doctrines of *precedent* and *stare decisis* necessarily require access to the decisions of the courts and resulted in their publication under the generic term of *law reports*. To "find the law," then, a lawyer has to search the law reports for opinions of the courts that arose from a similar fact situation to the one at hand and then determine if the cases located can serve as a precedent for the present case.

While the development of case law was predominant, the role of statutes cannot be ignored. The earliest statutes were enacted by the King with the concurrence of his Council, and then gradually the role of statute-making was assumed by Parliament. It was not until after the passage of the *Reform Act of 1832* that statutes played a significant role in the English legal system. The real growth of statutory law reflected the impact of the industrial revolution on society as it became apparent that a jurisprudence based only on judicial decisions could not meet the needs of a growing dynamic society. Situations soon developed where answers were needed that were not found in the court reports, or the answers found no longer met current needs, or resulted in actions that were felt to be unjust. To remedy this, Parliament began to pass statutes which changed the prior rules for circumstances not found in any decisions of the court. A statute has been defined as:

> "An act of the legislature declaring, commanding, or prohibiting something; a particular law established by the will of the legislative department of government * * * according to the forms necessary to constitute it the law of the state." [4]

> "The word is used to designate the written law in contradistinction to the unwritten law." [5]

The sources of law, then, in common law jurisdictions derive from the enactments of their legislative bodies and from the decisions of their courts.[6] The authorities of law in all common law jurisdic-

---

[4] BLACK'S, *supra* at 1581.

[5] *Id.*

[6] For a more detailed discussion of the sources of the common law, *see* R. JACKSON, THE MACHINERY OF JUSTICE IN ENGLAND 10–18 (6th ed. 1972). *See also* L. FRIEDMAN, A HISTORY OF AMERICAN LAW 17–25 (1975).

tions [7] are separated into two divisions—primary [8] and secondary. Primary law is found in: a) written constitutions and the enactments of legislatures (and in those adopted in some jurisdictions through the vote of the electorate), and b) the body of law found in the written opinions of the courts. In form of publication, the former are found in statute books, and the latter in sets of court reports. All other written expressions of the law are known as secondary authorities.

The term "sources of the law" has been variously defined. In relation to legal research, the phrase is employed to denote: (1) the literature of the law, (2) the authoritative organ of the state which formulates the legal rules or (3) the derivation of the concepts or ideas expressed in the body of the law. These meanings do not exhaust the definitions of the term; however, the present discussion will be limited to the concepts they impart.

2. The Literature of the Law

It is axiomatic to describe the law libraries as containing the literature of the law. This material includes statutes, administrative rules, judicial decisions, digests of case law, treatises, encyclopedias and other publications.

American law libraries contain large, diffused collections since, pursuant to the common law, much of our law is "found" or "made" by judicial decisions. Determining the decisions of present cases on the basis of past precedents results in legal literature accumulating and assuming large proportions. Another factor resulting in the growth of American legal collections is the multiple system of state and federal laws which makes necessary the acquisition and maintenance of primary sources for fifty states as well as those of the Federal government.

3. The Authoritative Organ of the State

The officials or bodies of officials whose acts give validity to the law are descriptive of another meaning of its source. In the democratic countries, there are two types of officials with such authority. They are legislators and judges. The latter group includes ordinary judges and administrative hearing officials. The former covers legislators and administrative rule-makers. These officials produce two authoritative forms of law: legislation and case law.

---

[7] "Jurisdiction" in this sense is used to describe the territory over which a government or subdivision thereof has control.

[8] Primary sources are also frequently designated as either mandatory or persuasive. The former, such as statutes or decisions of highest courts of a jurisdiction must be followed by all lower courts within the jurisdiction. The latter consists of appellate court opinions of other jurisdictions, or of writings in legal periodicals or treatises.

4. The Derivation of Legal Concepts

The third meaning given to the sources of the law relates to the derivation of its preceptual contents. Thus, the modern law of vicarious liability is considered by some as having its origin in the slave laws of the Romans.[9] The famous article by Warren and Brandeis was a source of the American law of the right to privacy.[10] The writings of Blackstone, Kent and Story contributed significantly to the early development of American law.

SECTION B. THE LEGAL SYSTEM OF THE UNITED STATES

As a result of our federal system, any particular legal transaction may be governed solely by state law, or solely by federal law, or perhaps both. Although the question of determination of jurisdiction is beyond the scope of this book, its significance, however, cannot be overlooked in determining the answer to a legal question and knowledge is needed of both federal and state law.

As previously indicated, the United States is a common law jurisdiction. The federal system of government in this country, however, has made its legal system extremely complex. Under our federal constitution, each state, except for those powers delegated to the federal government, is a sovereign state. This means that, in fact, there is not one legal system in this country, but fifty-one.

1. Federal Government

The primary sources of the United States Government are found in its Constitution, the Acts of Congress, and in the decisions of the Supreme Court of the United States and other inferior federal courts.

2. States

In addition to the above, the primary sources for each of the fifty states are found in each state's constitution as adopted by the people, the enactments of the legislature (and those initiated and enacted directly by the electorate) and the written decisions of its highest court of appeal, and in the law of England as delineated in its reception statute.[11]

[9] O. HOLMES, COMMON LAW 16–17 (1881).

[10] Warren and Brandeis, *The Right to Privacy*, 4 HARV.L.REV. 193 (1890).

[11] All states (except Louisiana, whose legal system is based on the civil law) have adopted the English common law as the basis of their jurisprudence. *See* 1 POWELL ON REAL PROPERTY § 45 (1969). For representative statutes adopting the English common law as part of their law, *see* SMITH–HURD, ILL.ANN.STAT. Ch. 28 § 1 (1969) ; TEX.REV.CIV.STAT., Art. 1 (1969).

SECTION C.   THE LEGAL SYSTEMS OF OTHER COUNTRIES

The doctrine of judicial precedent is not recognized by the European countries,[12] whose legal systems are derived from the Roman law, to the degree followed by common-law countries. Justinian, in codifying the law for the Roman state, declared that his code was to be the exclusive source of the law "on penalty of forgery," [13] thus attempting to discourage reference to earlier sources. Codification as a legal instrument was later adopted by the countries which followed the Roman law. However, in recent years, on the continent of Europe, judicial decisions are assuming a more significant authoritative role, claiming recognition with commentaries in interpreting the civil law. Modern European codes also recognize that no codification scheme can be all-inclusive and complete; thus, courts may be required to go outside the code, when its text is silent, obscure or deficient, for the solution to controversies.

The Latin American courts have followed a modified procedure. If a rule has been applied several times in different cases by the highest court, it is considered as binding. The French practice is also a compromise between the rule of *stare decisis* and the civil-law concept. A single decision by a court is not binding on it or on subordinate courts. While another lower court in a comparable case is not bound to follow the highest court's twice-told precedent, in practice the lower courts are prone to follow the precedent. Further, a uniform pattern of decisions is considered as binding in all courts in a manner similar to that of the highest courts in the United States.[14]

SECTION D.   LEGAL RESEARCH

The short summary so far presented on the structure of the legal system must be understood before one can approach the methods of doing legal research. What is involved in this process is a search for authorities. When engaged in legal research (more properly, legal search) a lawyer is seeking to find those authorities in the pri-

[12] For articles on judicial precedent in Europe, *see* Von Mehren, *Judicial Process: A Comparative Analysis*, 5 AM.J.COMP.L. 197 (1956); Dietze, *Judicial Review in Europe*, 55 MICH.L.REV. 539 (1957).

[13] A. KOCUREK, AN INTRODUCTION TO THE SCIENCE OF LAW 162 (1930).

[14] Goodhart, *Precedents in English and Continental Law*, 50 LAW Q.REV. 40 (1934). *See also* J. DAWSON, *supra* note 2 at 100; J. MERRYMAN, THE CIVIL LAW TRADITION: AN INTRODUCTION TO THE LEGAL SYSTEMS OF WESTERN EUROPE AND LATIN AMERICA (1969).

mary sources of the law that are applicable to a particular legal situation. In short, he/she is seeking to find the applicable statutes or court decisions (or both)[15] from the particular jurisdiction wherein the legal situation has occurred or will occur. The search is always first for mandatory primary sources, that is, constitutional or statutory provisions of the legislature, and court decisions of the jurisdiction involved. If these cannot be located, then the search focuses on locating persuasive primary authorities, that is, decisions from courts of other common law jurisdictions. Statutes are never considered persuasive authority. When in the legal search process primary authorities cannot be located, the searcher will seek for secondary authorities. These usually are considered to be the writings of lawyers as found in treatises or law reviews, or the publications of law reform organizations such as the American Law Institute and the law revision commissions of the various states.

This conglomerate mass and the diffusion of secondary American legal publications indicate the need for the organized study of the use of legal materials in our law schools. In addition, the systematized study of legal research reflects an increasing emphasis in law school curricula on training students in the professional crafts. But this is not suggestive of a pedagogical deemphasis of legal evaluation and theory. On the contrary, the modern curriculum also attempts to impart to the student the reasonings, the insights, and the principles which characterize the law. Without instruction in legal analysis and policy insights as well as training in legal skills, the modern lawyer is ill-prepared to meet the responsibilities of his profession.

1. Professional Responsibility

The *Code of Professional Responsibility* of the American Bar Association states that a lawyer must maintain high standards of professional conduct, and Canon 6 of this Code requires a lawyer to represent a client competently. For such representation, it is clear that a lawyer must be able to research the law, and all lawyers are expected to know "those plain and elementary principles of law which are commonly known by well-informed attorneys, *and to discover the additional rules which, although not commonly known, may readily be found by standard research techniques*" [16] (emphasis ours). The ability to find the law, to locate the applicable ruling authorities, and to ascertain their current status must become part and parcel of every lawyer's training if he/she is to uphold the standards of the legal profession.

[15] The place of administrative regulations and rulings will be covered in Chapter 13.

[16] Smith v. Lewis, 13 C.3d 349, 118 Cal.Rptr. 621, 520 P.2d 589 (1975). In this case, the plaintiff received a judgment of $100,000 in a malpractice action based on the negligence of the defendant lawyer in researching the applicable law.

2. Law Book Publishing

To engage in effective legal research, one must have an understanding not only of the organization of the legal system, but also of how law books are published and organized.

In the American Colonial period, law books were extremely scarce. At the time of the Revolution, only about thirty of the one hundred and fifty English reports were generally accessible in the Colonies. There were even fewer treatises in use. Law books were not found in the colleges for, at that time, the law was not an integrated academic study. The most extensive law collections of attorneys numbered from fifty to one hundred volumes.[17]

This situation did not prevail for long. As the economy of the country changed from an agrarian to an industrial society and greater demands were made upon the courts and the legislatures, the repositories of the law proportionately grew.

Over the years, there have been various statistics used by legal authorities on quoting the tremendous volume of reported decisions in the American legal system. The preface to the Century Edition of the American Digest System states that the courts made 500,000 decisions during the period 1658–1896.[18]

In trying to determine the number of cases reported since the Century opinion, the editors of this book in cooperation with the editors of West Publishing Company determined that up to 1975 there were approximately three million reported decisions in the United States.

In 1975 the National Reporter System, including State and Federal volumes, reported 44,000 cases. In 1950 there were 21,000 cases. Thus in a 25 year period, the number of cases just about doubled. Congress and state legislatures produce about 50,000 pages of statutory law per year, and the Federal Register annually publishes about 60,000 pages of federal administrative regulations.[19]

This flood of court decisions has from early times caused concern to the legal profession.[20] But despite all efforts to control the ever increasing number of court opinions, they continue to proliferate. Moreover, all fifty states as well as the Federal government publish their own statutes and administrative regulations. To help

[17] A. HARNO, LEGAL EDUCATION IN THE UNITED STATES 19 (1953); L. FRIEDMAN, *supra* note 6 at 538–546.

[18] 1 Cent.Dig. iii (1897).

[19] The Federal Register for 1975 contained 60,221 pages.

[20] For a discussion of the problem of excessive court reporting, *see* Jacobstein, *Some Reflections on the Selective Publication of Appellate Court Opinions*, 27 STAN. L.REV. 791 (1975).

lawyers cope with this multitude of primary sources, private publishers publish numerous types of secondary sources, such as treatises, periodicals, citators, digests, and annotations to assist lawyers in finding and understanding the law. A short discussion of the law book publishing industry will be helpful in understanding the use of law books, the subject of remaining chapters.

The largest law book publisher is the West Publishing Company of St. Paul, Minnesota. This company primarily publishes court reports and statutes but also offers many secondary sources. The next largest law book publishing company is that of the Lawyers Cooperative Publishing Company of Rochester, New York and its affiliate, the Bancroft-Whitney Company of San Francisco, California. Both emphasize the publications of primary sources. The Commerce Clearing House Company, the Bureau of National Affairs, and the Prentice-Hall Company are publishers of loose-leaf publications which emphasize areas of law requiring frequent updating. The Matthew Bender Company and Callaghan Law Book Publishing Company specialize in publishing treatises for practicing lawyers. Many other smaller companies also publish legal materials most useful in legal research.[21]

The important point to remember, however, is that both legal finding aids and primary repositories of the law are products of the private law book publishing industry.[22]

When engaged in legal research, searching for the law may involve the statutes and the court reports of many states as well as countless numbers of secondary sources.

SECTION E. SUMMARY

The sources of American law are found in the Constitution and statutes of the Congress and the states, and in the appellate court decisions of the courts. Statutes and court decisions are primary authority. Other law books are secondary sources of the law and may be categorized into two types.

---

[21] A thorough discussion of the law book publishing industry may be found in M. MAYER, THE LAWYERS 417–450 (1966). *See also* Lamson, *For Lawyers, West Isn't a Direction—It's a Way of Life*, 4 JURIS DOCTOR 28 (1974); Sandza, *Lawbook Publishing: A $145 Million-a-Year Business*, 4 JURIS DOCTOR 31 (1974).

[22] The reliance of lawyers on private law book publishers has led the Federal Trade Commission to promulgate standards for the law book trade. *See* U. S. FEDERAL TRADE COMMISSION, GUIDES FOR THE LAW BOOK INDUSTRY (Promulgated August 8, 1975).

Books of Search

Books of search may be subdivided into the following groups:

Annotated Reports and Annotated Statutes, with the annotations being secondary authority.

Encyclopedias.

Loose-Leaf Services and Reporters.

Books of search are cited as persuasive authority, for they serve in collating, describing and explaining the law.

Books of Index

This category includes the following types of legal publications:

Books of Definition, such as dictionaries.

Citators.

Digests.

Form-Books.

Indexes.

Tables.

Books of index serve primarily as aids in obtaining information. Most of these aids are not cited as persuasive authority. Thus, a dictionary, in certain circumstances, will be cited, but digests and citators are never cited as sources of the law.

Chapter 2

PRELIMINARY PROCEDURE IN LEGAL RESEARCH

Let us begin our study by surveying the procedure which is preliminary to the actual use of research publications. This entails three steps: Step 1, The determination and integration of facts. Step 2, The determination of the legal issues. Step 3, The procedure to be applied in searching for the law. Now we will consider each of these steps in order.

SECTION A. THE DETERMINATION AND INTEGRATION OF FACTS

A clear understanding of a legal problem, relating either to litigation or to counselling, requires a careful screening and ascertaining of the relevant facts. The application of various fact-situations may result in different conclusions although the principle of law remains the same. Since the facts are determinative of the results, their derivation through incisive interrogation and resourceful investigation assumes paramount importance and may mean the difference between success and failure.

After the facts are assembled, the mass of information must be screened, integrated, and evaluated. Although screening, integrating, and evaluating the facts are not necessarily distinct, separate processes, each possesses sufficiently discrete characteristics to be identifiable. Thus, screening entails the eliminating of nonessential facts; integration is the process of assembling the pertinent data; and evaluation gives direction to the research.

The process of factual appraisal of litigious or nonlitigious issues calls for recognizing and weighing the following four factors:

T—*Thing* or subject matter

A—Cause of *Action* or ground of defense

R—*Relief* sought

P—*Persons* or parties involved

This analysis can be quickly learned as the TARP rule, and the process embodies these considerations:

1. *Thing or subject matter.* The place or property involved in a problem or controversy may be a significant element. Thus, where

a passenger is injured in a skidding automobile, the personal property, the automobile, becomes an essential factor in the dispute.

2. *Cause of action or ground of defense.* A claim is asserted or a defense is made. The action centers around a point of controversy or a circumstance relating to the problem. The cause of action may be a breach of contract, negligence, or some other claim.

3. *Relief sought.* This relates to the purpose of the lawsuit or the claim. It may be a civil suit for damages, an equity matter seeking affirmative or injunctive relief, or a criminal action being brought by the state.

4. *Persons or parties involved in the problem; their factual and legal status and relationship to each other.* The parties or persons may fit within a group or class which is salient to the solution of the problem or the outcome of the lawsuit. Thus, infancy or insanity may have an important bearing on a result.

The commercial or professional activities of the parties or persons may be significant. For example, banking or medicine.

The relationship between the parties or persons may be of special importance, such as exists between a husband and wife or an employer and an employee.

An analysis of the facts in a problem, through the use of the TARP rule, should provide suggestive headings to be examined in an index of a publication, *e. g.*, the descriptive-word index of a digest, or the table of contents. References to the applicable sections of the publication may be found under the appropriate headings.

SECTION B. THE DETERMINATION OF THE LEGAL ISSUES

When the facts have been determined and integrated, the legal issues should then be ascertained. Legal controversies frequently involve more than one point of law. In such cases, the issues should be interrelated, not merged, and should be given separate treatment.

If introductory, general information is required to orient the researcher to the topic, some secondary sources are helpful at this stage. They include treatises, periodical articles, and general and local encyclopedias.

As the methods of research vary greatly with the problems and the subject matter, no single example can illustrate adequately all phases of research methodology. However, to facilitate the present

study and to illustrate the handling of a problem, an example case is analyzed below:

Example Case

A built a new home in Anycity, Iowa, and rented it to B for a period of three years. B personally arranged for the water service with the Acme Water Company, a privately owned local corporation. B moved out when his lease (containing no provision as to water supply) expired and left unpaid a six-months water bill of $30.00. A moved into the house and had the account changed to her own name. Now, six months after A moved in, the Acme Company is threatening that unless A pays the delinquent account of $30.00, it will discontinue the supply of water to the house. A, feeling that she should not have to pay the bill, seeks to have the threatened shut-off enjoined.

First, let us analyze the case for A.

(1) *Thing or subject matter.* Here the subject matter is the water supply. Or, it might be expanded to include all utilities. A case similar to our example case but involving the supply of gas would certainly help in the solution. But when the elements are thus expanded, caution must be used to avoid changing the issues.

(2) *Cause of action or ground of defense.* The suit here is based on the threat to turn off the water, which would cause property damage as well as personal inconvenience, discomfort, and injury. The defense would be non-payment of bills.

(3) *Relief sought.* A seeks a court injunction to stop Acme's intended cessation of water service.

(4) *Persons or parties involved.* There does not seem to be any particular class or group that includes A, except that she is now a consumer and was the owner and landlord at the time B consumed the water.

The Acme Company's status here is very important. It is a public utility and, of course, a water-works or water supply company. A further distinguishing feature is that it is a private rather than a governmental utility.

In this particular case, it would be dangerous to discard immediately any of the related elements as being unimportant.

The next question is: What is the primary law on the subject and where can it be found? You, no doubt, have assumed that this is essentially a problem on the state or local level, but it is not safe to disregard completely the federal legislation on the subject without some thought. Apparently, the Acme Company is doing business only in Anycity; hence, it would not be subject to the Congressional authority over interstate commerce. Therefore, in our particular example, it is

fairly safe to proceed to the state and local levels, for the company is private and is not subject to the Fourteenth Amendment.

After determining the facts and legal issues in a case, we are ready to proceed in the search for the law. At this point, the decision must be made on whether to start the search in Books of Search or Books of Index, as described in Chapter One.

SECTION C. SEARCH FOR THE LAW

Let us take our water problem through the next step. This may be done by applying one or more of four methods of legal research procedure. They are:

1. The Index Method

This technique requires the initial use of the subject index to a book. This may be done after an analysis of the facts in a problem through the use of the TARP rule. For example, under the appropriate topical or factual headings of a descriptive-word index to a digest or to the index to an encyclopedia, references may be found to the sections of the publication which provide cases or discussion in point.

Applying this procedure to the *American Digest System*, we may check the Descriptive-Word Index to the *Fifth Decennial* under the headings:

> → **PUBLIC WATER SUPPLY** (Cont'd)
> → INJUNCTION (Cont'd)
>   Jurisdiction of United States courts.
>   **Courts 262.9(10)**
>   Rates. **Courts 262.9(21)**
>   → To prevent shutting off water supply.
>   **Waters 203(12)**
>   Town directed to remove fence erected
>   around land in which town had easement.
>   **Waters 197**

Referring to volume 44 of the *Fifth Decennial*, under the heading Waters 203(12), we find a 1944 Vermont Supreme Court decision in point. In Hall v. Village of Swanton, 113 Vt. 424, 35 A.2d 381, the court held that an injunction is the proper remedy to prevent the shutting off of water where a consumer denies in good faith either his liability or the amount of the charge on the basis of irreparable injury to convenience and health which might result, notwithstanding that an action at law would lie for damages.

Applying the same technique to the legal encyclopedia, *Corpus Juris Secundum,* we examine its General Index under the following headings:

> → **WATERS**—Continued
> → Injunctions—Continued
>   Service, joinder of parties in suit to restrain dis-
>   continuance, **Injun** § 176, **p. 832**
>   → Supply,
>   Breach of contract, **Injun** § 86
>   Interference, **Injun** § 149, **p. 759, n. 82**
>   Issuance resulting in cutting off, **Injun** § 31
>   → Preventing shutting off, **Injun** § 124, **p. 671,**
>   **n. 14**
> Injuries, see **Title Index to Waters**
> Innkeepers, watering place, hotelkeeper as innkeeper,
>   **Inn** § 2, **p. 1135**

Referring to volume 43, under the title, Injunctions, section 124, p. 671, footnote 14 gives a related reference. Bienville Water Supply Co. v. Mobile, 112 Ala. 260, 20 So. 742, held that an injunction may be a proper remedy to prevent the shutting off of a water supply required for *public* or *municipal* purposes. But this is not a direct answer; however, we need not carry the problem further.

This research procedure is considered the easiest for the tyro, but many practicing lawyers also prefer it to the other research techniques. However, proficiency in the case of the Index Method is attained only through experience and familiarity with the factual or topical headings used in legal publications.

2.   The Topic or the Analytic Method

After analyzing the issues and points of law in a problem, the researcher can go directly to a table of contents or topical outline of a publication in quest of cases or other law in point. Instead of using the index, he approaches the problem by analyzing the law and searching the section lines of a topical outline to find the appropriate subdivision under which the material appears. Under the topic is an analytical note or scope-note which describes the coverage of the topic. A careful reading of the note should indicate whether it is the correct topic. Scanning the outline of the section lines should elicit the appropriate section number under that topic. Then an examination of the material under that section in the body of the publication should provide the law in point.

Outlines of the topics relating to the water problem, appearing in the *Fifth Decennial* and *Corpus Juris Secundum,* are given below.

Illustrations

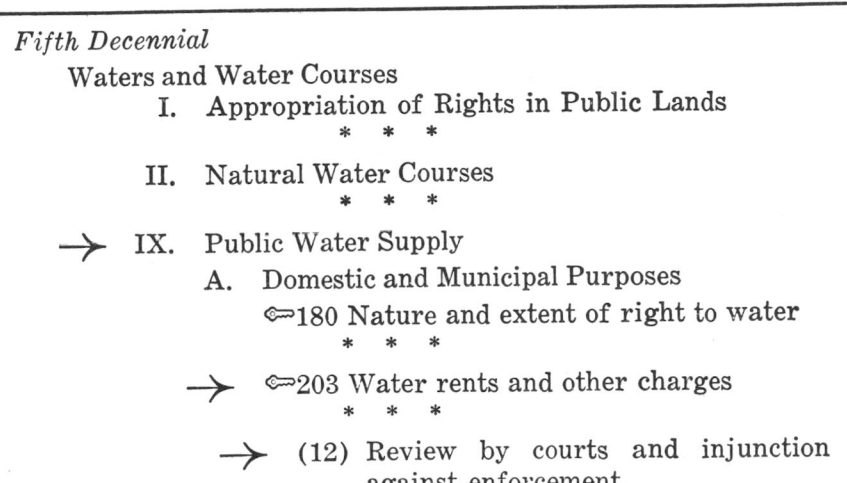

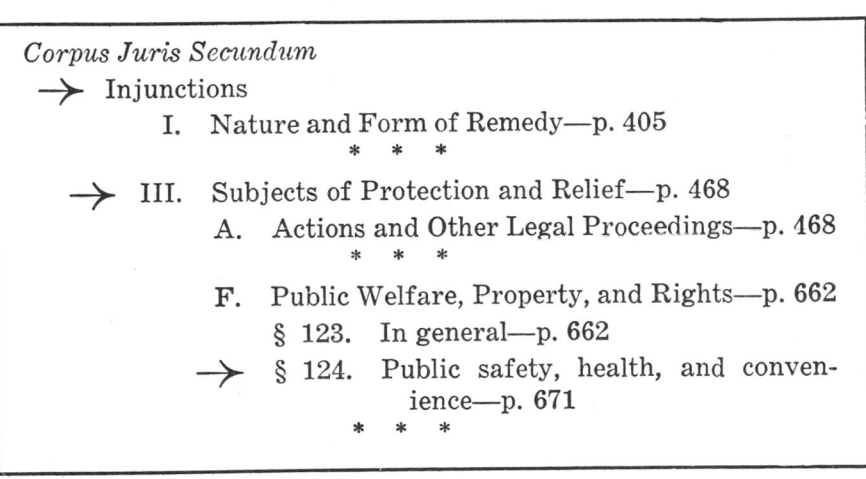

Some lawyers find the Topic Method difficult to apply, since legal headings are numerous and their meanings are elusive. But if a lawyer is familiar with the subject matter and can cogently analyze the legal issues, this method is a quick device in searching for the law.

3. The Case Method

When the name of an applicable case is known, this method of finding the law is useful. The case may be located in a treatise, an encyclopedia, an annotated report, a casebook or some other source. This procedure eliminates consulting an index or a topical outline. The specific case may be checked in a table of cases of an appropriate pub-

lication.   The reference following the name of the case in the table is to the section of the set containing information on the law in the case.

In relation to the water problem, let us assume that we know of the Hall v. Village of Swanton case.   Applying the Case Method for other applicable cases, we can look up the Hall case in the Table of Cases of the *Fifth Decennial,* and the reference would cite us to the appropriate sections of the *Digest* where the case is digested with other pertinent cases.   It also would provide the citations to the case. The listing follows:

> Hall v. Village of Swanton, 113 Vt. 424, 35 A.2d 381—App & E
>   1009(1); Electricity 11; Equity 39(1, 2), 46; Gas 13(2);
>   Mun.Corp. 57, 271, 272; Waters 202, 203(6, 12).

4.   The Definition Method

This method of approach is used only when the solution of a problem depends in whole or in part on the meaning of a legal or non-legal word or phrase.   The word or phrase is sought in a publication, such as *Words and Phrases* (West Pub. Co.), some state digests or an encyclopedia. These sources give references to court decisions which have defined the words or phrases.   Statutes and other publications, apart from cases, also provide definitions.

Although the water problem is not one in which definitions are a central issue, if the researcher were interested in locating the meanings of some pertinent phrases, such as private corporation, *Words and Phrases* could be examined under the appropriate terms.

The remaining chapters of this book will be devoted to charting a path through the law publications which must be used in finding the law.

Chapter 3

COURT REPORTS

SECTION A. THE REPORTING OF COURT DECISIONS

1. Introduction

The editing and publishing of court decisions have assumed special characteristics in American law. These manifestations were influenced significantly by the doctrine of judicial precedent or *stare decisis*. Since past decisions play such an important role in our law, the tremendous growth and inclusiveness of court reports are quite understandable. However, this extensive development in turn has created problems for the legal profession—problems relating to the informational content of case law, publication costs, absorption of office space and related issues.

As indicated previously, there are over three million reported judicial opinions in the United States, and over 40,000 American cases are published each year. These mostly include decisions of federal and state appellate courts. As a general rule, decisions of trial courts are not reported. A few states, such as New York, Ohio and Pennsylvania, do publish some trial court opinions but those so selected are few in number and represent only a very small proportion of the total cases heard by the trial courts.

It does not follow, however, that all appellate court decisions are published or that publication practices are identical in every state.[1] It should be noted that, notwithstanding this selectivity in the publication of trial and appellate cases, far too many opinions are written and reported which do not merit the treatment of permanent publication.[2]

The point is that a significant number of reported decisions relate merely to prosaic problems and make no doctrinal advancements. Although these cases are of value in resolving individual controversies, they add little or nothing to existing law. However, where the facts of cases are distinguishable, their precedential value is ascertainable. Therefore, the extensive publication of judicial decisions is a culmination of doctrinal development and fact differentiation.

But the problem which extensive case reporting presents is not serious. It has been reduced significantly through the availability of

[1] Chanin, *A Survey of the Writing and Publication of Opinions in Federal and State Appellate Courts*, 67 LAW LIB.J. 362 (1974).

[2] A full discussion of this may be found in Jacobstein, *Some Reflections on the Control of the Publication of Appellate Court Opinions*, 27 STAN.L.REV. 791 (1975).

secondary sources.   Also, as an ancillary matter, earlier decisions chiefly perform a historical function.   As Holmes observed, "It is a great mistake to be frightened by the ever-increasing number of reports.   The reports of a given jurisdiction in the course of a generation take up pretty much the whole body of the law, and restate it from the present point of view. We could reconstruct the corpus from them if all that went before were burned.   The use of the earlier reports is mainly historical   *   *   *".[3]

2.   Court Organization

Each jurisdiction has its own system of court organization, and although there may be differences in detail, the general structure is the same.   In general, there are trial courts and appellate courts.   The former are the courts where the trial is first held (courts of the first instance).   It is here where the parties appear, witnesses testify, and the evidence is presented.   The trial court usually determines any questions of fact that may be in dispute and then applies the applicable rules of law.

Once the trial court reaches its decision, the losing party has a right of appeal to an appellate court.   Generally, the appellate court can only decide questions of law and its decision in each case is based on the record made below.   Appellate courts do not receive new testimony or decide questions of fact and in most jurisdictions only the appellate courts issue written opinions.   Each state has a final court of appeal (usually called the Supreme Court) and some states have intermediate courts of appeal.   [see Illustration 1]

3.   Methods of Court Reporting

When a case has been appealed to an appellate court, both parties submit written briefs which contain a summary of the facts and arguments on the points of law involved, and the court may hear oral arguments by the attorneys.   The court then writes an opinion in which it states the reasons for its decision.   Technically speaking, the decision of a court only indicates the action of the court and is indicated by the words *Affirmed,* or *Reversed,* or *Remanded,* or similar words and phrases.   The reasons for this action are then stated in the opinion of the court.   However, in actual practice, the use of *opinion* and *decision* has become interchangeable and the word *decision* herein will be used to describe both.[4]

---

[3] Holmes, *The Path of the Law*, in COLLECTED LEGAL PAPERS 167, 169 (1975).

[4] For a discussion of the difference between "decision of the court" and "opinion of the court", *see* Rogers v. Hill, 289 U.S. 582, 587 (1933).

SECTION B. THE ELEMENTS OF COURT DECISIONS

The elements of an American court decision are as follows:

1. Name or Title of the Case

Cases generally are identified by the names of the parties to a lawsuit:

Payne v. *Green*—in table of cases as *Payne* v. *Green.*

In re Payne—in table of cases as *Payne, In re.* Judicial proceedings in which there are no adversary parties. Such designations usually denote a bankruptcy case, a probate case, a guardianship matter, a contempt case, a disbarment, or a habeas corpus case.

Ex parte Payne—in tables of cases as *Payne, Ex parte*—This is a special proceeding.

State on the relation of Payne v. *Green*—in tables of cases as *State ex rel. Payne* v. *Green.* These cases involve the extraordinary legal remedies, viz.: Mandamus, prohibition, certiorari, quo warranto, or habeas corpus.

State v. *Payne*—in tables of cases as *State* v. *Payne.* Suit by the state in its collective capacity as the party wronged by a criminal deed. In some sets the criminal cases are arranged in alphabetical order under the names of the respective states. "People" or "Commonwealth" are used in some states instead of "State."

In maritime law, a suit may be brought against the ship, e. g., The Caledonia.

Cases involving the seizure of commodities are brought in their names, e. g., *United States* v. *45 Barrels of Whisky.*

Usually, the plaintiff-defendant names remain in that order when cases are appealed by a defendant; however, in some states, they are reversed and the defendant on appeal becomes the plaintiff in error.

2. Docket Number

A docket number is the numerical designation assigned to each case by a court. It is the means of identifying the case as the suit progresses. Also, it is a convenient method for filing briefs in cases in libraries.

3. Date of Decision

This is the date on which the decision was rendered, and generally it appears after the docket number in the reported case.

4. Prefatory Statement

The prefatory statement explains the nature of the case, its disposition in the lower court, the name of the lower court and some-

times its judge, and the disposition of the case in the appellate court as being affirmed or reversed.

5. Syllabus or Headnote

In most court reports, the headnotes or syllabi, which are brief summaries of the legal rules or significant facts in a case, are drafted by the editors; however, in some jurisdictions, they are prepared by the judges who rendered the decisions. In the latter cases, the syllabi of the judges are printed in the official reports and reprinted in the unofficial publications which reprint the decisions. The syllabi are intended merely as indexes to the points of law in the opinions and that is equally true where the judges write them. It has been held, in the latter instances, that, when the syllabus conflicts with the opinion, the latter shall control. The United States Supreme Court has stated, "We look to the opinion for the original and authentic statement of the grounds of decision." [5] In view of this, the headnotes should be used merely as indexes to the law stated in the opinions of the cases and not as the law itself.[6]

To the extent that the syllabus culls the rule of law from the opinion, it is useful. Unfortunately, too often its use has been extended to give to the common law an unrealistic measure of certitude. This, in part, is an attempt to "bring certainty and order out of the wilderness of precedent." [7]

Admittedly, there is great value to certainty in a legal system. This principle applies with equal vigor to American law and is underscored by the demands of our legal practice. The practicing lawyer is frequently called upon to act as a forecaster of the law. Mr. Justice Holmes took special notice of this when he observed that the lawyer often prophesies as to the future decisions of courts on specific sets of facts. But, as the legal realists have convincingly demonstrated, the stating of legal rules alone is inconclusive of the judicial results. Judge Jerome Frank has elaborated at length upon this

---

[5] Burbank v. Ernst, 232 U.S. 162, 165 (1914).

[6] The Ohio Supreme Court has gone farther than most courts in that it gives to the syllabus a special status in relation to the law. Rule VI of the Court has been interpreted to mean that the syllabus and not the opinion is the law of the case. State ex rel. Donahey v. Edmondson, 89 Ohio St. 93, 105 N.E. 269 (1913). However, this ruling has been broadened by the Ohio Supreme Court to mean that the syllabus must be read in the light of the facts of the specific case, thus demonstrating an awareness as to the importance of the facts in controversies. In re Poage, 87 Ohio St. 72, 100 N.E. 125 (1912).

See Fenneberg, *The Rule of the Syllabus in Ohio*, 31 OHIO BAR 1105 (1958).

[7] B. CARDOZO, THE GROWTH OF THE LAW 1 (1924); B. CARDOZO, SELECTED WRITINGS OF BENJAMIN NATHAN CARDOZO 186 (M. Hall ed. 1947). Mr. Justice Cardozo used the phrase here in relation to the need of some restatement of the common law.

point, contending that the failure of the legal rules to perform their principal function—to guide and predict the decisions of the courts— is due primarily to the uncertainty as to which facts were applied to the rules by the judges in reaching their decisions.   Since the inclusion or exclusion of certain facts materially affects the results in a case, the mere exposition of the applicable rule is inconclusive.   This proposition can be stated another way: the operative facts may influence the judicial result in favor of one party or the other, so the stating of a rule of law alone is indeterminative of the judicial findings in specific cases.   This point was forcefully made by Holmes when he said, "General propositions do not decide concrete cases," [8] for a judge could admit any general rule that anyone might lay down and decide the case either way.[9]

Obviously, therefore, the use of the syllabus should be restricted merely to its identifying and indexing functions.

The number of headnotes to a case is determined by the variety of legal propositions and factual statements it embodies, each of which is individually digested.

6.   Names of Counsel
The names of counsel for both parties to a suit precede the opinion of the court.

7.   Synopsis of Briefs of Counsel
In the early period of reporting American cases, summaries of the briefs of counsel were given with almost all cases reported.   This aided researchers in locating cases in point and revealed the theories of law followed by counsel in support of their arguments.   With the increased volume of cases and the introduction of secondary aids, e. g., encyclopedias, digests, citators, annotated reports and text books, this practice has diminished.   However, some reports continue to provide abridged statements of the briefs of counsel, e. g., *United States Supreme Court Reports* (Lawyers' Edition), *New York Court of Appeals Reports*, etc.

8.   Statement of Facts
A statement of the facts in the case usually follows the briefs of counsel.

9.   Opinion of the Court
Although, as previously mentioned, a few trial court decisions are reported, most court opinions that are published are those of appel-

---

[8] Lochner v. N. Y., 198 U.S. 45, 76 (1905).

[9] 1 HOLMES–LASKI LETTERS 390 (M. Howe ed. 1953).

late courts. Every appellate court has at least three judges and in some jurisdictions the courts may have five, seven, or nine judges. The opinion of the court is the explanation of the court's decision, the latter being the conclusion or result in a controversy. The opinion is written by one member of the court after the majority has agreed to a decision. A member of the majority, while agreeing with a decision, may disagree with its reasoning; he then may write a concurring opinion which gives his reasons for the decision. The views of the minority generally are expressed by a dissenting opinion which is written by one of the dissenting judges. An opinion, in accord with the dissent, may be written by a dissenting judge when he agrees with the conclusions and result of the dissent but disagrees with its reasoning. Or several dissenting opinions may be rendered independently by the judges, each expressing different views. A *per curiam* opinion is an opinion of the whole court as distinguished from an opinion written by a specific judge. It may present a lengthy or a brief discussion of the issues in the case, e. g., New York Court of Appeals. In some courts, it may only give the conclusion without any reasoning, e. g., United States Supreme Court. A memorandum opinion is a brief holding of the whole court in which the opinion is limited or omitted.

Dissenting opinions are not the law in a case; nor are they binding as precedent. They assume the characteristics of *dicta* and serve merely as secondary authority. However, not infrequently the controlling opinion may later be overruled and the dissenting opinion is then accepted as the correct statement of the law.[10]

There are two additional elements of a case which merit brief attention. The first is the *ratio decidendi*, or the point in a case which determines the result. In other words, it is the basis of the decision, explicitly or implicitly, stated in the opinion. The second is *obiter dictum*. The latter is a collateral statement contained in the opinion which does not relate directly to the issues raised in the case. *Dictum*, therefore, is an official, incidental comment, not necessary to the formulation of the decision, made by the judge in his opinion which is not binding as precedent.

10. Decision, with Judgment or Decree

This refers to the actual disposition of the case by the court. Thus, a decision is noted by such terms as "affirmed," "reversed,"

---

[10] *E. g.*, in FTC v. R. F. Keppel & Bro., Inc., 291 U.S. 304 (1934), the United States Supreme Court adopted the dissenting opinion of Mr. Justice Brandeis in FTC v. Gratz, 253 U.S. 421, 429 (1920) as to the broad powers of FTC to declare trade practices unfair under Section 5 of the Federal Trade Commission Act. In FTC v. Brown Shoe Co., 384 U.S. 316 (1966), Mr. Justice Black, speaking for an undivided Supreme Court, again rejected the Gratz case as a precedent, indicating that the case had been decided shortly after the FTC Act was passed and that the view of the Court is now in line with Brandeis' dissent in Gratz.

volumes and advance sheets are consecutively numbered.   E. g., Federal Reporter and Federal Reporter, Second Series.

1.   Jurisdictional Reports

The decisions of a specific court or several courts within a system may be published in a set of volumes and kept current by advance sheets and new bound volumes.

Examples:

United States Supreme Court Reports

Minnesota Reports (reports cases of the Minnesota Supreme Court)

California Appellate Reports (reports cases of the District Courts of Appeal of California)

2.   Geographical Reports

Cases covering several courts of a state may be published in a reporter.

Examples:

New York Miscellaneous Reports

Ohio Opinions

Also, the decisions of small numbers of states, divided into geographical regions, are grouped together and published as units.   This grouping is called the National Reporter System.

Examples:

North Western Reporter (includes cases from Iowa, Michigan, Minnesota, Nebraska, North Dakota, South Dakota and Wisconsin)

South Western Reporter (includes cases from Arkansas, Kentucky, Missouri, Tennessee and Texas)

3.   Subject Reports

Another category of reports is that of subject reports, which are collections of decisions on specific legal subjects such as taxation, labor law and criminal law.   Since the standard sets of court reports include cases on all subjects, these special reports have found a ready market in lawyers who specialize in a particular area of the law.   For the most part, cases in these reports are reprints but some are not reported in the jurisdictional or geographical reports.

This feature has also been adopted by a number of the loose-leaf services.   A few examples of current special reports are:

a.   Commerce Clearing House, Trade Regulation Reporter (Trade Cases).

b.   Negligence and Compensation Cases, Annotated.

c.   Prentice-Hall, Tax Court Memorandum Decisions.

d.   Public Utilities Reports.

e.   U. S. Patents Quarterly.

SECTION F.   ILLUSTRATIONS

1.   **Court Organization Chart**

2.   **Statutory Provisions for the Publication of Court Decisions**

3.   **A Typical Case as Reported in an Official Set of Court Reports**

4.   **The Same Case as Reported in an Unofficial Set of Court Reports**

[Illustration 1]

COURT ORGANIZATION CHART

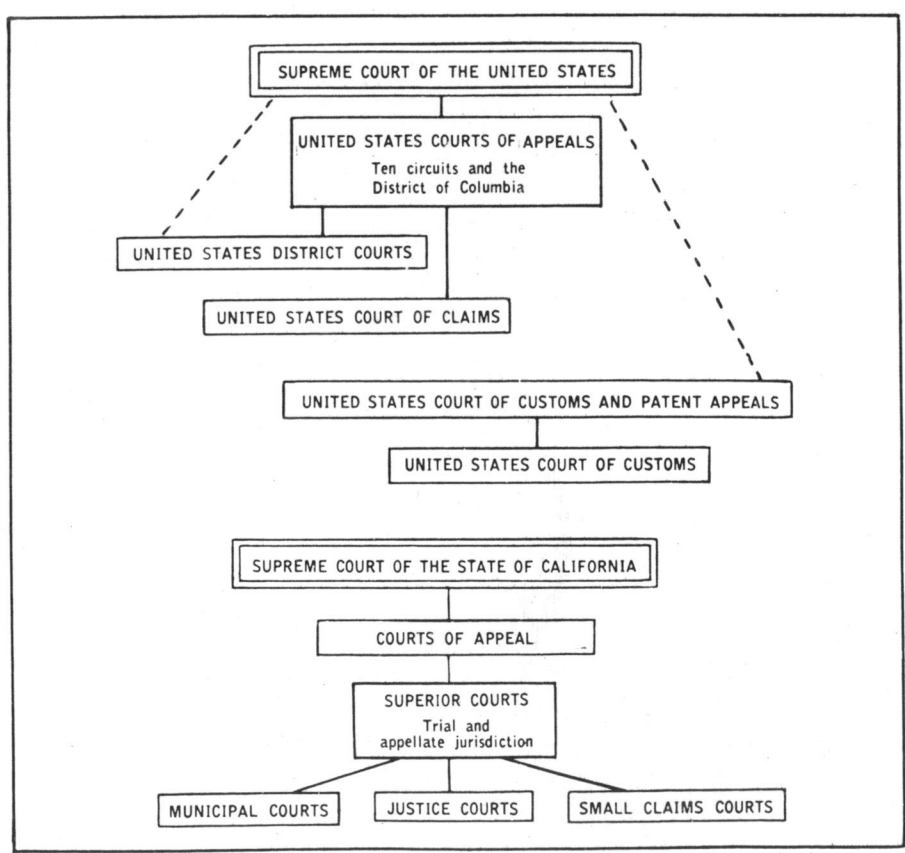

[Illustration 2]

TYPICAL STATUTORY PROVISIONS FOR PUBLICATION OF COURT REPORTS

Excerpt from West's Ann.Calif. Gov't Code

§ 68902. Publication of reports: Supervision by Supreme Court.

Such opinions of the Supreme Court, of the courts of appeal, and of the appellate departments of the superior courts as the Supreme Court may deem expedient shall be published in the official reports. The reports shall be published under the general supervision of the Supreme Court.

Excerpts from McKinney Consol.Laws of N.Y. Judiciary Law

§ 430. Law reporting bureau; state reporter

There is hereby created and established the law reporting bureau of the state of New York. The bureau shall be under the direction and control of a state reporter, who shall be appointed and be removable by the court of appeals by an order entered in its minutes. The state reporter shall be assisted by a first deputy state reporter and such other deputy state reporters and such staff as may be necessary, all of whom shall be appointed and be removable by the court of appeals.

§ 431. Causes to be reported

The law reporting bureau shall report every cause determined in the court of appeals and every cause determined in the appellate divisions of the supreme court, unless otherwise directed by the court deciding the cause; and, in addition, any cause determined in any other court which the state reporter, with the approval of the court of appeals, considers worthy of being reported because of its usefulness as a precedent or its importance as a matter of public interest.

Each reported decision shall be published as soon as practicable after it is rendered. Added L.1938, c. 494, § 1, eff. July 1, 1938.

Excerpt from Vernon's Ann.Mo.Stat.

§ 477.231. Designation of private publication as official reports

The supreme court may declare the published volumes of the decisions of the supreme court as the same are published by any person, firm or corporation, to be official reports of the decisions of the supreme court, and the courts of appeals may jointly make a similar declaration with respect to published volumes of the opinions of the courts of appeals. Any publication so designated as the official reports may include both the opinions of the supreme court and the courts of appeals in the same volume.

[Illustration 3]

A TYPICAL CASE AS REPORTED IN AN OFFICIAL SET OF COURT REPORTS

(68 Wis.2d 487, 1974)

8]   AUGUST TERM, 1974.   487

Calero v. Del Chemical Corp. 68 Wis. 2d 487.

Published opinions to the Wisconsin Supreme Court are printed in the official Wisconsin Reports. The headnotes or syllabi are prepared from the written opinions.

CALERO, Respondent, v. DEL CHEMICAL CORPORATION and another, Appellants.*

No. 463. Argued March 6, 1975.—Decided May 8, 1975.
(Also reported in 228 N. W. 2d 737.)

1. **Appeal—Alleged erroneous instructions—Failure to specifically raise on postverdict motion—Waiver.**
    In a libel and slander action by an ex-employee against his former employer arising from communications to prospective employers, defendants' allegations of errors in instructions were waived where postverdict motions asserted only the most general grounds for a new trial, because trial court error is not reviewable as a matter of right on appeal unless a motion for new trial specifying the alleged error with particularity has been made, so as to provide the court with an opportunity to correct the error and avoid an appeal. pp. 497, 498.

2. **Defamation—Communications between ex-employee and prospective employer—Conditional privilege—Plaintiff's burden of proof.**
    The social utility of encouraging a free flow of information between ex-employers and prospective employers as to the qualifications of employees requires that such communication be conditionally privileged, and an employee in a defamation action must overcome the privilege by proving by the greater weight of the evidence that the inter-employer communication was motivated by express malice. pp. 498, 499.

3. **Defamation—Malice—Difference between express malice and actual malice.**
    In a defamation action express or common-law malice is ill will, envy, spite, revenge or other bad or corrupt motive which actuates the defamatory communication and which must be

---

* Motion for rehearing denied, with costs, on July 8, 1975.

[Illustration 3–a]

SAMPLE PAGE FROM 68 Wis.2d 487, 1974

8] AUGUST TERM, 1974. 489

Calero v. Del Chemical Corp. 68 Wis. 2d 487.

APPEAL from a judgment and an order of the circuit court for Milwaukee county: ANDREW W. PARNELL, Reserve Circuit Judge, Presiding. *Affirmed.*

For the appellants there were briefs and oral argument by *Joseph P. Balistrieri* of Milwaukee.

For the respondent there was a brief and oral argument by *Jack L. Goodsitt* of Milwaukee.

DAY, J.   This is an appeal from a judgment of the trial court, following a jury trial, awarding damages to Mr. Mario Calero (plaintiff-respondent) against Robert C. Bagemihl (defendant-appellant) and his employer Del Chemical Corporation (Del Chemical—defendant-appellant). Mr. Bagemihl was found by the jury to have communicated defamatory oral or written statements about the plaintiff to prospective employers of the plaintiff. A judgment was entered for damages. The defendants also appeal from the decision and order denying the defendants' post-trial motions. The issues raised are discussed in this opinion.

At the time the case was tried the plaintiff was a married, fifty-year-old, college-trained public accountant, who was then living and working in Arizona. In November of 1964, the plaintiff, who had previously been employed as an accountant for various companies, applied

> The name of the judge writing the opinion is always given. All matter preceding this is editorial and not part of the opinion. It usually consists of (1) headnotes (2) summary of facts and judgment of court (indication, when appropriate, of concurring or dissenting opinion) (3) names of attorneys.

plaintiff designed and prepared an index file of purchasing records to guide him in his negotiations with suppliers. These were put on 11 by 8½ inch cards and contained pertinent information relating to the purchase of raw materials for the corporation. The plaintiff initiated this system and by the fall of 1967 there were approxi-

[Illustration 4]

A TYPICAL CASE AS REPORTED IN A SET OF UNOFFICIAL REPORTS
(228 N.W.2d 737, 1974)

CALERO v. DEL CHEMICAL CORP.   Wis.   **737**

Cite as 228 N.W.2d 737

of the sisters that a legal action commenced by their brother Chester had several stages and one appeal to pass through before the proper allocation of post-dissolution profits could be considered. We therefore find the defense of laches to be without merit.

Judgment reversed, and cause remanded for further proceedings not inconsistent with the opinion.

Mario CALERO, Respondent,

v.

DEL CHEMICAL CORPORATION and Robert C. Bagemihl, Appellants.

No. 463.

Supreme Court of Wisconsin.

May 8, 1975.

Former employee brought defamation action against ex-employer and one of the employer's representatives. The Circuit Court, Milwaukee County, Andrew W. Parnell, Presiding Judge of Outagamie County, rendered judgment for plaintiff for compensatory and punitive damages, and defendants appealed from judgment and order denying posttrial motions. The Supreme Court, Day, J., held that defendants waived claim errors in instructions by failure to state them in motions for a new trial with sufficient particularity, that defendants' communications to prospective employers, in response to the latters' inquiry as to plaintiff's job history, were entitled to a nonconstitutional qualified or conditional privilege, that to recover plaintiff was required to establish express malice by the greater weight of the evidence, that to recover punitive damages plaintiff was required to show express malice by a preponderance of the evidence, that evidence was

sufficient to support verdict, and that awards were not excessive.

Judgment and order affirmed.

1. Appeal and Error ⟨key⟩302(4)

Claimed errors in instructions, in defamation action, as to quantum of proof required to find express malice was waived for failure to state them in motions for a new trial with sufficient particularity to bring them to the attention of the trial judge.

2. Appeal and Error ⟨key⟩281(1)

No error of the trial court is reviewable as a matter of right on appeal without first moving for a new trial based on such error.

3. Appeal and Error ⟨key⟩302(4)

Assertion, in new trial motion, that verdict was contrary to law was insufficient to apprise trial court of particular errors alleged in instructions, i. e., quantum of proof required to find express malice, and was insufficient to preserve such claim of error for appellate review.

4. Libel and Slander ⟨key⟩44(3), 101(4)

Allegedly defamatory communications by plaintiff's former employer to prospective employers, in response to the latter's inquiry as to plaintiff's job history, were entitled to a qualified or conditional privilege; to recover in defamation, plaintiff was required to show express malice.

5. Libel and Slander ⟨key⟩44(3)

Communications between an ex-employer and prospective employer concerning a job applicant's work history are cloaked with a qualified or a conditional privilege; such privilege is based on the social utility in encouraging the free flow of information between such parties; however, the privilege is not absolute but is only conditional.

6. Libel and Slander ⟨key⟩51(1)

"Actual malice" in defamation cases refers to a constitutional standard that is

[Illustration 4–a]
SAMPLE PAGE FROM 228 N.W.2d 737, 1974

CALERO v. DEL CHEMICAL CORP.   Wis.   **739**
Cite as 228 N.W.2d 737

18. Libel and Slander ⟶112(2)

Evidence, including evidence that charges that plaintiff was going to start a competing business, hire away fellow employees and was helping himself to confidential corporate records were untrue and that employer's representative relied only on office hearsay in firing plaintiff and made no attempt to verify or investigate the charges, supported jury verdict against representative and employer in defamation action.

19. Appeal and Error ⟶1004.3

When there is any credible evidence which under any reasonable view supports the jury finding, especially when the verdict has the approval of the trial court, it should not be disturbed on appeal on ground of excessiveness.

20. Appeal and Error ⟶932(1)

In determining on appeal whether per-

made $5,600 and who unsuccessfully applied for many jobs in the $12,000 range, was not excessive.

24. Libel and Slander ⟶121(2)

Award of $9,000 punitive damages to former employee, who was defamed by ex-employer and who recovered $10,000 compensatory damages, was not excessive.

25. Damages ⟶87(1)

Purpose of punitive damages is to punish the wrongdoer for his malice and to deter others from like conduct.

Joseph P. Balistrieri, Milwaukee, for appellants.

Jack L. Goodsitt, Milwaukee, for respondent.

DAY, Justice.

This is an appeal from a judgment of the trial court, following a jury trial, awarding damages to Mr. Mario Calero (plaintiff-respondent) against Robert C. Bagemihl (defendant-appellant) and his employer Del Chemical Corporation [Del Chemical] (defendant-appellant). Mr. Bagemihl was found by the jury to have communicated defamatory oral or written statements about the plaintiff to prospective employers of the plaintiff. A judgment was entered for damages. The defendants also appeal from the decision and order denying the defendants' post-trial motions. The issues raised are discussed in this opinion.

At the time the case was tried the plaintiff was a married, 50-year-old, college-trained public accountant, who was then living and working in Arizona. In November of 1964, the plaintiff, who had previously been employed as an accountant for various companies, applied for a position with Del Chemical and was interviewed and hired by Mr. Bagemihl. Plaintiff began work on November 16, 1964, as a general accountant and assistant to Mr. Bagemihl at $135 a week. From November 16, 1964,

> **This is the same case as shown in illus. 3 as it appears in the North Western Reporter, an unofficial set of court reports. The headnotes are prepared by the publisher's editorial staff. Note how they differ from the headnotes for this case in the Wisconsin Reports (illus. 3).**
>
> **Although the material preceding the Opinion of the Court varies in the unofficial reports from the official reports, the text of the opinion is exactly the same.**
>
> **The difference between the official and unofficial reports and other features of court reports will be discussed in Chs. 4, 5, and 6.**

SECTION G. ABBREVIATIONS AND CITATIONS OF COURT REPORTS

1. Abbreviations

The first American decisions were reported by private reporters. The first American report published was Kirby's Connecticut Reports in 1789. Harris and McHenry's Maryland Reports contains the first American reported decision, dated 1658.

The early English and American reports were cited by the names of the reporters, such as Bunbury (English) and Cranch (American). The current policy is to cite reports by reference to the name of the set and not to the name of the reporter who edited the publication.

In judicial opinions, briefs, treatises and other legal publications the names of reporters and the reports are abbreviated in the citations. E. g., "Rich." for Richardson's Equity (S.C.); "Nev." for Nevada. A Table of Abbreviations, with references to the full names of reporters and reports, is given in Appendix B, below.

2. Methods of Citation

The objective of citations is to facilitate research through ready recourse to publications. The importance of accuracy, consistency and clarity in the citation of legal sources has increased with the steady flow of materials and the pressing need for brevity. From these demands certain standard forms and practices have evolved in citing legal publications.

The essence of legal citation is embodied in logical brevity and clear abbreviation. It avoids the brevity which confuses or misinforms and the minutia which embellishes and protracts.

Good form in a legal document is important not only for its communicative value but also for the favorable impression it creates in the mind of the reader, whether he be a judge, a lawyer or a teacher. As in other professions, the quality of the workmanship of an attorney inures to his reputation and influences eventual success or failure. It behooves the young lawyer, therefore, to form work-habits early in his career, as manifested in his legal writing, which will redound to his credit and help to enhance his reputation.

A guide to citation form for court reports may be found in Appendix A, at (I), (A), (3).

SECTION H. SUMMARY

To facilitate learning the essential features of the significant publications described in the chapters, a summary of them is provided

towards the end of the various chapters. The summaries are generally arranged with the following categories in mind: (1) scope—indicating coverage by subject matter and chronology, if any; (2) arrangement—for example, alphabetically by subject, by names or titles, or by chronology (following a time sequence); (3) index; and (4) supplementation.

1. Elements of a Court Decision

    a.   Name of the case.

    b.   Docket number.

    c.   Date of decision.

    d.   Synopsis, or Summary, of case.

    e.   Syllabus or headnote—brief summary of the legal rule or significant facts in a case.

    f.   Names of counsel.

    g.   Synopsis of briefs of counsel.

    h.   Statement of facts.

    i.   Opinion of the court—explanation of the court's decision.

Concurring opinion—opinion of a judge which agrees with the decision of the majority but disagrees with the reasoning.

Dissenting opinion—expressed disagreement of one or more judges of a court with the decision reached by the majority in a case before them.

Per curiam opinion—opinion of the whole court as distinguished from an opinion written by a specific judge.

Memorandum opinion—is a brief holding of the whole court in which the opinion (explanation) is very concise or totally absent.

Ratio decidendi—the point in a case which determines the result.

Obiter dictum—official, incidental comment, not necessary to the formulation of the decision, made by the judge in his opinion which is not binding as precedent.

    j.   Decision of the court—disposition of the case by the court.

2. Official and Unofficial Reports

    a.   Official reports—court reports directed by statute.

    b.   Unofficial reports—court reports published without statutory direction.

3. Elements of Judicial Reporting

    a.   "Slip" opinion—is an individual court decision published separately soon after it is rendered.

b.   Advance sheets—contain the decisions of a court or the courts of several jurisdictions decided just prior to publication and are in pamphlet format.

c.   Order of release of cases is determined by their decision dates and not by a logical arrangement, such as subject.

d.   A bound volume includes:

(1) Table of cases contained in the volume.

(2) Table of statutes interpreted by the decisions reported.

(3) Opinions (comprising of cases from preceding advance sheets)—written, *per curiam* or memorandum.

(4) Subject index or digest of the cases reported.

(5) Judicial definitions of words and phrases used in the cases reported.

(6) Court rules.

(7) Unofficial reports generally contain cross reference tables to the official reports.

4.   Organization of Court Reports

a.   Jurisdictional reports—decisions of a specific court or several courts within a system.

b.   Geographical reports:

(1) Cases from several courts of a state.

(2) Regional reporters.

c.   Subject reports—collections of cases on a specific subject.

Chapter 4

FEDERAL COURT DECISIONS

For present purposes, the federal court system can be described as consisting of three main divisions: The Supreme Court of the United States (the highest court), the Courts of Appeals (intermediate appellate courts), and the district courts (courts of original jurisdiction.)[1]

All written opinions of the Supreme Court of the United States are published in the official and unofficial reports. Most *per curiam* decisions also are reported. All written opinions designated "For publication" by the Courts of Appeals are unofficially published. Memorandum opinions are not published. As for the district court decisions, only selected opinions of those courts are unofficially reported. Typewritten unreported cases of the district courts generally are available through the court clerks.

SECTION A. UNITED STATES SUPREME COURT REPORTS

The decisions of the United States Supreme Court are published in five current reports:

1. United States Reports (official edition), cited "U. S."

2. United States Supreme Court Reports (Lawyers Cooperative Pub. Co.), cited "L.Ed." and "L.Ed.2d".

3. Supreme Court Reporter (West Publishing Co.), cited "Sup.Ct." or "S.Ct."

4. United States Law Week (Bureau of National Affairs), cited "U.S.L.W." or "U.S.L. Week."

5. Commerce Clearing House, United States Supreme Court Bulletin.

1. United States Reports (Official Ed.)

Prior to 1817, the United States Reports were published by private reporters. Since that date they have been published by official reporters. The reports were cited by the name of the reporters from

---

[1] For a more detailed description of the federal court system, *see* U. S. CONGRESS, HOUSE COMM. ON THE JUDICIARY, 92d CONG., 1st SESS., THE UNITED STATES COURTS: THEIR JURISDICTION AND WORK, by J. Spaniol. (Comm. Print, 1975).

Dallas through Wallace. The seven early reporters, with their abbreviations, are as follows:

Dallas (Dall.)	4 v.	v. 1– 4 U.S.	(1789–1800)
Cranch (Cranch)	9 v.	v. 5–13 U.S.	(1801–1815)
Wheaton (Wheat.)	12 v.	v. 14–25 U.S.	(1816–1827)
Peters (Peters)	16 v.	v. 26–41 U.S.	(1828–1842)
Howard (How.)	24 v.	v. 42–65 U.S.	(1843–1860)
Black (Black)	2 v.	v. 66–67 U.S.	(1861–1862)
Wallace (Wall.)	23 v.	v. 68–90 U.S.	(1863–1874)

The first ninety volumes, from Dallas through Wallace, were later numbered consecutively and beginning with volume 91 (1875) this method of numbering was adopted. 1 Dallas, although a volume of the U. S. Reports, contains only Pennsylvania decisions. The other volumes of Dallas contain U. S. Supreme Court and Pennsylvania decisions.[2]

It is the custom of the Supreme Court of the United States to have one term of court each year. The term starts in October and ordinarily adjourns in June. This is known as the October Term. The opinions of the Supreme Court are printed and sold by the United States Government Printing Office. They are initially issued separately as "slip" opinions and then subsequently published in advance sheets (called preliminary prints). The Reporter of Decisions of the Supreme Court prepares a summary of facts, syllabi and an index. After the end of the October Term each year, the advance sheets are replaced by bound volumes. There are usually three or four volumes per term.

Sample pages of an opinion are shown in Illustrations 5.

2.   United States Supreme Court Reports (Lawyers' Edition)

This set of the reports of the Supreme Court of the United States is privately published by the Lawyers Co-Operative Publishing Co. and the Bancroft-Whitney Co. It is presently in two series. The first series contains all of the opinions that appear in 1 U.S. through 349 U.S. The second series commences with 350 U.S. As this set uses smaller type than in the official reports, the opinions for each term are in fewer volumes. For example, the 1972 term required five volumes for the *United States Reports*, but only four for the *Lawyers' Edition*. The opinions in it are exactly the same as the opinions that appear in the official edition. The difference lies in the editorial treatment given to the opinions by the publishers who prepare their own

---

[2] Keeffe, *More Than You Want to Know About Supreme Courts Reports*, 62 A.B. A.J. 1057 (1976).

summary of cases and headnotes which precede the opinions. Additionally, an appendix to each volume contains, for selected important cases only, summaries of attorneys' briefs submitted to the Court and annotations written by the editorial staff of the publishers. Annotations are articles or essays on significant legal issues discussed in the reported cases. These are very useful in gaining an understanding of the impact and meaning of the decisions. Annotations will be discussed in more detail in Chapter Seven. A separate volume indexes the annotations through Volume 31 of the *Lawyers' Edition*, Second Series (1972). Starting with Volume 32 of the Second Series, each volume is provided with pocket supplementation in the back of the volume. Each year a cumulative supplement brings up to date the annotations in the volume.

Current decisions for each term of court are issued bi-weekly in advance sheets while the court is in session. Each advance sheet contains a cumulative table of cases. After the Court adjourns, bound volumes are issued replacing the advance sheets. Sample pages from the *Lawyers' Edition* are shown in Illustration Seven.

3. Supreme Court Reporter (West Edition)

This set is published by the West Publishing Co. and contains many of the editorial features common to their other sets of law reports. These will be discussed in detail in Chapter Five. This edition begins with volume 106 (1882) of the official set; therefore, it does not contain the cases reported in volumes 1–105 of the official reports. The full text of the opinions are reported with the publisher adding its own editorial features and headnotes. Decisions are first issued in advance sheets bi-weekly during the term of Court and after the adjournment of the Court, the advance sheets are replaced by two or more bound volumes containing all of the decisions of the Term. Sample pages from the *Supreme Court Reporter* are shown in Illustration Six.

4. Other Publications

As the decisions of the Supreme Court of the United States become the "law of the land" and must be followed as precedent by all other American courts, both Federal and state, it is rather obvious that lawyers as well as lay persons have a need for immediate access to the current decisions of the Supreme Court of the United States. Before opinions can be published in the advance sheets of the sets mentioned above, they must receive editorial treatment of preparing the summary and the headnotes resulting in a delay of several weeks from the date a decision is rendered and its appearance in advance sheets.

More rapid receipt of current U. S. Supreme Court decisions may be located in one of the two following publications. Each receives

the slip decisions on the day they are handed down, photocopies them, and mails them immediately to its subscribers. These sets of Supreme Court opinions do not have any editorial features added to them, but they do allow opinions to become available within a day or two after they have been released by the Supreme Court.

a. United States Law Week. This is published in two or more volumes by the Bureau of National Affairs, Inc. in Washington, D. C. Volume One contains the Supreme Court of the United States opinions in complete text and is in loose-leaf form. In addition to the current opinions, this volume contains the following features:

(1) Summary of Orders: This is a summary of cases finally acted upon as well as the lower court holdings that the Supreme Court consented to review with the questions present for review.

(2) Journal of Proceedings: This contains the minutes of all sessions of the court held during the week.

(3) Cases Docketed: This includes citations to opinions in the lower court, and the general subject matter of the case.

(4) Summary of Cases Recently Filed.

(5) Arguments Before the Court: A summary of the oral arguments of the more important cases argued each week.

(6) Cumulative Index and Table of Cases Pending Before the Court.

(7) Volume Two deals with other matters not connected with the Supreme Court of the United States and will be discussed in Chapter Five.

b. Commerce Clearing House Supreme Court Bulletin. This set is also in loose-leaf format. In addition to photocopies of the current opinions, it includes an index to opinions, an index to docket numbers and a status table of cases pending before the court.

5. Chamber Opinions of Supreme Court Justices

Each Supreme Court Justice is assigned at the beginning of each term the supervision of one or more federal judicial circuits. Frequently, when the Supreme Court is not in session, a petition may be directed to a Justice in his capacity as Circuit Justice. When an opinion is written on this, it is known as a "Chamber Opinion." Before the 1970 Term, these chamber opinions appeared only in *Lawyers'*

Edition and the *Supreme Court Reporter*. Starting with the 1970 Term, they also appear in the official *United States Reports*.[3]

6. Summary of United States Supreme Court Reports

The opinions of the Supreme Court of the United States are published in three sets: the official *United States Reports*, the *United States Supreme Court Reports, Lawyers' Edition*, and the *Supreme Court Reporter*. Each set first publishes the opinions in advance sheets. As proper citation practice calls for only citing to *United States Reports*, the two unofficial sets which have their own distinct pagination also show the pagination to the official reports so that the proper citation can be made to the *United States Reports*. This is sometimes denoted as "star-pagination." See Illustration 7–c. Both the *Lawyers' Edition* and the *Supreme Court Reporter* have in each volume a cross reference table listing the cases in the *United States Reports* and showing where they are reported in their volumes.

As the United States Government Printing Office is much slower in publishing their advance sheets, and as the two unofficial sets have editorial features facilitating their use, most lawyers and researchers prefer using them to the *United States Reports*.

United States Law Week and the *Commerce Clearing House Supreme Court Bulletin* are most useful for use during the current term of the Court. For older decisions it is preferable to use one of the three other sets.

SECTION B. LOWER FEDERAL COURT REPORTS

Although the Supreme Court of the United States is the highest court in the country, it actively deals with a small fraction of the total litigation within the Federal court system. With certain exceptions, the Supreme Court selects only the cases it wishes to hear on appeal [4] and they are relatively few in number. The bulk of the work of the Federal courts occurs in its trial courts—the Federal District Courts and in the appeals from them to the United States Courts of Appeals. These are divided geographically into 11 circuits.

In addition to the above-discussed courts, there exist federal courts with limited or specialized jurisdiction. The more important

---

[3] R. STERN AND E. GRESSMAN, SUPREME COURT PRACTICE 537–538 (4th ed. 1969); Wiener, *Opinions of Justices Sitting in Chambers*, 49 LAW LIB.J. 2 (1956); Boner, *Index to Chambers Opinions of Supreme Court Justices*, 65 LAW LIB.J. 213 (1972).

[4] Technically, cases reach the Supreme Court either by Writ of Certiorari or by Appeal. *See* R. STERN AND E. GRESSMAN, *id.* at Sec. 2.1 and 2.6.

ones are the Court of Claims, the Court of Customs and Patent Appeals, and the Tax Court.[5]

1. Privately Published Editions of Lower Federal Court Reports

a. Federal Cases. Prior to 1880, the decisions of the district courts and the circuit courts of appeals were published in many different sets of law reports. In 1880, the West Publishing Company reprinted all of the previously reported lower federal court decisions in one set of 31 volumes called *Federal Cases*. This set contains 18,-000 cases reported between 1789 and 1879. Unlike most sets of court reports where the cases are arranged chronologically, the decisions in this set are arranged alphabetically by name of case and are numbered consecutively. Volume 31 is the Digest volume, and includes Blue Tables which cross reference from the citations of the original volumes of reports to *Federal Cases*.

b. Federal Reporter. This set is published by the West Publishing Company and started in 1880. Until 1932 it included opinions from the Courts of Appeals and the Federal District Courts. The *Federal Reporter* consists of two series. The First Series stopped with Volume 300 and the Second Series started numbering anew from Volume 1. This scheme of starting a new series for the numbering of court reports is a common one as it serves to avoid long and unmanageable numbers.

Until recently, nearly all written opinions of the Courts of Appeals were published in the *Federal Reporter*. The increasing caseload placed on the Courts, however, has caused reconsideration of this practice[6] and eleven circuits have now adopted rules restricting the number of published opinions.[7]

Since Volume 34 of the Second Series (1929), the *Federal Reporter* includes the reports of the United States Court of Customs and Patent Appeals and in Volume 276 it began to include the decisions of the United States Court of Claims.

c. Federal Supplement. This set started publication in 1933 and is also published by the West Publishing Co. It contains selected opinions of the Federal District Courts. As these courts are the trial courts within the Federal court system, it is an exception to the general rule that only appellate court opinions are reported. It must, however, be emphasized that only a very small percentage of the cases heard in the Federal District Courts are ever reported in the *Federal*

---

5 For a history of the development of the Federal Judicial System, *see* C. WRIGHT, HANDBOOK ON THE LAW OF FEDERAL COURTS 1–5 (3d ed. 1976).

6 NLRB v. Amalgamated Clothing Workers, 430 F.2d 966, 971 (5th Cir. 1970).

7 Jacobstein, *Some Reflections on the Control of the Publication of Appellate Court Opinions*, 27 STAN.L.REV. 791, 796 (1975).

Supplement. From Volume 1 to Volume 181 it also contained the decisions of the United States Court of Claims and in Volume 135, it began to include the decisions of the United States Customs Court. Since 1880 there has not been officially published any sets of reports for the Federal Courts of Appeals and the Federal District Courts. The *Federal Reporter* and the *Federal Supplement* are relied on for these reports. Both of these sets are first issued in advance sheets and subsequently replaced by bound volumes.

   d.   Federal Rules Decisions. This set will be discussed in Chapter Twelve.

   e.   Officially Published Reports of Special Federal Courts.

Cases decided in the Court of Claims. Washington, Government Printing Office, 1863 to date. v. 1 et seq.

U. S. Court of Customs Appeals and U. S. Court of Customs and Patent Appeals. Reports. Washington, Government Printing Office, 1911 to date. v. 1 et seq. (Customs). 1929 to date, v. 1 et seq. (Patents).

U. S. Customs Court. Reports. Washington, Government Printing Office, July 1938 to date. v. 1 et seq.

Tax Court of the United States. Reports. Washington, Government Printing Office, Oct. 1942 to date. v. 1 et seq.

SECTION C. ILLUSTRATIONS

The opinion of Taylor v. Louisiana [419 U.S. 522, 95 S.Ct. 692, 42 L.Ed.2d 690] as it is published in:

5. Advance Sheets to the U. S. Reports (Official).

6. Advance Sheets to the Supreme Court Reporter (West Publishing Co.).

7. Sample pages from volume 42 2d of the Lawyers Edition of the United States Supreme Court Reports (Lawyers Co-operative Publishing Co.).

[Illustration 5]
TAYLOR v. LOUISIANA AS REPORTED IN THE ADVANCE SHEETS OF 419 U.S. 522

522   OCTOBER TERM, 1974

Syllabus   419 U. S.

TAYLOR *v.* LOUISIANA

APPEAL FROM THE SUPREME COURT OF LOUISIANA

No. 73–5744. Argued October 16, 1974—Decided January 21, 1975

Appellant, a male, was convicted of a crime by a petit jury selected from a venire on which there were no women and which was selected pursuant to a system resulting from Louisiana constitutional and statutory requirements that a woman should not be selected for jury service unless she had previously filed a written declaration of her desire to be subject to jury service. The State Supreme Court affirmed, having rejected appellant's challenge to the constitutionality of the state jury-selection scheme. *Held:*

1. Appellant had standing to make his constitutional claim, there being no rule that such a claim may be asserted only by defendants who are members of the group excluded from jury service. *Peters* v. *Kiff,* 407 U. S. 493. P. 526.

> This page is taken from the preliminary print (advance sheets) of the U.S. Reports. The syllabi (or headnotes) are prepared by the Reporter and are not part of the opinion. At the end of each term of the court, the advance sheets are replaced by bound volumes with the same pagination.

4. It can no longer be held that women as a class may be excluded from jury service or given automatic exemptions based solely on sex if the consequence is that criminal jury venires are almost all male, and contrary implications of prior cases, *e. g.,* *Hoyt* v. *Florida,* 368 U. S. 57, cannot be followed. Pp. 535–537.

282 So. 2d 491, reversed and remanded.

WHITE, J., delivered the opinion of the Court, in which DOUGLAS, BRENNAN, STEWART, MARSHALL, BLACKMUN, and POWELL, JJ., joined. BURGER, C. J., concurred in the result. REHNQUIST, J., filed a dissenting opinion, *post,* p. 538.

William McM. King argued the cause and filed a brief for appellant.

[Illustration 5–a]

SAMPLE PAGE FROM TAYLOR v. LOUISIANA, 419 U.S. 522

TAYLOR *v.* LOUISIANA   523

522   Opinion of the Court

Kendall L. Vick, Assistant Attorney General of Louisiana, argued the cause for appellee. On the brief were *William J. Guste, Jr.,* Attorney General, *Walter Smith,* and *Woodrow W. Erwin.*

MR. JUSTICE WHITE delivered the opinion of the Court.

When this case was tried, Art. VII, § 41,[1] of the Louisiana Constitution, and Art. 402 of the Louisiana Code of Criminal Procedure [2] provided that a woman should not be selected for jury service unless she had previously filed a written declaration of her desire to be subject to jury service. The constitutionality of these provisions is the issue in this case.

---

[1] La. Const., Art. VII, § 41, read, in pertinent part:
"The Legislature shall provide for the election and drawing of competent and intelligent jurors for the trial of civil and criminal

> The first page of the opinion, indicating the name of the Justice who authored the opinion. Note that the names of the attorneys participating in the case are given.

"A citizen of the state who has reached the age of majority is eligible to serve as a juror within the parish in which he is domiciled. The legislature may provide additional qualifications.
"(B) Exemptions.
"The supreme court shall provide by rule for exemption of jurors."
[2] La. Code Crim. Proc., Art. 402, provided:
"A woman shall not be selected for jury service unless she has previously filed with the clerk of court of the parish in which she resides a written declaration of her desire to be subject to jury service."
This provision has been repealed, effective January 1, 1975. The repeal, however, has no effect on the conviction obtained in this case.

[Illustration 6]
SAMPLE PAGE FROM 95 S.Ct. 692

---

692   95 SUPREME COURT REPORTER

Billy J. TAYLOR, Appellant,

v.

State of LOUISIANA.

No. 73–5744.

Argued Oct. 16, 1974.

Decided Jan. 21, 1975.

Defendant was convicted before the Twenty-second Judicial District Court for the Parish of St. Tammany of aggravated kidnapping, and he appealed. The Louisiana Supreme Court, 282 So.2d 491, affirmed, and defendant appealed. The Supreme Court, Mr. Justice White, held that defendant, a male, had standing to challenge constitutionality of Louisiana law excluding women from jury service unless they previously filed written declaration, that requirement that a petit jury be selected from a representative cross-section of the community is fundamental to the jury trial guaranteed by the Sixth Amendment, that such requirement is violated by the systematic exclusion of women from jury panels where in the judicial district involved women amounted to 53% of the citizens eligible for jury service, that such exclusion was not justified on ground that women as a class serve a distinctive role in society and jury service would substantially interfere with that function, that women as a class may not be excluded or given automatic exemption based solely on sex if the consequence is that criminal jury venires are almost totally male and that states remain free to prescribe relevant qualifications for jurors and to provide reasonable exemptions so long as the jury lists or panels are representative of the community.

Reversed and remanded.

Mr. Chief Justice Burger concurred in the result.

Mr. Justice Rehnquist dissented and filed opinion.

1. Constitutional Law ⚖️42.3(1)

Convicted male defendant had standing to challenge constitutionality of Louisiana jury selection system, which system excludes women from jury service unless they had previously filed written declaration; standing to make the constitutional challenge was not limited to female defendants. LSA–Const. art. 7, § 41; LSA–C.Cr.P. art. 402; U.S.C. A.Const. Amends. 6, 14.

> The first page of the Taylor opinion as it appears in the advance sheets of the Supreme Court Reporter, an unofficial set published by West Publishing Co. The summary is prepared by its editors.

Purpose of a jury is to guard against the exercise of arbitrary power, to make available common-sense judgment of the community as a hedge against the overzealous or mistaken prosecutor and in preference to the professional or perhaps overconditioned or biased response of a judge. U.S.C.A. Const. Amends. 6, 14.

5. Jury ⚖️33(1)

Community participation in administration of the criminal law is not only consistent with our democratic heritage but also critical to public confidence in fairness of the criminal justice system; restricting jury service to only special groups or excluding identifiable segments playing major roles in the community cannot be squared with the constitutional concept of jury trial. U.S.C. A.Const. Amends. 6, 14.

6. Jury ⚖️33(1)

Requirement that a petit jury be selected from a representative cross-section of the community was violated by the systematic exclusion of women, who amounted to 53% of the citizens eligible for jury service in the judicial district. LSA–Const. art. 7, § 41; LSA–C.Cr.P. art. 402; U.S.C.A.Const. Amends. 6, 14.

[Illustration 6–a]

SAMPLE PAGE FROM 95 S.Ct. 692

TAYLOR v. LOUISIANA   **693**

Cite as 95 S.Ct. 692 (1975)

7. Jury ⬤62(3)

Women cannot be systematically excluded from jury panels from which petit juries are drawn. U.S.C.A.Const. Amends. 6, 14.

13. Jury ⬤33(1)

The fair cross-section principle of jury selection must have much leeway in application; the states are free to prescribe relevant qualifications for their

---

Note how 16 headnotes have been assigned. These differ from the headnotes in the U.S. Reports and the L.Ed. Reports.

Note also how the syllabus as it appeared in the U.S. Reports is reproduced in this set.

---

jury service unless they had previously filed written declaration could not be justified on ground that women as a class serve a distinctive role in society and that jury service would substantially interfere with that function. LSA–Const. art. 7, § 41; LSA–C.Cr.P. art. 402; U.S.C.A.Const. Amends. 6, 14.

10. Jury ⬤75(1)

States are free to grant exemptions from jury service to individuals in case of special hardship or incapacity and to those engaged in particular occupations the uninterrupted performance of which is critical to the community's welfare. U.S.C.A.Const. Amends. 6, 14.

11. Jury ⬤33(1)

Administrative convenience in excluding women from jury service unless they file written declaration of their desire to be subject to such service is an insufficient justification for diluting the quality of community judgment represented by the jury in criminal trials. U.S.C.A.Const. Amends. 6, 14.

12. Jury ⬤33(1)

Women as a class may not be excluded from jury service or given automatic exemptions based solely on sex if the consequence is that criminal jury venires are almost totally male, disapproving Hoyt v. Florida, 368 U.S. 57, 82 S. Ct. 159, 7 L.Ed.2d 118. U.S.C.A.Const. Amends. 6, 14.

tory provisions exempting women from jury service unless they previously filed a written declaration of their desire to be subject to such service were unconstitutional as violating the fair cross-section requirements of the Sixth and Fourteenth Amendments. LSA–Const. art. 7, § 41; LSA–C.Cr.P. art. 402; U. S.C.A.Const. Amends. 6, 14.

15. Jury ⬤33(1)

Although petit juries must be drawn from a source fairly representative of the community, the juries actually chosen need not mirror the community and reflect the various distinctive groups in the population. U.S.C.A. Const. Amends. 6, 14.

16. Jury ⬤33(1), 79(3)

A defendant is not entitled to a jury of any particular composition; however, the jury wheels, pools of names, panels or venires from which juries are drawn must not systematically exclude distinctive groups in the community and thereby fail to be reasonably representative thereof. U.S.C.A.Const. Amends. 6, 14.

*Syllabus**

Appellant, a male, was convicted of a crime by a petit jury selected from a venire on which there were no women and which was selected pursuant to a system resulting from Louisiana constitutional and statutory requirements that

---

* The syllabus constitutes no part of the opinion of the Court but has been prepared by the Reporter of Decisions for the convenience of the reader. See United States v. Detroit Timber & Lumber Co., 200 U.S. 321, 337, 26 S.Ct. 282, 287, 50 L.Ed. 499.

[Illustration 7]
TAYLOR v. LOUISIANA AS REPORTED IN 42 L.Ed.2d 690

[419 US 522]
BILLY J. TAYLOR, Appellant,

v

STATE OF LOUISIANA

419 US 522, 42 L Ed 2d 690, 95 S Ct 692

[No. 5744]

Argued October 16, 1974. Decided January 21, 1975.

SUMMARY

Prior to trial on a kidnapping charge in the Twenty-Second Judicial District Court for the Parish of St. Tammany, Louisiana, the defendant, a male, sought to quash the petit jury venire from which his jury would be selected, contending that women had been systematically excluded from the venire, thus depriving him of his federal constitutional right to a fair trial by a properly selected jury. Of the persons eligible for jury service in the judicial district, 53 percent were female, but no more than 10 percent of the persons on the jury wheel were women, and none were selected for service on the defendant's venire. The discrepancy between females eligible for jury service and those actually included in the venire resulted from the operation of Louisiana constitutional and statutory provisions (later repealed) which excluded a woman from jury service selection unless she had previously filed a written declaration of her desire to be subject to jury service.

First page of Taylor decision as it appears in the bound volume of L.Ed.2d. Summary is by the publisher's editors.

an opinion by WHITE, J., expressing the view of seven members of the court, it was held that (1) the defendant had standing to object to the exclusion of women from his jury even though he was not a member of the excluded class, (2) the selection of a petit jury from a representative cross section of the community was an essential component of the Sixth Amendment right to a jury trial, (3) the exclusion of women from jury service unless they volunteered could not be sufficiently justified on the ground that jury service would interfere with the distinctive role of women in society, (4) the

Briefs of Counsel, 986, infra.

690

[Illustration 7–a]

SAMPLE PAGE FROM 42 L.Ed.2d 690

TAYLOR v LOUISIANA
419 US 522, 42 L Ed 2d 690, 95 S Ct 692

> Note references to other related publications of the publisher. These will be discussed in later chapters.

BURGER, Ch. J., concurred in the result.

REHNQUIST, J., dissented, expressing the views that (1) the fair cross section requirement should not be considered to be an essential component of the Sixth Amendment right to a jury trial, and (2) Louisiana should not be required to retry the defendant, since there was no suggestion that his trial was unlawfully conducted or that its result was unreliable.

TOTAL CLIENT-SERVICE LIBRARY® REFERENCES

47 AM JUR 2d, Jury §§ 104, 114, 117, 164, 171, 180

8 AM JUR PL & PR FORMS (Rev ed), Criminal Procedure, Form 264; 15 AM JUR PL & PR FORMS (Rev ed), Jury, Form 151

USCS, Constitution, 6th and 14th Amendments

US L ED DIGEST, Jury § 36.5

ALR DIGESTS, Jury §§ 66, 71.5, 106

L ED INDEX TO ANNOS, Jury; Sex; Women

ALR QUICK INDEX, Females; Jury and Jury Trial; Sex Discrimination

FEDERAL QUICK INDEX, Females; Jury and Jury Trial; Sex Discrimination

ANNOTATION REFERENCES

Group or class discrimination in selection of grand or petit jury as prohibited by Federal Constitution. 33 L Ed 2d 783.

Sex discrimination. 27 L Ed 2d 935.

What provisions of the Federal Constitution's Bill of Rights are applicable to the states. 18 L Ed 2d 1388, 23 L Ed 2d 985.

Violation of constitutional rights of defendant in criminal case by unfair practices in selection of grand or petit jury. 82 L Ed 1053.

Exclusion of women from grand or trial jury panel in criminal case as violation of constitutional rights of accused or as ground for reversal of conviction. 9 ALR2d 661.

Proof as to exclusion of or discrimination against eligible class or race in respect to jury in criminal case. 1 ALR2d 1291.

Eligibility of women as jurors. 157 ALR 461.

[Illustration 7–b]
SAMPLE PAGE FROM 42 L.Ed.2d 690

HEADNOTES

Classified to U. S. Supreme Court Digest, Lawyers' Edition

Appeal and Error § 1626; Jury § 36.5 — Sixth and Fourteenth Amendments — exclusion of women

1. A state court criminal defendant's right to an impartial jury trial under the Sixth and Fourteenth Amendments is violated by the operation of a state's constitutional and statutory provisions which exclude a woman from jury service unless she previously files a written

Jury § 36.5 — Sixth Amendment — representative cross section requirement — exclusion of women

5. Women are sufficiently numerous and distinct from men so that if they are systematically eliminated from criminal jury panels, the Sixth Amendment's requirement that the jury be selected from a representative cross section of the community cannot be satisfied.

> The headnotes are prepared by the publisher's editorial staff. They differ from the headnotes in the other two sets of the U.S. Supreme Court Reports.

Jury § 36.5 — exclusion of women — standing to challenge

2. A male defendant in a state criminal prosecution is entitled to tender and have adjudicated his claim that the exclusion of women from jury service deprived him of the kind of fact finder to which he was constitutionally entitled, even though the male is not a member of the excluded class.

Jury § 35 — petit jury — selection from representative cross section of community — Sixth Amendment

3. The selection of a petit jury from a representative cross section of the community is an essential component of the Sixth Amendment right to a jury trial in a criminal case.

Jury §§ 35, 36.5 — members — restrictions and exclusions

4. Restricting jury service in criminal cases to only special groups or excluding identifiable segments playing major roles in the community cannot be squared with the constitutional concept of jury trial; trial by jury presupposes a jury drawn from a pool broadly representative of the community as well as impartial in a specific case.

Jury § 36.5 — jury service — exclusion of women

7. The exclusion of women from jury service by the operation of a state's constitutional and statutory provisions which exempt a woman from jury service unless she previously files a written declaration of her desire to be subject to jury service may not be justified, so as to overcome the Sixth Amendment right to a proper jury in a criminal case, merely on the ground that subjecting women to jury service would substantially interfere with the distinctive role of women in society.

Jury § 36.5 — exemptions from jury service — exclusion of women

8. Although the states are free to grant exemptions from jury service to individuals in case of special hardship or incapacity and to those engaged in particular occupations the uninterrupted performance of which is critical to the community's welfare, nevertheless, a state's exclusion of all women from criminal jury service, in violation of the Sixth Amendment's requirement of selection of jurors from a fair cross section of the community, cannot be justified on the ground that it would be a special hardship for each and every woman to

692

[Illustration 7–c]

SAMPLE PAGE FROM 42 L.Ed.2d 690

U.S. SUPREME COURT REPORTS   42 L Ed 2d

art, Marshall, Blackmun, and Powell, JJ., joined. Burger, C. J., concurred in the result. Rehnquist, J., filed a dissenting opinion, post, p 538, 42 L Ed 2d, p 703.

APPEARANCES OF COUNSEL

William McM. King argued the cause for appellant.

Kendall L. Vick argued the cause for appellee.

Briefs of Counsel, p 986, infra.

OPINION OF THE COURT

[419 US 523]

Mr. Justice **White** delivered the opinion of the Court.

When this case was tried, Art VII, § 41,[1] of the Louisiana Constitution, and Art 402 of the Louisiana Code of Criminal Procedure[2] provided that a woman should not be selected for jury service unless she had previously filed a written declaration of her desire to be subject to jury service. The constitutionality of these provisions is the issue in this case.

→ [419 US 524]

I

Appellant, Billy J. Taylor, was indicted by the grand jury of St. Tammany Parish, in the Twenty-second Judicial District of Louisiana, for aggravated kidnapping. On April 12, 1972, appellant moved the trial court to quash the petit jury venire drawn for the special criminal term

beginning with his trial the following day. Appellant alleged that women were systematically excluded from the venire and that he would therefore be deprived of what he claimed to be his federal constitutional right to "a fair trial by jury of a representative segment of the community . . . ."

The Twenty-second Judicial District is comprised of the parishes of St. Tammany and Washington. The appellee has stipulated that 53% of the persons eligible for jury service in these parishes were female, and that no more than 10% of the persons on the jury wheel in St. Tammany Parish were women.[3] During the period from December 8, 1971, to November 3, 1972, 12 females were among the 1,800 persons drawn to fill petit jury venires in St. Tammany Parish. It was also stipulated that the discrepancy between females eligible for jury service and

Starting with the opinions of the court, the text is exactly the same as in the official reports. Note the reference to the pagination to U.S. Reports. Both the Supreme Court Reporter and the Lawyer's Edition include these cross references in the bound volumes. In the bound volumes of the Lawyer's Edition, an appendix contains summaries of briefs presented to the court, and annotations of selected decisions.

SECTION D. SUMMARY

1. **United States Supreme Court Reports**

   a. **United States Reports** (Official Ed.).

   (1) Text of all cases of the Supreme Court of the United States.

   (2) First ninety volumes are cited frequently by reporter, for, originally, they were not consecutively numbered.

   (3) Bound volumes and advance sheets have same volume and page numbers.

   (4) "Slip" opinions are initially printed.

   (5) No summaries of briefs of counsel; other standard reporting features are included.

   b. **United States Supreme Court Reports** (Lawyers' Edition).

   (1) Includes all Supreme Court cases—two series.

   (2) Bound volume combines several volumes of official edition.

   (3) Advance sheets and bound volumes have same volume and page numbers.

   (4) Reference table appears at the beginning of each volume unit which cross references from the official citations to Lawyers' Edition pages.

   (5) Briefs of counsel are summarized.

   (6) Annotations in increasing number since volume 92, 1st series.

   (7) **Index to Annotations**—subject index to annotations in *Lawyers' Edition* through 31 L.Ed.2d. Starting with Volume 32 2d; pocket supplements keep annotations up to date.

   (8) Star-pagination.

   (9) Standard reporting features are included.

   c. **Supreme Court Reporter** (West Edition).

   (1) Part of the National Reporter System; key-numbered sections of headnotes.

   (2) Begins with volume 106 of the official set.

   (3) Each volume contains several volumes of the official reports.

   (4) Advance sheets and bound volumes have same volume and page numbers.

   (5) Cross reference table from the official citations to the *Supreme Court Reporter* volume and pages.

   (6) Star-pagination.

(7) No summaries of briefs of counsel; other standard reporting features are included.

d.   United States Law Week.

(1) Supreme Court Sections—speedy publication of Supreme Court decisions and journal of cases.

(2) General Law Sections—include more important current federal statutes, summary of federal legal trends, some federal agency rulings and the texts of significant new court decisions; general topical index.

e.   Commerce Clearing House, U. S. Supreme Court Bulletin.

(1) Loose-leaf reporter of current Supreme Court decisions; provides fast service.

(2) Docket of Supreme Court cases.

f.   Chamber opinions of the Justices.   Until 1969, published only in *Lawyers' Edition* and *Supreme Court Reporter*; starting in 1970 are also published in the *United States Reports*.

2.   Federal Cases

a.   Reprinted reports of all available U. S. Circuit and District Courts decisions, 1789–1879.

b.   Cases are arranged alphabetically by case names and consecutively numbered.

c.   Cases are cited by number.

d.   Annotations are brief notes to the cases.

e.   Digest volume, volume 31, includes Blue Tables which cross-reference from the original reporter citations to the *Federal Cases* Numbers.

3.   Federal Reporter

a.   Part of *National Reporter System;* key-numbered sections of headnotes.

b.   Only current reporter for federal appellate cases.

c.   Reports cases from 1879 to date.

d.   Prior to 1932 included District Court decisions.

e.   Now reports cases of the Courts of Appeals, the U. S. Court of Customs and Patent Appeals and the Court of Claims (Court of Claims since 1960).

f.   Advance sheets and bound volumes have same volume and page numbers.

g.   No summaries of briefs of counsel; other standard reporting features are included.

4. Federal Supplement

a. Part of *National Reporter System;* key-numbered sections of headnotes.

b. Only current reporter of lower federal court cases.

c. Reports cases since 1932.

d. Now includes cases of the District Courts and the U. S. Customs Court (U. S. Customs Court since 1949).

e. From 1932 to 1960, included the Court of Claims cases.

f. Includes *selected* District Courts cases.

g. Advance sheets and bound volumes have same volume and page numbers.

h. No summaries of briefs of counsel; other standard reporting features are included.

5. Citations

Citation form for Federal cases is explained in Appendix A at (I), (A), (3).

Chapter 5

STATE COURT DECISIONS AND THE
NATIONAL REPORTER SYSTEM

SECTION A. STATE COURT REPORTS

As has been indicated previously, the laws of the several states generally provide the method of publishing state court decisions. Opinions published in accordance with such legislation are called "official" reports. Private companies also publish judicial decisions, with or without legislative directives. The private publications that are not legislatively endorsed are called "unofficial" reports, though no less accurate than the official reports. The unofficial reports may duplicate official reports or may be the only source of case publication. The unofficial opinions comprise three categories: (1) the *National Reporter System* and other private publications of similar coverage (2) the annotated reports and (3) the special reports. The latter two will be described in later chapters.

At one time, all states published their judicial decisions in bound volumes of reports such as the *Alabama Reports* or *Michigan Reports*.[1] Those states having immediate courts of appeals [2] may also have sep-

[1] While printing began in the Colonies in 1638, the first case reported appears to be the *Trial of Thomas Sutherland* for murder printed in 1692. About 30 of the 150 English reports were being used in this country prior to the American Revolution as the written case law because only about 35 to 40 legal books or pamphlets had been printed here. The first law book written by an American was printed in Virginia in 1736. Written by William Parks, the book was entitled, *The Office and Authority of a Justice of the Peace, and the Duty of Sheriffs, Constables, Coroners, Church Wardens, Surveyors of Highways, Constables and Officers of the Militia.*

Connecticut was the first state to publish an official law report after a 1784 statute entitled "An Act Establishing the Wages of the Judges of the Superior Court" was passed which required judges of the supreme and superior courts to file written opinions. The first volume, known as *Kirby's Reports*, was published in 1789 by Ephraim Kirby in Litchfield, Connecticut. In 1790 came Dallas' *Pennsylvania Cases*; in 1792 followed Hopkinson's *Admiralty Reports*; and Chipman's *Vermont Reports* in 1793. Through the early 1800's reports followed in North Carolina, Virginia, Kentucky, New Jersey, Maryland, Louisiana, New York, and Tennessee. The first volume of the *United States Reports* was published by Dallas in 1790.

For additional references to early law reporting in America *see*:
1. C. EVANS, AMERICAN BIBLIOGRAPHY VOLS. I, II, III (1893).
2. I. THOMAS, HISTORY OF PRINTING IN AMERICA VOL. VI.
3. AMERICAN ANTIQUARIAN SOCIETY, PROCEEDINGS (1874).
4. C. WARREN, HISTORY OF THE HARVARD LAW SCHOOL AND OF EARLY LEGAL CONDITIONS IN AMERICA VOL. I, CH. X (1908).
5. CONNECTICUT ACTS AND LAWS 1784, at p. 267.

[2] The following states have intermediate courts of appeal: Alabama, Arizona, California, Colorado, Delaware, Florida, Georgia, Illinois, Indiana, Louisiana, Mary-

arately bound sets of reports, such as the *Illinois Appellate Reports*. The decisions are published chronologically by terms of court. As in the case of the Supreme Court of the United States, the early state reports are frequently cited by the name of the reporter, e. g., *Binney's Reports, Pennsylvania*, cited "Binn". An increasing number of states, however, have discontinued publishing their official reports and are relying solely on the *National Reporter System*.[3] Set forth below are given the year of the first case decided in all of the states' or territories' highest appellate courts.

YEAR OF THE FIRST CASE DECIDED IN THE STATES' AND/OR TERRITORIES' HIGHEST APPELLATE COURTS

Alabama	1820
Alaska	1867
Arizona	1866
Arkansas	1837
California	1850
Colorado	1865
Connecticut	1785
Delaware	1814
District of Columbia	1801
Florida	1846
Georgia	1805
Hawaii	1847
Idaho	1866
Illinois	1819
Indiana	1820
Iowa	1839
Kansas	1858
Kentucky	1785
Louisiana	1809
Maine	1820
Maryland	1658
Massachusetts	1804
Michigan	1836

land, Massachusetts, Michigan, Missouri, New Mexico, North Carolina, New York, Ohio, Oklahoma, Oregon, Pennsylvania, Tennessee, Texas and Washington.

[3] About one-quarter of the states no longer publish their own official reports and either have officially adopted or rely on the decisions as reported in the regional reporters of the National Reporter System. These states are: Alaska, Delaware, Florida, Iowa, Kentucky, Louisiana, Maine, Mississippi, Missouri, North Dakota, Oklahoma, Tennessee, Texas, Utah and Wyoming. West Publishing Company also publishes separately the official reports of Alabama, Arizona, Idaho, New Jersey and Utah which makes it responsible for producing the court reports in more than one-third of the states.

YEAR OF THE FIRST CASE DECIDED IN THE
STATES' AND/OR TERRITORIES' HIGHEST
APPELLATE COURTS—Continued

Minnesota	1851
Mississippi	1820
Missouri	1821
Montana	1868
Nebraska	1854
Nevada	1865
New Hampshire	1802
New Jersey	1790
New York	1791
North Carolina	1778
North Dakota	1867
Ohio	1816
Oklahoma	1896
Oregon	1853
Pennsylvania	1754
Philippine Islands	1901
Puerto Rico	1905
Rhode Island	1828
South Carolina	1783
South Dakota	1867
Tennessee	1791
Texas	1840
Utah	1871
Vermont	1789
Virginia	1730
Washington	1854
West Virginia	1863
Wisconsin	1839
Wyoming	1870

Advance sheets or slip opinions precede the publication of the official reports in several states. The unofficial publications generally include advance sheets for the state cases.

A court or its reporter may have the power to select the decisions for publication in the official state reports. In the exercise of that power some less important cases may be eliminated from the official reports.[4]

In a general survey, such as this, it would be inappropriate to present a detailed study of the reporting systems of each state.[5] It is

[4] Chanin, *A Survey of the Writing and Publication of Opinions in Federal and State Appellate Courts*, 67 LAW LIB.J. 362 (1974).

[5] Several states have manuals devoted exclusively to the legal bibliography of the state. Inquiry should be made at a local law library for the availability of such a

sufficient to note that the Table of Abbreviations in Appendix C is adequate to direct the researcher to the specific unfamiliar publications for the occasional use which he will make of them.

SECTION B.   NATIONAL REPORTER SYSTEM

The *National Reporter System*, published by the West Publishing Company consists of two main divisions: (1) opinions of the state appellate and trial courts and (2) opinions of the federal courts. This system of state court reporting was initiated in 1879 with the *North Western Reporter*. The state reporting units consist of seven regional reporters arranged roughly by geographical divisions. The four federal units cover the various federal courts. There are also two state reports which are part of the *National Reporter System;* namely, *New York Supplement* and *California Reporter*. The entire system, with its coverage, is outlined below:

	Began in	Coverage
Atlantic Reporter	1885	Conn., Dela., Maine, Maryland, N. H., N. J., Penna., R. I., Vermont, and District of Columbia Municipal Court of Appeals.
North Eastern Reporter	1885	Ill., Ind., Mass., N. Y., and Ohio
North Western Reporter	1879	Ia., Mich., Minn., Nebr., N. D., S. D., and Wisc.
Pacific Reporter	1883	Alaska, Ariz., Calif. to 1960, Calif. S.Ct. since 1960, Colo., Hawaii, Idaho, Kan., Mont., Nev., N. M., Okla., Ore., Utah, Wash., and Wyo.
South Eastern Reporter	1887	Ga., N. C., S. C., Va., and W. Va.
South Western Reporter	1886	Ark., Ky., Indian Territory, Mo., Tenn., and Tex.
Southern Reporter	1887	Ala., Fla., La., and Miss.

---

manual, such as M. BONER, A REFERENCE GUIDE TO TEXAS LAW AND LEGAL HISTORY (1976), or D. HENKE, CALIFORNIA LEGAL RESEARCH HANDBOOK (1971).

Supreme Court Reporter	1882	Supreme Court of the United States.
Federal Reporter	1880	From 1880 to 1932: Circuit Courts of Appeals and District Courts of the U. S., U. S. Court of Customs and Patent Appeals, Court of Claims of the U. S., and Court of Appeals of the District of Columbia. From 1932 to date: U. S. Courts of Appeals, and U. S. Court of Customs and Patent Appeals. From 1942 to 1961: U. S. Emergency Court of Appeals. Since 1960: U. S. Court of Claims.
Federal Supplement	1932	U. S. District Courts, Court of Claims to 1960, U. S. Customs Court since Vol. 135 (1949).
Federal Rules Decisions	1940	District Courts of the U. S.
New York Supplement	1888	N. Y. (all state courts). Since 1932, the N. Y. Court of Appeals opinions are published here as well as in the North Eastern Reporter.
California Reporter	Dec. 1959	Calif.S.Ct., District Courts of Appeal and Appellate Dept. Superior Court.

The full text of the decisions of the courts are provided by this service. The editors prepare the headnotes which then are key-numbered to the American Digest classification system. This is a very significant and helpful feature, the nature of which is described in Chapter Six. However, cases in the early volumes of the units of the *National Reporter System*, although headnoted, are not integrated into the key-number system which was developed at the turn of the century.

The cumulation of decisions from several states promotes speedier publication of state cases by *Regional Reporters*.

The opinions first appear in advance sheets. The advance sheets are very useful for providing the text of recent opinions which have not yet been published in the official state reports. The pagination

of the opinions is the same in the bound volumes as in the advance sheets. [6]

The *National Reporters* list words and phrases as defined by judicial opinions. These definitions cover both legal and nonlegal words and phrases. Except for the *Supreme Court Reporter,* each bound volume provides two tables of cases: (1) a single alphabetical listing of all cases in the volume and (2) separate alphabetical listings of the cases by states or courts. The tables of cases in the advance sheets of the *Regional Reporters* are alphabetically arranged under the names of the states. Another significant feature is the Tables of Statutes Construed included in the bound volumes and the advance sheets. These lists cite the reported cases which interpret statutory law and are cumulated into some West's state digests. The *Reporter* units now publish the current revisions and amendments to appropriate court rules. Each advance sheet and bound volume includes a digest section comprising the key-numbered headnotes of the cases covered.

The publishers claim that the *National Reporter System* contains over 90,000 cases which are not in the official state reports.

The decisions of some but not all state intermediate appellate courts are included in the *National Reporter System.* Further, as to each intermediate court, the inclusion of its cases in the *Reporter System* began at different times. For example, Missouri appellate cases are included in the *South Western Reporter,* beginning with 93 Mo.App. (1902); Illinois appellate decisions are contained in the *North Eastern Reporter,* beginning with 284 Ill.App. (1936). Variations also exist between the *Reporters* as to general inclusion of state trial court cases, and the trial courts which are covered have different starting dates in each set. Thus, since 1887, nearly all reported court decisions are available in the seven regional reporters and the four sets of federal reporters that comprise the *National Reporter System.* This becomes significant in legal research as it provides a common editorial treatment to the syllabi which become the basis of locating court decisions through the use of the *American Digest System* which will be discussed in the next chapter.

---

[6] Occasionally after an opinion has been published in an advance sheet, the judge who wrote the opinion may, for one reason or another, recall the opinion and not publish it. In such instances, another opinion is published in the appendix of a subsequent advance sheet with the same pagination as the withdrawn case. By this means, the original pagination is preserved in the bound volume.

SECTION C.   CROSS REFERENCE TABLES

1.   To find the *National Reporter System* citation, when you have the official citation, refer to one of the following:

    a.   *National Reporter Blue Book.*   These tables refer the user from the official citation to the unofficial Reporter citation.   [Illustration 9]

    b.   *Shepard's Citations* for the state.

    c.   Table of Cases of the state digest.

2.   To locate the official citation, when given the *National Reporter System* citation, refer to one of the following:

    a.   *State Blue and White Book.*[7]   Consult the White Tables which cross-reference from the unofficial Reporter citation.   [Illustration 9]

    b.   *Shepard's Citations* for the Reporter.

    c.   Table of Cases of the state digest.

The *American Digest System, Shepard's Citations*, and state digests, which are listed above, will be discussed in greater detail in later chapters.

---

[7] Law libraries generally only have the *Blue and White Book* for the state in which they are located.

SECTION D.   ILLUSTRATIONS

8.   **Map of the National Reporter System.**

9.   **A page from the National Reporter Blue Book and Ohio Blue and White Book.**

[Illustration 8]

[Illustration 9]

This is an Excerpt from the National Reporter Blue Book

59 ILLINOIS REPORTS, SECOND SERIES

Ill.2d Pg.	N.E.2d Vol.	Pg.	Ill.2d Pg.	N.E.2d Vol.	Pg.	Ill.2d Pg.	N.E.2d Vol.	Pg.	Ill.2d Pg.	N.E.2d Vol.	Pg.	Ill.2d Pg.	N.E.2d Vol.	Pg.	Ill 2d Pg.	N.E.2d Vol.	Pg.
1	319	40	102	319	496	173	319	489	258	320	11	362	321	264	491	322	5
6	319	37	106	319	486	178	319	465	261	320	7	389	321	257	502	322	25
13	319	228	111	319	483	184	319	772	267	319	820	402	320	849	508	322	15
20	319	18	115	319	481	194	319	769	271	319	816	409	322	481	516	322	33
29	319	9	118	319	469	201	319	810	276	319	764	416	322	1	522	322	454
34	319	46	123	319	468	207	319	758	284	319	749	422	322	36	534	322	447
38	320	17	125	319	507	211	319	753	290	319	794	439	322	29	546	322	464
45	319	225	131	319	472	220	319	745	302	319	787	445	322	58	557	322	461
52	319	5	140	319	478	229	319	813	305	319	782	452	322	54	563	322	470
61	319	1	146	319	502	236	319	760	315	319	802	459	322	51	569	322	476
68	319	12	155	319	800	243	320	13	328	320	321	465	322	45	576	322	441
79	319	232	158	319	498	246	319	777	343	319	789	475	322	20	580	322	473
89	319	511	165	319	491	255	320	15	352	320	1	484	322	11	588	322	443
95	319	514															

The National Reporter Blue Book consists of a main bound volume, bound volume supplements, and an annual cumulative pamphlet. This Blue Book contains tables showing volume and page of the National Reporter volume for every case found in the corresponding state reports.

In this example, if one only had the citation to 59 Ill.2d 29, the table may be used to locate the citation of this case in the North East Reporter.

AN EXCERPT FROM THE WHITE TABLES IN OHIO BLUE AND WHITE BOOK

(Ohio References for North Eastern Cases)

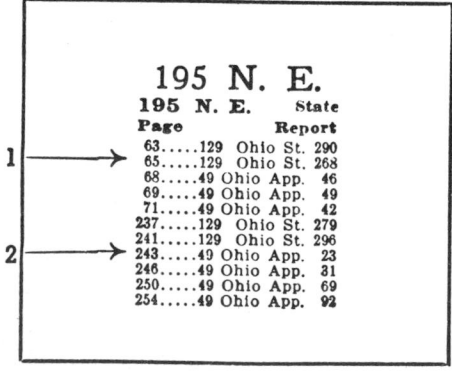

195 N. E.

195 N. E.	State
Page	**Report**
63.....129	Ohio St. 290
65.....129	Ohio St. 268
68.....49	Ohio App. 46
69.....49	Ohio App. 49
71.....49	Ohio App. 42
237.....129	Ohio St. 279
241.....129	Ohio St. 296
243.....49	Ohio App. 23
246.....49	Ohio App. 31
250.....49	Ohio App. 69
254.....49	Ohio App. 92

SECTION E. METHODS OF CITATION

1. State Decisions

a. Parallel Citations

Parallel citations to the official and the unofficial state reports are commonly provided in federal and state court briefs, treatises, and periodical articles. This practice is frequently modified by some state court briefs where the parallel citations are given for all state court reports except the forum, in which cases only the official citations are provided.

Oliver v. Robnett, 190 Cal. 51, 210 P. 408 (1922).

State ex rel. Fire District of Lemay v. Smith, 353 Mo. 807, 184 S.W.2d 593 (1945).

Standard v. Orleans Flour Co., 93 Neb. 389, 140 N.W. 636 (1913).

The abbreviations of the Regional Reporters are:

Atlantic Reporter cited "Atl." or "A." and "A.2d"

North Eastern Reporter cited "N.E." and "N.E.2d"

North Western Reporter cited "N.W." and "N.W.2d"

Pacific Reporter cited "Pac." or "P." and "P.2d"

South Eastern Reporter cited "S.E." and "S.E.2d"

South Western Reporter cited "S.W." and "S.W.2d"

Southern Reporter cited "So." and "So.2d"

New York Supplement cited "N.Y.Supp." or "N.Y.S." and "N.Y.S.2d"

California Reporter cited "Cal.Rptr."

b. Complete Citation

The state, the court, and the date are explicitly or implicitly given. Some information is clearly understood from the official citation and should not be repeated. When the court is not identified by the citation, the assumption is that it is a case reported by the highest court. Thus, in the examples noted above, the cases cover supreme court decisions.

c. Early State Reporters

Where the name of a reporter is used in citing an early state report, the favored practice is to indicate the state and the date.

Da Costa v. Shrewsbury, 1 Bay 211 (S.C.1791).

d. Recent Decisions

If the official report has not yet been published, cite the unofficial report, such as the *National Reporter System,* and indicate the jurisdiction and date.

Corsair v. Dempsey, 218 A.2d 478 (R.I.1966).

e.   National Reporter Reprint of State Cases

In the absence of an official state report, the reprints of cases of a state from the *National Reporter System* are cited by volume and page of the unit of the *National Reporter.* The state and court are explicitly or implicitly given with the date.

Arch Sellery, Inc. v. Simpson, 346 P.2d 1068 (Wyo.1959).

f.   Several Courts Included in a Report

If the decisions of several courts are included in a single report, the court rendering the decision and the date should be noted.

Kuebler v. Cleveland Short Line Ry., 10 Ohio N.P. (N.S.) 385
     (C.P.1910).

The method of citations for all types of law books is set forth in Appendix A.

SECTION F.   SUMMARY

1.   State Court Reports

a.   Official reports are court reports directed by statute.

b.   Unofficial reports are court reports published without statutory direction.

c.   Advance sheets and slip opinions are published in several states—most states rely on unofficial advance sheets, e. g., *National Reporter System* or other private publication.

2.   National Reporter System

a.   Opinions of state appellate and trial courts—7 regional reporters arranged roughly by geographical divisions and two state reporters.

b.   Opinions of the federal courts.

3.   Cross Reference Tables

a.   *National Reporter Blue Book* refers the user from the official citation to the unofficial *National Reporter* citation.

b.   White Tables in *State Blue and White Book* refer the user from the unofficial *National Reporter* citation to the official citation.

4.   Citation

Citation practice for State and National Reporter decisions is covered in Appendix A at (I), (A), (3).

Chapter 6

DIGESTS FOR COURT DECISIONS

Since our system of law follows the doctrine of *stare decisis*, the location of past cases in the reports, which we have just studied, is an essential requirement. We learned that the cases in the reports are published as rendered and follow no subject or systematic arrangement. It is compelling, therefore, that logical organization be applied to the search for the law in the cases. Otherwise, case law would be unwieldly and unmanageable. For example, assume that a client consults her lawyer about the following problem:

> She purchased an oriental rug for the price of $1,000.00 and placed it on the floor of her newly rented apartment. A week later there was a heavy rainstorm and the client, upon returning to her apartment, discovered that due to a leak in the roof, her oriental rug was ruined. She now wants to know if the landlord of the apartment can be made to pay for the rug.

Before answering this question, the lawyer must first determine what the issue is in this problem: *i. e.*, in a landlord-tenant relationship, is the landlord responsible for damages to personal property of the tenant caused by a defect in the premises? In order to find the law applicable to this fact situation, the lawyer has to research the law by searching for appellate court decisions and find cases with a similar fact situation. He/she must then determine from the cases what rules of law were set forth by the courts. Lawyers usually begin looking for cases decided in the jurisdiction where the problem arose; if none is found, they look for cases in other states. The search may start in either "books of index" or "books of search." The latter may be encyclopedias or treatises which present narrative statements of the law with footnote references to cases in point. "Books of search" will be discussed in subsequent chapters. This chapter will explain how cases in point may be located through the use of "books of index" and particularly through the use of digests. A digest is a case finder or an index to the law and is used only to find the law. It is never cited as legal authority.

As previously indicated, court decisions are arranged in the reports chronologically, and each separate volume may contain cases dealing with subjects ranging from abatement to zoning. If the hypothetical legal situation previously outlined existed in California and if only the *California Reports* and the *California Appellate Re-*

ports were available, a lawyer searching for cases involving landlords and tenants would have to examine several hundred individual volumes. In order to avoid this, digests were developed which arrange cases by subject rather than chronologically. However, instead of reprinting the entire decision, only an abstract or digest of each case is given.

There are various kinds of digests with different coverage. Some only include digests of cases of a particular state. Some include a group of neighboring states; some only federal cases; and one includes decisions from all courts, both federal and state. In this chapter, we shall discuss primarily the digests published by the West Publishing Company.

SECTION A. THE AMERICAN DIGEST SYSTEM

1. Key Number System

The *American Digest System* is a subject classification scheme whereby decisions that were reported chronologically in the various units of the *National Reporter System* are rearranged by subject, bringing together all cases on a similar point of law. Instead, however, of rearranging complete decisions, it rearranges digests (abstracts) of decisions. The West Publishing Co. has developed its own classification of law and classifies the digests of all cases to its system of classification. The system divides the subject of law into seven main classes. Each class is then divided into sub-classes and then each sub-class into topics. There are over 435 topics, each of which corresponds to a legal concept. [See Illustration 10]. The topics are then divided into subdivisions of the topic and each subdivision is given a paragraph number called a "Key Number." The Key Numbers vary from topic to topic from a few to many hundred.

With this outline in mind, it is then necessary to examine the actual steps involved in the making of the *American Digest System*. Basically, it all starts with a slip decision. After a decision is written, a copy of it goes to the West Publishing Company and is assigned to an editor. Keep in mind that all he has is the decision with no other information than the name of the case, the name of the judge who wrote it, and the name of the court. The editor reads the case and determines the headnotes. In theory, each headnote represents a particular point of law. The editor takes each point of law which he is about to make into a headnote and assigns to it a Topic and Key Number. He decides that a particular paragraph deals with, for example, negligence, and then turning to the *Table of Key Numbers* [Illustration 11] under *Negligence*, further decides that it specifical-

ly is involved with Business Visitors in Stores and thus gives it the Topic and Key Number *Negligence* 32 (2.8). Frequently a paragraph will deal with two points of law and will then get two Topics and Key Numbers.

Consequently, when the editor is finished with a case, all of the points of law covered in the case will be made into headnotes and placed at the beginning of the case, with each headnote assigned a Topic and Key Number. See Illustration 12. This procedure is followed for each case reported in the *National Reporter System*. The next step in the construction of the digest begins with each advance sheet. In the front of each advance sheet, all of the headnotes for all of the decisions reported are brought together in the *Key Number Digest*. In it, they are arranged alphabetically by Topic and then under each Topic, numerically by Key Number. Thus, through the *Key Number Digest* all decisions in an advance sheet pamphlet dealing with the same topic of law can be located.

2.   Units of the American Digest System

The next step is found in a publication called the *General Digest*. This is first issued monthly in *pamphlet* form. The January issue, for example, will consist of *all* the headnotes taken from *all* of the units of the *National Reporter System*. These again are arranged alphabetically by Topic and then numerically by Key Number under Topic. Thus, in the January issue of the *General Digest*, by looking under a particular Topic and Key Number, digests of all cases that dealt with that particular point of law reported in the January issue can be located.

From now on, the digest building becomes mechanical. The monthly issues of the *General Digest* are cumulated approximately every three months into bound volumes. This process has now been going on since 1896. If no further cumulation had taken place, digests of all the cases, arranged topically, would be in all of the bound volumes of the *General Digest*. In order to find all the cases dealing with a particular topic, it would be necessary to examine each one of hundreds of bound volumes. As this was not practical, the publishers in 1906 cumulated all the topics from all of the volumes from 1896 to 1906 into one alphabet. This is called the First *Decennial*. Now, by examining the volume containing a particular Topic and Key Number, all of the cases decided on that point during the years 1896–1906 may be located. This process has taken place since 1896 with a new *Decennial* every ten years. The latest one is the Eighth, covering the years 1966–76. All of the cases since 1976 are in the *General Digest*, 5th Series. Thus, given a Topic and Key Number, one can start with the First *Decennial* and then proceed through the

Eighth *Decennial* and then examine the individual bound volumes of the *General Digest*, and then the monthly issues and thereby locate all cases on a point of law under a particular Key Number from 1896 to approximately six weeks ago. See Illustrations 14–16.

It is actually possible to find all cases from 1658 as cases from 1658–1896 are in the *Century Digest*. However, the *Century Digest* did not use Key Numbers. This means that the numbering system in the *Century* is different than that of the *Decennials*. For example, Key Number *Negligence* 32 (2.8) in the *Decennials* stands for Business Visitors and Store and Restaurant Patrons, whereas in the *Century, Negligence* 32 stands for "Blasting" and cases dealing with Business Visitors are digested under *Negligence* 43 in the *Century*.

Thus, it is necessary when researching with a Key Number to translate this to the equivalent number in the *Century Digest*. This, however, is a simple matter. In the First *Decennial*,[1] at the beginning of each Key Number, reference is made to where that Key Number is located in the *Century*. See Illustration 16.

Should the search be started in the *Century Digest* under *Negligence* 43, a means of transfer from the *Century* paragraph number to the equivalent Key Number is needed. This is accomplished by using the *Table of Key Numbers Section for Century Digest*, located in the Table of Cases volume to the First and Second *Decennials*.

Law, of course, is constantly expanding. It is obvious that when the original classification was made in 1896 no provision was made for cases dealing with damages resulting from a jet plane breaking the sound barrier or cases subsequently to be decided under the *Labor Relations Management Act of 1937*. Consequently, in order to keep abreast of the law, new topics have to be added and old ones expanded. Thus, in the Sixth *Decennial* the following new titles were added: *Aviation, Labor Relations, Mental Health, Social Security*, and *Telecommunication*. Also, the titles of *Discovery* and *Divorce* had additional Key Numbers added to them. In the Seventh *Decennial* the topics *Arrest, Constitutional Law, Criminal Law, Insurance* and *Search and Seizure* were expanded; new topics added were *Secured Transactions, Trade Regulation* and *Zoning*. In the *General Digest*, 4th Series the following new topics were added or expanded: Volume 20, *Drugs and Narcotics* and *Securities Regulations*; Volume 21, *Civil Rights* (Revised); Volume 22, *Taxation* (Revised); Volume 24, *Product Liability;* Volume 25, *Public Contracts*; Volume 34, *Arbitration* (Expanded).

---

[1] In some printings, these cross references also appear in the *Second Decennial*.

When a new title is added, all cases previously digested under another title are re-digested under the new classification. Thus, for example, the *Labor Relations* topic in the Sixth *Decennial* digests *all* cases on that topic and not merely those for the years 1946–56.

The *American Digest System* consists of the following sets:

	Chronological Coverage	No. of Vols.
Century Digest	1658–1896	50 vols.
First Decennial	1897–1906	25 vols.
Second Decennial	1907–1916	24 vols.
Third Decennial	1916–1926	29 vols.
Fourth Decennial	1926–1936	34 vols.
Fifth Decennial	1936–1946	49 vols.
Sixth Decennial	1946–1956	36 vols.
Seventh Decennial	1956–1966	38 vols.
Eighth Decennial	1966–1976	42 vols.
General Digest (5th Series)	1976 to date	

From two to four bound volumes of the *General Digest* are published each year. They are preceded by unbound monthly supplements. A new Decennial appears each ten years and supersedes the *General Digest* for that period. Thus, the *Eighth Decennial* takes the place of the *General Digest,* 4th series, and covers the period 1966–1976. The *General Digest,* 5th series, will span the ten-year period, 1976–1986, and eventually will be superseded by the Ninth *Decennial.*

3. Finding the Key Number

The *American Digest System* as classified to the *Key Number System* provides a means to locate all decisions on the same point of law. Once it is determined to what Topic and Key Number a particular point of law has been classified, searching for cases can commence in the various units of the *American Digest System.*

The important matter is to learn how to find the Topic and Key Number. There are three common methods provided for within the *American Digest System.*

a. The Descriptive-Word Index to the American Digest System

The TARP rule as explained in Chapter 2, applies to the initial analysis of a problem in this situation, as in others. After the TARP

rule brings the facts and issues in focus, the *Descriptive-Word Index* to the *American Digest System* may be consulted to obtain digest-references to applicable cases. It is a convenient aid to the Index Method of searching for court decisions.

The *Descriptive-Word Index* is arranged alphabetically and includes: (1) all topics of the digest classification, (2) all key-number section lines and editorial reference lines in the *Decennial Digests*, and (3) "catch" words or descriptive words relating to parties to the suits who are members of a class, occupation, or legal relation; place names and physical objects; questions of law; constitutional and legislative provisions; and legal principles which relate to the subject matter of the suit.

In the *Descriptive-Word Index*, reference is made to topics and key-numbers under the "catch" words or other entries. After locating the appropriate key-number in the index, refer to the Digest volumes under the key-number designations.

There is a separate *Descriptive-Word Index* to each of the *Decennial* units as well as to the *General Digest*.

Let us examine a problem to see how the *Descriptive-Word Index* to the *Decennials* units of the *American Digest System* may be used to locate a Topic and Key Number. Assume this problem.

A, accompanied by her grandmother, was shopping in a supermarket. As A was waiting at the check-out counter, she suddenly remembered that she needed a pound of butter. She asked her grandmother to go to the dairy department for it. As the grandmother was returning to the check-out counter, she slipped, fell to the floor, and broke her hip. While A was assisting her grandmother, she noticed a piece of lettuce was attached to her grandmother's shoe.

The grandmother brings suit against the supermarket.

Using the TARP method as described in Chapter Two, this problem may be analyzed as follows:

T (*Thing* or subject matter)	Supermarket or Store
A (Cause of *action* or grounds for defense)	Negligence; duty of care of defendant to plaintiff.
R (*Relief* sought)	Money damages for injury suffered.
P (*Persons* or parties involved—legal status to each other)	Status of plaintiff to store owner.

In starting the search, it is best to start with the *Descriptive-Word Index* to the *General Digest*, or the latest *Decennial* unit. When using the index method, the first entry looked under should be the *least common denominator* to the problem being researched. In this instance, it may be *vegetable* or *lettuce;* if no suitable index entry is found, then try *stores* or *supermarket;* if still no entry is located, then broaden the search and if necessary use legal concepts such as *personal injuries* or *negligence.* Illustration 13 demonstrates the use of the *Descriptive Word Index* method. After the Topic and Key Number is located, the digest paragraphs under it should then be consulted to locate those cases analogous to the problem being searched.

b. Analysis or Topic Approach

As the *American Digest System* is based on a classification system, it is possible to analyze a fact situation and to determine from this analysis what Topic and Key Number would cover the point of law. In the problem used to illustrate the *Descriptive-Word Index* approach, *supra,* one could determine that the topic of law involved is *Negligence* and then check the *Analysis and Outline* that appears immediately after the Topic *Negligence* in the Seventh *Decennial* and then locate Key Number 32 (2.8). Illustration 11.

This method requires a certain amount of legal sophistication and should not be used without having a fairly good knowledge of law. Moreover, there is always the danger inherent in this approach that the researcher may arrive at one analysis which leads to a specific Topic and Key Number, whereas the Editors in their analysis assigned a different Topic and Key Number. Hence, it is recommended that this method be used with care and only after one has had considerable experience in legal research.

c. Table of Cases Method

Each *Decennial* unit and each volume of the *General Digest* have an alphabetical table of cases by plaintiff. Each case listed gives its citation and what Topics and Key Numbers the case has been digested under. Thus, if one knew, for example, that *McKenney v. Quality Foods* dealt with the question of care due to a business visitor, by consulting the Table of Cases volumes of the Seventh *Decennial* the citation and Topics and Key Numbers can easily be located. Illustration 18.

d.   Table of Cases by Popular Names

When only the popular name of a case is known, such as the *Dred Scott case* the best sources to use to find the actual citation are:

(1) *Shepard's Acts and Cases by Popular Name.* See Illustration 20.

(2) The Sixth *Decennial* of the *American Digest System* contains a cumulative *List of Popular Name Titles* in the *American Digest System.* This feature has been discontinued in the Seventh *Decennial.*

(3) Most special digests contain a Table of Cases by Popular Name.

————

SECTION B.   SPECIAL DIGESTS

As the *American Digest System* with its Key Number classification is made up from the *National Reporter System*, it is all-inclusive and most useful when one is interested in locating decisions from all American jurisdictions. Frequently, however, when engaged in legal research, one is primarily interested in locating decisions from a particular state or region or only those decisions from the Federal Courts.

The West Publishing Company publishes Key Number digests that are less inclusive than the *American Digest System.* As these are published in one alphabet (rather than chronologically as in the *American Digest System*) and they are kept up-to-date by pocket supplements, it is frequently easier to start the search in one of the following. Each has its own *Descriptive-Word Index* and Table of Cases volumes. Once a Topic and Key Number is located in a Key Number Digest, search for decisions can proceed in any other Key Number Digest.

1.   U. S. Supreme Court Digest (West Pub. Co.)

This 17-volume digest (25 physical volumes) of all decisions of the Supreme Court of the United States is classified under the *Key-Number System,* and duplicates the Supreme Court cases in the *American Digest System.* It is kept up-to-date by cumulative annual pocket supplements and includes the following:

(1) Volumes 1, 1A and 1B of the Digest comprise the *Descriptive-Word Index.*

(2) Volume 14, *Table of Cases.*

2. U. S. Supreme Court Reports Digest (Lawyers Co-op. Pub. Co.)

This is a 20-volume digest (26 physical volumes), with cumulative annual pocket supplements, to all U. S. Supreme Court decisions. Since this set is not published by the West Publishing Co., it does not employ the *Key-Number System* and follows the publisher's own distinct classification.

(1) Volume 16 is the *Word Index*, used in the first instance when applying the Index Method.

(2) Volumes 15 and 15A include the *Table of Cases*.

(3) Volumes 17, 18 and 19 cover *Court Rules* (to be discussed in Chapter 12, Court Rules and Procedure).

(4) Volume 17 contains the text of the U. S. Constitution, with references to topics in the *U. S. Supreme Court Reports Digest* (Lawyers Co-op.) covering the subject matter.

(5) In 1975, Volume 20 was added to this set. It contains the complete text of the recently adopted new Rules of Evidence for United States Courts and Magistrates, with Annotations and the Legislature History of these new rules.

3. West's Federal Practice Digest, 2d; Modern Federal Practice Digest; Federal Digest

These three sets are Key-Number digests and are published by the West Publishing Company. The *Federal Digest* was published in 1940 and for twenty years served as a basic source for locating federal court decisions. By 1960, however, significant changes in both statutory and case law had occurred. This led the publisher to publish a new digest of federal court decisions under the title, *Modern Federal Practice Digest*. The *Federal Digest* contains the digests of all federal cases decided prior to 1939. The *Modern Federal Practice Digest* has the digests of federal cases decided from 1939 to 1961. Decisions handed down since 1961 are in the *West's Federal Practice Digest, 2d*.[2] This set is kept up to date by annual pocket supplements and subsequent pamphlet supplements. The *Descriptive Word Index* volumes index all three sets. Other features of these digests are:

(a) Cases are arranged under each Key-Number: (1) Supreme Court of the United States, (2) Court of Appeals, alphabetically by

[2] This set started publication during 1976, and will not be completed for several years. As each volume is published, the cumulative supplements for the *Modern Federal Practice Digest* corresponding volume are removed. As indicated in the text, when completed, Federal cases will be digested as follows: 1789–1938 in the *Federal Digest*, 1939–1960 in the *Modern Federal Practice Digest*, and 1961 to date in *West's Federal Practice Digest 2d*.

jurisdiction, (3) District Courts, alphabetically by jurisdiction. Cases are listed chronologically with latest case listed first.

(b) Case histories—the *Digest* paragraphs include information as to whether a case has been affirmed, reversed or modified.

(c) "Library references" in each section note other general secondary sources in point, *e. g., Corpus Juris Secundum; Davis, Administrative Law.*

(d) *Table of Cases* volumes for cases within each set.

(e) *Defendant-Plaintiff Table* indexes for each set.

(f) *Words & Phrases* volumes also index each set.

(g) A complete numerical listing of all patents adjudicated is included under the topic "Patents", Key-Number 328.

(h) An alphabetical table of all *Trade-Marks and Trade-Names Adjudicated* is included in the *Trade-Mark* volume.

4. Regional Digests (West Pub. Co.)

The units of the *National Reporter System* have separate digests. These digests presently follow the *Key-Number* classification and cover all the reports of each state in the regions. Each regional digest includes a *Descriptive-Word Index*. The digest paragraphs under the key-numbers are arranged alphabetically by states. The publisher in recent years has expanded some of the reporter digests to include synopses of the early court decisions not covered by the *National Reporter System*. These expanded services are the *North Western Digest, Pacific Digest, Southern Digest* and *South Eastern Digest*. The *Atlantic Digest* does not contain summaries of the early Pennsylvania, New Hampshire, Maryland and Vermont opinions. The other state reports are included in the *Atlantic Digest* from their inception.

The regional digests are:

Atlantic Digest, First and Second Series
North Western Digest, First and Second Series
Pacific Digest, First and Second Series
South Eastern Digest
Southern Digest

The *Reporters* covered by the digests began publication between 1879 and 1887.

5. State Digests

Digests to the court decisions of the several states have been published by the West Publishing Co. and other publishers. The West's state digests follow the *Key-Number* scheme. In fact, the various

digests published by the West Publishing Co. are segments of the *American Digest System* with divisions into the *Federal* and *regional digests* and further subdivision of these units, with some minor variances, into the *U. S. Supreme Court* and *state digests*. This can be illustrated by the following chart:

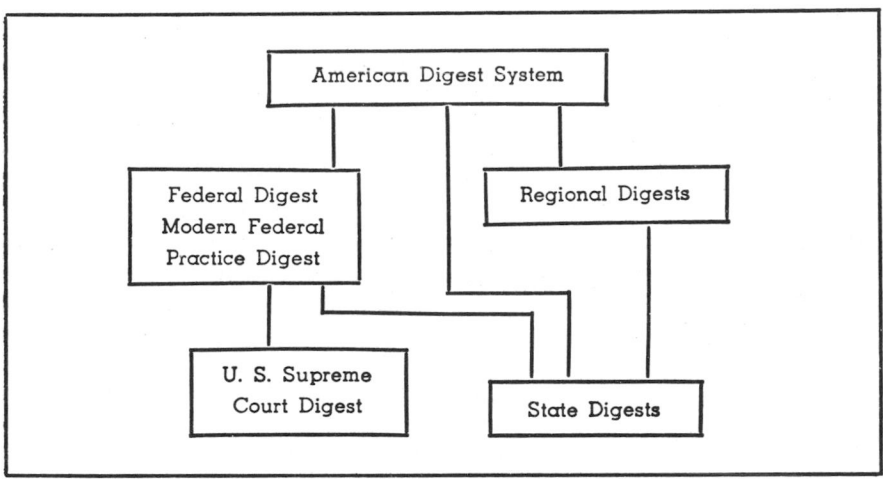

Features Common to Most
State Digests

As with other legal publications, the characteristics common to most state digests [3] may be surveyed in relation to their: (1) scope, (2) arrangement, (3) special features and (4) supplementation.

The state digests usually cover all reported state decisions and the Supreme Court of the United States and other federal cases arising in each state or applying state law, from the earliest period to date. The digests are arranged by a subject classification, with titles, sections, scope-notes and analyses. The most common additional features are: (1) a descriptive-word and topical index, (2) a table of the digested cases and (3) words and phrases judicially defined by the digested cases. The state digests are kept up-to-date by replacement volumes and cumulative periodic pocket and pamphlet supplements.

The characteristics of the various state digests, regardless of the publishers, are sufficiently uniform to make the methods of use of one generally applicable to the others. But each state digest should be examined for any special features.

---

[3] The West Publishing Co., publishes *Key-Number* digests for nearly every state and for the District of Columbia. Some states also have state digests of other publishers. Although not *Key-Number* digests, the method of use is similar.

SECTION C. WORDS AND PHRASES AS AIDS IN THE USE OF THE DEFINITION METHOD

We have observed that at times the meaning or definition of a legal or non-legal word or phrase plays a significant role in the solution to a problem. Occasionally, the English language dictionaries are helpful in providing definitions of words whose interpretations and meanings influence the results in decisions. Legal dictionaries are also useful aids in providing informational content to the meaning of words. These will be discussed in Chapter 19.

The need extended to include the meaning given words and phrases by judges. This resulted in specialized publications devoted to words and phrases judicially defined.

Further, by using the Definition Method in research it became possible to deconceptualize problems and depart from subject fields in eliciting word meanings. Thus, a definition of a word framed in a negligence case could be applied with equal significance to a contracts problem where it was correspondingly applicable. To have limited the search for the definition of the word to the confines of the subject matter, contracts, would have eliminated the possibility of locating its definition in a different area, torts. The advantage of this extensive approach to definition research is obvious. To illustrate, "good faith" is defined in bankruptcy, corporation, landlord and tenant and family law.[4]

The most significant set for use in this technique is:

1. Words and Phrases

The West Publishing Co. has compiled words and phrases which have been defined judicially by federal and state courts in a comprehensive publication called *"Words and Phrases"* (Permanent edition). This 46-volume set includes over 350,000 court definitions of *legal* and *non-legal* terms, arranged alphabetically by the words or phrases. When there are numerous definitions under a word or a phrase, they are arranged and subdivided by topics. The publication is kept up-to-date by cumulative annual pocket supplements and replacement volumes. To obtain supplemental down-to-the-minute definitions, consult the Tables of Words and Phrases in the current volumes and advance sheets of the *National Reporter System*. The back of the title page of each pocket supplement to *Words and Phrases* indicates the volumes of the *Reporter System* covered by the set. See Illustration 19.

Tables of Words and Phrases also appear in most of the special digests discussed *supra*.

---

[4] *See* Fenneberg, *A Short Cut in Legal Research*, 29 OHIO BAR 523 (1956).

SECTION D. ILLUSTRATIONS

10. Sample page from Alphabetical List of Digest Topics used in Key Number System.

11. Pages from Topic Negligence from Seventh Decennial Digest.

12. Sample pages from the Pacific Reporter.

13. Sample pages from Descriptive Word Index to the Seventh Decennial Digest.

14. Sample page from the Seventh Decennial Digest.

15. Sample page from the General Digest, Fourth Series.

16. Sample page from Second Decennial Digest.

17. Sample page from the Century Edition Digest.

18. Sample page from Table of Cases Volume of the Seventh Decennial Digest.

19. Sample page from Volume of Words and Phrases.

20. An excerpt from a page of Shepard's Federal and State Cases by Popular Names.

[Illustration 10]

SAMPLE PAGE FROM ALPHABETICAL LIST OF DIGEST TOPICS USED IN KEY NUMBER SYSTEM

DIGEST TOPICS

Navigable Waters
Ne Exeat
Negligence
Neutrality Laws
Newspapers
New Trial
Notaries
Notice
Novation
Nuisance
Oath
Obscenity
Obstructing Justice
Officers
Pardon and Parole
Parent and Child
Parliamentary Law
Parties
Partition
Partnership
Party Walls
Patents
Paupers
Pawnbrokers and Money Lenders
Payment
Penalties
Pensions
Perjury
Perpetuities
Physicians and Surgeons
Pilots
Piracy
Pleading
Pledges
Poisons
Possessory Warrant
Post Office
Powers
Principal and Agent
Principal and Surety
Prisons
Private Roads
Prize Fighting
Process

Quo Warranto
Railroads
Rape
Real Actions
Receivers
Receiving Stolen Goods
Recognizances
Records
Reference
Reformation of Instruments
Reformatories

Rewards
Riot
Robbery
Sales
Salvage
Schools and School Districts
Scire Facias
Seals
Seamen
Searches and Seizures
Seduction
Sequestration
Set-Off and Counterclaim
Sheriffs and Constables
Shipping
Signatures
Slaves
Social Security and Public Welfare
Sodomy
Specific Performance
Spendthrifts
States

Subscriptions
Suicide
Sunday
Supersedeas
Taxation
Telecommunications
Tenancy in Common
Tender
Territories
Theaters and Shows
Threats

There are over 435 Topics in the American Digest System. **Each Topic is subdivided into "Key-Numbers".** See next Illustration.

Trespass to Try Title
Trial
Trover and Conversion
Trusts
Turnpikes and Toll Roads
Undertakings
United States
United States Commissioners
United States Marshals
Unlawful Assembly
Use and Occupation
Usury
Vagrancy
Vendor and Purchaser
Venue
War and National Defense
Warehousemen
Waste
Waters and Water Courses
Weapons
Weights and Measures
Wharves
Wills

[Illustration 11]
FIRST PAGE OF TOPIC NEGLIGENCE FROM SEVENTH DECENNIAL DIGEST

NEGLIGENCE

SUBJECTS INCLUDED

Failure to use due care, either in respect of acts or of omissions, in performance or observance of a duty not founded on contract, which failure is the proximate cause of unintended injury to the person to whom such duty is owing

Nature and extent of liability for such injuries in general

Nature and effect of negligence or other fault on the part of the person injured contributing to his injury

> **In each unit of the Decennial and General digests, each topic has a list of subjects included and excluded and of the Key-Number classification for the Topic.**

SUBJECTS EXCLUDED AND COVERED BY OTHER TOPICS

Death, actions for damages for, see DEATH

Manslaughter by negligence, see AUTOMOBILES, HOMICIDE

Particular kinds of property, negligence in care and use of, see MINES AND MINERALS, WATERS AND WATER COURSES, ANIMALS, SHIPPING, COLLISION, and other specific topics

Particular kinds of works, public improvements, etc., negligence in construction and use of, see RAILROADS, BRIDGES, HIGHWAYS, MUNICIPAL CORPORATIONS, and other specific topics

Particular personal relations, occupations, employments, contracts, etc., negligence in respect of duties incident to, see ATTORNEY AND CLIENT, MASTER AND SERVANT, PHYSICIANS AND SURGEONS, CARRIERS, LANDLORD AND TENANT, BAILMENT, and other specific topics

For detailed references to other topics, see Descriptive-Word Index

---

Analysis.

I. ACTS OR OMISSIONS CONSTITUTING NEGLIGENCE, ☞1–55.
    A. PERSONAL CONDUCT IN GENERAL, ☞1–15.
    B. DANGEROUS SUBSTANCES, MACHINERY, AND OTHER INSTRUMENTALITIES, ☞16–27.
    C. CONDITION AND USE OF LAND, BUILDINGS, AND OTHER STRUCTURES, ☞28–55.

[Illustration 11–a]

SAMPLE PAGE OF TOPIC NEGLIGENCE—Cont'd

NEGLIGENCE

I. ACTS OR OMISSIONS CONSTITUTING NEGLIGENCE—Continued.

C. Condition and Use of Land, Buildings, and Other Structures.

    ⊨28. Care required in general.
    29. Duty to use care.
    30. Customary methods and acts.
    31. Requirements of statutes or ordinances.
    32. Care as to licensees or persons invited.
        (1).   In general.
        (2).   Who are licensees, and status of person going on land of another in general.
        (2.1).   Classes of licensees, and distinction between them in general.
        (2.2).   Bare licensees.
        (2.3).   Invitees in general.
        (2.4).   Implied invitation in general.
        (2.5).   Automobile service stations and parking service.
        (2.6).   Bill collectors.
        (2.7).   Buildings in process of construction, alteration, or demolition.
    →(2.8).   Business visitors, and store and restaurant patrons.
        (2.9).   Deliverymen and haulers.
        (2.10).   Employees and contractors.
        (2.11).   Frequenters.
        (2.12).   Gratuitous licensees.
        (2.13).   Guests in private homes.
        (2.14).   Meter readers.
        (2.15).   Persons accompanying invitees.
        (2.16).   Postmen.
        (2.17).   Public officials in general.

> **Immediately following the summary and analysis, there appears a detailed listing of the Key-Numbers, each representing a minute point of law. Each time a headnote deals with business visitors in a store or restaurant and involves negligence it will receive the Topic Negligence and Key-Number 32(2.8)**

    35. Care as to persons on adjacent highway.
    36. Private grounds in general.
    37. Places open to public.
    38. Places abutting on or near highways.
    39. Places attractive to children.
    41. Streams, ponds, and wells.
    42. Excavations.
    43. Embankments and piling of materials.
    44. Buildings and other structures.
    45. Elevators, hoistways, and shafts.
    46. Use of property.
    47. Traps, pitfalls, and harmful devices.
    48. Knowledge of defect or danger.
    49. Precautions against injury.
    50. —— In general.

[Illustration 12]
SAMPLE PAGE FROM THE PACIFIC REPORTER

450 Cal.   319 PACIFIC REPORTER, 2d SERIES

his failure to exercise ordinary care in remedying the defect after he has discovered it or as a man of ordinary prudence should have discovered it."

[4–7] As to the first issue, it is conceded that here the plaintiff was a business invitee and to whom the defendant owed a duty to exercise reasonable care in keeping the premises safe. Oldenburg v. Sears, Roebuck & Co., 152 Cal.App.2d ——, 314 P. 2d 33; Raber v. Tumin, 36 Cal.2d 654, 226 P.2d 574. Plaintiff in order to recover must establish that the defendant breached that duty and that such breach was the proximate cause of the injury. Palmer v. Crafts, 16 Cal.App.2d 370, 60 P.2d 533. The burden is on the plaintiff to prove every essential fact on which she relies. McKellar v. Pendergast, 68 Cal.App.2d 485, 156 P.2d 950. As no inference of negligence arises based simply upon proof of a fall on the owner's floor (Vaughn v. Montgomery Ward & Co., 95 Cal.App.2d 553, 213 P.2d 417; Thomas v. Moore, 146 Cal.App. 2d 59, 303 P.2d 624), we must turn to the record to discover if there are any facts from which the inference may be drawn that defendant was responsible for the presence of the lettuce on the floor.

The record reveals that defendant's market is one of several businesses occupying a common building and served with a common terrazzo corridor. Defendant is the only tenant of the building who sells vegetables. While all of the tenants participated in the cleaning of the corridor, defendant had assumed the duty of removing vegetable and other matter which fell thereon from the checkstands, a portion of which extended to the corridor.

Before entering defendant's market plaintiff and her companions had not been in the other area where vegetables were sold. They did not enter defendant's vegetable department. Plaintiff went through defendant's usual checking-out procedure which is as follows: the customer places his purchases on the revolving package platform extending beyond the entrance to the checkstand; the customer has nothing further to do with the

handling of his purchases until the attendant has completely packaged them and handed them to the customer at the far end of the checkstand.

On the date in question, defendant carried five or more types of lettuce, of which only the Los Angeles head lettuce was sold in a sealed cellophane bag. The other kinds of lettuce were sold in bulk tied with a flexible wire band. There was some evidence that the piece of vegetable matter found on plaintiff's shoe may have been of the Los Angeles type. The packaging and handling of the lettuce was done in defendant's basement. It was the custom of defendant's checkstand operators to remove

> This is a typical page from a case reported in the National Reporter System. It illustrates how headnotes are developed. The bracketed numbers are inserted by the editors. Each number has been rewritten into a headnote. See next Illustration.

its employees at the checkstand would fall from the counter to the floor, and therefore instructed its checkers that spilled greens were to be cleaned immediately after they fell and to inspect and sweep customers' aisles and the common corridor whenever necessary. Brooms and dustpans for this purpose were located between checkstands numbers 5 and 6. Defendant's janitor was employed only until 12:00 noon. After the janitor left, it was the duty of the checkers and baggers to sweep if they had the time.

Defendant's manager had no personal knowledge whether the area in question had been swept in the three hours preceding the fall but had inspected the area about fifteen minutes before the accident and had seen no lettuce leaves. Defendant's assistant manager had been delegated the duty of seeing that the corridors and aisle walk by the checkstands were clean but had not inspected the area in question for several hours before the fall. One of

[Illustration 12–a]

SAMPLE PAGE FROM THE PACIFIC REPORTER

418   Cal.   319 PACIFIC REPORTER, 2d SERIES

Beryl McKENNEY, Plaintiff and
Respondent,

v.

QUALITY FOODS, Inc., a corporation,
et al., Defendant and Appellant.

Civ. 17528.

District Court of Appeal, First District,
Division 2, California.

Dec. 26, 1957.

Action for customer's personal injuries allegedly resulting from fall in defendant's supermarket. The jury returned a verdict for plaintiff. The Superior Court, City and County of San Francisco, Edward Molkenbuhr, J., rendered judgment, and defendant appealed. The District Court of Appeal, Kaufman, P. J., held that evidence raised questions for jury as to whether defendant was responsible for vegetable matter on floor and whether fall was caused by slipping on such matter and whether defendant had actual or constructive notice of the presence of vegetable matter on the floor.

Affirmed.

1. Appeal and Error ☞930(1)

On appeal from judgment on verdict for plaintiff, the District Court of Appeal was required to accept the evidence most favorable to plaintiff.

2. Negligence ☞136(22, 25)

In action for injuries sustained by customer who fell in defendant's supermarket, evidence raised question for jury as to whether defendant was responsible for vegetable matter on floor and whether fall was caused by slipping on such matter.

3. Negligence ☞136(16)

In action for injuries sustained by customer who fell in defendant's supermarket, evidence raised question for jury as to whether defendant had actual or constructive notice of presence of vegetable matter on floor.

4. Negligence ☞32(2.8)

Customer in defendant's supermarket was a business invitee to whom defendant

owed duty to exercise reasonable care in keeping the premises safe.

5. Negligence ☞121(1, 5)

Customer suing for injuries sustained when she fell in defendant's supermarket must establish that defendant breached duty to exercise reasonable care in keeping premises clean and that such breach was proximate cause of injury.

6. Negligence ☞121(1)

In personal injury action, burden is on plaintiff to prove every essential fact on which she relies.

7. Negligence ☞121(3)

No inference of negligence of storekeeper arises based simply on proof of fall of customer on the storekeeper's floor.

8. Negligence ☞3

The quantum of care which the law

Note how the wording of the headnotes are paraphrased from the opinion. See Illustration 12.

10. Trial ☞260(1)

The refusal of proposed instruction was not error where other instructions covered the matter adequately.

11. Appeal and Error ☞1067

In action for injuries sustained by customer who allegedly fell in defendant's supermarket when she slipped on vegetable matter on the floor, the refusal to instruct on unavoidable accident was not prejudicial.

———

Hadsell, Murman & Bishop, San Francisco, for appellant.

Hoberg & Finger, L. Chas. Gay, San Francisco, for respondent.

KAUFMAN, Presiding Justice.

Plaintiff brought this action to recover for personal injuries resulting from a fall in defendant's grocery store. The cause was tried before a jury which returned a

[Illustration 13]

SAMPLE PAGE FROM THE DESCRIPTIVE WORD INDEX TO THE SEVENTH DECENNIAL DIGEST

NEGLIGENCE   36–7th D—294

NEGLIGENCE—Cont'd
Product liability—Cont'd
  Wheel chair, defective fork stem.
    Torts 1
  Wooden box—
    Neglig 136(18)
    Sales 445(1)
Propane gas—
  Explosion. **Gas 17, 20(4)**
  Heater installation. **Gas 17**
Questions for jury—
  Injury from escape or explosion of
    gas. **Gas 20(4)**
  Parking truck hitting lessee's wall—
    Fall on pedestrian on sidewalk.
    Land & Ten 169(11)
  Personal injuries on pier. **Wharves
    21**
  Statutory violations, evidence of
    negligence. **Neglig 6**
  Town's negligence. **Towns 45**
Reformation of instruments relief as
  barred by. **Ref of Inst 25**
Religious organizations and societies—
  Abolishing immunity. **Relig Soc 3**
Religious society's employees injuring
  patrons, liability of society. **Relig
  Soc 30**
Repudiation, absolute liability rule.
  Torts 1
Rescue doctrine. **Neglig 74**
  Conduct constituting negligence.
    Neglig 74
  Overturned vehicle, injuries warn-
    ing overtaking vehicles, action
    against overturned driver. **Autos
    246(33)**
Safety inspections, workmen's compen-
  sation insurance carrier. **Neglig 2**
Safety pilot valve, gas water heater,
  malfunction—
  Gas 10, 20(2, 5)
  Neglig 27
School districts, softball playing during
  recess. **Schools 5**

NEGLIGENCE—Cont'd
Superseding cause, defined. **Neglig 62
  (3)**
Surgical nail becoming stuck in leg
  during operation, liability for mis-
  branding. **Drug 9**
Swimming pool operated by city. **Mun
  Corp 747(2)**
Swimming pools, municipal corporation
  operating. **Mun Corp 734**
Taxicabs, inference or presumption from
  happening of accident. **Carr 316(4)**
Teachers—
  Personal liability for injuries to
    pupils. **Schools 147**
Third person—
  Insulating negligence of third per-
    son. **Neglig 62(3)**
Tools, defective and dangerous tools—
  Product liability. **Neglig 27**
Tractor-trailer, test. **Autos 146**
Trees, low hanging branches, infants.
  Neglig 32(4)
Unavoidable accident, instruction to
  jury. **Neglig 140**
United States, weapons, reckless use on
  United States property, tort liability.
  U S 78(15)
University employee causing injury to
  patron, liability of university. **Col-
  leges 5**
Violation of law—
  Causal connection, violation and in-
    jury. **Neglig 136(25)**
  Negligence per se. **Neglig 6**
Visible and obvious hazards, duty to
  warn. **Neglig 52**
Voluntary violation of standards of
  due care. **Neglig 138(1), 145(4)**
Volunteer. **Neglig 2**
  Firemen, fire district liability. **Au-
    tos 187**
  Standard of care. **Neglig 2**
Warnings—

NEGOTIABLE INSTRUMENTS—C't'd
Cross-action for rescission, summary
  judgment. **Judgm 181(10)**
Divorce, award of homestead. **Divorce
  249(6)**
Income tax—
  Capital gains, new note for old.
    Int Rev 410.1
Judgment, setting aside, authority of
  trial court. **Judgm 67(2)**
Pawn ticket as not. **Pawnb 5**
Reformation, third party rights. **Ref
  of Inst 6**
Summary judgment, reversible error in
  changing cause from one on nego-
  tiable instrument to one based
  upon quantum meruit—
  App & E 1073(1)
  Judgm 186
Trade acceptances, non-licensed foreign
  corporation payee—
  Assignee as holder in due course,
    jury question. **Bills & N 537(6)**
  Enforcement. **Corp 657(7)**
Trading stamps, negotiable character.
  Insurance 506.5
United States bonds. **U S 91**

NEGOTIATIONS
Enticement of nonresident into jurisdiction for service of process. **Proc
  65**

NEGRO CANDIDATES
Race designation, discrimination. **Const
  Law 215**

NEGROES
Adoption of children—
  Negro by white parents, application,
    mandamus to compel acceptance.
    Mand 166(4)
Airports—
  Preliminary injunction against ex-
    clusion from waiting room. **Inj
    136(2)**
  Regulation and use in general.
    Aviation 234
  Separate facilities for whites and
    Negroes—
    Aviation 234
    Commerce 62
Amusement parks—
  Refusal to leave park which did
    not admit Negroes—
    Arrest and convicting defend-
      ants as violative of equal pro-
      tection. **Const Law 217**
    Disorderly conduct. **Disorderly
      C 9**
  Right to entry or tickets—
    Const Law 217
    Theaters 4
Amusement places—
  Denial of admission, damages—
    Civil R 4, 6
    Inj 7
  Picket lines, segregation. **Inj 128**
  Anti-miscegenation statutes, constitu-
    tionality—
    Const Law 250, 258
    Misceg 1
Apartment houses—
  Civil rights, entrapment. **Civil R 1**
  Discrimination. **Civil R 3**
  Appeal, order directing board of edu-
    cation to submit desegregation plan.
    Courts 405(12.1, 12.23)

We can now start to illustrate how Topics and Key-Numbers can be located using the Descriptive Word Index for the fact situation as set forth on page 70. The first step is to choose a word or concept.

If the search is started under Negligence, it quickly becomes apparent that this entry is too broad to locate a specific topic and key-number applicable to the problem being researched.

Statutory standard of care. **Neglig 6**
Stevedores, breach of warranty of
  workmanlike service—
  Recovery over from vessel from
    stevedore for liability to injured
    longshoreman. **Ship 84(6)**
Stopping motor vehicle without warn-
  ing. **Autos 158, 169**
Storekeeper, accumulation of slush.
  Neglig 134(5)
Stores and storekeepers, injury to pa-
  tron, attractive display doctrine.
  Neglig 67
Subrogation, automobile accident, ac-
  crual of right, time. **Subrog 35**
Sudden emergency rule. **Neglig 12, 72**
Suntan lotion, skin irritation. **Neglig
  27**

Autos 168(1), 246(36)

NEGLIGENT HOMICIDE
Burden of proving affirmative defense.
  Autos 353

NEGOTIABLE INSTRUMENTS
Assignment to secure money, usury,
  evidence. **Usury 117**
Attachment, jurisdiction of court. **At-
  tach 62**
Certificate of savings account in savings
  and loan association. **B & L Assoc
  40**
Chattel mortgages providing for maturity without notice on customer's default as not negotiable. **Chat Mtg 203**
Corporations, dissolution of. **Corp 617
  (3)**

Appeal to race prejudice by district at-
  torney in argument to jury. **Crim
  Law 723(5), 1171(1)**
Appeal to racial discrimination in criminal
  prosecution. **Crim Law 723(5), 730
  (14)**
Apprentices—
  Aptitude test. **Civil R 3**
  Qualifications. **Civil R 1**
Apprenticeship classes, union discrimi-
  nation. **Civil R 1**
Arguments and conduct of counsel—
  Retaliatory statement of prosecutor
    elicited by defense counsel's re-
    marks. **Crim Law 726**
Assault with automobile, asserting civil
  rights, federal court pendent juris-
  diction. **Courts 263**

[Illustration 13–a]

EXCERPTS FROM THE DESCRIPTIVE WORD INDEX TO THE SEVENTH DECENNIAL DIGEST

STORES AND STOREKEEPERS—C't'd

Customers—
  Assault and battery by employee—
    Course of employment. **Mast & S 302(3)**
    Pleading. **Mast & S 329**
  Class suit, recovery, tax collections by retailer. **Parties 10**
  Falling on onion stalk on floor. **Neglig 134(7)**
  Friend as invitee of licensee. **Neglig 32(2.8)**
  Injuries, falling over stock truck in aisle, questions for jury, sufficiency of evidence. **Neglig 136(22)**
  → Invitees. **Neglig 32(2.8)**
  Use of reasonable care. **Neglig 67, 80**
Damages for loss of view by extension of building over sidewalk area. **Mun Corp 671(4)**

35—7th D—1221

INVITATION
Assumption, normal or obvious risks. **Neglig 105**
Assumption of risk, invitee. **Neglig 106**
Care as to invited person in respect to condition and use of land, buildings or other structures—
  Knowledge of dangerous condition. **Neglig 48**
  Pupils, private school. **Schools 5**
  Slipping on waxed floor. **Neglig 121(3)**
Church premises, member of public injured on portion of premises to which not invited, jury question. **Relig Soc 30(6)**
Clinic door identical to basement door, invitee falling **Neglig 50**
Contributory negligence of invitee. **Neglig 65**
Custom concerning movement of motor vehicles—
  Duty of invitee to inform self concerning custom. **Autos 152**
  Effect of custom on invitee's liability for another's injuries in collision. **Autos 170(3)**
→ Customer's friend as invitee of licensee. **Neglig 32(2.8)**
Docks—

    This illustrates how by looking under either Stores and Storekeepers or INVITATION subentries will lead to Topic Negligence and Key-Number 32(2.8) which stands for "Business Visitor, and Store and Restaurant Patron". While not shown in illustrations, this Topic and Key-Number could also have been located in the Descriptive Word Digest index to the Seventh Decennial under the entries: Business Invitee; Fall or Floors. After locating the Topic and Key-Number the next step is to search all units of the American Digest System under Negligence 32(2.8) as shown in Illustrations 14–17.

[Illustration 14–a]

SAMPLE PAGE FROM THE SEVENTH DECENNIAL DIGEST

NEGLIGENCE ☞32(2.8)

tempted to descend after finishing playing.—West v. Shizuko Tan, 208 F.Supp. 708.

D.C.La. 1962. Generally, one who is on premises in the performance of his duty occupies the status of an invitee or a business visitor with respect to degree of care owed by him to owner or person in charge.—Hurst v. Point Landing, Inc., 212 F.Supp. 160, quoting 65 C.J.S. Negligence § 43(4).

D.C.S.C. 1964. Relationship between storekeeper and customer is that of invitor and invitee.—Rikard v. J. C. Penny Co., Columbia Division, 233 F.Supp. 133.

Cal.App. Customer in defendant's supermarket was a business invitee to whom defendant owed duty to exercise reasonable care in keeping the premises safe.—McKenney v. Quality Foods, Inc., 319 P.2d 448.

Cal.App. A patron of a tavern is a business invitee and proprietors thereof owe patron a duty of exercising ordinary care to keep premises in a safe condition.—Shaw v. Colonial Room, 1 Cal.Rptr. 28.

Cal.App. Adult accompanying friend into store where friend intended to make purchase was an invitee rather than a mere licensee.—Farrier v. Levin, 1 Cal.Rptr. 742.

Cal.App. Customer in a store was an invitee to whom the store owed the duty to exercise ordinary care to keep the premises in reasonably safe condition or to warn of danger, and duty was not limited to conditions actually known to be dangerous but extended also to conditions which might have been found dangerous by reasonable care.—Iloff v. Purity Stores, Limited, 2 Cal.Rptr. 735.

Cal.App. In order to be an invitee or business visitor, it is not necessary that visitor should himself be on land for purpose of possessor's business, but it is sufficient that he be on premises for convenience or necessity of one who is on land for such purpose.—Beeston v. Lampasona, 6 Cal.Rptr. 531.

Cal.App. 1962. Store patron was business invitee while walking on parking lot adjacent to store as well as while in store itself, and storekeeper owed invitee duty of exercising ordinary care to avoid injury to her.—Perez v. Ow, 19 Cal.Rptr. 372.

Cal.App. 1963. Generally, "invitee" or "business visitor" is person who is invited or permitted to enter or remain in possession of another for a purpose directly or indirectly connected with business dealings between them.—Clawson v. Stockton Golf and Country Club, 34 Cal.Rptr. 184.

Invitation to an invitee or business visitor may be implied from such circumstances as conduct of possessor, arrangement of premises, or local custom.—Id.

Colo. 1964. Plaintiff's driver while on shipper's premises in connection with plaintiff's business was an invitee.—Colorado-Wyoming Ry. Co. v. Wheelock Bros. Inc., 395 P.2d 1.

Del. A storekeeper is not an insurer of his patrons, and has only duty to exercise same standard of care reasonably prudent storekeepers would exercise under like circumstances to keep premises in reasonably safe condition for customers' use.—Robelen Piano Co. v. Di Fonzo, 169 A.2d 240.

D.C.Mun.App. An adult daughter who accompanied her mother who desired to purchase a rake needed in house where daughter lived with her mother was an "invitee" of store from the time she entered store because she was a potential customer.—Sears, Roebuck & Co. v. Donovan, 137 A.2d 716.

Under Maryland law an adult daughter who accompanied her mother for purpose of buying a rake was "invitee" of store notwithstand-

> After locating the Topic and Key-Number as shown in Illustration 13, the digest paragraphs should be consulted to select cases in point with the problem under research.
>
> The Seventh Decennial Digest covers cases reported from 1956–1966.

service station premises for purpose of paying a bill for oil previously purchased was a "business invitee", and persons in control of premises had duty to exercise ordinary care for customer's safety and to warn customer of latent or concealed defects which should have been known to such persons; however, the persons in control had no duty to warn customer against patent or obvious conditions which were not dangerous per se.—Andrews v. Goetz, 104 So.2d 653.

Fla.App. Incidental motives of the visit of a social guest, other than purely social, or minor services performed by guest for host during visit will not be sufficient to change status of visitor from licensee to invitee or business visitor.—Cochran v. Abercrombie, 118 So.2d 636.

Fla.App. In absence of showing of reason why can fell from shelf and struck patron on leg and foot, patron could not recover for her injuries from store owners.—Food Fair Stores, Palm Beach, Inc. v. Spinelli, 122 So.2d 41.

Fla.App. 1962. An "invitee" is normally considered to be one who enters upon premises of another for purposes connected with business of owner or occupant of premises.—North Broward Hospital Dist. v. Adams, 143 So.2d 355.

Fla.App. 1964. Plaintiff who was injured when sacks of cow feed stacked in defendants' barn struck plaintiff on the back and head at a time when he was engaged, with permission of defendants, in removing bags of feed from their barn to plaintiff's truck for transportation to ranch on which he worked for another, was, while he was in the barn, a "licensee."—Jerrell v. Whitehurst, 164 So.2d 875.

Fla.App. 1966. Plaintiffs, as customers of defendants' cocktail lounge, were invitees of defendants' place of business.—Carter v. Parker, 183 So.2d 3.

Ga.App. While there must be at least some mutuality of interest in the subject matter to which the visitor's business relates, the particular subject of the visit need not be for the benefit or the profit of the occupant.—Knudsen v. Duffee-Freeman, Inc., 109 S.E.2d 339.

A mere permissive use of premises is sufficient to raise an implied invitation to those having business with the permittee to come upon the premises and the existence of the relation of landlord and tenant as between the owner and the person visited is not essential to the owner's liability.—Id.

[Illustration 15]

SAMPLE PAGE FROM GENERAL DIGEST, FOURTH SERIES

NEGLIGENCE 🔑32(2.13)

owes duty to avoid willfully, intentionally or recklessly injuring him.—Id.

N.Y.A.D. 1969. School district employee

> After consulting the 7th Decennial, the individual volumes of the General Digest should be checked for cases handed down after 1966. Each volume contains all the cases for a three-month period. In all of the Decennial Digests, cases under a Key-Number are arranged alphabetically with Federal courts listed first. In 1977, it is anticipated that all of the volumes of the General Digest 4th Series will be cumulated into the Eighth Decennial Digest.

status, whether that of a trespasser, a licensee, a social guest, or a mere passerby only duty to avoid willfully, intentionally or recklessly injuring him.—Lemon v. Busey, 461 P. 2d 145.

An "invitee" on premises to whom owner owes duty to exercise ordinary care for his safety is either a public invitee or a business visitor.—Id.

A "public invitee" to whom owner of property owes duty to exercise ordinary care for his safety is person who is invited to enter or remain on land as member of public for purpose for which land is held open to public.—Id.

Fact that someone is invited to visit does not make him a "public invitee" to whom owner of land owes duty to exercise ordinary care for his safety; rather purpose of his visit determines his status.—Id.

Meaning of "invitee" to whom owner of property owes duty to exercise ordinary care for his safety is more limited than meaning of term "invitation" in popular sense and not all of those who are invited to enter on land are invitees.—Id.

Place and purpose of visit determine whether person on premises is invitee to whom owner owes duty to exercise ordinary care for his safety or merely licensee to whom owner owes duty to avoid willfully, intentionally or recklessly injuring him.—Id.

Miss. 1969. Lady who paid admission charge to go upon historical site controlled and maintained by county historical society was "public invitee", toward whom society owed duty of reasonable care including reasonable inspection to discover actual condition of premises and any latent defects, followed by such repairs as might be reasonably necessary for protection under circumstances.—Alexan-

der v. Jackson County Historical Soc., Inc., 227 So.2d 291.

🔑**32(2.8). Business visitors, and store and restaurant patrons**

Kan. 1969. A "business visitor" to whom owner of property owes duty to exercise ordinary care for his safety is a person who is invited to enter or remain on land for purpose directly or indirectly connected with business dealings with possessor of land.—Lemon v. Busey, 461 P.2d 145.

Minn. 1969. A "business visitor" is a person who is invited or permitted to enter or remain on land in possession of another for a purpose directly or indirectly connected with business dealings between them.—Berry v. Haertel, 170 N.W.2d 558.

Where city employees had entered garden-supply dealer's building to help load hay used by city on municipal projects and none of city's employees had ever been instructed or warned not to enter building, employee, who entered building for purpose of loading hay and sustained injury when board gave way and he slipped into hole up to his hip, was a business visitor as a matter of law.—Id.

🔑**32(2.10). Employees and contractors**

C.A.Miss. 1969. The United States, which engaged independent contractor to remove debris from lake and against which suit was brought to recover for death of contractor's employee who, while returning by boat from work to base camp, struck submerged highway bridge turntable located in center of lake and suffered fatal heart attack in attempting to rescue coemployee who was thrown overboard by impact, owed the contractor-invitee, under Mississippi law, a duty to (1) use ordinary care to have the premises in reasonably safe condition for uses consistent with the snagging operations, (2) not expose the contractor to unreasonable risks, and (3) give the contractor adequate notice of latent perils known to the United States.—Market Ins. Co. v. U. S., 415 F.2d 459.

🔑**32(2.13). Guests in private homes**

Ala. 1969. Where mother went to home of her son at invitation of son's wife, mother was a mere social guest and son and remodeling contractor owed her only the duty to refrain from putting traps in her way and were under no duty to take affirmative care to prepare premises for her reception and were not liable for injuries she sustained when wooden block, serving as temporary step, turned over under her weight with result that she fell and suffered fracture.—Deese v. Espy, 226 So.2d 332.

Ill.App. 1969. Care owed a business invitee by owner of a private home is less than that required by owner of a business establishment. —Hunter v. Alfina, 251 N.E.2d 303.

Kan. 1969. An owner of property owes an invitee a duty to exercise ordinary care for his safety but owes a person having any other status, whether that of a trespasser, a licensee, a social guest, or a mere passerby only duty to avoid willfully, intentionally or recklessly injuring him.—Lemon v. Busey, 461 P. 2d 145.

N.J.Super.A.D. 1969. At time niece and her husband were in process of proceeding from

[Illustration 16]

SAMPLE PAGE FROM THE SECOND DECENNIAL DIGEST

◆⟶32(1)   NEGLIGENCE   [17—2d Dec. Dig., Page 56]

I. Acts or Omissions Constituting Negligence.   (C) Condition and Use of Land, Buildings, and Other Structures.

One can search for cases under a Key-Number back to 1897 by consulting the earlier Decennials. Illustrated here is the Second Decennial Digest which covers all cases reported from 1897–1906.

For cases prior to 1897, it is necessary to consult the Century Digest. Note the cross reference in this illustration indicating that cases on this topic will be found in the Century Digest under Negligence § 43.

aua, not receiving any answer to her knock, she started along the hall to enter the back room in order to secure attention. As she did so she fell into the trap, the door of which had been left open by a plumber employed by the owner of the house, a few minutes before. *Held*, that there was no negligence of defendant, except that it had failed to open the shutter by which the hall could have been adequately lighted.—Donohue v. Western Union Telegraph Co., 57 Pa. Super. Ct. 251.

A telegraph company is not bound to supply its patrons a safe place to do business, but only a reasonably safe place.—Id.

(**Tex.**1910) Invitation, license, or allurement of others to come on premises may give rise to responsibility on the part of the owner which, without it, would not exist, for injuries sustained by them from dangerous things there on against which he has not exercised ordinary care to guard them.—Stamford Oil Mill Co. v. Barnes, 128 S. W. 375, 103 Tex. 409, 31 L. R. A. (N. S.) 1218, Ann. Cas. 1913A, 111, reversing judgment (Civ. App. 1909) 119 S. W. 871.

(**Tex.Civ.App.**1907) Where a railway track is constructed and used through a smelter company's premises by its permission and for its benefit, it is the duty of the smelter company to exercise ordinary care to avoid injury to the employés of the railway company rightfully upon its premises in the discharge of their duties. —Consolidated Kansas City Smelting & Refining Co. v. Binkley, 99 S. W. 181, 45 Tex. Civ. App. 100.

(**Tex.Civ.App.**1907) Defendant owed a customer's employé on its premises the legal duty to exercise at least ordinary care to protect him from injury.—Waters-Pierce Oil Co. v. Snell, 106 S. W. 170, 47 Tex. Civ. App. 413.

(**Utah,**1912) A gas company maintaining an office for the payment of gas bills *held* only bound to exercise ordinary care to provide a reasonably safe place for customers.—Quinn v. Utah Gas & Coke Co., 129 P. 362, 42 Utah, 113, 43 L. R. A. (N. S.) 328.

(**Wash.**1911) Defendant engaged in removing a rock bluff, incident to the construction of its railroad, contracted with plaintiff to drive a tunnel in the face of the bluff in which to explode powder. A heavy blast in another tunnel, for the purpose of loosening part of the face of the bluff, brought down a quantity of rock immediately in front of plaintiff's tunnel, blocking the entrance to it. Plaintiff, at the direction of defendant's foreman, commenced to remove the débris, but being alarmed by the fall of a rock, ceased work, and reported

fall to defendant's foreman who said he ɟ make the bluff safe. Plaintiff did not n to work till the next morning, after oreman had assured him that he had causɪe wall and slope to be made safe. *Held* even if plaintiff was an independent conor, and not an employé, defendant having him the wall would be made safe, and asl him that this had been done, owed him luty of making it safe, in so far as this be done by inspection and barring down ɔse rock; so that, plaintiff having a right ly on the assurance that it had been made defendant was liable for injury to him gh the falling of a rock, caused by negliɪ in not making the place safe.—Gibson v. ɪgo, M. & P. S. Ry. Co., 112 P. 919, 61 ɪ. 639.

ash.1914) Where defendant's servant, ɔed the skip of a derrick on deceased, who on defendant's premises after refusal of ɔyment, *held* that defendant was not liable. ɔeger v. Grays Harbor Const. Co., 145 P. 3 Wash. 68.

.Va.1914) A property owner owes a highgree of care in keeping the premises reaɔly safe, to persons entering by his inɪent or by his invitation, than to persons wno are mere licensees.—Smith v. Sunday Creek Co., 82 S. E. 608, 74 W. Va. 606.

(**Wis.**1911) Maintenance of an open stairway in part of a store not intended for use by customers, but merely for storage, is not negligence, so as to create a liability to a customer falling down the stairway, unless he was expressly or impliedly invited there.—Lehman v. Amsterdam Coffee Co., 131 N. W. 362, 146 Wis. 213.

(**Wis.**1913) A manufacturing company maintaining in its yard a switch track owes the duty to the members of a railroad switching crew, switching on the track, of removing obstructions on the track.—Landry v. Great Northern Ry. Co., 140 N. W. 75, 152 Wis. 379.

◆⟶32(2). *Who are licensees, and status of persons going on land of another.*

See 37 Cent. Dig. Neglig. § 43.

(**U.S.C.C.A.Ga.**1914) One who goes on the premises of another for the benefit, real or supposed, of the owner or occupant, or in a matter of mutual interest, or in the ordinary course of their business, or for the performance of some duty, is an invitee.—Middleton v. P. Sanford Ross, 213 F. 6, 129 C. C. A. 622, reversing order (D. C. 1913) 202 F. 799.

The rule that an owner or occupant of premises is required to use ordinary care to keep them in safe condition for invitees' use is applicable to a servant of an independent contractor.—Id.

(**U.S.C.C.A.Neb.**1913) Plaintiff accompanying a friend owning an automobile to defendant's garage, where he was injured by falling down a cellar stairway, *held* a mere licensee for whose injury defendant was not liable, where the place was lighted, with a door at the head of the stairway.—Rhode v. Duff, 208 F. 115, 125 C. C. A. 343.

(**U.S.C.C.A.N.Y.**1914) Employé of seller of oil, who went upon buyer's tank to measure the oil therein before and after delivery, *held* an invitee, and it was the buyer's duty to exercise ordinary care to keep the premises in a safe condition.—New York Lubricating Oil Co. v. Pusey, 211 F. 622, 129 C. C. A. 88.

(**U.S.C.C.A.Pa.**1908) Where defendant had consented to the use of a crane runway in defendant's mill by plaintiff, a servant of an independent contractor, in moving scaffolding from one truss in an addition to the mill to another, plaintiff in so using the runway was not a trespasser, but was within the class of persons present in dangerous premises by the

[Illustration 17]

SAMPLE PAGE FROM THE CENTURY EDITION DIGEST

377 (§ 42)   NEGLIGENCE.   (§ 43) 378
Cent. Ed.]   I. Acts or Omissions Constituting Negligence.   (C) Condition and Use of Land, Buildings, and Other Structures.   1. In General.

[p] (N. J. 1871) It is well settled that the mere permission to pass over lands which are dangerous, either naturally or by reason of the use which is made of them, imposes no duty or obligation upon the owner of such lands, except to refrain from acts which are willfully injurious or knowingly in the nature of a trap, and except, also, where there are hidden dangers, the concealment of which would be in the nature of a fraud. He who enjoys the permission or passive license is only relieved from the responsibility of being a trespasser, and must assume all the ordinary risk attached to the nature of the place or the business carried on there.—Vanderbeck v. Hendry, 34 N. J. Law (5 Vroom) 467.

> Century Digest **covers all reported cases from 1658–1896.**
>
> **Note this is not a "key-number" digest and classifications differ from the** Decennial Digests.

who unnecessarily follows a clerk to that part of the store, and in so doing stumbles over the truck.—Hart v. Grennell, 122 N. Y. 371, 25 N. E. 354.

[s] (N. Y. 1892) While plaintiff was on premises adjoining her own, seeking her children, who were accustomed to play there, she was injured by the breaking of a decayed stairway. *Held*, that she could not recover from the owner of such premises on the ground that he negligently permitted the stairs to remain in an unsafe condition, because, she being on the premises without invitation and as a mere licensee, the owner owed her no duty of protection.— Sterger v. Vansiclen, 132 N. Y. 499, 30 N. E. 987, 28 Am. St. Rep. 594, 16 L. R. A. 640, affirming (1890) 55 Hun, 605, 7 N. Y. Supp. 805.

[t] (Ohio, 1884) Where a lot is left unfenced, a person who goes upon it by bare permission, because there is no obstruction to keep him off, goes at his own risk; and the owner is not liable for injuries resulting to him from the unsafe or dangerous condition of the lot.—Kelley v. City of Columbus, 41 Ohio St. 263.

[u] (S. C. 1873) The plaintiff was in the store of the defendant as a customer. A clerk invited her to walk into a dark part of the store, in which there was an open trapdoor, through which she, without negligence on her part, fell and broke her arm. *Held*, that the defendant was liable.—Freer v. Cameron, 4 Rich. Law, 228, 55 Am. Dec. 663.

[v] (Vt. 1875) Plaintiff went to defendant late in the evening to buy oats. Defendant had no oats to sell, but, yielding to plaintiff's importunity, he consented to sell him the oats, to accommodate him. Defendant always kept his granary locked, but he obtained the key by sending some distance for it, and went with plaintiff to the upper floor of the granary, where the oats were, and, while defendant stepped back to get a measure, plaintiff walked about the floor in the dark, and fell through an aperture therein, and was injured. *Held*, defendant was not liable for the injury.—Pierce v. Whitcomb, 48 Vt. 127, 21 Am. Rep. 120.

[w] (Wis. 1895) Plaintiff alleged that his intestate was invited by defendant into an uncompleted building, to make certain estimates. At the head of the stairs there was a hallway, in which there was a partially open window. Deceased followed defendant up the stairs, thrust his head through the window, without knowledge that the window was part of the

elevator shaft, and was struck by the descending elevator. *Held*, that defendant was not guilty of any breach of duty to the deceased, and therefore the facts alleged did not constitute a cause of action.—Peake v. Buell, 90 Wis. 508, 63 N. W. 1053, 48 Am. St. Rep. 946.

§ 43. —— Who are licensees.
Places open to public, see post, § 53 [b].

[a] (Ill. 1892) A person who breaks into a building to protect property from fire is a mere licensee, to whom the owner owes no duty to keep the premises in safe repair.—Gibson v. Leonard, 143 Ill. 182, 32 N. E. 182, 36 Am. St. Rep. 376, 17 L. R. A. 588, affirming (1890) 37 Ill. App. 344.

[b] (Ind. 1893) In an action for personal injuries caused by falling through an open cellarway in a college building, there was evidence that plaintiff was a visitor, but had previously been a student; that he was in attendance at a literary society at the invitation of a student; that circulars had been prepared, advertising the society as a feature of the college; that the students were authorized to send out the circulars; that plaintiff received one by mail; and that he was personally asked by the superintendent to visit the building. *Held*, that plaintiff was in the building at the invitation of the college authorities.—Howe v. Ohmart, 7 Ind. App. 32, 33 N. E. 466.

[c] (Ind. 1893) Where plaintiff came into defendant's store without invitation on part of defendant, and solely on plaintiff's own business, and fell into an elevator shaft in a part of the store unfrequented by visitors, whereby he sustained injuries, defendant cannot be held liable for negligence, as plaintiff can only be regarded as a licensee.—Faris v. Hoberg, 134 Ind. 269, 33 N. E. 1028, 39 Am. St. Rep. 261.

[d] (Ind. 1893) A fireman in the course of his duty goes on the roof of a building on fire as a mere licensee, and not as of right or by invitation of the owner.—Woodruff v. Bowen, 136 Ind. 431, 34 N. E. 1113, 22 L. R. A. 198.

[e] (Mass. 1880) If a religious society gives notice of a meeting to be held at its house of worship, and invites the members of other societies to attend, a member of a church so invited, while on the land of the society, is not a mere licensee, and may maintain an action against the society for a personal injury sustained, while in the exercise of due care, from the dangerous condition of the defendant's premises.—Davis v. Central Congregational Soc., 129 Mass. 367, 37 Am. Rep. 368.

[f] (Mass. 1892) A person who enters a building containing offices, to inquire about a servant of the occupier of one of the offices, who keeps no servant's registry and who has no connection with such business, the building not being used or designed in any part for such purpose, is a mere licensee therein; and the owner is not liable for injuries received by her through the unsafe condition of the building.— Plummer v. Dill, 156 Mass. 426, 31 N. E. 128, 32 Am. St. Rep. 463.

[g] (Mich. 1893) A teamster, after delivering merchandise at the back door of a store, started towards the desk for a receipt, and fell through an open trapdoor. *Held*, that the proprietor was not liable for the injuries; it not appearing that there had been any express or implied invitation to the teamster to pass to the desk, but that it was the custom of truckmen to make their presence known by calling, when no one was at the door.—Pelton v. Schmidt, 97 Mich. 231, 56 N. W. 689.

[h] (N. Y. 1890) Plaintiff having gone, in the course of his business, to defendant's factory, to find an employé of defendant who usually attended to the business, went, through a passageway not generally used for that purpose,

[Illustration 18]

SAMPLE PAGE FROM TABLE OF CASES VOLUME OF THE SEVENTH DECENNIAL DIGEST

McKENNEY   38–7th D—38

References are to Digest Topics and Key Numbers

McKenney v. Buol, Or, 329 P2d 664—Account 3; Action 6; App & E 781 (1); Judgm 829(3).

McKenney v. F C C, CADC, 324 F2d 444—Tel 398.

McKenney v. McKenney, Md, 135 A2d 423—Equity 219; Ex & Ad 43, 85 (1); Ten in C 11; Wills 627(3), 741.

McKenney v. Oregon Am Lumber Co, Or, 304 P2d 426—App & E 78(3, 4), 103, 870(5); Judgm 195.

McKenney v. Quality Foods, Inc, Cal App, 319 P2d 448—App & E 930(1), 1067; Neglig 3, 32(2.8), 121(1, 3, 5), 136(16, 22, 25, 26); Trial 260 (1).

McKenney Logging Co v. Buffelen Mfg Co, CAOr, 232 F2d 5. See McKenney v. Buffelen Mfg Co.

McKennon v. Anderson, Wash, 298 P 2d 492—App & E 766; Evid 384, 417(7), 455, 461(1); Frds St of 129 (6); Land & Ten 24(1), 25(1), 31, 180(4); Licens 44(2).

Mackensworth v. Mathiasen's Tanker Industries, Inc, DCPa, 203 FSupp 316—Adm 82; Seamen 12, 26, 30.

Mackenzie, Application of, Sup, 164 NYS2d 319, aff In re Mackenzie, 170 NYS2d 987, appeal den 178 NYS 2d 594, motion dism 179 NYS2d 857, 154 NE2d 137—Trusts 272(3).

McKenzie v. Albaeck, CalApp, 32 Cal Rptr 762—App & E 948, 962; Dismissal 60(1, 2).

McKenzie v. Arthur T McIntosh & Co, IllApp, 200 NE2d 138—App & E 714 (5); Const Law 70(1); Counties 21½; Offic 103; Plead 360(10).

McKenzie v. Atlantic Manor, Inc, Fla App, 181 So2d 554—Land & Ten 150 (1), 152(3), 169(11); Trial 178.

McKenzie v. Brixite Mfg Co, NJ, 166 A2d 753—Work Comp 673, 1983.

McKenzie v. Brixite Mfg Co, NJSuper AD, 161 A2d 276, rev 166 A2d 753 —Work Comp 51, 230, 673, 676, 1357, 1562.

McKenzie v. Campbell & Dann Mfg Co, Tenn, 354 SW2d 440—Evid 501 (2); Work Comp 546, 836, 854, 862, 1336, 1638, 1643, 1644, 1855.

McKenzie v. Carte, TexCivApp, 385 SW2d 520, ref n r e—App & E 758 (1), 1175(7); Contracts 141(1); Elect of Rem 1, 7(1); Land & Ten 42(3), 105, 180(1, 3, 4, 6); Plead 427; Trial 392(1), 404(1).

McKenzie v. City of Florence, SC, 108 SE2d 825—Mun Corp 54, 57, 59, 189(1), 723, 724, 745½, 747(3); Princ & S 66(1).

McKenzie v. Com for Use and Benefit of Hicks, Ky, 373 SW2d 595—Bankr 198, 216; Execution 110, 116; Interest 39(3); Sheriffs 120½, 138 (3).

McKenzie v. Cutter, Wis, 117 NW2d 249. See Schmitz' Estate, In re.

MacKenzie v. Fritzinger, Mich, 121 NW2d 410—Trusts 103(3), 107, 110.

McKenzie v. International Ladies Garment Worker's Union, AFL-CIO, Local No 371, SC, 141 SE2d 834. See Bouchette v. International Ladies Garment Worker's Union, AFL-CIO, Local No 371.

McKenzie v. Kirkpatrick, DCCal, 141 FSupp 49—Armed S 3; Courts 265; Decl Judgm 272.

McKenzie v. McKenzie, FlaApp, 105 So2d 614—Divorce 227(1), 312.4.

McKenzie v. McKenzie, Mich, 84 NW 2d 333—Divorce 246.

MacKenzie v. MacKenzie, Mich, 115 NW2d 326—Divorce 27(18), 49(2), 50, 135.

McKenzie v. McKenzie, Mich, 132 NW 2d 73—App & E 927(7); Autos 245 (24).

McKenzie v. McKenzie, MoApp, 306 SW2d 588—Contin 22; Divorce 1, 164, 172, 179, 225, 255, 298(3, 4); Infants 19.2(2); Parent & C 2 (3.2, 3.3).

McKenzie v. Nelson, Mich, 91 NW2d 15—Autos 244(6, 36), 245(72); Judgm 199(3.2); Neglig 136(26); Trial 178.

Mackenzie v. Newton, TexCivApp, 341 SW2d 498, ref n r e—Licens 39.45; Trial 350(3).

McKenzie v. North River Ins Co, Ala, 58 So2d 581—Insurance 599.3.

McKenzie v. Ohio State Racing Commission, Ohio, 215 NE2d 397—Admin Law 676; App & E 2; Theaters 3.

McKenzie v. Ohio State Racing Commission, Ohio App, 204 NE2d 569, rev 215 NE2d 397—Admin Law 676; Theaters 2.

McKenzie v. Pacific Gas & Elec Co, CalApp, 19 CalRptr 628—App & E 927(3), 989; Electricity 14(1, 2), 19(3, 5, 9, 10, 12); Neglig 10, 121 (2); Torts 1.

McKenzie v. Porter, Idaho, 386 P2d 363—Joint Adv 5(2).

McKenzie v. Racing Commission, Ohio App, 204 NE2d 569, rev 215 NE2d 397.

MacKenzie v. Reesey, Md, 201 A2d 848—Autos 160(1), 217(3), 227(3); Neglig 65, 83.1.

A page from the Table of Cases volume of the Seventh Decennial.

When a case is known to deal with a topic of law, Key-Number can be located by the use of a Table of Cases.

Mackenzie v. Soden Mineral Springs Co 27 AbbNC 402, 18 NYS 240—Trade Reg 436.

McKenzie v. State, AlaApp, 177 So2d 110—Crim Law 1076(5), 1081, 1099 (6), 1106(1), 1109(1), 1182.

McKenzie v. State, Md, 187 A2d 885—Crim Law 260(11), 566, 901, 1044.

McKenzie v. State, Md, 204 A2d 678 —Const Law 250, 257; Crim Law 511(1), 586, 589(1), 590(2), 594(3), 595(4), 627.5(2), 742(1), 747, 1171 (1); Sod 6.

McKenzie v. State, Miss, 101 So2d 651—Const Law 268(3); Crim Law 641(1), 641.6(3), 641.12(1, 2), 1163 (2).

MacKenzie v. State, CtCl, 166 NYS2d 408—Em Dom 136, 149; States 184.-5; Stip 14(11).

McKenzie v. State, TexCrApp, 383 S W2d 177—Crim Law 13, 739(1), 814(8), 1036(1), 1038(3); Poisons 4, 9.

McKenzie v. State, TexCrApp, 390 SW 2d 281—Crim Law 1028, 1170½(2); Poisons 9.

MacKenzie v. Sullivan 40 Erie 216—Land & Ten 167(2), 168(1), 169 (11); Neglig 67.

Mackenzie v. Sun Choo Choi, Hawaii, 387 P2d 475—App & E 78(7), 801 (1); Dismissal 24, 42.

MacKenzie v. Town Planning and Zoning Commission of Town of Trumbull, Conn, 183 A2d 619—Const Law 93(1); Evid 43(3); Int Liq 46½, 59(1), 75(7); Statut 265; Zoning 324.

McKenzie v. U S, DCMunApp, 158 A2d 912—Weap 11(1).

McKenzie v. U S, CAOkl, 266 F2d 524 —Crim Law 452(2), 456, 493, 570 (2), 740, 753(2).

MacKenzie v. U S, CAOr, 244 F2d 712, rev Simpson v. U S, 78 SCt 14 —Crim Law 1134(3); Witn 297 (8).

McKenzie v. Western Greenbrier Bank, Va, 124 SE2d 234—App & E 1062(1); Fixt 7, 14; Land & Ten 37, 152(3), 154(3), 160(2).

McKenzie Const Co v. Pittman, Tex CivApp, 288 SW2d 527, error dism—Venue 7.

McKenzie Const Co v. U S, DCTex, 214 FSupp 738—Int Rev 550.

McKenzie Elec Co-op, Inc v. Eklund Bros Transport, Inc, DCND, 225 F

Supp 940. See White v. McKenzie Elec Co-op, Inc.

McKenzie Mach Shop v. Western Fire Ins Co, DCMinn, 161 FSupp 115. See Richard v. Western Fire Ins Co.

McKenzie Sand & Gravel Co v. State, CtCl, 166 NYS2d 408. See MacKenzie v. State.

McKenzie's Estate, In re, CalApp, 18 CalRptr 680—Ex & Ad 497, 501, 502, 506(3), 507(1), 510(4, 10), 513(9); Wills 728, 734(1), 753.

McKenzie's Estate, In re, CalApp, 38 CalRptr 496—Char 1, 10, 18, 21(1); Perp 8(1, 8); Trusts 160(2).

Mackenzie's Estate, In re, Sur, 230 NYS2d 63—Corp 123(10).

McKenzie's Estate, In re, Ohio Prob, 139 NE2d 505—Des & Dist 75; Ex & Ad 3(1), 7, 43.

McKenzie, State ex rel, v. La Driere, MoApp, 294 SW2d 610. See State ex rel McKenzie v. La Driere.

Mackenzie's Will, In re, Sur, 227 NYS2d 561, adhered to In re Mac-

Estop 72; Ex & Ad 456(1).

McKeon v. Goldstein, Del, 164 A2d 260—Land & Ten 169(11); Neglig 56(1), 60, 62(1), 136(25).

McKeon v. Highway Truck Drivers and Helpers, Local 107, of Intern Broth of Teamsters, Chauffeurs, Warehousemen and Helpers of America, DCDel, 223 FSupp 341—Courts 289; Labor 123, 140.

McKeon v. Highway Truck Drivers and Helpers, Local 107, of Intern Broth of Teamsters, Chauffeurs, Warehousemen and Helpers of America, DCDel, 28 FRD 592—Fed Civ Proc 1275, 1483, 1512.

McKeon v. Northeast Service Corp, Mass, 166 NE2d 733—App & E 1064 (1); Death 58(1); Trial 295(6).

McKeon v. Santa Claus of Cal, Inc, CalApp, 41 CalRptr 43—App & E 882(9), 1010(1); Equity 38; Evid 448, 450(5), 455; Spec Perf 28(1), 121(2); Trial 404 (5), 412.

McKeon v. State for Use of Conrad, Md, 127 A2d 635—Death 9, 18(3), 58(1); Statut 181(1), 235.

McKeon v. Unemployment Compensation Bd of Review 195 PaSuper 69, 169 A2d 332—Social S 388, 399.

McKeon v. U S, DCNJ, 152 FSupp 427. See Gordon v. U S.

McKeon's Estate, In re, Sur, 199 NYS 2d 158—Des & Dist 43.

McKeon Unemployment Compensation Case 195 PaSuper 69, 169 A2d 332. See McKeon v. Unemployment Compensation Bd of Review.

McKeone, Appeal of, IllApp, 204 NE 2d 611. See Rakus v. Black.

Mackerman, Ex parte, TexCrApp, 376 SW2d 350—Evid 590; Extrad 36; Hab Corp 85.8(1).

McKernan v. Mutual of Omaha 31 LehLJ 201—Insurance 536, 583(1), 583.1.

McKeough v. Witman, DelSuper, 127 A2d 234—Autos 245(40, 72); Judgm 181(2); Neglig 122(1).

McKeown v. Wheat, CAGa, 231 F2d 540—Courts 359; Judgm 564(2), 675(1), 678(2), 828(3:31, 3.32).

McKeown's Estate, In re 394 Pa 186, 147 A2d 331—App & E 1008(1); Infants 83.

McKerley v. U S Fidelity & Guaranty Co, GaApp, 101 SE2d 103—Work Comp 1433, 1939.

[Illustration 19]

SAMPLE PAGE FROM VOLUME OF WORDS AND PHRASES

BUSINESS INVITEE

Corp. v. Morse, D.C.Minn., 222 F.Supp. 645, 652.

"Store patron" was a "business invitee". Stewart v. George B. Peck Co., 135 S.W.2d 405, 408, 234 Mo.App. 864.

Independent contractor employed to put a new surface on roof was on the premises as a "business invitee." U. S. Steel v. Warner, C.A.Utah, 378 F.2d 995, 997.

Paying patron of skating rink was a "business invitee". Noble v. Park Enterprise, 47 N.E.2d 947, 949, 313 Mass. 454.

One who enters retail store for purpose of making a purchase is a "business invitee". Little v. Butner, 348 P.2d 1022, 1028, 186 Kan. 75.

A member of crew of fishing trawler whose owner paid wharfage for right to unload vessels was "business invitee" of pier operator. Hayes v. Boston Fish Market Corp., 66 N.E.2d 713, 715, 319 Mass. 556.

Where plaintiff's intestate went to defendants' funeral home to attend wake of his father, intestate was a "business invitee". Watts v. Rhodes, 91 N.E.2d 925, 926, 325 Mass. 697.

A master pilot who was assigned to take charge of shifting of steamship was a "business invitee". Mason v. U. S., D.C.N.Y., 77 F.Supp. 921, 922.

A registered guest of a hotel is a "busi-

Truck driver, delivering lumber for his employer to lumber yard of buyers, was a "business invitee" of lumber yard operators. Nowell v. Harris, 68 So.2d 464, 467, 219 Miss. 363.

Where United States as owner of vessel contracted with engineering company for removal of contents of life boats, rigger employed by company was a 'business invitee". Mack v. U. S., D.C.Mass., 105 F.Supp. 149, 152.

A motel guest is a "business invitee" to whom operator of motel owes a duty to use ordinary or reasonable care to provide the guest with reasonably safe premises. Winer v. Walo, Inc., Fla.App., 105 So.2d 376, 377.

Woman attending evening bingo games at incorporated school was "business invitee" of school and was entitled to protection accorded such invitees. Garofoli v. Salesianum School, Inc., Del.Super., 208 A.2d 308, 310.

Society newspaper reporter, who was given complimentary membership by country club was its "business invitee" so that club owed her duty to keep its premises in reasonably safe condition. Country Club of Coral Gables v. McHale, Fla.App., 188 So.2d 405, 407.

Bowler at bowling alley was "business invitee" or proprietors, and they owed him duty to use ordinary care to keep bowling alley reasonably safe for his use. Guidani v. Cumerlato, 207 N.E.2d 1, 6, 59 Ill.App.2d 13.

ness [...] was
of c[...] l but
Irwi[...] ation
[...] s in-
latio[...] ty &
party[...] So.2d
is im[...]
"busi[...] erat-
ing elevator in building under control of
S. F. R. Co., 392 P.2d 873, 876, 193 Kan. 223.   landlord during evening after landlord's reg-

A page from Words & Phrases. The paragraphs are essentially the same as they appeared as headnotes in the volumes of the National Reporter System. The pocket supplement of the volumes of Words & Phrases should always be checked.

One entering strafing range at army camp pursuant to contract with the United States for recovery of scrap metal from range was a "business invitee". White v. U. S., D.C.Cal., 97 F.Supp. 12, 13, 14.

A minor child, accompanying mother, when she went to store, on business errand, was "business invitee". Takashi Kataoka v. May Dept. Stores Co., 140 P.2d 467, 470, 60 Cal.App.2d 177.

ular operator had left was a "business invitee" of tenant. Peay v. Reidy, 73 N.E.2d 737, 738, 321 Mass. 455.

Painters on service station premises with permission of operator and for purpose in which he had beneficial interest would be his "business invitees" even though they were not under contract with him or in his employ. Bates v. Callahan, 198 N.E.2d 644, 646, 347 Mass. 772.

[Illustration 20]

AN EXCERPT FROM A PAGE OF SHEPARD'S FEDERAL AND STATE CASES BY POPULAR NAMES

D-E   TABLE OF CASES CITED BY POPULAR NAMES

302 US 134, 82 LE 155, 58 SC 208;
114 F2d 242; 312 US 678, 85 LE
1117, 61 SC 450; 312 US 714, 85
LE 1144, 61 SC 620

1→ **Dred Scott Case**
60 US 393, 15 LE 691

Drive-It-Yourself Case
144 Md 223, 125 At 69

Driven-Well Cases
8 Fed 269
15 Fed 109; 122 US 40, 30 LE 1064,
7 SC 1073
2→ 16 Fed 387; 123 US 267, 31 LE 160,
8 SC 101; 124 US 694, 31 LE 557,
8 SC 676
FC No. 371

Driver's License Revocation Case
(Cal) 187 P2d 421; 32 Cal2d 226, 195
P2d 792

Drover's Pass Cases
84 US 357, 21 LE 627
95 US 655, 24 LE 535
67 Fed 209, 14 CCA 368
73 Fed 519, 19 CCA 551
200 Fed 197, 118 CCA 383
40 Ark 298
6 Del 469
160 Ill 40, 43 NE 809; 57 IllApp 538
174 Ill 13, 50 NE 1019; 69 IllApp 363
184 Ill 294, 56 NE 331; 81 IllApp 137
47 Ind 471
71 Ind 271

Drummer Cases—Cont'd
102 Ark 314, 144 SW 211; 227 US 401,
57 LE 569, 33 SC 298
57 Md 251; 120 US 502, 30 LE 699,
7 SC 655
167 Mich 417, 132 NW 1071; 232 US
665, 58 LE 786, 34 SC 476
127 NC 521, 37 SE 138; 187 US 622,
47 LE 336, 23 SC 229
143 PaSt 642, 22 At 893; 153 US 289,
38 LE 719, 14 SC 829
81 Tenn 303; 120 US 489, 30 LE 694,
7 SC 592
105 Tenn 412, 58 SW 1061; 185 US 27,
46 LE 785, 22 SC 576
23 TexCrim 662, 5 SW 91; 128 US 129,
32 LE 368, 9 SC 1
113 Va 562, 75 SE 1135; 236 US 697,
59 LE 795, 35 SC 479

Dry Ice Case
25 F2d 730; 38 F2d 62; 281 US 711,
74 LE 1133, 50 SC 347; 283 US
27, 75 LE 819, 51 SC 334; 283
US 794, 75 LE 1419, 51 SC 483;
283 US 420, 75 LE 1153, 51 SC
496

Duck Lake Case
223 La 47, 64 So2d 839

Dud Fireworks Bomb Case
273 AppDiv 939, 78 NYSupp2d 4; 298
NY 409, 84 NE2d 38

Notes to Illustration 20:
1. Popular name of case.
2. Several different cases may go by the same popular name.

Drowned Child Liability Case
(Tex) 200 SW2d 699; 146 Tex 434,
208 SW2d 843

Druggists Cases
85 Tenn 449, 3 SW 490

Drugless Healer Case
36 Wash2d 482, 219 P2d 79; 340 US
892, 95 LE 646, 71 SC 208

Drummer Cases
16 DC 489; 129 US 141, 32 LE 637,
9 SC 256
95 Ark 464, 130 SW 569; 227 US 389,
57 LE 565, 33 SC 294

58 SC 300

Dulles Case
123 Fed 371, 59 CCA 499; 139 Fed
510; 139 Fed 513, 71 CCA 500

Duncan Iron Works Case
136 PaSt 478, 20 At 647

Duplex Case
247 Fed 192; 252 Fed 722, 164 CCA
562; 254 US 443, 65 LE 349, 41
SC 172

Du Pont Trust Case
188 Fed 127; 273 Fed 869

SECTION E.   CITING DIGESTS

Digests are *indexes* to cases and indexes, because they are merely finding aides with no legal authority as such, are never cited.   Therefore, *do not cite* digests.

In connection with the use of digests, a further caveat is appropriate at this time.   Do not rely on the text of the digest-paragraphs for the essence or the theory of a case.   They are intended to serve merely as guide-posts and not as edifices.   Since the paragraphs are necessarily brief, they can be misleading, can fail to suggest a nuance or shading of the case or can omit an element which may have specific bearing on your problem.   Thus, the digest is not the final repository of the law, and when research is important, it should not be the singular source of research.   Such perfunctory practice, in matters requiring deliberateness, could be embarrassing to you and catastrophic to your client.

SECTION F.   SUMMARY

1.   Index books—digests

a.   Digest—is an index to case law, giving brief, unconnected statements of court holdings or facts of cases, and is classified by subject.

2.   Types of Digests

a.   All courts, federal and state.

b.   A region, a group of neighboring states.

c.   A state.

d.   A specific court or court system.

3.   American Digest System

a.   Scope.

(1)   Digest which purports to cover every reported case, federal, state or local, from 1658 to date.

(2)   Consists of a *Century Digest* (1658–1896), eight *Decennial Digests* (1897–1906, 1907–1916, 1916–1926, 1926–1936, 1936–1946, 1946–1956, 1956–1966, and 1966–1976), and the *General Digest, 5th Series* (1976 to date).

b.   Arrangement.

(1)   Key-Number System—(topic and number) subject classification, e. g., Corporations ⟳343.

(2) Corresponding key-numbers used in all *Decennial Digests*, *General Digest* and other West digests.

(3) Scope-note (delimits and identifies the content of a topic).

(4) Analysis (conceptual breakdown of a topic).

(5) Section lines, preceded by the key-numbers, indicate the content of each key-number under a topic.

(6) Digest-paragraphs arranged under key-numbers by: Supreme Court of the United States, other federal courts, and state cases listed alphabetically by names of states. The name and citation of each case follows the digest-paragraph.

(7) Expanded topics are periodically added, e. g., Trade Regulation.

   c.   Century Digest (1658–1896).

(1) Not classified by Key-Number System.

(2) To refer from *Century Edition* to the *Decennials*, use the pink reference table in volume 21 of the *First Decennial.*

(3) When a key-number is known and one wishes to locate the corresponding section in the *Century Edition,* refer to the cross reference included in the *First* or *Second Decennials* under the appropriate key-number. The references in the *Second Decennial* are more complete.

   d.   Use of the Index Method with the *American Digest System.*

(1) Each Decennial and the *General Digest* have a *Descriptive-Word Index.*

(2) Since recent cases are preferred, begin research with the latest Decennial's *Descriptive-Word Index.* After locating a key-number, check it in all Decennials and the *General Digest* for cases in point. Then consult the cross reference under the key-number to the *Second Decennial* to identify the corresponding section in the *Century Edition.* Examine the *Century Edition,* under that section number, for early cases. This research will disclose cases in point from 1658 to date.

   e.   Using the Topic Method with the *American Digest System.*

(1) Avoids use of the *Descriptive-Word Index.*

(2) Examine the scope-note and analysis under the appropriate title. Select the key-number and proceed as above.

4.   U. S. Supreme Court Reports Digests (see Section B2 *supra*)

5.   West's Federal Practice Digest 2d
   a.   Scope.

(1) Index to federal cases since 1961.

(2) Covers decisions of the Supreme Court of the United States, the *Federal Reporter, 2d Series,* the *Federal Supplement,* and the *Federal Rules Decisions.*

(3) Kept up to date with cumulative pocket supplements.

6. **Modern Federal Practice Digest**

a. Scope.

(1) Index to modern federal practice cases between 1939 and 1960.

(2) Covers decisions of the Supreme Court of the United States, the *Federal Reporter, 2d Series,* the *Federal Supplement* and the *Federal Rules Decisions.*

b. Arrangement.

(1) Under the Key-Number System.

(2) Descriptive-Word Index to *Federal Digest* and to *Modern Federal Practice Digest.*

(3) *Tables of Cases* in volumes 53, 53A and 54.

(4) Words and Phrases in volumes 57 and 58.

(5) Case history.

(6) Library references.

(7) The cases of a jurisdiction, which are digested under a key-number, are listed chronologically, beginning with the latest case.

(8) Cumulative annual pocket and pamphlet supplements keep the *Digest* current.

7. **Federal Digest**

a. Scope.

(1) Indexes federal case law of historical significance, some of which is no longer controlling, from the foundation of the Government to 1939.

(2) Covers *Federal Cases,* the U. S. Supreme Court decisions, the *Federal Reporter* and the *Federal Supplement.*

b. Arrangement.

(1) By the Key-Number System.

(2) Descriptive-Word Index to the *Modern Federal Practice Digest* also covers the *Federal Digest.*

(3) Tables of Cases in volumes 66–68.

(4) Words and Phrases in volumes 71 and 72.

(5) Volume 72 has a *Table of Popular Name Titles,* covering cases in the *Digest.*

8. Regional Digests

a.   Segments of the *American Digest System,* arranged by states which form the units of the *National Reporter System.*

b.   Some *Regional Digests* do not include cases prior to the unit of the *National Reporter.*

c.   Classified under the Key-Number System.

d.   Contain standard digest features, e. g., Descriptive-Word Index, Table of Cases, etc.

9. State Digests

a.   West state digests follow the Key-Number System and are fragments of the *American Digest System.*

b.   Standard features common to many state digests:

(1) Cover all reported state decisions and federal cases arising in each state or applying state law from the earliest period to date.

(2) Classified by subject, with titles, sections, scope-notes and analyses.

(3) Descriptive-Word Index.

(4) Table of Cases.

(5) Words and phrases judicially defined by the digested cases.

(6) Kept up-to-date by replacement volumes and cumulative pocket and pamphlet supplements.

Chapter 7

ANNOTATED LAW REPORTS

The *National Reporter System* with its *Key-Number Digest System* provides for the comprehensive reporting of all reported decisions. Another private publishing company, the Lawyers Co-operative Publishing Co. (and its related company, the Bancroft-Whitney Co.) publish court reports on a selective basis. Their theory is that only a small portion of the total number of cases handed down each year is of interest to most lawyers, as most cases deal with either strictly local matters, or cover an area of law so well settled that they add very little to an understanding of the law. What would serve lawyers better, they claim, is reporting only significant court decisions, those that deal with points of law not previously decided, or that indicate a change in the law, or indicate a new trend in legal thinking. By this manner of selective reporting a lawyer could have all important decisions and not have to burden his bookshelves with thousands of cases that really add nothing to the corpus of the law.

Although selective law reporting was the basis for their first venture in publishing court reports, they realized that lawyers would have to be able also to locate other decisions not reported in their publication and also have a method of locating current decisions. To provide this service they began to publish auxiliary sets, all related to each other, and all aimed to assist the lawyer in finding answers to all of his legal questions through the use of their publications. These sets gradually grew into what they now call *The Total Client Service Library*,[1] which consists of seven distinctive sets of law books. This chapter will discuss its annotated law reports.

SECTION A.   AMERICAN LAW REPORTS (A.L.R.)

The *American Law Reports* is a selective reporter of appellate court decisions. Its editors scan all current decisions and select those that in their opinion are or will become "leading" cases. There are no advance sheets to this set and several volumes are published each

---

[1] *The Total Client-Service Library consists of: American Jurisprudence 2d; American Jurisprudence Legal Forms 2d; American Jurisprudence Pleading and Practice Forms, Annotated, Revised; American Jurisprudence Trials; American Law Reports Annotated (A.L.R.; A.L.R.2d; A.L.R.3d; A.L.R.Fed.); American Jurisprudence Proof of Facts; United States Code Service; United States Supreme Court Reports, Lawyers Edition;* and *Federal Procedural Forms, Lawyers Edition.*

year. *A.L.R.*, however, is significant not for the decisions it reports but for the editorial service that follows each reported decision, or for what the publishers call *Annotations*. These are expository encyclopedic essays of varying length on the significant legal topics embodied in the reprinted cases with each case followed by an annotation. *A.L.R.* annotations contain: (1) statements and reasons for general rules; (2) discussion of supposedly all cases on the point annotated, with jurisdictional analyses and emphases; (3) consideration of the application of rules to specific facts, as well as distinctions, differentiations and commentaries; and (4) definitions of words and phrases.

The annotations are very helpful in providing discussions on detailed points of law, thus obviating exploratory research in locating and analyzing cases. Annotations may also cover topics of such currency as not to be found in encyclopedias, treatises or periodical literature. The annotations on overriding cases add to the usefulness of the set. The manner in which *A.L.R.* is published and the role of annotations can be made clear by example.

In the case of *Low v. Siewert*, 55 Wis.2d 251, 195 N.W.2d 451, 66 *A.L.R.3d* 198 (1972), the plaintiff had parked her car in her employer's parking lot. She worked late that evening and upon leaving, noticed that the parking lot was unlighted due to a burned out bulb. As she neared her car, she stumbled or fell over some unknown object and severely injured herself. She brought suit alleging negligence on the part of the employer in failing to keep the parking lot well lighted. The editors of *A.L.R.* decided that this decision was suitable for publication in *A.L.R.* but in terms of legal research this is not significant, as this decision will also be published in the official *Wisconsin Reports* and in the *North Western Reporter*. What is significant is what *A.L.R.* furnishes *in addition to* the decision, which is a 162-page annotation that immediately follows the decision in the *A.L.R.* volume. In legal research, *A.L.R.* is used not for the reported decision, but for the annotation that follows. The decision is merely a basis for an annotation on a particular point of law. The case of *Low v. Siewert*, as in nearly every reported case, involves more than one point of law. This case, for instance, dealt with the issues of trial procedure, negligence, and landlord and tenant. It was chosen by *A.L.R.* for the issues involving the law of landlord and tenant and it uses these for the subsequent annotation. Thus, the annotation following the *Siewert* decision is entitled:

> **Liability of landlord for personal injury or death due to inadequacy or lack of lighting on portion of premises used in common by tenants.**

Although the decision itself is only three pages, the annotation is not restricted to its limited fact situation but is written on the generalized

topic. The editor assigned to it researches this area of law and locates all previous decisions from all jurisdictions that dealt with this topic. It cites and summarizes the facts and holdings of every reported case in point and presents an analysis and synthesis of the cases. In short, what *A.L.R.* designates as an "Annotation" is in fact a legal memorandum on a particular topic of law which covers all sides of every question, presents general principles deduced from the cases, and gives their exceptions, qualifications, distinctions, and applications.

The usefulness of locating an *A.L.R.* annotation should be evident, since it presents in an organized fashion a commentary and discussion of all previously reported decisions and saves the searcher the task of locating the cases and then analyzing and synthesizing them.

A.L.R., in summary, consists of bound volumes containing selected appellate decisions, each of which has an annotation on a point of law decided in the case. An annotation may vary from one page to over a hundred. See Illustration 23 for example of a typical *A.L.R.* Annotation.

1. A.L.R. Series

The American Law Reports are published in four series.[2]

First Series (cited "*A.L.R.*") 1919–1948, 175 v.

Second Series (cited "*A.L.R.2d*") 1948–1965, 100 v.

Third Series (cited "*A.L.R.3d*") 1965 to date.

Federal (cited "*A.L.R.Fed.*") 1969 to date.

The latter set started in 1969 and includes only court decisions from the federal courts. As mentioned in Chapter 3, the Lawyers Cooperative Publishing Company publishes an annotated set of the U. S. Reports. Although decisions from the Federal Courts of Appeals previously have appeared in *A.L.R.*, litigation has, however, been increasing in both amount and importance and the publishers felt that federal cases now deserved special treatment.

A.L.R.-Fed. is published in a format similar to *A.L.R.* Leading decisions of the federal courts are published followed by an annotation in the same manner as described *supra*.

2. A.L.R. Upkeep Service

Once an *A.L.R.* annotation has been found in a volume, further steps must be taken to determine cases subsequent to those found in the *A.L.R.* annotation. For example, after Volume 1 of *A.L.R.* was published in 1919, the publishers were immediately faced with the

---

[2] The *American Law Reports Annotated* replaced the *Lawyers Reports Annotated* (*L.R.A.*). For a description of the set and other earlier sets of annotated reports, *see* E. POLLACK, FUNDAMENTALS OF LEGAL RESEARCH 116 (3d ed. 1967).

problem of providing their subscribers with a means of alerting them to cases that were handed down after Volume 1 was published and that related to the annotations in it and would have been cited had they been handed down before Volume 1 had been published. They accomplished this by providing their subscribers a supplementary set to *A.L.R.* Each of the *A.L.R.* Series is now supplemented as follows.

(a) *A.L.R.* (First). Volume 1 of *A.L.R.* was published in 1919. The publishers then started a companion set to *A.L.R.*, which they called the *A.L.R. Blue Book of Supplemental Decisions.* This service is correlated to *A.L.R.* annotations and lists citations to all decisions on the same topic as the annotations. Thus, if one located an Annotation in 117 *A.L.R.* 606–639, all that is necessary is to turn to that citation in *A.L.R. Blue Book of Supplemental Decisions* and find citations to all cases on that topic handed down after the Annotation in 117 *A.L.R.* 606–639 was written. The *A.L.R. Blue Book of Supplemental Decisions* is now in four volumes and is kept current by a semiannual cumulative pamphlet. [See Illustration 26]

(b) *A.L.R.2d.* After the publication of 175 *A.L.R.* in 1948, the publishers decided to stop this series and the next volume published was 1 *A.L.R.2d*, being the second series of the *American Law Reports.* Actually, each volume of the second series appears nearly the same as the first series. The most fundamental change was in the method of keeping annotations published in *A.L.R.2d* up-to-date. For this purpose it abandoned the use of the *A.L.R. Blue Book of Supplemental Decisions* (although still publishing it for use with *A.L.R.* [first series]). In its place, a new set called *A.L.R.2d Later Case Service* was started. This provides the same service for *A.L.R.2d* that *A.L.R. Blue Book of Supplemental Decisions* does for the first series, but instead of merely listing citations to later cases, it provides digests of these cases and then keys them directly to each section of the *A.L.R. 2d* annotations. In using *A.L.R.2d* then, after the annotation has been read, the set of *A.L.R.2d Later Case Service* must be consulted. [See Illustration 25]

(c) *A.L.R.3d.* After 100 volumes of *A.L.R.2d* were published, the publishers again decided to change the method of up-keep. In 1965, *A.L.R.3d* started and the most significant difference from the previous two series is that it is no longer necessary to examine an auxiliary set, such as the *A.L.R. Blue Book of Supplemental Decisions,* or *A.L.R.2d Later Case Service.* Rather, each volume of *A.L.R. 3d* has an annual cumulative pocket supplement. When using *A.L.R. 3d* and after reading the annotations, it is only necessary to check the pocket supplement to locate later cases. [See Illustration 24]

(d) *A.L.R.Fed.* This is kept up-to-date by pocket supplements the same as *A.L.R.3d.*

3. Supplementing and Superseding Annotations.

Frequently after an annotation on a particular topic has been published, the law outlined in the annotation undergoes rapid development and the number of subsequent decisions become quite substantial. In such instances, one of two methods are utilized.

(a) Supplementing annotations. This is accomplished by taking all of the cases in point and handed down since the original annotation was written and writing a new annotation. This supplementary annotation is to be read in connection with the original annotation. The original and supplementing annotation are kept up-to-date in the appropriate up-keep service only under the citation to the supplementing annotation.

(b) Superseding annotations. There are times when the topic of law covered in an *A.L.R.* annotation is subsequently completely changed. For example, an annotation in an early volume of *A.L.R.* may have dealt with the right to recover damages for emotional distress when there was no physical impact. Subsequently, this rule is changed by the courts and they start allowing damages in such instances. The editors of *A.L.R.* may decide that the current status of law on a topic covered in an earlier annotation is such that it is better to rewrite the annotation completely. This is known as a *superseding annotation.*

Thus, any *A.L.R.* annotation may subsequently be *supplemented* or *superseded.* In the former instance, the supplemented and supplementing annotations must be read; in the latter, only the superseding annotation has to be read.

(c) Two means are used to alert users of *A.L.R.* to the fact that an annotation has been either supplemented or superseded. One is notation of this in the appropriate upkeep service. The other is through the *Annotation History Table* located in the back of both the bound volume and pocket supplement of the *A.L.R.2d & 3d Quick Index* volume.[3] Its use may best be described graphically:

Assume that one has a reference to an annotation to 12 *A.L.R.* 111–144, this citation is then checked in the *Historical Table.* As the illustration below indicates, the annotation at 12 *A.L.R.* 111–144 is now supplemented in 37 *A.L.R.2d* 453.

---

[3] These tables do not include supplementing or superseding annotations published in the first series of *A.L.R.* To determine if an annotation in 1–175 *A.L.R.* was supplemented or superseded in a subsequent volume of the first series, consult the *A.L.R. Blue Book of Supplemental Decisions.*

HISTORICAL TABLE

10 ALR 321–336 Superseded 75 ALR2d 633	**11 ALR 1325–1328** Superseded 50 ALR2d 143	**13 ALR 151–156** Superseded 46 ALR2d 1227
10 ALR 409–410 Superseded 84 ALR2d 1017	**11 ALR 1401–1402** Superseded 24 ALR2d 194	**13 ALR 225–247** Supplemented 43 ALR2d 1291
10 ALR 429–435 Superseded 17 ALR3d 705	**11 ALR 1405–1407** Superseded 20 ALR2d 1053	**13 ALR 324–340** Superseded 8 ALR3d 235
10 ALR 488–494 Superseded 92 ALR2d 570	**12 ALR 111–144** Supplemented 37 ALR2d 453	**13 ALR 346–355** Superseded 19 ALR3d 1227
10 ALR 783–809 Supplemented 40 ALR2d 1407	**12 ALR 333** Superseded 7 ALR2d 226	**13 ALR 372–383** Superseded 35 ALR2d 124

This means that 12 *A.L.R.* 111–140 and 37 *A.L.R.2d* 453 should be read together as if they were a single annotation, and then searching for later decisions as previously outlined in *A.L.R.2d Later Case Service.*

Assume, however, that the reference was to 15 *A.L.R.* 244–245 instead of 12 *A.L.R.* 111–144, as in our first assumption. When this citation is checked in the *Historical Table* we note that 15 *A.L.R.* 244–45 has been superseded by an annotation in 32 *A.L.R.3d* 589, as indicated below.

HISTORICAL TABLE

13 ALR 1414–1419 Superseded 41 ALR2d 329	**14 ALR 1300–1328** Supplemented 26 ALR2d 1139	**16 ALR 984–996** Superseded 87 ALR2d 407
14 ALR 240–249 Superseded 51 ALR2d 331	**14 ALR 1350–1352** Superseded 6 ALR3d 297	**16 ALR 1162–1165** Superseded 91 ALR2d 618
14 ALR 316–318 Superseded 11 ALR3d 1074	**15 ALR 244–245** Superseded 32 ALR3d 589	**16 ALR 1273–1286** Supplemented 24 ALR2d 1161
14 ALR 344–347 Superseded 77 ALR2d 1307	**15 ALR 437–446** Superseded 2 ALR3d 1151	**16 ALR 1316–1322** Superseded 31 ALR2d 713
14 ALR 409–411 Superseded 33 ALR2d 145	**15 ALR 569–575** Superseded 69 ALR2d 203 (civil liability) and 73 ALR2d 960 (criminal liability)	**17 ALR 170–179** Superseded 39 ALR2d 209

This means that the Annotation in 15 *A.L.R.* 244 should be ignored and only the annotation in 32 *A.L.R.3d* 589 has to be read, and its pocket supplement checked for later cases.

SECTION B.   FINDING A.L.R. ANNOTATIONS

1. Index Method

Each of the four sets has a one-volume index entitled *Quick Index*. These are alphabetically arranged indexes to the annotations

in the *A.L.R.* volumes, and are subdivided by topics and facts, and the annotations are listed by their titles. Presently, the indexes available are as follows:

> *Quick Index* to *A.L.R.2d* and *A.L.R.3d* (with cumulative pocket supplement kept inside front cover). Second edition. (1 Vol.)
>
> *Quick Index* to *A.L.R.Fed.* (1 Vol.)[4]

2. Digest Method

A.L.R. and *A.L.R.2d* were both provided with additional sets entitled *A.L.R.* Digests. This is no longer provided for *A.L.R.3d*. For use of *A.L.R.* Digests, see Pollack, Fundamentals of Legal Research, 3d ed. 1967 p. 132, *et seq.*

3. Table of Cases

An alphabetical listing of all cases reported in *A.L.R.* (first series) may be found in Volume 12 of the *A.L.R. Permanent Digest* and Volume 7 of the *A.L.R.2d* Digest. For *A.L.R.3d* and *A.L.R.Fed.* a *Table of Cases* appears in the bound volumes of the *Quick Index* for these sets and are supplemented in the pocket supplement. It is important to note that this Table lists decisions reported in *A.L.R.* and not the cases cited in the annotations.

---

[4] This index is called *Federal Quick Index to The Total Client-Service Library.* It indexes *A.L.R.Fed.* as well as all matter on federal law in the other sets of *The Total Client-Service Library.* There were also published for the first and second series of *A.L.R.* separate indexes called *Word Indexes.* The annotations were indexed in much greater depth in these indexes. The *Word Index* for the first series is in four volumes and in three volumes for the second series. These have now been replaced by the *Quick Indexes.*

SECTION C.   ILLUSTRATIONS

Illustrative Problem on Use of A.L.R.

We will now show how to find an *A.L.R.* annotation for a fact situation where an employee is injured in an employer's unlit parking lot.

Illustrations

21. **Quick Index**

22. **Historical Table**

23. **An A.L.R. Annotation**

24. **A.L.R.3d Supplement**

25. **A.L.R.2d Later Case Service**

26. **A.L.R. (First) Blue Book of Supplemental Decisions**

[Illustration 21]

SAMPLE PAGE FROM AN A.L.R. QUICK INDEX

→ **Lights**   ALR2d-3d

Casting of light on another's premises as con-stituting actionable wrong, 5 ALR2d 705

Electricity and Electric Companies (this index)

→ Landlord's liability for personal injury or death due to inadequacy or lack of lighting on portion of premises used in common by tenants 25 ALR2d 496

Municipal corporation's liability for injury or death occurring from defects in, or negli-gence in construction, operation, or main-tenance of its electric street-lighting equip-ment, apparatus, and the like, 19 ALR2d 344

Premises Liability (this index)

Proprietor of store, office, or similar business premises, liability for fall due to improper lighting of steps or stairway, 66 ALR2d 443

tions to damage actions against public ac-countants for negligence in performance of professional services, 26 ALR3d 1438

Amendment of Pleading (this index)

Appeal

– amendment of judgment as affecting time for taking or prosecuting appellate review proceedings, 21 ALR2d 285

– motion or petition for rehearing in court below as affecting time within which appellate proceedings must be taken or instituted, 10 ALR2d 1075

– portion of verdict: appellate court's power to remit portion of verdict or judgment covering period barred by statute, 26 ALR2d 956

– retroactive effect on appeal from judgment previously entered of statute shortening time allowed for appellate review, 81 ALR2d 417

The first step is to check the A.L.R. Quick Index 2d
and 3d. When the term "Lights" is consulted, note the
reference to an Annotation on the problem being researched at 25 A.L.R.2d 496.

Excessiveness or adequacy of damages awarded to injured person for injuries to organic systems and processes of body, 12 ALR3d 475

Future pain: sufficiency of evidence, in personal injury action, to prove future pain and suffering and to warrant instructions to jury thereon, 18 ALR3d 10.

Permanent injury: sufficiency of evidence, in personal injury action, to prove perma-nence of injuries and to warrant instruc-tions to jury thereon, 18 ALR3d 170

LIMITATION OF ACTIONS

As to particular actions, proceedings, or is-sues, see more specific topics

§ 1. Generally
§ 2. Interruption of statute
§ 3. Defenses to application of statute
§ 4. New action

---

§ 1. Generally.

Abuse of Process (this index)

Accountants: application of statute of limita-

– validity of contractual time period, shorter than statute of limitations, for bringing action, 6 ALR3d 1197

– waiver: contractual waiver of statute of limi-tations, validity of, 1 ALR2d 1445

– what constitutes a contract in writing within statute, 3 ALR2d 809

Copyright infringement: construction and ap-plication of provision of Federal Copyright Act (17 USCS (§ 115(b)) requiring that civil action arising out of copyright in-fringement be commenced within 3 years after claim accrued, 13 ALR Fed 922

Demurrer: raising defense of statute by demur-rer, equivalent motion to dismiss, or by motion for judgment on pleadings, 61 ALR2d 300

Encroachment

– statute of limitations applicable to action for, 24 ALR2d 903

– when does cause of action accrue, for pur-poses of statute of limitations, against action based upon encroachment of building or other structure upon land of another, 12 ALR3d 1265

Executors and Administrators (this index)

[Illustration 21–a]

SAMPLE PAGE FROM A.L.R. QUICK INDEX

QUICK INDEX   **Landlord and Tenant**

§ 3. Liability for injury or death.

Animals: liability of landlord to tenant or member of tenant's family, for injury by animal or insect, 67 ALR2d 1005

Fire escape: liability of landlord to one using fire escape for other than intended purpose, 12 ALR2d 217

Appliances
– liability for injury or death due to defects in appliances supplied for use of different tenants, 25 ALR2d 576
– liability for injury to tenant's person or property caused by water overflowing from defective appliances in other premises of landlord, 26 ALR2d 1044

Business patron: landlord's liability to tenant's business patron injured as a result of defective condition of premises, 17 ALR3d 422

Children
– guest: liability for injury or death of child of social guest, 20 ALR3d 1127
– lead poisoning: landlord's liability for injury or death of tenant's child from lead poisoning resulting from peeling paint, 43 ALR3d 1268

Criminal activities: landlord's obligation to protect tenant against criminal activities of third persons, 43 ALR3d 331

ity for personal injury or death of tenant or his privies from, 86 ALR2d 791

Ice or snow
– landlord's liability to tenant or tenant's invitees for injury or death due to ice or snow in areas or passageways used in common by tenants, 49 ALR3d 387
– liability of tenant occupying abutting premises for injury from ice formed on sidewalk by discharge of rain or melted snow thereon because of condition existing on premises, 22 ALR2d 738

Invitee status of lessor: duty and liability of lessee of building to lessor for personal injuries occasioned by condition of premises, 47 ALR2d 1439

Latent defect: modern status of rule requiring actual knowledge of latent defect in leased premises as prerequisite to landlord's liability for injury resulting therefrom, 88 ALR2d 586

Lease obligation: tenant's obligation under lease as basis of tort liability to third persons, 44 ALR3d 943

Lights: liability of landlord for personal injury or death due to inadequacy or lack of lighting on portion of premises used in common by tenants, 25 ALR2d 496

> As is generally true when using indexes, answers can be found under different entries. Note in the instance how the same Annotation may also be located under the entry Landlord and Tenant. One could logically expect to also find a citation to this Annotation under Parking Lots. Although this term is used in the index, it does not refer to 25 A.L.R.2d 496. This illustrates the need to consult an index under other entries when not successful with the first choice.

– duty owed by landlord to, and status of, social guest of tenant's employee on tenant's business premises, 78 ALR2d 142
– landlord's liability to social guest of tenant, 25 ALR2d 598
– liability of landlord to tenant's social guest injured otherwise than by condition of premises, 79 ALR2d 990

Heating system or equipment, landlord's liabil-

ant or purchaser for injury resulting from condition of premises, 3 ALR3d 976

Public use: what constitutes a "public" use affecting landlord's liability to tenant's invitees for defects in leased premises, 17 ALR3d 873

Refrigerant: liability for injury or damage from escaping refrigerant, 74 ALR2d 894

Res ipsa loquitur in actions against owner or

Consult POCKET PART for later annotations

495

[Illustration 22]

PAGE FROM A.L.R. HISTORICAL TABLE

[ALR3d]   HISTORICAL TABLE

154 ALR 1592–1406
Superseded 56 ALR3d 815

4 ALR2d 348–385
§ 12 superseded 56 ALR3d 1109

18 ALR2d 1225–1230
Superseded 68 ALR3d 546

Illustration 21 indicated that an Annotation on the subject under research can be located at 25 A.L.R.2d 496. Before reading this Annotation, the Historical Table in the pocket supplement to the Quick Index to A.L.R.2d and 3d should be checked.

This indicates that the Annotation in 25 A.L.R.2d 496 has been superseded by the Annotation in 66 A.L.R.3d 202. It is now only necessary to read this Annotation.

159 ALR 854–857
Superseded 58 ALR3d 1241

160 ALR 287–289
Superseded 53 ALR3d 848

161 ALR 382–383
Superseded 9 ALR Fed 279

162 ALR 581–605
Superseded 66 ALR3d 1115

163 ALR 1124–1128
Superseded 67 ALR3d 26

166 ALR 675–701
Superseded 61 ALR3d 511

168 ALR 446–467
Supplemented 57 ALR3d 16

170 ALR 721–728
Superseded 59 ALR3d 488

173 ALR 836–844
Superseded 64 ALR3d 1251

173 ALR 999–1008
Superseded 59 ALR3d 767

2 ALR2d 489–511
Superseded 13 ALR Fed 6

3 ALR2d 212–214
Superseded 65 ALR3d 656

4 ALR2d 276–285
Superseded 63 ALR3d 527

14 ALR2d 550–559
Superseded 49 ALR3d 934

14 ALR2d 750–774
§§ 10–12 superseded 57 ALR3d 16

14 ALR2d 1369–1372
Superseded 65 ALR3d 1222

15 ALR2d 785–798
§ 6 superseded 50 ALR3d 1311, 56
ALR3d 386

15 ALR2d 1064–1076
§§ 3–5 superseded 55 ALR3d 349
§§ 6–7 superseded 55 ALR3d 477

16 ALR2d 979–1014
§§ 4–5 superseded 55 ALR3d 1254

16 ALR2d 1304–1306
Superseded 66 ALR3d 601

16 ALR2d 1404–1407
Superseded 65 ALR3d 541

17 ALR2d 832–867
Superseded 46 ALR3d 680, 46 ALR3d
733, 47 ALR3d 909, 47 ALR3d 971,
and 52 ALR3d 1289

17 ALR2d 872–880
Superseded 46 ALR3d 680, 46 ALR3d
733, 47 ALR3d 909, 47 ALR3d 971,
and 52 ALR3d 1289

18 ALR2d 725–755
Superseded 56 ALR3d 14, 56 ALR3d
138, and 57 ALR3d 279

22 ALR2d 427–451
Superseded 63 ALR3d 816

23 ALR2d 1306–1311
§ 6 superseded 53 ALR3d 1005

25 ALR2d 364–437
Superseded 67 ALR3d 587

25 ALR2d 444–487
Superseded 65 ALR3d 14

25 ALR2d 496–565
Superseded 66 ALR3d 202

25 ALR2d 576–592
Superseded 66 ALR3d 374

26 ALR2d 468–603
§§ 14–16 superseded 65 ALR3d 14
§§ 25–38 superseded 65 ALR3d 14
§§ 12, 13, 17–24 superseded 68 ALR3d
382

28 ALR2d 287–343
§§ 2–7, 10 superseded 63 ALR3d 74
§§ 15–17 superseded 60 ALR3d 1
§ 8 superseded 61 ALR3d 729
§ 11 superseded 62 ALR3d 429
§§ 13–14 superseded 61 ALR3d 686
§§ 18, 19, 21, and 22 superseded 62
ALR3d 304
§ 20 superseded 62 ALR3d 375

29 ALR2d 171–205
§§ 4, 5, 6, 9, 10 superseded 64 ALR3d
398

29 ALR2d 1074–1140
§ 4.135 superseded in 44 ALR3d 306

155

[Illustration 23]

FIRST PAGE OF ANNOTATION OF 66 A.L.R.3d 202

ANNOTATION

LIABILITY OF LANDLORD FOR PERSONAL INJURY OR DEATH DUE TO INADEQUACY OR LACK OF LIGHTING ON PORTION OF PREMISES USED IN COMMON BY TENANTS

by

Allan E. Korpela, LL.B.

> This is the first page of the Annotation for 66 A.L.R.3d 202. Immediately preceding it is reprinted the case of Low v. Siewart, 55 Wis.2d 251, 195 N.W.2d 451 (1972). Although this case dealt specifically with lighting in an employer's parking lot, note how the Annotation deals with lighting in all situations where injury occurred at or near property under the control of a landlord.
>
> After the title of each Annotation, a detailed analysis of it is given with citation to paragraph number within the Annotation.

202

[Illustration 23–a]

PAGE FROM 66 A.L.R.3d 204

LANDLORD'S LIABILITY—ADEQUACY OF LIGHT   66 ALR3d
66 ALR3d 202

[b] Not liable
§ 22. Drives and parking lots
§ 23. Other outside areas:
    [a] Liable
    [b] Not liable

B. Injury to Persons Other Than Tenant or Occupant

1. Interior Areas

§ 24. Entrance or exit area
§ 25. Steps or stairs:
    [a] Liable
    [b] Not liable
§ 26. Halls and passageways:
    [a] Liable
    [b] Not liable
§ 27. Other interior areas:
    [a] Liable
    [b] Not liable

2. Exterior Areas

§ 28. Entrance or exit areas:
    [a] Liable
    [b] Not liable
§ 29. Porches
§ 30. Steps and walks:
    [a] Liable
    [b] Not liable
→ § 31. Drives and parking lots:
    [a] Liable
    [b] Not liable
§ 32. Other outside areas

> Page 203 of this Annotation (not illustrated) indicates that Part IV deals with "Landlord's Breach of Duty as to Particular Area." This Illustration shows that cases arising out of inadequate lighting in parking lots to persons other than tenants are covered in § 31.

sup-

orta-

    [a] Finding of contributory negligence or assumption of risk not supportable or not required
    [b] Finding of contributory negligence or assumption of risk supportable or required
§ 35. Outside steps, walks, or entry areas:
    [a] Finding of contributory negligence or assumption of risk not supportable or not required

[Illustration 23-b]

PAGE FROM 66 A.L.R.3d 206: INDEX TO ANNOTATION

> After the Analysis, a detailed index to the Annotation is given.

[Illustration 23–c]

PAGE FROM 66 A.L.R.3d 202, SHOWING TABLE OF JURISDICTIONS REPRESENTED

§ 1[a]   LANDLORD'S LIABILITY—ADEQUACY OF LIGHT   66 ALR3d
66 ALR3d 202

	17[b], 28[a], 30[a], 33[b], 34[a], 38[a]	Minn	§§ 5[a], 18[a], 21[b], 25[a], 34[a], 35[b], 36, 38[a]
Canal Zone	§§ 5[a], 21[a], 35[a]	Mo	§§ 2[a], 3[a], 4[a–c], 5[a–c], 6[a, b], 8[a], 10[a, b] 17[a],
Colo	§§ 2[b], 3[a], 4[a], 5[a], 26[b], 28[b], 33[b], 39[a], 40[b]		25[a], 26[a, b], 31[a], 33[a], 34[a], 38[a, b]
Conn	§§ 2[b], 3[b], 7, 8[a, b], 10[b], 11[a], 13–15, 17[a, b], 18[b], 19[a], 21[a], 25[a], 33[a, b], 35[a], 38[a]	Neb	§§ 17[b], 39[b]
		Nev	§§ 21[b], 27[a], 35[b], 39[a]
		NH	§§ 3[a], 4[a], 5[a], 17[b]
DC	§§ 2[b], 3[b], 6[a, b], 8[a], 15, 17[a, b], 21[a], 25[b], 28[a], 33[a], 39[a]	NJ	§§ 3[a], 4[a–c], 5[a, b], 6[a, b], 8[a], 9[b], 10[a], 11[a, b], 17[a, b], 25[a], 26[b], 28[a], 30[a], 33[a, b], 38[a, b], 39[b], 41
Fla	§§ 3[a], 6[b], 8[a], 10[b], 16, 17[a], 28[b], 33[a], 34[b],	NY	§§ 2[a], 3[a, b, d], 4[a], 5[a–c], 6[a, b], 8[a, b], 9[a, b], 10[a,

---

After the Analysis, there is always a Table of Jurisdictions Represented. **Note how only Missouri and Wisconsin had cases cited in § 31 of the Annotations.**

Note also how § 1 of an Annotation outlines its scope.

	9[b], 13–15, 17[a, b], 18[a], 25[a, b], 26[b], 33[a, b], 34[a], 38[a], 39[a]	Pa	§§ 2[a], 3[b], 5[b], 17[a], 28[b], 33[a, b], 36, 38[a, b], 40[a, b]
La	§§ 3[a], 5[a], 12, 25[a], 28[b], 33[b], 38[b]	RI	§§ 3[a], 4[a, c], 5[a, c], 25[a]
		Tenn	§ 33[b]
Me	§§ 3[a], 5[a], 25[a], 26[b], 38[a], 39[b]	Tex	§§ 4[a, c], 34[b]
		Utah	§§ 6[b], 9[a], 17[a], 33[a]
Md	§§ 3[b], 17[b], 21[a], 35[b]	Vt	§§ 3[a], 4[a, c], 5[a, b], 38[a]
Mass	§§ 3[a], 4[a–c], 5[a–c], 6[b], 9[a, b], 10[a, b], 11[a], 12, 13, 15, 17[a, b], 18[a], 19[a, b], 21[b], 22, 25[a, b], 26[a, b], 28[a], 30[a], 33[a], 34[a, b], 38[a], 39[a,], 40[a]	Va	§§ 3[a], 4[a, c], 13, 17[b], 25[a]
		Wash	§§ 3[a], 4[a], 5[a], 30[a], 32, 33[a], 40[a]
		Wis	§§ 2[a], 13, 15, 18[b], 31[b], 33[a]

I. Introduction

§ 1. Prefatory matters

[a] Scope

This annotation[1] collects those cases in which it is determined

whether and to what extent a landlord is required to illuminate portions of premises used in common by tenants and retained under the landlord's control, so as to render him liable for personal injury or death allegedly caused by the absence of light. The annotation is limited to cases in which the alleged failure to light, and the injury or death, occur-

---

1. It supersedes the annotation at 25 ALR2d 496.

[Illustration 23–d]

PAGE FROM 66 A.L.R.3d 202 SHOWING RELATED
ANNOTATIONS AND SUMMARY

§ 1[b]   Landlord's Liability—Adequacy of Light   66 ALR3d
66 ALR3d 202

Related Annotations

ant's invitees for defects in leased premises. 17 ALR3d 873.

Effect, on nonsigner, of provision of lease exempting landlord from liability on account of condition of property. 12 ALR3d 958.

Liability of proprietor of business premises for injury from fall on exterior walk, ramp, or passageway connected with the building in which the business is conducted. 81 ALR2d 750.

Breach of lessor's agreement as ground of liability for personal injury to tenant or one in privity with latter. 78 ALR2d 1238.

Statute requiring property to be kept in good repair as affecting landlord's liability for personal injury to tenant or his privies. 17 ALR2d 704.

◆

Quinn and Phillips, The Law of Landlord-Tenant: A Critical Evaluation of the Past with Guidelines for the Future. 38 Ford L Rev 225 (1969).

§ 2. General comment

[a] Summary

It appears that most jurisdictions adhere to, or at least have not expressly rejected, the common-law rule that an owner of a building does not owe a duty to his tenants or their invitees to provide with artificial light the common ways retained under his control,[4] in the absence of defective conditions, or conditions of peculiar

danger, that may call for special warning.[5] Symmetry of reasoning would appear to require that a landlord's duty with respect to lights in a common area be measured by the same yardstick as is used to define his duty with respect to the general maintenance of such areas, namely, where the owner of premises leases parts thereof to different tenants and expressly or impliedly reserves other parts for the common use of different tenants, it is his duty to exercise ordinary care to keep reasonably safe the common areas of which he reserves control.[6] It would appear that in areas retained under the landlord's control, a tenant or his invitee generally has no more power over lighting facilities than he has over the condition of floors, stairways, railings, or exterior grounds or walks. It has been said that the common-law rule absolving the landlord from a duty to light common areas evolved when artificial lighting meant gaslighting and when the feudal nature of the landlord-tenant relationship had not yet begun to be questioned.[7]

A few courts have apparently adopted the position that the landlord's general duty to use ordinary care to keep common areas retained under his control in reasonably safe condition applies also to illumination of such areas, illumination being considered but one aspect of the general condition of the premises,[8] with the position of a few jurisdictions appar-

---

Paragraph 1b of Annotations lists related Annotations and these should always be consulted to see if problem under research is not better covered elsewhere in A.L.R.

Paragraph 2 always gives a summary of the Annotations.

[Illustration 23–e]

FIRST PAGE OF TEXT OF ANNOTATION AT 66 A.L.R.3d 317

66 ALR3d   Landlord's Liability—Adequacy of Light   § 31[b]
66 ALR3d 202

without merit unless the particular circumstances required the defendants to furnish such illumination. In finding no such other circumstances, the court affirmed judgment for the defendant, distinguishing the present case from one in which a petition was held to have stated a cause of action where the injured person was in a grandstand and was injured while attempting to leave in the dark, where the lights were turned off by the defendant during a performance and were not turned back on after the performance, the plaintiff in that case being placed in the situation of either having to remain in the rain in the open grandstand or attempting to leave in the dark. In the instant case, the court said, the injured person was not placed in such a situation.

§ 31. Drives and parking lots

[a] Liable

In the following case in which recovery was sought by a person other than a tenant or an occupant of leased premises for injuries allegedly suffered because of inadequate lighting, by the landlord or owner, of a common parking lot retained under the control of the landlord or owner, a finding for plaintiff on the issue of defendant's primary negligence was held supportable under the particular facts and circumstances of the case.

In Swanson v Godwin (1959, **Mo**) 327 SW _____ of the _____ tenant _____ firmed, _____ the gue _____ of the _____ injury _____ semidarkness, fell over a dropoff between defendant's parking lot and an adjacent lot, and that after the building had been converted from an apartment house into an office build-

ing, the landlord had continued to provide one light, controlled and serviced by him, to light the rear portions of the building, including the new parking lot, and where there was evidence that the light provided was wholly inadequate for the purpose of providing night illumination to those persons who the landlord knew used the parking lot at night.

[b] Not liable

In the following case in which recovery was sought by a person other than a tenant or occupant of leased premises for injuries allegedly suffered because of inadequate lighting, by the landlord or owner, of a parking lot retained under the control of the landlord or owner, a finding for the defendant on the issue of primary negligence was held required under the particular facts and circumstances of the case.

The action of an employee of a tenant against the owner of the building was dismissed, in Low v Siewert (1972) 54 **Wis** 2d 251, 195 NW2d 451, 66 ALR3d 198, where there was evidence that the employee, who had been working late for her employer in the defendant's office building, was injured when she fell in a parking lot at 10 p.m. in May, that on leaving the office she reached the front door of the building and noticed that the adjacent parking lot was unlighted, that ____ ____ from ____ her car ____ ien she ____ umbled ____ and in- ____ so evi- ____ cing lot was to be left on 24 hours a day, that the janitor left the building in daylight at 5:30 p.m. and did not notice whether the light was on or off, that the injured employee came to work at

The beginning of § 31. This Annotation contains 167 pages. An Annotation may vary from one page to several hundred.

317

[Illustration 24]

PAGE FROM SUPPLEMENT TO 66 A.L.R.3d 202

AMERICAN
LAW REPORTS

THIRD SERIES

1976 Supplement

VOLUME 66 ALR3d

66 ALR3d 145–186

§ 1   [66 ALR3d 148]

[b] Related matters

Use of goods by buyer as constituting acceptance under UCC § 2-606(1)(c). 67 ALR3d 363.

66 ALR3d 190–197

§ 1   [66 ALR3d 191]

[b] Related matters

Use of goods by buyer as constituting acceptance under UCC § 2-606(1)(c). 67 ALR3d 363.

66 ALR 202–364

§ 1   [66 ALR3d 208]

[b] Related matters

Landlord's liability for personal injury or death due to defects in appliances supplied for use of different tenants. 66 ALR3d 374.

Landlord's liability for injury or death due to defects in exterior steps or stairs used in common by tenants. 67 ALR3d 490.

Landlord's liability for injury or death caused by defective condition of interior steps or stairways used in common by tenants. 67 ALR3d 587.

66 ALR3d 374–416

§ 1   [66 ALR3d 377]

[b] Rel
Liab
death
portior
ants. 6
Lanc
defects
mon by
Land
by defe

ways used in common by tenants. 67 ALR3d 587.

66 ALR3d 472–504

§ 7   [66 ALR3d 495]

Plaintiff husband was not entitled to new trial on issue of plaintiff wife's medical expenses, despite fact that wife recovered for injuries suffered in fall and that medical expenses were stipulated, where stipulation as to medical expenses did not acknowledge that such expenses were attributable to accident in question, where only medical evidence offered by plaintiffs was that of neurologist concerning treatment and hospitalization of wife three years after accident, and where defendant contended that neurologist's services were not made necessary by reason of accident three years previously. Oulman v Minneapolis **(Minn)** 227 NW2d 822.

66 ALR3d 532–597

§ 2   [66 ALR3d 537]

[a] Generally

For later Michigan decision see Manistee Bank & Trust Co. v McGowan, 394 **Mich** 655, 232 NW2d 636, infra § 5.

For later Ohio decision see Primes v Tyler, 43 **Ohio** St 2d 195, 72 Ohio Ops 2d 112, 331 NE2d 723, infra § 5.

§ 3   [66 ALR3d 541]

anistee
:h 655,

distin-
other

anistee

3

> **After reading the Annotation, a search should be made for later cases. When using A.L.R.3d, this is done by checking in the annual cumulative supplement in the back of the volume.**
>
> **Note how this pocket supplement is keyed to the paragraph numbers of the main Annotation.**

[Illustration 25]

PAGE FROM A.L.R.2d LATER CASE SERVICE

63 ALR2d 108–175

Liability for injury occasioned by backing of motor vehicle from private premises into public street or highway.

§ 1. Scope, p. 114.
3 Am Jur Pl & Pr Forms, Automobiles and Highway Traffic, Forms 480, 481.

extremely careful, and if he is backing onto highway he must use an even higher degree of care. Morgan v Southern Farm Bureau Casualty Ins. Co. (DC La) 223 F Supp 996, affd (CA5) 339 F2d 755 (applying Louisiana law).

[b] Right of way and lookout.

Also recognizing duties of backing drivers:

Iowa.—Sayre v Andrews (Iowa) 146 NW2d 336 (duty to exercise high degree of care, keep proper lookout, stop, and yield right of way to approaching vehicles).

La.—State Farm Mut. Auto. Ins. Co. v C. & C. Oil Field Servicing Co. (La App) 168 So 2d 918 (statutory duty to yield right of way, and duty to exercise unusual degree of care); Deville v Aetna Ins. Co. (La App) 191 So 2d 324 (duty to exercise high degree of care, stop at curb or sidewalk, and yield right of way), writ refused 250 La 13, 193 So 2d 527.

Miss.—Baxter v Rounsaville (Miss) 193 So 2d 735 (statutory duty to yield right of way).

Okla.—Turner v Gallagher (Okla) 371 P2d 733 (duty to keep proper lookout while

§ 3. Generally; lookout and right of way, p. 116.

[a] Generally.

Automobile operator who drives from private driveway onto highway must be

imposed upon backing motorist; remaining half of duty is to maintain proper lookout during continuing maneuver. Smith v Hearn (La App) 181 So 2d 433.

§ 4. Warning signals; lights, p. 120.

Also recognizing duty to signal or to warn of presence:

Ky.—Nolan v Nally (Ky) 342 SW2d 400 (duty to warn that truck backed across highway at night near curve was blocking road).

§ 5. In general; action against owner or operator of backing vehicle, p. 122.

[b] Questions of negligence of one responsible for backing automobile.

In action for injuries to plaintiff when car she was driving was struck by defendant's car, being backed from private driveway into street, evidence supported finding that defendant's negligence proximately caused accident, and that plaintiff was not contributorily negligent. Alessi v Farkas (Fla App) 118 So 2d 658.

Where plaintiffs, motorist and passenger, testified that defendant backing from driveway at night had stopped car with its

---

When using an Annotation in A.L.R.2d a different method of locating later cases must be used as A.L.R.2d did not use pocket supplements. Rather, a separate 11 volume set called A.L.R.2d Later Case Service is provided. The citation of the A.L.R.2d Annotation should be checked in this set. While not shown in this Illustration, the pocket supplement to A.L.R.2d Later Case Service must also be checked.

[Illustration 26]

EXCERPTS FROM A.L.R. BLUE BOOK OF SUPPLEMENTAL DECISIONS

VOL. 1

117 A.L.R. 606–639.
Richardson v. D. (Ala.) 187 So. 176.
Norgard v. N. 54 CalApp(2d) 82, 128 P(2d) 566.
Morrison v. N. 311 IllApp 411. 36 NE(2d) 581.
Loeser v. S. (Ind) 39 NE(2d) 945.
Re Gollobit (Iowa) 3 NW(2d) 191.
Crawford v. C. (Iowa) 15 NW (2d) 633.
Re Stephenson (Iowa) 14 NW (2d) 684.
Simpson v. S. 276 Ky. 223, 123 S.W.(2d) 816.
Leitner v. G. (Ky) 177 SW (2d) 903.
Re Boese (Minn) 7 NW(2d) 355.

VOL. 2

117 ALR 606–639
Livingston v. P. (Ala) 57 So2d 521.
Cross v. P. (Ark) 221 SW2d 24.
Guyot v. F. (Ark) 243 SW2d 639.
Black v. B. 91 Cal App2d 328. 204 P2d 950
Johnson v. B. (Ga App) 67 SE2d 189.
Re Conner's Estate (Iowa) 36 NW2d 833.
Boggess v. C. E. (Mo App) 207 SW2d 814.
Re Haas' Estate, 10 NJ Super 581, 77 A2d 523.
Santos v. M. (Tex Civ App) 195 SW2d 927.
Logan v. T. (Tex Civ App) 199 SW2d 210. error granted.

VOL. 3

117 ALR 583–599
General Motors Acceptance Corp. v M. (Kan) 311 P2d 339.

117 ALR 606–639
Berendsen v. Mcl. 126 Cal App2d 347. 272 P2d 76.
Seeba v B. (Fla) 86 So2d 432.
Fuller v F. (Ga) 97 SE2d 306.
Hays v I. I. H. (Ill) 147 NE2d 287.
Re Guardianship of Anderson (Iowa) 78 NW2d 788.
Reidinger v. A. (Mo) 266 SW2d 610.
Grimm v G. (Mo) 303 SW2d 43.
Ellison v. S. (ND) 62 NW2d 95.
Theadgill v A. (Okla) 303 P2d 297.
Chandler v W. (Tex) 294 SW2d 801.
Leach v C. E. (Tex Civ App) 279 SW2d 630.
Chandler v W. (Tex Civ App) 282 SW2d 940
Chamberlain v R. (Tex Civ App) 305 SW2d 817.

VOL. 4

117 ALR 606–639
Ala.—Taylor v F. N. B. 189 So 2d 141
Alaska—Re Hewett's Estate. 358 P2d 579
Ky.—Cook v B. 346 SW2d 725
Neb.—Olsen v B. 92 NW2d 531
N. J.—Moss v G. (Co) 146 A2d 227
N. Y.—Lindsay v L. 22 Misc 2d 1071, 203 NYS2d 705
Tex.—Connor v P. (Civ App) 360 SW2d 438

117 ALR 649
Superseded 130 ALR 272+

LATEST PAM. SUPPL.

117 ALR 470–484
Supplemented 168 ALR 581+

117 ALR 496–498
Superseded 95 ALR2d 585+

117 ALR 522–538
Mo.—Swiastyn v S. J. L. & P. Co. (App) 459 SW2d 24 (citing anno)

117 ALR 563–565
Superseded 53 ALR2d 224+

117 ALR 571–572
U. S.--Doyle v N. J. Const. Co. (CA Wis) 382 F2d 735

117 ALR 606–639
Fla.—Roberts v B. (App) 201 So 2d 811
S. C.—Havird v S. 166 SE2d 801
Tex.—Gibson v A. (Civ App) 463 SW2d 277

Note how A.L.R. Blue Book of Supplemental Decisions also indicates when an Annotation has been supplemented or superseded. It is simpler to use the Historical Table.

After using an Annotation in A.L.R. (First Series), later cases may be found in the A.L.R. Blue Book of Supplemental Decisions. There are four Blue Books that contain references decided after the original annotation was written. Vol. 1 covers 1919–46; Vol. 2, 1946–52; Vol. 3, 1953–58; Vol. 4, 1959–67. A semi-annual pamphlet lists citations since 1967.

SECTION D. SUMMARY

A.L.R. may be used to locate court decisions on a topic of law. If, through its indexes, an *A.L.R.* annotation is located, it will cite all previous court decisions on the topic, and the up-keep services pro-

vided will locate cases subsequent in time to the writing of the *A.L.R.* annotation.

It is important to keep in mind that *A.L.R.* is primarily a *case finding tool* and all decisions located through its use should be read.

Summary of Finding A.L.R. Annotations

Step 1.   Start search in *Quick Index* to *A.L.R.3d.*

    (a.) If reference in index to an appropriate annotation is located, proceed to Step 2; if not:

        (1) search *Quick Index* to *A.L.R.2d*; if reference located, proceed to Step 2, if not,

        (2) search Index to *A.L.R.* (1st); if applicable reference found, proceed to Step 2, if not:

            (a) subject being researched probably not covered by *A.L.R.*; start search for cases using other techniques outlined in Ch. 21.

Step 2.   Check *Historical Table* in Pocket *Supplement in Quick Index to A.L.R.2d* and *3d* to determine if annotation(s) located through Step 1 have been *superseded* or *supplemented*:

    (a) If superseded, note superseding annotation, ignore original, and proceed to Step 3;

    (b) if supplemented, note supplementary annotation and proceed to Step 3;

    (c) if annotation not listed in *Historical Table,* proceed to Step 3.

Step 3.   Read annotation(s) found through Steps 1 and 2.

    After reading annotation(s) check for later cases in:

        (a) If *A.L.R.* (1st) annotation in *A.L.R. Blue Book of Supplemental Decisions*;

        (b) If *A.L.R.2d* annotation in *Later Case Service to A.L.R.2d*;

        (c) If *A.L.R.3d* annotation in pocket supplement to *A.L.R. 3d* volume.

Other methods of locating *A.L.R.* annotations will be discussed in Chapters 15 and 16.

Citation form for *A.L.R.* annotations may be found in Appendix A at (I), (D), (1).

Chapter 8

CONSTITUTIONS

This chapter will discuss the role of constitutions for both the federal and state governments. As these documents are the charters adopted by the people, they are the highest primary authority.

SECTION A. FEDERAL CONSTITUTION

The Constitution of the United States, in a formal sense, is the written document which was drafted at Philadelphia in the summer of 1787 plus the amendments that have since been added. It was not the intention of the framers that the Constitution be static but rather, as noted by Chief Justice Marshall, it should "endure for the ages to come and consequently, be adapted to various crises in human affairs." [1] More recently, a noted constitutional scholar commented that "The proper point of view from which to approach the task of interpreting the constitution is that of regarding it as a living statute, palpitating with the purpose of the hour, reenacted with every waking breath of the American people, whose primitive right to determine their institutions is its sole claim to validity as law and as the matrix of laws under our system." [2]

It follows from this that to research problems in federal constitutional law, one must not only consult the document itself, but all of the sources that will assist in the interpretation of the Constitution. Such sources will include the background and record of the Constitutional Convention, the interpretation of the Constitution by the Supreme Court of the United States in the over 400 volumes of its reports, and the commentaries on the Constitution which appear in treatises, legal periodicals and encyclopedias. Recent events [3] have once again shown the vitality of the Constitution and how lawyers, when faced with grave constitutional questions of interpretation, refer back to the

[1] McCullock v. Maryland, 17 U.S. (4 Wheat.) 316, 415 (1819).

[2] U. S. LIBRARY OF CONGRESS. CONGRESSIONAL RESEARCH SERVICE, THE CONSTITUTION OF THE UNITED STATES OF AMERICA; ANALYSIS AND INTERPRETATION: ANNOTATIONS OF CASES DECIDED BY THE SUPREME COURT OF THE UNITED STATES TO JUNE 29, 1972, S.DOC. NO. 92–82, 92d Cong., 2d Sess. VII (1973), p. VIII.

[3] United States v. Nixon, 418 U.S. 683 (1974).

117

sources of constitutional interpretation.[4]   How to locate and use such sources will be discussed in this chapter.

1.   Historical Sources

When faced with interpreting the meaning of a provision or clause of the Constitution, it is frequently useful to ascertain the meaning given to the words used by the "founding fathers."   At times, it may be necessary to check into sources that preceded the adoption of the Constitution, such as documents of the Continental Congress or the Articles of Confederation.   These may be easily located in *Documents Illustrative of the Formation of the Union of the American States*.[5]

While the Constitutional Convention did not keep official records of its secret session, several sources exist that provide an insight into the debates that took place and should be consulted when researching an historical interpretation of the Constitution.[6]

2.   Judicial Interpretation: Annotated Editions of the Federal Constitution

When determining the meaning of the United States Constitution, it is also necessary to search for the interpretations of constitutional provisions by the courts, and especially those of the Supreme Court of the United States.   Some of the most useful sources for these are the various annotated editions of the United States Constitution, which set forth each article, section and clause of the Constitution and provide digests (and, in some instances, commentary) on court decisions.

a.   *United States Code Annotated.   Constitution of the United States Annotated.*   (West)

[4] *Id.* at 705 n. 15.

[5] U. S. LIBRARY OF CONGRESS.   LEGISLATIVE REFERENCE SERVICE, DOCUMENTS ILLUSTRATIVE OF THE FORMATION OF THE UNION OF THE AMERICAN STATES, H.DOC. 398, 69th Cong., 1st Sess. (1935).   *See also:* S. BLOOM, FORMATION OF THE UNION UNDER THE CONSTITUTION (1935).

[6] J. MADISON, THE PAPERS OF JAMES MADISON (H. Gilpin ed. 1840); THE FEDERALIST (P. Ford ed. 1898) (This is one of several editions.); U. S. BUREAU OF ROLLS AND LIBRARY OF THE DEPARTMENT OF STATE, DOCUMENTARY HISTORY OF THE CONSTITUTION OF THE UNITED STATES OF AMERICA, 1786–1870 (1894–1905); M. FARRAND, THE RECORDS OF THE FEDERAL CONVENTION OF 1787 (1934–1937); J. ELLIOT, THE DEBATES IN THE SEVERAL STATE CONVENTIONS ON THE ADOPTION OF THE FEDERAL CONSTITUTION TOGETHER WITH THE JOURNAL OF THE FEDERAL CONVENTION (1937, Supp.: DEBATES ON THE ADOPTION OF THE FEDERAL CONSTITUTION IN THE CONVENTION HELD AT PHILADELPHIA IN 1787, 123–565, Madison papers revised and newly arranged); THE DOCUMENTARY HISTORY OF THE RADIFICATION OF THE CONSTITUTION, 1976–(to be completed in 12 volumes).   When finished this set will be the most complete and up-to-date source for the history of the United States Constitution.

The United States Constitution volumes are a separate unit of the *United States Code Annotated* and consist of eight unnumbered volumes, including a separate index to the Constitution. After each article, section or clause of the Constitution, digests from all courts that have interpreted a constitutional provision are set forth. For example, Article 1 is followed by 101 digests of cases while Article 1, Section 8, Clause 3 is followed by 1187 digests of cases. To assist in the location of the digests, indexes to them are provided. The means of locating a constitutional provision and the annotations to it are shown in Illustrations 28 and 29.

b. *United States Code Service. Constitution Volumes.* (F.C.A. Edition)

These volumes are a separate unit of the *United States Code Service* published by the Lawyers Cooperative Publishing Company and the Bancroft-Whitney Company which is part of their *Total Client Service Library*.[7] It is organized similarly to the *United States Code Annotated* and is used in a like manner.

c. *The Constitution of the United States of America; Analysis and Interpretation.* (Library of Congress Edition, 1973)[8]

This one-volume edition of the annotated Constitution was prepared by the Congressional Research Service of the Library of Congress, as authorized by a joint Congressional Resolution.[9] It sets forth each article, section and clause of the Constitution; immediately following each of them, in smaller typeface, appear an analysis and commentary prepared by the editorial staff. Important decisions of the Supreme Court of the United States are discussed in the analysis, and citations to them are given in the footnotes. (See Illustration 30.) Frequently the commentary will quote from the proceedings of the Constitutional Convention, the opinions of dissenting justices, and other documents. This volume, unlike the ones discussed above, does not attempt to cite or comment on all decisions of the Supreme Court of the United States, but refers only to the significant ones. It has a detailed index and includes the following useful tables:

Proposed Amendments Pending Before the States.

Proposed Amendments Not Ratified by the States.

Acts of Congress Held Unconstitutional in Whole or in Part
    by the Supreme Court of the United States.

State Constitutional and Statutory Provisions and Municipal
    Ordinances Held Unconstitutional on Their Face or As
    Administered (1789–1972).

---

[7] *See* Chapter 7, Section A.

[8] For the complete citation of this *see* note 2.

[9] 2 U.S.C. § 168 (1970 ed.).

Supreme Court Decisions Overruled by Subsequent Decisions.

Table of Cases.

This is a very useful volume, and it is often the preferred starting point for research on constitutional questions. The Congressional Research Service plans to keep the volume up to date by periodic issuance of pocket supplements.

d. *Digests.*

The following digests of federal cases provide additional judicial interpretations to the Constitution. These publications are discussed in detail in Chapter Six.

United States Supreme Court Reports Digest (Lawyers Co-op. Pub. Co.).

Volume 17 includes the text of the constitution reference under its provisions to related sections in the Digest.

United States Supreme Court Digest (West Pub. Co.).
Federal Digest, Modern Federal Practice Digest, and *West's Federal Practice Digest 2d.*

e. *Encyclopedias.*

The general legal encyclopedias (*American Jurisprudence 2d* and *Corpus Juris Secundum*) may treat the topic and provide reference to pertinent cases. The use of encyclopedias is described in Chapter Sixteen.

f. *Annotations.*

The annotations in A.L.R.Fed. and the *U. S. Supreme Court Reports* (L.Ed.) may contain discussion, with case analysis, on a phase of the Constitution which is being studied.

3.   Treatises and Periodical Literature

Voluminous literature has been written by legal scholars on the interpretation of constitutional provisions. A listing of such publications would be disproportionately long and would have little immediate value.[10] It is sufficient to point out that research in constitutional

---

[10] A few useful titles are: C. ANTIEAU, MODERN CONSTITUTIONAL LAW (1969); P. BREST, PROCESSES OF CONSTITUTIONAL DECISIONMAKING (1975); T. COOLEY, A TREATISE ON THE CONSTITUTIONAL LIMITATIONS WHICH REST UPON THE LEGISLATIVE POWER OF THE STATES OF THE AMERICAN UNION (8th ed. 1927); W. CROSSKEY, POLITICS AND THE CONSTITUTION IN THE HISTORY OF THE UNITED STATES (1953); G. GUNTHER, CASES AND MATERIALS ON CONSTITUTIONAL LAW (9th ed. 1975); B. SCHWARTZ, A COMMENTARY ON THE CONSTITUTION OF THE UNITED STATES (1963–68); J. STORY, COMMENTARIES ON THE CONSTITUTION OF THE UNITED STATES (5th ed. 1891). For more detailed listings of treatises *see*: NEW YORK UNIVERSITY SCHOOL OF LAW LIBRARY, A CATALOGUE OF THE

law can seldom be successfully completed without consulting the writings of constitutional scholars in either treatises or legal periodicals. The latter are especially important for matters of contemporary interest and can easily be located through the use of periodical indexes.[11]

4. Amending the Federal Constitution

The provisions for amending the Constitution are set forth in Article 5. Under it, amendments may be proposed by: (1) the initiative of Congress by two-thirds vote in each house, or (2) by convention on application of two-thirds of the state legislatures. Congress, in proposing amendments, may specify that ratification shall be either by three-quarters of the state legislatures or by conventions in three-fourths of the states.[12] To date there have been 26 amendments proposed, ratified, and incorporated into the Constitution. Six amendments proposed by Congress have not been ratified by the states, and only one of these is still pending before them.[13]

LAW COLLECTION AT NEW YORK UNIVERSITY (1953); J. JACOBSTEIN & M. PIMSLEUR, LAW BOOKS IN PRINT, and ASSOCIATION OF AMERICAN LAW SCHOOLS, 2 LAW BOOKS RECOMMENDED FOR LAW LIBRARIES: CONSTITUTIONAL LAW (1968).

[11] Discussed in Chapter Seventeen.

[12] To date none of the adopted or proposed constitutional amendments have been adopted by the convention method. For a discussion of unanswered questions that may arise if this method is used, *see*: AMERICAN BAR ASSOCIATION. SPECIAL CONSTITUTIONAL STUDY COMMITTEE, AMENDMENT OF THE CONSTITUTION BY THE CONVENTION METHOD UNDER ARTICLE V (1974); Comment, *Amendment by Convention: Our Next Constitutional Crisis?* 53 N.C.L.REV. 491 (1975).

[13] Equal Rights Amendment, Proposed Amendment XXVII, H.J.RES.NO.208, 92d Cong., 1st Sess. (1971). For more detailed information on proposed and unratified amendments, *see*: U. S. CONGRESS. HOUSE, THE CONSTITUTION OF THE UNITED STATES OF AMERICA: AS AMENDED THROUGH JULY 1971; ANALYTICAL INDEX: UNRATIFIED AMENDMENT, H.DOC.NO.93–215, 93d Cong., 2d Sess. (1974); U. S. CONGRESS. SENATE LIBRARY, PROPOSED AMENDMENTS TO THE CONSTITUTION (69th Congress—87th Congress), SEN.DOC.NO. 163, 87th Cong., 2d Sess. (1963), and (88th Congress—90th Congress), SEN.DOC.NO. 91–38, 91st Cong., 1st Sess. (1939); U. S. CONGRESS. SENATE, COMMITTEE ON THE JUDICIARY, SUBCOMMITTEE ON CONSTITUTIONAL AMENDMENTS, ANNUAL REPORTS (*e. g.*, SEN.R.NO.93–1423, 93d Cong., 2d Sess. (1974)).

SECTION B. ILLUSTRATIONS: FEDERAL CONSTITUTION

Problem: Does the United States Constitution prohibit Congress from reducing the compensation paid to judges?

Illustrations

28. Page from Index to U.S.C.A.

29. Pages from Constitution volumes of U.S.C.A.

30. Pages from the Constitution of the United States of America: Analysis and Interpretations [Library of Congress Ed. 1972].

[Illustration 28]
PAGE FROM INDEX VOLUMES OF U.S.C.A.

INDEX

COMMANDER-IN-CHIEF
President to be, Art. 2, § 2, cl. 1.

COMMERCE
Interstate and Foreign Commerce, generally, this index.

COMMERCIAL REGULATIONS
Port preferences forbidden, Art. 1, § 9, cl. 6.

COMMON DEFENSE
Provision for by Congress, Art. 1, § 8, cl. 1.
Purpose of Constitution to promote, Preamble.

COMMON LAW
No fact tried by jury shall be re-examined except according to, Am. 7.
Rules adhered to, Am. 7.
Trial by jury, actions exceeding $20, Am. 7.

COMPACT
States with each other or foreign powers, Art. 1, § 10, cl. 3.

COMPENSATION
→Judges, Art. 3, § 1.
Justices of Supreme Court, Art. 3, § 1.
Members of Congress, Art. 1, § 6, cl. 1.
President, Art. 2, § 1, cl. 6.
Private property not to be taken for public use without, Am. 5.

> Consult index volumes to U.S.C.A. (or U.S.C.S.).
> Note reference to Art. 3, § 1.

CONFEDERATE STATES
Debts, assumption prohibited, Am. 14, § 4.

CONFEDERATIONS
Debts contracted before adoption of Constitution valid, Art. 6, cl. 1.
States not to enter into, Art. 1, § 10, cl. 1.

CONFESSION
Persons convicted for treason on confession in open court, Art. 3, § 3, cl. 1.

CONFRONTATION
Accused persons by witnesses, Am. 6.

CONGRESS
Adjournment of Congress, generally, this index.
Composition, Art. 1, § 1.
Consent, this index.
Constitutional amendments, proposing, Art. 5.
Exclusive Legislation, this index.
Extra sessions, President's power, Art. 2, § 3.
House of Representatives, generally, this index.
Information and recommendations by President, Art. 2, § 3.
Journals,
　　Each house to keep. Art. 1, § 5, cl. 3.
　　Entries in, Art. 1, § 7, cl. 2.
Legislative power vested in, Art. 1, § 1.
Members,
　　Compelling attendance, Art. 1, § 5, cl. 1.

596

[Illustration 29]

PAGE FROM CONSTITUTION VOLUMES OF U.S.C.A.

THE JUDICIARY   **3 § 1**

ARTICLE III.—THE JUDICIARY

Section 1.   The judicial Power of the United States, shall be vested in one supreme Court, and in such inferior Courts as the Congress may from time to time ordain and establish. The Judges, both of the supreme and inferior Courts, shall hold their Offices during good Behaviour, and shall, at stated Times, receive for their Services, a Compensation, which shall not be diminished during their Continuance in Office.

Section 2.   The judicial Power shall extend to all Cases, in Law and Equity, arising under this Constitution, the Laws of the United States, and Treaties made, or which shall be made, under their Authority;—to all Cases affecting Ambassadors, other public Ministers and Consuls;—to all Cases of admiralty and maritime Jurisdiction;—to Controversies to which the United States shall be a Party;—to Controversies between two or more States;—between a State and Citizens of another State;—between Citizens of different States,—between Citizens of the same State claiming Lands under Grants of different States, and between a State, or the Citizens thereof, and foreign States, Citizens or Subjects.

Text of Article 3, § 1.

Crimes shall have been committed, but when not committed within any State, the Trial shall be at such Place or Places as the Congress may by Law have directed.

Section 3.   Treason against the United States, shall consist only in levying War against them, or in adhering to their Enemies, giving them Aid and Comfort. No Person shall be convicted of Treason unless on the Testimony of two Witnesses to the same overt Act, or on Confession in open Court.

The Congress shall have Power to declare the Punishment of Treason, but no Attainder of Treason shall work Corruption of Blood, or Forfeiture except during the Life of the Person attainted.

Section 1.   Judicial Power, Tenure and Compensation

Section 1.   The judicial Power of the United States, shall be vested in one supreme Court, and in such inferior Courts as the Congress may from time to time ordain and establish. The Judges, both of the supreme and inferior Courts, shall hold their Offices during good Behaviour, and shall, at stated Times, receive for their Services, a

7

[Illustration 29–a]

PAGE FROM CONSTITUTION VOLUMES—U.S.C.A.

---

3 § 1   **CONSTITUTION**

Compensation, which shall not be diminished during their Continuance in Office.

Cross References

Customs Court, declaration as court established under this article, see 28 U.S.C.A. § 251.

Notes of Decisions

Immediately after the text, there is an index to all the annotations (digests) of cases interpreting this Section. Cases dealing with compensation will be found under Notes 31–60. See next Illustration.

[Illustration 29–b]

PAGE FROM CONSTITUTION VOLUMES—U.S.C.A.

JUDICIAL POWER, TENURE, ETC.   3 § 1
Note 34

D.C.N.Y.1964, 226 F.Supp. 593, affirmed 371 F.2d 79.

A territorial court is not a court of the United States in the sense of the Constitution, but, with its judges, is a creation of Congress, subject to the will of that

31. Hold office

Under this clause, person appointed to office of United States district judge becomes entitled to draw salary of office so long as he continues to "hold office," and he "holds office" until he voluntarily

---

Digests of court decisions concerning compensation of judges, with diminution of compensation covered in Notes 33–41. While not shown in this Illustration, pocket supplement to the volume must also be checked. The U.S.C.S. is similarly organized.

---

12. Retirement for disability

The acceptance by the President of a certificate concerning the disability of a district court judge presented by the Judicial Council of the particular circuit pursuant to 28 U.S.C.A. § 372(a), does not accomplish the retirement of a judge under this section, which provides for removal of judges only by impeachment, and, therefore, when the President finds it necessary to appoint an additional judge for the efficient dispatch of business, in the case of a disabled judge who does not retire because he has not had the required service for retirement at full pay he may continue to receive full pay. 1965, 44 Comp.Gen. 544.

II. COMPENSATION

Subdivision Index

33. Diminution—Generally

Apart from this section pertaining to vesting of the judicial power, neither tenure nor salary of federal officers is constitutionally protected from impairment by Congress. Glidden Co. v. Zdanok, N. Y. & App.D.C.1962, 82 S.Ct. 1459, 370 U. S. 530, 8 L.Ed.2d 671, rehearing denied 83 S.Ct. 14, 371 U.S. 854, 9 L.Ed.2d 93.

Prohibition of this clause against the diminishing of compensation of "judges" applies only to judges of a constitutional court. Charles v. U. S., 1938, 21 F.Supp. 366, 86 Ct.Cl. 168.

The mere performance of judicial duties is not the test as to whether officer is one whose compensation cannot be diminished under this clause. Id.

Judges of all federal constitutional courts are protected as to tenure of office and compensation by specific constitutional provision as well as by fact that they are constitutional courts, while judges of legislative courts have no constitutional protection from legislative power of Congress as to tenure or compensation. Gorham v. Robinson, 1936, 186 A. 832, 57 R.I. 1.

34. —— Laws affecting

26 U.S.C.A. [I.R.C.1939] § 22(a) is not unconstitutional, since a nondiscriminatory tax laid generally on net income is not when applied to the income of a federal judge, a "diminution of salary" within prohibition of Constitution. O'Malley v. Woodrough, Neb. 1939, 59 S. Ct. 838, 307 U.S. 277, 83 L.Ed. 1289, 122 A.L.R. 1379.

The exemption of a federal judge's salary from taxation is not affected by the fact that the taxing statute was passed before his salary was fixed, and he was

[Illustration 30]

PAGE FROM LIBRARY OF CONGRESS EDITION—
ANNOTATED CONSTITUTION

JUDICIAL DEPARTMENT

ARTICLE III

SECTION 1. The judicial Power of the United States, shall be vested in one supreme Court, and in such inferior Courts as the Congress may from time to time ordain and establish. The Judges, both of the supreme and inferior Courts, shall hold their Offices during good Behaviour, and shall, at stated Times, receive for their Services, a Compensation, which shall not be diminished during their Continuance in Office.

ORGANIZATION OF COURTS, TENURE, AND COMPENSATION OF JUDGES

The Constitution is almost completely silent concerning the organization of the federal judiciary. "That there should be a national judiciary was readily accepted by all." [1] But whether it was to consist of one high court at the apex of a federal judicial system or a high court exercising appellate jurisdiction over state courts which would initially hear all but a minor fraction of cases raising national issues was a matter of considerable controversy. [2] The Virginia Plan provided for a "National judiciary [to] be established to consist of one or more supreme tribunals, and of inferior tribunals to be chosen by the National Legislature . . . ." [3] In the Committee of the Whole, the proposition "that a national judiciary be established" was unanimously adopted, [4] but the clause "to consist of One supreme tribunal,

---

This one volume edition sets forth the text of each Section of the Constitution. Immediately following, in smaller type, is an analysis and commentary of the Section. Footnotes give the sources to citations in the analysis.

[Illustration 30–a]

PAGE FROM LIBRARY OF CONGRESS EDITION— ANNOTATED CONSTITUTION

ART. III—JUDICIAL DEPARTMENT 587

> The analysis of the compensation provision as it appears in Section 1 of Article 3.
>
> This edition is very useful for the scholarly analysis given to each section and clause of the Constitution.

to the district courts.

Compensation

The prohibition against the diminution of judicial salaries has presented very little litigation. In *Evans* v. *Gore* [1] the Court invalidated the application of the income tax law to a federal judge, over the strong dissent of Justice Holmes, who was joined by Justice Brandeis. This ruling was extended in *Miles* v. *Graham* [2] to exempt the salary of a judge of the Court of Claims appointed subsequent to the enactment of the taxing act. *Evans* v. *Gore* was disapproved and *Miles* v. *Graham* in effect overruled in *O'Malley* v. *Woodrough*,[3] where the Court upheld section 22 of the Revenue Act of 1932 which extended the application of the income tax to salaries of judges taking office after June 6, 1932. Such a tax was regarded neither as an unconstitutional diminution of the compensation of judges nor as an encroachment on the independence of the judiciary.[4] To subject judges who

---

[7] Thus, John Taylor of Caroline, upon whom the Jeffersonians in Congress relied: "The Constitution declares that the judge shall hold his office during good behavior. Could it mean that he should hold this office after it was abolished? Could it mean that his tenure should be limited by behaving well in an office which did not exist? It must either have intended these absurdities or admit of a construction which will avoid them. This construction obviously is that an officer should hold that which he might hold, namely an existing office, so long as he did that which he might do, namely his duty in that office; and not that he should hold an office which did not exist or perform duties not sanctioned by law. If, therefore, Congress can abolish the courts, as they did by the last law, the officer dies with the office, unless you allow the Constitution to admit impossibilities as well as absurdities." W. Carpenter, *Judicial Tenure in the United States* (New Haven: 1918), 63–64. The controversy is recounted in id., 58–78.

[8] 1 Cr. (5 U.S.) 299 (1803).

[9] The Court was created by the Act of June 18, 1910, 36 Stat. 539, and repealed by the Act of October 22, 1913, 38 Stat. 208, 219. *See* F. Frankfurter & J. Landis, *The Business of the Supreme Court* (New York: 1928), 153–174; W. Carpenter, *Judicial Tenure in the United States* (New Haven: 1918), 78–94.

[1] 253 U.S. 245 (1920).

[2] 268 U.S. 501 (1925).

[3] 307 U.S. 277 (1939).

[4] Id., 278–282.

SECTION C. STATE CONSTITUTIONS

Each of the fifty states has adopted its own constitution, and many states have adopted several different constitutions over the years. The procedure for adopting a new constitution is usually accomplished by the convening of a state constitutional convention.[14] The state constitution, except for those issues covered by the supremacy clause of the United States Constitution,[15] is the highest primary legal authority for the state.

When doing research involving a state constitution, it may also be necessary to check the historical documents that led to its adoption and to consult the state and federal court decisions interpreting it.

1. Texts of State Constitutions

a. The most common source for the text of a state constitution is the constitution volume of the state code.[16] This ordinarily will contain the current text, the text of previously adopted versions, and annotations similar in format to those of the United States Constitution as described in Section A *supra*. The volume or volumes containing your state constitution should be examined carefully, and distinctive bibliographic features should be noted. Many states also print and distribute an unannotated edition of the state constitution in pamphlet form.

b. Columbia University. Legislative Drafting Research Fund. *Constitutions of the United States: National and State* (2d ed. 1974).[17]

This two-volume, looseleaf set collects the text of the Constitutions of all fifty states and is kept current by supplements.

---

[14] A. STURM, A BIBLIOGRAPHY ON STATE CONSTITUTIONS AND CONSTITUTIONAL REVISION, 1945–1975 (1975).

[15] U.S.CONST. art. VI; Gibbons v. Ogden, 22 U.S. (9 Wheat.) 1 (1824); National Labor Relations Bd. v. Jones & Laughlin Steel Corp., 301 U.S. 1 (1937); United States v. Darby, 312 U.S. 100 (1941); Perez v. United States, 402 U.S. 146 (1971).

[16] State codes are discussed in Chapter Eleven.

[17] The following older titles are also useful in tracing the historical development of state constitutions: B. POORE, CHARTERS AND CONSTITUTIONS (1877); F. STIMSON, THE LAW OF THE FEDERAL AND STATE CONSTITUTIONS OF THE UNITED STATES (1908); F. THORPE, FEDERAL AND STATE CONSTITUTIONS (1909); C. KETTLEBOROUGH, STATE CONSTITUTIONS (1918); NEW YORK CONSTITUTIONAL CONVENTION COMMITTEE, 3 REPORTS: CONSTITUTIONS OF THE STATES AND UNITED STATES (1938). Although Thorpe and Poore are out-of-date, they are useful for their parallel study of state constitutions. The last item, although never brought up-to-date, is still useful for its index volume to the constitutions of all of the states.

2. Historical Sources of State Constitutions

The records, journals, proceedings, and other documents relating to state constitutional conventions provide valuable information on the intended meanings and interpretations given to state constitutions by their framers.[18] Some state codes also contain historical introductions to the constitutions printed therein. Local encyclopedias and treatises should also be consulted.

3. Judicial Interpretation of State Constitutions

In addition to consulting the annotations to the constitution in the appropriate volumes of the state code, the state digest should also be consulted, using the index to the constitution to locate the relevant sections of the digest.

4. Comparative Sources of State Constitutions

Frequently, a provision of a particular state constitution has not received any judicial interpretation or has not been recently discussed by a state court. In such instances, the interpretation of similar provisions in other state constitutions may be useful. The most useful and quickest method for locating similar provisions is through the use of the *Index Digest of State Constitutions*.[19] This set is a "comparative statement of the provisions of all the (state) constitutions arranged by subject." Under each subject are listed the various constitutional provisions listed alphabetically by state. For example, under the topic "Elections" and the subdivisions thereto, are listed digests of state constitutional provisions with citations. See Illustration 31. This set is a companion to the *Constitutions of the United States: National and State*, discussed in 1b *supra*.

[18] *See* note 14.

[19] COLUMBIA UNIVERSITY. LEGISLATIVE DRAFTING RESEARCH FUND, INDEX DIGEST OF STATE CONSTITUTIONS (2d ed. 1959).

[Illustration 31]

PAGE FROM INDEX DIGEST TO STATE CONSTITUTIONS

INDEX DIGEST 517

Issued in name and by authority of state, sealed with great seal, signed by governor and countersigned by secretary of state. **Ala** V 135; **Ark** VI 10; **Cal** V 14; **Fla** IV 14; **Ida** IV 16; **Iowa** IV 21; **Mont** VII 18; **Nev** V 16; **NC** III 16; **Ohio** III 13; **SC** IV 19; **Utah** VII 21.

Issued in name and by authority of state, sealed with great seal, signed by governor or person administering the government and countersigned by secretary of state. **NJ** X 2.

GRASSLANDS

See PUBLIC LANDS.

Grasslands and other replenishable resources belonging to state to be utilized, developed and maintained on sustained yield principle, subject to preferences among beneficial uses. **Alas** VIII 4.

For special provisions relating to lease of grazing land, *see* PUBLIC LANDS—LEASE. **Ariz** X 3, 8–10.

Legislature to prevent destruction by fire of grasses on public lands or on lands of public domain of which Congress may give state control. **Mont** XIX 3.

Board of land commissioners to classify public lands into grazing lands and other specified types of land; reclassification may be made whenever necessary because of increased facilities for irrigation or otherwise. **Mont** XVII 2.

Educational and charitable lands to be leased for pasturage, meadow, farming, growing of grain and general agricultural purposes, after notice as for sale, in tracts of not over one section; rent payable in advance; lease not valid unless approved by governor, unless leasing entrusted to county. **SD** VIII 9, 12.

GUARANTY COMPANIES

See CORPORATIONS.

Duly organized and responsible foreign or domestic guaranty companies, lawfully doing business in state, may be sureties on bonds of state, county and municipal officers. **Fla** XVI 13.

HABEAS CORPUS, WRIT OF

Granting Provided for 517
Suspension 517

For power of courts and judges to issue, hear and determine, *see various classes of courts and judges under title* COURTS.

GRANTING PROVIDED FOR

To be granted freely, without cost, speedily and of right. **Fla** DR 7.

To be granted speedily and cheaply, easily, expeditiously and in in an ample manner. **Mass** VI 7; **NH** II 91.

Issuable of right. **Vt** II 33.

Persons restrained of liberty entitled to remedy to inquire into lawfulness thereof. **NC** I 18.

Legislature to render remedy speedy and effective. **Tex** I 12; **Vt** II 33.

SUSPENSION

Privilege not to be suspended. **Ala** 117; **Ariz** II 14; **Ga** I Sec I 11; **Mo** I 12; **NC** I 21; **Okla** II 10; **Tex** I 12; **Vt** II 33; **W Va** III 4.

Privilege not to be suspended, unless when, in case of rebellion or invasion, public safety requires it. **Cal** I 5; **Colo** II 21; **Del** I 13; **Fla** DR 7; **Ill** II 7; **Ind** I 27; **Iowa** I 13; **Kan** BR 8; **Ky** 16; **La** I 13; **Me** I 10; **Mich** II 11; **Minn** I 7; **Mont** III 21; **Nev** I 5; **NJ** I 14; **NM** II 7; **NY** I 4; **ND** I 5; **Ohio** I 8; **Ore** I 23; **Pa** I 14; **SD** VI 8; **Utah** I 5; **Va** IV 58; **Wash** I 13; **Wis** I 8; **Wyo** I 17.

Same; adds "insurrection". **SC** I 23.

Privilege not to be suspended, unless when in cases of rebellion or actual or imminent invasion, public safety requires it. **Alas** I 13.

Privileges not to be suspended, unless when in case of rebellion or invasion, public safety may require it; nor in any case but by legislature. **Conn** I 14; **H** I 13; **Miss** III 21; **RI** I 9.

Privilege not to be suspended, except by legislature in case of rebellion, or invasion, when public safety may require it. **Ark** II 11.

> This volume presents comparative provisions of state constitutions arranged by subject.

partment and bank commission to protect stockholders and depositors. **Okla** XIV 1.

requires it, and then only in manner prescribed by law. **Ida** I 5; **Nebr** I 8.

SECTION D.   STATE CONSTITUTIONS: RESEARCH PUBLICATIONS

The state constitutions are published with the state codes, in pamphlets and in appropriate local treatises.   The usual source to locate a state constitution is the code or compilation of statutes for a specific state.   Such publications generally include the text of the state constitution and annotations to it.   As in the case of the Federal Constitution, they are separately indexed.   However, the general indexes of some state codes also cover the state constitution.   The indexes are generally topically arranged without factual analyses.   Thus, a modified topic method is frequently used to ascertain cases in point, for the index must be topically analyzed.   In some state publications, subdivision analyses precede the annotations.   A few of the state codes include not only annotated state constitutions but also the Federal Constitution with annotations.   An example of the latter is the *Iowa Code Annotated*, volume 2.   Examples of annotated state constitutions are:

Florida Statutes Annotated, vols. 25, 26 and 26A.

Michigan Statutes Annotated, vol. 1 (1965 Revision).

New Jersey Statutes Annotated, Constitution vol.

Vernon's Annotated Texas Constitution, 3 vols.

The records, journals, proceedings and other documents relating to the state constitutional conventions provide valuable source data on the intended meanings and interpretations given to the state constitutions, as amended, by their framers.   An array of these publications are available for the several states.   Consult your library catalog for its holdings for your state.

Popular names by which provisions of individual state constitutions have been referred are indicated in *Shepard's Federal and State Acts and Cases by Popular Names, 1968.*   Its cumulative pamphlet supplement keeps it current.

SECTION E.   FOREIGN CONSTITUTIONS

There are occasions when it is necessary to locate the constitutions of foreign countries.   A publication has now made research in this area relatively simple.   This is:

Blaustein, A. P. and Flanz, C. H. (eds.) *Constitutions of the Countries of the World.* Permanent Edition. Dobbs Ferry, N. Y., Oceana Publications, Inc., (1971) (to be completed in 12 volumes).

This set is published in looseleaf format, with a separate pamphlet for each country. For those countries where there is not an official English version, an English translation is provided. The constitutions for each country are preceded by a constitutional chronology and followed by an annotated bibliography.

Periodically supplements are issued, keeping each constitution up-to-date.

The Introduction in Chapter One should be consulted for bibliographical references to previous compilations of constitutions.

A companion set is A. Blaustein and E. Blaustein, *eds., Constitions of Dependencies and Special Sovereignties.* The first of two volumes was published in 1975 and contains pamphlets on the world's associated states, dependent territories, and areas of special sovereignty. Each pamphlet contains constitutional status data and an annotated bibliography. When a "territory" in this set achieves the status of a nation-state, it will be incorporated into the *Constitutions of the Countries of the World.*

SECTION F. SUMMARY

1. **Federal Constitution**
    a. Text in:
        (1) *United States Code.*
        (2) *United States Code Annotated.*
        (3) *United States Code Service-F.C.A. Edition.*
        (4) *U. S. Supreme Court Reports Digest* (Lawyers Co-op.).
        (5) *Library of Congress, Constitution of the United States of America* (1973).
    b. Interpretation.
        (1) Historical (see list of historical sources in Section A1, *supra*).
        (2) Judicial.
            (a) U.S.C.A.: (i) index is to the text of the Constitution; does not cover interpretative cases; (ii) topic analysis precedes digests of cases; (iii) digests of interpretative federal and state cases and Attorneys General opinions under constitutional provisions, subdivided by topic analysis (Notes to Decisions); (iv) parallel citation; and (v) cumulative annual pocket and subsequent pamphlet supplements.
            (b) U.S.C.S.: (i) index is to the text of the Constitution; does not cover interpretative cases; (ii) topic analysis precedes

digests of cases; (iii) digests of interpretative federal and state cases and Attorneys General opinions under constitutional provisions, subdivided by topic analysis (Notes to Decisions); (iv) parallel citation; and (v) cumulative annual pocket and later pamphlet supplements.

(c) *Library of Congress. Constitution of the United States of America* (1973): (i) partially indexes cases as well as the text of the Constitution; (ii) discussion of selected cases of the Supreme Court of the United States; documents; views of writers; (iii) no provision is made for keeping this publication up-to-date.

(d) *U. S. Supreme Court Reports Digest:* (i) volume 17 provides text and references to sections of the *Digest* covering the Constitution and (ii) volume 14 contains a Table of Constitutional Provisions with citations to U. S. Supreme Court decisions which construe them.

(e) Digests (see Section A2d), above.

(f) Encyclopedias: *Am.Jur.2d* and *C.J.S.* may treat the topic.

(g) Annotations: *A.L.R.Fed.* and the *U. S. Supreme Court Reports (L.Ed.)* may discuss the problem.

(h) Shepard's Citations: (i) *U. S. Citations* for federal court cases and (ii) *State Citations* for state cases interpreting U. S. Constitution. Also Shepardize cases.

c. Treatises and periodical literature (see Section A3, above).

2. Amending the Federal Constitution

a. *U. S. Congress. House, The Constitution of the United States of America: As Amended Through July 1971; Analytical Index; Unratified Amendments, H.Doc.No.93–215, 93d Cong., 2d Sess. (1974).*

b. *U. S. Congress. Senate Library, Proposed Amendments to the Constitution (69th Congress—87th Congress), Sen.Doc.No.163, 87th Cong., 2d Sess. (1963), and (88th Congress—90th Congress), Sen.Doc.No.91–38, 91st Cong., 1st Sess. (1969).*

3. State Constitutions

a. Published with state code.

b. Separate indexes and general indexes which are topically and not factually analyzed.

c. Annotated.

4. Sources of Comparative Information about State and Federal Constitutions

a. See Section E, above.

b. *Index Digest of State Constitutions*, 2d ed., 1959.

(1) Comparative statement of the provisions of all state constitutions arranged by subject.

(2) Analysis is not evaluative and is limited to the terms of the provisions.

(3) Most recent comprehensive, comparative study of constitutional provisions.

(4) Pocket supplement.

c. *Constitutions of the United States: National and State.*

(1) Looseleaf edition.

(2) Texts of the constitutions of the U. S. and the 50 states.

(3) Companion publication to the *Index Digest*.

5. Citation

Citation form for Constitutions may be found in Appendix A, at (I), (A), (1).

Chapter 9

FEDERAL LEGISLATION

Article I, Section 8, of the *United States Constitution* enumerates the powers of Congress, and provides the authority for Congress to make all laws necessary and proper for carrying into execution the enumerated powers, as well as other powers vested in the Congress.

A Congress meets in two year periods with each such period known as a *Congress*. The period in which Congress met, for example, during the years 1971–72, is known as the 92nd Congress, the First Congress being 1789–91. Under the Constitution, Congress must meet at least once a year.

SECTION A. THE ENACTMENT OF FEDERAL LAWS

Before discussing the various ways the laws of Congress are published, a brief description of the legislative process is necessary.[1] At the beginning of each Congress, any member of the House of Representatives or the Senate may introduce legislation in his respective house of Congress. Each proposed law is called a "bill"[2] when introduced. The first bill in the House of Representatives is labeled "H.R. 1" with all subsequent bills numbered sequentially. Similarly, the first bill introduced into the Senate is labeled "S. 1". After a bill passes the house in which it was introduced, it is sent for consideration to the other house. If approved, it is then sent to the President for his signature. If he signs it, it then becomes a law. If the President vetoes it, it may become law if approved by two-thirds of both houses of Congress. Under the Constitution, a bill sent to the President may also become law if the President does not either sign or veto

---

[1] For more detailed statements on the enactment of federal laws *see*: C. ZINN, HOW OUR LAWS ARE MADE, H.R.DOC.NO.377, 93d Cong., 2d Sess. (1974) ; F. R. VALEO AND M. ZWEBEN, ENACTMENT OF A LAW: PROCEDURAL STEPS IN THE LEGISLATIVE PROCESS. S.DOC.NO.94–152, 94th Cong., 2d Sess. (1975). *See also* CONGRESSIONAL QUARTERLY SERVICE, GUIDE TO THE CONGRESS OF THE UNITED STATES, ORIGINS, HISTORY, AND PROCEDURE (1971).

[2] A *bill* is the form used for most legislation. *Joint resolutions* may also be used, but there is no practical difference between the two and the two forms are used indiscriminately. *Concurrent resolutions* are used for matters affecting both Houses, but are not legislative. *Simple resolutions* are used for matters concerning the operation of either house. The first three forms are published in the *Statutes at Large*, the latter in the *Congressional Record*. C. ZINN, *supra* note 1, at 7.

it within ten days of receiving it.[3]   Bills introduced but not passed during a specific Congress do not carry over to the subsequent Congress but must be reintroduced.

The first law to pass a Congress is designated either Public Law No. 1 or Private Law No. 1.[4]   Each succeeding law is then numbered in sequence throughout the two-year life of a Congress.   A distinction is also made between permanent laws and temporary laws.   A *permanent* law remains in effect until repealed.   A *temporary* law continues in force only as long as explicitly or implicitly stated within the language of the law.   Examples of the latter are laws appropriating monies for a specific period of time or laws containing language which states that the law is no longer in force after a specified date.

1. Current Laws

During a session of Congress, each law as passed is first issued by the U. S. Government Printing Office as a *slip law*.   See Illustration 32.   This means that each law is separately published and may be one page or several hundred pages in length.   There are four sources commonly consulted for the text of current laws.

a.   *Slip laws*.   These are available at all libraries that are depositories for U. S. Government publications [5] and in certain law libraries.

b.   *U. S. Code Congressional and Administrative News Service*. This set is published by the West Publishing Co. in connection with the *United States Code Annotated*.   During each session of Congress it is issued monthly in pamphlet form and prints in full text all of the public laws.   Each issue contains a cumulative subject index and a cumulative *Table of Laws Enacted*.   After each session of Congress the pamphlets are re-issued in bound volumes.

c.   *Advance Sheets, United States Code Service, Lawyers Edition*.   This is published by the Lawyers Co-operative Publishing Company in connection with the *United States Code Service, L.Ed.*   It contains similar information as that described in b. *supra*.

d.   *U. S. Law Week*.   This weekly looseleaf service, which is published by the Bureau of National Affairs, includes the

[3] U.S.CONST. art. I, § 7.

[4] This is done by the Office of the Federal Register, General Services Administration.   Letter from Fred J. Emery (Office of the Federal Register) to J. Myron Jacobstein, Nov. 13, 1972.

[5] A list of such libraries is published each year in the September issue of the *Monthly Catalog of Government Publications*.   Government Depository collections may be consulted by the public.

text of the more important laws passed during the previous week.

2. U. S. Statutes at Large

At the end of each session of Congress, all of the slip laws are published in numerical order as part of the set called the *United States Statutes at Large*. Thus all of the laws enacted since 1789 are contained in the many volumes of this set.[6]

It is important to keep in mind that the laws are arranged in chronological order rather than by subject. Moreover, amendments to a previously passed law will appear in different volumes from the law being amended. For example, a law passed in 1900 is in volume 31 of the *Statutes at Large*. If Congress amended it in 1905, the amendment will appear in the volume for that year. Some laws have been amended many, many times and in order to obtain the full and current text of such a law, the *Statutes at Large* volume containing the original law must be examined in context with subsequent volumes in which amendments to the law appear.

Each volume of the *Statutes at Large* has its own subject index and contains tables listing how each public law in it affects previous public laws.

SECTION B. CODIFICATION OF FEDERAL LAWS

The chronological method of publication of Congressional laws created obvious problems for the process of determining the statutory provisions on any given subject. In order to better accomplish this, the laws passed by Congress have to be rearranged in a manner that will do three things: (1) collate the original law with all subsequently passed amendments by taking into consideration the deletion or addition of language changed by the amendments; (2) bring all laws on the same subject or topic together, and (3) eliminate all repealed, superseded, or expired laws. This process is called codification.[7]

1. United States Revised Statutes

The first codification [8] of the *Statutes-at-Large* was authorized by the Congress in 1866 and resulted in the publication of the *Revised Statutes of 1875*.

---

[6] Until 1936, each volume of the *Statutes at Large* covered a two-year period.

[7] For articles dealing with codification *see*: Donald, *Codification in Common Law Systems*, 47 AUST.L.J. 160 (1973); McClellan, *Codification, Reform and Revision: The Challenge of a Modern Federal Criminal Code*, 1971 DUKE L.J. 663; Tucker, *Tradition and Technique of Codification in the Modern World: The Louisiana Experience*, 25 LA.L.REV. 698 (1965); Zinn, *Revision of the United States Code*, 51 L.LIB.J. 388 (1958).

[8] Dwan and Feidler, *The Federal Statutes, Their History and Use*, 22 MINN.L. REV. 1008 (1938).

The Commissioners authorized by Congress to prepare this revision began by extracting from the volumes of the *Statutes at Large* all public laws that met the following two criteria: (1) they were still in force, and (2) they were of a general and permanent nature. They eliminated all appropriation laws and those that did not have general applicability. The next step was to take each public law and all its amendments and rewrite the law in one sequence by incorporating amending language and eliminating deleting language. All of the laws on one topic were then arranged in a chapter. Chapter 35, for example, contained all legislation passed by Congress, and still in force, on taxation; Chapter 70 all legislation in force on criminal law. All of the chapters were then bound in one volume, a subject index prepared, and the volume issued as the *Revised Statutes of 1875*.

This volume as prepared by the Commissioners was then submitted to Congress, introduced as a bill, and went through the legislative process of becoming a public law. Within the bill before Congress there was a section specifically repealing each previously passed public law that had been incorporated into the *Revised Statutes of 1875*.[9] Thus, when it passed Congress and was signed by the President, all of the laws passed since 1789, in force and of a general and public nature, were codified in the *Revised Statutes of 1875*. Moreover, as the act of codification repealed all the previous *Statutes at Large* citations, the *Revised Statutes of 1875* became *positive law* and it was no longer necessary to refer back to the *Statutes at Large* volumes.

Unfortunately, this volume, known as the first edition, was subsequently discovered to contain many inaccuracies and unauthorized changes in the law.[10] In 1878, a second edition of the *Revised Statutes* was authorized to be published which would include legislation passed since 1873, delete sections that were repealed since 1873, and also correct the errors that had inadvertently been incorporated into the first edition.

The second edition indicated changes to the text of the first edition by the use of brackets and italics. It is important to note, however, that the second edition of the *Revised Statutes* was never reenacted by Congress and all changes indicated in it are only *prima facie* evidence of the law. There were no further codification of federal laws until 1926.

2. United States Code

Prior to 1926, the positive law for federal legislation was contained in the one volume of the *Revised Statutes of 1875* and then in

---

[9] Revised Statutes of the United States, 1873–1874, Act of June 22, 1874, Title LXXIV, Repeal Provisions, §§ 5595–5601, pp. 1091–1092 (1875).

[10] *Id.* note 8.

each subsequent volume of the *Statutes at Large*. In 1925, Congress authorized the preparation of the *United States Code*. This was prepared by a Revisor of Statutes appointed by Congress, who extracted all sections of the *Revised Statutes of 1875* that had not been repealed and then all of the public and general laws from the *Statutes at Large* since 1873 that were still in force. These were then rearranged into fifty titles and published as the *United States Code*, 1926 ed., in four volumes. Each year thereafter a cumulative supplement containing the laws passed since 1926 was published. In 1932 a new edition was issued which incorporated the cumulated supplements to the 1926 edition, and this became the *United States Code*, 1932 ed. Every six years a new edition of the *U. S. Code* is published with cumulative supplement volumes being issued during the intervening years. The *United States Code* differs from the *Revised Statutes of 1875* in one important aspect. It was never submitted to Congress and re-enacted in its entirety. Instead the Committee on the Judiciary of the House of Representatives is engaged in revising the *United States Code* title by title, each of which is then submitted to Congress for legislative approval. To date, nineteen titles have been enacted into law.[11] Thus, in using the *United States Code* it is important to ascertain if the title being consulted is one that has been enacted into positive law. Those titles not so enacted are *prima facie* evidence of the law.[12] Should there be a conflict between the wording in the *United States Code* and the *Statutes at Large*, the latter will govern.[13]

[11] The titles so enacted are 1, 3, 4, 5, 6, 9, 10, 13, 14, 17, 18, 23, 28, 32, 35, 37, 38, 39, 44. Preface, U.S.C. p. IX (Supp. IV, 1974). In 1974, Congress established the Office of Law Revision Counsel (2 U.S.C. 285a–e, 1974 Supp.). The principal duty of this Office is "to develop and keep current an official and positive codification of the laws of the United States" and "to prepare * * * one title at a time, a complete compilation, restatement and revision of the general and permanent laws of the United States * * *." The Law Revision Counsel has indicated that his office plans to reenact the remaining titles of the U. S. Code as soon as possible, but could not indicate an exact schedule. It will probably be several years before this assigned task will be completed. (Memo of telephone conversation of authors with Mr. Edward Willett, September 13, 1976, on file at the Tarlton Law Library, University of Texas, Austin.)

[12] 1 U.S.C. § 204(a) (1970) provides that "The matter set forth in the edition of the Code of Laws of the United States current at any time shall, together with the then current supplement, if any, establish prima facie the laws of the United States, general and permanent in their nature, in force on the day preceding the commencement of the session following the last session the legislation of which is included: *Provided, however*, that whenever titles of such Code shall have been enacted into positive law the text thereof shall be legal evidence of the laws therein contained in all the courts of the United States, the several States, and the Territories and insular possessions of the United States."

[13] *See* an interpretation of 1 U.S.C. § 204(a) (1970) in *U. S. v. Welden*, 377 U.S. 95, 98 n. 4 (1964).

3.   Annotated Editions of the U.S. Code

The *United States Code* is designated as the official edition, and is printed and sold by U. S. Government Printing Office.   As is frequently the case with such publications, it is slow in being published, particularly in the issuance of the supplements, which are seldom available until several months after a session of Congress is over. Furthermore, the meaning of a law passed by a legislative body is not always clear and the intent of the language used must frequently be interpreted by a court.   Consequently, access to the court decisions interpreting statutes is frequently as important as the text of the statute itself.   This has led to the publication of annotated codes where digests of court decisions interpreting a code section are given. There are two privately published annotated editions of the *United States Code*.

Both of these sets have many advantages over the official edition of the *United States Code* and are usually consulted in preference to it.   These advantages are (1) each title is published in one or more separate volumes; (2) the entire set is kept up to date by annual cumulative pocket supplements; (3) pamphlets are issued during the year bringing up-to-date the pocket supplements; (4) more detailed indexing is provided in both bound volumes and supplements; (5) each Code section contains annotations of court decisions which have cited and interpreted it.

a.   *United States Code Annotated* (U.S.C.A.)   This set is published by the West Publishing Company.   In addition to annotating relevant cases, the notes following each code section make reference to other West publications and frequently refer to the Topic and Key Numbers where additional cases may be located.   In addition to a separate eight volume index, each title has an individual, detailed index.

b.   *United States Code Service, Lawyers Edition* (U.S.C.S.)

This set was originally published by the Bobbs-Merrill Company as the *Federal Code Annotated*.   Several years ago it was purchased by the Lawyers Cooperative Publishing Company/Bancroft-Whitney Company.   Originally bound in red, the new publishers have now re-issued the entire set in black binding and are in the process of revising each of the fifty titles.   This is not being done title by title sequentially but rather by choosing individual titles which reflect both active legislative changes and the flow of federal decisions.   The revised volumes have entirely new annotations prepared by the new publishers, as well as new editorial notes and comments.   An important new feature are the citations, when appropriate, to the *Code of Federal Regulations*.[14]   The new volumes have a blue label on the

---

[14] Discussed in Chapter Thirteen.

spine with the abbreviation USCS L ED while the volumes not yet replaced have red labels with USCS FCA. It also has a new five volume index to the entire set. When all of the volumes are replaced, the *United States Code Service, Lawyers Edition,* will become an integral part of their Total Client Service Library. A one volume *U. S. Code Guide* is part of this set and relates the entire Code to the other related publications of this company.

Illustrations 32–38 show the use of the various editions of the United States Code.

SECTION C.   POPULAR NAMES OF FEDERAL ACTS

It is common practice to refer to a federal act by a popular name. Generally, this is the name which the public or media give the statute, and it may describe its subject matter (*e. g.,* Gold Clause Act) or refer to its authors (*e. g.,* the Taft-Hartley Act).

The tables of popular names of federal acts are designed to provide the citations to acts when only the popular names are known.

There are a number of such tables. They are:

1.   *Shepard's Federal and State Acts* and *Cases by Popular Names,* Vol. 1, 1968, and Cumulative Supplement. See Illustration 41.

2.   *United States Code Annotated* contains a table of acts cited by popular name in volume 5 of the Index and in its pocket supplement. See Illustration 40.

3.   The popular names for federal acts for those still in force are also listed alphabetically in the general indexes to the *U. S. Code Annotated* and the *United States Code Service, Lawyers Edition.*

4.   The *United States Code* in the *General Index* volume has an *Index of Acts by Popular Name.*

5.   *United States Code Service, Lawyers Edition.* Table volumes contain a *Table of Acts by Popular Name.*

6.   *U. S. Code Congressional and Administrative News* provides tables of *Popular Name Acts* for each session of Congress, beginning with the 77th Congress, 2d Session, 1942. These tables are for each session, are not cumulated, and cite the acts in the pages of the *News.*

SECTION D.   ILLUSTRATIONS

[Illustration 32]

SLIP LAW—93RD CONGRESS

Public Law 93-473
93rd Congress, S. 3234 ◄—— 1.
October 26, 1974

An Act

2. ——► 88 STAT. 1431

To authorize a vigorous Federal program of research, development, and demonstration to assure the utilization of solar energy as a viable source for our national energy needs, and for other purposes.

Be it enacted by the Senate and House of Representatives of the United States of America in Congress assembled, That this Act may be cited as the "Solar Energy Research, Development, and Demonstration Act of 1974".

Solar Energy Research, Development, and Demonstration Act of 1974. 42 USC 5551 note. 42 USC 5551.

DECLARATION OF FINDINGS AND POLICY

SEC. 2. (a) The Congress hereby finds that—
(1) the needs of a viable society depend on an ample supply of energy;
(2) the current imbalance between domestic supply and demand for fuels and energy is likely to persist for some time;
(3) dependence on nonrenewable energy resources cannot be continued indefinitely, particularly at current rates of consumption;
(4) it is in the Nation's interest to expedite the long-term development of renewable and nonpolluting energy resources, such as solar energy;
(5) the various solar energy technologies are today at widely differing stages of development, with some already near the stage of commercial application and others still requiring basic research;
(6) the early development and export of viable equipment utilizing solar energy, consistent with the established preeminence of the United States in the field of high technology products, can make a valuable contribution to our balance of trade;
(7) the mass production and use of equipment utilizing solar energy will help to eliminate the dependence of the United States upon foreign energy sources and promote the national defense;
(8) to date, the national effort in research, development, and demonstration activities relating to the utilization of solar energy has been extremely limited; therefore
(9) the urgency of the Nation's critical energy shortages and the need to make clean and renewable energy alternatives commercially viable require that the Nation undertake an intensive research, development, and demonstration program with an estimated Federal investment which may reach or exceed $1,000,000,000.
(b) The Congress declares that it is the policy of the Federal Govern-

42 USC 5552.

> This is a typical "slip" law. At the end of the year, all of the slip laws are published in a bound volume of the Statutes at Large.
>
> Marginal notes are not part of the law but editorial aids. The code citations in the margin indicate where the Statute at Large citations in the text are found in the U.S. Code.
>
> Notes: 1. Bill number in Senate.
> 2. Statute at Large citation.

[Illustration 33]

A PAGE FROM U.S.C.A. SHOWING CONVERSION TABLE FOR STATUTE AT LARGE CITATION TO U.S. CODE CITATION

STATUTES AT LARGE   **1974**

1974—93rd Cong.—88 Stat.				U S C A		
Oct.	P.L.	Sec.	Page	Tit.	Sec.	Status
23	92–463	103(a)	1392	7	6, 6c–6g, 6i, 7, 7a, 8, 9, 11, 12, 12—1, 12a, 12b, 13b	
		103(b)	1392	7	7b, 8, 9, 12a, 13b, 13c	
		103(c)	1392	7	8	
		103(d)	1392	7	15	
		103(e)	1392	7	7a, 12, 12—1, 12a	
		103(f)	1392	7	6, 6g, 6i, 7, 7a, 12—1	
		103(g)	1392	7	7	
		104	1392	7	4a nt	
		105	1392	7	12—2, 12—3	
		106	1393	7	18	
		107	1395	7	19	
		201, 202	1395	7	2	
		203	1396	7	6j	
		204(a)	1396	7	6k	
		204(b)	1397	7	9	
		204(c)	1397	7	12a	
		205(a)	1397– 1400	7	6l–6o	
		205(b)	1400	7	9	
		205(c)	1400	7	12a	
		206	1400	7	6p	
		207	1400	7	7	
		208–210	1400	7	7a	
		211	1402	7	13a—1	
		212(a)(1), (2)	1403	7	9	
		212(a)(3)	1403	7	9a	
		212(b)	1403	7	13a	
		212(c)	1404	7	13b	
		212(d)	1404	7	13	
		213–215	1404	7	12a	
		216	1405	7	12c	
		217	1405	7	15a	
		301	1406	7	21	
		401	1412	7	13	
		402	1412	7	6c	
		403	1413	7	6a	
		404	1413	7	6a, 6a nts	
		405	1413	7	6b	
		406, 407	1413, 1414	7	7a	
		408(a)	1414	7	9	
		408(b)	1414	7	9, 15	
		409	1414	7	13	
		410	1414	5	5108	
		411–413	1414	7	4a nts	
		414	1414	7	20	
		415	1415	7	6g	
		416	1415	7	22	
		417	1415	7	4a nt	
		418	1415	7	2 nt	
24	93–464	—	1416	7	1314b	
	93–466	1	1420	16	450bb	
		2	1420	16	450bb—2	
		3	1420	16	450bb nt	
	93–468	1	1422	22	263a	
	93–469	—	1422	10	prec. 3741 nt	
26	93–470	1	1422	19	1202	
		2	1422	19	1202 nt	
	93–471	208(e)	1429	7	361a	
		407	1430	7	361a nt	
	93–472	—	1430	33	1420	
➤	93–473	1	1431	42	5551 nt	
		➤ 2	1431	42	5551	
		3	1431	42	5552	
		4	1432	42	5553	
		5	1433	42	5554	
		6	1433	42	5555	
		7	1434	42	5556	
		8	1435	42	5557	
		9	1436	42	5558	
		10	1436	42	5559	
		11	1437	42	5560	

37

[Illustration 34]

PAGE FROM THE INDEX VOLUME TO THE U.S.C.A.

TAXATION   726

FINDING A FEDERAL STATUTE

Problem: Are stocks and bonds issued by the United States Government exempt from taxation by the states?

Step 1.   Check index volumes to U.S.C., U.S.C.A., or U.S. C.S.

This will indicate that there is a code section covering this topic at Title 31, § 742.

[Illustration 35]
PAGE FROM U.S. CODE, 1952 EDITION

§ 741a. Sale and disposition of bonds, notes, and other securities.

(a) Notwithstanding the provisions of section 302 of Title 40, the Secretary of the Treasury is authorized to sell, exchange, or otherwise dispose of any bonds, notes, or other securities, acquired by him on behalf of the United States under judicial process or otherwise, or delivered to him by an executive department or agency of the United States for disposal, or to enter into arrangements for the extension of the maturity thereof, in such manner, in such amounts, at such prices, for cash, securities, or other property, or any combination thereof, and upon such terms and conditions as he may deem advisable and in the public interest. No such bonds, notes, or other securities of any single issuer having at the date of disposal an aggregate face or par value, or in the case of no-par stock an aggregate stated or book value, in excess of $1,000,000, which may be held by the Secretary of the Treasury at any one time, shall be sold or otherwise disposed of under the authority of this section.

(b) Nothing contained in this section shall be construed to supersede or impair any authority otherwise granted to any officer or executive department or agency of the United States to sell, exchange, or otherwise dispose of any bonds, notes, or other securities, acquired by the United States under judicial process or otherwise. (Apr. 3, 1945, ch. 51, § 5, 59 Stat. 48.)

REFERENCES IN TEXT

Section 302 of Title 40, referred to in the text, was repealed by act Oct. 31, 1951, ch. 654, § 1 (95), 65 Stat. 705, and is now covered by sections 483 and 484 of Title 40, Public Buildings, Property and Works.

→§ 742. Exemption from taxation.

Except as otherwise provided by law, all stocks, bonds, Treasury notes, and other obligations of the United States, shall be exempt from taxation by or under State or municipal or local authority. (R. S. § 3701.)

DERIVATION

Act Feb. 25, 1862, ch. 38, § 2, 12 Stat. 346; act Mar. 3, 1863, ch. 73, § 1, 12 Stat. 710; act Mar. 3, 1864, ch. 17, § 1, 13 Stat. 13; act June 30, 1864, ch. 172, § 1, 13 Stat. 218; act Jan. 28, 1865, ch. 22, § 1, 13 Stat. 425; act Mar. 3, 1865, ch. 77, § 2, 13 Stat. 469; act July 14, 1870, ch. 256, § 1, 16 Stat. 272.

CROSS REFERENCES

United States obligations and evidences of ownership issued after March 27, 1942, as subject to Federal taxation, see section 742a of this title.

This is a page from the United States Code 1952 edition. Ordinarily one would use the latest edition of the U.S.C., or one of the two annotated editions which are kept current by pocket supplements.

This edition is shown to illustrate how this section of the Code appeared before it was amended.

Note the reference to the Revised Statutes. All sections of the Revised Statutes not repealed are still in force.

After each code section, citation is given either to the Revised Statutes or the Statutes at Large where the section first appeared as passed by Congress.

[Illustration 36]

PAGE FROM VOLUME 73 OF THE STATUTES AT LARGE

622   **PUBLIC LAW 86-346—SEPT. 22, 1959**   [73 STAT.

bond shall be includible in gross income in the taxable year in which the obligation is finally redeemed or in the taxable year of final maturity, whichever is earlier."

Paying agents.
Relief from liability.
57 Stat. 63.

SEC. 103. Subsection (i) of section 22 of the Second Liberty Bond Act, as amended (31 U.S.C., sec. 757c(i)), is amended by inserting after the third sentence thereof the following: "Relief from liability shall be granted in all cases where the Secretary of the Treasury shall determine, under regulations prescribed by him, that written notice of liability or potential liability has not been given by the United States, within ten years from the date of the erroneous payment, to any of the foregoing agents or agencies whose liability is to be determined: *Provided*, That no relief shall be granted in any case in which a qualified paying agent has assumed unconditional liability to the United States."

SEC. 104. The following provisions of law are amended by striking out the words "on original issue at par" and inserting in lieu thereof the words "on original issue at the issue price":

53 Stat. 1226.

(1) Section 6(g)(5) of the Act of March 24, 1934, as amended (22 U.S.C., sec. 1393 (g)(5)), relating to the trust account for

R.S. 3701 (31 U.S.C. 742) was amended in 1959. Frequently, as in this instance, a public law amends many different sections of the U.S. Code.

(4) Section 15(b) of the Railroad Retirement Act of 1937 (45 U.S.C., sec. 228o(b)), relating to the Railroad Retirement Account.

70 Stat. 397.
23 USC 120 note.
Tax exemption.

(5) Section 209(e)(2) of the Highway Revenue Act of 1956 (23 U.S.C., sec. 173(e)(2)), relating to the Highway Trust Fund.

SEC. 105. (a) Section 3701 of the Revised Statutes (31 U.S.C., sec. 742) is amended by adding at the end thereof the following: "This exemption extends to every form of taxation that would require that either the obligations or the interest thereon, or both, be considered, directly or indirectly, in the computation of the tax, except nondiscriminatory franchise or other nonproperty taxes in lieu thereof imposed on corporations and except estate taxes or inheritance taxes."

Repeals.

(b) The following provisions of the Second Liberty Bond Act, as amended, relating to the tax-exempt status of obligations of the United States, are repealed, without changing the status of any outstanding obligation:

46 Stat. 19, 775.

(1) Subsections (b) and (d) of section 5 (31 U.S.C., sec. 754 (b) and (d));

40 Stat. 291, 1309.

(2) The second and third sentences of section 7 (31 U.S.C., sec. 747);

(3) Subsection (b) of section 18 (31 U.S.C., sec. 753(b));

55 Stat. 7.

(4) The first sentence of subsection (d) of section 22 (31 U.S.C., sec. 757c(d)).

TITLE II—INCOME TAX TREATMENT OF CERTAIN EXCHANGES OF UNITED STATES OBLIGATIONS

68A Stat. 302.
26 USC 1031-1036.

SEC. 201. (a) Part III of subchapter O of chapter 1 of the Internal Revenue Code of 1954 (relating to common nontaxable exchanges) is amended by adding at the end thereof the following new section:

[Illustration 37]

PAGE FROM U.S. CODE, 1970 EDITION

any bonds, notes, or other securities, acquired by him on behalf of the United States under judicial process or otherwise, or delivered to him by an executive department or agency of the United States for disposal, or to enter into arrangements for the extension of the maturity thereof, in such manner, in such amounts, at such prices, for cash, securities, or other property, or any combination thereof, and upon such terms and conditions as he may deem advisable and in the public interest. No such bonds, notes, or other securities of any single issuer having at the date of disposal an aggregate face or par value, or in the case of no-par stock an aggregate stated or book value, in excess of $1,000,000, which may be held by the Secretary of the Treasury at any one time, shall be sold or otherwise disposed of under the authority of this section.

(b) Nothing contained in this section shall be construed to supersede or impair any authority otherwise granted to any officer or executive department or agency of the United States to sell, exchange, or otherwise dispose of any bonds, notes, or other securities, acquired by the United States under judicial process or otherwise. (Apr. 3, 1945, ch. 51, § 5, 59 Stat. 48.)

REFERENCES IN TEXT

Section 302 of Title 40, referred to in the text, was repealed by act Oct. 31, 1951, ch. 654, § 1 (95), 65 Stat. 705, and is now covered by sections 483 and 484 of Title 40, Public Buildings, Property and Works.

§ 742. Exemption from taxation.

Except as otherwise provided by law, all stocks, bonds, Treasury notes, and other obligations of the United States, shall be exempt from taxation by or under State or municipal or local authority. This exemption extends to every form of taxation that would require that either the obligations or the interest thereon, or both, be considered, directly or indirectly, in the computation of the tax, except nondiscriminatory franchise or other nonproperty taxes in lieu thereof imposed on corporations and except estate taxes or inheritance taxes. (R.S. § 3701; Sept. 22, 1959, Pub. L. 86-346, title I, § 105 (a), 73 Stat. 622.)

DERIVATION

Acts Feb. 25, 1862, ch. 33, § 2, 12 Stat. 346; Mar. 3, 1863, ch. 73, § 1, 12 Stat. 710; Mar. 3, 1864, ch. 17, § 1, 13 Stat. 13; June 30, 1864, ch. 172, § 1, 13 Stat. 218; Jan. 28, 1865, ch. 22, § 1, 13 Stat. 425; Mar. 3, 1865, ch. 77, § 2, 13 Stat. 469; July 14, 1870, ch. 256, § 1, 16 Stat. 272.

AMENDMENTS

1959—Pub. L. 86-346 added second sentence.

CROSS REFERENCES

United States obligations and evidences of ownership issued after March 27, 1942, as subject to Federal taxation, see section 742a of this title.

§ 742a. Same; by Federal tax Acts.

(a) Interest upon obligations, and dividends, earnings, or other income from shares, certificates, stock, or other evidences of ownership, and gain from the sale or other disposition of such obligations and evidences of ownership issued on or after March 28, 1942, by the United States or any agency or instrumentality thereof shall not have any exemption, as such, and loss from the sale or other disposition of such obligations or evidences of ownership shall not have any special treatment, as such, except as pro-

vided under the Internal Revenue Code of 1954; except that any such obligations which the United States Maritime Commission or the Federal Housing Administration had, prior to March 1, 1941, contracted to issue at a future date, shall when issued bear such tax-exemption privileges as were, at the time of such contract, provided in the law authorizing their issuance. For the purposes of this subsection a Territory, a possession of the United States, and the District of Columbia, and any political subdivision thereof, and any agency or instrumentality of any one or more of the foregoing, shall not be considered as an agency or instrumentality of the United States.

(b) The provisions of this section shall, with respect to such obligations and evidences of ownership, be considered as amendatory of and supplementary to the respective Acts or parts of Acts authorizing the issuance of such obligations and evidences of ownership, as amended and supplemented.

(c) Nothing contained herein shall be construed to amend or repeal sections 114 and 115 of the

> Here is 31 U.S.C. 742 as amended.
> Note how citation is given to original R.S. citation and amending public law.

(1), respectively, of Title 26, Internal Revenue Code of 1939, and were repealed by section 7851 of Title 26, Internal Revenue Code of 1954.

Sections 42 and 117 were repealed by section 7851 of Title 26, I. R. C. 1954. Section 42 is now covered by sections 451 and 454 of Title 26, I. R. C. 1954. Section 117 is now covered by sections 1221 and 1222 of Title 26, I. R. C. 1954. For provision deeming a reference in other laws to a provision of I. R. C. 1939, also as a reference to corresponding provision of I. R. C. 1954, see section 7852 (b) of Title 26.

AMENDMENTS

1959—Subsec. (a). Pub. L. 86-346 substituted "except as provided under the Internal Revenue Code of 1954" for "under the Internal Revenue Code, or laws amendatory or supplementary thereto."

1947—Subsec. (a). Act June 25, 1947, substituted "the

> Effect of amendment stated.

EFFECTIVE DATE OF 1959 AMENDMENT

Amendment of section by Pub. L. 86-346 effective for taxable years ending after Sept. 22, 1959, see section 203 of Pub. L. 86-346, set out as a note under section 1037 of Title 26, Internal Revenue Code.

ABOLISHMENT OF COMMISSION AND TRANSFER OF FUNCTIONS

The United States Maritime Commission was abolished by 1950 Reorg. Plan No. 21, eff. May 24, 1950, 15 F. R. 3178, 64 Stat. 1273, set out in the Appendix to Title 5, Government Organization and Employees, which transferred part of its functions and part of the functions of its Chairman to the Federal Maritime Board and the Chairman thereof, the Board having been created by that Plan as an agency within the Department of Commerce with an independent status in some respects, and transferred the remainder of the Commission's functions and the functions of its Chairman to the Secretary of Commerce, with power vested in the Secretary to authorize their performance by the Mari-

[Illustration 38]

PAGE FROM TITLE 31, U.S.C.A. POCKET SUPPLEMENT

MONEY AND FINANCE   **31 § 742**

Conditions for relief

(c) No relief shall be granted on account of interest coupons claimed to have been attached to a security unless the Secretary is satisfied that such coupons have not been paid and are in fact destroyed or will not become the basis of a valid claim against the United States.

Definition of "security"

(d) The term "security" means any direct obligation of the United States issued pursuant to law for valuable consideration, including bonds, notes, certificates of indebtedness, and Treasury bills, and interim certificates issued for any such security.
As amended May 27, 1971, Pub.L. 92–19, 85 Stat. 74.

1971 Amendment. Subsec. (a). Pub.L. 92–19, in revising the provisions, substituted former subsec. (d) provisions em-   or official, State or local government, Federal Government corporation, foreign government, or Federal Reserve bank.

This is the text of 31 U.S.C. 742 in an annotated code. Note how the text and notes are the same as in the U.S.C.

The difference is the case annotations that are added. They start immediately after the notes.

See next Illustration.

---

sec. (c) of this section.
Subsec. (b). Pub.L. 92–19, in revising the provisions, made it clear that indemnity bond is required whether relief is provided before, at, or after maturity, and deleted provision excepting certain classes of cases from the requirement of an indemnity bond where not essential in public interest, namely, where loss, theft, destruction, etc. occurred without fault of owner; where substantially entire security is surrendered and any missing portion is insufficient to form basis of a valid claim against the United States; where the security is transferable only by operation of law; and where owner of the security is the Federal Government

security and also meaning any bond issued under section 780 of Title 26, I.R.C. 1939, provision now covered in subsec. (d) of this section.
Subsec. (d). Pub.L. 92–19 substituted definition of "security", formerly included in former subsec. (c) defining "interest-bearing security of the United States" or "security" for former provision empowering Secretary of Treasury to make rules and regulations for administration of section, now incorporated in subsec. (a) of this section.
Legislative History. For legislative history and purpose of Pub.L. 92–19, see 1971 U.S.Code Cong. and Adm.News, p. — .

—→ **§ 742. Exemption from taxation** ←—

Except as otherwise provided by law, all stocks, bonds, Treasury notes, and other obligations of the United States, shall be exempt from taxation by or under State or municipal or local authority. This exemption extends to every form of taxation that would require that either the obligations or the interest thereon, or both, be considered, directly or indirectly, in the computation of the tax, except nondiscriminatory franchise or other nonproperty taxes in lieu thereof imposed on corporations and except estate taxes or inheritance taxes. As amended Sept. 22, 1959, Pub.L. 86–346, Title I, § 105(a), 73 Stat. 622.

1959 Amendment. Pub.L. 86–346 amended section to add second sentence.
Legislative History: For legislative history and purpose of Pub.L. 86–346, see 1959 U.S.Code Cong. and Adm.News, p. 2769.

Library references
Municipal Corporations ⊂⊃956(1).
Taxation ⊂⊃7.
C.J.S. Municipal Corporations § 1978 et seq.
C.J.S. Taxation § 209.

4a. Generally
Obligations of federal government cannot be taxed, either directly or indirectly, by state, municipal or local authorities. Peter Kiewit Sons' Co. v. Douglas County, 1955, 72 N.W.2d 415, 161 Neb. 93.

Supplementary Index to Notes

Generally **4a**
Mortgages **18**

[Illustration 38–a]

PAGE FROM TITLE 31, U.S.C.A.

---

31 § 742   MONEY AND FINANCE

5. "Other obligation"

Principle that obligations of federal government are immune from state taxation embraces indirect taxation of such obligations through their inclusion in tax imposed on all property of a taxpayer, and it is quite immaterial that state tax does not discriminate against the federal obligations. Society for Savings in City of Cleveland, Ohio, v. Bowers, Ohio 1955, 75 S.Ct. 607, 349 U.S. 143, 99 L.Ed. 959.

Mortgages, executed by mortgagors who were lessees of federal land to be used for construction of military housing projects, though guaranteed by United States, did not constitute direct obligations of United States within provisions of this section exempting from state or local taxation, except as otherwise provided by law, all stocks, bonds, treasury notes, and other obligations of United States. Application of S. S. Silberblatt, Inc., 1958, 180 N.Y.S.2d 210, 6 A.D.2d 603.

6. Stocks and securities

Federal securities owned by corporation for profit were properly included in franchise taxes in determining franchise taxes notwithstanding this section exempting federal securities from taxation. Raymond Bag Co. v. Bowers, 1955, 126 N.E.2d 321, 163 Ohio St. 275, appeal dismissed 76 S.Ct. 648, 350 U.S. 1003, 100 L.Ed. 866, rehearing denied 76 S.Ct. 777, 351 U.S. 928, 100 L.Ed. 1457.

10. Franchise tax

New Jersey statute imposing on each domestic corporation an annual franchise tax measured by corporation's net worth, which is defined as sum of corporation's issued and outstanding capital stock, paid in or capital surplus, earned surplus and undivided profits, other surplus accounts, which will accrue to shareholders, not including depreciation reserves, and debts owed to shareholders owning 10 per cent or more of corporation's stock, is valid despite the inclusion of tax-exempt federal bonds in the determination of net worth. Werner Mach. Co. v. Director of Division of Taxation, Dept of Treasury, State of N. J., N.J.1956, 76 S.Ct. 534, 350 U.S. 492, 100 L.Ed. 634.

12. National bank notes

As exception to general rule of immunity of federal government obligations from property taxation by states, tax may be levied upon shareholders of state or national banks though tax is measured by corporate assets which include federal obligations and though payment of tax by corporation as collecting agent is required. Society for Savings in City of Cleveland, Ohio v. Bowers, Ohio 1955, 75 S.Ct. 607, 349 U.S. 143, 99 L.Ed. 950.

18. Mortgages

Arrangement, whereby successful bidder on military housing project became sole stockholder of corporations which obtained leases of federal land and gave mortgages under National Housing Act, section 1748–1748h of Title 12 in order to procure necessary private financing for construction of project with payment of mortgages guaranteed by United States, was designed to relieve government of obligation to provide housing for its military personnel and at same time avoid increasing the national debt, government did not pledge its credit in the usual sense and mortgages were not exempt from mortgage recording tax under this section exempting stocks, bonds, treasury notes and all other obligations of the United States from local taxation. S. S. Silberblatt, Inc. v. Tax Commission of State of N. Y., 1959, 159 N.E.2d 195, 5 N.Y.2d 635, 186 N.Y.S.2d 646, certiorari denied 80 S.Ct. 253, 361 U.S. 912, 4 L. Ed.2d 183.

Where contractor, who was successful bidder on military housing project, was sole stockholder of corporations which obtained leases of federal land and gave mortgages under National Housing Act, section 1748–1748h of Title 12 in order to procure necessary private financing for construction of project with mortgage payments guaranteed by United States, it would not be assumed, in absence of statute, that the government function was involved, so as to exempt mortgages from New York mortgage recording tax. Id.

Where contractor, who was successful bidder on military housing project, was sole stockholder of corporations which obtained leases of federal land and gave mortgages under National Housing Act section 1748–1748h of Title 12 in order to procure necessary private financing for construction of project with mortgage payments guaranteed by United States, contractor and corporate mortgagors were not exempt from state and local taxation or state mortgage recording tax as instrumentalities of federal government or its agencies, notwithstanding fact that all of capital stock of each corporation would ultimately be owned by federal government. Id.

> Every time a court cites or interprets a code section, a digest of the case appears in the annotations.

---

cept as provided under the Internal Revenue Code of 1954; except that any such obligations which the United States Maritime Commission or the Federal Housing Administration had, prior to March 1, 1941, contracted to issue at a future date, shall when issued bear such tax-exemption privileges as were, at the time of such contract, provided in the law authorizing their issuance. For the purposes of this subsection a Territory, a possession of the United States, and the District of Columbia, and any political subdivision thereof, and any agency or instrumentality of any one or more of the foregoing, shall not be considered as an agency or

150

[Illustration 39]

A SAMPLE PAGE FROM UNITED STATES CODE SERVICE— LAWYERS EDITION

15 USCS § 70   COMMERCE AND TRADE

CODE OF FEDERAL REGULATIONS

16 CFR Parts 1, 14, 15, 303.
19 CFR Part 11 (especially § 11.12b).

CROSS REFERENCE

Federal Trade Commission, 15 USCS § 41 et seq.
Territories and possessions of United States, 48 USCS §§ 1 et seq.
This section is referred to in 15 USCS §§ 70a–70e, 70g–70k.

RESEARCH GUIDE

Am Jur:

55 Am Jur 2d, Monopolies, Restraints of Trade, and Unfair Trade
Practices §§ 879, 880.

Am Jur Proof of Facts:

Textile Identification and Clothing Hazards, 13 Am Jur Proof of Facts
649.

INTERPRETIVE NOTES AND DECISIONS

1. Purpose
2. Relation to other statutes

1. Purpose

Textile Fiber Products Identification Act is intended to protect producers and consumers against misbranding and false advertising of fiber content of textile fiber products. Bigelow-Sanford Carpet Co. v Federal Trade Com. (1961) 111 App DC 89, 294 F2d 718.

Textile Fiber Products Identification Act is disclosure bill, for protection of consumer. Cour-

taulds (Alabama) Inc. v Kintner (1960, DC Dist Col) 182 F Supp 207.

2. Relation to other statutes

Textile Fiber Products Identification Act (15 USCS §§ 70-70k) was enacted in tradition of Wool Labeling Act of 1939 and Fur Products Labeling Act of 1951. Courtaulds (Alabama) Inc. v Kintner (1960, DC Dist Col) 182 F Supp 207.

§ 70a.   Misbranding and false advertising declared unlawful

(a) The introduction, delivery for introduction, manufacture for introduction, sale, advertising, or offering for sale, in commerce, or the transportation or causing to be transported in commerce, or the importation into the United States, of any textile fiber product which is misbranded or falsely or deceptively advertised within the meaning of this Act [15 USCS §§ 70 et seq.] or the rules and regulations promulgated thereunder, is unlawful, and shall be an unfair method of competition and an unfair and deceptive act

> Those volumes of the U.S.C.S. with Blue Labels have been recompiled by the publishers with new notes and Annotations. Note how references are given after each section of the Code of Federal Regulations. The Research Guide, when appropriate, also cites to A.L.R. Annotations and relevant law review articles. Annotations then follow.

412

[Illustration 40]
PAGE FROM THE POPULAR NAME TABLE U.S.C.A.

POPULAR NAME TABLE　　　　　　　　　　　**616**

Legislative Reorganization Act of 1970
　　Pub.L. 91–510, Oct. 26, 1970, 84 Stat. 1140 (**Title 2, §§ 28, 29, 60–I,
　　　　61–I, 72a, 88b–I, 166, 190a–190d, 190f, 190h–190k, 198, 281–
　　　　281b, 282–282e, 331–336, 411–417, 2107, 8332; Title 5, §§ 2107,
　　　　5533, 8332; Title 8. § 1106 note; Title 31, §§ 11, 1151–1157,
　　　　1171–1176; Title 40, §§ 166 note, 166b–Ia–166b–If, 184a,
　　　　193m–I, 851**)
　　Pub.L. 91–522, § 1(1), (3)–(5), Dec. 16, 1970, 84 Stat. 1440

Leprosy Act
　　Mar. 3, 1905, ch. 1443, 33 Stat. 1009

Lesinski Pension Increase Act
　　June 6, 1940, ch. 246, 54 Stat. 237

Lever Act (Food Control)
　　Aug. 10, 1917, ch. 53, 40 Stat. 276
　　Oct. 22, 1919, ch. 80, 41 Stat. 297

Liberty Loan Acts
　　(First)
　　Apr. 24, 1917, ch. 4, 40 Stat. 35 (**Title 31, §§ 745, 746, 755, 755a,
　　　　759, 764, 768, 774, 804**)
　　(Second)
　　Sept. 24, 1917, ch. 56, 40 Stat. 288 (**Title 31, §§ 745, 747, 752–754b,
　　　　757, 757b–757e, 758, 760, 764–766, 769, 771, 773, 774, 801**)
　　(Third)
　　Apr. 4, 1918, ch. 44, 40 Stat. 502 (**Title 31, §§ 752, 752a, 754, 765,
　　　　766, 771, 774**)
　　(Fourth)
　　July 9, 1918, ch. 142, 40 Stat. 844 (**Title 31, §§ 750, 752, 772, 774**)
　　(Supplement to Second)
　　Sept. 24, 1918, ch. 176, 40 Stat. 965 (**Title 12, §§ 84, 95a; Title 31,
　　　　§§ 757, 774; Title 50 App., § 5**)
　　(Victory)
　　Mar. 3, 1919, ch. 100, 40 Stat. 1309 (**Title 31, §§ 750, 753, 754, 763,
　　　　767, 774, 802, 803**)
　　Mar. 2, 1923, ch. 179, 42 Stat. 1427 (**Title 31, § 767**)

Library of Congress Police Act
　　Aug. 4, 1950, ch. 561, §§ 1 to 11, 64 Stat. 411 (**Title 2, §§ 167 to
　　　　167j**)
　　June 17, 1970, Pub.L. 91–281, 84 Stat. 309 (**Title 2, § 167j**)

Library of Congress Trust Fund Board Act
　　Mar. 3, 1925, ch. 423, 43 Stat. 1107 (**Title 2, §§ 154–163**)

Library Services Act

```
                                                              3)
          This Table of Popular Name Table is from           2,
      the U.S.C.A.
          There is a similar Table in the  U.S.C.            3,

Li
```

　　Pub.L. 89-511, §§ 2–10, 12(a), (b), July 19, 1966, 80 Stat. 313 (**Title
　　　　20, §§ 351–353, 355–355b, 355e to 355e–3, 355f to 355f–7,
　　　　356–358**)
　　Pub.L. 90–154, § 1, Nov. 24, 1967, 81 Stat. 509 (**Title 20, §§ 355e–2,
　　　　355f–2, 355f–3, 355f–6, 355f–7, 358**)
　　Pub.L. 91–600, § 2(b), Dec. 30, 1970, 84 Stat. 1660–1669 (**Title
　　　　20, §§ 351–354, 355a–355c, 355e to 355e–2**)

Library Services and Construction Act Amendments of 1966
　　Pub.L. 89–511, July 19, 1966, 80 Stat. 313 (**Title 20, §§ 351–353,
　　　　355–355b, 355e to 355e–3, 355f to 355f–7, 356–358**)

Library Services and Construction Amendments of 1970
　　Pub.L. 91–600, Dec. 30, 1970, 84 Stat. 1660 (**Title 20, §§ 351–354,
　　　　355a–355c, 355e to 355e–2, 1204, 1211**)

[Illustration 41]

PAGE FROM SHEPARD'S FEDERAL AND STATE ACTS CITED BY POPULAR NAME

FEDERAL AND STATE ACTS CITED BY POPULAR NAMES   Bon

Bond Act of 1915 (Improvement Bonds)
Cal. Streets and Highways Code §8500
et seq.

Bond Act of 1918
N. J. Rev. Stat. 1937, 2:60-207 to 2:60 211

Bond Act of 1935 (Revenue)
N. C. Public Laws 1935, Ch. 473

Bond Act of 1938 (Revenue)
N. C. Gen. Stat. 1943, §160-413 et seq.

Bond Act of 1946 (Veterans)

> All laws are listed in this volume by popular name.

Bond Act of 1951 (Veterans)
Cal. Military and Veterans Code §996
et seq.

Bond Act of 1962 (State Construction Program)
Cal. Statutes 1962, 1st Ex. Sess., Ch. 23,
p. 193

Bond Act of 1962 (State School Building Aid)
Cal. Education Code 1959, §19891 et seq.

Bond Act of 1962 (Veterans)
Cal. Military and Veterans Code §996.87
et seq.

Bond and Coupon Collection Law
Cal. Government Code §16311

Bond and Coupon Registration Law
Cal. Statutes 1935, p. 994

Bond and License Act (Citrus Fruits)
Fla. Stat. 1965, 601.55 et seq.

Bond and Lien Collateral Act of 1949
Az. Rev. Stat. 1956, §30-191 et seq.

Bond and Mortgage Act
N. J. Rev. Stat. 1937, 2A:50-1 et seq.

Bond and Warrant Acts
N. J. Rev. Stat. 1937, 2:27-266 to 2:27-277, 22:
1-13
Tex. Rev. Civ. Stat. 1948, Art. 2368a

Bond Assumption Acts (Highways)
Tex. Rev. Civ. Stat. 1948, Arts. 6674q-1 to
6674q-11a

Bond Certification Law
Cal. Water Code §20000 et seq.

Bond Compromise Law (Municipal)
Cal. Statutes 1903, p. 164

Bond Curative Act (Municipalities)
Wis. Stat. 1065, 67.02

Bond for Deed Act
La. Rev. Stat. 1950, 9:2041 et seq.

Bond Guarantors Protection Law
Cal. Government Code §5100 et seq.

Bond Investment Act
Ohio Rev. Code 1953, 3949.01 et seq.

Bond Issue Acts (Roads)
Ill. Rev. Stat. 1965, Ch. 121, §6-510 et seq.

Bond Limitation Act
U. S. Code 1964 Title 31, §757b
May 26, 1938, c. 285, 52 Stat. 447
Kan. Stat. Anno. 10-301 et seq.

Bond Plan Enabling Act (Industrial Locations)
Ala. Code 1958, Title 37, §511(20)

Bond Purchase Act
U. S. Code 1964 Title 31, §741
Mar. 3, 1881, c. 133, §2, 21 Stat. 435

Bond Refinancing Act (Revenue)
W. Va. Code 1931, Ch. 13, Art. 2A, §1 et seq.

Bond Refinancing Act of 1937
Ark. Stat. 1947, 19-4301 et seq.

Bond Refunding Act
Ark. Pope's Digest 1937, §§11237-11367

Bond Refunding Act (Municipal)
Mich. Comp. Laws 1948, 136.1 et seq.

**Bond Refunding and Special Assessment Law
of 1939**
Cal. Government Code §59100 et seq.

Bond Registration Act
Mo. Rev. Stat. 1959, 108.240 et seq.

Bond Registration Act (Municipal)
Kan. Stat. Anno. 10-601 et seq.
N. C. Gen. Stat. 1943, §160-406 et seq.

Bond Retirement Fund Act
Okla. Stat. 1961, Title 62, §217.1 et seq.

Bond Sinking Fund Law of 1943
Cal. Statutes 1943, Ch. 611, p. 2225

Bond Surrender Act
Okla. Stat. 1961, Title 62, §341 et seq.

Bond Trust Fund Act
Nev. Rev. Stat. 1957, 282.230 et seq.

Bond Validating Acts
Fla. Stat. 1965, 75.01 et seq.
Ida. Laws 1935, First Extra Session, Ch. 3
Ida. Laws 1937, Ch. 232

Continued

SECTION E. INDEXES TO FEDERAL STATUTES

At times it is necessary to locate federal statutes that are no longer in force. The indexes listed here cover *all* public, permanent laws, including those that were inoperative as of dates of publication.

1. *Index Analysis of Federal Statutes*, 1789–1873 (Beaman and McNamara, 1911).

This index to the *Revised Statutes* and the *Statutes at Large*, for the period 1789 to 1873, was published in 1911. Although covering an earlier period, it supplemented Scott & Beaman's Index Analysis of the Federal Statutes, 1873–1907 (since superseded). The Beaman and McNamara edition indexes the federal public, permanent laws from 1789 to 1873 and includes laws enacted which were inoperative when the *Revised Statutes* became law.

2. *Index to the Federal Statutes, 1874–1931*, compiled by McClenon and Gilbert (1933).

This is a revision of the early *Scott & Beaman, Index Analysis of the Federal Statutes*, 1873–1907. The *Index* includes references to public, permanent laws, which were operative and inoperative, appearing in the *Revised Statutes, Statutes at Large* and the *United States Code* for 1874–1931. It contains a list of statutory definitions and a list of treaties and conventions.

Obsolete provisions (expressly repealed or otherwise superseded) are cited in italics. Where all the provisions cited for an entry appear to be obsolete, an asterisk "*" has been placed at the beginning of the entry.

Where a provision appears to be amended, or superseded in part, by subsequent legislation, this is identified by a note "a" following the citation. Provisions which have become obsolete through the lapse of time, in the absence of specific superseding legislation, are assigned the designation "b".

The *Index* also includes a Table of Repeals and Amendments of Statutory Provisions Indexed. The Table lists the provisions by their Revised Statutes section numbers or Statutes at Large citations with references and explanations to the amending or superseding Statutes at Large provisions.

If the problem involves a federal act which is in effect, refer to one of the annotated editions of the text of the law, which includes its history and digests of cases interpreting it. When only the text of the law and all amendments are needed, consult the *United States Code*. For the text of acts prior to amendments, or the text of amendments, consult the *Statutes at Large*.

SECTION F.   ADDITIONAL SOURCES OF INTERPRETATION OF FEDERAL STATUTES

1.   Current Statutes

a.   Digests.   In addition to the annotations available in the annotated editions of the *United States Code,* decisions interpreting federal statutes may be located by the use of the various digests of the U. S. Supreme Court, the *Federal Digest,* the *Modern Federal Practice Digest,* or the *Federal Practice Digest 2d.*

b.   The *Table of Statutes* cited in each volume of *Am.Jur.2d* [15] indicates where provisions of the *United States Code* are cited within the volume.

c.   Annotations in the *Lawyers Edition, U. S. Supreme Court Reports, A.L.R.* and *A.L.R.Fed.* frequently are decisions involving federal statutes.

d.   Treatises [16] and encyclopedias [17] provide expository discussions on federal statutory law.

e.   Periodical articles [18] treat federal statutory law analytically and with some detail.

f.   Legislative histories of federal acts.[19]

2.   Early Federal Statutes

The following selected compilations of earlier federal laws, since superseded, have been published.   They are useful historical sources.

a.   *Laws of the United States, 1789–1815.*   Fowell edition.   12 vols.   Chronological compilation.

b.   *Laws of the United States, 1785–1839.*   Bioren and Duane edition.   10 vols.   Chronological compilation.

c.   *Public and General Statutes,* 1789–1827 (1st ed.);   1789–1836 (2d ed.);   1789–1847 (3d ed.).   Story and Sharswood editions.   Chronological compilations.

d.   *United States Compiled Statutes* (West Pub. Co.) (1st ed.) 1789–1901, 3 vols., Unannotated;   (2d ed.) 1916 and two cumulative supplements, 1919 and 1923, 12 vols., + 4 vols., Annotated.   This publication is arranged like the *Revised Statutes.*

[15] Chapter 16,

[16] Chapter 18, Sec. A.

[17] Chapter 16.

[18] Chapter 17.

[19] Chapter 10.

e.   *Federal Statutes Annotated* (Edw. Thompson Co.).   (1st ed.) 1906, 10 vols., (2d ed.) 1916, 12 vols., with annual supplements. The arrangement is encyclopedic by topics.

f.   *Barnes' Federal Code* (Bobbs-Merrill Co.).   Published in 1919 with a 1925 cumulative supplement.   Its arrangement is similar to the *Revised Statutes*.

g.   *Mason's United States Code Annotated.*   Published in 1926. 3 vols. with supplements.   It is arranged like the *United States Code.*

SECTION G.   TABLES OF FEDERAL STATUTES

Tables, providing cross references and other information, are published with the current federal codes to facilitate their use.   These tables are in the *United States Code* (*Tables* volume and *Supplement* volumes), the *United States Code Annotated* (*Tables* volume) and the *United States Code Service, Lawyers Edition* (*Tables* volume). The tables provide such information as references from the *Revised Statutes* or *Statutes at Large* citations to the corresponding sections of specific titles for the *U. S. Code*, parallel tables from former Title 18 U.S.C. (Criminal Code) to the new section numbers, parallel tables from former Title 28 U.S.C. (Judicial Code) to the new section numbers, and tables of statutes repealed or eliminated.   See Illustration 33.

U.S.C.A. and U.S.C.S. also show the disposition of all sections of former titles by tables in the titles volumes.

The *Tables* volume of the *United States Code* contains the following tables:

1.   Table I—Revised Titles; these tables show where former sections of titles of the *United States Code*, which have been revised, are incorporated in U.S.C.

2.   Table II—*Revised Statutes 1878*; this table shows where sections of the *Revised Statutes of 1878* are found in U.S.C.

3.   Table III—*Statutes at Large*; this table shows where the Acts of Congress are found in U.S.C.

4.   Table IV—Executive Orders; this table lists the Executive Orders "that implement general and permanent law as contained in U.S.C."

5.   Table V—Proclamations; this table lists the Proclamations that are cited in U.S.C.

6.   *Table VI—Reorganization Plans*; this table lists the *Reorganization Plans* that are provided in U.S.C.

The tables in U.S.C.A. and U.S.C.S. cover relatively the same materials as listed above for U.S.C.

SECTION H. FEDERAL LEGISLATION: RESEARCH PROCEDURE

1. Federal Law in Force

To trace the origin of an act and its amendments, consult the parenthetical references following the code section in the *United States Code Annotated* and the *United States Code Service, Lawyers Edition.* Reference also should be made to the historical notes which follow the parenthetical references.

If the *Statutes at Large* citation is given, an act can be located in a code by using the *Tables* volume. Check the parallel tables from the *Statutes at Large* citation to the code title and sections.

The titles and section numbers of the *United States Code*, the *United States Code Annotated* and the *United States Code Service, Lawyers Edition* are the same; therefore, if a searcher has the citation to an act in one set, he can locate it equally well in the others by the use of the same reference.

To determine whether the act has recently been amended or repealed, check the pocket and pamphlet supplements to the *United States Code Annotated* or the *United States Code Service, Lawyers Edition.* *Shepard's United States Citations* also provides a history of the act with citations to the latest changes.

For additional cases interpreting the act, consult *Shepard's United States Citations.*

The *Statutes at Large* tables in U.S.C.A. and U.S.C.S. also give the history of all acts passed (operative and inoperative) since the *Revised Statutes* (1875).

To determine the existence of federal legislation on a given point, the following procedure may be used:

(1) *The Index Method.* Analyze the facts and the law. Check the general index or the title or volume indexes to a current federal code, using a fact or topical analysis. Consult the general index pocket part for the latest information, for it supplements the general index and the title or volume index.

(2) *The Topic or Analytic Method.* Federal law is divided into fifty titles which are alphabetically arranged into codes. Select the appropriate topic. Then consult the analysis of the topic to locate the specific section number. The *Table of Titles* is useful in locating the proper topic if one is unfamiliar with the title designations. For an analysis of the cases interpreting the section, refer to the subdivision

index (U.S.C.A.) or "analysis" (U.S.C.S.) which follows the text of the law and precedes the notes to decisions. The figures following the headings in the subdivision index refer to case and note numbers.

(3) *The Definition Method.* If the definition of a word is in point, consult the general index to the code under the heading, "Definitions." The defined words are listed alphabetically. Reference is given to the title and section of the code which defines the word as used in the statute. Words are also defined under the subjects in the indexes.

2. Inoperative Federal Law

To locate an act no longer in force, passed between 1874 and 1931, consult the *Index to Federal Statutes.* For acts in force prior to 1873, and inoperative when the *Revised Statutes* was enacted, refer to the *Index Analysis of the Federal Statutes* (Beaman and McNamara, ed. 1789–1873).

The *Revised Statutes*, an earlier edition to the *United States Code* or *a superseded code* (see Section F2 above) may provide the text to a law which is no longer in effect. Each has an index.

The statutes tables in U.S.C.A. and U.S.C.S. give the history of all acts passed since the *Revised Statutes* (1875). For annotations to statutes that never appeared in the *Revised Statutes* or the *United States Code*, consult the uncodified volume of U.S.C.S. This volume also has a separate section of annotations to all laws on American Indians.

3. Private, Temporary and Local Laws

The preceding sections relate to the search for permanent, public, general laws. Less frequently, the lawyer is confronted with the problem of locating a private, temporary or local law which is not included in the codes or indexes previously discussed. The latter federal laws are published in the *Statutes at Large.* If the date is known, the law can be located easily in the *Statutes at Large.* However, if the date of enactment is not known, the act cannot be readily found. The *Consolidated Index to the Statutes at Large*, covering the period 1789 to 1903, should be consulted for acts passed during those dates. After that period, each volume of the *Statutes at Large* must individually be checked. Public temporary and local laws are published in the *United States Code Congressional and Administrative News.*

For annotations to private, special and temporary acts, refer to U.S.C.S., *Uncodified Laws* volume.

4. Use of Tables

Tables in the *United States Code* (*Tables* volume and supplement volumes) the *United States Code Annotated* (*Tables* volume) and the *United States Code Service* (*Tables* volumes) provide useful parallel information. They can be consulted for the following significant, as well as other, purposes:

To refer from the *Revised Statutes* or *Statutes at Large* citations to the corresponding sections in the code.

To cross-reference from former Title 18 U.S.C. (Criminal Code) to the new section numbers.

To cross-reference from former Title 28 U.S.C. (Judicial Code) to the new section numbers.

To locate sections of the Bankruptcy Act of 1898, as amended in the code.

To refer from provisions of Title 26 of the *United States Code*, 1925 and 1934 editions, to Title 26, Internal Revenue Code.

To locate sections of the Interstate Commerce Act of 1887, as amended in Title 49 of the code.

To locate statutes repealed and eliminated.

5. Public Law Citations

When only the public law number is known, consult the *Statutes at Large Tables* in U.S.C.A. or U.S.C.S. to obtain the citation to an act (from 32 Statutes at Large, 1902 to date). The List of Public Laws in each volume of the *Statutes at Large* also cross-references to the *Statutes at Large* citations. The *United States Code Congressional and Administrative News* is another source of obtaining statutory citations when only the public law numbers are known (consult the Table of Public Laws table).

SECTION I. SUMMARY

1. Statutes at Large

a. Published after each session of Congress.

b. Arrangement—by chapters and chronologically by date of passage of act.

c. Grouped into public and private laws.

d. Volumes 1–8 were published some time after the acts were passed.

(1) Volumes 1–5 contain public laws and are arranged in chronological order.

(2) Volume 6 consists of private laws.

(3) Volume 7 relates to Indian treaties.

(4) Volume 8 contains foreign treaties.

   e.   For various periods Public and Private Laws were published in two parts. Part two covered Private laws and resolutions, concurrent resolutions, treaties and proclamations. Since 1959, they are published in a single volume after each session of Congress.

   f.   Since 1950, treaties are not published as a part of the *Statutes at Large.*

   g.   Marginal notes since Volume 33 give House or Senate bill number, Public Law number and date.

   h.   Each volume includes a chronological and numerical list of laws and a very complete subject index.

2.   Methods of Codification (see Section B, above)

3.   Features Common to Codes
   a.   Constitutions.

   b.   Text of statutes.

   c.   Historical notes.

   d.   Annotations.

   e.   Tables.

   f.   Indexes.

   g.   Popular names of acts.

   h.   Pocket and pamphlet supplementation.

4.   United States Revised Statutes

   a.   1875 edition—rewritten and reenacted, with inaccuracies and unauthorized changes.

   b.   1878 edition—evidence of the law to December 1, 1873.

      (1) Rewritten and classified.

      (2) Some case annotations and marginal notes.

5.   United States Code, 1976 Ed.
   a.   Current official code.

   b.   Covers public and permanent laws in force.

   c.   Arranged alphabetically under 50 titles.

   d.   Supplemented by cumulative bound volumes.

   e.   Complete index.

   f.   Many tables.

g.   *Prima facie* evidence of law; is a recompilation of the law and not a re-enactment, except for titles listed in 1 U.S.C. 201.

h.   New editions every six years.

6.   United States Code Annotated

a.   Text of public, permanent laws in force.

b.   Arranged under the 50 titles of U.S.C.

c.   Annotations are complete, covering federal and state court decisions and Attorney General opinions.

d.   Historical notes.

e.   About 135 volumes with one or more separate volumes for each code title.

f.   Kept current by cumulative pocket and pamphlet supplements and replacement volumes.

g.   Five-volume Index and title indexes in recompiled volumes.

h.   Tables.

i.   Index includes a *Table of Acts* by popular names.

j.   Federal Court Rules.

7.   United States Code Service

a.   Formerly called *Federal Code Annotated*, new publication replacing older volumes title by title.

b.   Covers public and permanent laws in force.

c.   Annotations include federal and state court decisions and Attorney General's opinions.

d.   Historical notes.

e.   Volume of Uncodified Laws.

f.   Tables volumes.

g.   General Index and each individual volume also has an index covering its subject matter.

h.   Research aid references.

i.   Federal acts by popular names.

j.   Kept up-to-date by cumulative annual pocket and pamphlet supplements and replacement volumes.

k.   Federal court rules.

l.   Advance pamphlets issued for current materials.

8.   Additional Sources of Interpretation of Federal Statutes (see Section F, above)

9. Early Federal Statutes (see Section F2, above)

10. Indexes to Federal Statutes

a. Beaman and McNamara, *Index Analysis of Federal Statutes, 1789–1873.*

    (1) Public and permanent laws.

    (2) Includes obsolete and superseded laws.

b. *Index to the Federal Statutes,* 1874–1931 (ed. McClenon and Gilbert).

    (1) Public and permanent laws.

    (2) Includes operative and inoperative laws.

11. Popular Names of Federal Acts Tables

a. *Shepard's Federal Acts and Cases by Popular Name—Federal and State.* Supplemented by the paper-covered cumulative supplement to *Shepard's United States Citations* (Statutes and Dept. Reps.).

b. *United States Code Annotated;* table in volume (5) of the General Index.

c. *United States Code Service, Tables* volumes.

d. The popular names for federal acts also are listed in the general indexes to U.S.C.A. and U.S.C.S.

e. *United States Code, General Index* volumes and *Supplement* volumes.

f. *U. S. Code Congressional and Administrative News.*

12. Functions of Tables of Federal Statutes

a. Refer from *Revised Statutes* and *Statutes at Large* to specific code; also give history of acts.

b. Parallel tables from former title to current sections.

c. Lists of Executive Orders and Proclamations that implement or cite federal laws.

13. Citation

Citation form for federal legislation may be found in Appendix A, at (I), (A), (2), (a).

Chapter 10

FEDERAL LEGISLATIVE HISTORIES

SECTION A. LEGISLATIVE HISTORIES IN LEGAL RESEARCH

A law is the means by which a legislative body expressed its intent to declare, command, or prohibit some action. A legislative history is the term used to designate the documents that contain the information considered by the legislature prior to reaching its decision to enact a law. A legislative history of a statute is consulted in order to better understand the reasons for the enactment of the statute. Since an act of the legislature is prospective and is not always drafted with the most precise language, courts constantly look to extrinsic aids in determining the intent of a legislative body.[1] This intent may be found in the language of the bill introduced into the legislature, the subsequent amendments to the bill, the reports of legislative committees to which the bill was assigned, and other legislative documents issued in consideration of the submitted bill.

There has been some difference of opinion as to the extent to which legislative histories should be used to determine the meaning of legislation.[2] But this conflict is more academic than it is practical, for the use of legislative histories is a very essential technique of contemporary litigation.

[1] "But, while the clear meaning of statutory language is not to be ignored, 'words are inexact tools at best,' *Harrison v. Northern Trust Co.*, 317 U.S. 476, 479 (1943), and hence it is essential that we place the words of a statute in their proper context by resort to the legislative history." Tidewater Oil Co. v. United States, 409 U.S. 151, 157 (1972).

[2] Note, *e. g.*, the language of Mr. Justice Jackson, "Resort to legislative history is only justified where the face of the Act is inescapably ambiguous, and then I think we should not go beyond Committee reports, which presumably are well considered and carefully prepared * * *. But to select casual statements from floor debates, not always distinguished for candor or accuracy, as a basis for making up our minds what law Congress intended to enact is to substitute ourselves for the Congress in one of its important functions * * *. Moreover, it is only the words of the bill that have presidential approval, where that approval is given. It is not to be supposed that, in signing a bill, the President endorses the whole Congressional Record. For us to undertake to reconstruct an enactment from legislative history is merely to involve the Court in political controversies which are quite proper in the enactment of a bill but should have no place in its interpretation." Schwegmann Bros. v. Calvert Distillers Corp., 341 U.S. 384, 395–396 (1951). *See also*: R. DICKSON, THE INTERPRETATION AND APPLICATION OF STATUTES (1975). Ch. 10, The Uses and Abuses of Legislative Histories.

Once the concept of what is contained in a legislative history is understood, the location and compilation of the history of a federal act becomes relatively simple. The techniques for locating legislative documents which assist in the interpretation of a statute or statutory provision will be discussed in the following sections of the Chapter.

SECTION B. THE ELEMENTS OF A LEGISLATIVE HISTORY

Before compiling a legislative history, it is necessary to be familiar with the documents that are relevant to establishing the legislative intent of a federal law: [3]

1. Congressional Bills

Prior to its enactment as law, a proposed piece of legislation is first introduced as a bill into either the House of Representatives or the Senate and is assigned either an H.R. or S. number. This number stays with the bill until passed or until the adjournment of the Congress. When a bill is amended, it is usually reprinted with the amending language. The comparison of the language of the bill as introduced with that of the final language of the law as passed may frequently reveal legislative intent.[4]

2. Committee Reports

After a bill is introduced into either the House or the Senate, it is assigned to a committee which has jurisdiction over the subject matter of the bill. It is then the committee's obligation to consider the bill and to decide whether or not to recommend its passage. If passage is not recommended or if no action is taken during the life of the Congress in which the bill was introduced, the latter "dies in committee." If the committee recommends passage it does so in a written report which usually sets forth the rationale behind the recommendations. When the bill is approved by the house in which it was introduced, it is then sent to the other house and again assigned to an appropriate committee where it receives similar consideration. When a bill has been passed by both houses, but in different versions, a "conference" committee is appointed which consists of Representatives and Senators who must reconcile differing language in the respective versions of the bill. Their recommendation is issued in a conference report.

[3] As legislative histories consist primarily of documents produced during the consideration of the bill or law by Congress, the documents cited in Chapter 9, Footnote 9, should be consulted.

[4] United States v. St. Paul M. & M. R. Co., 247 U.S. 310, 318 (1918).

Committee reports are usually considered the most important documents in determining the legislative intent of Congress.[5]

3. Congressional Debates

After a bill has been reported out of the committees to which it had been assigned, it may be debated upon the floor of the House or Senate.[6] Some authorities claim that floor statements of Congressmen on the substance of a bill under discussion are not to be considered by courts as determinative of Congressional intent.[7] The courts, however, generally do give some merit to such statements, especially when they are made by the bill's sponsors, whose stated intention is to clarify or explain the bill's purpose.[8] Such statements are published in the *Congressional Record* and are usually included as an integral part of legislative histories.

4. Committee Hearings

After a bill is assigned to a Congressional committee, a hearing is frequently scheduled. The primary function of a hearing is to provide committee members with information which may be useful in their consideration of the bill. Interested persons or experts on the subject of the bill may be requested to express their opinions on the bill's purpose or effect and may suggest changes or amendments to its language. In most instances transcripts of the hearings are published. Committee hearings are technically not part of a legislative history since they do not contain Congressional deliberations but rather the views of non-legislators of what the bill under consideration should accomplish. But in practice, hearings should be consulted when available because they frequently contain information helpful to understanding why Congress adopted or did not adopt certain language.

5. Other Documents

There are occasions when other documents are relevant to obtaining the legislative intent of a law. These may consist of Presidential messages, committee hearings on other bills, or reports and documents of other federal agencies. The location and use of these, however, are beyond the scope of this chapter. Ordinarily, the documents discussed are sufficient to help determine the legislative intent

[5] G. FOLSOM, LEGISLATIVE HISTORY: RESEARCH FOR THE INTERPRETATION OF LAWS 33 (1972). *See also*, Zuber v. Allen, 396 U.S. 168, 186 (1969).

[6] Most public laws are passed without ever being debated on the floor of Congress. It is usually only bills of great public interest which receive such debate.

[7] S. & E. Contractors, Inc. v. United States, 406 U.S. 1, 13 & n. 9 (1971).

[8] Jacques Isler Corp. v. United States, 306 F.Supp. 452, 454 (1969).

of a federal statute. When not sufficient, the researcher must then pursue the matter further.[9]

SECTION C. THE SOURCES OF LEGISLATIVE HISTORIES

In beginning the research for a legislative history, it must be kept in mind that one rarely finds all of the documents pertaining to the passage of a particular law together in one or more volumes.[10] Rather, a legislative history has to be compiled from various documentary sources such as the following:

1. Bills

    a. The bill as originally introduced in the House or Senate.

    b. The bill as amended.

    c. The bill as it passed in the originating body and as introduced into the other. (At this point, it is called an "act").

    d. The "act" as amended.

    e. The "act" as amended by Joint Conference Committee of the House and Senate.

2. Reports

    a. The reports of the committee to which the bill was assigned.

    b. The reports of the committee to which the "act" was assigned.

    c. The report of the Joint Conference Committee of the House and Senate. This is usually issued as a House report.[11]

---

[9] G. Folsom, *supra* note 5.

[10] Occasionally a compilation of a legislative history is published. But in most instances researchers have to compile their own. An example of a compiled legislative history is the following published by the Government Printing Office: HOUSE EDUCATION AND LABOR COMM., 91st CONG., 2d SESS., LEGISLATIVE HISTORY: FEDERAL COAL MINE AND SAFETY ACT (Comm.Print 1970).

The Information Handling Services also has published in microfilm a *Legislative History Service for Selected Acts of Congress*, 82d Congress to date. It has also published, in microform, the *Legislative Histories of Internal Revenue Acts, 1909–1950*. Many law libraries subscribe to both of these sets.

[11] Under the rules of Congress, the Conference Report is also to be printed as a Senate Report. This requirement is frequently waived by the unanimous consent of the Senate. F. VELEO AND M. ZWEBEN, ENACTMENT OF LAW; PROCEDURAL STEPS IN THE LEGISLATIVE PROCESS, S.DOC.NO.94–152, 94th Cong. 2d Sess. (1975), p. 12.

3.   Debates

The debates, if any, on the floor of Congress that appear in the *Congressional Record.*

4.   Hearings

The hearings, if any, held by the committees to which the bill or "act" had been assigned.

5.   The Public Law resulting from all of the above

SECTION D.   HOW TO COMPILE A LEGISLATIVE HISTORY

The compilation of a legislative history is a two-step process in which first the citations to the documents listed in Section C, *supra*, have to be located and then the documents examined in the various sets in which they are published.

1.   Legislative Histories, 1970–

The publication of a new set commencing in 1970 by the Congressional Information Service, Inc., called CIS, has simplified the method of compiling legislative histories.   This service is first issued in monthly pamphlets and then each year is reissued in two cumulative bound volumes.   Part (Volume) One contains abstracts of hearings, reports, committee prints,[12] and other Congressional publications such as House and Senate Documents.   Part (Volume) Two contains detailed indexes of the subjects of reports, documents, and hearings, lists of witnesses, official and popular names of laws, reports, and bills, and names of committee and subcommittee chairmen.

Each CIS Annual volume has a section on legislative histories for the public laws passed during the year.   Each public law is listed and citations are given to the bill number, the committee reports, hearings, the *Congressional Record*, and other documents that may be relevant to a legislative history such as committee prints, Congressional documents, and hearings held under related bills.[13]   Ref-

[12] Special studies in specific subject areas are often prepared for Congressional committees.   These are known as committee prints.   Often, only limited numbers, for the use of the committee members, are printed.   Historically these have been difficult to obtain.   Only recently have some become available through the Depository Program and indexing is often incomplete.   The Depository Program is a system whereby approximately 1400 libraries throughout the country are issued a copy of selected U. S. government publications.   For further information, *see* JOINT COMM. ON PRINTING, 94th CONG., 2d SESS., GOVERNMENT DEPOSITORY LIBRARIES (Comm.Print 1976).   Since 1970, committee prints have been made available on microfiche by the Congressional Information Service, Inc.

[13] In order to speed measures through, identical or similar bills are frequently introduced into both Houses, so that House and Senate Committees may work on

erences are also given to the abstracts of these documents within CIS. Through the use of the indexes in Part Two, references to public laws may be found by the name or title of a public law, by the subject matter of the law, or by bill number.

Because of the frequency of publication, the thoroughness of the indexing, the citation to all relevant documents, the CIS, since 1970, is now the quickest and most efficient method of locating citations to documents that make up a legislative history.

2.　Legislative Histories, before 1970

Prior to 1970, or when CIS may not be available, the key to locating the citations of the various documents is the bill number under which a public law was introduced into either the House or Senate. This bill number may be located by the use of one of the following sources:

a.　*Daily Digest. Annual Cumulation.*

The *Daily Digest* appears in each issue of the *Congressional Record* and highlights the daily activities of Congress. After each annual session of Congress, it is cumulated and contains a *History of Bills Enacted into Public Law*, arranged by public law number.

b.　*Guide to Legislative History of Bills Enacted Into Public Law.*

Beginning with Volume 77 (1963) of the *Statutes at Large*, each volume contains this guide which lists all laws passed during the year with corresponding bill number, report numbers, and citations to consideration and passage in the *Congressional Record*.

c.　*CCH Congressional Index.*

This is a privately published loose-leaf service which issues weekly supplements while Congress is in session and covers its legislative work. New volumes are issued for each Congress. One section contains a list of public laws passed and gives the bill number for each. This set lists all bills introduced, contains a history of all Senate and House bills introduced, and includes a detailed subject index. Because of its weekly supplements, this is the best set to use to obtain information about current laws.

d.　*Digest of General Bills.*

This is published by the Library of Congress and contains brief summaries of public bills for each Congress. The *Digest* is normally issued in five cumulative issues during each session of Congress.

---

the measure at the same time. Ordinarily, at some point in the legislative process, one House agrees to drop its bill and the legislative process continues on the other bill. The Companion Bills Table should be consulted in the CCH Congressional Index. It lists all companion bills.

Among its many tables is a Public Law listing with corresponding bill numbers for each law.

After the bill number has been ascertained, it is then necessary to check a status table, which presents a chronological history of the bill as it has moved through the various legislative steps toward enactment. From such tables it is possible to determine if committee reports were issued, if debates on the bill took place in Congress, and if hearings were held and printed. Tables of histories of bills may be found in all of the publications listed *supra*.

———

SECTION E. HOW TO OBTAIN ACCESS TO THE DOCUMENTS OF LEGISLATIVE HISTORIES

After using the indexes previously described, the bills with amendments, the committee reports, the debates on the bills, and the committee hearings now have to be located and consulted. The means of access to these will vary because libraries shelve U. S. government documents in different ways.[14] The various documents that must be consulted, and the tools for gaining access to them are set forth below:

1. **Bills.** These are usually kept together by Congress, with all different stages of each bill collected together.

2. **House and Senate reports** are included as part of the "Serial Set" [15] and assistance from the library staff is usually needed to locate them. Some law libraries maintain these reports in separate series. Many reports are also reprinted in both the pamphlets and bound volumes of the *United States Code Congressional and Administrative News Service*.

3. **Transcripts** of debates on the floor of Congress are bound in the *Congressional Record*. For each session of Congress, there is an Index volume which contains a *History of Bills Table*. Under the bill number, one is directed to the pages in the *Congressional Record* where the bill was debated.

---

[14] If the research for the compilation of a legislative history is being done in a law library, the researcher should ascertain how the law library organizes and indexes government documents. If a researcher is not near a law library, or the law library does not collect government documents, access to needed documents may be had at any public or college libraries which are depositories for the publications of the U. S. Government Printing Office. A list of such libraries is published in the September issue of the *Monthly Catalog of Government Publications*. Each such depository collection may be consulted by the public.

[15] The "Serial Set" is a bound compilation of *House Documents, Senate Documents, House Reports, and Senate Reports*. They are arranged in one continuous numerical sequence.

4. **Hearings.** The *CCH Congressional Index, CIS,* the *Monthly Catalog of Government Documents,* and *Cumulative Index of Committee Hearings* (issued by the Library of the United States Senate) all indicate when Committee hearings have been printed.

Hearings are usually shelved according to the Government Printing Office classification scheme. This number is always given in the *Monthly Catalog of Government Publications.* In some law libraries, hearings are catalogued separately and may be located either through the name of the committee or by subject.

5. Citation

The citation form for the elements of a legislative history may be found in Appendix A at (I), (A), (2).

The next section consists of illustrations demonstrating the procedure for compiling a legislative history of a federal law.

SECTION F.   ILLUSTRATIONS

The illustrations in this section demonstrate the two steps ordinarily required to compile a legislative history.   Step 1 involves using index volumes to obtain citation to documents.   Step 2 requires the obtaining of the documents from various sets of government documents.

For purposes of demonstration, the procedures required to compile a legislative history for the 1975 amendment to the National Environment Act of 1969 are shown.

---

1.   Indexes to Consult in Compiling a Legislative History

Illustrations

42.   Page from 42 U.S.C.A.

43.   Page from Congressional Information Service for 1975.

44.   Page from CCH Congressional Index.

45.   Page from 1975 Congressional Record—History of Bills.

2.   Locating documents cited in Indexes

Illustrations

46.   First page of H.R. 3130.

47.   First page of House Hearing on H.R. 3130.

48.   First page of House Report 94–144.

49.   First page of H.R. 3130 as amended by House Committee.

50.   Page from Congressional Record, April 21, 1975.

51.   First page of H.R. 3130 as an Act in the Senate.

52.   First page of Senate Hearing on H.R. 3130.

53.   First page of H.R. 3130 as amended by Senate Committee.

54.   First page of Senate Report on H.R. 3130.

55.   First page of Conference Report on H.R. 3130.

56.   Public Law 94–83.

[Illustration 42]
PAGE FROM 42 U.S.C.A. 4332

42 § 4332　PUBLIC HEALTH AND WELFARE
Note I

(ii) the responsible Federal official furnishes guidance and participates in such preparation,

(iii) the responsible Federal official independently evaluates such statement prior to its approval and adoption, and

(iv) after January 1, 1976, the responsible Federal official provides early notification to, and solicits the views of, any other State or any Federal land management entity of any action or any alternative thereto which may have significant impacts upon such State or affected Federal land management entity and, if there is any disagreement on such impacts, prepares a written assessment of such impacts and views for incorporation into such detailed statement.

The procedures in this subparagraph shall not relieve the Federal official of his responsibilities for the scope, objectivity, and content of the entire statement or of any other responsibility under this chapter; and further, this subparagraph does not affect the legal sufficiency of statements prepared by State agencies with less than statewide jurisdiction.

(E) study, develop, and describe appropriate alternatives to

Step 1. Researcher needs legislative history of 42 U.S.C. 4332D. Note that end of Section 4332 indicates that this Section was added by P.L. 94–83. The next step is to consult an index to locate citations to the bills, reports, and hearings related to P.L. 94–83.

1975 Amendment. Subpar. (D). Pub.L. 94–83 added subpar. (D). Former subpar. (D) redesignated (E).
Subpars. (E) to (I). Pub.L. 94–83 redesignated former subpars. (D) to (H) as (E) to (I).

Legislative History. For legislative history and purpose of Pub.L. 94–83, see 1975 U.S.Code Cong. and Adm.News, p. —.

Supplementary Index to Notes

Appropriation requests 48a
Assessment statement 89
Attorney's fees 139
Benefit-cost ratio, determination of 40a
Class actions 113a
Construction with other laws 1a
Contents of statement
　Benefits to costs ratio 80a
Costs 140
Description in statement 81a
Designation of agency 31a
Dissolution 173
Guidelines 15
Hearings
　Exhaustion of administrative remedies 36a
Intra-agency coordination and review
　Generally 41a
　Comments and views of other agencies 41b

Deference to reviewing agency's evaluation 41c
　Time schedule 41d
Law of the case 130a
Mitigation of environmental impacts 44a
Modification 174
Necessity of statement
　Statement of reasons 73a
On-site investigations 44b
Persons liable 112a
Prerequisites to suit 141
Records 88a
Rules and regulations 14
Scope 170a
Sovereign immunity 112b
Substitutes for statements
　Misleading statement 86a
Sufficiency of statements
　Poststatement developments 83a
Withdrawal of request for funds 49a

---

1. Construction
Where non-federal action cannot lawfully begin or continue without prior approval of a federal agency, then if this chapter is construed to mandate that the agency decision be enlightened by and grounded on an environmental impact statement, it is beyond cavil that the district court may then enjoin the nonfederal actors pending completion of an impact statement; indeed, were such non-

[Illustration 43]

PAGE FROM 1975 VOLUME—CONGRESSIONAL INFORMATION SERVICE (C.I.S.)

PL94–85

PL94–78 COUNCIL ON WAGE AND PRICE STABILITY ACT AMENDMENTS OF 1975.
Aug. 9, 1975. 94-1. 2 p. •
CIS/MF/3 •Item 575.
89 STAT. 411.

"To increase the authorization for the Council on Wage and Price Stability, and to extend the duration of such Council."

Requires Senate confirmation of the director; au-

Also allows congressional franking privileges for Commission mailings.

Legislative history: (S. 2073):

1975 CIS/Annual:
House Report: H443-15 (No. 94-426).

Congressional Record Vol. 121 (1975):
July 9, considered and passed Senate.
July 31, considered and passed House, amended; Senate concurred in House amendment.

Congressional Record Vol. 121 (1975).
June 16, considered and passed House.
July 28, 29, considered and passed Senate, amended.
July 30, House concurred in Senate amendments.

PL94–83 ENVIRONMENTAL IMPACT STATEMENTS, preparation.
Aug. 9, 1975. 94-1. 1 p. •
CIS/MF/3 •Item 575.
89 STAT. 424.

"To amend the National Environmental Policy Act of 1969 in order to clarify the procedures therein with respect to the preparation of environmental impact statements."

Clarifies extent States may participate with EPA in statement preparation.

Legislative history: (H.R. 3130 and related bills):

1975 CIS/Annual:
House Hearings: H561-22; H641-10.
Senate Hearings: S641-38; S641-39.
House Reports: H563-2 (No. 94-111, Pt. 2, accompanying H.R. 3787); H563-3 (No. 94-144); H563-15 (No. 94-388, Conference Report); H643-2 (No. 94-111, Pt. 1, accompanying H.R. 3787).
Senate Reports: S443-17 (No. 94-152); S443-32 (No. 94-331, Conference Report).

Congressional Record Vol. 121 (1975):
Apr. 21, considered and passed House.
May 22, considered and passed Senate, amended.
July 25, Senate agreed to conference report.
July 29, House agreed to conference report.

> ### Step 2. Using CIS
>
> The CIS/INDEX volume for 1975 has a section containing legislative histories for all Public Laws enacted in 1975. This cites to all Congressional documents related to the Public Laws. The citations refer to pages in CIS where they are abstracted. In most instances, however, the full documents should be examined. The researcher should note the citations to the Reports.

PL94–79 NUCLEAR REGULATORY COMMISSION, appropriation authorization.
Aug. 9, 1975. 94-1. 2 p. •
CIS/MF/3 •Item 575.
89 STAT. 413.

"To authorize appropriations to the Nuclear Regulatory Commission in accordance with section 261 of the Atomic Energy Act of 1954, as amended, and section 305 of the Energy Reorganization Act of 1974, and for other purposes."

Authorizes funding for FY76 and transition quarter. Restricts shipment by air of plutonium in any form except in medical devices until a safe container has been developed and tested as crash and explosion proof.

Legislative history: (S. 1716 and related bills):

1975 CIS/Annual:
House Report: J803-11 (No. 94-260, accompanying H.R. 7001).
Senate Report: J803-10 (No. 94-174).

Congressional Record Vol. 121 (1975):
June 17, considered and passed Senate.
June 20, considered and passed House, amended, in lieu of H.R. 7001.
July 31, Senate concurred in House amendment.

PL94–80 AMERICAN INDIAN POLICY REVIEW COMMISSION, voluntary contributions of services.
Aug. 9, 1975. 94-1. 2 p. •
CIS/MF/3 •Item 575.
89 STAT. 415.

"To authorize the American Indian Policy Review Commission to accept voluntary contributions of services and for other purposes."

PL94–82 POSTAL SERVICE, SAFETY PROGRAMS; Federal executive salary adjustments.
Aug. 9, 1975. 94-1. 5 p. •
CIS/MF/3 •Item 575.
89 STAT. 419.

"To amend title 39, United States Code, to apply to the United States Postal Service certain provisions of law providing for Federal agency safety programs and responsibilities, to provide for cost-of-living adjustments of Federal executive salaries, and for other purposes."

Extends to USPS coverage under the Occupational Safety and Health Act; allows pay increases for executive, judicial, and congressional employees heretofore frozen at certain levels.

Legislative history: (H.R. 2559 and related bills):

1973 CIS/Annual:
House Hearings: H621-19.

1974 CIS/Annual:
House Hearings: H341-4.2.

1975 CIS/Annual:
House Document: H620-2.
Senate Hearings: S621-1.
House Committee Print: H622-8.
House Report: H623-9 (No. 94-271).
Senate Report: S623-5 (No. 94-333).

PL94–84 JOHN C. KLUCZYNSKI FEDERAL BUILDING, ILL., designation.
Aug. 9, 1975. 94-1. 1 p. •
CIS/MF/3 •Item 575.
89 STAT. 425.

"To designate the John C. Kluczynski Federal Building."

Refers to Federal office building in Chicago, Ill.

Legislative history: (H.R. 4241):

1975 CIS/Annual:
House Report: [Public Works and Transportation] (No. 94-186).
Senate Report: [Public Works] (No. 94-348).

Congressional Record Vol. 121 (1975):
May 19, considered and passed House.
Aug. 1, considered and passed Senate.

PL94–85 CARGO VESSELS, passengers.
Aug. 9, 1975. 94-1. 1 p. •
CIS/MF/3 •Item 575.
89 STAT. 426.

"To amend the Merchant Marine Act, 1920, in order to permit cargo vessels to carry more than sixteen passengers when emergency situations arise."

Affects ferrying of vehicles and passengers across the mouth of the Chesapeake Bay during emergency periods when tunnel is closed to traffic, as determined by the Coast Guard.

Legislative history: (H.R. 5405):

[Illustration 44]

PAGE FROM THE CCH CONGRESSIONAL INDEX

62　3-24-76　　　　　　**Status of House Bills**　　　　　**5061**
For digest, see "House Bills" Division.

3118
Hearing in H. (printed) 3/13/75
Reptd., with amend., H. Rept.
94-575 .... 10/28/75

3128
Hearing in H. (printed) 4/7/75

3129
Hearing in H. (printed) 3/5/75

★ 3130
Hearing in H. (printed) 4/7/75
Reptd., with amend., H. Rept.
94-144 .... 4/11/75
Passed H. as reported [Roll-call] ... 4/21/75
To S. Interior and Insular Affairs ......
.... 4/22/75
Hearing in S. (printed) 5/5/75
Reptd., with amend., S. Rept. 94-152 ...
.... 5/21/75
Passed S. as reported [Voice] 5/22/75
H. appoints conferees 6/9/75
S. appoints conferees 6/19/75
Conf. Rept. submitted to H., H. Rept.
94-388 .... 7/24/75
Conf. Rept. submitted to S., S. Rept.
94-331 .... 7/24/75
Conf. Rept. agreed to by S. 7/25/75
Conf. Rept. agreed to by H. 7/29/75
To President 7/30/75
Approved [Public Law 94-83] 8/9/75

3214
Hearing in H. (printed) 4/22/75

3215
Hearing in H. (printed) 4/22/75

3228
Hearing in H. (printed) 3/10/75

3246
Hearing in H. (printed) 4/8/75

3247
Hearing in H. (printed) 2/25/75

3251
Hearing in H. (printed) 6/3/75

★ 3260
Reptd., no amend., H. Rept. 94-17 ......
.... 2/20/75
Passed H.., with amend. [Roll-call] .....
.... 2/25/75
To S. Appropriations 2/26/75
Reptd., with amend., S. Rept. 94-24 ....
.... 2/27/75
Passed S., further amend. [Roll-call] ....
.... 3/17/75
S. appoints conferees 3/17/75
H. appoints conferees 3/20/75
Conf. Rept. submitted to H., H. Rept.
94-112 .... 3/24/75
Conf. Rept. agreed to by H 3/25/75

Step 2a.　**Using CCH Congressional Index**

This loose-leaf set has a status table giving the history of each bill introduced during Congress. In order to obtain the Bill Number, obtain the P.L. number from the Statutes at Large volume, or in the Daily Calendar in the History of Bills section of the Congressional Record for the year in which the law was enacted.

Note that this CCH Index lists when Hearings have been printed, but does not cite to the Congressional Record.

3211
Hearing in H. 2/25/75

3212
Hearing in H. 4/8/75

3327
Hearing in H. (printed) 3/13/75

3333
Hearing in H. (printed) 9/10/75

Congressional Index — 1975-1976

[Illustration 45]

PAGE FROM HISTORY OF BILLS SECTION, CONGRESSIONAL RECORD—1975

H.B. 8

CONGRESSIONAL RECORD INDEX

H.R. 3130—Continued
procedures therein with respect to the preparation of environmental impact statements.
Mr. LaFalce; Committee on Merchant Marine and Fisheries, H744.
Reported (H. Rept. 94–144), with amendment, H2738.
Debated, H3001.
Rules suspended. Amended and passed House, H3009.
Referred to Committee on Interior and Insular Affairs, S6456.
Reported with amendment (S. Rept. 94–152), S8829.
Amended and passed Senate, S8928.
House disagreed to Senate amendment and asked for a conference. Conferees appointed, H5105.
Senate insisted on its amendments and agreed to a conference. Conferees appointed, S11075.
Conference report (H. Rept. 94–388), submitted in House and agreed to, H7450, H7739
Conference report submitted in Senate and agreed to, S13758.
Examined and signed, H7821, S14080.
Presented to the President, H7934.
Approved (Public Law 94–83), H8201.

H.R. 3474—To authorize appropriations to the Energy Research and Development Administration in accordance with section 261 of the Atomic Energy Act of 1954, as amended, section 305 of the Energy Reorganization Act of 1974, and section 16 of the Federal Nonnuclear Energy Research and Development Act of 1974, and for other purposes.
Mr. Price and Mr. Teague (by request); Joint Committee on Atomic Energy; Committee on Science and Technology, H993.
Reported with amendment (H. Rept. 94–294), H5467.
Made special order H. Res. 554, H5719.
Debated, H5755, H5833.
Amended and passed House, H5887.
Ordered held at desk, S11397.
Amended and passed Senate (in lieu of S. 598), S14776.
House disagreed to Senate amendments and asked for a conference. Conferees appointed, H8354.
Senate insisted on its amendments and agreed to a conference. Conferees appointed, S15572.
Additional conferees appointed, H8664.

H.R. 3884—To terminate certain authorities with respect to national emergencies still in effect, and to provide for orderly implementation and termination of future national emergencies.
Mr. Rodino, Mr. Flowers, Mr. Danielson, Miss Jordan, Mr. Mazzoli, Mr. Pattison of New York, and Mr. Fish; Committee on the Judiciary, H1260.
Reported with amendment (H. Rept. 94–238), H4577.
Made special order H. Res. 524, H5259.
Debated, H8327.
Amended and passed House, H8341.
Referred to Committee on Government Operations, S15373.

H.R. 4222—To amend the National School Lunch and Child Nutrition Acts in order to extend and revise the special food service program for children and the school breakfast program, and for other purposes related to strengthening the school lunch and child nutrition programs.
Mr. Perkins, Mr. Quie, Mr. Thompson, Mr. Meeds, Mr. Dominick V. Daniels, Mr. Peyser, Mr. Dent, Mr. Sarasin, Mr. Brademas, Mr. Pressler, Mr. O'Hara, Mr. Goodling, Mr. Hawkins, Mr. Ford of Michigan, Mrs. Mink, Mrs. Chisholm, Mr. Biaggi, Mr. Andrews of North Carolina, Mr. Lehman, Mr. Benitez, Mr. Blouin, Mr. Cornell, Mr. Risenhoover, and Mr. Zeferetti; Committee on Education and Labor, H1380.
Reported with amendment (H. Rept. 94–68), H1868.
Made special order H. Res. 352, H2133.

Debated, H2237, H2279, I13350.
Amended and passed House. Title amended, H3371.

H.R. 4241—To designate the John C. Kluczynski Federal Building.
Mr. Rostenkowski, Mr. Jones of Alabama, Mr. Harsha, Mr. Annunzio, Mrs. Collins of Illinois, Mr. Crane, Mr. Derwinski, Mr. Findley, Mr. Hall, Mr. Hyde, Mr. McClory, Mr. Madigan, Mr. Metcalfe, Mr. Michel, Mr. Mikva, Mr. Murphy of Illinois, Mr. O'Brien, Mr. Price, Mr. Railsback, Mr. Russo, Mr. Shipley, Mr. Simon, and Mr. Yates; Committee on Public Works and Transportation, H1380.
Reported (H. Rept. 94–186), H3609.
Passed House, H4145.
Referred to Committee on Public Works, S8663.
Reported (S. Rept. 94–348), S14477.
Passed Senate, S14886.
Examined and signed, H8202, S15097.
Presented to the President, H8255.
Approved (Public Law 94–84), H8201.

H.R. 4415—To amend the Intergovernmental Personnel Act of 1970 to provide more effective means to improve personnel administration in State and local governments; to correct certain inequities in the law; and to extend coverage under the law to the Trust Territory of the Pacific Islands.
Mr. Henderson and Mr. Derwinski; Committee on Post Office and Civil Service, H1462.
Reported with amendment (H. Rept. 94–242), H4696.
Made special order H. Res. 549, H5634.
Debated, H8207.
Amended and passed House. Title amended, H8226.
Referred to Committee on Government Operations, S15240.

H.R. 4723—Authorizing appropriations to the National Science Foundation for fiscal year 1976.
Mr. Teague, Mr. Mosher, and Mr. Symington; Committee on Science and Technology, H1630.
Reported (H. Rept. 94–66), H1787.
Recommitted to Committee on Science and Technology, H1794.
Reported (H. Rept. 94–99), H2132.
Made special order H. Res. 368, H2344.
Debated, H2575.
Amended and passed House, H2607.
Referred to Committee on Labor and Public Welfare, S5788.
Reported (S. Rept. 94–112), S7778.
Amended and passed Senate, S7930.
Objection heard to unanimous consent request that House disagree with Senate amendment and ask for a conference, H3995.
House disagreed to Senate amendments and asked for a conference, H5597.
Motion to reconsider laid on the table, H5600.
Conferees appointed, H5600.
Senate insisted on its amendments and agreed to a conference. Conferees appointed, S10878.
Conference report (H. Rept. 94–422), submitted in House, H7826.
Made special order H. Res. 654, H7935.
Conference report submitted in Senate and agreed to, S14329.

Conference report agreed to in House, H8070, H8072.
Examined and signed, H8184, S15098.

> **Step 2b.** If CCH Congressional Index or CIS/INDEX are not available, use History of Bills section in Congressional Record. Note that this does not give citations to Hearings.

Presented to the President, H7821.
Approved (Public Law 94–74), H8201.

H.R. 5328—To authorize the Smithsonian Institution to plan museum support facilities.
Mr. Mahon; Committee on House Administration, H2198.
Reported with amendment (H. Rept. 94–258), H4921.
Reported (H. Rept. 94–258 Pt. II), H6307.
Made special order H. Res. 94–361, H6862.
Amended and passed House, H8205.
Proceedings vacated. Laid on the table (S. 907 passed in lieu), H8207.

H.R. 5405—To amend the Merchant Marine Act, 1920, in order to permit cargo vessels to carry more than sixteen passengers when emergency situations arise.
Mr. Downing; Committee on Merchant Marine and Fisheries, H2268.
Reported with amendment (H. Rept. 94–182), H3535.
Rules suspended. Passed House, amended, H3619.
Referred to Committee on Commerce, S7475.
Reported (S. Rept. 94–344), S14374.
Passed Senate, S14677.
Examined and signed, H8202, S15097.
Presented to the President, H8255.
Approved (Public Law 94–85), H8201.

H.R. 5447—To amend the Act of August 16, 1971, as amended, which established the National Advisory Committee on Oceans and Atmosphere, to increase and extend the appropriation authorization thereunder.
Mrs. Sullivan, Mr. Ruppe, Mr. Murphy of New York, and Mr. Mosher; Committee on Merchant Marine and Fisheries, H2345.
Reported with amendment (H. Rept. 94–222), H4290.
Rules suspended. Amended and passed House, H4176.
Referred to Committee on Commerce, S8663.
Reported with amendment (S. Rept. 94–268), S12100.
Amended and passed Senate. Title amended, S12378.
House concurs in Senate amendment, H7445.
Examined and signed, H7583, S13679.
Presented to the President, H7718.
Approved (Public Law 94–69), H8201.

H.R. 5522—To give effect to the International Convention for the Conservation of Atlantic Tunas, signed at Rio de Janeiro May 14, 1966, by the United States of America and other countries, and for other purposes.
Mr. Leggett; Committee on Merchant Marine and Fisheries, H2374.
Rules suspended. Amended and passed House, H5506.
Reported with amendment (H. Rept. 94–295), H5573.
Referred to Committee on Commerce, S10724.
Reported with amendment (S. Rept. 94–269), S12100.
Amended and passed Senate, S12378.
House concurs in Senate amendment, H7184.

[Illustration 46]
FIRST PAGE OF H.R. 3130—94th CONGRESS, 1st SESSION

94TH CONGRESS
1ST SESSION

H. R. 3130

IN THE HOUSE OF REPRESENTATIVES

FEBRUARY 13, 1975

Mr. LaFALCE introduced the following bill; which was referred to the Committee on Merchant Marine and Fisheries

A BILL

To amend the National Environmental Policy Act of 1969 in order to clarify the procedures therein with respect to the preparation of environmental impact statements.

1   *Be it enacted by the Senate and House of Representa-*

2   *tives of the United States of America in Congress assembled,*

3   That section 102 of the National Environmental Policy Act

4   of 1969 (42 U.S.C. 4332) is amended—

5   (1) by inserting " (a) " immediately after "Sec.

6   102."; and

7   (2) by

8   new subsect

9   " (b) The p

I

> From the Indexes described, researcher should now have citations to (1) Bill Number, (2) Congressional Record, (3) Reports, (4) Hearings. These must all be separately obtained and examined.
>
> This illustration shows the first page of H.R. 3130 as first introduced into the 94th Congress.

[Illustration 47]
FIRST PAGE OF HOUSE HEARING ON H.R. 3130

ENVIRONMENT MISCELLANEOUS—PART 1

HEARINGS
BEFORE THE

SUBCOMMITTEE ON FISHERIES AND WILDLIFE CONSERVATION AND THE ENVIRONMENT
OF THE

COMMITTEE ON MERCHANT MARINE AND FISHERIES HOUSE OF REPRESENTATIVES
NINETY-FOURTH CONGRESS

FIRST SESSION

ON

ENVIRONMENTAL IMPACT STATEMENTS AMENDMENT

H.R. 3128, H.R. 3130, H.R. 3787, H.R. 3968, H.R. 4159, H.R. 4912

BILLS TO AMEND THE NATIONAL ENVIRONMENTAL POLICY ACT

———

APRIL 7, 8, 1975

———

A committee may hold hearings on a bill. Most, but not all, hearings are published. Frequently, as in this case, hearings may be held on related bills.

———

Printed for the use of the Committee on Merchant Marine and Fisheries

U.S. GOVERNMENT PRINTING OFFICE
WASHINGTON : 1975

55-638

[Illustration 48]

FIRST PAGE OF HOUSE OF REPRESENTATIVES REPORT NO. 94–144 ON H.R. 3130

94TH CONGRESS } HOUSE OF REPRESENTATIVES {   REPORT
 1st Session }   { No. 94–144

STATE PARTICIPATION IN ENVIRONMENTAL ANALYSES

APRIL 11, 1975.—Committed to the Committee of the Whole House on the State of the Union and ordered to be printed

---

Mrs. SULLIVAN, from the Committee on Merchant Marine and Fisheries, submitted the following

REPORT

together with

MINORITY VIEWS

[To accompany H.R. 3130]

> A committee to which a Bill has been assigned issues
> a report which states the purpose of the Bill.

---

and recommend that the bill as amended do pass.

The amendment is as follows:

Strike line 9 on page 1 and all that follows and insert the following:

(b) A statement prepared after January 1, 1970, shall not be deemed to be legally insufficient solely by reason of having been prepared by a state agency or official if the responsible Federal official furnishes guidance and participates in such preparation and independently evaluates such statement prior to its approval and adoption. This procedure shall not relieve the Federal official of his responsibilities for the scope, objectivity, and content of the statement, nor of any other responsibilities under this Act.

PURPOSE OF THE BILL

The purpose of this bill is to clarify the application of the National Environmental Policy Act of 1969 to certain projects, where the environmental impact statement was drafted, or there was extensive

38–006

[Illustration 49]

FIRST PAGE OF H.R. 3130, AS AMENDED BY THE HOUSE COMMITTEE

Union Calendar No. 62

94TH CONGRESS
1ST SESSION

H. R. 3130

[Report No. 94–144]

IN THE HOUSE OF REPRESENTATIVES

FEBRUARY 13, 1975

Mr. LaFALCE introduced the following bill; which was referred to the Committee on Merchant Marine and Fisheries

APRIL 11, 1975

Reported with an amendment, committed to the Committee of the Whole House on the State of the Union, and ordered to be printed

[Omit the part struck through and insert the part printed in italic]

A BILL

To amend the National Environmental Policy Act of 1969 in order to clarify the procedures therein with respect to the

---

After a Bill is introduced, it is referred to a committee which may amend it. When it does, it reprints the Bill with the deleted language lined out and amended language printed in italics.

---

8   new subsection:

9   "(b) The preparation of any detailed statement required

10   under subsection (a) (C) (i) may be accomplished by the

I

[Illustration 50]

EXCERPT FROM CONGRESSIONAL RECORD

April 21, 1975   CONGRESSIONAL RECORD — HOUSE   H 3001

Transportation and passed by the House on April 10, temporarily waiving certain Federal matching and categorical requirements restricting the use of funds in the interest of accelerating construction.

H.R. 3786 would be cold consolation for the three States unable to take advantage of those provisions between now and June 30, 1975, the date by which funds must be obligated for projects qualifying under those provisions and under guidelines for availability of the $2 billion.

This bill also has the virtue of targeting the legislative response precisely to the problem raised by this single court

---

A Bill may be debated or discussed in the House.

---

and ambiguous, and would indirectly amend NEPA.

As to the first two points, we fully agree that this is a limited bill in terms of its application to the highway program in three States, but would argue that this is a virtue of the legislation. It tailors the solution to the problem, offers no potential for disruption of environmental procedures and offers the best prospects for speedy enactment by both Houses of the Congress.

There is a great deal of merit to arguments that legal problems raised by the second circuit decision can be resolved by the Supreme Court, which is being petitioned for certiorari. Therefore, our committee is content to limit action to the immediate problem on an emergency basis.

I would cite in this connection prepared testimony of Chairman Russell W. Peterson of the Council on Environmental Quality to the effect that, if the Congress deems a legislative remedy advisable, H.R. 3787 is the way to go.

As to specific intent, I would argue that H.R. 3787, as amended makes abundantly clear that the intent is to clarify and reaffirm what has traditionally been considered the intent of NEPA since its enactment as to preparation of environmental impact statements. The reported bill itself, the report of the Committee on Public Works and Transportation, and extensive colloquy in the hearing record leave no grounds for misinterpretation.

Specifically, the bill was amended to assure that there be no encroachment on the ultimate responsibility of the Federal agency under NEPA to evaluate, analyze and adopt a State-prepared EIS.

This legislative history, also reaffirming the holdings in five Federal circuits other than the second, also makes clear that highway procedures under NEPA are not being legislatively altered.

Aside from the merits of this legislation and the deficiencies of the adverse report, certain other considerations merit your attention.

The standing of the Committee on Public Works and Transportation to legislate in this matter is beyond dispute. The bill was referred initially to the committee, which took it up with dispatch. The fact of sequential referral in no way diminishes that standing.

Since every piece of legislation considered by this body has the possibility of impacting the environment, if we decide to adopt the reasoning of our good friends in Merchant Marine and Fish- contention. To determine otherwise would frustrate the orderly progress of legislation to the floor, for which this committee has traditionally exhibited a high regard.

To conclude, H.R. 3787 is an emergency measure in which time is the critical factor, and which stands the best chance of passage. It fully deserves favorable consideration by the House.

The SPEAKER pro tempore (Mr. O'NEILL). The question is on the motion offered by the gentleman from New Jersey (Mr. HOWARD) that the House suspend the rules and pass the bill (H.R. 3787) as amended.

The question was taken.

Mr. THONE. Mr. Speaker, I object to the vote on the ground that a quorum is not present, and make the point of order that a quorum is not present.

The SPEAKER pro tempore. Pursuant to the provisions of clause 3(b) of rule XXVII and the prior announcement of the Chair, further proceedings on this motion will be postponed.

Does the gentleman from Nebraska withdraw his point of order that there is no quorum?

Mr. THONE. Yes, I do, Mr. Speaker.

GENERAL LEAVE

Mr. HOWARD. Mr. Speaker, I ask unanimous consent that all Members may have 5 legislative days in which to revise and extend their remarks on the legislation just considered.

The SPEAKER pro tempore. Is there objection to the request of the gentleman from New Jersey?

There was no objection.

PARLIAMENTARY INQUIRY

Mr. PEYSER. Mr. Speaker, a parliamentary inquiry.

The SPEAKER pro tempore. The gentleman will state his parliamentary inquiry.

Mr. PEYSER. Mr. Speaker, do I understand that we will now vote on this particular suspension at the end of the day; is that the procedure to be followed on the particular bill (H.R. 3787)?

The SPEAKER pro tempore. There is one more suspension. When that is completed, the Chair will put the question.

STATE PARTICIPATION IN ENVIRONMENTAL ANALYSES

Mr. LEGGETT. Mr. Speaker, I move to suspend the rules and pass the bill (H.R. 3130) to amend the National Environmental Policy Act of 1969 in order to clarify the procedures therein with respect to the preparation of environmental impact statements, as amended.

The Clerk read as follows:

H.R. 3130

Be it enacted by the Senate and House of Representatives of the United States of America in Congress assembled, That section 102 of the National Environmental Policy Act of 1969 (42 U.S.C. 4332) is amended—

(1) by inserting "(a)" immediately after "Sec. 102."; and

(2) by adding at the end thereof the following new subsection:

"(b) A statement prepared after January 1, 1970, shall not be deemed to be legally insufficient solely by reason of having been prepared by a State agency or official if the responsible Federal official furnishes guidance and participates in such preparation and independently evaluates such statement prior to its approval and adoption. This procedure shall not relieve the Federal official of his responsibilities for the scope, objectivity, and content of the statement, nor of any other responsibilities under this Act."

The SPEAKER pro tempore. (Mr. O'NEILL) Is a second demanded?

Mr. FORSYTHE. Mr. Speaker, I demand a second.

The SPEAKER pro tempore. Without objection, a second will be considered as ordered.

There was no objection.

Mr. LEGGETT. Mr. Speaker, I yield myself such time as I may consume.

(Mr. LEGGETT asked and was given permission to revise and extend his remarks.)

Mr. LEGGETT. Mr. Speaker, I rise in support of H.R. 3130. This legislation would amend the National Environmental Policy Act of 1969 to clarify certain procedures dealing with the preparation of environmental impact statements. It is the intent of this legislation to simply restate in statutory form what is presently the policy and practice established by the Council on Environmental Quality in its guidelines to Federal agencies.

The need for this statutory clarification stems from a recent decision in the Second Circuit Court of Appeals which held that certain actions taken by the State of Vermont Highway Department, with some Federal participation, were not in compliance with the requirements of the National Environmental Policy Act. This decision was interpreted by the Federal Highway Administration as requiring the halting of all federally

[Illustration 51]
FIRST PAGE OF H.R. 3130 AS AN "ACT" IN THE SENATE

94TH CONGRESS
1ST SESSION
H. R. 3130

IN THE SENATE OF THE UNITED STATES

APRIL 22 (legislative day, APRIL 21), 1975
Read twice and referred to the Committee on Interior and Insular Affairs

AN ACT

To amend the National Environmental Policy Act of 1969 in order to clarify the procedures therein with respect to the preparation of environmental impact statements.

1   *Be it enacted by the Senate and House of Representa-*

2   *tives of the United States of America in Congress assembled,*

3   That section 102 of the National Environmental Policy Act

4   of 1969 (42 U.S.C. 4332) is amended—

5   (1) by inserting " (a) " immediately after "SEC.

6   102."; and

8

9

10

> After a Bill passes the House in which it was introduced, it is reprinted with all adopted amendments incorporated into the text and introduced into the other House as an "Act."

[Illustration 52]
FIRST PAGE OF SENATE HEARING ON H.R. 3130

RESPONSIBILITY FOR PREPARATION OF ENVIRONMENTAL IMPACT STATEMENTS

JOINT HEARING

BEFORE THE

SUBCOMMITTEE ON TRANSPORTATION

OF THE

COMMITTEE ON PUBLIC WORKS

AND THE

ENVIRONMENT AND LAND RESOURCES SUBCOMMITTEE

OF THE

COMMITTEE ON INTERIOR AND INSULAR AFFAIRS

UNITED STATES SENATE

NINETY-FOURTH CONGRESS

FIRST SESSION

ON

H.R. 3130

AN ACT TO AMEND THE NATIONAL ENVIRONMENTAL POLICY ACT OF 1969 IN ORDER TO CLARIFY THE PROCEDURES THEREIN WITH RESPECT TO THE PREPARATION OF ENVIRONMENTAL IMPACT STATEMENTS

Hearings may be held on the "Act."

Printed for the use of the Committees on Public Works and Interior and Insular Affairs

U.S. GOVERNMENT PRINTING OFFICE
WASHINGTON : 1975

54–037 O

[Illustration 53]

FIRST PAGE OF H.R. 3130 AS AMENDED BY THE
SENATE COMMITTEE

Calendar No. 147

94TH CONGRESS
1ST SESSION

H. R. 3130

[Report No. 94–152]

IN THE SENATE OF THE UNITED STATES

APRIL 22 (legislative day, APRIL 21), 1975
Read twice and referred to the Committee on Interior and Insular Affairs

MAY 21, 1975
Reported by Mr. HASKELL, with an amendment

[Strike out all after the enacting clause and insert the part printed in italic]

AN ACT

To amend the National Environmental Policy Act of 1969 in
order to clarify the procedures therein with respect to the
preparation of environmental impact statements.

1   *Be it enacted by the Senate and House of Representa-*

2   *tives of the United States of America in Congress assembled,*

3   ~~That section 102 of the National Environmental Policy Act~~

4   ~~of 1969 (42 U.S.C. 4332) is amended—~~

5   ~~(1) by inserting "(a)" immediately after "SEC.~~

6   ~~102."; and~~

7

8   The Act may be amended by the Committee
      or on the floor of the Senate. When it is, it
9   is reprinted.

10

II

[Illustration 54]

FIRST PAGE OF SENATE REP. 94–152 ON H.R. 3130

Calendar No. 147

94th Congress *2d Session*	SENATE	Report No. 94–152

AMENDING THE NATIONAL ENVIRONMENTAL POLICY ACT TO CLARIFY THE FEDERAL AND STATE ROLES IN THE PREPARATION OF ENVIRONMENTAL ANALYSES ON CERTAIN FEDERAL PROGRAMS

May 21, 1975.—Ordered to be printed

Mr. Haskell, from the Committee on Interior and Insular Affairs, submitted the following

REPORT

[To accompany H.R. 3130]

The Committee on Interior and Insular Affairs, to which was referred the Act (H.R. 3130) to amend the National Environmental Policy Act of 1969 in order to clarify the procedures therein with respect to the preparation of environmental impact statements, having considered the same, reports favorably thereon with an amendment and recommends that the Act, as amended, do pass.

The amendment is as follows:

Strike all after the enacting clause and insert in lieu thereof the following:

That section 102(2)(C) of the National Environmental Policy Act of 1969 (83 Stat. 852) is amended by striking the semicolon at the end thereof and inserting a period and the following new paragraph:

"Any detailed statement prepared after January 1, 1970, on a major Federal action funded under a program of grants to states shall not be deemed to be legally insufficient solely by reason of having been prepared by a state agency

---

A Committee Report is then published. Discussion or debate may also be held on it. In this instance, the Act was not discussed on the floor of the Senate.

38–010 O

[Illustration 55]

FIRST PAGE OF CONFERENCE REPORT ON H.R. 3130

94TH CONGRESS	HOUSE OF REPRESENTATIVES	REPORT
1st Session		No. 94–388

When an Act is passed, and the language differs from the Bill as passed by the other House,
a Conference Committee of both Houses is appointed to reconcile the differences. The Conference Committee issues a Report which must
be approved by both Houses without changes.

This Conference Report was also issued as a
Senate Report.

Mrs. SULLIVAN, from the committee of conference,
submitted the following

CONFERENCE REPORT

[To accompany H.R. 3130]

The committee of conference on the disagreeing votes of the two
Houses on the amendment of the Senate to the bill (H.R. 3130) to
amend the National Environmental Policy Act of 1969 in order to
clarify the procedures therein with respect to the preparation of
environmental impact statements, have agreed to recommend and do
recommend to their respective Houses as follows:

That the House recede from its disagreement to the amendment of
the Senate and agree to the same with an amendment as follows:

In lieu of the matter proposed to be inserted by the Senate amendment insert the following:

*That section 102(2) of the National Environmental Policy Act of 1969
(83 Stat. 852) is amended by redesignating subparagraphs (D), (E),
(F), (G), and (H) as subparagraphs (E), (F), (G), (H), and (I),
respectively; and by adding immediately after subparagraph (C) the
following new subparagraph:*

*"(D) Any detailed statement required under subparagraph (C)
after January 1, 1970, for any major Federal action funded under
a program of grants to States shall not be deemed to be legally
insufficient solely by reason of having been prepared by a State
agency or official, if:*

*"(i) the State agency or official has statewide jurisdiction
and has the responsibility for such action,*

*"(ii) the responsible Federal official furnishes guidance
and participates in such preparation,*

57–006 O

[Illustration 56]

FIRST PAGE OF PUBLIC LAW 94-83

Public Law 94-83
94th Congress, H. R. 3130 ←
August 9, 1975

An Act

To amend the National Environmental Policy Act of 1969 in order to clarify the procedures therein with respect to the preparation of environmental impact statements.

Be it enacted by the Senate and House of Representatives of the United States of America in Congress assembled, That section 102(2) of the National Environmental Policy Act of 1969 (83 Stat. 852) is amended by redesignating subparagraphs (D), (E), (F), (G), and (H) as subparagraphs (E), (F), (G), (H), and (I), respectively; and by adding immediately after subparagraph (C) the following new subparagraph:

Environmental impact statements, preparation. 42 USC 4332.

"(D) Any detailed statement required under subparagraph (C) after January 1, 1970, for any major Federal action funded under a program of grants to States shall not be deemed to be legally insufficient solely by reason of having been prepared by a State agency or official, if:

"(i) the State agency or official has statewide jurisdiction and has the responsibility for such action,

"(ii) the responsible Federal official furnishes guidance and participates in such preparation,

"(iii) the responsible Federal official independently evaluates such statement prior to its approval and adoption, and

"(iv) after January 1, 1976, the responsible Federal official provides early notification to, and solicits the views of, any other State or any Federal land management entity of any action or any alternative thereto which may have significant impacts upon such State or affected Federal land management entity and, if there is any disagreement on such impacts, prepares a written assessment of such impacts and views for incorporation into such detailed statement.

The procedures in this subparagraph shall not relieve the Federal official of his responsibilities for the scope, objectivity, and content of the entire statement or of any other responsibility under this Act; and further, this subparagraph does not affect the legal sufficiency of statements prepared by State agencies with less than statewide jurisdiction.".

Approved August 9, 1975.

P.L. 94-83 as passed and signed by the President will be published in the Statutes at Large.

Chapter 11

STATE AND MUNICIPAL LEGISLATION

There is much similarity between the organization and publication of federal and state statutes. While there are differences between the fifty states, this is mostly in nomenclature rather than substance. Each state has a state legislature, and with the exception of Nebraska, each has an upper and lower house similar to the House of Representatives and the Senate of the United States Congress. In general, the legislative process for the passage of state laws is similar to that previously described for federal laws.

State legislatures meet in either annual or biennial sessions.[1] Information for individual states as to nomenclature, frequency of session, and other pertinent information on state legislatures may be obtained by consulting the latest edition of *The Book of the States*.[2]

SECTION A. SESSION LAWS

Each state publishes all of the laws passed during each session of its legislature in volumes with the generic name, "session laws," although in some states they may have other names, such as acts and resolves, or statutes or laws. The session laws are published in chronological order comparable to those in the *U. S. Statutes at Large*. See Illustrations 57 and 58. Most states also publish their laws in "slip" form soon after they are passed. In some states current laws are found in the pamphlet or advance sheet services to privately published state codes.

SECTION B. CODIFICATION OF STATE LAWS

Since each volume of the session laws for a state contains the laws passed by the state legislature during an annual, biennial or spe-

[1] COUNCIL OF STATE GOVERNMENTS, LEGISLATIVE SESSION SHEET.

[2] COUNCIL OF STATE GOVERNMENTS, THE BOOK OF THE STATES, 1974–1975 (1974). This chapter is devoted to the location of state statutes. It must be noted, however, that after a relevant statute has been located, it is frequently necessary to determine its proper application. For these purposes, consult R. DICKSON, THE INTERPRETATION AND APPLICATION OF STATUTES (1975) or J. SUTHERLAND, STATUTES AND STATUTORY CONSTRUCTION (4th ed. by C. Sands, 1972).

cial session, and since the laws passed are arranged chronologically in each volume, it is necessary to have the laws rearranged by title or subject as they are in the *United States Code*. Each state does, in fact, have a set of statutes which have been extracted from its session laws. The terms "revised", "compiled", "consolidated", and "code" are often used indiscriminately to describe such sets of books.[3] In some instances compilations are accomplished under the official auspices of a state, in others by private publishers, and in some states there are both official and unofficial sets of codes. Some are unannotated, while others are fully annotated. Some state codes have been enacted into positive law, others are only *prima facie* evidence of the law with the positive law being in the volumes of the session laws. The important thing to note is that each state has a set of session laws and a current code. The set or sets for the state being used should be carefully examined to note its features, its method of publication, and the way it is kept up to date.

The following features are common to most sets of state statutes:

1. **Constitutions**

   The constitution of the state currently in force as well as the text of previous constitutions.

2. **Text of Statutes**

   Each state code contains the public laws of a general nature and still in force and arranged by subject.

3. **Historical Notes**

   Historical references showing the derivation of each section of the code at the end of each statutory section. As many state codes have several completely new codifications during the history of the state, citations are frequently given to the present provision in a previous codification.

4. **Annotations**

   Most state codes have an annotated edition. Some are very similar in appearance to the U.S.C.A. or the U.S.C.S. Frequently, citations are given to law review articles and to legal encyclopedias.

5. **Tables**

   Each state code will have tables that cross-reference from session law to the code and many will have tables that refer

---

[3] Methods of compilation differ from state to state. One state may simply reissue the session laws in chronological order but with temporary and repealed acts not included. A second may arrange the laws still in effect in a classified order but with the text kept intact as originally enacted. A third may rewrite, rearrange, and re-enact the laws in a new classified order. *See* Chapter 9, Footnote 7.

from an older codification to the current one.   (See Illustration 59 for examples of a state annotated code.)

SECTION C.   INDEXES AND GUIDES TO STATE LEGISLATION

There is no comprehensive indexing service providing a convenient means to locate citations to all state statutes on the same topic.[4] When comparative state statutes are needed, the following may be of use:

1.   Looseleaf services.   These are described in detail in Chapter 14.   Many looseleaf services provide either full texts, digests, or tables of citations to state laws on a specific subject.   For example, the CCH *All-State Tax Reporter* provides charts and digests of comparative state tax provisions;   the Prentice-Hall *Wills, Trusts, and Estates Reporter* reproduces the text of all state laws on these subjects.   Before using other methods, a check should be made to see if there is a looseleaf service on the subject or for other methods of locating comparative state legislation.[5]

2.   Martindale-Hubbell Law Directory.   This is an annual publication which includes a volume titled *Law Digests* providing a digest of state laws on many subjects.

SECTION D.   FINDING STATE LEGISLATION

When researching state legislation, one is usually attempting to ascertain if there is a current state statutory provision on a particular legal subject, *e. g.*, at what age may one be issued a driving license? The first step is to examine carefully the code for the state in question and familiarize oneself with the way the code is organized.   Consulting the index provided should lead to the citation of a provision in the code which will set forth the current statutory law on the subject. Next, all of the notes set forth below the statutory provision should be consulted.   Many codes have references to legislative reports and

---

[4] For the period 1925–1948, the Library of Congress published the State Law Index on a biennial basis, but unfortunately this work has the following limitations: (1) the laws of each two-year period are indexed separately, (2) the indexes are not cumulated, and (3) the work is out of date.   The Aspen Systems Corporation had provided a computer-generated index to current session laws for the years 1964 to 1971.   This is now defunct.   Letter from Aspen Systems Corporation to Stanford Law Library, September 14, 1972.

[5] *See* J. SCHULTZ, COMPARATIVE STATE LEGISLATION (1974).

give citations to law reviews and other secondary sources. The method of supplementation should then be noted (*e. g.*, pocket supplements, bound cumulative supplements, or advance pamphlets). If the set is annotated, the appropriate case annotations should be checked. Frequently it will also be helpful to use the appropriate Shepard's Citator. This will be discussed in Chapter 15.

1. Inoperative State Law

At times the problem being researched may involve an act which has been repealed or is no longer in force. It will then be necessary to consult this law in the code volume that was available when the law was in force, or to consult the session volumes which contain the text of the act as originally passed by the legislature.

SECTION E. MUNICIPAL OR LOCAL GOVERNMENT LEGISLATION

Traditionally the various forms of local government are known as "municipal corporations". Municipalities are instruments of the state and have only such power as granted to them by the state. This will vary from state to state,[6] and the constitution and statutes of the state wherein the municipality is located must be examined.

1. Municipal Charters

In general, municipalities operate under a charter which is the basic document setting forth its power. Usually the charter has been adopted by the voters of a municipality and is analogous to a state constitution. The form of publication will vary, and in the larger cities, may be available in bound volumes.

a. *Ordinances.* Ordinances are the legislative enactments of local jurisdictions, as passed by its legislative body, *e. g.*, the city council or board of supervisors. They are to municipalities what acts are to the state legislatures and the United States Congress. In larger cities, ordinances are first published in an official journal and may be separately published in "slip" form. In smaller communities they are frequently published in the local newspaper.

b. *Codes.* Municipal codes are codifications of ordinances. As with state codes, they generally contain only those ordinances in force at the time of publication and are usually classified and arranged according to a logical plan.

[6] C. ANTIEAU, MUNICIPAL CORPORATION LAW § 12 (1975).

2. Features Common to Most City Codes

a. City Charters

Most city codes include the text of city charters. They usually are unannotated.

b. Text of Ordinances

The texts of city ordinances are the basic information contained in municipal codes. They are rarely annotated with digests of cases.

c. Topical Analyses; Historical Notes; Cross References

In some of the new city codes a topical analysis may precede each chapter. The history of the sections, references to pertinent state law and notations to related provisions in the city code may be given after the text of each ordinance or in footnotes.

d. Indexes

The codes are indexed according to various schemes. Some index the charter and ordinances together and some contain separate indexes to each of these units. In a few cities, where the codes are divided into separately bound parts, each part may have a detailed index and/or a broad general index covering all the ordinances.

e. Tables

In some municipal codes, tables are included which show the disposition of the sections of an earlier code and the location of earlier provisions in the current compilation.

3. Interpretations of Municipal Charters and Ordinances

Most city codes are unannotated and do not include annotations of cases interpreting the charters and ordinances. The following are useful in obtaining court decisions for municipal legislation:

a. State Digests.

The reported cases interpreting an ordinance or a charter are included in a state digest. The location of the appropriate key number or paragraph numbers under which such cases are digested may be located through the use of the index or topical outlines to the digest.

b. Treatises.

Both *McQuillin on Municipal Corporations* and *Antieau on Local Government Law* will be helpful in locating court decisions.

c. *Shepard's State Citations.*[7]

This is most useful for finding court decisions which have cited and interpreted municipal laws. See Illustration 61.

d. *Shepard's Ordinance Law Annotations.*

This set is arranged by subject and has annotations on court decisions arising out of city charters and ordinances. See Illustration 61–b.

[7] Shepard's Citations are discussed in Chapter Fifteen.

SECTION F. ILLUSTRATIONS

57. Page from 1973 Missouri Session Laws.

58. Page from the Illinois Session Laws amending a previous session law.

59. Page from an Index volume of West's Wisconsin Statutes Annotated.

60. Pages from West's Wisconsin Statutes.

61. Page from Shepard's Missouri Citations—Ordinance Section, and Municipal Ordinance Digest.

[Illustration 57]

A PAGE FROM THE 1973 MISSOURI SESSION LAWS

370   LAWS OF MISSOURI, 1973

SECTION
   1. Enacting clause.

SECTION
208.150. Maximum monthly benefits—adjustment to cost of living standards.

Be it enacted by the General Assembly of the State of Missouri, as follows:

Section 1. Enacting clause.—Section 208.150, RSMo 1969, is repealed and a new section is enacted in lieu thereof to be known as section 208.150, to read as follows:

208.150. Maximum monthly benefits—adjustment to cost of living standards.—1. Except as provided in subsection 2, the maximum amount of monthly public assistance money payment benefits payable to or on behalf of a needy person shall not exceed the following:

(1) Old age assistance for each person in an amount not to exceed eighty-five dollars;

(2) Aid to the permanently and totally disabled for each person in an amount not to exceed eighty dollars;

(3) Aid to a dependent child, or children, and needy eligible relative caring for a dependent child, or children, in an amount not to exceed thirty-eight dollars for the needy eligible relative, forty-eight dollars for the first child and twenty-nine dollars for each additional child;

(4) Aid or public relief to an unemployable person not to exceed seventy dollars;

(5) To any of the above recipients who do not reside in a licensed nursing home and are completely bedfast and totally disabled, total payment not to exceed one hundred ten dollars per month.

2. The division of welfare shall make a survey of the cost of living needs of recipients of aid to dependent children as of July 1, 1969, and shall adjust standards or budgetary guides for determining minimum costs of meeting needs of such recipients to reflect fully changes in living costs since such standards were last established pursuant to subdivision (19), subsection 1 of section 207.020, RSMo. Upon the adjustment of the living cost standards, the amounts fixed by subdivision (3) of subsection 1 hereof shall be proportionately adjusted.

Approved June 27, 1973.

> A typical state session law. Note how this act specifically refers to the R.S.Mo. (Revised Statutes of Missouri which is its codification of the Missouri session laws) which it is amending.
>
> This is the most common way for states to amend their codes.

new section enacted in lieu thereof, to be known as section 208.151, to read as follows:

Section 208.151. Persons eligible to receive medical assistance.—For the purpose of paying medical assistance on behalf of needy persons and to comply with Title XIX, Public Law 89-97, 1965 amendments to the federal Social Security Act

[Illustration 58]

A PAGE FROM THE 1973 ILLINOIS SESSION LAWS

1239   [LAWS OF ILLINOIS]   PUBLIC ACT 78-407.

PUBLIC ACT 78-407

CHARITIES AND PUBLIC WELFARE.

PUBLIC AID CODE—STANDARDS OF ASSISTANCE—EFFECTIVE
DATE.

(Senate Bill No. 901. Approved August 28, 1973.)

AN ACT to amend Section 12–4.11 of "The Illinois Public Air Code",
approved [ILL. SESS. LAWS] as amended.

*Be it enacted by the People of the State of Illinois, repre-
sented in the General Assembly:*

Section 1. Section 12-4.11 of "The Illinois Public Aid
Code", approved April 11, 1967, as amended, is amended, to read
as follows:
(Ch. 23, par. 12-4.11)
§ 12-4.11.   Standards   of   Assistance-Contents-Limitations.)
Establish standards by which need for public aid will be determined and amend such standards from time to time as circumstances may require.
The standards shall provide a livelihood compatible with
health and well-being for persons eligible for financial aid under

> Another typical state session law. Note, however, how
> this law refers to and amends a previous session law
> rather than a specific section of the Illinois Revised Stat-
> utes (its codification of session laws). With only a cita-
> tion to this session law, a transfer table must be used
> to find where this session law has been codified.

established for care in a group facility appropriate to the person's
condition. Standards established to determine the eligibility of
medically indigent persons for aid under Articles V or VII shall
take into account the requirements of the spouse or other dependent or dependents of the applicant for medical aid.
    The quantity and quality of the items included in the stand-
ards established for food, clothing, and other basic maintenance
needs shall take account of the buying and consumption patterns
of self-supporting persons and families of low income, as determined from time to time by the United States Department of Agriculture, the United States Bureau of Labor Statistics, and other

Changes or additions indicated by *italics* deletions by ~~strikeout.~~

[Illustration 59]
A PAGE FROM THE INDEX TO WEST'S WISCONSIN STATUTES ANNOTATED

L

LA CROSSE, CITY OF
See, also, Municipalities, generally, this index
Educational television facilities, 39.11

LABOR AND EMPLOYMENT—Cont'd
Air conditioning, places of employment, 101.12
Fees for inspection, 101.19

> When doing research in state legislation, the search is started in the index volumes of the state code.
>
> Assume problem under search is whether Wisconsin has a statute prohibiting discrimination in employment due to age.
>
> This illustration shows how statute is located in the Wisconsin Statutes Annotated at Sec. 111.31.

LA POINTE COUNTY
See, also, Counties, generally, this index
Bayfield County, generally, this index
Judicial circuit, Const. Art. 7, § 5

LA SOCIETE DES 40 HOMMES ET 8 CHEVAUX
Generally, 188.12

LABELS
Brands, Marks and Labels, generally, this index

▶**LABOR AND EMPLOYMENT**
Abrogation of defenses, employe's personal injuries, 895.37
Actions and proceedings,
Avoiding, 101.24
Children and minors, street trades, back wages, 103.32
Discrimination, 111.33, 111.36
Employe welfare funds, depletion of assets, 211.14
Unfair labor practices, 111.07
Adverse examination at trial, employe of party to action, 885.14
Advertisements,
Children and minors, 103.81
Disputes, lawful conduct, 103.53
Foreign labor, 103.43
▶Age,
Children and minors, post
▶Discrimination, 111.31 et seq.
Agents. Employment Agents and Agencies, generally, this index
Agricultural Labor and Employment, generally, this index

Unfair labor practices proceedings, 111.07
University of Wisconsin system teachers, termination of employment, 37.31
Veterans, actions to force re-employment, 45.50
Apprentices, generally, this index
Arsenic poisoning, notice by physician treating, 69.53
Assignment of wages,
Discharge of employe, support of wife or children, 247.265
Support of persons, 247.232
Support of wife or children, 52.055, 247.265
Assumption of risk, defense abrogated, 895.37
Bill of human rights, 66.433
Blacklists, 101.24, 134.02
Blind persons, procuring employment, 101.23
Blind-made goods, labels, etc., 47.07
Bond of employe, deposit, 895.41
Books and papers, time book, 103.85
Bootblacks, 103.21 et seq.
Bribery, 134.05
Burden of proof, unfair labor practices proceedings, 111.07
Bus drivers, alcoholics, 346.64
Calculations, places of employment, 101.12
Fees, inspection, 101.19
Cash bond of employes, trust, 895.41
Certificates of age, children and minors, 103.75
Fees, 103.805

[Illustration 60]
A PAGE FROM WEST'S WISCONSIN STATUTES ANNOTATED

111.17   EMPLOYMENT RELATIONS

Library References

Statutes ⊜223.2(19).   C.J.S. Statutes §§ 366, 368.

Notes of Decisions

I. In general

This section did not apply to subsequently enacted section 108.02 where it did not appear that it was legislative intent that prior law should prevail over later enacted law. Salerno v. John Oster Mfg. Co. (1967) 155 N.W.2d 66, 37 Wis.2d 433.

Employment relations board had jurisdiction to determine union's demand for order to pay money in connection with alleged unfair labor practice arising by reason of claimed breach of expired employment contract and had power to make order for payment of money not-withstanding fact that claimed practice arose after termination of contract which was allegedly violated. General Drivers and Helpers Union Local 662 v. Wisconsin Employment Relations Bd. ₁1963) 124 N.W.2d 123, 21 Wis.2d 242.

This subchapter and National Labor Relations Act, 29 U.S.C.A. § 151 et seq., are not so inconsistent on their face as to require holding that the state act has been suspended by the national act. International Brotherhood of Electrical Workers, Local No. 953, A. F. of L., v. Wisconsin Employment Relations Board (1944) 15 N.W.2d 823, 245 Wis. 532.

After locating the citation in the Index, the Section cited to must be read carefully.

Care must be taken to check any supplement that may have been published. In this set, annual pocket supplements are available.

Library References

Labor Relations ⊜47.   C.J.S. Labor Relations § 25 et seq.

SUBCHAPTER II
FAIR EMPLOYMENT

111.31   **Declaration of policy**

(1) The practice of denying employment and other opportunities to, and discriminating against, properly qualified persons by reason of their age, race, creed, color, handicap, sex, national origin or ancestry, is likely to foment domestic strife and unrest, and substantially and adversely affect the general welfare of a state by depriving it

388

[Illustration 60–a]

A PAGE FROM WEST'S WISCONSIN STATUTES ANNOTATED

EMPLOYMENT RELATIONS   **111.31**

of the fullest utilization of its capacities for production. The denial by some employers, licensing agencies and labor unions of employment opportunities to such persons solely because of their age, race, creed, color, handicap, sex, national origin or ancestry, and discrimination against them in employment, tends to deprive the victims of the earnings which are necessary to maintain a just and decent standard of living, thereby committing grave injury to them.

(2) It is believed by many students of the problem that protection by law of the rights of all people to obtain gainful employment, and other privileges free from discrimination because of age, race, creed, color, handicap, sex, national origin or ancestry, would remove

---

Note how citations are given to the session laws from which Section 111.31 was codified.

Also note cross reference to the Sections of the code where discrimination is prohibited.

---

liberally construed for the accomplishment of this purpose

Historical Note

Source:

L.1945, c. 490, § 3.
St.1945, § 111.31.
L.1959, c. 149, § 1.

L.1961, c. 529, § 1.
L.1965, c. 230, § 1.
L.1967, c. 234, § 1, eff. Dec. 21, 1967.

Cross References

Civil rights, generally, see 42 U.S.C.A. § 1981 et seq.
Discriminations prohibited,
 Accommodations or amusements, see § 942.04.
 Automobile insurance, see §§ 631.36, 942.04.
 Blighted area law, see § 66.43.
 Civil service, see § 16.14.
 Handicapped teachers, see § 118.195.
 Housing, see §§ 66.432, 101.22.
 Housing authorities, see § 66.395 et seq.
 Metropolitan transit authority, see § 66.94.
 National guard, see §§ 21.145, 21.35.
 School pupils, see § 118.13.
 Teacher employment, see § 118.20.
 Urban redevelopment projects, see § 66.405.
 Veterans' housing, see § 66.39.
Equal protection, see U.S.C.A.Const. Amend. 14, § 1.
Equal rights for women, see § 246.15.
Equality and inherent rights of man, see Const. Art. 1, § 1.
Maintenance of free government, see Const. Art. 1, § 22.
Religious tests for public office prohibited, see Const. Art. 1, § 19.

389

[Illustration 60–b]

A PAGE FROM WEST'S WISCONSIN STATUTES ANNOTATED

111.31   EMPLOYMENT RELATIONS

Law Review Commentaries

Discrimination concerning migrant farm workers in Wisconsin. 1951 Wis. L.Rev. 344, 349.

Effect of state statute upon federal requirement for collective bargaining. 1966 Wis.L.Rev. 538 (Spring).

Racial discrimination in denial of union membership. 1958 Wis.L.Rev. 294.

Library References

Civil Rights ⚷9.10 et seq.
Labor Relations ⚷1 to 8.

C.J.S. Master and Servant § 14.

Notes of Decisions

In general I
Racial discriminations 2
Remedies, in general 3

I. In general

Purpose of the Fair Employment Practices Act would clearly not be effectuated if Industrial Commission could do no more than enter an order to cease and desist. Murphy v. Industrial Commission (1968) 155 N.W.2d 545, 37 Wis. 2d 704, rehearing 157 N.W.2d 568, 37 Wis.2d 704.

objection, on racial grounds, of members already there. Ross v. Ebert (1957) 82 N.W.2d 315, 275 Wis. 523.

3. Remedies, in general

Agreement whereby employer was to reemploy complainant conditioned on his ability to perform duties of available work and complainant was to dismiss complaint as to Equal Rights Division of state of Wisconsin did not encompass liability under federal law so as to bar complainant from bringing an action in

> At the end of each Section of the Code, citations are given to Law Review articles published in the state; to the Topic and Key Numbers where cases on this subject are digested, and annotations of all Federal and Wisconsin cases which cited and interpreted this Section.
>
> Most annotated codes are similar to this one.

Vehicle Workers of America, Local No. 25 (1920) 177 N.W. 867, 171 Wis. 532.

2. Racial discriminations

The Fair Employment Code did not give to a colored applicant an enforceable right to union membership over

Circuit court had jurisdiction over action by female employees against employer for back pay based on employer's alleged discrimination because of sex. Murphy v. Miller Brewing Co. (1971) 184 N.W.2d 141, 50 Wis.2d 323.

390

[Illustration 61]

PAGE FROM SHEPARD'S MISSOURI CITATIONS—
ORDINANCE SECTION

E-I   **INDEX TO ORDINANCES**

Elevators
Operator
Requirement ....Kansas City

Employees
Compensation
Kansas City, Adm. Code 56, §202 et seq.
Overtime ....Kansas City
Sick Leave ....St. Louis, Rev. Code 60, 44.230
Working Hours ....Kansas City

Employment
Racial Discrimination
Prohibition
St. Louis, Rev. Code 60, 482.020 Subd. a

F

Fair Housing
Definitions
Discrimination

Disc
O

Fire D
Resp
Sala
Wor
In

Fire I
Buil
W

Firem
Sala

Pen:
Co

Pers
W

St. Louis, Rev. Code 60, 335.280
Retirement
Allowance
St. Louis, Rev. Code 60, 335.230

Flag
Desecration
Penalty ..Kansas City, Gen. Ord. 67, §26.125

Food
Sunday
Closing—Bakeries
St. Louis, Rev. Code 60, 479.020

Fortune Tellers
Prohibition
Kansas City, Gen. Ord. 67, §26.18

Franchises
Cablevision ....Columbia

G

Gambling
Devices
Possession—Penalty
Kansas City, Rev. Ord. 56, §23.050

Garbage
Collection and Disposal
Regulations ....Higginsville
Equipment
Restrictions ....Frontenac
Franchise Agreement
Authorization ....Higginsville
Removal
Franchise—Amendment ....St. Joseph

Gas
Gross Receipts
Taxes—Payment
St. Louis, Rev. Code 60, 155.010

Gasoline Business
Zoning
Building Permit—Requirements ..St. Louis

General Provisions
Newspaper
Publications
Kansas City, Rev. Ord. 56, §1.170

H

Health
Lead-bearing Substances
Prohibition ....St. Louis

Health and Sanitation

§18.152

§18.172

ington

illivan

sailles

191.040

ubd. d

Occupancy—Regulations
St. Louis, Rev. Code 60, 390.080

I

Improvements
Special Tax Bills
Issuance—Lien against Property
Springfield City Code 61, §19-18

Insurance
Personal Injury
Settlement—Authorization ...Independence

Intoxicating Liquors
Beer
Sunday Sale—Prohibition
North Kansas City, Code 60, §8-12
General Regulations
St. Louis, Rev. Code 60, 372.010 et seq.
License
Revocation—Cancellation—Suspension
St. Louis, Rev. Code 60, 372.020
—Disorderly Place
St. Louis, Rev. Code 60, 372.100
Licensed Premises
Accessibility
St. Louis, Rev. Code 60, 372.170
Licenses
St. Louis, Rev. Code 60, 374.010 et seq.
Number—Limitation—Increase ..St. Robert
Package Sales
Regulation—Limitation ....Fairfax
Sale
Closed Hours ....Maryville
Possession—Prohibition ....Kirksville
(Continued)

See note on first page of this division. See 1963 and 1963-1972
Bound Volumes for additional references

288

Each state unit also has a section on City Charters and Ordinances. This "Shepardizes" the charters and ordinances of the major cities within the state.

This section is followed by an index.

Thus, if one is interested in the regulations of fortune tellers, the index indicates which cities have ordinances. The next Illustration gives citations to cases interpreting the ordinance.

[Illustration 61–a]

PAGE FROM MISSOURI SHEPARD'S CITATIONS—
ORDINANCE SECTION

KANSAS CITY ORDINANCES

§ 4.61 Alcoholic Beverages Retail–License– Discretion of Issuance 533SW652	Prohibition 477SW736 518SW38 **§ 11.2** Taxation Cigarettes– Retail Sales–Rate 499SW501	**§ 18.97** Air Pollution Control– Mainte- nance 39KCR74	**§ 20.2** Residential Structures Purpose 495SW68 **§ 20.5** Subd. c	Motels– Rentals– Tax–Use 499SW501 **§ 22.1** Munici- Cour. Trial by Court	ment– Hearing 42KCR13 **§ 25.21** Fortune Tellers Prohibition 30MB283	Public Street 393FS24 **§ 26.35** Offenses Police– Resistance –Obstruc- tion	421US926 44LE83 95SC1650 Subd. a Obscenity Offenses– Sale 421US925 44LE83 95SC1650
§ 4.68 Subd. k Alcoholic Beverages Retail–Dis- orderliness –Indecency –Obscenity –Prohibi- tion 487SW556 **§ 4.69** Subd. e Alcoholic Beverages Retail–By- the-drink –Minors –Prohibited C476SW538 487SW556	**§ 18.** Air Pollut Control– Enforce I 39KCF Subd. Air Polluti Control– Violatic Hearing 39KCR59 **§ 18.94** Air Pollution Control– Board of Appeals 39KCR71						

> This indicates that there is an article in the Journal of the Missouri Bar in which the Kansas City ordinance on Fortune-telling is cited. The bound volumes of Shepard's Missouri citations should be checked first. It will indicate if any cases cited this Section.

§ 4.74 Alcoholic Beverages Retail– Minors– Entry–Pro- hibition 487SW556 **§ 6.50** Dogs Dangerous Disposition –Possession –Prohibi- tion 526SW385 **§ 6.52** Dogs Dangerous Disposition –Public Streets– Prohibition 526SW385 **§ 6.54** Dogs Running at Large– Prohibition 526SW385 **§ 7.9** Auctions Sunday–	Subd. B Air Pollution Control– Board of Appeals– Variances 39KCR74 **§ 18.95** Air Pollution Control– Confiden- tial Records 39KCR76 **§ 18.96** Air Pollution Control– Circumven- tion 39KCR76	Air Pollution Control– Nuisance 39KCR77 **§ 18.102.** 2 Air Pollution Control– Actionable Rights 39KCR77 **§ 18.152** Health and Sanitation Drugs– Possession –Restric- tions 507SW51 525SW337 **§ 18.172** Health and Sanitation Weeds and Noxious Plants– Nuisance 42KCR12 **§ 20.1** et seq. Residential Structures Minimum Standards 495SW71 381FS1364	**§ 20.8** Residential Structures Regulations –Violation 495SW68 **§ 20.24** Subd. d Housing Sanitation –Water Supplies 481SW575 **§ 21.36** Licenses Definitions –Gross Annual Business 512SW916 **§ 21.86** Licenses Construc- tion Com- pany–Fee –Ratio 512SW916 **§ 21.95** Licenses Restau- rants– Gross Receipts– Tax–Use 499SW501 **§ 21.162** Licenses Hotels–	Court City Counselor– Appeal 509SW44 **§ 25.2** Subd. a Nuisances Enumera- tion– Noxious Odors– Substances 42KCR13 Subd. e Nuisances Enumera- tion– Noxious Odors–Es- tablish- ments 42KCR13 Subd. g Nuisances Enumera- tion– Noxious Odors– Vegetables 42KCR13 **§ 25.3** Nuisances Burning– Noxious Odor 42KCR13 **§ 25.15** Nuisances Abatement– Enforce–	468SW23 393FS23 Subd. a Offenses Disorderly Conduct– Offensive Language 524SW119 Subd. c Disorderly Conduct Streets– Congrega- tion C499SW455 39MoL277 **§ 26.13** Offenses Disturbing the Peace– Misde- meanor 502SW411 **§ 26.13.1** Offenses Bodily Injury– Attempt 513SW415 **§ 26.18** Nuisances Enumera- tion– Noxious 42KCR12 **§ 26.25** Offenses Intoxicating Liquor–	**§ 26.68** Offenses Race Dis- crimination Preven- tion–Hotels –Motels– Restau- rants 518SW38 **§ 26.125** Flag Desecration –Penalty Up507SW [385 63FRD677 **§ 26.141** et seq. Obscenity Offenses C510SW689 C515SW488 421US925 44LE83 95SC1650 **§ 26.141** Subd. a Obscenity Offenses– Definitions C510SW692 421US925 44LE83 95SC1650 **§ 26.142** Obscenity Offenses– Provisions	Dissemina- tion 421US925 44LE83 95SC1650 **§ 26.143** Subd. a Obscenity Exceptions– Justified Possession C510SW692 Subd. b Obscenity Exceptions– Noncom- mercial Dissemina- tion C510SW692 **§ 26.144** Obscenity Adjudica- tion 510SW697 C515SW488 **§ 26.159** Offenses Prostitu- tion–Pro- curers– Prohibi- tion 468SW717 **§ 26.160** Offenses Prostitu- tion–Pur- poses–So- licitation 468SW719

See Index to Ordinances. See 1963 and 1963-1972
Bound Volumes for earlier citations

273

[Illustration 61-b]

PAGE FROM SHEPARD'S MUNICIPAL ORDINANCE DIGEST

FORTUNETELLING

EDITORIAL COMMENT. The word "fortunetelling" evokes all kinds of images of witchcraft, sorcery, and magic. At this place, however, we are not concerned with such exotic images, but only with the prosaic matter of local regulations that attempt to see that fortunetellers do not cheat or defraud the gullible. Some cities license them, and others regulate advertising and solicitation.

§ 1. Regulating
§ 2. Prohibiting
§ 3. —Advertising
§ 4. —Soliciting
§ 5. —Where Licensed by State

§ 6. As Fraudulent Device or Practice
§ 7. Not Offense Where Defined but Not Prohibited

• • •

§ 1. Regulating

An ordinance forbidding, and providing a fine for, fortunetelling is a valid enactment in the interest of the peace, good order and safety of the community, and does not offend the right of freedom of religion.

Mo   St Louis v Hellscher (1922) 295 Mo 293, 242 SW 652.

An ordinance making it unlawful to engage in fortunetelling is a valid exercise of delegated police power under charter authority to regulate practices detrimental to the public morals or general welfare.

Mo   Turner v Kansas City (1945) 354 Mo 857, 191 SW2d 612.

§ 2. Prohibiting

This six volume set, published by Shepard's is actually a Digest rather than a Citator.

It is topically arranged and digests all appellate court decisions that have interpreted a city ordinance.

E. g., if research involved the power of a city to regulate Fortunetelling, this set, under that heading, will digest all cases wherein such regulation was the subject of litigation.

It is kept current by annual pocket supplements.

SECTION G. STATE LEGISLATIVE HISTORIES

Generally, state legislatures do not publish their debates, committee reports, or transcripts of hearings held before legislative committees. It is not, therefore, possible to compile a legislative history for a state law as was described in Chapter 10 for federal laws. Yet the need for them in state legislation is just as great as for federal laws since state laws have provisions which are also vague and ambiguous. In most states the only official documents available are the bills as introduced and the Senate and House Journals. These, however, contain only a history of the voting records on the bills and lack explanatory provisions. A few states [8] may have reports of a State Law Revision Commission or the reports of special committees of the legislature for selected laws. If a state has an annotated code, the notes should be carefully examined to see if reference is made to such documents. In most instances, however, extrinsic aids for determining legislative intent are not available and reliance must be made on the language of the act by using the ordinary rules of statutory construction.[9]

SECTION H. SUMMARY

1. Session laws are published after adjournment of the state legislatures for the regular or special sessions and cover the laws enacted during that period.

2. State statutes are compiled, in single or multi-volume editions, under a logical arrangement with the obsolete and revoked laws eliminated.

3. Features Common to Most State Statutes

    a. Constitutions.

        (1) State—usually annotated.

        (2) Federal—usually unannotated.

    b. Text of statutes.

    c. Historical notes.

    d. Comparative legislation.

    e. Annotations.

    f. Tables.

---

[8] Examples of states which publish an annual report are Michigan and California. Louisiana is a state which publishes a biennial report.

[9] *Id.*, Footnote 2.

g.   Research aids.

h.   Cross references to related sections.

i.   Indexes.

j.   Forms.

k.   Popular names of state acts.

l.   Supplementation—cumulative annual pocket parts, pamphlet supplements and replacement volumes.

4.   Martindale-Hubbell Law Directory

a.   *Law Digests* volume contains brief synopses of some statutory laws of all states and selected statutory laws of many foreign countries.

b.   Revised annually.

5.   Inoperative State Law

a.   Consult earlier state code or session laws.

6.   Popular Names of State Acts

a.   In *Shepard's Acts and Cases by Popular Names.*

b.   General index of the state code.

7.   Private, Temporary, Local and Appropriation Acts

a.   Generally, consult session laws.

8.   Municipal Charters—variously published

9.   Municipal Ordinances are the legislative enactments of local jurisdictions

10.   Municipal Codes are codifications of ordinances

11.   Features Common to Most City Codes

a.   Classified.

b.   City charters.

c.   Text of ordinances.

d.   Topical analysis; historical notes; cross references.

e.   Indexes.

f.   Tables.

g.   Supplementation—not always up-to-date.

h.   Annotations in codes are a rarity.

12.   Interpretations to Municipal Charters and Ordinances

a.   Shepard's State Citations.

b.   *Shepard's Ordinance Laws Annotated.*

13. Status and History of a City Charter and Ordinances

    a.   Check Shepard's State Citations.

    b.   Check city code and its supplement.

14. Citation

    a.   Citation form for state and municipal legislation may be found in Appendix A, at (I), (A), (2), (b).

Chapter 12

COURT RULES AND PROCEDURE

This chapter is concerned with the procedures and rules for the conduct of lawsuits in the courts. After the substantive rights of a party have been determined, the lawyer involved may then decide it is necessary to institute an action in court on behalf of the client. The publications discussed herein deal with the procedures for bringing and defending a court suit, and the procedures and methods of appellate courts. Such publications include legislation pertaining to judicial proceedings, the rules promulgated by courts for the conduct of their business, and legal forms used in court proceedings.

SECTION A. COURT RULES IN GENERAL

Rules of courts are legislative in effect, since they control the operation of the court and the conduct of the litigants appearing before it. Court rules relate to such matters as the issuance of complaints, assignment of cases, method of appeal, and the proper method of making motions which are required during the many phases of a court proceeding. In general, the purposes of court rules are (1) to aid the court in performing its business, (2) to establish uniform procedures, and (3) to provide the parties to a lawsuit with information and instruction on matters pertaining to judicial proceedings.

The power of a court to promulgate court rules is found either in its inherent authority or in a constitution or statutory provision.

SECTION B. FEDERAL COURT RULES OF GENERAL APPLICABILITY

Federal court rules are in three categories: (1) the rules of general application such as the Rules of Civil Procedure, the Rules of Criminal Procedure; (2) the Federal Rules of Appellate Procedure; and (3) the individual rules of the various federal courts.

1. Rules of General Application: Unannotated

The Supreme Court of the United States has the authority to issue rules for the other federal courts. The Supreme Court pursuant

to this authority has promulgated rules of criminal and civil procedure for use in the federal district courts and rules pertaining to proceedings in matters of bankruptcy, admiralty, and copyright. The text of the Rules of Criminal Procedure may be found in 18 U.S.C. Appendix. The Rules of Civil Procedure and Appellate Procedure are in 28 U.S.C. Appendix, as well as in volumes 16 and 17 of the *U. S. Supreme Court Digest* (Lawyers Co-op Pub. Co.).

2.   Federal Rules: Annotated

After the promulgation of rules, there frequently is litigation concerning the meaning of the rules and their applicability to specific fact situations. When involved in research of federal procedure, one must often locate court decisions which interpret the rules. The following are useful for this purpose:

a.   *Federal Rules Decisions* (F.R.D.).

This is a unit of the *National Reporter System* and contains cases of the federal district courts since 1940 which construe the Rules of Civil Procedure and cases since 1946 decided under the Rules of Criminal Procedure. Similar to other units of the *National Reporter System*, it first appears in the form of advance sheets and then in bound volumes with headnotes which are classified to the West Key-Number System. In addition to court decisions, it also includes articles on various aspects of federal courts and federal procedure.

b.   *Federal Rules Service* (Callaghan & Co.).

This is a most useful service to use when searching for court decisions construing the Federal Rules of Civil Procedure and the Federal Rules of Appellate Procedure. It is in four sections:

(1) *Federal Rules Service* (First and Second Series). This contains the full text on all federal court decisions construing the Federal Rules of Civil Procedure.

(2) *Federal Rules Digest* (3d ed. 1973).

This seven volume set digests all court decisions from 1955 to date which appear in the *Federal Rules Decisions*. Digests of decisions from 1938 to 1954 are located in the four volumes of *Federal Rules Digest* (2d ed.).

(3) *Federal Local Court Rules.*

(4) *Finding Aids Volume.* This includes a Word Index to the Federal Rules of Civil Procedure and the full text of all the rules. This volume also contains an outline on how to use the entire *Federal Rules Service* set.

3.   Annotated Codes

Both the U.S.C.S. and the U.S.C.A. have volumes which contain the Rules of Federal Procedure, Civil, and Criminal.

a. *United States Code Service, Lawyers Edition.*

This set has several unnumbered volumes of Court Rules. In organization they are similar to the other volumes of the set. The text of each rule is given and then followed by annotations of decisions under the rule. The notes include comments from the Advisory Committee of the Federal Rules, and references to other appropriate sections in other sets of the *Total Client Library Service.*

b. *United States Code Annotated.*

The Rules of Civil Procedure are in volumes following Title 28, and the Rules of Criminal Procedure are in volumes following Title 18. Each rule is followed by editorial annotations and Advisory Committee notes.

4. Treatises

There are many treatises pertaining to the practice and procedure of the federal courts. They generally contain the text of appropriate statutes and the Rules of Federal Civil and Criminal Procedure. The text of each rule is followed by an analysis of the rules, and citations to court decisions are given in the footnotes. The following multivolume sets are most useful in obtaining commentary on federal practice:

a. *Cyclopedia of Federal Procedure.*

b. *Moore's Federal Practice.*

c. *West's Federal Practice Manual.*

d. *Wright's Federal Practice and Procedure.*

5. Form Books

Model instruments or forms used in federal practice have also been published and keyed to the Federal Rules. They contain proper terms, phrases, and other essential details needed by an attorney to compose formally correct legal documents. These are practice form books. Other types of form books are discussed in Chapter Nineteen.

a. *Bender's Federal Practice Forms.*

This is a looseleaf publication with annotations and cross references to *Moore's Federal Practice.* The forms cover civil and criminal rules.

b. *Nichols Cyclopedia of Federal Procedure Forms.*

The forms are annotated and cover civil and criminal rules and some administrative agencies.

c. *West's Federal Forms.*

d. U.S.C.S. *Federal Procedural Forms.*

Additional treatises and books of forms may be located by checking the catalog in a law library or in the subject volume of Jacobstein & Pimsleur *Law Books in Print* (1976).

SECTION C. LOCAL COURT RULES FOR FEDERAL COURTS

All federal district courts, the eleven courts of appeal, and the Court of Appeals for the District of Columbia have promulgated court rules. These rules apply only to the court issuing them and are mainly concerned with its operation. They contain rules for filing motions and the preparation of briefs, as well as other rules dealing with the procedure of the court. Rules for the federal district courts may be found in the following publications:

1.   Federal Rules Service. Local Rules Volume

This is a looseleaf volume which contains all of the rules of district courts currently in force. It is arranged in alphabetical order by state, and the volume is kept up to date as amendments and new rules are issued.

2.   Other Sources

Local district court rules may also be found in (a) the court rule volume of the *U. S. Supreme Court Digest* (Lawyers Co-op Pub. Co.), (b) the appendix volumes following 28 U.S.C.A., and (c) individual pamphlets published by each court. However, since these sources are usually only supplemented annually, the *Federal Rules Service* volume discussed above should be consulted for the most current status of the rules.

3.   Rules for the Courts of Appeal

(a). *Federal Rules Service. Local Rules Volume.*

(b). The rules volume following 28 U.S.C.A. contains the federal rules for the courts of appeal.

(c). Each court also issues its rules in pamphlet form, which are available from the clerk of the court.

SECTION D.   FEDERAL RULES OF EVIDENCE

In 1974, the United States Congress enacted Public Law 93–595 which created for the first time a uniform code of evidence providing uniform standards for the admission of evidence in all United States courts. Prior to this enactment, the law of evidence was scattered throughout the court decisions with the law varying from circuit to

circuit. The Federal Rules of Evidence may be found in the following publications:

1. *Rules of Courts Act,* 28 U.S.C. § 2076 (1975).

2. *Federal Rules* (West Pub. Co. ed. 1975).

3. K. Redden & S. Saltzburg, *Federal Rules of Evidence Manual* (1975).

4. P. Rothstein, *Understanding The New Federal Rules of Evidence* (Suppl.1975).

5. J. Weinstein and M. Berger, *Weinstein's Evidence.* 1975.

SECTION E. COURT RULES FOR STATE COURTS

The method of publication of the rules of court varies from state to state.[1] In most states, they are published in the state code or in the state reports.

Treatises on state civil and criminal practice have been published for a number of states. They may be located in the catalog of a local law library or in the subject volume of Jacobstein & Pimsleur, *Law Books in Print* (1976).

SECTION F. SUMMARY

1. **Purposes of court rules**

   a. Aid the court in expediting and performing its business.

   b. Establish uniform procedure for the conduct of the court's business.

   c. Provide parties to a suit with procedural information and instructions on matters pertaining to judicial proceedings.

2. **Publication of Federal Court Rules**

   a. Rules of General Application.
   U.S.C., 18 Appendix and 28 Appendix.
   U. S. Supreme Court Digest, volumes 17 and 18 (not annotated).
   Federal Rules Service.

   b. Rules and Annotations.
   Federal Rules Service (Callaghan).
   Federal Rules Decisions (West).
   U.S.C.A. and U.S.C.S.

---

[1] Checklists of state court rules are found in Klein, *Rules of Court,* 52 LAW LIB. J. 206 (1959) and Blau & Clark, *Sources of Rules of State Courts,* 66 LAW LIB.J. 37 (1973).

    c. Treatises.
Cyclopedia of Federal Procedure.
Moore's Federal Practice.
West's Federal Practice Manual.
Wright's Federal Practice and Procedure.

    d. Form Books.
Bender's Federal Practice Forms.
Nichols Cyclopedia of Federal Procedure Forms.
West's Federal Forms.
U.S.C.S. Federal Procedural Forms.

    e. Local Federal Court Rules.
Federal Rules Service.   Local Rules Volume.

    f. Courts of Appeal Rules.
28 U.S.C.A. *Rules Volumes.*

    g. Federal Rules of Evidence.
See Section D.

    h. State Courts.
Check local card catalog.

Chapter 13

ADMINISTRATIVE LAW

SECTION A. FEDERAL ADMINISTRATIVE REGULATIONS AND DECISIONS: INTRODUCTION

Administrative law has been defined as:

> "The law concerning the powers and procedures of administrative agencies, including especially the law governing judicial review of administrative action. An administrative agency is a governmental authority, other than a court and other than a legislative body, which affects the right of private parties through either adjudication or rule making." [1]

The purpose of this chapter is to explain the manner in which the rules and the adjudication of federal adminstrative bodies are published and how they may be located.

The power of issuing regulations [2] and of adjudication is delegated to administrative bodies by Congress.[3] The increasingly complex problems of security and economy of the last forty years have brought about a tremendous increase in the number of administrative agencies and in the documents produced by them for publication. The normal procedure is for Congress to delegate to an administrative office or agency the power to issue rules or regulations, and in some instances the power to hear and settle disputes arising from the statute. Once an administrative body has been established, the issuance of rules or regulations is fairly simple, unlike the enactment of a statute which must go through the legislative process of Congress. Some agencies, such as the National Labor Relations Board, not only promulgate regulations, but are also authorized to adjudicate disputes between management and labor unions, and the results of their adjudication are published in a format similar to court reports.

All regulations by administrative agencies are issued either under authority delegated to them by a federal statute or by a Presidential Executive Order.

---

[1] 1 K. DAVIS, ADMINISTRATIVE LAW TREATISE § 1.01 (1958).

[2] *See id.* § 2.01, *et seq.*, for a discussion of Congressional authority to delegate legislative power to administrative agencies.

[3] For example, 16 U.S.C. § 824(f) (1970) provides that whenever the Federal Power Commission " * * * shall find that any interstate service of any public utility is inadequate * * *, the Commission shall determine the * * * adequate * * * service to be furnished, and shall fix the same by its order, rule, or regulation * * *."

The types of actions taken by federal agencies may be classified as: (a) rules or regulations, (b) orders, (c) licenses, (d) advisory opinions, and (e) decisions. Each of these may be defined as follows: [4]

a. Rules or regulations. These are statements by an agency of general or particular applicability and which are designed to implement, interpret, prescribe law or policy. Properly promulgated rules and regulations have the same legal effect as statutes.

b. Orders. These are used to describe the final dispositions of any agency matters (other than rule making but including licensing).

c. Licenses. These include any permits, certificates, or other forms of permission.

d. Advisory opinions. Although containing advice regarding contemplated action, they are not binding and serve only as authoritative interpretations of statutes and regulations.

e. Decisions. Federal agencies authorized by law use decisions to adjudicate controversies arising out of the violation or interpretation of statutes and administrative regulations or rules. This function is performed by special boards of review, hearing examiners, and other officers through administrative decisions.

SECTION B. PUBLICATION OF FEDERAL RULES AND REGULATIONS

1. Federal Register

Before 1936, there was no official source for publication of rules and regulations of federal agencies nor indeed were such agencies required to make them available to the public. This resulted in much confusion, as there was no way of determining if a proposed action by a person or company was prohibited by some federal agency. In fact, in one well-known instance, the federal government prosecuted a corporation for violations of an administrative regulation. This case [5] reached the Supreme Court of the United States before the Attorney-General realized that the action was based on a regulation that had been revoked prior to the time the original action had begun.[6]

[4] 5 U.S.C. § 551 (1970).

[5] Panama Ref. Co. v. Ryan, 293 U.S. 388 (1935).

[6] 1 K. DAVIS, *supra* note 1, at 2.06 n. 5.

As a result of the *Panama* case, Congress passed the *Federal Register Act, 49 Stat.* 500, 44 U.S.C. § 1504, *et seq.* (1976). This provided for the publication of the *Federal Register.* It started in 1936 and is published daily (except Saturday, Sunday, or days following official holidays). For any administrative ruling or regulation to be legally effective it must be published in the *Federal Register.* The definition of what is considered to have general applicability and legal effect is as follows:

> " * * * any document issued under proper authority prescribing a penalty or a course of conduct, conferring a right, privilege, authority, or immunity, or imposing an obligation, and relevant or applicable to the general public, members of a class, or persons in a locality, as distinguished from names of individuals or organizations * * *." (1 C.F.R. 1.1, January 1, 1974).

Thus, since 1936, the *Federal Register* contains within it every regulation having legal effect, and amendments thereto, that have been issued by any federal agency authorized by Congress or the President to issue rules or regulations. It now consists of several hundred volumes.

There is no comprehensive index to the *Federal Register.* Indexes are issued in monthly, quarterly, and annual cumulations.

Although the *Federal Register* is the source for publication of regulations, it alone is insufficient to locate the present status of a particular regulation. It is analogous to the *Statutes at Large.* Although the latter contains every law ever passed by Congress, it is not useful in locating a statute on a particular subject. For this, of course, the *U. S. Code* must be consulted. In order to give subject access to federal regulations in a similar manner, the *Code of Federal Regulations* was also established. This bears the same relationship to the *Federal Register* as the *U. S. Code* does to the *Statutes at Large.*

2.   Code of Federal Regulations (C.F.R.)[7]

This set is a codification of the *Federal Register* wherein all regulations, and amendments thereto, in force, are codified and brought together by subject. It is in fifty titles similar to the arrangement of the *U. S. Code* and published in pamphlet form. Each year, the pamphlet volumes of the *Code of Federal Regulations* are revised at

---

[7] For a more detailed history of the publication of the earlier editions of the *Code of Federal Regulations, see* E. POLLACK, FUNDAMENTALS OF LEGAL RESEARCH 366–72 (3d ed. 1967).

least once and are issued on a quarterly basis approximately as follows:

Title 1 through Title 16.................as of January 1
Title 17 through Title 27 ....as of April 1
Title 28 through Title 41...................as of July 1
Title 42 through Title 50.................as of October 1

Each new volume when issued contains the text of regulations still in force, incorporating those promulgated during the preceding twelve months, and deleting those revoked. Through this process, all of the regulations first published chronologically in the *Federal Register* and currently in force are rearranged by subject and by agency in the fifty titles of the *Code of Federal Regulations*. For example, all of the regulations issued by the Federal Communications Commission, and still in force, may be located in Title 47 of the *CFR* and are up-to-date through October 1st of the current year.

The contents of the *Federal Register* are required to be judicially noticed [8] while the *Code of Federal Regulations* is *prima facie* evidence [9] of the original documents which were published in the *Federal Register*.

3. Up-Dating The Code of Federal Regulations

After a title of the *CFR* has been newly published as explained above, an agency may issue new regulations or amend or revoke a regulation. These changes will be published in the *Federal Register*. Thus, whenever using a volume of the *CFR*, it is always imperative to ascertain if the section of the *CFR* being consulted has been changed in any way subsequent to the effective date of the regulations in the particular volume of the *CFR*. To accomplish this, two tables must be consulted:

  a. *Cumulative List CFR Sections Affected.* This is a monthly pamphlet which indicates the changes made since the latest publication of the *CFR* volumes. The December issue cumulates all changes for Titles 1–16, the March issue contains all changes for Titles 17–27, the June issue changes for Titles 28–41, and the September issue for Titles 42–50.

  b. *Cumulative List of Parts Affected.* As the list described in 3a above is issued monthly, a further check must be made for any later changes. This is accomplished by checking in the latest issue of the daily *Federal Register* in the section entitled *Cumulative List of Parts Affected*.

[8] 44 U.S.C. § 1507 (1970).

[9] *Id.* § 1510 (1970).

4. Finding Federal Regulations

    a. Index Method. Each year a new index to the *CFR* is issued. This includes in one alphabet both subject items and the names of administrative agencies. The index will refer to the appropriate title and to a specific part within a title. At the beginning of each Part a more specific listing leads one to the Section covering the subject under research.

    b. Parallel Table of Statutory Authorities and Rules. If the citation is known to be a statute or Presidential Executive Order, this table will indicate where administrative regulations promulgated under the authority of the statute or Executive Order will be found in the *CFR*. This Table is located in a separate *Finding Aids* volume of the *CFR*.

    c. Current Regulations. For regulations which may have been promulgated subsequent to the latest volumes of the *CFR*, it is necessary to check the current indexes to the *Federal Register*. Current regulations may also be listed in the *United States Code Congressional and Administrative News Service* or the Advance Pamphlets to the *United States Code Service*. Both of these are discussed in Chapter Nine.

If none of the above techniques are successful in locating a desired regulation, the separately issued and annually revised volume to the *CFR* entitled *Finding Aids* should be consulted for other possibilities.

See Section C for examples of the use of the *Federal Register* and the *Code of Federal Regulations*.

SECTION C.   ILLUSTRATIONS FOR FEDERAL
REGISTER & CFR

Problem: How does one obtain copies of records or documents from the U.S. Department of State?

[Illustration 62]

PAGE FROM ANNUAL INDEX VOLUME TO C.F.R.

Index

STATE DEPARTMENT—Con.

Books, maps, newspapers, etc., 22 Part 132

Certificates of authentication, 22 Part 131

Civil aviation, 22 Part 102

Claims, tort, 22 Part 31

Conduct standards, employees, 22 Part 10

STATE DEPARTMENT—Con.

Vessels, 22 Parts 81, 82, 86–88
  Abroad, transfers, 22 Part 87
  Services fees, 22 Part 88
  Status, 22 Part 81
  U.S., in foreign ports, 22 Part 82
Visas to immigrants and aliens, 22 Parts 41–46

Step 1

Consult latest annual index to the C.F.R. This index is not easy to use as it frequently lacks specific entries.

Note reference to 22 Part 6.

Part 11

Foreign students, 22 Part 62

Gifts and decorations from foreign governments, 22 Part 3

Import controls, 22 Part 91

➤ Information availability. *See* Records, *below.*

Insignia of rank, 22 Part 1

International educational and cultural exchange program, 22 Parts 61–63

Maritime disasters, awards, and seizures, 22 Part 86

Marriages, 22 Part 52

Nationality procedures, 22 Part 50

Nondiscrimination, Federally-assisted programs, 22 Part 141

Notarial and related services, 22 Part 92

Organization, 22 Part 5

Passports, 22 Part 51

Personnel, 22 Parts 10, 13, 14

Presidential functions delegated, 3 E.O. 11609

Procurement, 41 Parts 6-1—6-60

Protection and welfare, American citizens; deaths, estates, property, etc., 22 Parts 71, 72

➤ Records:
  ➤ Availability, 22 Part 6
  Classified information, 22 Part 9

Reparations, World War II, 22 Part 112

Seamen, deceased, effects, relief and repatriation, etc., 22 Parts 83–85

Stolen property, Mexico treaty, 22 Part 32

Surplus property located in foreign areas, 22 Part 133

Travel control in time of war or national emergency, 22 Part 53

Peanuts, 7 Part 1300

Steel

Hair and bobby pins, trade practices, 16 Part 39

Manufacturing, effluent guidelines, 40 Part 420

Scrap, trade practices, 16 Part 76

Stocks

See Securities.

Stockyards

See Packers and Stockyards Administration.

Stone

Industry trade practices. *See* Masonry.

Storm Doors and Windows

Industry trade practices, 16 Part 25

Strategic Materials

General Services Administration, 41 Parts 101–14, 101–15

Straw

Standards, 7 Part 57

Strawberries

See also Berries.

Freezing, 7 §§ 51.4435–51.4444

Fresh, grades, 7 §§ 51.3115–51.3124

Frozen, 7 §§ 52.1981–52.1993

Manufacture, grades for 7 §§ 51.4415–51.4426

147

[Illustration 62–a]

PAGE FROM ANNUAL INDEX VOLUME—C.F.R.

Index

→ **Information Availability—Con.**
Social Security Administration, 20 Part 401
Soil Conservation Service, 7 Part 661
→ State Department, 22 Parts 6, 9
Tenessee Valley Authority, 18 Part 301
Trade Information Committee, 15 § 2003.7
Transportation Department, 49 Parts 7, 8
Treasury Department, 31 Parts 1, 2
United States Arms Control and Disarm-

Insignia—Continued
Public Health Service, 42 §§ 21.232–21.242
State Department, rank, 22 Part 1
Veterans Administration, 38 § 1.9

Insular Possessions and Territories
See also Puerto Rico; Virgin Islands; Wake Island.
Air pollution prevention implementation plans:

As with most indexes, references can be found under different entries.

Wage and Hour Division, 29 Parts 516, 850
Wage and Price Stability Council, 6 Part 702
Water Resources Council, 18 §§ 701.200–701.204

Inhalants
Amphetamine and methamphetamine, 21 § 250.101
Amyl nitrate, 21 § 250.100

Injuries
See Accidents.

Insecticides
See Pesticides.

Insects
Honeybees:
Imports, 7 Part 322; 19 § 12.32
Pesticide indemnity payments, 7 §§ 760.100–760.118
Import restrictions, injurious insects, 19 § 12.31
Pesticide programs:
See also Environmental Protection Agency.
Indemnity payments, 7 Part 760
Plant quarantine, 7 Parts 301, 318–320, 330, 351, 352

Insignia
See also Seals; Symbols.
Armed forces, 32 Parts 53, 57
Civil Defense, official, 32 Part 1806
Coast Guard Auxiliary, 33 § 5.63
Federal Home Loan Bank System, 12 § 523.25
4–H Club emblem, 7 Part 8
National Aeronautics and Space Administration, 14 Part 1221

Guam:
Air pollution prevention, 40 §§ 52.2670–52.2673
Apra Harbor, 33 §§ 110.129a, 110.238, 127.1401, 128.1401
Employee compensation, 20 § 25.27
Trade with, 46 Part 277
Water quality standards, 40 § 120.22
Health planning and service, 42 Part 51
Immigration, 8 Part 101
Liquor and articles sent to U.S., 27 Part 250
Navy jurisdiction, 32 Part 761
Panama Canal. See Canal Zone.
Quarantine notices:
Foreign, 7 Part 319
Territorial, 7 Part 318
Sugar industry controls, 7 Parts 801–896
Tax on income from sources within, 26 §§ 1.931—1.934–1
Trade with Guam, Wake, and Midway, 46 Part 277

Insulin
Certification, packaging, labeling, 21 §§ 201.50, 201.51 Part 429
Definition, 21 § 200.15

Insurance
Aged, blind, disabled, black lung, etc. See Social Security Administration.
Aircraft:
Liability insurance; air carriers, air taxis, 14 §§ 208.10–208.15, 296.51, 298.41–298.45
War risk insurance, 14 Part 198
Companies, financial statements, 17 §§ 210.7–01—210.7a–06, 210.12–23—210.12–31a
Credit Union accounts, 12 Parts 740–746
Crime insurance, 24 Parts 1930–1934

[Illustration 63]

PAGE FROM PARALLEL TABLE OF STATUTORY AUTHORITIES AND RULES

5 U.S.C. 552   **Finding Aids**

United States Code	Code of Federal Regulations
5 U. S. C. 552 _____	15 CFR Part 911
	Part 950
	16 CFR Part 14
	17 CFR Part 140
	Part 200
	18 CFR Part 3
	19 CFR Part 103
	21 CFR Part 2
	22 CFR Parts 5–6
	Part 212
	Parts 302–303
	Parts 503–504
	Parts 602–603
	Part 1002
	24 CFR Part 15
	26 CFR Part 601
	27 CFR Part 71
	28 CFR Part 16
	29 CFR Part 2
	Part 14
	Parts 70–71
	Part 570
	Parts 1401–1404
	Parts 1610–1801
	Part 1913
	31 CFR Part 1
	Part 256
	Part 270
	Part 323
	32 CFR Part 64
	Part 66
	Part 75
	Part 100
	Part 138
	Parts 168–169a
	Part 213
	Part 245
	Part 275
	Parts 286–287
	Parts 290–293
	Part 295
	Part 518
	Part 735
	Parts 806–806a
	Part 813a
	Part 1285
	Part 1480
	Part 1701
	Part 1705
	Part 1813
	Part 1900
	33 CFR Part 1
	Part 3
	Parts 85–91
	Part 96
	Part 136
	35 CFR Part 9
	36 CFR Part 200
	37 CFR Part 1
	39 CFR Part 111
	Part 262
	Part 601
	Part 3002

> **Step 1–a: Alternative Method of Finding C.F.R. Regulations.**
>
> When the U.S.C. citation which delegates power to issue regulations to an agency is known, this Table in the Finding Aids volume of C.F.R. can be used to locate citations to regulations in the C.F.R. E.g., 5 U.S.C. 552 is the statutory authority for agencies to issue regulations for release of their records.

14

[Illustration 64]
PAGE FROM TITLE 22 OF C.F.R.

Chapter I—Department of State   § 6.1

Subject matter	Office	Address
Appointment of Foreign Service Officers.	Board of Examiners for the Foreign Service.	Department of State, Annex 8, 1900 E Street NW., Washington, D.C. 20520.
Authentication and other services____	Records Services Division___	Department of State, Room 1237, 2201 C Street NW., Washington, D.C. 20520.
Claims and stolen property_____	Legal Adviser_____	Department of State, 2201 C Street NW., Washington, D.C. 2052?.
International educational and cultural exchange program.	Bureau of Educational and Cultural Affairs.	Department of State, 2201 C Street NW., Washington, D.C. 20520.
International traffic in arms_____	Office of Munitions Control.	Department of State, Annex 6, Room 103, 2121 Pennsylvania Avenue NW., Washington, D.C. 20520.
Nationality and passports_____	Passport Office_____	Department of State, Annex 17, Room 102, 17th and H Streets NW., Washington, D.C. 20524.
Protection and welfare of U.S. citizens, shipping and seamen, and other consular services abroad.	Office of Special Consular Services.	Department of State, 2201 C Street NW., Washington, D.C. 20520.
Visa issuance_____	Visa Office_____	Department of State, Annex 2, 515 22d Street NW., Washington, D.C. 20520.

§ 5.4 Substantive rules of general applicability adopted as authorized by law, and statements of general policy or interpretation of general applicability formulated and adopted by the agency.

(16) Department of State Procurement. 41 CFR 6–1 et seq.

(c) These regulations are supplemented from time to time by amendments appearing initially in the FEDERAL REGISTER.

PART 6—FREEDOM OF INFORMATION POLICY AND PROCEDURES [1]

Sec.
6.1 Definitions.
6.2 Availability of records.
6.3 Executive Order 11652.
6.4 Records which may be exempt from disclosure.
6.5 Classified records and information from other agencies.
6.6 Authority to release and certify; authority to withhold records.
6.7 Time limits.
6.8 Appeals.
6.9 Public reading room.
6.10 Manner of requesting records.
6.11 Requests addressed to Foreign Service posts.
6.12 Closing requests.
6.13 Subsequent requests for same records.
6.14 Schedule of fees and method of payment for services rendered.
6.15 Opening of records for nonofficial research.
6.16 Activities of advisory committees.

AUTHORITY: Sec. 4 of the Act of May 26, 1949, as amended (63 Stat. 111) (22 U.S.C. 2658); E.O. 11652, 37 FR 5209 (5 U.S.C. 552) (Pub. L. 93–502).

SOURCE: Dept. Reg. 108.711, 40 FR 7256, Feb. 19, 1975, unless otherwise noted.

§ 6.1 Definitions.

As used in this part, the following definitions shall apply:

(a) The term "identifiable" means, in the context of a request for a record, a

[1] 37 F.R. 18616, Sept. 14, 1972.

Step 2

Refer to the Part indicated in the Index. After each Part, a detailed list of sections of the Part is given. In this instance, section 6.6 is probably the relevant one.

Note how at the end of the listing of the sections, the statutory authority for this regulation is given as well as the citation where this regulation originally appeared in the Federal Register.

This information is given for each Part in the C.F.R.

---

(11) Other Consular Services Abroad. 22 CFR 91 et seq.
(12) Economic, Commercial and Civil Air Functions Abroad. 22 CFR 101 et seq.
(13) International Traffic in Arms. 22 CFR 121 et seq.
(14) Certificates of Authentication. 22 CFR 131 et seq.
(15) Civil Rights. 22 CFR 141 et seq.

[Illustration 64–a]

PAGE FROM TITLE 22 OF C.F.R.

Chapter I—Department of State § 6.6

clearly unwarranted invasion of personal privacy.

(7) Investigatory records compiled for law enforcement purposes, but only to the extent that the production of such records would: (i) Interfere with enforcement proceedings; (ii) deprive a person of a right to a fair trial or an impartial adjudication; (iii) constitute an unwarranted invasion of personal privacy; (iv) disclose the identity of a confidential source and, in the case of a record compiled by a criminal law enforcement authority in the course of a criminal investigation, or by an agency

ity of the classification to the maximum extent feasible within the time limits for a denial under § 6.7.

(b) When a request for a Departmental record encompasses classified information originated by another department or agency, the request for that information shall be referred to the originator. The requester should be advised of the date and the addressee of the referral. Classified information involving intelligence sources and methods is subject to the control of the Director, Central Intelligence Agency; FBI information (whether or not classified) is sub-

---

Step 3

Read the specific section. Sec. 6.6 sets forth who in the State Dept. has authority to release department records.

When the cover of the Pamphlet (22 C.F.R.) from which this illustration is taken is consulted, it will be seen that it is "Revised as of April 1 (of current or past year)". Hence, it must be ascertained if any changes have subsequently occurred. This is accomplished by checking the pamphlet: C.F.R. Cumulative List of C.F.R. Sections Affected.

See next illustration.

---

a portion of a record shall be considered reasonably segregable when segregation can produce an intelligible record which is not distorted out of context and does not contradict the record being withheld.

§ 6.5 **Classified records and information from other agencies.**

(a) The applicability of the exemption for classified information (§ 6.4(a)(1)) requires a determination that the record in question is specifically authorized under the criteria established by Executive Order 11652 to be kept classified and is in fact properly classified pursuant to that order. This determination shall be made whenever possible before the initial denial under § 6.6(b). It must, in any case, be made prior to the decision of an appeal under § 6.8. No denial should be based solely on the existence of a classification marking on the record, and there shall be a substantive review of the valid-

priate department or agency whether or not classified. The requester shall be advised of the date and the addressee of the referral.

§ 6.6 **Authority to release and certify; authority to withhold records.**

(a) Except as provided in § 6.15, the FOI Director is authorized to furnish copies of any record requested under these regulations which is not the subject of a denial letter under paragraph (b) of this section, and this authority shall include the authority to declassify any such record. The FOI Director is also authorized upon request to provide certified copies of any such record in accordance with Part 131 of this chapter. In order to determine whether a record requested under this Part may be furnished, the FOI Director shall refer the request to the bureau, office, or other unit

13

[Illustration 65]

PAGE FROM C.F.R. CUMULATIVE LIST OF C.F.R. SECTIONS
AFFECTED

Step 4
This List is issued monthly with the December, March,
June and September issues
consisting of the annual cumulation for the titles indicated on the cover.

Cumulative List of CFR Sections Affected

MARCH 1976

SAVE THIS ISSUE
for Annual Cumulation
of Titles 17–27*

CONTAINING:

TITLES 1–16
Changes January 2, 1976
through March 31, 1976

TITLES 17–27
*Changes April 1, 1975
through March 31, 1976

TITLES 28–41
Changes July 1, 1975
through March 31, 1976

TITLES 42–50
Changes October 1, 1975
through March 31, 1976

PARALLEL TABLE OF U.S.C.–C.F.R.

[Illustration 65–a]

PAGE FROM C.F.R. CUMULATIVE LIST OF C.F.R. SECTIONS AFFECTED

MARCH 1976   37

(CHANGES APRIL 1, 1975 THROUGH MARCH 31, 1976)

	Page
701	40682, 44570
	△7514
950	25916, 29954, 52051
951	25916, 29554, 52051
952	2591, 29554, 52051
1000	42749, 58151
	△13367, 13368
1002	△13367
1003	40682, 44570
1004	40682, 44570
1010	44846
	△13367
1020	24528,
	24909, 25830, 26277, 28095, 33828
	△7957, 13368
1030	23877, 27038
1040	25830
1210	40682, 44570
1301	16082 47514
1303	△8078, 8794
1304	30117
	△1498
1308	16082, 23306, 24216, 26676
1401	20542

TITLE 22—FOREIGN RELATIONS

Chapter I—Department of State

6.14	(a) and (b) revised	48503	
➤ 6a	Added	45606	
	Heading corrected	47419	
6a.3	Corrected	51194	
8	Added	28606	
15	Added	50027	
21.1	Table amended	39859	
22.1	(a) CFR correction	36116	
41.6	(b) revised	33444	
	Technical correction	36116	
42.91	(a)(15) revised	42532	

Chapter II—Agency for International Development, Department of State

201.11	(b)(4) amended	34113
203	Revised	△6066
205	Heading and text revised	31754
214	Revised	33205
214.11	(c) revised	54777
214.13	(b)(8) revised	54778
214.33	(a)(2) revised	54778
214.37	Revised	54778
215	Added	45679

Chapter V—United States Information Agency

505	Added	49278

Chapter VI—United States Arms Control and Disarmament Agency

601	Redesignated as Part 606	
	(dated 2–18–76)	△8168
	Revised (dated 1–30–76)	△9318

	Page
602 Heading and text revised	56661
602.16 (e) amended	△8168
602.20 (b) amended	△8168
602.21 Amended	△8168
603 Redesignated as Part 601	△8168
606 Redesignated from Part 601	△8168

Chapter VII—Overseas Private Investment Corporation

707 Added		46284

Chapter XI—International Boundary and Water Commission, United States and Mexico, United States Section

Chapter established		32116
1100 Added		32116
1102 Added		△8475

> **Step 4 (con't.)**
> In this illustration, note how Sec. 6a has been added. This should be checked in the Federal Register at the page indicated to see if it is relevant to the problem under research.

602	36381
603	39663
606	39663
707	36878
1003	36264
1101	△5292

TITLE 23—HIGHWAYS

Chapter I—Federal Highway Administration, Department of Transportation

1.8	Removed	△8168
1.12	Removed	△8168
1.25	Removed (provisions recodified in Part 646 Subpart B)	16057
1.29	Removed	24519
130.403	Amended	△10430
140.603	Amended	△10430
140.604	(c) and (d) amended	△10430
140.606	Amended	△10430
140.607	(a) amended	△10430
140.802	Amended	△10430

Note: Symbol (△) refers to 1976 page numbers

[Illustration 66]

PAGE FROM CUMULATIVE LIST OF PARTS AFFECTED DURING JULY

FEDERAL REGISTER

20 CFR
401_____ 27314
405_____ 27961

21 CFR
5_____ 28261
193_____ 28951
310_____ 28261
510_____ 28264
520_____ 27722, 28264
522_____ 27033, 27316, 28265
558_____ 28513
561_____ 28790, 28951
640_____ 27034
1002_____ 27316
1220_____ 27316
1303_____ 28514
1304_____ 28514
1308_____ 28515

PROPOSED RULES:
128d_____ 28990
436_____ 29413
440_____ 27082
444_____ 29151
448_____ 29413
452_____ 27083
540_____ 28313

22 CFR
➤ 6_____ 29100

29 CFR
40_____ 27318
95_____ 29378
96_____ 29378
403_____ 27318
524_____ 29378
1952_____ 28788

PROPOSED RULES:
1910_____ 27744, 29425
1928_____ 27378, 28797
1952_____ 28313

30 CFR
55_____ 28266
56_____ 28266
57_____ 28266
250_____ 27319
251_____ 27319

31 CFR
103_____ 27831
520_____ 27963

32 CFR
251_____ 27963
286_____ 27074
296_____ 27074
297_____ 27074
705_____ 29101
707_____ 29119

39 CFR
111_____ **28478**, **29136**
244_____ **27353**

40 CFR
35_____ 27966
52_____ 27833, 28491, 28492
60_____ 27967
61_____ 27967
86_____ 29389
124_____ 28493
125_____ 28493
141_____ 28402
180____ 27035, 27355–27358, 28790, 29121
430_____ 27732
454_____ 27968
459_____ 29078

PROPOSED RULES:
128_____ 29156
129_____ 29156
141_____ 28991
180_____ 27741, 28804, 28998
418_____ 29429
430_____ 27741
454_____ 27976

41 CFR
1–1_____ 27723
1–2_____ 27725
1–16_____ 27723
1–18_____ 27725
3–4_____ 27834
Ch. 5A_____ 27037

PROPOSED RULES:
101–20_____ 29188

42 CFR
54_____ 29379
56b_____ 29379
57_____ 29380
101_____ 28686

PROPOSED RULES:
101_____ 28690

43 CFR
419_____ 29084
1720_____ 29122
2110_____ 29122
2530_____ 29122
2550_____ 29122
2560_____ 29122
2740_____ 29123
2760_____ 29123
2812_____ 29123
2820_____ 29123
2860_____ 29122
2910_____ 29123
3100_____ 29122
3810_____ 29122
3600_____ 29122

PUBLIC LAND ORDERS:
5590_____ 27830
5591_____ 27837
5592_____ 28954
5593_____ 28954

PROPOSED RULES:
6220_____ 27380

45 CFR
160_____ 29280
196_____ 29123
250_____ 27300

Step 5

After checking the issues of Cumulative List of C.F.R. Sections Affected, the Cumulative List of Parts Affected should be checked in the Federal Register for the latest changes.

This illustration shows that in July that some change was made to Section 6 starting at page 29100 of the Federal Register.

PROPOSED RULES:
41_____ 27082

26 CFR
Ch. I_____ 28478
PROPOSED RULES:
1_____ 28517, 28523, 28792, 29411
31_____ 28517
301_____ 28523

27 CFR
72_____ 27034

28 CFR
42_____ 28478
45_____ 27317
PROPOSED RULES:
16_____ 27972

PROPOSED RULES:
133_____ 27978

36 CFR
7_____ 27723, 29120
292_____ 29379
PROPOSED RULES:
7_____ 28291

37 CFR
1_____ 27832

38 CFR
3_____ 29120
PROPOSED RULES:
3_____ 27391, 29188
4_____ 27086

SECTION D. PRESIDENTIAL DOCUMENTS

Although most of the contents of the *Federal Register* and the *Code of Federal Regulations* result from the activities of Federal agencies operating under delegated powers from Congress, the President also has the authority to issue regulations that have legal effect. This authority is both constitutional and statutory. The publications of Presidential documents are issued in the following forms.

1. Proclamations

While there is no legal difference between Presidential Proclamations and Executive Orders, the former is customarily used for Presidential action that has no legal effect, such as Proclamation 4352 in which the President (See Illustration 67) designated March, 1975 as Red Cross Month.

    a. Publication of Proclamations.

        (1) *Statutes at Large.*

        (2) *Federal Register.*

        (3) *C.F.R.* Title 3 and compilation volumes of Title 3.

        (4) *U. S. Code Congressional and Administrative News.*

        (5) *U. S. Code Service. Advance Pamphlets.*

2. Executive Orders [10]

These are generally used by the President to direct and govern activities of government officials and agencies.

    a. Publications of Executive Orders. 1a *supra*,[11] except for the *Statutes at Large.*

3. Reorganization Plans

By the provisions of 5 U.S.C. 901 *et seq.* (1976) the President is authorized to examine the organization of all agencies and make changes that provide for the better management of the executive branch of the government. The President is authorized to submit proposed reorganization plans to both houses. If after 60 days neither house has passed a resolution opposed to the plan, it goes into effect.

    a. Publication of Reorganization Plans. The President issues his proposed changes as Executive Orders. In addition to their pub-

---

[10] For a detailed study, *see* HOUSE COMM. ON GOVERNMENT OPERATIONS, 85th CONG., 1st SESS., EXECUTIVE ORDERS AND PROCLAMATIONS: A STUDY OF A USE OF PRESIDENTIAL POWERS (Comm.Print 1957).

[11] To locate Executive Orders issued prior to the publication of the *Federal Register* in 1936, *see* HISTORICAL RECORDS SURVEY, PRESIDENTIAL EXECUTIVE ORDERS (1944).

lication in the sources indicated at 1a *supra,* reorganization plans are published as approved in 5 U.S.C. Appendix.

4. Weekly Compilation of Presidential Documents

This Office of the Federal Register publication is published every Monday and contains statements, messages and other presidential materials released by the White House. It includes an Index of Contents at the front of each issue for documents in it and a quarterly cumulative index at the back. The quarterly indexes are cumulated semi-annually. Other finding aids are: lists of laws approved by the President, nominations submitted to the Senate, and a checklist of White House releases. Similar materials are published in annual volumes entitled *Public Papers of the Presidents.*

SECTION E. U. S. GOVERNMENT MANUAL

This is an annually published directory of general information about the federal government, with emphasis upon the executive branch and regulatory agencies. Each department and agency is described in concise form with citations to the statutes creating the department or agency; a description of functions and authority, names and functions of major officials; organization charts and bibliographies of major publications. Another important feature is the section that gives the history of all agencies no longer in existence and sets forth which agencies, if any, now have jurisdiction over the same subject matter. It is one of the most important reference books for administrative law research. An example of its importance can be ascertained by examining the information it gives for the Civil Aeronautics Board and the Federal Aviation Administration and their predecessor agencies.

SECTION F. FEDERAL ADMINISTRATIVE DECISIONS

1. Agency Decisions

Many federal administrative agencies also serve in a quasi-judicial manner and in performing this function issue decisions. The Federal Communications Commission, for example, is authorized by Congress to license radio and television stations. It also has the authority to enforce its regulations covering the operations of these stations. When stations allegedly violate the terms of the statute or the regulations, the Federal Communications Commission will hear the charges and issue decisions.

Decisions of administrative agencies are not published in the *Federal Register* but in separately published sets of volumes. They are available in two forms: (1) official publications of the Government Printing Office and (2) unofficial publications of commercial publishers. The latter will be discussed in Chapter 14.

a. Official Publications of Federal Administrative Agencies. These are available in most law libraries, and in public and university libraries that are official depositories of the U. S. Government Printing Office. The format, frequency, and method of publications vary from agency to agency. Generally, they are issued on an infrequent schedule, and poorly indexed. Some sets have separate volumes of indexes and digests and it is often necessary to check the indexes in the individual volumes of decisions. Some sets of federal administrative agencies do provide an advance sheet service.

2. Judicial Review of Agency Decisions

After an agency has issued a decision, it may, in most instances, be appealed to the federal courts. These decisions may be found by consulting the following sets:

a. *West's Federal Practice Digest 2d; Modern Federal Practice Digest; Federal Digest.*

b. *U. S. Supreme Court Digest.*

c. *American Digest System* in the absence of the preceding digests.

d. *Shepard's U. S. Administrative Citations.*
(Discussed in Chapter 15).

e. Treatises on administrative law.
(Discussed in Chapter 18).

3. Representative Examples of Currently Published Official Decisions of Federal Administrative Tribunals

a. Civil Aeronautics Board. *Reports,* vol. 2 *et seq.* (1940 to date).

b. Comptroller General. *Decisions,* vol. 1 *et seq.* (1921 to date).

c. Federal Communications Commission. *Reports,* vol. 1 *et seq.* (1934 to date).

d. Federal Power Commission. *Reports,* vol. 1 *et seq.* (1931 to date).

e. Federal Trade Commission. *Decisions,* vol. 1 *et seq.* (1915 to date).

f. National Labor Relations Board. *Decisions and Orders,* vol. 1 *et seq.* (1935 to date).

    g.   Securities and Exchange Commission. *Decisions*, vol. 1 *et seq.* (1934 to date).

    h.   *Treasury Decisions*, vol. 1 *et seq.* (1899 to date).

SECTION G. ILLUSTRATIONS FOR PRESIDENTIAL DOCUMENTS

[Illustration 67]
PAGE FROM TITLE 3A, CODE OF FEDERAL REGULATIONS

Chapter I—Proclamations	Proc. 4352

Proclamation 4352   •   February 24, 1975

Red Cross Month, 1975

By the President of the United States of America

A Proclamation

Since the first settlement on these shores, we Americans have worked together voluntarily to conquer problems and to care for one another in time of adversity. This neighbor-helping-neighbor approach is still with us today and is exemplified by an organization that has become known as the Good Neighbor—the American National Red Cross.

We can all be grateful that the Red Cross is here in time of need. When disasters occur, this Good Neighbor responds with quick and openhanded assistance to help the injured and homeless. When the need is blood, the Red Cross provides this precious fluid from volunteer donors to more than half of this nation's medical facilities. This Good Neighbor, through its first aid and water safety training programs, arms us with the knowledge and skill to save our own and the lives of others. Veterans and members of the military services, often separated far from their loved ones, also turn to the Red Cross for help in time of personal crisis.

> **A Presidential Proclamation issued under the inherent authority of the President.**

than half of the 3,100 Red Cross chapters will be asking Americans to be Good Neighbors by making contributions. In communities where the Red Cross is in partnership with United Way, these chapters will be asking us to lend our time and skills as volunteers in one of their many service programs.

NOW, THEREFORE, I, GERALD R. FORD, President of the United States of America, and Honorary Chairman of the American National Red Cross, do hereby designate March, 1975, as Red Cross Month.

IN WITNESS WHEREOF, I have hereunto set my hand this twenty-fourth day of February, in the year of our Lord nineteen hundred seventy-five, and of the Independence of the United States of America the one hundred ninety-ninth.

GERALD R. FORD

23

[Illustration 67–a]

PAGE FROM TITLE 3A, CODE OF FEDERAL REGULATIONS

Chapter I—Proclamations	Proc. 4360

Proclamation 4360   •   March 29, 1975

Terminating Registration Procedures Under the Military Selective Service Act, as Amended

By the President of the United States of America

A Proclamation

Under authority vested in the President by the Military Selective Service Act (62 Stat. 604), as amended, procedures have been established for the registration of male citizens of the United States and of other male persons who are subject to registration under section 3 of said act, as amended (85 Stat. 348).

In order to evaluate an annual registration system, existing procedures are being terminated and will be replaced by new procedures which will provide for periodic registration.

NOW, THEREFORE, I, GERALD R. FORD, President of the United States of America, by virtue of the authority vested in me by the Constitution and the statutes of the United States, including the Military Selective Service Act, as amended, do hereby revoke Proclamations No. 2799 of July 20, 1948, No. 2937 of August 16, 1951, No. 2938 of August 16, 1951, No. 2942 of August 30, 1951, No. 2972 of April 17, 1952, No. 3314 of September 14, 1959, and No. 4101 of January 13, 1972; thereby terminating the present procedures for registration under the Military Selective Service Act, as amended.

IN WITNESS WHEREOF, I have hereunto set my hand this twenty-ninth day of March in the year of our Lord nineteen hundred seventy-five, and of the Independence of the United States of America the one hundred ninety-ninth.

GERALD R. FORD

> A Presidential Proclamation issued by the President under Congressional authority.

33

[Illustration 68]
PAGE FROM TITLE 3A, CODE OF FEDERAL REGULATIONS

Chapter II—Executive Orders   **E.O. 11884**

Executive Order 11884   •   October 7, 1975

Prescribing the Official Coat of Arms, Seal, and Flag of the Vice President of the United States

By virtue of the authority vested in me as President of the United States, it is hereby ordered as follows:

SECTION 1. The Coat of Arms of the Vice President of the United States shall be of the following design:

SHIELD: Paleways of thirteen pieces argent and gules, a chief azure; upon the breast of an American eagle displayed holding in his dexter talon an olive branch proper and in his sinister a bundle of thirteen arrows gray, and in his beak a gray scroll inscribed "E PLURIBUS UNUM" sable.

CREST: Behind and above the eagle a radiating glory or, on which appears an arc of thirteen cloud puffs gray, and a constellation of thirteen mullets gray.

SEC. 2. The Seal of the Vice President of the United States shall consist of the Coat of Arms encircled by the words "Vice President of the United States."

SEC. 3. The Color and Flag of the Vice President of the United States shall consist of a white rectangular background of sizes and proportions to conform to military custom, on which shall appear the Coat of Arms of the Vice President in proper colors within four blue stars. The proportions of the element of the Coat of Arms shall be in direct relation to the hoist, and the fly shall vary according to the customs of the military services.

SEC. 4. The Coat of Arms, Seal, and Color and Flag shall be as described herein and as set forth in the illustrations and specifications attached hereto and made a part of this Order. These designs shall be used to represent the Vice President of the United States exclusively.

SEC. 5. This Order shall become effective immediately. Executive Order No. 10016 of November 10, 1948, is hereby revoked.

GERALD R. FORD

THE WHITE HOUSE,
October 7, 1975.

A Presidential Executive Order issued under the inherent power of the President.

[Illustration 68–a]

PAGE FROM TITLE 3A, CODE OF FEDERAL REGULATIONS

Chapter II—Executive Orders   E.O. 11851

Executive Order 11851   •   April 10, 1975

Delegation of Authority To Issue Regulations Limiting Imports of Certain Cheeses

By virtue of the authority vested in me by section 204 of the Agricultural Act of 1956, as amended (7 U.S.C. 1854), and section 301 of ⬅
Title 3 of the United States Code, and as President of the United States, it is ordered as follows:

SECTION 1. The Secretary of the Treasury, with the concurrence of the Secretary of State and the Special Representative for Trade Negotiations, in order to implement an agreement concluded in December 1974 with the Commission of the European Communities designed to prevent the transshipment to the United States of certain cheeses on which restitution payments have been made, is authorized to issue regulations:

(a) to prevent the importation into the Customs Territory of the United States, except for the Commonwealth of Puerto Rico, of certain cheeses, originating in member states of the European Communities, upon which restitution payments have been made for export to (1) Puerto Rico, the Virgin Islands, other United States possessions and territories or (2) any country other than the United States;

(b) to prevent the importation of such cheeses into the Commonwealth of Puerto Rico if such cheeses are imported into the Commonwealth of Puerto Rico for transshipment to other areas of the Customs Territory of the United States.

SEC. 2. Heads of departments and heads of agencies are hereby authorized to redelegate within their respective departments or agencies the functions herein assigned to them, except that the function of issuing regulations delegated to the Secretary of the Treasury by Section 1 of this order may be redelegated only to officials required to be appointed by and with the advice and consent of the Senate, as provided by 3 U.S.C. 301.

GERALD R. FORD

A Presidential Executive Order issued by President under Congressional authority.

151

SECTION H.   FEDERAL REGISTER: OTHER FEATURES

In addition to the publication of the rules and regulations from the Office of the President and the executive agencies, issues of the *Federal Register* contain the following features.

1. *Highlights.*   On the front page of each issue, the more important documents are summarized.

2. *Reminders.*   This lists *Rules Going Into Effect Today, Next Week's Deadlines for Comments on Proposed Rules, Next Week's Public Hearings,* and *Next Week's Meeting.*

3. *Proposed Rules.*   This section contains notices of proposed issuance of rules and regulations.   Its purpose is to give interested persons an opportunity to participate in the rule-making process prior to the adoption of final rules.

4. *Notices.*   This section of the *Federal Register* contains documents other than rules or proposed rules that are applicable to the public.

SECTION I.   OTHER METHODS OF FINDING
FEDERAL REGULATIONS

As discussed in the previous sections of this chapter, the rules and regulations and other documents that serve as the written sources for administrative law can all be located through the use of the *Federal Register,* the *Code of Federal Regulations,* and other publications of administrative agencies.   But it is frequently an awkward and time-consuming task necessitating the constant checking of these sources.   In the next chapter, looseleaf services are discussed.   Most of these services consist primarily of documents that appear in the *Federal Register,* or in the publications of administrative agencies.   They are usually better indexed and contain other features facilitating the location of information.   Consequently, when the necessity to research a problem of administrative law arises, it is frequently better practice to ascertain if a looseleaf service covering the topic under research exists and to use that service rather than the official publications discussed above.

SECTION J.   STATE ADMINISTRATIVE REGULATIONS
AND DECISIONS

1.   State Regulations

The regulations and decisions of state agencies are variously published by the states.   In about fifteen states, the administrative regu-

lations are officially codified and published in sets similar to the *Code of Federal Regulations.* In other states, each agency issues its own regulations and it is necessary that inquiries be directed to the pertinent agency.

2. State Administrative Decisions

Many state agencies also publish their decisions. These more commonly are those of the Unemployment Compensation Commissions, Tax Branches, and Public Utility Commissions.

3. Research in State Administrative Law

    a. Check the state code to determine if the state has an Administrative Procedure Act, and if the method of publication for regulations is prescribed.

    b. Check the state's organization manual to determine the agencies which issue regulations or decisions.

    c. Many states have local legal encyclopedias or local administrative law treatises. These should be consulted.

SECTION K. SUMMARY

1. Federal Register

    a. Types of federal documents published in it

        (1) Regulations and Rulings of Federal Agencies.

        (2) Proposed Regulations and Rules.

        (3) Notices of Agencies.

        (4) Presidential Executive Orders.

    b. Indexes

        (1) Monthly, Quarterly, Annually.

        (2) *Cumulative List of Parts Affected.*
        This table brings up to date the monthly issues of *Cumulative List of CFR Sections Affected.*

    c. Frequency of Publication
        Began in 1936. Published Monday through Friday, except on the day following an official federal holiday.

    d. Publications in the *Federal Register* must be judicially noted.

2. Code of Federal Regulations

    a. Contains all regulations which first appeared in the *Federal Register*, are of a general and permanent nature, and are still in force.

b. Arranged by subject in 50 titles similar to the *U. S. Code.*

c. Each title is subdivided into Chapters, Subchapters, Parts, and Sections. It is cited by Title and Section.

d. Each title is in separate pamphlets. Each title is re-published once a year, in which new material is added, and repealed or obsolete regulations are deleted.

e. Regulations published in CFR are *prima facie* evidence of the text.

f. Indexes.

   (1) Annual subject and agency index.

   (2) *Monthly List of CFR Sections Affected.*
       This list indicates any changes in the annual volumes of the CFR.

g. The Finding Aids volume has Parallel Tables of Authorities or Rules, and other aids for assisting in the location of federal administrative documents.

3. U. S. Government Manual

a. Annual Handbook.

b. Describes administrative organizations whose regulations are published in the *Federal Register.*

c. Information on Congress, the federal judiciary and important agency personnel.

d. Subject index.

4. Federal Administrative Decisions

a. Official publications published by U. S. Government Printing Office.

b. Unofficially published by commercial publishers.

5. State Administrative Regulations and Decisions

a. A few states have codified their administrative rules.

b. Some states publish the decisions of administrative agencies.

6. Citation

a. Citation form for Federal and State administrative rules and regulations may be found in Appendix A, at (I), (A), (2), (c).

b. Citation form for Federal and State administrative decisions may be found in Appendix A, at (I), (A), (3).

Chapter 14

LOOSELEAF SERVICES

SECTION A. INTRODUCTION TO LOOSELEAF SERVICES

The rapid growth of statutory and case law has caused a major change in the literature of the law, but it is the expansion of the administrative agency as an arm of the executive branch that has created the greatest obstacle to effective legal research. This is especially true in the area of public law where administrative regulations and rulings play so large a role. Over the past forty years such rules and regulations have shown phenomenal growth, both in numbers and complexity. Thus while cases and statutes can still be located through the traditional means of digests, annotations and citators, research that involves the publications of administrative agencies demands a broadening of the research focus. For example, to adequately research a problem in the law of taxation, a researcher must locate not only relevant statutes and court decisions, but regulations of the Internal Revenue Service and the Treasury Department, rulings of the Commissioner of Internal Revenue, news releases, technical information bulletins, tax court decisions, and other agency documents. A researcher attempting to find the answer to a tax problem using only the *U. S. Code*, the digests, the *Federal Register* and the *Code of Federal Regulations* would find it not only cumbersome but at times impossible.

It was the inaccessibility, complexity and bulk of administrative regulations and decisions that prompted the publication of looseleaf services or reporters by private publishers.[1] As the name indicates, looseleaf services consist of separate, perforated pages in special binders that simplify the insertion, removal and substitution of individual pages. This characteristic allows the publisher to update continuously the material in a process of constant editing, introducing what is new, removing what is superseded. The speed and accuracy afforded by this on-going revision are two of the looseleaf services' greatest values.

The looseleaf format allows for creativity in organizational approach. Most, however, attempt to consolidate into one source the statutes, court decisions and commentary on a particular legal topic. By this means a researcher can find all relevant material, both primary and secondary, in one place. Further, most services provide current awareness notices on the topic, which can include news of

[1] Neal, *Loose-Leaf Reporting Services*, 62 L.L.J. 153 (1969).

proposed legislation, pending agency decisions and even informed rumor.

The convenience, currentness, and excellent indexing of looseleaf services make them the best place to begin researching most administrative law problems. It should be noted that in many rapidly developing areas of the law, like poverty, the environment, consumer protection and others, the looseleaf service may be the only research tool available.

Looseleaf services vary in content and coverage, reflecting both the subject area of the service and the editorial policy of the publisher. This chapter can describe only those features that are common to most services. When using any looseleaf service, one should be alert to its individual characteristics, and special attention should be paid to the introduction and/or prefatory materials supplied by the publisher.[2]

SECTION B. USING LOOSELEAF SERVICES

1. In general

Most looseleaf services have the following common elements:

a. Full text of the statutes on the topic, with significant legislative history.

b. Full text of administrative regulations, and either full text or digests of all relevant court and agency decisions.

c. Editorial comment and explanatory notes.

d. Subject or Topical indexes.

e. Tables of cases and statutes.

f. Indexes to current materials.

g. Current Reports summarizing recent developments. Such reports are issued either weekly, bi-weekly, or monthly.

2. Using Commerce Clearing House or Prentice-Hall looseleaf services

Commerce Clearing House (CCH) and Prentice-Hall (P-H) are two of the major publishers of looseleaf services. Although their publications run the full spectrum of form and content, the underly-

---

[2] This is particularly necessary when using looseleaf services on taxation or labor law. Because of the magnitude of materials, looseleaf services on these subjects are very complex. For more detailed information on taxation, *see* Altman, *How to Make More Effective Use of the Tax Research Tools That Are Available*, 1 TAXATION FOR LAWYERS 366 (1973).

ing organizational principle of each publisher is the same. This allows them to be discussed together.

CCH and P-H services range from those complete in one binder, to those that fill a dozen or more. Regardless of size, they commonly share similar features. They begin with an introductory section that discusses the use and organization of the service. The importance of this feature cannot be over-emphasized. A careful reading of it may save the researcher both time and frustration. The volume(s) will be divided into sections by tab cards. These offer quick access to major topic headings. Typically there will be a comprehensive index to the entire service (Topical Index in CCH, Master Index in P-H). In addition, some services have special indexes to particular topics or volumes. The quality of the indexing is generally quite high, since both publishers strive to provide as many access points as possible.

The indexes are made more useful by the unique, dual numbering system employed in these services. Under this system, in addition to normal pagination, there is a "paragraph" number assigned to each topic area. These numbers may encompass one paragraph or fifty pages. This flexibility of format allows for constant additions and deletions to the text without a total disruption of the indexing system. Research can begin by consulting one of the indexes, which will refer to the appropriate paragraph number. By turning to the correct paragraph number one can locate the pertinent material. In looseleaf services, page numbers are often used only for filing purposes.

The full texts of new court decisions and agency rulings, often supplied as part of the looseleaf service, are generally placed in a separate volume or section. Each case or ruling is commonly assigned its own paragraph number, and can be located in any one of several ways. Most services have tables of cases, statutes, and administrative regulations. When a citation to one of these is encountered, research can begin by consulting the appropriate table and obtaining the paragraph number where the citation is discussed. Both services have special indexes which cross-reference from materials found under the paragraph numbers to materials concerning current developments.

Materials on current developments are generally presented in the form of weekly bulletins that accompany the pages to be filed. These bulletins are often retained as part of the service, and constitute valuable research tools in themselves.

In general, the successful use of CCH or P-H looseleaf services requires the following three steps:

a. Locate where topic or topics under research are dealt with in the service by consulting the Topical or Master Index.

b. Read carefully all materials under paragraph numbers referred to by the Index. When digests of cases are given, note citations to cases so that the full text of decisions may be read.

c. Consult appropriate index or indexes to current materials.

Illustration 69 demonstrates the use of a CCH Service.

3. Bureau of National Affairs, Inc.

.The Bureau of National Affairs (BNA) is the third major publisher of looseleaf services. Its organizational principle differs from that of CCH and P-H. BNA's typical format consists of one or more three-ring binders in which periodic issues (or releases) are filed. Unlike CCH and P-H, the issues do not contain individual pages to be interfiled with existing text, but instead consist of pamphlet-size inserts numbered sequentially and filed chronologically. Thus there is no provision for revision of earlier issues. This format allows for greater speed of issue generation, at the expense of the comprehensiveness guaranteed by the interfiling system.

Each issue contains several separate components, usually including a summary and analysis of major developments, the text of pertinent legislation, and the text or digest of court and agency actions. Such features as important speeches, government reports, book reviews and bibliographies may also be included. Each of these components is generally filed behind its own tab card. Thus each issue is an attempt to keep the practitioner fully informed of all developments in the subject area of the service.

BNA services feature cumulative indexes which offer topic access to the material. Since current issues supplement earlier ones there is no need for paragraph numbers, and simple pagination is used. There are also case tables for each service. BNA periodically supplies special storage binders for old issues, so that the main volumes can always contain current material.

Illustration 70 shows the use of a typical BNA Reporter.

4. Other features of looseleaf services

Looseleaf services aim at providing complete information on a subject. Thus they frequently contain forms, reports on current Congressional activities, summaries of professional meetings, and other news deemed relevant to the researcher or practicing attorney. Those services which include state laws are generally arranged by states with the same paragraph number being assigned uniformly to the same topic for each state. In some instances, "all-state" charts are published which give citations to the various state codes. See Illustration 71.

Many looseleaf services, as already indicated, report the full text of current court decisions that fall within the scope of a particular service. These are filed in a separate section volume since they usually arrive with each mailing. In many instances, at the end of the year, the publisher will send to the subscriber a bound volume of the decisions for permanent reference. The looseleaf pages containing the decisions for the year can then be discarded. As an example, subscribers to Commerce Clearing House *Standard Federal Tax Reports* will receive bound volumes with the title *U. S. Tax Cases*. The latter contain decisions previously sent in looseleaf format. Similarly, subscribers to the BNA's *Labor Relations Reporter* will receive bound volumes called *Labor Relations Reference Manual(s)*, which contain all cases on federal labor law. In all cases, headnotes and other editorial aids are prepared by the publishers. Some of these case series have come to be recognized as standard reference units. Of course, the decisions usually can also be found in official reporters or the *National Reporter System,* but some of these looseleaf sets have become so widely recognized for the speed, accuracy and ease of access that they are cited by the courts.

CCH, BNA and P-H are not the only publishers of looseleaf services, but most services will conform to either the interfiled or supplemented format. If the principles that underlie these forms are understood, any service should be usable. The most vital step will always be a careful reading of the publisher's introductory material. Section C lists looseleaf services by subject.

SECTION C. SELECTED LOOSELEAF SERVICES ARRANGED BY SUBJECT

BNA—Bureau of National Affairs

CCH—Commerce Clearing House

P–H—Prentice Hall

ACCOUNTING

(CCH) SEC Accounting Rules

(CCH) Cost Accounting Standards Guide

(CCH) Accounting Articles

(CCH) Accountancy Law Reports

ADMINISTRATIVE LAW

(Pike and Fischer) Administrative Law, Second Series

ADMIRALTY

(Pike and Fischer) Shipping Regulation.

ANTITRUST AND TRADE REGULATION

(BNA) Antitrust and Trade Regulation Report
(CCH) Trade Regulation Reports

ATOMIC ENERGY

see Nuclear Energy

AVIATION

(CCH) Aviation Law Reports

BANKRUPTCY

(CCH) Bankruptcy Law Reports

BANKS AND BANKING

(BNA) Washington Financial Reports
(CCH) Federal Banking Law Reports
(P–H) Federal Aids to Financing
(P–H) Federal Control of Banking

CARRIERS

(CCH) Federal Carrier Reports
(CCH) State Motor Carrier Guide
(CCH) Federal and State Carrier Reports

COLLEGES AND UNIVERSITIES

(CCH) College and University Reports

COMMON MARKET

(BNA) Foreign Import and Exchange Controls and Common Market
    Manual
(CCH) Common Market Reports

COMMUNICATIONS

see Radio and Television

COMPUTERS

(Callaghan) Computer Law Service

COPYRIGHT

(BNA) Copyright Laws and Treaties of the World

(BNA) BNA's Patent, Trademark & Copyright Journal
(BNA) U. S. Patents Quarterly

CORPORATIONS

(CCH) Corporation Law Guide
(P–H) Corporation Forms Service
(P–H) Corporation Guide
(P–H) Corporation Service
(P–H) Professional Corporation Guide

CREDIT

(CCH) Consumer Credit Guide
(P–H) Consumer & Commercial Credit—Credit Union Guide
(P–H) Installment Sales

CRIMINAL LAW

(BNA) Criminal Law Reporter

DOMESTIC RELATIONS

see Family Law

ENERGY

[see also Nuclear Energy]

(BNA) Energy Users Report
(CCH) Energy Management
(Matthew Bender) Federal Power Service
(P–H) Energy Controls

ENVIRONMENT

(BNA) Environment Reporter
(BNA) Noise Regulation Reporter
(CCH) Pollution Control Guide
(Environmental Law Institute, Wash., D. C.) Environmental Law Reporter

ESTATE PLANNING

(P–H) Estate Planning Ideas & Methods

FAMILY LAW

(BNA) Family Law Reporter

FOOD, DRUGS & COSMETICS

(CCH) Food Drug Cosmetic Law

FOUNDATIONS

see Taxation—Foundations

GOVERNMENT CONTRACTS

(BNA) Federal Contracts Report
(CCH) Government Contract Reports
(CCH) Contract Appeals Decisions

GOVERNMENT EMPLOYEES

(BNA) Government Employee Relations Report
(BNA) The Government Manager

FAIR EMPLOYMENT

(BNA) Fair Employment Practice Service
(CCH) EEOC Compliance Manual
(CCH) Employment Practices Guide

HEALTH AND SAFETY

(BNA) Occupational Safety & Health Reporter
(CCH) Employment Safety and Health Guide

HOUSING

(BNA) Housing and Development Reporter
(CCH) Urban Affairs Reports
(P–H) Equal Opportunity in Housing

INSURANCE

(CCH) Automobile Insurance Law Reports
(CCH) Fire and Casualty Insurance Law Reports
(CCH) Life-Health and Accident Insurance Reports
(P–H) Insurance Guide

INTERNATIONAL TRADE

(BNA) International Trade Reporter

LABOR RELATIONS

(BNA) Policy and Practice Series
(BNA) Collective Bargaining Negotiations & Contracts
(BNA) Construction Labor Report
(BNA) Daily Labor Report
(BNA) Labor Arbitration Report
(BNA) Labor Relations Reporter
(BNA) Manpower Information Service

(BNA) Retail/Services Labor Report
(BNA) Union Labor Report
(BNA) White Collar Report
(CCH) Labor Law Guide
(CCH) Labor Law Reports
(CCH) Labor Arbitration Awards
(P–H) Labor Relations
(P–H) Labor Relations Guide: Occupational Safety & Health
(P–H) Personnel Management
(P–H) Policies & Practices for Personnel
(P–H) Union Contract—Collective Bargaining
(P–H) American Labor Arbitration

LEGISLATION

(CCH) Congressional Index

LIQUOR CONTROL

(CCH) Liquor Control Law Reports

NUCLEAR ENERGY

(CCH) Nuclear Regulation Reports

OIL AND GAS—TAXATION

see Taxation—Oil and Gas

PATENTS

(BNA) Patent, Trademark & Copyright Journal
(BNA) U. S. Patent Quarterly

PENSIONS

(BNA) Pension Reporter
(CCH) Pension Plan Guide
(P–H) Pension and Profit Sharing

POLLUTION

see Environment

POVERTY LAW

(CCH) Poverty Law Reports

PRODUCTS LIABILITY

(BNA) Product Safety & Liability Reporter
(CCH) Consumer Product Safety Guide
(CCH) Products Liability Reports

PUBLIC UTILITIES

(CCH) Utilities Law Reports

RADIO AND TELEVISION & COMMUNICATIONS

(Pike & Fischer) Radio Regulation 2nd series
(laws, FCC rules and regulations, FCC decisions, court decisions, and digest of the decisions)
(P–H) Communications Service

SAFETY

see Health & Safety

SECURITIES REGULATIONS

(BNA) Security Regulation & Law Report
(CCH) Federal Securities Law Reports
(CCH) Blue Sky Law Reports
(CCH) Federal and State Securities Law
(P–H) Securities Regulation Service

SOCIAL SECURITY

(CCH) Unemployment Insurance—Social Security Federal and All-States
(P–H) Social Security-Unemployment Compensation

STOCKS AND BONDS

(CCH) Mutual Fund Guides
(CCH) Stock Transfer Guides
(CCH) New York Stock Exchange Guide
(CCH) American Stock Exchange Guide
(CCH) PBW Stock Exchange Guide
(CCH) Pacific Stock Exchange Guide
(CCH) NASD Manual
(CCH) Midwest Stock Exchange Guide
(CCH) Boston Stock Exchange Guide
(CCH) Chicago Board Options Exchange Guide
(CCH) Commodity Futures Law Reports

TAXATION

(BNA) Primary Sources
(CCH) Federal Tax Guide
(CCH) Federal Tax Guide Reports—Control Ed.
(CCH) Standard Federal Tax Reports (income, excise, estate & gift taxes)

(CCH) Internal Revenue Manual
(CCH) Code and Regulations
(CCH) Federal Income Tax Regulations
(P–H) Attorney's Federal Tax Guide
(P–H) Cumulative Changes in the Internal Revenue Code
(P–H) Federal Tax Citator
(P–H) Federal Tax Guide
(P–H) Federal Tax Service
(P–H) Tax Ideas

TAXATION—BIBLIOGRAPHY

(CCH) Federal Tax Articles

TAXATION—CORPORATIONS

(CCH) Professional Corporation Handbook
(CCH) Pension Plan Guide

TAXATION—COURT DECISIONS

(CCH) Tax Court Decision Reports
(CCH) Tax Court Reports
(P–H) American Federal Tax Reports
(P–H) Tax Court Service

TAXATION—ESTATE AND GIFT

(BNA) Estates, Gifts, and Trusts
(CCH) Federal Estate and Gift Tax Reports
(CCH) Estate Planning Review
(CCH) Provincial Inheritance and Gift Taxes
(CCH) New York Estates Wills Trusts
(P–H) Inheritance Taxes

TAXATION—EXCISE

(CCH) Federal Excise Tax Reports
(P–H) Excise Taxes

TAXATION—FOREIGN

(BNA) Foreign Income
(CCH) Income Taxes Worldwide

TAXATION—FORMS

(BNA) Foreign Income
(CCH) Federal Tax Forms
(P–H) Federal Revenue Forms—With Official Instructions
(P–H) Annotated Tax Forms

TAXATION—FOUNDATIONS

(CCH) Private Foundations Report

TAXATION—INCOME

(BNA) U. S. Income

TAXATION—INTERNATIONAL

(BNA) International Taxation
(P–H) U. S. Taxation of International Operations

TAXATION—MISCELLANEOUS

(P–H) Tax-Exempt Organizations
(P–H) Tax Ideas
(P–H) Wage-Hour Guide

TAXATION—OIL AND GAS

(P–H) Oil and Gas Taxes

TAXATION—PROPERTY

(P–H) Real Estate Federal Tax Guide
(P–H) Property Tax

TAXATION—STATES

(CCH) State Tax Reports
(CCH) State Tax Guide
(CCH) State Tax Case Reports
(CCH) State Tax Guide and State Tax Cases Reports
(CCH) All State Sales Tax Reports
(CCH) Puerto Rico Tax Reports
(CCH) State Personal Income Tax Forms
(CCH) State Corporate Income Tax Forms
(CCH) Unemployment Insurance—Social Security
    Federal and All-States
(P–H) Sales Taxes
(P–H) State and Local Taxes
(P–H) State Income Taxes
(P–H) State Tax Guide

TAXATION—TREATIES

(CCH) Tax Treaties
(P–H) Tax Treaties

TRADE REGULATIONS

see Antitrust & Trade Regulation

TRADEMARKS

(BNA) Patent, Trademark & Copyright Journal
(BNA) U. S. Patents Quarterly

TRUSTS

(P–H) Wills and Trust Forms
(P–H) Wills, Estates & Trust Service

UNEMPLOYMENT COMPENSATION

[see also Social Security]

(P–H) Social Security-Unemployment Compensation

U. S. SUPREME COURT

(BNA) The U. S. Law Week
(CCH) U. S. Supreme Court Bulletin

WILLS

(P–H) Wills, Estates & Trust Service
(P–H) Wills & Trust Forms

WORKERS' COMPENSATION

(CCH) Workmens' Compensation Law

MISCELLANEOUS

(BNA) Daily Report for Executives
(BNA) Executive Compensation
(BNA) Security and Loyalty Reporter
(CCH) Capital Changes Reports
(CCH) Payroll Management Guide
(CCH) Secured Transaction Guide
(CCH) Medicare-Medicaid Guide
(CCH) Consumerism
(CCH) Balance of Payment Reports
(CCH) Urban Affairs Reporter
(CCH) Federal Policy Positions
(P–H) Capital Adjustment Services
(P–H) Executive Report
(P–H) Manual for Managing the Law Office
(P–H) Payroll Guide

SECTION D.   ILLUSTRATIONS

69.   Illustrations showing use of CCH Standard Federal Tax Reporter.

70.   Illustrations showing use of BNA Energy Users Reports.

71.   Page from CCH Employment Practices Reporter.

[Illustration 69]

INDEX PAGE FROM CCH STANDARD FEDERAL TAX REPORTER

Topical Index   **6609**

Labor apprenticeship committee, exempt status 3037.044

Labor liens, priority under state law 5362.8955-5362.9584

Labor management relations examiner, law school course costs 1360.32

LABOR ORGANIZATIONS
. business income of 3237.01
. dues, deductibility 1338.229; 1338.2301
. exemption from tax 3001: 3036:

Laundry trailer, bonus depreciation allowance 1996F.38

Law firms serving public interest, exempt status 3033.4537

Law libraries—see Libraries

Law reporters, withholding of tax on wages 4939.3969

Law school courses, educational expenses .... 1360.25-1360.35 ⬅

Lab
Lab
Lak
  s1
Lak
LAf
. .
. .
. .
. .
. .
LAf
F.

> **Problem:** Can a person who is employed but attending evening law school deduct the tuition and other costs as an education expense?
>
> **Step 1.** Check CCH Topical Index. Note under "Law School Courses" citation to 1360.25–1360.35. These are references to paragraph numbers in the main compilation volumes. Paragraph numbers appear on the bottom of the page. While not shown in these illustrations the same references can be found in the Topical Index under "Education Expense—law school courses."

LAND CONTRACTS
. closing of transaction, year gain
   reported 2831.063
. discount purchases 4085.10
. gain or loss 2831.063; 4460.0101; 4460.0106;
                               4460.0339
. . installment or deferred payment
   contracts 4460.163
. interest included in purchase price ...
                         4460.0101
. Michigan, discount purchases 4085.10
. sale by dealer 4717.5947
. valuation 4460.1643

Land damage awards 932.213

Land purchase contract, price adjusted downward 670.019

LAND TRUSTS
. association status 5950.1092
. Illinois, fiduciary capacity of
   trustee 5670.03
. lien for taxes against 5357.12

Landlord and tenant—see Leases and leaseholds

Landlord-tenant trusts, returns 5017.716

Landscaping improvements in dispute, legal expenses 2006.3362

Last-in, first-out rule of inventory—see Inventories

Lasts, depreciation 1715.161

Late returns—see also Returns 5018; 5520;
                             5522

Laterite, percentage depletion 3554;
                          3557B.016

Laundry, accounting methods 2765.23

Laundry agency, self-employment tax ...
                           4866.198

LAUNDRY AND VALET EXPENSES 1350.144
. traveling expenses 1350.021

. . depreciation deduction 1715.362
. tax planning 244.16
. trust-leaseback, rental deduction 259.12

Leased wires, tax on—Fully covered in the Federal Excise Tax Reporter

Lease-purchase agreements 668.542;
                           1382.5522

LEASES AND LEASEHOLDS
. abandonment 1535.463-1535.468
. acquired for stock, valuation 3510.50;
                     4460.3925-4460.3945
. . bonus value 4460.3932
. . capital stock tax valuation 4460.3925
. . dissolution of corporation,
   reacquisition 4460.3932
. . expenditures capitalized 4460.3932
. . opinion testimony as to value ... 4460.3935
. . par value of stock as basis 4460.3937
. . sales as basis 4460.394
. . savings in rent as basis 4460.3943
. . transferor's basis 4460.3945
. . value of leasehold more than par
   value of stock 4460.393
. acquisition of leases, cost of 1348.441;
        1382.01; 1382.0636; 1382.395; 2219.3093
. ad valorem taxes paid for lessor 1382.525
. adjustments between lessor and
   lessee 1382.50
. advance payments on execution of
   lease 668.506; 668.508
. advances by lessor
. . bad debts 1619.3298
. . capitalization of 2219.30
. agreement determined to be sale
. . capital expenditures 2219.301
. allocation of basis 4512.058
. amortization of cost of lease 1382.01;
            1996.02; 1996.81-1996.88
. anticipated profits 4460.397
. apportionment of depletion between
   lessor and lessee 3558.012
. assigned lease 938.36; 1382.056
. . interest paid 1416.113

[Illustration 69–a]

PAGE FROM CCH STANDARD FEDERAL TAX REPORTER

17,122   TRADE OR BUSINESS EXPENSES—Sec. 162 [page 17,007]

[¶ 1360]   Deduction of Expenses for Education

• • *CCH Explanation*_____

    .01   Rule has been liberalized.—The Commissioner in his regulations has liberalized his rules on the deductibility of expenses for education. Reg. § 1.162-5 at ¶ 1359 will not be applied in asserting deficiencies or denying claims for refund for taxable years beginning before January 1, 1968. Taxpayers may rely on either the new regulations or the prior regulations to claim deductions for such taxable years. Reg. § 1.162-5 as amended by T. D. 6918 applies to all expenses for education for taxable years beginning on or after January 1, 1968 (Rev. Rul. 68-191, 1968-1 CB 67, and T. I. R. 964, January 23, 1968, 687 CCH ¶ 6555). The general rule is that a taxpayer can deduct expenses for education (including research activities) undertaken for the purpose of

    (1) maintaining or improving skills required in his employment or other trade or business, or

    (2) meeting the express requirements of his employer, or the requirement of applicable law or regulations imposed as a condition to the retention by the taxpayer of an established employment relationship, status, or rate of compensation.

> **Step 2:**
>   Obtain volume that contains paragraph number 1360. Although the Index referred to 1360.25–1360.35, one should always turn first to the whole number to the left of the decimal point. This usually contains editorial explanatory matter. Note on top of the page reference to Sec. 162 at p. 17,007. This sets forth the full text of the relevant Internal Revenue Sections. Paragraph 1359 has the full text of relevant regulations.

test, under which educational expenses were deductible if the taxpayer could show that his primary purpose in taking the courses was to maintain or improve skills.)

    The minimum education necessary to qualify for a position or other trade or business is determined from a consideration of such factors as requirements of the employer, applicable laws or regulations, and the standards of the profession, trade, or business involved. The fact that the taxpayer is already performing service in an employment status does not mean that he has met the minimum requirements for qualification in that employment so as to be entitled to a deduction under the improving of skills test.

    Example (1): A taxpayer, who has completed two years of a three-year course leading to an LL.B. degree, is hired by a law firm to do legal research and perform other functions on a full-time basis. As a condition to continued employment, he is required to obtain an LL.B. degree and pass the state bar examination. He completes his law school education by attending night school, and he takes a bar review course in order to prepare for the state bar

¶ 1360.01   Reg. § 1.162-5   © 1975, Commerce Clearing House, Inc.

[Illustration 69–b]

PAGE FROM CCH STANDARD FEDERAL TAX REPORTS

Sec. 162 [page 17,007]—LAW SCHOOL COURSES **17,129**

Similarly, as to expenses incurred by a clinical psychologist in studying to become a psychoanalyst.

S. H. Markham, (DC) 65-2 ustc ¶ 9574, 245 F. Supp. 505.

Similarly, as to expenses incurred by a psychiatrist for psychoanalytic training as a condition to accepting the directorship of a child study center.

H. G. Gianakon, (CA-3) 66-1 ustc ¶ 9355, 358 F. 2d 731.

However, when a psychiatric residency was undertaken to qualify the taxpayer for a new profession, expenses were consequently nondeductible.

However, a licensed attorney, who conducted lectures and demonstration on hypnosis and psychology at a resort hotel, was not entitled to deduct educational expenses incurred in obtaining a Master's degree in general psychology and a Doctor of Philosophy degree in general psychology. His principal purpose in undertaking his education was to become a licensed psychologist rather than for the purpose of maintaining or improving skills required in his work or to meet the express requirements of his employer.

N. Fleischer, (CA-2) 68-2 ustc ¶ 9638, 403 F. 2d 403.

A licensed attorney, who conducted lec-

Step 3:

After reading the CCH explanation, turn to the paragraph numbers to the right of 1360. Starting with .25 are digests of cases and other relevant documents. Caution: full text should be read in the sources cited!

Law School Courses

.25 Accountant.—A practicing accountant could not deduct the cost of books and a law correspondence course. There was no showing that the course was necessary for one who was already a practicing accountant.

A. E. Spitaleri, 32 TC 988, Dec. 23,703.

To the same effect, where the law school expenses of a junior accountant were incurred to obtain a substantial advance in position.

H. A. Huene, (DC) 65-2 ustc ¶ 9488, 247 F. Supp. 564.

To the same effect, where an accountant's primary purpose in entering law school was to become a practicing attorney, which he, in fact, did.

D. Roeberg, 29 TCM 1007, Dec. 30,295(M), TC Memo. 1970-236.

Since an accountant's legal education would lead to qualifying him for a new trade or business, the deduction was disallowed under the 1967 amendment of Reg. § 1.162-5.

M. S. Taubman, 60 TC 814, Dec. 32,111.
P. L. O'Donnell, 62 TC 781, Dec. 32,767, aff'd under CA-7 unpublished opinion rules, 7/23/75.

See, also, .15, above.

⫸→ *Caution: The following cases, under .25, involved years that were not governed by amended Reg. § 1.162-5.* ←⫷

However, law school expenses were deductible where a CPA obtained a law

degree for purposes of improving his skills as an accountant.

W. T. Charlton, 23 TCM 420, Dec. 26,688(M), TC Memo. 1964-59.

Similarly.

F. Kilgannon, 24 TCM 619, Dec. 27,370(M), TC Memo. 1965-118.
C. W. Berry, 30 TCM 465, Dec. 30,785(M), TC Memo. 1971-110.

.26 Air Force employee.—Law school expenses of a civilian Air Force employee were deductible where his legal education improved his skill in writing regulations and policy and procedure documents.

D. P. Frazee, 22 TCM 1086, Dec. 26,261(M), TC Memo. 1963-217.

.27 Chemical engineer.—A chemical engineer employed as a patent liaison engineer could not deduct law school expenses where his primary purpose was to become a lawyer rather than to improve his skills as a patent liaison engineer.

D. H. Pfeffer, 22 TCM 785, Dec. 26,173(M), TC Memo. 1963-163.

Similarly.

J. J. Condit, (CA-6) 64-1 ustc ¶ 9317, 329 F. 2d 153.
J. Lezdey, 23 TCM 485, Dec. 26,714(M), TC Memo. 1964-78.
R. H. Montgomery, 23 TCM 599, Dec. 26,754(M), TC Memo. 1964-101.
J. C. Martin, (CA-4) 66-2 ustc ¶ 9531, 353 F. 2d 35.
R. F. Weiszmann, (CA-9) 71-1 ustc ¶ 9312, 443 F. 2d 29.
N. K. Baker, 51 TC 243, Dec. 29,226.

Reg. § 1.162-5 ¶ 1360.27

[Illustration 69–c]

PAGE FROM NEW MATTERS VOLUME, CCH STANDARD FEDERAL TAX REPORTER

70,314   Cumulative Index to 1976 Developments   20 4-20-76
(Through Report 17)
See also Cumulative Index at page 70,251.

From Compilation   **To New Development**
Paragraph No.   **Paragraph No.**

1352	.1502	*Kowalski*, TC (¶7053)—Overnight test used to determine amount spent. Taxpayer on appeal to CA-9.
	.153	*Kammerer*, TCM—Meal expenses of physician on standby call were nondeductible 7215
	.153	*Liang*, TCM—Resident physician could not deduct cost of meals and sleeping room 7130
	.155	Rev. Rul. 54-497 superseded in part by Rev. Rul. 75-432 .... 6252H
1354	.01	Income tax rules for clergymen—*Rewrite* 8270
	.01	Travel and entertainment expenses—*Illustrative Case* 8301
	.027	Rev. Rul. 56-25 superseded and Rev. Rul. 63-100 revoked by Rev. Rul. 75-380 .... 6250 O

> **Step 4:**
> Each week new materials are filed in a separate volume behind a "New Matter" tab. These are all correlated to materials in the main volume through a Cumulative Index keyed to the Paragraph numbers of the main volumes.
>
> Note all the new matters relating to Paragraph 1360. These will be found under the indicated paragraph numbers in the separate "New Matters" volume. Also, note reference at top of page to "Cumulative Index at Page 70,251." This supplements this index and must be checked.
>
> **Step 5** would be to read the pertinent materials found in the Cumulative Index.

	.2872	Deductibility of sawyer's equipment maintenance expenses—Rev. Rul. 6255S
→1360→	.01	Job-related law courses noncompensatory business expenses—Rev. Rul. 6451
	.01	*Randick*, TCM—Educational expenses were not deductible since not related to existing trade or business 7273
→.01		*Reinhard*, TCM—Hospital administrator's law school expenses not deductible 7139
	.01	Southeast Asian refugees and sponsors—News Release 6255A
	.01	*Stroope*, TCM—Real estate courses 7118
	.05	*Antzoulatos*, TCM—Weiszmann and Weiler applied to pharmacy student's expenses 7083
→	.05	*Melnik*, CA-9—IRS agent's law school costs 9002.4
	.305	Law school courses for foreign lawyer—Rev. Rul. 6257
→	.315	*Melnik*, CA-9—IRS agent's law school costs 9002.4
	.43	*Davis*, TC—Ph.D. study led to permanent faculty appointment 7269
	.43	*Shepherd*, TCM—Education did not improve employment skills 7276
	.48	Treatment of reimbursed expenses.—*Rewrite* (¶8235).
	.55	Educational expenses by employees on job-related educational leave deductible—Rev. Rul. 6454
	.615	*Davis*, TC—Permanent faculty position was trade or business 7269
	.68	*Davis*, TC—Ph.D. study expenses nondeductible because job depended on doctorate 7269
	.688	*Garwood*—Taxpayer's appeal to CA-6 dismissed for lack of jurisdiction 1/28/76.
	.721	*Gino*—Taxpayer and gov't on appeal to CA-9.
1362	.04	*Liang*, TCM—Automobile and office expenses unsubstantiated 7130
	.07	*Kellner*, TCM—Teacher was permitted to deduct cost of professional magazines 7304
	.22	*Kellner*, TCM—Payments made to substitutes not deductible since not made out of teacher's taxable income 7304
1370	.029	*Crescent Wharf & Warehouse Co.* rev'd and rem'd, CA-9—Reasonably estimated accrued self-insurance liability deductible though not paid. *Rewrite* (¶8277).
	.059	*Freeport Transport, Inc.*, TC—Payment for truck route plus seller's services was partly capitalized and partly deductible. *Rewrite* (¶8292)
	.106	*American Foundry*—Taxpayer on appeal to CA-9.
	.125	*Kammerer*, TCM—Resident physician's stipend was compensation 7215
	.125	*Watson Electrical Construction Co.*, TCM—Additional compensation to corporate officer nondeductible because Code Sec. 274 supervened 7206
	.247	*Watson Electrical Construction Co.*, TCM—Corporation's payments to its president were nondeductible because he was not its employee 7206
	.3341	*Saia*—Taxpayer on appeal to CA-5.

¶ 1352   ©1976, Commerce Clearing House, Inc.

[Illustration 70]

USING A BUREAU OF NATIONAL AFFAIRS SERVICE

The BNA Energy Users Reports is typical of many of its services. Its primary purpose is to keep those concerned with energy up to date by providing the text or digests of relevant statutes, regulations, administrative rulings or decisions, and other important information. This service consists of three looseleaf volumes. One is labeled Reference File and contains (1) a master index, (2) policy statements as issued by the President and various agencies, (3) Federal Energy Administration regulations, (4) programs of the various agencies concerned with energy, (5) full text of statutes and Presidential Executive Orders on energy matters. Thus, this volume provides all current primary sources.

The other two volumes contain weekly reports for the current year. Each issue contains summaries of important court decisions, regulations, and other matters concerning energy. This illustration shows how information on petroleum may be obtained.

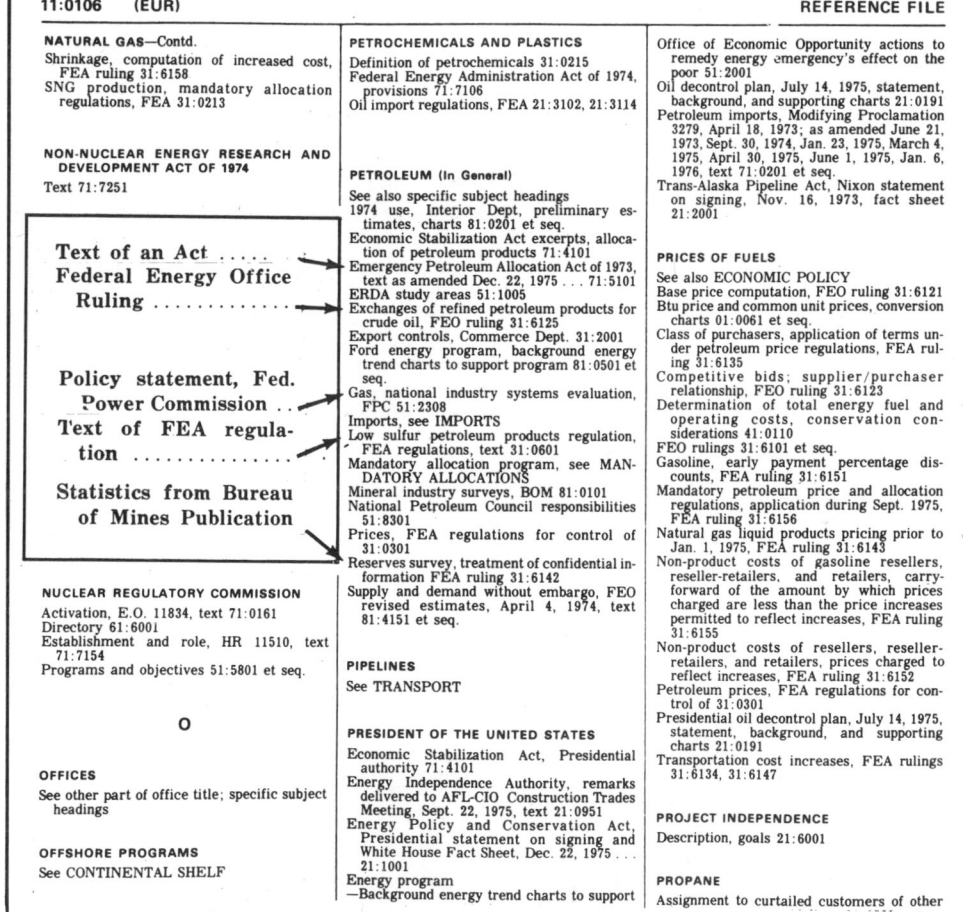

11:0106　(EUR)　　　　　　　　　　　　　　　　**REFERENCE FILE**

NATURAL GAS—Contd.
Shrinkage, computation of increased cost, FEA ruling 31:6158
SNG production, mandatory allocation regulations, FEA 31:0213

NON-NUCLEAR ENERGY RESEARCH AND DEVELOPMENT ACT OF 1974
Text 71:7251

Text of an Act .....
Federal Energy Office Ruling ....

Policy statement, Fed. Power Commission ..
Text of FEA regulation ....

Statistics from Bureau of Mines Publication

NUCLEAR REGULATORY COMMISSION
Activation, E.O. 11834, text 71:0161
Directory 61:6001
Establishment and role, HR 11510, text 71:7154
Programs and objectives 51:5801 et seq.

O

OFFICES
See other part of office title; specific subject headings

OFFSHORE PROGRAMS
See CONTINENTAL SHELF

PETROCHEMICALS AND PLASTICS
Definition of petrochemicals 31:0215
Federal Energy Administration Act of 1974, provisions 71:7106
Oil import regulations, FEA 21:3102, 21:3114

PETROLEUM (In General)
See also specific subject headings
1974 use, Interior Dept, preliminary estimates, charts 81:0201 et seq.
Economic Stabilization Act excerpts, allocation of petroleum products 71:4101
Emergency Petroleum Allocation Act of 1973, text as amended Dec. 22, 1975 ... 71:5101
ERDA study areas 51:1005
Exchanges of refined petroleum products for crude oil, FEO ruling 31:6125
Export controls, Commerce Dept. 31:2001
Ford energy program, background energy trend charts to support program 81:0501 et seq.
Gas, national industry systems evaluation, FPC 51:2308
Imports, see IMPORTS
Low sulfur petroleum products regulation, FEA regulations, text 31:0601
Mandatory allocation program, see MANDATORY ALLOCATIONS
Mineral industry surveys, BOM 81:0101
National Petroleum Council responsibilities 51:8301
Prices, FEA regulations for control of 31:0301
Reserves survey, treatment of confidential information FEA ruling 31:6142
Supply and demand without embargo, FEO revised estimates, April 4, 1974, text 81:4151 et seq.

PIPELINES
See TRANSPORT

PRESIDENT OF THE UNITED STATES
Economic Stabilization Act, Presidential authority 71:4101
Energy Independence Authority, remarks delivered to AFL-CIO Construction Trades Meeting, Sept. 22, 1975, text 21:0951
Energy Policy and Conservation Act, Presidential statement on signing and White House Fact Sheet, Dec. 22, 1975 ... 21:1001
Energy program
—Background energy trend charts to support

Office of Economic Opportunity actions to remedy energy emergency's effect on the poor 51:2001
Oil decontrol plan, July 14, 1975, statement, background, and supporting charts 21:0191
Petroleum imports, Modifying Proclamation 3279, April 18, 1973; as amended June 21, 1973, Sept. 30, 1974, Jan. 23, 1975, March 4, 1975, April 30, 1975, June 1, 1975, Jan. 6, 1976, text 71:0201 et seq.
Trans-Alaska Pipeline Act, Nixon statement on signing, Nov. 16, 1973, fact sheet 21:2001

PRICES OF FUELS
See also ECONOMIC POLICY
Base price computation, FEO ruling 31:6121
Btu price and common unit prices, conversion charts 01:0061 et seq.
Class of purchasers, application of terms under petroleum price regulations, FEA ruling 31:6135
Competitive bids; supplier/purchaser relationship, FEO ruling 31:6123
Determination of total energy fuel and operating costs, conservation considerations 41:0110
FEO rulings 31:6101 et seq.
Gasoline, early payment percentage discounts, FEA ruling 31:6151
Mandatory petroleum price and allocation regulations, application during Sept. 1975, FEA ruling 31:6156
Natural gas liquid products pricing prior to Jan. 1, 1975, FEA ruling 31:6143
Non-product costs of gasoline resellers, reseller-retailers, and retailers, carryforward of the amount by which prices charged are less than the price increases permitted to reflect increases, FEA ruling 31:6155
Non-product costs of resellers, resellerretailers, and retailers, prices charged to reflect increases, FEA ruling 31:6152
Petroleum prices, FEA regulations for control of 31:0301
Presidential oil decontrol plan, July 14, 1975, statement, background, and supporting charts 21:0191
Transportation cost increases, FEA rulings 31:6134, 31:6147

PROJECT INDEPENDENCE
Description, goals 21:6001

PROPANE
Assignment to curtailed customers of other

[Illustration 70–a]

PAGE FROM BNA ENERGY USERS REPORT

INDEX—SUMMARY — REPORTS 125 through 137   (EUR)   15

PENNSYLVANIA—Contd.

Natural gas, intervention requested by state in mandamus suit to require FPC regulation of intrastate sales (CA DC) 125:A-11

PEOPLES REPUBLIC OF CHINA

Japan to increase imports of crude oil from China in 1976, situation analysis 125:A-1

PETROCHEMICALS AND PLASTICS

Baltimore Gas & Electric Co. new SNG plant will require 13 percent of total naphtha used by petroleum industry in 1972, Petrochemical Group views, reactions 132:A-23

PETROLEUM (In General)

See also ENERGY POLICY; PETR ALLOCATIONS; and specific headings
Decontrol of wholesale and retail m of all oil refined products would s sumers billions of dollars annuall views 127:A-5
Defense Dept.'s oil-purchasing prac policies scored by Proxmire (D Jackson (D-Wash) based on GAO formation 126:A-18
Demand, FEA four-week period rep
—Dec. 26 . . . 127:G-2
—Jan. 23 . . . 131:G-1
—Feb. 6 . . . 133:G-1
—Feb. 20 . . . 134:G-1
—March 12 . . . 137:G-5
Drilling activities during 1975, API report summary 129:G-2
Petroleum Data System developed and maintained by Oklahoma Univ., functions 129:C-2
Recovery
—Enhanced oil recovery cutback in ERDA budget proposed, Sharp views 133:E-6
—Increased oil production of oil wells rather than efforts to boost energy supplies by developing shale oil and synthetic fuels may be environmentally favorable, CEQ 134:C-1
—Tar sands, ERDA seeks proposals for demonstration recovery methods 134:E-2
—Waterflooding, ERDA seeks proposals for field demonstration projects utilizing improved techniques 132:E-6
Refiner, reseller, and retailer prices, FEA issues regulations as required by Title IV of EPCA 130:A-15
Reserves
—Development, see LEGISLATION, HR 49
—Naval Petroleum Reserve No. Four federal lands are under authority of Interior Dept. rather than Navy (CA 9) 132:A-24
—Strategic petroleum reserves storage requirements, FEA funding shortages for FY 1976 cited, Zausner and others 135:A-19; OMB seeks cutbacks in FY 1977 budget, situation overview 136:A-31; FEA and OMB remain deadlocked over regulatory programs and policies, status 137:A-31
—Undiscovered recoverable reserve estimates to Jan. 1975, Exxon study findings 137:G-1
Stripper well leases, regulation adopted allowing oil in unitized field to be priced at upper tier levels, FEA 130:A-5

PETROLEUM ALLOCATIONS

See also names of specific resources
Assessment of federal and criminal penalties, FEA proposes revised regulations 128:A-4
Canadian crude-oil imports to U.S., FEA issues allocation regulations 130:A-1

Compliance with federal allocation regulations does not constitute complete defense to breach of contract action for failure to deliver fuel (DC NY) 134:A-10
FEA's authority to promulgate and amend regulations and issue orders under Energy Petroleum Allocation Act of 1973 extended, provisions 127:C-1
Mandatory allocation program, FEA
—Administrative Procedures and Sanctions, temporary stay relief adopted 130:C-3
—Affirmative defense in antitrust litigation eliminated where alleged offense was caused by compliance with Emergency Petroleum Allocation Act of 1973, regulatory amendment 127:A-2
—Amerada Hess' Virgin Islands refinery, foreign treatment proposals rejected 134:A-20
—Crude-oil supplier purchaser freeze rule amendment proposed to reflect changes in domestic crude oil pricing structure under allocation and price control regulations dismissed (US SupCt; rev den) 133:A-14
—Puerto Rican oil firm exempted from refiner rule, FEA decision requiring three major mainland U.S. oil firms to pay cost-equalization relief upheld (TECA) 132:A-18
—Refiner, reseller and retailer prices, revisions to regulations proposed as required by Title IV of Energy Policy and Conservation Act, provisions, text 127:A-1, B-1
—Refiners' profit margins, elimination of regulatory limit proposed 126:A-22
—Residual fuel oil exemption proposed 132:A-20; contingency on proposed entitlement amendments acknowledged, Butler 133:A-38; oil-industry representatives support FEA views and exemption proposal, testimonies 135:A-1f
—Small refiners get limited exemption of obligation to purchase entitlements to cheaper "old" oil under crude-oil price-equalization program, provisions 126:A-14; repeal of provision requested 129:A-23; rule change proposed to modify exemptions and create equitable competitive situation for all refiners 135:A-9; disagreements continue at FEA hearing on proposed change in EPCA provision 137:A-11
—Supplemental fee regulations revised, summary 128:A-3

PIPELINES

See also specific entries under NATURAL GAS
Alaskan natural gas transportation system, FPC and Canadian counterpart should decide by Dec. 1976 on definite system for construction, testimonies before Senate Commerce and Interior Committees 132:A-5; see also LEGISLATION, S 2510, S 2778, S 2950, S 3167
Coal pipeline transportation technology status and feasibility, Keller and others 131:E-1
Treaty initiated by Canada and U.S. to insure free and unrestricted movement of Alaskan oil and natural gas through Canada 130:A-20

Water pipelines, construction of interstate networks with periodic turbine stations to generate electric power proposed, Shoaf 133:E-1

POLLUTION

See AIR QUALITY STANDARDS; ENVIRONMENT (In General)

POWER PLANTS

See specific entries under ELECTRIC POWER; NUCLEAR POWER; UTILITIES

PRESIDENT OF THE UNITED STATES

Congress chided for failure to adopt Admn.'s energy proposals, Ford announces three new programs, summary of statements 134:A-19

PROJECT INDEPENDENCE

See also specific entries under ENERGY POLICY
Failure to meet goals to 1985 without resolution of production and use problems predicted, FEA analysis 135:A-23
FEA second valuation, demand for coal, and consumption of electricity, gas, and oil estimated through 1985 . . . 128:A-2

PROPANE

Export quotas set for first quarter of 1976, Commerce Dept. 127:A-6
Supply-demand "imbalance" shows significant improvement through 1980, Jensen Associates, Inc. report summary 133:A-7

PUBLICATIONS

Coal
—"Energy From Coal: Guidelines for the Preparation of Environmental Impact Statements" 129:C-1
Coal conversion
—Technical publications issued, ERDA, listing 128:D-1
Conservation
—"Energy Requirements for Environmental Control in the Iron and Steel Industry," Commerce Dept. 137:C-1
—"Guide to Energy Conservation for Food Service," FEA 127:C-2
Electric power
—Magnetohydrodynamics bibliography published, ERDA 131:E-2
—"Systems Engineering for Power: Status and Prospects," EPRI proceedings published 131:E-5
—"Typical Electric Bill," FPC 131:G-5
"Energy Information in the Federal Government," FEA 130:C-1
Energy policy
—"National Energy Outlook," FEA 135:A-23

> After checking the Index in the Reference File (previous illustration), the indexes in the two current volumes should be checked for current information.

[Illustration 70–b]

PAGE FROM BNA ENERGY USERS REPORTS

ENERGY USERS REPORT
A weekly review of energy policy, supply, and technology

Number 148   **June 10, 1976**

HIGHLIGHTS OF CURRENT REPORT

AN INFLATIONARY IMPACT STATEMENT on proposed energy efficiency targets for appliances is requested of the Federal Energy Administration by the Council on Wage and Price Stability. The council maintains that FEA has not completed an adequate statement. FEA's choice of 1972 as a base year from which to measure improvement is challenged and it is suggested that price increases resulting from energy-efficiency improvements may cause consumers to shift to less energy-efficient alternatives. A representative of appliance manufacturers urges FEA to reveal the methodology used in developing its proposals (A-35).

THE UNEMPLOYMENT EFFECT OF OIL IMPORTS is inadequately appreciated, an official of a valve manufacturers association tells FEA hearings on the third stage of the agency's new oil price-control program. The witness tells of adverse effects on valve manufacturers of failure to spur domestic oil production and refinery expansion (A-19) . . . FEA Chief Frank Zarb tells the National Industrial Energy Council that FEA plans to submit a proposal to Congress for decontrol of middle distillates during the week of June 13 and a gasoline deregulation proposal by late September (C-2).

AN INVESTIGATION OF AN ALLEGEDLY FORGED MEMO stirs up FEA, and the
Federal Bure   emo suggested expan   ooklet which
later became   **The first page of a weekly**   . . . The
compromise   **report. Each report has be-**   s $5.2
billion durin;   **tween 30 to 40 pages.**   Congressional
Research Se: uthorizes
an interstate   ck trailer
manufacture:

FPC CAN CONSIDER ANTICOMPETITIVE PRACTICES and discriminatory treatment by wholesale power suppliers in establishing wholesale electric-power rates under a June 7 Supreme Court ruling (A-32) . . . Officials of five federal agencies testify against a Senate bill to break up the largest U.S. oil companies. Anticompetitive problems are seen as behavioral rather than structural (A-23) . . . The Temporary Emergency Court of Appeals upholds a court order that an integrated oil company which sold a marketing subsidiary must supply the former subsidiary's gasoline purchasers directly to alleviate inequities (A-34).

THE CALIFORNIA NUCLEAR SAFETY INITIATIVE is defeated by a two-to-one margin. The vote is seen as a setback for nuclear opponents elsewhere (A-28) . . . A large excess uranium-enrichment capacity is seen possibly resulting from a bill to permit Energy Research and Development Administration agreements for developing a competitive private industry (A-30) . . . Glass containment is proposed as the long-sought solution to nuclear waste-disposal problems (A-12) . . . Uranium production must increase fivefold over the next 10 years and by a factor of 13 over the next 25 years, according to a study by The Atlantic Council (A-13).

[Illustration 71]

PAGE FROM CCH EMPLOYMENT PRACTICES REPORTER

101 2-76 **Charts** **8 0 1 5**

Equal Employment Opportunities—Cont'd

¶ 20,080

Broad FEP Law may contain what is separate law in another state, i. e., Equal Pay or Union Discrimination Law	Iowa	Kansas	Kentucky	Louisiana	Maine
CCH Comment	¶ 22,798	¶ 22,998	¶ 23,198	¶ 23,548	¶ 23,598
Fair Employment Practices, Civil Rights or Human Rights Law	¶ 22,800	¶ 23,000	¶ 23,200		¶ 23,600
Equal Pay			¶ 23,300		¶ 23,725
Sex Discrimination	¶ 22,807	¶ 23,008	¶ 23,204—23,208		¶ 23,611
Religious Discrimination	¶ 22,807	¶ 23,008	¶ 23,204—23,208, 23,320		¶ 23,611
Age Discrimination	¶ 22,807		¶ 23,204—23,208	¶ 23,550	¶ 23,611
Union Discrimination	¶ 22,807	¶ 23,008	¶ 23,206		¶ 23,611
Employment Agencies	¶ 22,807	¶ 23,008	¶ 23,205		¶ 23,611

> Several looseleaf services include coverage for
> state laws. In some, the sections containing the full
> text of the state laws are preceded with a chart out-
> lining where the laws on a topic may be found for
> the various states.

Police Records					
Photographs					
Reports—Records—Posters		¶ 23,011, 23,051	¶ 23,250, 23,296		
Affirmative Action Programs					
Defense Contracts					
Administration—Commissions—Agencies	¶ 22,803—22,805	¶ 23,003—23,004	¶ 23,212—23,215, 23,226—23,231		¶ 23,609
Guides—Checklists—Questions and Answers	¶ 22,875	¶ 23,050, 23,055, 23,091—23,093			
Rules—Regulations	¶ 22,885	¶ 23,075	¶ 23,275		
Practice—Procedure—Policies	¶ 22,885	¶ 23,075	¶ 23,275		
Enforcement					
Hospitals					
Utilities					

[The next page is 8015-3.]

Employment Practices ¶ **20,080**

SECTION E.   SUMMARY

1. Each service relates to a special subject.

2. Includes all relevant sources—both primary and secondary.

3. Frequent reports keep contents up-to-date.

4. Contents

    a. Text of statutes on the topic, with significant legislative history.

    b. Text of relevant administrative regulations as published in the *Federal Register*.

    c. Full text, or digests, of all court or agency decisions on the subject.   Some services also provide permanent bound volumes for decisions.

    d. Tables of cases, statutes and regulations.

    e. Indexes to subjects—including indexes to the most current material.

    f. Some services cover state law, with comparative analysis.

5. Best place to start research for subjects governed by administrative regulations and rulings.

6. Citation form for looseleaf services may be found in Appendix A, at (I), (D), (2).

Chapter 15

SHEPARD'S CITATIONS

SECTION A. CASE CITATORS

The previous chapters were directed toward enabling one to locate court decisions relevant to a particular point of law. In most instances, this step is preliminary toward a more concrete goal—a trial or appellate brief has to be written, or an opinion letter composed, or an article authored. Locating cases is undertaken to find rules of law as determined from the reading of the cases, which can then be cited in another document as authority. But before this can be done with any degree of confidence, one further step must be taken. This is to determine that any given case that is to be relied on as authority is indeed still good authority. The decision must be checked to make positive that it has not been reversed by a higher court, or overruled by a subsequent decision of the same court.[1] This is accomplished by the use of *Shepard's Citations*.

These sets of law books provide a means by which any reported case (cited decision) may be checked to see when and how another court (the citing decision) has cited the first decision. For example, assume the problem under research was the constitutionality of a state statute denying the right to vote to ex-felons. During the course of the research the case of *Ramirez v. Brown,* 9 Cal.3d 199, 507 P.2d 1345, 107 Cal.Rptr. 137 (1973) has been found. In this case, the California Supreme Court held such a statute unconstitutional under the Fourteenth Amendment of the United States Constitution. Although this case is exactly in point, it cannot be cited as yet as authority. One must first determine if this case had been appealed to the Supreme Court of the United States, and if so, whether it was affirmed or reversed. If the latter, it is no longer authority and must not be cited as if it were.

---

[1] The failure to properly "Shepardize" can lead to embarrassing situations. One court commented on such an instance as follows: " *   *   * unfortunately, counsel for the defendant quoted extensively from *   *   * the Matter of Newins' Will, 29 Misc. 614, 213 N.Y.S.2d 255 (Sur.Ct., Suffolk County 1961) ; that case was cited as the authority which required plaintiff herein to prove every possible and conceivable fact imaginable before a court of law will declare a marriage null and void. *The court was astounded to find that that case upon which so much reliance was placed by defendant's counsel was reversed by the Appellate Division *   *   * on the point in question and this reversal was affirmed by the Court of Appeals *   *   *.*" (emphasis ours, eds.) Rosenstiel v. Rosenstiel, 43 Misc.2d 462, 475, 251 N.Y. S.2d 565, 578 (Sup.Ct.1964).

Another factor that must be ascertained is whether the California Supreme Court in a subsequent case overruled its decision in the *Ramirez* case (assuming it had not been reversed). Again, if it did so, it can no longer be cited as authority.

This is determined by checking in the *California Shepard's Citations*, or *Pacific Shepard's Citations*. As they list every case subsequently written in which the cited case was mentioned, it can be determined easily if the cited case has been reversed or overruled.

As *Shepard's Citations* presents all citing cases for a cited case, it is evident that its usefulness goes beyond only checking to see if a cited case has been reversed or overruled. The value of a precedent for any given decision also depends to a large extent on the treatment subsequently given to it by courts deciding whether the cited case is in fact applicable to the case under consideration. Whether a cited case has subsequently been followed, distinguished, limited, or questioned may be of vital importance in determining the present value of the cited case as a precedent. Thus, *Shepard's* may be used to determine how a given case has been treated in subsequent decisions.

The court decisions are listed by volume and page in black letter (bold face) type. Under the citation of the case in point subsequent decisions, which have cited the case, are listed by volume and page with letter-form abbreviations indicating the *judicial history* of the case in point and its *treatment* by subsequent decisions. See Illustrations 75–76.

The *history of the case* is indicated by abbreviations showing whether the case was affirmed, reversed, dismissed or modified on appeal. Parallel citations of the cited case in the standard reports are also provided. In like manner, the nature of the *treatment of the case* in point in subsequent decisions is indicated by abbreviations. The introductory pages of each *Shepard's Citations* explain the abbreviations used in the volume. Some illustrative abbreviations of case citations are given below:

History of Case [2]

a (affirmed)	Same case below affirmed on appeal.
cc (connected case)	Different case from case cited but arising out of same subject matter or intimately connected therewith.

---

[2] These abbreviations and their descriptions are embodied in the pamphlet HOW TO USE SHEPARD'S CITATIONS, published by Shepard's Citations, Inc.

D (dismissed)	Appeal from same case below dismissed.
m (modified)	Same case below modified on appeal.
r (reversed)	Same case below reversed on appeal.
s (same case)	Same case as case cited.
S (superseded)	Substitution for former opinion.

Treatment of Case

c (criticized)	Soundness of decision or reasoning in cited case criticized for reasons given.
d (distinguished)	Case at bar different either in law or fact from case cited for reasons given.
e (explained)	Statement of import of decision in cited case. Not merely a restatement of the facts.
f (followed)	Cited as controlling.
h (harmonized)	Apparent inconsistency explained and shown not to exist.
j (dissenting opinion)	Case cited in dissenting opinion.
L (limited)	Refusal to extend decision of cited case beyond precise issues involved.
o (overruled)	Ruling in cited case expressly overruled.
p (parallel)	Citing case substantially alike or identical with law or facts of cited case.
q (questioned)	Soundness of decision or reasoning in cited case questioned.

There is a separate set of *Shepard's Citations* for every set of court reports. Consequently, there are sets of *Shepard's* for each of

the fifty states; separate sets for each of the Regional Reporters of the *National Reporter System*; one set for the *Federal Reporter* and the *Federal Supplement*; and one for the reports of the Supreme Court of the United States.

As most court decisions are reported in two sets, one has to make a determination of which set of *Shepard's* is to be used in *Shepardizing* [3] a case. For example, a case reported in 9 Cal.3d 199 is also reported in 507 P.2d 1345. It can be *Shepardized* in the *California Shepard's Citations* or the *Pacific Shepard's Citations*. When one should be selected over the other will be discussed *infra*.

1. State Shepard's Citations

These are to be used in connection with state reports. As most reported decisions cover more than one point of law, *Shepard's* through the use of superscript figures, keys each citing case to the headnotes of the cited case. For example, the case of *Ramirez v. Brown* as published in the *California Reports* has seven headnotes, each on a different point of law. A citing case may cite *Ramirez* only for the point of law in its third headnote. In order to allow a researcher to find all citing cases which cite *Ramirez* only for the point in its third headnote, *Shepard's* add the superscript "3" to the citing case. By this means, one can find in the *California Shepard's Citations* all subsequent cases that cited *Ramirez* for that point of law.

The state *Shepard's* gives citing cases only from courts within the jurisdiction or cases that originated in a federal court within the state. Additionally, state *Shepard's* gives citations to any legal periodical published in the state (plus 20 national law reviews) that cite the cited cases. It also gives a citation to the reports of the state Attorney-General's opinion that cite the cited cases. State *Shepard's* also have a section or a separate volume arranged by the regional reporter citation. By this means, when only a state unit *Shepard's* is available, it may be *Shepardized* under the state citation, or the regional reporter citation. In both instances, citing cases are given only for the courts within the state.

2. Regional Shepard's Citations

In the example of *Ramirez v. Brown*, this case could also be *Shepardized* in the *Pacific Shepard's* under 507 P.2d 1345. In such instances, that volume has to be examined to determine which headnote or headnotes are of interest. In the *Pacific Reporter*, there are five headnotes and each can be followed in citing cases in the same method as described *supra*. In our example, if the *California Shep-*

---

[3] The term "Shepardizing" is the trade-mark property of Shepard's Citations, Inc. and is used here with reference to its publications only and with its express consent.

ard's is used all of the citing cases given are to the *California Appellate Reports* or *California Reports* or federal cases heard in California. In the *Pacific Shepard's*, all citations to the same citing cases are to the *Pacific* or *California Reporter*. The regional *Shepard's*, unlike the state *Shepard's*, also gives citations to any case throughout the *National Reporter System*. Thus, if a New York case cited *Ramirez v. Brown*, it can be found in the *Pacific Shepard's* but not in the *California Shepard's*. However, the regional *Shepard's* do not give citations to legal periodicals or to Attorney General's opinions.

The choice, then, of when to use a state or regional *Shepard's* is dependent on the research in hand. Illustrations 72–76 demonstrate the *Shepardizing* of the *Ramirez* case in both sets of reports.

3. Shepard's Citations for federal cases

When a case with a *F.Supp., Fed. (F.2)*, or *U. S. Citation* is to be *Shepardized, Federal Shepard's Citations* are used for the first two, and *U. S. Shepard's Citations* for the last.

4. Other Uses of Shepard's Citations

In addition to citing all cases that cite a given case, *Shepard's* also indicates when a case is cited in one of the following:

A.L.R. Annotations,

Legal periodicals articles, (state citators only)[4]

---

[4] Most state units, in addition to the legal periodicals for the particular state, include citations to each of the following law reviews:

American Bar Association Journal
California Law Review
Columbia Law Review
Cornell Law Quarterly
Cornell Law Review
Georgetown Law Journal
Harvard Law Review
Law and Contemporary Problems
Michigan Law Review
Minnesota Law Review
New York University Law Review
Northwestern University Law Review
Stanford Law Review
Texas Law Review
University of California at Los Angeles Law Review
University of Chicago Law Review
University of Illinois Law Forum
University of Pennsylvania Law Review
Virginia Law Review
Wisconsin Law Review
Yale Law Journal

5. Using Shepard's Citations to Find Parallel Citations

In Chapter 5 it was pointed out how, given a state report citation, the *National Reporter System* regional citations could be found through the use of the *National Reporter Blue Book*. *Shepard's* may also be used for this and, additionally, to find the state citation from the regional reporter citation. It always includes the parallel citation as the first citation under the page number the first time the case is listed. When a case has also been reported in *A.L.R.* that is also listed. See Illustration 75.

6. Shepard's Citations as a Research Aid

Although *Shepard's Citations* are very useful research aids, they should not be stretched beyond their normal function.

The editors' use of the letter-form abbreviations to indicate the treatment of cases is intelligently conservative. The essence of a citing case may go beyond its expressed language. The inclusiveness of a case is not identified by the abbreviations unless its expression is clearly stated in the opinion. Therefore, a case which implicitly overrules a cited case will not be marked with the symbol "o" for "overruled." This can be determined only by a careful reading of the case. In other words, although these guides immeasurably facilitate a lawyer's research, there are no substitutes for reading and "squeezing the juices" from cases.

In addition, cases dealing with the same subject matter, which do not cite each other, are not covered by *Shepard's Citations*. Or contrariwise, since the *Shepard* editions are not selective, the citing cases may be so numerous as to create a formidable research problem. A further limitation is that *Shepard's Citations* perpetuate the inaccuracies created by judges who inappropriately cite cases. But these are minor defects which the general utility, comprehensiveness and accuracy of the citators effectively overbalance.

SECTION B. ILLUSTRATIONS: SHEPARD
CASE CITATIONS

[Illustration 72]

PAGE FROM 9 C.3d 199

---

200   Ramirez *v.* Brown
9 C.3d 199; 107 Cal.Rptr. 137, 507 P.2d 1345

Headnotes

Classified to McKinney's Digest

(1)   **Elections § 145—Mandamus to Enforce Obedience to Election Laws —Registration.**—Mandamus to compel election officials to register them as voters was an appropriate procedure for ex-felons by which to seek reconsideration, by the Supreme Court, of the question of the constitutionality of provisions of California law excluding, from the franchise, all persons who have been convicted of an "infamous crime."

(2)   **Courts § 144—Supreme Court—Original Jurisdiction—Validity of Election Laws.**—Challenges to the validity of election laws come particularly within the rule that exercise of the Supreme Court's inherent discretion to resolve an issue which is of broad public interest, which is likely to recur, and which should receive uniform resolution throughout the state, is appropriate even though an event occurring during its pendency would normally render the matter moot.

(3)   **Elections § 22—Electors—Right of Suffrage—Persons Convicted of Infamous Crime—Effect of Changes in Constitutional Provisions.**—There is no difference in substance between the provision in former Cal. Const., art. II, § 1, prohibiting persons convicted of an infamous crime from voting, and the provision of Cal. Const., art. II, § 3, d⎡   ⎤ldi-

ti| |ter-

Headnotes of case from California Reports. There are two more headnotes on the next page.

p rity
w ⸴rn-
n

(4)   **Elections § 22—Electors—Right of Suffrage—Persons Convicted of Infamous Crime—Effect of Changes in Constitutional Provisions.**—No change in legal effect resulted from the fact that Proposition 7, as passed at the November 7, 1972, general election, in substituting Cal. Const., art. II, § 3, for the provision of former Cal. Const., art. II, § 1, declaring that, among others, no person convicted of any infamous crime shall "ever" exercise the privileges of an elector, deleted the word "ever."

(5)   **Elections § 22—Electors—Right of Suffrage—Restrictions in Limitations of Right to Vote.**—A state-imposed limitation on the right to

[Mar. 1973]

[Illustration 73]

FIRST PAGE FROM 507 P.2d 1345

RAMIREZ v. BROWN   Cal. **1345**

Cite as 507 P.2d 1345

107 Cal.Rptr. 137

Abran RAMIREZ et al., Petitioners,

v.

Edmund G. BROWN, Jr., as Secretary of State, etc., et al., Respondents.

S. F. 22916.

Supreme Court of California,
In Bank.

March 30, 1973.

Proceeding for writ of mandate brought by three ex-felons to compel election officials to register them as voters.

Headnotes from the Pacific Reporter.

forcement of modern statutes regulating the voting process and penalizing its misuse, rather than outright disfranchisement of persons convicted of crime, is the method of preventing election fraud which is the least burdensome on the right of suffrage, and which should be followed.

Alternative writ discharged, petition for peremptory writ denied.

1. Courts ⬅207.4(3)

Prayer of ex-felons seeking mandamus to compel election officials to register them as voters was for the appropriate remedy, and case fell within limited category in which the Supreme Court deemed it proper to exercise original jurisdiction.

2. Courts ⬅209(2)

It was appropriate for the Supreme Court to exercise its inherent jurisdiction to resolve the issue of whether ex-felons may vote, even where election officials in three counties involved had decided not to contest the issue and advised the Court that they would hereafter register all such ex-felons who applied, where the case

507 P.2d—85

posed a question which was of broad public interest, was likely to recur, and which should receive uniform resolution throughout the state.

3. Statutes ⬅158

Repeals by implication are not favored.

4. Elections ⬅18

Where at time petitioning ex-felons were not permitted to register to vote the Constitution stated, inter alia, that " * * * no person convicted of any infamous crime * * * shall ever exercise the privilege of an elector in the State * * *," new constitutional article which stated, inter alia, that "The Legislature shall prohibit improper practices that affect elections and shall provide that no * * * person convicted of an infamous crime shall exercise the privileges of an elector in this state.", contained no differences in substance by reason of fact that the words "The Legislature shall provide," were added, and by reason of the deletion of the word "ever" from the provision of the former constitutional section. West's Ann.Const. art. 2, §§ 1, 3.

5. Constitutional Law ⬅211
   Elections ⬅18

As applied to all ex-felons whose term of incarceration and parole have expired, provisions of the Constitution denying the right of suffrage to persons convicted of crime, together with the several sections of the Election Code implementing that disqualification, violate the equal protection clause of the Fourteenth Amendment; the enforcement of modern statutes regulating the voting process and penalizing its misuse, rather than outright disfranchisement of persons convicted of crime, is the method of preventing election fraud which is the least burdensome on the right of suffrage and which should be followed. West's Ann.Const. art. 2, §§ 1, 3; West's Ann.Elections Code, §§ 310, 321, 383, 389, 390, 14240, 14246; U.S.C.A.Const. Amend 14.

[Illustration 74]

TITLE PAGE: CALIFORNIA SHEPARD'S CITATIONS

Vol. 57	MAY, 1976	No. 3

(In Two Parts) PART 1

SHEPARD'S
CALIFORNIA CITATIONS

CASES

A COMPILATION OF CITATIONS TO

CALIFORNIA CASES REPORTED IN THE VARIOUS SERIES OF CALIFORNIA RE-
PORTS, IN THE PACIFIC REPORTER AND IN THE CALIFORNIA REPORTER

THE CITATIONS
which include affirmances, reversals and dismissals by the California courts and the United States
Supreme Court

APPEAR IN

CALIFORNIA SUPREME COURT REPORTS
CALIFORNIA APPELLATE REPORTS
CALIFORNIA REPORTER
PACIFIC REPORTER (California Cases)
CALIFORNIA UNREPORTED CASES
LABATT'S DISTRICT COURT REPORTS
MYRICK'S PROBATE COURT REPORTS
COFFEY'S PROBATE DECISIONS
UNITED STATES SUPREME COURT
  REPORTS

LOYOLA OF LOS ANGELES LAW
  REVIEW
PACIFIC LAW JOURNAL
SAN DIEGO LAW REVIEW
SANTA CLARA LAWYER
SOUTHERN CALIFORNIA LAW REVIEW
STANFORD LAW REVIEW
UNIVERSITY OF CALIFORNIA AT LOS
  ANGELES LAW REVIEW

> Each volume of Shepard's in each of its units has a title
> page indicating which court reports and law reviews are cov-
> ered for citing cases.

CALIFORNIA COMPENSATION CASES
OPINIONS AND ORDERS OF THE RAIL-
  ROAD COMMISSION OF CALIFORNIA
OPINIONS AND ORDERS OF THE PUBLIC
  UTILITIES COMMISSION OF
  CALIFORNIA
CALIFORNIA LAW REVIEW
CALIFORNIA WESTERN LAW REVIEW
HASTINGS LAW JOURNAL
JOURNAL OF THE STATE BAR OF
  CALIFORNIA

TEXAS LAW REVIEW
UNIVERSITY OF CHICAGO LAW REVIEW
UNIVERSITY OF ILLINOIS LAW FORUM
UNIVERSITY OF PENNSYLVANIA LAW
  REVIEW
VIRGINIA LAW REVIEW
WISCONSIN LAW REVIEW
YALE LAW JOURNAL
AMERICAN BAR ASSOCIATION
  JOURNAL

and in annotations of

LAWYERS' EDITION, UNITED STATES SUPREME COURT REPORTS
AMERICAN LAW REPORTS

also, for California cases reported prior to the Pacific Reporter or not reported in either the Cali-
fornia Reporter or the Pacific Reporter as cited in all units of the National Reporter System and in
Vols. 1—283 Illinois Appellate Court Reports, Vols. 1—19 Ohio Appellate Reports and Vols. 1—101
Pennsylvania Superior Court Reports

SUBSCRIPTION $58.00 PER YEAR

SHEPARD'S CITATIONS, Inc.

Post Office Box 1235
Colorado Springs, Colorado 80901 — (303) 633-5521

[Illustration 75]

PAGE FROM CALIFORNIA SHEPARD'S CITATIONS—CASES

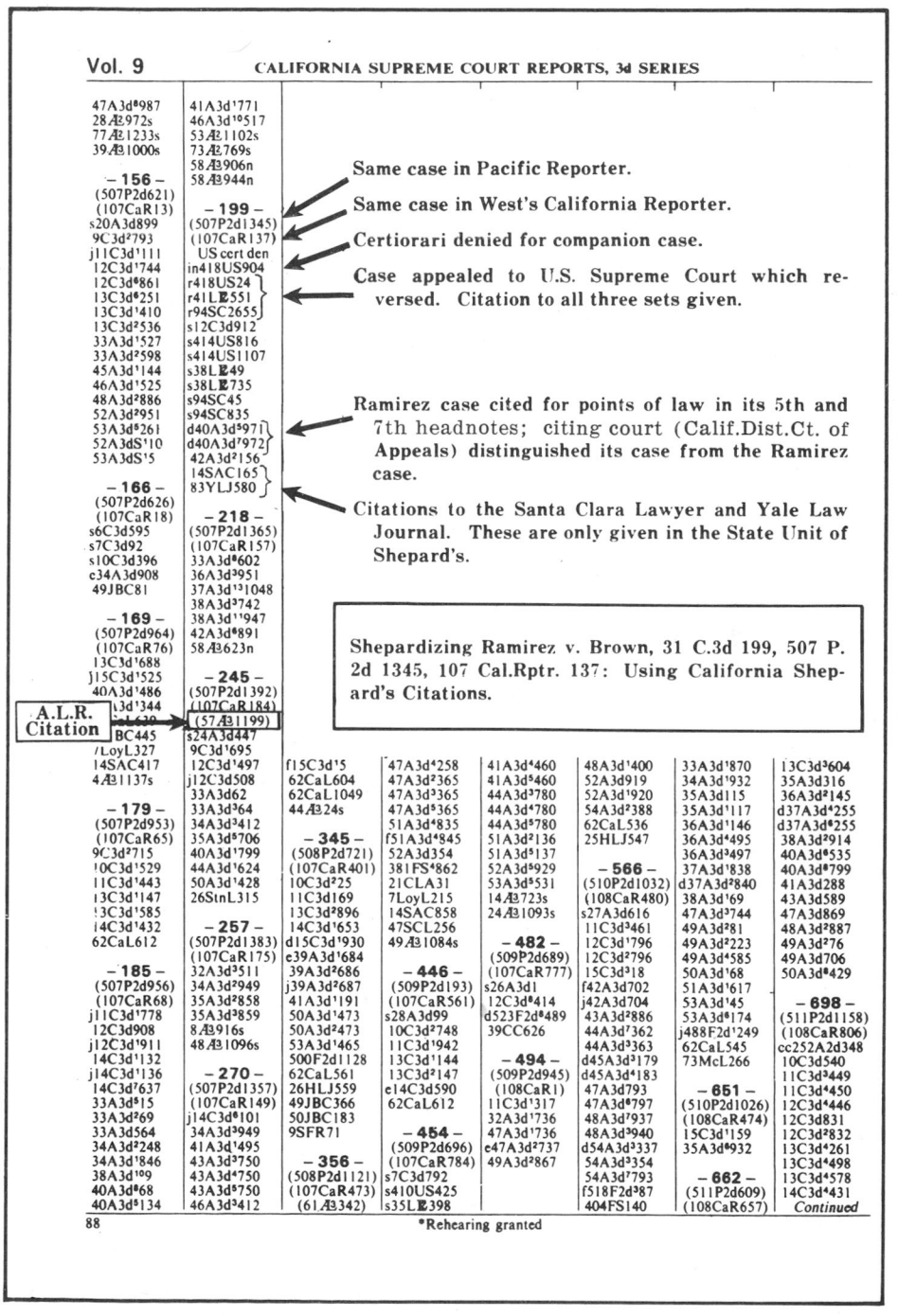

Vol. 9   **CALIFORNIA SUPREME COURT REPORTS, 3d SERIES**

Same case in Pacific Reporter.

Same case in West's California Reporter.

Certiorari denied for companion case.

Case appealed to U.S. Supreme Court which reversed. Citation to all three sets given.

Ramirez case cited for points of law in its 5th and 7th headnotes; citing court (Calif.Dist.Ct. of Appeals) distinguished its case from the Ramirez case.

Citations to the Santa Clara Lawyer and Yale Law Journal. These are only given in the State Unit of Shepard's.

Sheperdizing Ramirez v. Brown, 31 C.3d 199, 507 P. 2d 1345, 107 Cal.Rptr. 137: Using California Shepard's Citations.

A.L.R. Citation

88   *Rehearing granted

[Illustration 76]

PAGE FROM PACIFIC SHEPARD'S CITATIONS—CASES

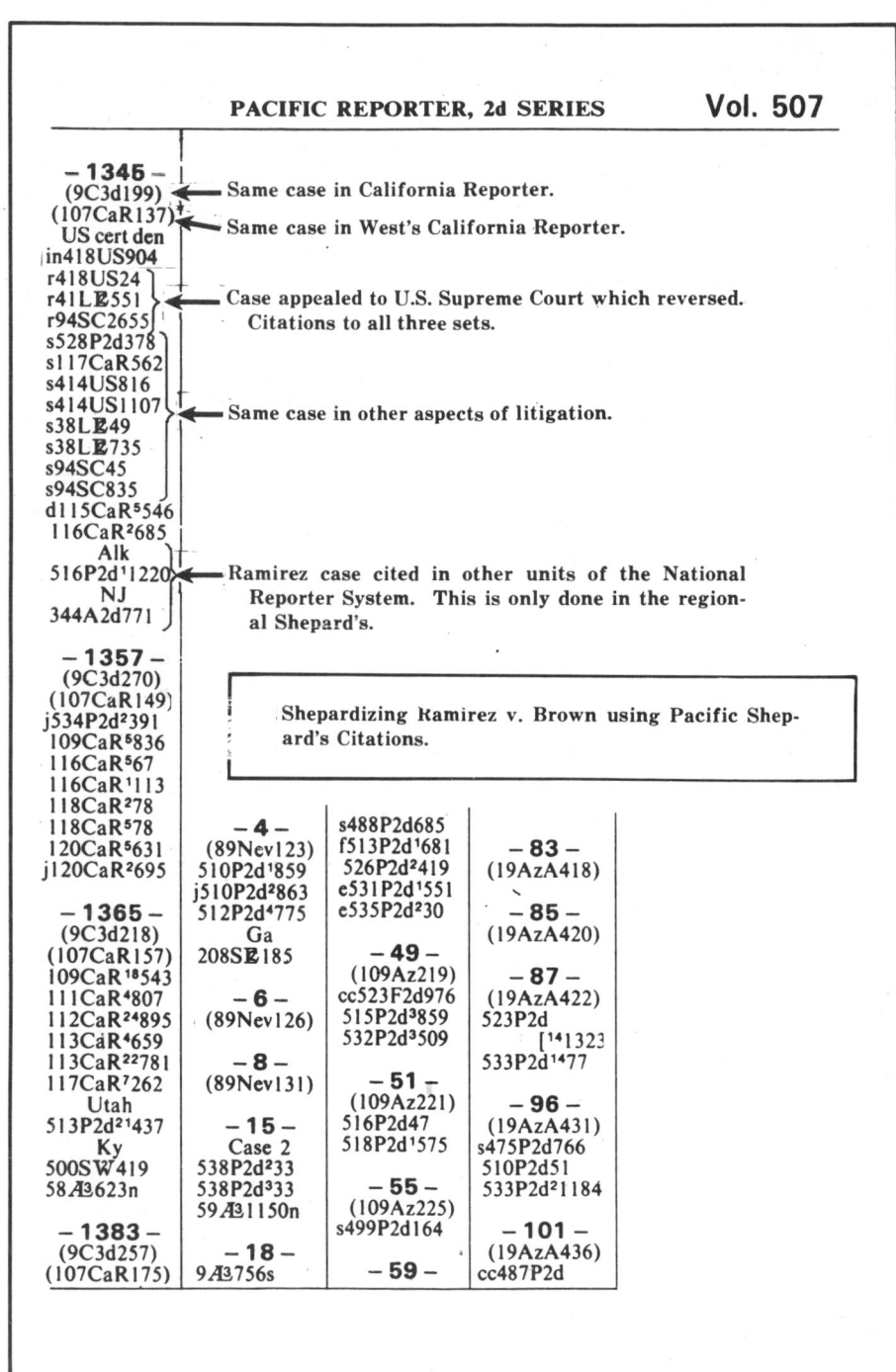

PACIFIC REPORTER, 2d SERIES   **Vol. 507**

– 1345 –
(9C3d199) ◄——— Same case in California Reporter.
(107CaR137) ◄——— Same case in West's California Reporter.
US cert den
in418US904
r418US24
r41LE551 ◄——— Case appealed to U.S. Supreme Court which reversed.
r94SC2655   Citations to all three sets.
s528P2d378
s117CaR562
s414US816
s414US1107 ◄——— Same case in other aspects of litigation.
s38LE49
s38LE735
s94SC45
s94SC835
d115CaR⁵546
116CaR²685
Alk
516P2d¹1220 ◄——— Ramirez case cited in other units of the National
NJ   Reporter System. This is only done in the region-
344A2d771   al Shepard's.

– 1357 –
(9C3d270)
(107CaR149)
j534P2d²391
109CaR⁵836
116CaR567
116CaR¹113
118CaR²78
118CaR⁵78
120CaR⁵631
j120CaR²695

– 1365 –
(9C3d218)
(107CaR157)
109CaR¹⁸543
111CaR⁴807
112CaR²⁴895
113CaR⁴659
113CaR²²781
117CaR⁷262
Utah
513P2d²¹437
Ky
500SW419
58A3623n

– 1383 –
(9C3d257)
(107CaR175)

– 4 –
(89Nev123)
510P2d¹859
j510P2d²863
512P2d⁴775
Ga
208SE185

– 6 –
(89Nev126)

– 8 –
(89Nev131)

– 15 –
Case 2
538P2d²33
538P2d³33
59A31150n

– 18 –
9A3756s

s488P2d685
f513P2d¹681
526P2d²419
e531P2d¹551
e535P2d²30

– 49 –
(109Az219)
cc523F2d976
515P2d³859
532P2d³509

– 51 –
(109Az221)
516P2d47
518P2d¹575

– 55 –
(109Az225)
s499P2d164

– 59 –

– 83 –
(19AzA418)

– 85 –
(19AzA420)

– 87 –
(19AzA422)
523P2d
[¹⁴1323
533P2d¹477

– 96 –
(19AzA431)
s475P2d766
510P2d51
533P2d²1184

– 101 –
(19AzA436)
cc487P2d

Sheshardizing Ramirez v. Brown using Pacific Shepard's Citations.

SECTION C.   STATUTE CITATIONS

Statutes are dealt with by *Shepard's Citations* in a manner similar to cases.   The notations cover the form and operation of the law by the legislature and the courts.   Its operation is identified by abbreviations denoting legislative changes (amendments, repeals, revisions, re-enactments, etc.) and judicial interpretations (constitutional, unconstitutional, invalid, etc.).

Some abbreviations used for notations in *Shepard's Citations* to statutes are given below:[5]

Form of Statute

Amend.	Amendment.
App.	Appropriation Act.
Art.	Article.
C or Ch.	Chapter.
Cl.	Clause.
Ex.	Extra Session.
Loc.	Local Acts or Laws.
No.	Number.
p.	Page.
Res.	Resolution.
Sp.	Special Session.
Subd.	Subdivision.
Subsec.	Subsection.
Tit.	Title.
§	Section.
¶	Paragraph.

The form of statutes vary, depending on the plan adopted by a jurisdiction.   The Table of Abbreviations in each unit of *Shepard's Citations* should be examined specifically to determine the local scheme.

Operation of Statute

Legislative

A (amended)	Statute amended.
Ad (added)	New section added.
E (extended)	Provisions of an existing statute extended in their application to a later statute, or allowance of additional time for perform-

---

[5] *Id*. note 2.

	ance of duties required by a statute within a limited time.
L (limited)	Provisions of an existing statute declared not to be extended in their application to a later statute.
PA (proposed amendment)	Future action necessary to confirm or reject amendment.
PR (proposed repeal)	Future action necessary to confirm or reject repeal.
R (repealed)	Abrogation of an existing statute.
Re-en (re-enacted)	Statute re-enacted.
Rn (renumbered)	Renumbering of existing sections.
Rp (repealed in part)	Abrogation of part of an existing statute.
Rs (repealed and superseded)	Abrogation of an existing statute, and substitution of new legislation therefor.
Rv (revised)	Statute revised.
S (superseded)	Substitution of new legislation for an existing statute, not expressly abrogated.
Sg (supplementing)	New matter added to an existing statute.
Sp (superseded in part)	Substitution of new legislation for new part of an existing statute, not expressly abrogated.

Judicial

    C Constitutional.

    U Unconstitutional.

    V Void or invalid.

    Up Unconstitutional in part.

    Va Valid.

    Vp Void or invalid in part.

The "Citations to Statutes" units of *Shepard's Citations* cover the following areas: citations to the United States Constitution and

state constitutions; the United States Code and Acts of Congress (not included in the United States Code); the various state codes, legislative enactments and court rules; and various municipal charters and ordinances.

The information contained in the statutes units is presented in accordance with this arrangement: Statutory amendments, repeals, etc., are listed first, followed by state and federal court citations and citations in the attorneys general opinions, legal periodicals and acts of the legislature.

1. Constitutions

The federal and state constitutions are covered by the *Statute Editions to Shepard's Citations*. A constitution section in a *Statute Edition* is arranged under the articles and amendments to the constitution. Citing sources are listed under these provisions. See Illustration 78.

2. City Charters and Ordinances

The municipal charters and ordinances are part of the *State Citations*. Reference should be made to the citator of the state in which the city is located for citations to the city's charter or ordinances.

The section under "Municipal Charters" in the *Statute Citations* is arranged alphabetically by cities in many state editions and subdivided by topics. The unit may have a separate *Index to Municipal Charters*. The Ordinances section also may be arranged alphabetically by cities and subdivided by topics. It, too, may have a separate *Index to Ordinances*. In some citators, the citations to the ordinances of the larger cities are separately arranged. To meet editorial requirements, the citations to ordinances may be indexed by section numbers as well as topically. See Illustration 61–a.

3. Shepard's Ordinance Law Citations

This six-volume set is actually a digest rather than a citator. It is arranged under broad subjects, with each subject subdivided into subentries. Under each subentry annotations of court decisions are listed. This set is useful when legal research requires the locating of cases on the same aspect of local government law in different cities. See Illustration 61–b.

4. Court Rules

Citations to court decisions interpreting court rules are also covered by *Shepard's Citations*. The Court Rules section is arranged by courts (final, intermediate and original jurisdiction), and is subdivided by rule numbers.

SECTION D. ILLUSTRATIONS: STATUTE CITATIONS

[Illustration 77]

PAGE FROM U.S. SHEPARD'S CITATIONS—STATUTES

UNITED STATES CODE '70 Ed. & '71 Supp.　T. 26 § 4411

| Subd. 3
Ad83St487
A84St1836 | § 4231
400F2d982
413F2d181 | 430F2d986
454F2d136
269FS274 | § 4253
R85St251 | Subsec. 3
388F2d305
265FS68 | 88SC710
88SC717
89SC392 | 298FS1358
5ARF185n
§ 4402 | 390F2d616
391F2d230
391F2d255 |

"Sheppardizing" a U.S. Code provision. This unit of Shepard's gives citations to each Court decision citing the U.S. Code. It also indicates when a code section has been amended or repealed.

1. 26 U.S.C. 4221c amended by 85 Stat. 497.

2. 26 U.S.C. 4251 repealed by 82 Stat. 251.

3. 26 U.S.C. 4401 held Constitutional in cases cited.

A85St497 389F2d634	426F2d833	§ 4243	§ 4271 Ad84St219	¶ A 446F2d323	408F2d112 408F2d1017	§ 4403 390US43	414F2d761 422F2d1246
§ 4217 371F2d831	436F2d1068 448F2d179 264FS952	Subsec. b 405F2d1233	§ 4272 Ad84St219	¶ B 446F2d323	411F2d505 414F2d761	19LE895 88SC700	423F2d629 425F2d1335
§ 4218 296FS633 329FS1273	279FS419 285FS681 293FS51	277FS669 277FS749 280FS534	§ 4281 Ad84St219	¶ C 446F2d323	416F2d921 422F2d1246 423F2d629	373F2d33 416F2d921 446F2d1006	427F2d1028 428F2d103 431F2d914
Subsec. a 371F2d832 389F2d633 461F2d1268 299FS1357 329FS1274	§§ 4232 to 4234 426F2d834	Subsec. c 405F2d1232 Subd. 1 405F2d1233 Subd. 2	§ 4282 Ad84St219 § 4291 A84St219 371F2d442	¶ D 446F2d320 311FS141 § 4401 et seq.	427F2d1028 431F2d914 432F2d900 435F2d23 437F2d93 437F2d737	447F2d914 309FS469 § 4404 1ARF797n § 4411 et seq.	434F2d628 435F2d23 437F2d737 443F2d372 445F2d642 445F2d869
Subsec. b 387F2d662	§ 4232 426F2d834 264FS953 319FS634	449F2d906 284FS503 Subd. 3	28LE426 91SC1165	401US702	445F2d642 445F2d1070	294FS335	445F2d1070 446F2d182 446F2d1251
Subsec. c 329FS1274	Subsec. b 381F2d982 406F2d906	405F2d1233 Subd. 4 405F2d1233	319FS419 325FS487 § 4292	378F2d757 406F2d404 406F2d1167	446F2d1251 446F2d857 447F2d915	§ 4411 U396F2d220 C425F2d817	447F2d857 447F2d914 451F2d1032
Subsec. e 389F2d634	264FS952 279FS4__ 319FS6_	A84St219 § 4293 A84St219	411F2d923 426F2d985	451F2d [1354 456F2d153	C441F2d [1337 388US903	456F2d153 457F2d1355 462F2d488		
§ 4220 Subsec. 1 412F2d1203	§ 4241 370F2d202 422F2d1059	§ 4251 R82St251 404F2d405 411F2d606	§ 4294 Subsec. a A84St219	449F2d1321 451F2d1028 458F2d762 264FS182	457F2d1355 462F2d488 270FS396 280FS345	390US39 390US62 393US963 394US570	264FS395 270FS396 276FS396 280FS345
Subsec. 2 412F2d1203	430F2d986 430F2d1327 454F2d136	449F2d906 319FS419 325FS487	Subsec. b A83St487	325FS359 329FS761 41FRD353	282FS635 285FS148 286FS643	395US13 396US78 401US670	282FS635 282FS979 283FS904
§ 4221 284FS287	269FS274 269FS309	Subsec. a 449F2d912	§ 4301 et seq.	42FRD587 17LE984s	289FS642 292FS35	401US715 18LE1343	285FS148 285FS791
Subsec. a 284FS287	273FS756 279FS587	319FS419 Subd. 1	265FS71 266FS230	89A2540s 1ARF795n	296FS984 299FS258	19LE889 19LE906	286FS544 286FS643
Subd. 1 284FS287	280FS534 301FS1151	319FS420 Subd. 2	57ABA53 § 4401	1ARF801n 5ARF170n	302FS452 306FS889	21LE376 22LE553	288FS57 289FS642
Subsec. c A85St497	207FS1081	A82St92 395F2d1006	C402F2d3 C441F2d	308FS518 313FS1035	23LE68 24LE275	291FS762 292FS35	
Subsec. d	Subsec. a 399F2d883	446F2d___	[1337 C442F2d405	322FS157 326FS960	28LE407 28LE436	293FS789 296FS984	
Subd. 5 A83St487	405F2d1232 269FS274	A84St1836 Subsec. b	266FS_	C309FS469 388US904	330FS596 332FS1277	87SC2094 88SC697	298FS1358 299FS258
Subd. 6 284FS287	301FS1153 305FS983 100A2739s	A82St251 A83St487 A84St1836	§ 4361 391F2d610 301FS22	390US42 390US62 393US963	333FS408 338FS273 338FS1109	88SC710 89SC392 89SC1251	300FS1387 302FS452 306FS889
§ 4222 390US80 19LE919 88SC720	Subd. 1 381F2d383 430F2d986 277FS749	Subsec. c A82St92 A82St251	§ 4362 301FS22	395US13 401US669 402US454	341FS1152 342FS833 343FS1279 4ARF632n	89SC1536 90SC364 91SC1041 91SC1160	308FS518 309FS469 313FS1035 322FS156
Subsec. d A85St497	284FS494 Subd. 2 383F2d10	§ 4252 Subsec. a R82St251	§ 4371 265FS68	18LE1343 19LE894 19LE906 21LE377	Subsec. a 423F2d1207 447F2d912 291FS762	369F2d106 372F2d698 373F2d33 379F2d394	326FS960 332FS1277 338FS341 338FS1109
§ 4223 Subsec. a 420F2d907 284FS287	422F2d1056 § 4242 370F2d202 422F2d1059	319FS419 Subsec. b 319FS419	Subsec. 1 265FS72 Subsec. 2 265FS72	23LE69 28LE407 29LE33 87SC2097 88SC697	1ARF795n Subsec. c 411F2d923 291FS762	379F2d946 381F2d133 381F2d559 385F2d489 386F2d177	341FS1152 342FS833 343FS1279 346FS1002 *Continued*

See note on preceding half title page

[Illustration 78]
PAGE FROM FLORIDA CONSTITUTION IN THE FLORIDA SHEPARD'S CITATIONS—STATUTES

1968, Art. VII			FLORIDA CONSTITUTION, 1968	
§ 1	**§ 12**	**§ 6**	257So2d274	**§ 2**
231So2d1	229So2d842	261So2d2	24MiL335	229So2d842
2468o2d741	234So2d651	325FS495	24MiL591	234So2d655
261So2d1	235So2d1	Subd. a	**§ 6**	261So2d5
Subd. a	257So2d26	261So2d4	238So2d678	**§ 6**
261So2d3	260So2d497	Subd. b	239So2d628	257So2d273
33F1S178	26180206	261So2d2	239So2d878	32F1S203
C410F2d	399US213	33F1S116	23MiL349	Subd. a
[1067	26LE530	33F1S178	24MiL578	223So2d37
Subd. c	90SC1996	Subd. c	3643806n	33F1S178
239So2d1	U317FS859	33F1S116	Subd. a	**§ 7**
257So2d10	Subd. a	Subd. d	238So2d163	229So2d846
Subd. d	235So2d2	251So2d1	245So2d286	257So2d273
239So2d3	**§ 13**	33F1S123	253So2d910	Subd. b
243So2d574	235So2d4	Subd. e	34F1S62	229So2d841
257So2d10	**§ 14**	230So2d131	35F1S72	**§ 8**
§ 2	23FLR478	245So2d80	23FLR490	229So2d841
C410F2d	70C70-270	261So2d137	23MiL355	**§ 9**
[1067	70 p1517	450F2d563	**§ 7**	A Nov. 4,
21FLR324		Subd. f	234So2d666	[1969
§ 3	**Art. VIII**	224So2d688	**§ 8**	(69HJR
248So2d3	261So2d2	230So2d131	Subd. a	1851)
Subd. a	**§§ 1-5**	240So2d505	243So2d149	238So2d830
233So2d184	261So2d5	245So2d114	247So2d54	239So2d7
§ 4	**§ 1**	425F2d1142	Subd. b	69C69-299
240So2d884	245So2d113	**§ 11**	243So2d148	69HJR
34F1S183	245So2d295	Subd. 1	**§ 9**	[1851
21FLR324	251So2d5	¶ f	401US737	1972HJR
Subd. a	23FLR660	239So2d635	28LE448	[3576
232So2d390	Subd. c		91SC1052	Subd. a
257So2d538	23FLR659	**Art. IX**	**§ 10**	1971C369
§ 5	Subd. d	**§ 1**	232So2d58	1972SJR
243So2d574	261So2d5	34F1S89	259So2d505	[292
1971C20	440F2d339	**§ 3**	23FLR651	Subd. c
§ 6	33F1S116	247So2d305	**§ 11**	246So2d102
222So2d424	21FLR324	**§ 4**	23FLR493	¶ 4
Subd. a	23FLR659	Subd. b	24MiL588	69C69-304
24MiL581	Subd. e	231So2d1	70 p1516	¶ 5
§ 7	23FLR664		70HJR792	246So2d102
229So2d588	Subd. f	**Art. X**	**§ 12**	249So2d423
§ 9	251So2d1	238So2d831	235So2d1	261So2d813
231So2d1	33F1S116	**§ 1**	Subd. b	**§ 10**
246So2d738	1971C629	238So2d830	238So2d833	223So2d35
261So2d1		339FS1260	Subd. d	

> In each Shepard's Citations state unit, there is a statute section which includes a section on the state's Constitution.
>
> This illustration is from the Florida Shepard's. Each time a section of the Florida Constitution has been cited by a Florida Court, or a Federal Court sitting in Florida, the citation appears in this section of the Florida Shepard's.
>
> Note how Art. VII, section 2 has been held Constitutional.

246So2d737	Subd. a	246So2d575		
247So2d304	261So2d803	Subd. c	**§ 4**	
257So2d10	70C70-735	237So2d217	238So2d831	
261So2d6	Subd. b	239So2d525	**§ 5**	
Subd. c	244So2d536	254So2d777	243So2d575	
247So2d305	261So2d129	258So2d450	1971C20	
249So2d7	261So2d803	24MiL578		
250So2d875	**§ 3**	**§ 5**	**Art. XII**	
§ 11	261So2d498	217So2d585	234So2d655	
245So2d863	**§ 4**	234So2d3	261So2d5	
246So2d102	261So2d5	247So2d41	69C69-230	
257So2d10	1971C629	251So2d15	**§ 1**	
	§ 5	252So2d826	32F1S203	
	261So2d5	254So2d777		

272

[Illustration 79]

PAGE FROM CALIFORNIA SHEPARD CITATIONS—STATUTES

ELECTIONS CODE (1961 C 23) § 3569

§ 6
57AG114
§ 17
101CaR441
§ 20
A1971C724
3C3d123
265A2d905
14A3d964
89CaR603
92CaR886
101CaR443
474P2d417
54AG9
57AG409
§ 21
263A2d306
265A2d905
101CaR443
57AG409
§ 22
410US763
36LE10
93SC1253
§ 23
3C3d268
90CaR182
101CaR439
475P2d213
§ 28
57AG409
§ 31
56AG42
§§ 33 to 35
52AG9
§§ 35 to 38
56AG42
§ 35
56AG15
56AG42
§ 36
56AG42
§ 41
415US734
39LE726
94SC1274
§ 45
A1971C1219
265A2d908
§ 45.1
Ad1971C724
§ 45.5
28A3d176
104CaR493
§ 46
A1971C1219
A1974C1543
265A2d904
32A3d444
77CaR689
108CaR317
§ 46.5
Ad1971
[C1219
§ 48
117CaR631
415US722
39LE712
94SC1323
§ 49
A1969C75

§ 56
A1970C294
§ 58
Ad1969C511
§ 60
A1970C164
← 1.
Ad1970C789
§ 100
2C3d225
C79CaR
[646
85CaR21
466P2d244
54AG9
§ 200
et seq.
57AG409
§ 200
2C3d225
85CaR21
466P2d244
§ 201
A1973C385
A1973C885
5C3d578
96CaR697
488P2d1
§ 203
A1972C1356
Up7C3d18
11A3d1038
→ 2.
93SC1253
53AG243
22StnL188
§ 203.5
Ad1973C23
12C3d55
115CaR249
524P2d377
§ 205.5
Ad1971C724
§ 206
4A3d293
84CaR256
§ 207
C35A3d900
C111CaR
[238
§ 213
5C3d578
96CaR697
488P2d1
55AG128
§ 213.1
A1969C810
A1971C1219
A1974C1135

§ 214
23HLJ237
§ 215
23HLJ237
§ 217
4A3d293
11A3d1038
84CaR256
90CaR263
§ 220
9C3d215
4A3d295
35A3d901
84CaR253
107CaR148
111CaR238
507P2d1345
418US80
41LE586
94SC2683
§ 224
Rs1969C870
§ 226
Ad1971
[C1274
§ 280
A1972C1053
§ 282
A1972C1053
§ 282.5
Ad1972
[C1356
§ 284
A1970C726
§ 287
A1970C342
§ 310
A1969C402
A1969C1543
A1970C148
A1972C1053
A1974C74
Up9C3d204
C34A3d448
Up107CaR
[137
C110CaR78
Up507P2d
[1345
C418US28
C41LE556
C94SC2655
53AG43
Subd. b
C34A3d450
C11(
23I
S
C79(
S
C41
C41
C94
S
(19
2C
85C
466
S
U9C
14A
92C
U107CaR
[140

U507P2d
[1348
§ 311
A1973C444
410US763
415US741
36LE10
39LE730
93SC1253
94SC1275
22StnL167
§ 312
410US763
36LE10
93SC1253
§ 315
A1974C1410
A1974C1445
265A2d911
§ 316
4A3d293
84CaR256
§ 321
A1969C402
A1969C1543
A1970C148
A1971C1760
A1972C1053
A1973C444
A1974C74
Up9C3d204
265A2d911
Up107CaR
[137
Up507P2d
[1345
C418US28
C41LE556
C94SC2655
53AG43
Subd. 1
265A2d911
Subd. 10
14A3d964
92CaR886
C418US28
C41LE556
C94SC2658
§ 321.5
Ad1970C148
55AG126
§ 321.7
Ad1970C148
418US31
41LE558

94SC2660
53AG43
§ 380
265A2d911
§ 381
A1969C870
4A3d295
84CaR255
468F2d1219
§ 383
A1969C810
Up9C3d204
4A3d295
84CaR253
Up107CaR
[137
Up507P2d
[1345
C418US28
C41LE556
C94SC2655
468F2d1218
53AG45
Subd. b
7C3d144
101CaR564
496P2d465
Subd. c
14A3d964
92CaR886
§ 385
A1972C579
468F2d1219
§ 388
468F2d1219
60CaL470
§ 388.2
60CaL470
§ 388.4
60CaL470
§ 388.6
60CaL470
§ 389
Up9C3d204
Up107CaR
[137
Up507P2d
[1345
C418US28
C41LE556
C94SC2655
265A2d907

§ 450
A1970C341
A1972C1053
A1974C74
§ 453.1
Ad1973C403
§ 454
7C3d25
101CaR534
496P2d445
§ 455
A1972C1356
7C3d18
101CaR534
496P2d445
§ 456
A1974C337
§ 456.5
A1969C607
A1970C859
A1972C1356
7C3d18
101CaR534
496P2d445
§ 456.6
A1969C607
A1970C859
A1972C1356
7C3d18
101CaR534
496P2d445
§ 459
A1969C151
A1972C1356
7C3d18
101CaR534
496P2d445
§ 460
A1970C267
§ 751
Rs1971
[C1453
11A3d1041
90CaR263
§ 752.5
R1971C1453
§ 753
A1971C1453
§ 754
A1971C1453
§ 755
A1971C1453
§ 758
A1970C615
§ 1618.5
Ad1973C352

§ 2500
415US747
39LE733
94SC1287
§ 2501
415US747
39LE733
94SC1287
§ 2502
→ 3.
[C1146
§ 2504
(1973C1146)
A1974C68
L1974C385
L1974C404
A1974C469
L1974C506
1974C866
[§9
L1974C1157
A1974C1386
57AG90
57AG110
57AG408
§ 2504.5
Ad1974C907
§ 2505
264A2d290
§ 2601
A1970C615
A1973C271
A1974C1165
17CLA152
§ 2603
A1969C159
§ 2605
Ad1971C129
§ 3500
et seq.
55AG219
§ 3500.1
Ad1973C800
§ 3506
A1974C1410
A1974C1445
§ 3507
A1970C81
A1973C1125
11C3d343
85CaR816
467P2d537

§ 3520
A1973C1125
A1974C1543
11C3d343
113CaR477
521P2d469
55AG219
§ 3520.5
Ad1974
[C1543
§ 3522
R1974C1543
§ 3523
55AG219
§ 3524
Ad1973C547
§ 3527
A1971C1775
A1974C1389
§ 3527.1
A1974C1389
§ 3527.3
A1974C1389
§ 3527.4
A1974C1389
§§ 3558 to 3574
7C3d25
101CaR534
496P2d445
§ 3560
A1974C1389
101CaR452
§ 3561
A1974C1389
101CaR452
§ 3563.5
A1973C1177
§§ 3564 to 3574
11A3d1049
90CaR479
§ 3565.5
Ad1969
[C1520
A1974C1389
§ 3566
Rs1973
[C1177
2C3d242
7C3d25
85CaR34
101CaR538
103CaR555
466P2d244
d445
66.3
)
C1383
1stEx
[C1
1stEx
[C2
3
C1177
567
C994
568
C978
C1177
569
C978
Rs1973
[C1177

Shepardizing a state statute

1. Sec. 20. Amended by 1972 Calif. session law, page 724.
2. Sec. 310 held unconstitutional in part by Calif. Supreme Court in the Ramirez case. Held constitutional by U. S. Supreme Court.
3. Sec. 3522 repealed in 1974.

See note on first page of this division. See 1970 Bound Volume, Statute Edition for earlier citations

233

[Illustration 80]

PAGE FROM GEORGIA SHEPARD'S CITATIONS— COURT RULES SECTION

GEORGIA COURT RULES

Supreme Court 1965	Supreme Court 1971 Revision	Court of Appeals 1971 Revision		Superior Court 1936	Rules of Procedure, Pleading and Practice in Civil Actions 1947	Rules and Regulations of the State Bar 1963
(220Ga909)	(226Ga905)	(122GA885)	125GA366 187SE563 Subd. b ¶ 1 124GA831 186SE323 Subd. c ¶ 2 123GA284 123GA856 124GA515 125GA666 184SE489 188SE831 ¶ 3 123GA102 123GA568 125GA199 186SE781 Cl. i 123GA856 Cl. ii 123GA856 Cl. iv 123GA102	Rule 23 228Ga114 184SE158	(1946p761)	(219Ga873)
Rule 14 227Ga18 227Ga223 227Ga463 227Ga525 227Ga831 227Ga832 124GA68 183SE41 183SE384 183SE466	**Rule 11** Subd. c Ad227Ga847	**Rule 1** et seq. 125GA204 186SE783		**Rule 41** 124GA549 184SE665	**Rule 1** 125GA399 188SE158	**Rule 1-501** 125GA42 186SE448
Rules 15 to 23 449F2d127	**Rule 14** 228Ga193 184SE583 Subd. a A227Ga847	**Rule 8** 124GA452 184SE362		**Rule 84** 23Mer250	**Rule 21** 124GA825 186SE318	**Rule 3-106** 228Ga13 125GA145 183SE749 186SE560
Rule 16 Subd. 2 228Ga143 184SE578 Subd. 3 227Ga248 227Ga291 227Ga430 Subd. 4 227Ga248	**Rule 9** 330FS291 **Rule 10** 330FS291 **Rule 11** 126GA115 190SE88 Subd. c AdMar. 2, [1972					**Rule 4-215** Subd. b 22Mer175
Rule 18 227Ga248 **Rule 20** 227Ga18 227Ga345 227Ga463 227Ga525	228Ga92 228Ga99 228Ga156 228Ga192 228Ga193 228Ga251 228Ga253 228Ga270 228Ga372 228Ga393 184SE156 184SE347 184SE457 184SE580	**Rule 33** 23Mer241 Subd. f 125GA534 188SE240 **Rule 34**				

> Each state unit of Shepard's citations has a section in the Statutes Division which "Shepardizes" the Court Rules of the state Appellate Courts.

Supreme Court 1965	Supreme Court 1971	Court of Appeals 1971
227Ga831 227Ga832 124GA68 183SE41 183SE384 183SE466	Subd. a 229Ga11 189SE86	183SE41 184SE519 Subd. a A Mar. 2, [1972 124GA452 125GA541 184SE362 188SE400 23Mer327
Rule 35 23Mer241	**Rule 18** Subd. c ¶ 2 228Ga812 229Ga65 188SE504 189SE439	Subd. c 125GA199 186SE780
Rule 45 227Ga345	**Rule 37** Subd. j A227Ga847 ¶ 1 228Ga675 187SE665	Subd. e AdMar. 2, [1972 126GA180 126GA249 190SE139 190SE445
Rule 54 227Ga264		**Rule 16** 124GA68 124GA545 183SE41 184SE519 Subd. a 23Mer327
		Rule 18 123GA612

SECTION E.   OTHER UNITS OF SHEPARD'S CITATIONS

Some units of *Shepard's Citations* have additional or different features than state and *National Reporter System* regional units. These are discussed below.

1.   Criminal Justice Citations

In 1963 the American Bar Association established a project on the Standards Relating to the Administration of Criminal Justice. Between 1964 and 1973 these Standards were issued in 18 separate pamphlets.   Each Standard deals with a specific aspect of criminal procedure, such as "The Prosecution Function"; "The Defense Function"; "Speedy Trial"; and "Trial By Jury."   In 1974 all of the 18 separately adopted Standards were published in one volume entitled *Standards Relating to the Administration of Criminal Justice*.   While these Standards have no official status, they are frequently cited by courts.   In 1975, *Shepard's Citations* published *Shepard's Criminal Justice Citations*, which lists each of the Standards and then gives citations to those cases which have cited sections of the Standards.

2.   Federal Circuit Table

In order to determine the circuit or district for *Federal Reporter* or *Federal Supplement* citations, *Shepard's Federal Circuit Table* has been published.   This Table identifies the circuit or district of any reference since 1960 of the *Federal Reporter* or the *Federal Supplement* shown in any edition of *Shepard's Citations*.

3.   Shepard's Federal Labor Law Citations

Shepard's Citations, Inc. has expanded its activity to include a new concept of citation service, which embodies the principle of applying the citation scheme to a subject area.   *Shepard's Federal Labor Law Citations* permits a researcher to trace any National Labor Relations Board Decision as well as any federal court labor decision through all later applications.   The coverage also includes labor decisions since 1935 (the inception of the NLRB) in Supreme Court of the United States and lower federal court reports and analyses of statutory labor provisions in the *United States Code*.

The volume divisions of the cited sources are:

a.   *Case Edition 1959:*   NLRB decisions and federal courts.

b.   *Statutes Edition 1959:* U. S. Code.

c.   *Cross Reference Edition 1959:* cross references from NLRB decisions and orders to Bureau of National Affairs, Commerce Clearing House and Prentice-Hall services.

d. Supplement, 1959–1963: cases, statutes, and cross references.

The citing sources referred to are:

a. Reports of decisions and orders of the NLRB, all federal court reports, all state reports, all units of the *National Reporter System*, with cross references to any reports or digests of the same cases in the several loose-leaf labor law services and reports.

b. Labor relations periodicals, such as *Labor Law Journal* and *Arbitration Journal*.

c. Law Journals.

d. Annotations in *U. S. Supreme Court Reports (L.Ed.)* and the *American Law Reports*.

The citations concept is applied in this service. Thus, it provides (1) *the complete history* (affirmed, amended, dismissed, reversed or superseded) of any reported decision of the NLRB, covering both further action by the Board and action by the courts on appeal from the Board's decision, and (2) *subsequent treatment* (criticised, distinguished, explained, followed, harmonized, dissented, limited, overruled or questioned) accorded the decision by the Board and the courts. The *Case Edition* (1959) volume covers these decisions.

e. Many labor cases are decided in federal district courts and are not reported in the *Federal Supplement*. At times some of these unreported decisions are cited in the labor looseleaf services or law reviews. Occasionally, an unreported federal district court case is appealed to a federal court of appeals. *Shepard's Federal Labor Law Citations* has a section entitled *Miscellaneous Federal Court Decisions by Labor Cases*. This section lists cited unreported decisions by the name of the case in alphabetical order. Under the name of each unreported decision, citations indicate where it has been cited in the various sets of court reports and law reviews.

4. Federal Law Citations in Select Law Reviews

This unit will be discussed in Chapter 17.

5. Shepard's Law Review Citations

This unit will be discussed in Chapter 17.

6. United States Citations

a. (Case Edition).

This Case Edition of *Shepard's United States Citations* consists of a main volume and three bound supplements. The first volume contains citations to the U. S. Reports through 1943 and the history and treatment of Supreme Court of the United States cases appear

only under the official (U. S.) citations. The *Lawyer's Edition* and the *Supreme Court Reporter* units only provide parallel references from their unofficial citations to the official citation. The cases must then be *Shepardized* under the official citations.

In all volumes after the 1943 volume, citations are given under both the official set and the two unofficial sets.

   b.   Statute and Department Reports Editions.

This part provides citations to all cases citing the U. S. Constitution, *U. S. Code*, and *Statutes at Large*, that have not been included in the *U. S. Code* and those cases citing U. S. Supreme Court Rules.

   c.   United States Administrative Citations, 1967, 1 vol. and pamphlet supplements.

This publication extends the coverage of *Shepard's United States Citations*, citing administrative decisions reported in twenty-two series of reports of federal administrative departments, courts, boards and commissions. Examples are the Securities and Exchange Commission Decisions and Reports, the Federal Trade Commission Decisions and the Federal Communications Commission Reports. The coverage includes history (affirmed, dismissed, modified or reversed on appeal) and treatment (criticized, distinguished, followed, questioned or overruled in later administrative or court decisions). Parallel citations and cited references in periodical articles also are noted. *Shepard's Administrative Citations* also provides direct and reverse cross reference tables which correlate decisions of agencies as reported in official government reports and in loose-leaf services and reporters. The cross references are for decisions reported in *Federal Carrier Cases, Public Utilities Reports, Radio Regulation, Utilities Law Reporter-Federal Decisions, Trade Regulation Reporter and Federal Securities Law Reporter.*

   d.   Patents and Trademarks.

This unit of the *United States Shepard's Citations* is a compilation of citations to U. S. patents, trademarks, and copyright.

   (1) The patents section lists each patent by number and then lists all citations to a patent by a court or administrative agency.

   (2) The copyright section. This lists titles of copyrighted works and lists citations to all court and administrative decisions involving the title.

   (3) The trademark section lists all trademarks alphabetically and then lists all citations to court and administrative decisions involving the trademark.

   (4) A separate section contains all citations to decisions published in the *United States Patent Quarterly.*

(5) Various cross-reference tables from sets of reports to other sets.

6. Shepard's Restatement Citations

This unit will be discussed in Chapter 18.

7. Shepard's Federal Tax Locator

This three volume set started publication in 1974. It is unlike other Shepard publications in that it is not a citator. Rather, it is an index to current sources of law relating to federal taxation. It attempts in one alphabet to cite all sources on federal tax law. Main entries are listed on the top of the page, and sub-entries are then alphabetically listed under each main entry. Each sub-entry cites to the relevant Internal Revenue Code provision, Treasury regulations, Tax Court Rules, Treatises, Treasury Decisions and other applicable administrative regulations. It also cites court decisions, the various tax looseleaf services, and articles from over 120 legal periodicals.

It is kept up-to-date by quarterly cumulative pocket supplements.

8. Shepard's Other Locators

Shepard's also publishes multi-volume sets in digest form to locate the law in three major states. Illinois, New York, and Texas each have a set of law locators which are divided into two parts. The first part is the locator itself which is an elaborate subject index with relevant cases summarized and cited. The second part is textual matter summarizing the law of the state on selected subjects. State law found in the volumes includes court opinions, administrative regulations, rules of court, state statutes, state constitution, and law reviews published in the state. The sets are kept up-to-date by annual cumulative pocket supplements.

SECTION F. ILLUSTRATIONS: OTHER UNITS OF SHEPARD'S

[Illustration 81]

UNITED STATES PATENTS (Original)						No. 3,714,696	
3,713,523 co913OG794	3,713,699 co910OG1457	3,713,876 co911OG762	3,714,077 co913OG1044	3,714,151 co928OG888	3,714,243 co913OG5 co920OG1020	3,714,375 co910OG1457	3,714,501 co915OG1166
3,713,524 co916OG3	3,713,710 co912OG397	3,713,883 co913OG5	3,714,078 co912OG2	3,714,156 co913OG794	3,714,245 co913OG4	3,714,378 co915OG2	3,714,510 co913OG5
3,713,541 co911OG1132	3,713,711 co911OG3 co919OG404	3,713,908 co917OG4	3,714,079 co923OG806	3,714,160 co913OG794	3,714,249 co914OG394	3,714,385 co912OG397	3,714,512 co911OG365
3,713,554 co913OG794	3,713,713 Re28,431	3,713,910 co915OG1562	3,714,080 co914OG394	3,714,165 co913OG4	3,714,259 co911OG762	3,714,391 9200OG286 9200GT88	3,714,515 co915OG380
3,713,556 co914OG4	3,713,715 co913OG1044	3,713,920 co915OG2	3,714,088 co911OG3	3,714,167 co916OG806	3,714,260 co912OG397	3,714,396 co913OG1044	3,714,518 co913OG5
3,713,557 co911OG11?		3,713,921	3,714,095	3,714,172			3,714,537 :o913OG4 :o915OG1166
3,713,55? co916OG3							3,714,545 o913OG4

An excerpt from Shepard's United States Citations: Patents.

This illustrates how decisions on a specific patent may be located.

Basketmaster

TRADEMARKS

Basketmaster 9240GT [151	9210GT [109	Bathtub Buddies 8950GT [306	Bauder Fashion College 181PQ275	B. B. 9180GT [152	Beach Party 9140GT71 [152	"Beanie" Beans 9380GT [142	Beau 9230GT [200
Basodur 9420GT [103	Batchelors 9170GT [234	Bath-Valet 9430GT57	Bauer 9320GT [332	B B i 9270GT [330	Beach Peach 9010GT [266	Bear 58PA982 178PQ428	Beau-Bra 9090GT [322
Basol 9020GT [100	Batch-Pak 9130GT [136	Bath Wand 9420GT [404	Bavarian 345FS1402 173PQ421	B Bonded 9020GT [250	Beachville USA 9240GT73	Bear Brand 9020GT [250	Beau Breck 9360GT [206
Bass Anglers Sportsman Society 185PQ43	Bathanal 9170GT53	Batik 9180GT [152	Bavarian Alpine Inn 9410GT [197	BBQ-Lites 9270GT [330	Beach-wagon 9230GT [141	Bearcat 177PQ344	Beau-Bunt 8880GT [218
Bass Bagger 185PQ192	Bath Buddy 9380GT [142	Batman 9370GT [191 9190GT [181	B C 8930GT60 9270GT [266		Beach Warmer 9090GT [322	Be a Social Lion 9030GT [307	Beauchaine 9290GT [247
Bass Buggy 8980GT [412	Bath-Gard 9070GT [112	Bat-Man, The 9280GT [220	Baybrook 9320GT80	B C A 9120GT [307		Beast Brand 9410GT [197	Beau Chalet 9310GT52
Bass Buster 185PQ192	Bathhouse Brass 9250GT68		Bay City Sight 9120GT [307		Beacon 9300GT [242		Beau/Craft 9030GT [306
Bass-Buzzer 185PQ192	Bathique 9330GT		Bay Sound Bay Sound, The 9270GT62	b c g 9310GT52	9310GT52		Beau de Cologne 9090GT [251

An excerpt from United States Shepard's Citations: Patents.

This is from the Trademarks Section and illustrates how a trademark may be Shepardized.

[Illustration 82]

EXCERPTS FROM OTHER UNITS OF SHEPARD'S CITATIONS

FEDERAL CIRCUIT IDENTIFICATION TABLE

Pages	Circ	Pages	Circ	Pages	Circ	F2d Vol. 466		Pages	Circ	Pages	Circ
379–380	5	891–928	PT	1338–1350	5			573–577	7	1163–1177	7
380–381	7	929–932	9	1350–1366	10			577–578	6	1177–1191	6
381–382	9	933–933	5	1366–1369	8	Pages	Circ	578–583	5	1191–1193	9
382–388	5	934–939	9	1369–1372	2			583–588	10	1193–1194	5
388–392	8	940–943	5	1373–1376	6	1–6	10	588–593	3	1194–1200	9
392–395	7	943–950	9	1376–1382	9	6–11 ←	7	593–600	7	1200–1201	5
396–402	9	950–956	5	1382–1389	8	11–17	5	601–611	3	1201–1202	8
402–406	7	956–958	10	1389–1394	10	17–24	2	611–612	9	1203–1205	10
406–407	9	958–964	9	1394–1395	5	24–35	6	613–618	7	1205–1206	9
408–415	5	964–966	10	1395–1397	9	35–42	10	618–621	10	1206–1209	8
416–418	8	966–969	9	1398–1398	2	42–53	9	621–625	8	1209–1210	10
419–420	5	969–970	6	1398–1398	3	53–59	6	626–672	7	1210–1212	8
420–421	10	970–973	5	1398–1399	5	59–65	5	672–674	9	1213–1226	5
422–423	4	974–978	9	1399–1399	2	65–69	10	675–679	7	1226–1229	3
423–425	5	978–982	5	1399–1400	3	69–76	6	679–689	5	1230–1233	5
425–427	6	982–991	7	1400–1400	5	76–80	10	689–694	7	1234–1239	3
427–428	9	991–992	5	1401–1401	3	80–83	3	694–701	6	1239–1246	5
428–432	7	993–994	10	1401–1402	5			702–714	7	1246–1249	6

Excerpt from Shepard's Federal Circuit Identification Table.

This Table may be used to determine the circuit or district for Fed., F.2d, or F.Supp. citations.

Note how 466 F.2d 6 is indicated that it was heard in the Seventh Circuit.

SPEEDY TRIAL (1968)

1.1	Kan	Colo
et seq.	502P2d742	484P2d1222
Iowa	Mich	525P2d469
195NW356	194NW138	532P2d784
1.1	Mont	Kan
255Ark545	516P2d375	528P2d1192
16MdA312	Nebr	Mass
457Pa508	202NW609	326NE326
Ark	Pa	Pa
502SW484	303A2d486	329A2d265
Iowa	**2.2**(a)	**2.3**(d)(i)
215NW264	468F2d1134	418F2d469
Md	391FS121	**2.3**(d)(ii)
295A2d782	456Pa428	Mass
Pa	Alk	326NE326
327A2d18	486P2d946	**2.3**(e)
1.2	Iowa	420F2d364
373FS827	207NW776	174Col568
210Kan556	Pa	Colo
448Pa322	321A2d640	484P2d1222
66Wis2d361	**2.2**(c)	**2.3**(f)
Kan	163Mt214	Colo
502P2d742	4TnCr669	525P2d469
Pa	Iowa	Pa
292A2d402	224NW235	329A2d265
Wis	Mont	**3.1**
225NW465	516P2d375	36CA3d114
1.3	Tenn	176Col292
	475SW206	

Excerpt from Shepard's Criminal Justice. This unit compiles citations to the American Bar Association's Standards Relating to the Administration of Criminal Justice.

This illustrates how citations to court decisions which have cited Section one of the Standard on Speedy Trial may be located.

SECTION G.   KEEPING SHEPARD'S CITATIONS CURRENT

1.   Supplements

As with any set of law books, there must be a method of keeping the set up to date.   Since *Shepard's Citations* are used to determine the current status of a case or statute, the method of supplementation is of the utmost importance to *Shepard's*.   This is accomplished in the following manner.   Each separate unit of *Shepard's* is available in at least one bound volume.   Every two months a cumulative paper supplement is issued, covering all decisions and other changes since the date of the bound volume.   For some sets, in addition to the bi-monthly cumulative supplement, an interim monthly supplement is issued in the form of a white pamphlet.   Some sets now have a bound volume, one or more bound supplements, and then a cumulative bi-monthly supplement.   Before using *Shepard's Citations*, it is extremely important to ascertain that all of the volumes and supplements are at hand.

In all cases, the bound volume or volumes plus the paper supplement or supplements must be used.

2.   Shepard's Special Citation Service

A special up-dating service is now available to subscribers of any unit of *Shepard's Citations*.   By writing or calling the publisher, information to citing cases subsequent to the latest supplement may be obtained.   Detailed information about this service is available upon request.

SECTION H.   SUMMARY

1.   Shepard's Citations.   Cases.
a.   States.
(1) There is a separate *Shepard's* unit for each of the fifty states.   In some states there are separate volumes for cases and statutes; in others they are combined.

(2) In each state unit, all of the sets of reports are listed in separate sections.   For each state case listed in dark type, the columns thereunder reveal (a) the history of the case in the same or higher courts, and (b) citations to all cases within the state that have cited the cited case.

(3) Citations are given to legal periodicals published within the state and to 21 national law reviews.

(4) Citations in Attorney-General's Opinions to state cases are given.

b.   **National Reporter System.**

There is a *Shepard's* unit corresponding to each of the units of the *National Reporter System*.

For any given *National Reporter* decision, citations to it are listed whenever the given citation is cited in any unit of the *National Reporter System*.

2.   **Shepard's Citations.   Statutes.**

a.   **States.**

(1) Each state unit of *Shepard's Citations* has either separate volumes or separate sections in which the state constitutions and the current code are listed, with citations to cases that have cited each section.

(2) Reference is also made to any constitutional amendment, or statutory clause which has been cited in court decisions.

(3) City Charters and Ordinances.   These are in separate parts of the statute volumes or sections of the state units.

(4) Court Rules.   These are in separate sections in the statute volumes or sections of the state units.

3.   **Shepard's Citations for Federal Cases.**

a.   **United States Citations.**   Separate volumes for (1) Supreme Court reports;   (2) Constitution, *U. S. Code* and *Statutes at Large*, and (3) Administrative agency decisions.

b.   **Federal Citations.**   Separate volumes for (1) *Federal Reporter*, First and Second Series and (2) *Federal Supplement, Federal Rules Decisions*, and *Court of Claims Reports*.

4.   **Other Units of Shepard's Citations.**

a.   **Shepard's Criminal Justice Citations.**   Citations to Standards Relating to the Administration of Criminal Justice.

b.   **Shepard's Federal Circuit Table.**   Indicates circuit or district for Federal Reporter or Federal Supplement citations.

c.   **Shepard's Federal Labor Law Citations.**

d.   **Shepard's Federal Law Citations in Select Law Reviews.**

e.   **Shepard's Law Review Citations.**

f.   **Shepard's Ordinance Law Citations.**

g.   **Shepard's Federal Tax Locator.**

h.   **Shepard's Restatement of the Law Citations.**

5. **Other Uses of Shepard's Citations.**
    a.   Indicates when a case is cited in:
        (1) A.L.R. Annotations
        (2) Legal periodical articles (state and U. S. editions only)
    b.   Finds parallel citations.

Chapter 16

LEGAL ENCYCLOPEDIAS

SECTION A. INTRODUCTION

In the previous chapters we have discussed the primary sources
of the law: court decisions, constitutions, statutes, legislative histories, court rules, and the indexes, digests, and other sets of law
books which enable a researcher to find both the source and status
of the law. In the remaining chapters we shall discuss the secondary
sources of the law. The mass of primary source materials has reached
such voluminous proportions that secondary publications have assumed significant roles in identifying and explaining the law. As
will be pointed out, it is frequently much better practice to start one's
research with secondary publications rather than the sets containing
the primary sources which were studied in the previous chapters.
The secondary sources to be discussed consist of legal encyclopedias,
treatises, periodicals, Restatements, and other miscellaneous sets of
law books.

Legal encyclopedias are written in narrative form, arranged by
subject and contain supporting footnote references to cases in point.
In most instances, they are noncritical in approach and do not attempt
to be analytical or evaluative. Instead, they simply state the propositions of law, with introductory explanations of an elementary nature.
The legal encyclopedia, because of these features, is a popular and
useful research tool. Its utility, however, as a secondary source, has
frequently been abused by both courts and attorneys. In particular,
it is often cited as a final authoritative source rather than as an expository introduction to case authority.

In many research problems, it is necessary to go beyond such
rudimentary sources. It is not wise to stop one's research without
reading the cases cited in the footnotes because cited references frequently will not fully reflect the propositional ramifications for which
they stand, or because the facts of the immediate problem will be distinguishable and different from those in the cited cases.

This criticism should not be interpreted as being directed at the
function of the encyclopedia. It is an excellent index and introductory
guide to the law, and as long as this is kept in mind, and it is not relied upon as the final authority for a proposition of law, it is a valuable publication to be consulted initially. In most instances, the
cases cited will have to be read, analyzed and Shepardized; statutory

sources must be checked to ascertain whether the rules of law have changed in any particular jurisdiction.

Three types of legal encyclopedias are distinguished by dealing with: (1) general law, (2) local or state law, and (3) special subjects. Each is discussed below.

SECTION B.   CURRENT GENERAL ENCYCLOPEDIAS

1.   Corpus Juris Secundum (cited "C.J.S.")

Corpus Juris Secundum, published by the West Publishing Company, is an attempt to restate the entire body of American case law from the first reported case to date. It includes both adjective and substantive law, and its publisher aims at citing all reported decisions. This revision, begun in 1936, was completed in 101 volumes and has a five-volume general index. It supersedes the text of *Corpus Juris*, its earlier edition, and the footnotes cite all reported federal and state cases rendered since the publication of the corresponding titles in *Corpus Juris*. Where there are earlier cases in point, footnote references are given to the *Corpus Juris* page and note numbers which list them; therefore, although the text of *Corpus Juris* has been superseded by the text of C.J.S., the *Corpus Juris* footnotes are still useful for references to the earlier cases. If there is no footnote reference back to *Corpus Juris*, it may be assumed that there are no earlier applicable cases. If there are no new cases on a subject and the statement in *Corpus Juris* is still the law, the original text in *Corpus Juris* is repeated, giving a few representative early case citations from *Corpus Juris*.

Cross-references from C.J.S. titles and sections to corresponding West topics and key-numbers (section numbers) also are provided, permitting easy entry to the *American Digest System*. The West topics and key-numbers and other secondary authority sources are noted under "Library References," which precede the texts of the sections, in the C.J.S. replacement volumes published since 1961 and in the annual cumulative pocket supplements.

Thus, C.J.S. provides the complete text and recent cases and representative early cases in the absence of new ones in point. *Corpus Juris* should be consulted only for the earlier cases when a footnote reference to it is given in C.J.S.

As previously noted, C.J.S. has a five-volume general index. Each volume also has a separate index to the topics contained in it. Where the topic is covered in more than one volume, the topic index appears in the concluding volume of the topic.

The set is kept up-to-date by replacement volumes and annual cumulative pocket supplements. Replacement volumes appear when significant sections of the text require rewriting or when the recent pocket references become very extensive and unwieldy. The pocket references may cover rewritten text, citations to cases rendered since the publication of the original volume, and secondary sources.

Judicial and other definitions of *words and phrases* and *legal maxims* are interfiled alphabetically with the essay topics. They also are listed in each appropriate volume preceding the index, with references to the pages containing the definitions.

Corpus Juris Secundum provides some discussion on federal and local statutory law, including court interpretation of these enactments.

A "Law Chart" of the topical arrangement of *Corpus Juris Secundum* is included at the beginning of the first volume of the General Index and a "List of the Titles in Corpus Juris Secundum" precedes the text of each volume of the set. The Law Chart is a guide to the titles under seven major divisions with numerous subheads. All related titles are so grouped as to enable comparison and discrimination in their correct selection. To use a topical approach when you do not know the title under which your question is discussed, first select the major division in the Law Chart that covers the problem. Then choose the pertinent subhead and the most specific title under that subhead. The last step is to consult the text of C.J.S. under the selected title.

2. American Jurisprudence

American Jurisprudence is published by the Lawyers Cooperative Publishing Co. and the Bancroft-Whitney Co. It began publication in 1936 and was completed in 58 volumes, superseding *Ruling Case Law*, an earlier encyclopedia. In 1962, the publishers initiated *American Jurisprudence 2d* which was completed in 1976 in 82 volumes, replacing *American Jurisprudence*.

American Jurisprudence 2d is a textual statement of substantive and procedural law, arranged alphabetically under more than 400 topics. It differs from *Corpus Juris Secundum* in that this set does not cite all reported decisions in support of its textual statement of the law. Rather, *American Jurisprudence 2d*, cites only selected decisions in its footnotes but does give citations to *A.L.R.* annotations. In using *American Jurisprudence 2d*, reported cases may be located through its footnotes and by consultation of the cited *A.L.R.* annotations.

American Jurisprudence 2d also gives in its footnotes references to treatment of a topic in the other sets of the Total Client Library

Service.   Since *American Jurisprudence 2d* has a detailed multi-volume index, it is much more inclusive in entries than the indexes to *A.L.R.*   It is frequently easier to locate an *A.L.R.* annotation by starting in the *American Jurisprudence 2d* index, reading the section cited to, and then locate the appropriate *A.L.R.* citation in *American Jurisprudence 2d's* footnotes.

The publishers describe *American Jurisprudence 2d* as giving the law in breadth and *A.L.R.* as the law in depth.   The former is very useful to obtain a quick answer to a problem which then may be explored in depth through the use of *A.L.R.*   In use one may go directly to the volume containing the topic being researched.   For example, if one is interested in the law of *Copyright*, the index volumes may be by-passed and the search started immediately by consulting the volume that contains the title *Copyright*.   If the broad topic of the law under which the subject is included is not familiar to the researcher (e. g., restrictive covenants), the search should start first in the index volumes.

Some features of *American Jurisprudence 2d* are:

(1) Greater emphasis is placed on statutory law, federal procedural rules, and uniform state laws.   The federal statutory law germane to a topic is covered, while state statutory law is covered in general but without reference to the specific laws of each state.

(2) *Federal Taxation* Volumes 33 and 34 are replaced annually and contain substantially the same text found in the current year editions of the Research Institute of America (RIA) *Tax Guide*.   This is a looseleaf service with weekly supplements.   The volumes as printed in *American Jurisprudence 2d* are supplemented during the year only for major Federal tax law changes.   As rules, regulations, and new court decisions occur so frequently in tax law, the user of these *Am.Jur.2d* volumes should always check for the most current materials in the RIA *Tax Guide*, or the other taxation services described *supra* in Chapter 14, Section B.

(3) *Am.Jur.2d New Topic Service* This looseleaf volume started in 1973 and covers (1) new topics of the law which have developed after the printing of the main volumes and (2) new and substantial changes in already published articles.

(4) *American Jurisprudence* Desk Book

Another feature of Am.Jur.2d is its *Desk Book* which functions as a "legal" almanac, containing miscellaneous data and information. The *Desk Book* is divided into seven main categories: (1) governmental documents and historical matters, (2) the courts (the canons of judicial ethics and the business and organization of the courts), (3) lawyers and the legal profession (the canons of professional

ethics, minimum requirements for admission to legal practice in the
U. S. and professional data), (4) statutes and statutory material
(text of the ancient statutes and tabulated statutory material—e. g.,
marriage laws, record of passage of Uniform and Model Acts), (5)
statistical matters (financial and mathematical tables, etc.), (6)
tables of law reports (abbreviations), and (7) miscellaneous information (selected legal (Latin) maxims and phrases, freely translated, etc.).

(5) *American Jurisprudence 2d* is kept up-to-date by annual
pocket supplements.

(6) Words, phrases and definitions are interfiled alphabetically
in the index to each volume.

3. American Jurisprudence Proof of Facts (AM.JUR.P.O.F.)

This set was published in 1959, and is now in 30 volumes. Its
purpose is to provide lawyers with a compilation of materials that
will guide the lawyer in organizing his fact material, in preparing
for trial, and in the examination of witnesses. It attempts to show
the elements required in presenting or defending a *prima facie* case.
This is done through a text discussion of the area followed by an outline in question and answer form, demonstrating the facts discussed
in the text. It is designed to assist a lawyer in obtaining information
from his client, in interviewing witnesses, in preparing for the taking of depositions, in preparation of briefs, and other steps lawyers
need to take in preparing a case for trial.

The set has its own index and access to it may also be obtained
by references to it from *A.L.R.* and *American Jurisprudence.* It is
kept up-to-date by annual pocket supplements. Each topic included
in the set is usually written by an experienced lawyer.

3A. American Jurisprudence Proof of Facts 2d (Am.Jur. Proof of Facts 2d)

a. In 1974 the publishers issued volume one of the *American
Jurisprudence Proof of Facts 2d.* Succeeding volumes will be issued
periodically until the set is completed. The articles in the Second
Series are shorter and more specific in scope. Consequently, each
volume will contain more articles and will have its own separate index. The set will be kept current by annual pocket supplements.

b. *American Jurisprudence Proof of Facts 2d, Quick Index
volume.* This new volume serves as an index to volumes 1–30 of the
first series. The cumulative pocket supplement in this volume will
also index *Am.Jur. Proof of Facts 2d.*

4.   American Jurisprudence Trials (AM.JUR. TRIALS)

This set, which started in 1964 and is now in 20 volumes, is essentially a treatise on trial practice.   The first six volumes cover what the publishers describe as practice, strategy and control, and include matters that are common to all types of problems in trial practice. The remaining volumes are called *Modern Trials* and deal with the handling of trials for a specific topic.   *American Jurisprudence Trials* is written by over 250 experienced trial lawyers.   As with *American Jurisprudence Proof of Facts 2d* it has its own index and is referred to in the footnotes of the other sets of the Total Library Client Service.

5.   American Jurisprudence Pleading and Practice Forms, Annotated (AM.JUR. P & P)

This set is essentially a collection of forms designed to assist a lawyer in preparing the procedural aspects of a law suit.   Other than the references in its footnotes to the other sets of the publishers, it is typical of other sets containing legal forms.

6.   American Jurisprudence Legal Forms 2d

This set is similar to *American Jurisprudence* P & P, but contains forms lawyers need in their practice other than pleading and practice forms.[1]

SECTION C.   ILLUSTRATIONS: ENCYCLOPEDIAS USING CORPUS JURIS SECUNDUM

In Chapter Six, Section A, in discussing the use of the *Key Number System* and the *American Digest System* we had the problem of finding cases dealing with the facts of the status of a person who enters a store and is injured therein.   We found cases by using the *Key Number System.*

Another approach would have been to start our search in *Corpus Juris Secundum* as shown in the following illustrations.

83.   Page from General Index to C.J.S.
84.   Page from Index to Volume 65–A, C.J.S.
85.   Page from Volume 65, C.J.S.

USING AMERICAN JURISPRUDENCE AND RELATED SETS

PROBLEM: In Chapter 7, it was shown how cases dealing with the liability of a landlord for personal injuries on portion of premise used in common by tenants, may be found by using *A.L.R.*   Another approach would be to use *American Jurisprudence 2d,* as shown in the following illustrations.

86.   Page from Index to American Jurisprudence 2d.
87.   Page from 49 American Jurisprudence 2d.
88.   Pages from American Jurisprudence Proof of Fact.
89.   Page from American Jurisprudence Trials.

[1] Form books will be discussed in more detail in Chapter 19.

[Illustration 83]

PAGE FROM GENERAL INDEX TO C.J.S.

SHOPPING GUIDE

SHOPPING GUIDE
Injunctions, newspaper, publication as violation of agreement not to publish newspaper, **Injun** § 84, p. 568, n. 49

> This page is from a volume of the General Index to C.J.S.
>
> This is an index to the entire 100 volumes of C.J.S. and thus must be more general than specific in its entries. No entry, for example, will be found in the General Index for Customers.
>
> If one looks under Stores and Storekeepers, a "See" reference is found to Shops and Shopkeepers. Under this heading, note sub-entry Negligence with "See" reference to Title Index to Negligence. This means that one should consult the index to the topic Negligence in the appropriate volume of C.J.S.

SHOPS AND SHOPKEEPERS—Continued
Industrial co-operative societies,
    Members' liability for debts of, **Indust Co-op** § 7, p. 16, n. 33
    Organization for purpose of operating, **Indust Co-op** § 2
Injunctions, restrictive covenant, use of premises, **Injun** § 87, p. 595
Insurance, nonoccupancy avoiding fire policy, **Ins** § 556, p. 306
Internal revenue,
    Bonded warehouses, custody, **Int Rev** § 584
    Compensation, distiller's bond to reimburse government for wages paid, **Int Rev** § 574, p. 816, n. 30
Labor and employment,
    Bailments, return of article intrusted to customer to, **Bailm** § 38
    Injuries to third persons, liability for injuries inflicted by employee, **Mast & S** § 570, p. 314
    Liability for injuries to customers, **Mast & S** § 575, p. 335
Liability insurance, excepted risks or liabilities, **Ins** § 834, p. 908
Licenses and permits,
    Power to license, municipalities, **Licen** § 10, p. 489
    Subject to license or tax, **Licen** § 30, p. 584
Limitations of actions, store account, **Lim of Act** § 72, p. 1039
Machine Shops, generally, this index
Machines, excise tax on sale or use, **Int Rev** § 528
Mechanics' liens, building within meaning of lien law, **Mech Liens** § 21, p. 513
Milk distributing plants, as, **Food** § 10, n. 39
Mortgages, land appurtenant as included, **Mtg** § 188
Motor vehicles, maintenance tax on motor vehicles used, **Motor V** § 63, n. 54
→Negligence, see **Title Index to Negligence**
Nuisances, **Nuis** § 41, p. 793; § 75, p. 822
    Junk store, **Nuis** § 75, p. 824
    Residential zoned area, **Nuis** § 41, p. 793
Owner's liability for detective agency's extortion, **Threats** § 27, p. 808, n. 48
Pleading, statement of separate causes of action for conduct of store manager as regards need for paragraphing, **Plead** § 88, p. 211, n. 33
Purposes, restrictions, **Deeds** § 165, p. 1132
Registers, jury room, allowance in during deliberations, **Crim Law** § 1369
Repair Shops, generally, this index
Residential districts, ordinances prohibiting as denial of due process, **Const Law** § 703, p. 1186
Robbery, sufficiency of evidence, **Rob** § 47, p. 495
Segregation of goods, asportation as resulting, **Larc** § 6, p. 803
Self-service store, acceptance of goods offered for sale on shelves of, **Sales** § 28, p. 641
Snow and ice on sidewalk, duty to keep free from, **Mun Corp** § 862, p. 231, n. 87
Warrants, search of as requiring, **Searches and Seizures** § 66, p. 834
Weapons, criminal responsibility for carrying or possessing in, **Weap** § 9, p. 503

[Illustration 84]

PAGE FROM INDEX TO VOLUME 65-A, C.J.S.

NEGLIGENCE

This page is from the index to the topic Negligence as found in Vol. 65-A of C.J.S.

Note the sub-entry Customers and under it the sub-sub-entry Business visitor or invitee, 63 (119).

This leads one to where that matter is discussed within C.J.S.

[Illustration 85]

PAGE FROM VOLUME 65, C.J.S.

§§ 63(118)–63(119) NEGLIGENCE   65 C. J. S.

The proprietor is liable only for his negligence;[14] and he is not liable for wrongful or negligent acts of third persons not under his control which he could not reasonably have anticipated and guarded against,[15] at least in the absence of some special relationship between him and such third persons.[16]

The proprietor may be held free from liability for acts of an employee which are not wrongful or negligent.[17]

b. Stores

→ **§ 63(119). In General**

A person who enters a store for the purpose of trade occupies the status of an invitee or business visitor.

Library References
Negligence ⊂⇒32(1), (2.8).

A person who enters a store for the purpose of trade occupies the status of an invitee or business visitor,[18] and in this connection it is not necessary that the person entering should have a definite purpose of making any particular purchase, but it is

---

This is the Reference found in the Index to the Topic Negligence in Vol. 65–A.

This is a typical page from C.J.S. Note how most of it is given over to citations supporting the statements of the text.

Note footnote 18 and the citation to McKenney v. Quality Foods, Inc., 319 P.2d 448. This is the case located using the American Digest System. See Illustration 17–a.

Also note how C.J.S. through its "Library Reference" refers to Negligence ⊂⇒32(1), (2.8) which was also located by use of the American Digest System.

This set is kept up-to-date by pocket supplements.

Rush v. Townsend & Wall Co., 343 S.W.2d 44, 50—Gregorc v. Londoff Cocktail Lounge, Inc., 314 S.W.2d 704.
N.Y.—Booth v. Sears, Roebuck & Co., 68 N.Y.S.2d 26.
Ohio.—Scott v. Allied Stores of Ohio, 122 N.E.2d 665, 96 Ohio App. 532.
Tenn.—Gargaro v. Kroger Grocery & Baking Co., 118 S.W.2d 561, 22 Tenn.App. 70.

Wis.—Radloff v. National Food Stores, Inc., 121 N.W.2d 865, 20 Wis.2d 224, rehearing denied 123 N.W.2d 570, 20 Wis.2d 224.
Anticipation of negligence of patrons
Proprietor of business establishment cannot usually anticipate negligence of his patrons.
La.—Alfortish v. Massachusetts Bonding & Ins. Co., App., 171 So.2d 705.
16. La.—Alfortish v. Massachusetts Bonding & Ins. Co., supra.
17. N.Y.—Greene v. Sibley, Lindsay & Curr Co., 177 N.E. 416, 257 N.Y. 190.
18. U.S.—Montgomery Ward & Co. v. Lamberson, C.C.A.Idaho, 144 F.2d 97—Baskin v. Montgomery Ward & Co., C.C.A.N.C., 104 F.2d 531—Montgomery Ward & Co. v. Snuggins, C.C.A.Minn., 103 F.2d 458.
   Rikard v. J. C. Penny Co., Columbia Division, D.C.S.C., 233 F.Supp. 133—Lucas v. City of Juneau, D.C.Alaska, 168 F.Supp. 195—Rankin v. S. S. Kresge Co., D.C.W.Va., 59 F.Supp. 613, affirmed, C.C.A., 149 F.2d 934.
Ala.—Ten Ball Novelty & Mfg. Co. v. Allen, 51 So.2d 690, 255 Ala. 418.
Cal.—Neel v. Mannings, Inc., 122 P.2d 576, 19 C.2d 647.
   Iloff v. Purity Stores, Limited, 178 C.A.2d 1, 2 Cal.Rptr. 735—McKenney v. Quality Foods, Inc., 319 P.2d 448, 156 C.A.2d 349—Lundin v. Shumate's Pharmacy, 221 P.2d 260, 98 C.A.2d 817—Sheridan v. Ravn, 204 P.2d 644, 91 C.A.2d 112—Locke v. Red River Lumber Co., 150 P.2d 506, 65 C.A.2d 322—Thompson v. B. F. Goodrich Co., 120 P.2d 693, 48 C.A.2d 723—Colombo v. Axelrad, 114 P.2d 425, 45 C.A.2d 439—Strong v. Chronicle Pub. Co., 93 P.2d 649, 34 C.A.2d 335.
Colo.—**Corpus Juris Secundum quoted in** Nettrour v. J. C. Penney Co., 360 **P.2d** 964, 966, 146 Colo. 150.
Conn.—Lunny v. Pepe, 165 A. 552, 116 Conn. 684.
D.C.—Custer v. Atlantic & Pacific **Tea Co., Mun.App., 43** A.2d 716.
Ga.—Townley v. Rich's, Inc., 67 S.E.2d 403, 84 Ga.App. 772—Bray v.

Barrett, 65 S.E.2d 612, 84 Ga.App. 114—Bryant v. S. H. Kress & Co., 46 S.E.2d 600, 76 Ga.App. 530.
Ill.—Olinger v. Great Atlantic & Pacific Tea Co., 167 N.E.2d 595, 26 Ill.App.2d 88, affirmed 173 N.E.2d 443, 21 Ill.2d 469—Wesbrock v. Colby, Inc., 43 N.E.2d 405, 315 Ill.App. 494—Todd v. S. S. Kresge Co., 24 N.E.2d 899, 303 Ill.App. 89.
Ind.—Clark Fruit Co. v. Stephan, 170 N.E. 558, 91 Ind.App. 152.
Iowa.—Crouch v. Pauley, 116 N.W.2d 486, 254 Iowa 14—Anderson v. Younker Bros., Inc., 89 N.W.2d 858, 249 Iowa 923—Atherton v. Hoenig's Grocery, 86 N.W.2d 252, 249 Iowa 50—Osborn v. Klaber Bros., 287 N.W. 252, 227 Iowa 105.
Kan.—Marietta v. Springer, 392 P.2d 858, 193 Kan. 266—Little v. Butner, 348 P.2d 1022, 186 Kan. 75—**Corpus Juris cited in** Thogmartin v. Koppel, 65 P.2d 571, 152, 145 Kan. 347.
Ky.—Winn-Dixie Louisville, Inc. v. Smith, 372 S.W.2d 789—Winebarger v. Fee, 205 S.W.2d 1010, 305 Ky. 814—Lyle v. Megerle, 109 S.W.2d 598, 270 Ky. 227—F. W. Woolworth Co. v. Brown, 79 S.W.2d 362, 258 Ky. 29.
La.—Burns v. Child's Properties, Inc., App., 156 So.2d 610, writ denied 159 So.2d 284, 245 La. 567—Provost v. Great Atlantic & Pacific Tea Co., App., 154 So.2d 597—Cannon v. Great Atlantic & Pacific Tea Co., App., 146 So.2d 804—Grelle v. Patecek, App., 74 So.2d 349.
Mass.—Boehm v. S. S. Kresge Co., 145 N.E.2d 691, 336 Mass. 320—Greenfield v. Freedman, 103 N.E.2d 242, 328 Mass. 272.
Mich.—Muth v. W. P. Lahey's Inc., 61 N.W.2d 619, 338 Mich. 513—Steggall v. W. T. Knepp & Co., 217 N.W. 16, 241 Mich. 260.
Miss.—Louisiana Oil Corporation v. Davis, 158 So. 792, 172 Miss. 126.
Mo.—Wilkins v. Allied Stores of Missouri, 308 S.W.2d 623—Happy v. Walz, 213 S.W.2d 410, 358 Mo. 56.
   Cayer v. J. C. Penney Co., App., 326 S.W.2d 413—Sullivan v. S. S. Kresge Co., 163 S.W.2d 811, 236 Mo.App. 1191—Stewart v. George

[Illustration 86]

PAGE FROM INDEX TO AMERICAN JURISPRUDENCE 2d

AM JUR 2d

LANDLORD AND TENANT—Cont'd

Common use by tenants, responsibility of landlord as to part of premises maintained for, L & T §§ 805-827

Concealment, liability of landlord to tenant and persons in right of tenant as to, L & T §§ 787-792

Conditional seller to tenant, priority of landlord's lien as against, L & T §§ 719-721

Condition, repair, and improvement of premises

- common use, liability of landlord for defects in premises maintained for, L & T §§ 818-827
- contracts or agreements, infra
- damages, infra

LANDLORD AND TENANT—Cont'd

Condition, repair, and improvement of premises—Cont'd

- unsanitary or defective condition of premises as defense to action for rent, L & T §§ 597-599
- use and enjoyment of demised premises, infra

Conditions. Covenants and conditions, infra

Condominiums, Condomin §§ 6-20

Consent
- assignment of leasehold, consent to, L & T §§ 421-424
- holding over, assent of landlord as to tenancy on, L & T §§ 1143-1145
- subletting, consent to, L & T §§ 495-499

Step 1.

Use index volume to AM JUR2d. The entry noted in this illustration indicates that the topic under research is discussed in the AM JUR volume on Landlord and Tenant starting at Section 805.

- eviction, making repairs or failure to make repairs, improvements, or alterations as constituting, L & T §§ 314-317
- independent contractor employed for making repairs or improvements, effect on landlord's liability, L & T §§ 874-877
- nuisance or dangerous condition existing at time of lease, landlord's liability to person outside demised premises for, L & T §§ 903-907
- particular conditions, landlord's liability to tenant or persons in right of tenant as to, L & T §§ 878-897
- payment for repairs and improvements
- - agreement of landlord to pay for repairs or improvements by tenant, L & T §§ 860-868
- - duty of landlord to make or pay for, L & T §§ 774-779
- persons outside demised premises, duties and liabilities of landlord to, L & T §§ 898-921
- tenant and persons in right of tenant, duties and liabilities of landlord to, L & T §§ 767-897
- third person, duties and liabilities of tenant as to, L & T §§ 981-989

- damages, L & T §§ 176-190
- enforcement of provisions of lease, L & T §§ 176-190
- extension or renewal provisions in lease, L & T §§ 1160-1167
- extrinsic facts, L & T §§ 145-153
- leases, construction of, generally, L & T §§ 141-190
- modification and discharge of lease, L & T §§ 166-174
- option to terminate or provision for termination, construction of, L & T §§ 1000,1001
- parol evidence rule, L & T §§ 145-153
- renewal or extension provisions in lease, construction as to, generally, L & T §§ 1160-1167
- repairs or improvements, contracts as to
- - express provision as to liability of tenant for condition of property at expiration of term, L & T §§ 963-968
- - landlord's agreement to make repairs, construction of, L & T §§ 832-837
- - tenant's agreement to make repairs or improvements, construction of, L & T §§ 945-949

312

[Illustration 87]
PAGE FROM 49 AM.JUR.2d

49 Am Jur 2d   LANDLORD AND TENANT   § 817

There is authority to the effect that assumption of risk by a tenant, relied upon as a defense against the landlord's responsibility for the consequences of his failure to make repairs, must be specially pleaded.[9]

§ 817. — Unlighted premises.

Where the accident is alleged to have been due to the unlighted condition of the halls and stairways of premises used in common by different tenants, the question of the contributory negligence of the plaintiff arises.[10]   The question is presented in three different aspects: (1) where the injured person was familiar with the premises, and there were no defects in the hall or stairway; (2) where there were other defects in the hall or stairway, and the injured person, with knowledge thereof, ventured to use the hall or stairway when it was unlighted; and (3) where a stranger, with no knowledge of the condition of the premises, undertook to use the same when they were in a darkened condition.[11]   It has been said that while it is generally held that one who is accidentally injured while proceeding in the dark in

> Step 2. Section 817 deals specifically with unlighted premises. Note how AM JUR uses fewer footnotes than C.J.S. as it cites to A.L.R. annotations. 25 A.L.R.2d 496 cited in footnote 11 is on the same subject as the annotation shown in Illustration 23. That annotation supersedes the one at 25 A.L.R.2d 496.
>
> The next step, after reading Sec. 817 and 66 A.L.R.3d 323 is to check the pocket supplement in the AM JUR volume for later cases.

Co. 211 **Mass** 54, 97 NE 745.

Generally, as to contribtuory negligence of infants, see NEGLIGENCE (1st ed § 204).

9. Ziulkowski v Kolodziej, 119 **Conn** 230, 175 A 780, 96 ALR 1065.

10. Gibson v Hoppman, 108 **Conn** 401, 143 A 635, 75 ALR 148; Donnelly v Larkin, 327 **Mass** 287, 98 NE2d 280, 25 ALR2d 487; Gallagher v Murphy, 221 **Mass** 363, 108 NE 1081; Rhodes v Fuller Land & Improv. Co. 92 **NJL** 569, 106 A 400; Truax v Knox, 188 App Div 61, 175 NYS 772.

Annotation: 25 ALR2d 496, 543–565, §§ 12–15; 25 ALR 1273, 1335, s. 39 ALR 294, 305, 58 ALR 1411, 1422, 75 ALR 154, 171, 97 ALR 220, 242.

Practice Aids.—Expert testimony as to adequate lighting of common staircase or hallway. 7 AM JUR PROOF OF FACTS 239, 244, LIGHTS, Proof 1.

11. Gallagher v Murphy, 221 **Mass** 363, 108 NE 1081 (in which the evidence was held to be sufficient to show that the injured person

guilty of contributory negligence, as a matter of law, where she undertook to use an unlighted hallway which she did not know to be unlighted until she had closed the doors from her apartment, and she fell after taking the first step from the threshold of her door); Rhodes v Fuller Land & Improv. Co. 92 NJL 569, 106 A 400; Truax v Knox, 188 App Div 61, 175 NYS 772.

Annotation: 25 ALR2d 496, 543–565, §§ 12–15; 25 ALR 1273, 1335, s. 39 ALR 294, 305, 58 ALR 1411, 1422, 75 ALR 154, 171, 97 ALR 220, 242.

11 U of Pittsburgh L Rev 513 et seq.

The contributory negligence of the guest of a tenant in a tenement building who, in the dark, attempts to enter a water closet, which he assumes to be in the same location on the floor where he is as is a water closet of which he has knowledge on another floor, opens a closed door, and steps through the opening from the hall into an elevator shaft to his injury, will prevent his holding the owner of the building liable for the injury. Steger v Immen, 157 **Mich** 494, 122 NW 104.

781

[Illustration 88]
PAGE FROM AM.JUR. PROOF OF FACTS

LIGHTS

Proof No.

1 Adequate Lighting in Common Staircase or Hallway of Multiple Dwelling—Testimony of Expert
2 Glare From Headlights of Approaching Vehicle Creating Emergency
3 Effect of Glare From Headlights on Vision—Testimony of Ophthalmologist

---

COLLATERAL REFERENCES

For general text discussion
    see American J
      FIC §§ 25,
      AND TENA

For pleading for
    see American J
      3:391, 3:5

For ALR annota
    see those listed
      and ALR2
      AND HIGH
      AND TENA

> After status of law has been determined in Am.Jur.2d this set can be examined to determine the proof required in a case involving lights.
>
> This article in Am.Jur. Proof of Facts could be located from the index volume to the set; or from footnote reference in Am.Jur.2d. It consists of 95 pages and sets forth in detail all the elements a lawyer needs in preparing a case for trial.

CROSS-REFERENCE TABLE

(From American Jurisprudence to Am Jur Proof of Facts)

Am Jur	*Proof of Facts*	*Am Jur*	*Proof of Facts*
AUTOMOBILE AND		LANDLORD AND TENANT	LIGHTS
HIGHWAY TRAFFIC	LIGHTS	§§ 701, 702 1	
§ 332 .... 2, 3			
§§ 450, 707 2			

ANNOTATIONS

Liability of landlord for personal injury or death due to inadequacy or lack of lighting on portion of premises used in common by tenants. 25 ALR2d 496.

Violation of statute or ordinance as to lights in stairways and halls as creating or affecting liability for injuries. 132 ALR 863, 880.

[Illustration 88–a]

PAGE FROM AM.JUR. PROOF OF FACTS

LIGHTS   **Proof 1**

in the hallway in general.   These readings were taken on a plane between two and three feet above the floor with the light-sensitive cell maintained in a horizontal position.

Q.   How did these readings compare with the one on the railing of the staircase?

A.   Each one differed only slightly from it.   The average of all readings was 4.9 footcandles.

Q.   What is your occupation?

A.   Electrical engineer.

> A page showing how Am.Jur. Proof of Facts points out elements of proof necessary in trial.

Q.   How long have you been so engaged?

A.   15 years.

Q.   What degree, if any, have you in relation to this subject?

A.   Master of Science in physics.

Q.   Do you specialize in any particular field?

A.   Illumination engineering.

Q.   Are you engaged in practice in this field at the present time?

A.   Yes.

Q.   For how long have you been so engaged?

A.   Six years.

Q.   Did you at my request visit the residential premises known as 112 . . . . Street in this city?

A.   I did.

Q.   What did you do there?

A.   I made an examination with reference to a measurement of illumination of the back hallway and the staircase leading down from it.

[*Similarity of conditions affecting light at time of injury and*

245

[Illustration 89]

PAGE FROM VOLUME 10, AM.JUR. TRIALS

Article Outline

> After determining the law in Am.Jur. and methods of proof in Am.Jur. P.O.F., Am.Jur. Trials, may be used to prepare for the trial of the case.
>
> This set is in 19 volumes. Each volume consists of substantial articles on different topics written by experienced trial attorneys. These articles can be located by the index to Am.Jur. Trials or by footnote references in Am.Jur.2d or Am.Jur. P.O.F.

SECTION D. STATE ENCYCLOPEDIAS

Some states have encyclopedias devoted to their own laws. Five states have encyclopedias published by the Lawyers Cooperative Publishing/Bancroft-Whitney Co., and they follow the format of *American Jurisprudence 2d* while covering only the laws of a specific state. These are:

> *California Jurisprudence 3d*
> *Florida Jurisprudence*
> *New York Jurisprudence*
> *Ohio Jurisprudence 2d*
> *Texas Jurisprudence 2d*

Three states have encyclopedias published by the West Publishing Co. and these follow the format of *Corpus Juris Secundum.* These are:

> *Illinois Law and Practice*
> *Maryland Law and Practice*
> *Michigan Law and Practice*

A few other states have sets by other publishers.

1. Common Features of State Encyclopedias

   a. *Scope*: case and statutory law (substantive and procedural). The cases include both state and federal courts interpreting state law.

   b. *Arrangement*: alphabetically by topics.

   c. *Index*: general index and individual volume indexes. In some local encyclopedias, the titles included in a volume are separately indexed in the volume.

   d. *Supplementation*: cumulative annual pocket parts and replacement volumes.

   e. *Table of Statutes*: shows where code sections are cited in the local encyclopedia.

   f. *Words and Phrases*: definitions of words and phrases are indexed.

   g. *Research aids*: references to other secondary aids, such as A.L.R. annotations, periodical articles, etc., are often provided.

2. Shepard's Law Locators

See Chapter 15, Section E for a description of these sets.

SECTION E. SUMMARY

1. Corpus Juris Secundum

   a. *Scope*

     (1) Attempts to restate the entire body of American case law citing all reported cases since publication of the title in *Corpus*

Juris. Where there are earlier cases in point, footnote references are given to C.J.   The text supersedes the text of C.J.

(2) Includes some discussion of federal and state statutory law.

(3) Definitions of words and phrases and legal maxims are interfiled alphabetically with the essay topics.

b. *Arrangement*

(1) Alphabetically by titles.

(2) "Law Chart" is an outline of the titles, with all related topics grouped together under seven major divisions.   (General Index, vol. 1.)

(3) Scope-note—delimits and identifies the content of a title.

(4) Analysis—appears after scope-note, giving conceptual breakdown of the topic.

c. *Indexes*

(1) General Index—arranged alphabetically by broad descriptive and legal terms.

(2) Volume Indexes—more detailed subject and fact indexes.

d. *Supplementation*

(1) Cumulative annual pocket supplements to volumes.

(2) Replacement volumes.

2. American Jurisprudence 2d

a. *Scope*

(1) Textual statement of substantive and adjective law, with selected case references.   Supersedes *Am.Jur.*

(2) Greater emphasis on federal statutory laws, federal procedural rules and Uniform State Laws.

(3) State statutory law is treated broadly.

(4) Definitions of words and phrases are noted under the words and phrases which are interfiled alphabetically in a Volume Index.

(5) Footnote references to *A.L.R.* annotations and research aids.

(6) Table of Parallel References in each volume identifies the location of sections of the original edition in *Am.Jur.2d.*

(7) Table of Statutes Cited in each volume covers *United States Code,* Federal Rules of Procedure and Uniform Laws.

(8) *Desk Book.* (See Section B2(4) above).

b. *Arrangement*

(1) Alphabetically by titles.

(2) A scope-note, cross references, notations to federal aspects of the law and an analysis of the section headings precede the text pertaining to a title.

c. *Indexes*

(1) Multivolume Index.

(2) Volume Indexes arranged by topics in a volume with subheadings under each topic.

d. *Supplementation*

(1) Cumulative annual pocket supplements.

(2) Replacement volumes.

e. Citations to other sets of the Total Client Library Service.

3. Local Encyclopedias

For an outline of the generally applicable features of local encyclopedias, see Section D, above.

4. Citation

Citation form for Legal Encyclopedias may be found in Appendix A, at (I), (D), (1).

Chapter 17

LEGAL PERIODICALS

Legal periodicals are an important secondary source in legal research. During the nineteenth century they greatly contributed to improving the image of the legal profession in America.[1] With the ever increasing proliferation of legislation and court decisions, legal periodicals in the twentieth century are playing an increasingly important role in keeping lawyers current on developing areas of the law and in providing information on the specialized areas of the law. The function of a legal periodical may be described as "recording and critici[zing] of doings of legislators and judges, discussion of current case law, narration of lives of eminent lawyers, and the scientific study of * * * jurisprudence."[2] Legal periodicals may be classified into three groups: (1) law school publications, (2) bar association publications and (3) special subject and interest periodicals.

SECTION A. LEGAL PERIODICALS

1. Law School Reviews

The periodical publications of law schools are generally called "reviews" (as the *Harvard Law Review* or *Michigan Law Review*). Law school reviews play a unique role in legal research. One distinctive nature of law school reviews is the control of their editorial

---

[1] M. BLOOMFIELD, AMERICAN LAWYERS IN A CHANGING SOCIETY 1776–1876, at 142–143 (1976). For a brief account of legal periodicals in nineteenth-century America *see*, L. FRIEDMAN, A HISTORY OF AMERICAN LAW 546–548 (1973). Some additional references that deal with the early history of legal periodicals in the United States are as follows:

1. Brainerd, *Historical Sketch of American Legal Periodicals*, 14 L.LIB.J. 63 (1921).
2. Pound, *Types of Legal Periodicals*, 14 IOWA L.REV. 257 (1929).
3. *Digest of American Reports and American Law Periodicals*, 23 AM.JURIST 128 (1840).

A complete list of legal periodicals of the last century and their dates of publication may be found in L. JONES INDEX TO LEGAL PERIODICALS TO 1886, at vii–xiii (1888), and 1887–1899, at vii–xii.

[2] F. HICKS, MATERIALS AND METHODS OF LEGAL RESEARCH 210 (3d rev. ed. 1942).

policy and management by student editors. As one legal scholar has noted:

> There is not so far as I know in the world an academic faculty which pins its reputation before the public upon the work of undergraduate students—there is none, that is, except in the American law reviews.[3]

The students forming the board of editors are chosen entirely on the basis of their scholarship record or, in some instances, through a writing competition. Each year a new board is chosen and has the responsibility for the publication of the next volume.

The typical law review is in two or more sections. The first consists of solicited leading articles, usually written by law professors, on various legal topics. These articles are usually scholarly in nature and frequently have a substantial impact in changing the law or in charting the course for newly developing fields of law.[4] The second section is written entirely by the students and is devoted to surveys of selected subjects and critical analyses of current court decisions. In many law reviews the former are called "comments" and the latter "notes". Many reviews also publish book reviews. There are now published more than 200 law school reviews. The vast majority of law reviews are general in nature with no emphasis placed on any specific subjects,[5] but some continue to stress only the law of the state where they are published. A new trend in law schools is to publish more than one review; in such instances the publications are on specialized subjects, such as civil rights, constitutional law, environmental law or international law.[6]

---

[3] K. LLEWELLYN, THE BRAMBLE BUSH 105 (2d ed. 1951).

[4] *E. g.* Warren & Brandeis, *The Right to Privacy*, 4 HARV.L.REV. 193 (1890).

[5] During the 1950's and 1960's there was a trend for law reviews to change their format and devote their efforts toward covering a single area of the law. More recently, this trend appears to be abating. The following journals have changed titles and formats: *Wyoming Law Journal* to *Land and Water Law Review* (with v. 1, no. 1, 1966); *University of Detroit Law Journal* to *Journal of Urban Law* (with v. 44, no. 1, Fall 1966); *Journal of Public Law* to *Emory Law Journal* (with v. 23, no. 1, Winter 1974); *Law and the Social Order* to *Arizona State Law Journal* (with 1974, no. 1).

[6] The following are representative titles from seven American law schools:
Columbia University Law School:
> *Columbia Human Rights Law Review*
> *Columbia Journal of Environmental Law*
> *Columbia Journal of Law and Social Problems*
> *Columbia Journal of Transnational Law*
> *Columbia Law Review*

Harvard University Law School:
> *Harvard Civil Rights–Civil Liberties Law Review*
> *Harvard International Law Journal*

In general, the objectives of law school reviews are these:
"(1) To serve the practicing bar and the profession, and through
them the nation as a whole; (2) to educate students in the method
of legal research, analysis, and expression." [7]

The law school reviews have had a high degree of success in meeting these goals.[8]   The foremost legal scholars of this century have

> *Harvard Journal on Legislation*
> *Harvard Law Review*
> University of California, Hastings College of Law:
>> *Hastings Constitutional Law Quarterly*
>> *Hastings Law Journal*
> University of California School of Law (Berkeley):
>> *California Law Review*
>> *Ecology Law Quarterly*
> University of Michigan Law School:
>> *Michigan Law Review*
>> *University of Michigan Journal of Law Reform*
> University of Texas School of Law:
>> *American Journal of Criminal Law*
>> *Texas International Law Journal*
>> *Texas Law Review*
>> *Urban Law Review*
> Yale University Law School:
>> *Yale Law Review*
>> *Yale Review of Law and Social Problems*
>> *Yale Studies in World Public Order*

The following international legal periodicals are edited at American law schools:
> *Brooklyn Journal on International Law*
> *California Western International Law Journal*
> *Case Western International Law Journal*
> *Columbia Journal of Transnational Law*
> *Cornell International Law Journal*
> *Denver Journal of International Law and Policy*
> *Georgia Journal of International and Comparative Law*
> *Harvard International Law Journal*
> *Journal of International Law and Economics* (George Washington University)
> *Journal of Space Law* (University of Mississippi)
> *Law and Policy in International Business* (Georgetown University)
> *Lawyer of the Americas* (University of Miami)
> *New York University Journal of International Law and Politics*
> *Stanford Journal of International Studies*
> *Syracuse Journal of International Law and Commerce*
> *Texas International Law Journal*
> *Vanderbilt Journal of Transnational Law*
> *Virginia Journal of International Law*

[7] Cribbett, *Experimentations in the Law Reviews*, 5 J.LEGAL ED. 72, 74 (1952).

[8] *See, e. g.*, Douglas, *Law Reviews and Full Disclosure*, 40 WASH.L.REV. 227
(1965); Warren, *Upon the Tenth Anniversary of the UCLA Law Review*, 10 U.C.
L.A.L.REV. 1 (1962); Hughes, *Foreward*, 50 YALE L.J. 737 (1940); Edmunds,
Hail to Law Reviews, 1 JOHN MAR.J.PRAC. & PROC. 1 (1967); M. HALL,
SELECTED WRITINGS OF BENJAMIN NATHAN CARDOZO 190–192 (1947).

written for law reviews, and their articles have been instrumental in molding the course of many legal doctrines. Increasingly, courts have cited law review articles and student comments.[9] It is interesting to note that only as recently as the 1920's did the Supreme Court of the United States begin citing law review articles in its opinions,[10] while presently it is indeed a rare decision of the Court which does not cite or quote from a law review article.

But law school reviews have not been without their critics.[11] The substance of the criticism is aimed at their pedantic style and their similarity to each other. Indeed, some members of Congress have even attacked law reviews as having an insidious influence on the Supreme Court of the United States.[12]

Law school reviews do, however, play a significant role in the growth of the law and remain important to legal research. The typical review may be summarized as being subsidized by its parent institution, with its circulation usually limited to law libraries, its alumni, and members of the bar within the jurisdiction where it is published.[13] It is edited by a select group of law students and serves as an important vehicle for the publication of significant legal research as well as an incisive and effective teaching tool.

2. Bar Association Periodicals

Each state and the District of Columbia have bar associations. In some states membership is voluntary; in other states it is a prerequisite to the practice of law within the state. The latter have what is called an "integrated bar." [14] In addition, many counties and larger cities have their own local bar association. Most of the state bar associations and many of the local ones publish periodicals. They vary in scope from such distinguished periodicals as the American

---

[9] For a recent, scientific study of the citation patterns of the "major" law reviews *see*, Maru, *Measuring the Impact of Legal Periodicals*, 1 A.B.F.RES.J. 227 (1976).

[10] Newland, *The Supreme Court and Legal Writing: Learned Journals as Vehicles of an Anti-Trust Lobby?*, 48 GEO.L.J. 105, 127 (1959).

[11] *See e. g.*, Rodell, *Goodbye to Law Reviews*, 23 VA.L.REV. 38 (1936) and *Goodbye to Law Reviews—Revisited*, 48 VA.L.REV. 279 (1962); Miller, *The Law Journals*, 5 CHANGE 64 (1973).

[12] 103 CONG.REC. 16159–16162 (1957) (remarks of Representative Patman). *See also*, Douglas, *supra* note 8.

[13] The *Harvard Law Review* has the largest circulation at 10,000; *Yale Law Journal* has 4,500; *Minnesota Law Review*, 2,215; *North Carolina Law Review*, 1,900. Circulation figures are obtained from *Ulrich's International Periodicals Directory*. (16th ed. 1975–76).

[14] For a complete list *see*: AMERICAN BAR ASSOCIATION 1974/75 DIRECTORY 214A–219A.

Bar Association Journal [15] or the *Record of the Bar of the City of New York,* to those that are little more than newsletters.[16] The primary purposes of bar association publications are to inform the membership of the associations' activities, to comment on pending and recent legislation, and to review current local court decisions. When they do publish articles, they tend to stress the more practical aspects of the law, with emphasis upon problem-solving, rather than the theoretical ones. They are concerned more with the law as it is rather than with what it should be. Thus, they perform different functions than the law school reviews, where the emphasis is upon reform and scholarly legal research. As a consequence, bar association publications have less historical value but are more useful when researching subjects of current interest to practitioners.

3. Subject and Interest Legal Periodicals

As the literature of the law grows and reflects the increasing complexity of society, it has become ever more difficult for a lawyer to keep current not only with the general development of the law, but also with their particular legal interests. Concurrently with this law explosion, there has been developing a movement in the legal profession towards the interest of one particular sub-group within the legal profession. Some are published by law schools, edited by students, and follow the format of the traditional law review; others are published by non-profit associations; and still others are published by private publishing companies. Another recent develop-

---

[15] Allen, *A Preliminary Listing of Current Publications of A.B.A.—Approved Law Schools and Their Libraries,* 67 L.LIB.J. 79 (1974).

[16] A few states publish legal newspapers which serve as official reporters for certain state and district courts in their jurisdictions. Periodicals which daily compile opinions, legal notices, and various articles by legal scholars of the bench and bar include the following:

Chicago Daily Law Bulletin,
415 N. State Street
Chicago, IL   60610
Legal Intelligencer,
66 N. Juniper Street
Philadelphia, PA   19107
Los Angeles Daily Journal,
210 S. Spring Street
Los Angeles, CA   90012
New Jersey Law Journal,
240 Mulberry Street
Newark, NJ   07101
New York Law Journal,
New York Law Publ. Co.,
258 Broadway
New York, NY   10007

A complete list of legal newspapers is available in the *Ayer Directory,* West Washington Square, Philadelphia, Pennsylvania, 19106.

ment has been the publication of periodicals devoted to law and its interaction with another discipline. These reflect the increasing emphasis many law schools and legal scholars are placing on integrating the findings of the social and behavioral sciences with the legal process.

a. Subject Journals.

Journals devoted to one area of law vary in scope from the very practical to the very scholarly.[17] The *Insurance Law Journal* [18] or *Trusts and Estates*,[19] both published by private companies, are examples of periodicals aimed primarily at the practicing attorney specializing in particular fields of law. They contain articles written by well-known practitioners interpreting the impact of recent legislation and court decisions and may contain reviews of books within their subject area. The *American Journal of Legal History* [20] and the *American Journal of Comparative Law* [21] are examples of periodicals published under the auspices of learned societies, while the *Ecology Law Quarterly*,[22] published at the University of California, Berkeley, School of Law, and the *Urban Law Review*,[23] pub-

[17] A few publishers have begun the practice of collecting the best articles written and published over the course of each year, and combining them into a single volume which measures the development of the law in a particular subject area over the period. ADVERTISING LAW is an example of one such annual. Another annual which changed its approach to include original articles which update the law is the CRIMINAL JUSTICE REVIEW.

[18] *Insurance Law Journal,*
Commerce Clearing House, Inc.
4025 W. Peterson Ave.,
Chicago, IL   60646

[19] *Trusts and Estates,*
Communication Channels, Inc.,
461 8th Ave.,
New York, N.Y.   10001

[20] *American Journal of Legal History,*
Temple University School of Law,
1715 N. Broad St.,
Philadelphia, PA   19122

[21] *American Journal of Comparative Law,*
Boalt Hall,
University of California,
Berkeley, CA   94720

[22] *Ecology Law Quarterly,*
School of Law (Boalt Hall),
University of California
Berkeley, CA   94720

[23] *Urban Law Review,*
University of Texas Law School,
2500 Red River,
Austin, TX   78705

lished at the University of Texas School of Law, are typical of subject journals that are similar to law school reviews.

b.   Special Interest Periodicals.

These periodicals are aimed at those members of the bar who have similar interests and serve as a means to encourage writing and research within the special area of interest.   They include such journals as *Black Law Journal*,[24] the *Women Lawyers Journal*,[25] the *Catholic Lawyer*,[26] the *Christian Lawyer*,[27] and the *Judges' Journal*.[28]

c.   Interdisciplinary Journals.

Perhaps the most distinguished of this group is the *Journal of Law and Economics*,[29] published by the faculty of the School of Law at the University of Chicago.   Other representative titles are the *University of Michigan Journal of Law Reform*,[30] the *Journal of*

[24] *Black Law Journal*,
UCLA,
1228 Campbell Hall,
Los Angeles, CA   90024

[25] *Women Lawyers Journal*,
National Assoc. of Women Lawyers,
American Bar Center,
1155 E. 60th St.,
Chicago, IL   60637

[26] *Catholic Lawyer*,
St. Thomas More Institute for Legal
Research of St. John's Univ. School of Law,
Grand Central & Utopia Pkwys.,
Jamaica, N.Y.   11439

[27] *Christian Lawyer*,
Christian Legal Society,
P.O. Box 363,
Chicago, IL   60690

[28] *Judges' Journal*,
American Bar Assoc.,
Nat. Conf. of State Trial Judges,
Chicago, IL   60637

[29] *Journal of Law & Economics*,
Univ. of Chicago Law School,
111 E. 60th St.,
Chicago, IL   60637

[30] *Univ. of Michigan Journal of Law Reform*,
Univ. of Michigan Law School,
731 Legal Research Building,
Ann Arbor, MI   48104

Psychiatry and Law,[31] *Law and Society Review*,[32] and the *Journal of Legal Medicine*.[33]

SECTION B.   COMPREHENSIVE PERIODICAL INDEXES

As described in Section A the usefulness of legal periodicals to legal research depends almost entirely on the ability to find out what articles have been written and where they have been published. Generally, it is necessary to rely on indexes to the legal periodical literature for this purpose.

1.   Jones-Chipman Index to Legal Periodicals, 1886–1937, 6 vols.

This was the first index that attempted to provide a comprehensive and systematic index to English language legal periodicals. It is still necessary to consult this set to locate articles published between 1887 and 1908.

2.   Index to Legal Periodicals

The most comprehensive index is the *Index to Legal Periodicals*. This started publication in 1908 by the American Association of Law Libraries. In 1961, publication was assumed by the H. W. Wilson Co. Since then the Committee on the *Index to Legal Periodicals* of the American Association of Law Libraries has served in an advisory capacity to the publisher on indexing and editorial policy. This *Index* does not attempt to be all-inclusive but rather restricts its coverage to legal periodicals published in the United States, Canada, Great Britain, Ireland, Australia and New Zealand when such serials are regularly published, have legal content of high quality, and are of permanent reference value. The publisher relies almost entirely on the Committee for the inclusion or exclusion of titles. The *Index* also includes only articles which are at least five ordinary pages or two folio pages in length. Case notes, bibliographies, biographies, and book reviews must be at least two ordinary pages or one folio page in length.

31 *Journal of Psychiatry & Law*,
   Federal Legal Publications,
   95 Morton,
   New York, N.Y.   10014

32 *Law & Society Review*,
   Univ. of Denver College of Law,
   200 W. 14th Ave.,
   Denver, CO   80204

33 *Journal of Legal Medicine*,
   777 Third Ave.,
   New York, N.Y.   10017

Authors are listed only as cross-references to subjects, the only headings under which articles are fully indexed. Current issues are published monthly, except for September, and are cumulated semi-annually, annually, and triennially.[34] Each of the cumulations contains a "List of Subject Headings." In addition to indexing articles, there is a "Table of Cases Commented Upon" which gives the names of all cases (for the time period of the issue) that have had a note or comment written on them. Under the name of the case, citations are given to the periodicals. Each issue and cumulative volume also has a "Book Review Index," which lists by author all books reviewed in the periodicals indexed by the *Index to Legal Periodicals.* Under the author's name is the title of the book, followed by the citations to periodicals where the reviews appeared.

As the *Index to Legal Periodicals* is the most complete available index to legal periodicals for the major common law jurisdictions, it is indispensable when utilizing legal periodicals in legal research. A researcher should know, however, its several limitations.[35] These are summarized below:

    a.   Periodicals not indexed. Legal periodicals not published in the United States, Great Britain, Canada, Australia, or New Zealand are not included. Also coverage is limited strictly to legal periodicals; legal articles in journals similar to the *Stanford Journal of International Studies, Foreign Affairs,* or the *American Political Science Review* are not indexed in it. Moreover, the requirement of the *Index to Legal Periodicals* that indexed periodicals include "regularly published legal content of high quality and permanent reference value" results in many worthwhile articles not being covered. Finally, one must be aware that not all legal periodicals from the above named countries are covered in the *Index to Legal Periodicals.* Many of those omitted are publications of bar associations.

    b.   The limitation as to length of article results at times, in the omission of useful articles that are less than five pages long.

[34] A weekly newsletter style publication which supplements the *Index to Legal Periodicals* is the *Current Index to Legal Periodicals* published by the University of Washington Law Library and Washington Law Review. The subject headings are very broad and no master or cumulative indices are provided. It is a useful tool only for those researchers wishing to find articles published more recently than the last monthly edition of the *Index to Legal Periodicals.*

[35] G. Grossman, Report of the Subcommittee on the *Index to Legal Periodicals* (to the) Committee on Libraries (to the) Association of American Law Schools, December 1975 (unpublished report in Tarlton Law Library, University of Texas at Austin).

c.   Indexing Policy.

(1) Insufficient List of Subject Headings.   At times the lack of a sufficient number of subject terms makes the location of articles on specific subjects difficult.   For example, the 1970–1973 cumulative volume lists 98 titles under the subject "Legal Profession."   Since each title is listed alphabetically under subject, it is necessary to scan each one in order to locate all titles on the particular aspect of the legal profession that is being researched.   This can be both a time consuming and frustrating process.

(2) Inconsistent Subject Indexing.   The tendency for this *Index* to be less than precise in assigning the same subjects to similar articles makes it necessary to search frequently for articles covering the same topic under two or more subject terms.   Otherwise, important articles will be missed.   As an example, assume that a search for articles dealing with lost credit cards is being made.   In the 1970–1973 cumulative volume, under the subject "Consumer Protection" the article entitled "Consumer protection—credit card protection under the truth-in-lending act" will be found, while under the subject term "Credit" will be found "Apportionment of credit card fraud loss."

The inconsistency of the indexing makes it mandatory that a search be conducted under all possible subject headings.   The "List of Subject Headings" in the front of each volume should always be consulted, and all "See Also" references listed under each subject must be searched.

(3) Indexing of Survey Articles and Case Notes.   Case notes (since 1963) are listed as a subdivision under each title but only citations are given.   The omission of the title for each note means that it is not possible to ascertain the precise topic of the note.   In the latest triennial volume, 11 cases are cited under "Criminal Law", but there is no indication as to what aspect of criminal law the notes on these cases cover.

There has been considerable improvement over the years in the quality of the *Index to Legal Periodicals*, which is constantly under consideration by the Committee on the *Index to Legal Periodi-*

cals of the American Association of Law Libraries, and further improvement may be anticipated. It is also likely that better indexing will result from the increasing use of the computer in legal research. The *Index to Legal Periodicals*, however, remains as the most useful reference work for finding periodical articles when used with care. Section G (Illustrations) *infra* should be carefully examined in order to obtain the most efficient use of the *Index to Legal Periodicals*.

<hr>

SECTION C. OTHER INDEXES TO LEGAL PERIODICAL LITERATURE

The limitations of the *Index to Legal Periodicals* described above make necessary familiarity with other sources for locating periodical articles. These are:

1.   Index to Periodical Articles Related to Law [36]

This publication is issued quarterly and indexes all articles of a legal nature in English that, in the judgment of the editors, are of research value and appear in periodicals that are not covered by the *Index to Legal Periodicals* or the *Index to Foreign Legal Periodicals*. It is arranged in four parts: A Subject Index; an Index to Articles; a List of Journals Indexed; and an Author Index. The last issue of each volume is a cumulative one. There is a ten-year cumulation covering the years 1958–1968 and a five-year cumulation covering the years 1969–1973. Since legal subjects are assuming greater prominence in a variety of non-legal periodicals, this index is particularly useful in locating timely articles on newly developing areas which often first appear in non-legal journals. With fifteen or more different periodical indices being brought together in this publication, it is a useful tool as companion to the *Index to Legal Periodicals*.

2.   Annual Legal Bibliography

This is published by the Harvard Law School Library. It is issued first in a monthly pamphlet called *Current Legal Bibliography*, which is then cumulated annually. It is an index to selected books and articles received at the Harvard Law School Library. Unlike most indexes, it is arranged in a classified, rather than alphabetical, manner. Section A covers Common Law Jurisdictions; Section B, Civil Law and Other Jurisdictions; Section C, Private International Law; and Section D, Public International Law. Each section is classified hierarchically, i. e., there is a main class such as "Corpo-

<hr>

[36] *Index to Periodical Articles Related to Law*, Glanville Publishers, Inc., Dobbs Ferry, N. Y. 10522. Edited by R. M. Mersky and J. M. Jacobstein, this index started publication in 1958.

rations," and then all of the subdivisions within corporations are arranged under it. Since the Harvard Law Library is the largest law school library in the world and since this *Index* includes books as well as periodical articles, it is an extremely useful bibliographic reference tool, especially when searching for materials in international and comparative law. Its classified arrangement makes it more difficult to use and the lack of any cumulation of the annual volumes makes it cumbersome for retrospective searching.

3. Index to Foreign Legal Periodicals

Since 1960, the Institute of Advanced Legal Studies of the University of London, in cooperation with the American Association of Law Libraries, has published an *Index to Foreign Legal Periodicals*. It covers a wide range of journals dealing with International Law (Public and Private), Comparative Law and the Municipal Law of all countries of the world other than the United States, the British Isles and nations of the British Commonwealth whose legal systems are based on the common law. It mainly complements and, to a limited extent, duplicates the *Index to Legal Periodicals*.

The *Index to Foreign Legal Periodicals* is published quarterly with annual and triennial cumulations. Articles and book reviews of two or more pages in length are indexed in this publication. Titles of articles are given in the language of publication, transliterated for those languages not using the Roman alphabet. The subject headings are alphabetically arranged and reasonably follow the established headings of the *Index to Legal Periodicals*.

The publication is divided into the following units: (1) subject index; (2) geographical index; grouping, by country or region, the topics of the articles listed in the subject index; (3) book review index; and (4) author index. As in the *Index to Legal Periodicals*, the author-index entries refer to the subject index where the notations are complete.

4. Index to Indian Legal Periodicals

Since 1963 the Indian Law Institute (New Delhi, India) has issued this publication which indexes periodicals (including yearbooks and other annuals) pertaining to law and related fields published in India. Articles, case comments, notes and other material are included irrespective of the length of the material. Unbound issues appear semi-annually with bound, annual cumulations.

5. Index to Canadian Legal Periodical Literature

This ambitious index was started by the Canadian Association of Law Libraries in 1961 to cover the growing number of Canadian legal journals and to give access to two systems of law, Civil and

Common, in two languages, English and French. A cumulation volume for 1961–70 has appeared, and annual cumulations of bimonthly issues have subsequently been published. Series of audio-cassettes are also indexed.

6. Current Index to Commonwealth Legal Periodicals

This monthly publication began in September, 1974, and is issued by the Sir James Dunn Law Library, Dalhousi University, Halifax, Canada.

7. Contents of Current Legal Periodicals [37]

Published now by the Corporation Services Company, this monthly service reprints the table of contents for each currently issued legal periodical and includes an index of articles by field of law.

SECTION D.   INDEXES TO SUBJECT PERIODICALS

1. Tax Planning and Research Indices for Periodicals

Begun in 1974 by Pro-dex Publishers, this looseleaf service identifies and chronologically organizes all of the tax articles and other research materials appearing in the major American tax-oriented periodicals. The period covered is 1965 to date.

2. Index to Federal Tax Articles

Compiled by Gersham Goldstein of the University of Cincinnati Law School and published by Warren, Gorham and Lamont, this 3-volume, computer-produced work appeared in 1975. It covers the literature on federal income, estate and gift taxation contained in legal, specialized tax, and economic journals, as well as nonperiodical publications. Consisting of separate subject and author indexes, all of the entries are arranged in reverse chronological order so that the most recent entry appears first. A periodic updating service is planned.

3. Commerce Clearing House, Federal Tax Articles

This monthly looseleaf reporter of the Commerce Clearing House, Inc., which began publication in 1962, contains summaries of articles on federal (income, estate, gift and excise) taxes appearing in legal, accounting, business and related periodicals. Proceedings and papers delivered at major tax institutes are also noted. The con-

---

[37] Some law schools also publish reprints of current table of contents pages of those periodicals which their libraries receive. An example of one school which produces copies for its own use is the *Contents Pages of Legal Periodicals* compiled at the Tarlton Law Library, University of Texas at Austin.

tents are arranged by Internal Revenue Code section numbers. To find articles on federal tax problems refer to the division entitled "Articles by Code Section" using the section number of the Internal Revenue Code. Each item is preceded by a decimal number which combines with the Code section for referencing. Descriptions of recent articles are included under Code section numbers in the division entitled "Current Articles by Code Section." To locate articles on a subject, consult the "Index by Topic" and the "Current Index by Topic." Articles are listed by author names in the "Index by Author" and the "Current Index by Author." Each basic unit has a "Current" materials or a "Current" index section. To identify the publishers of the articles, check the periodicals covered in the Reporter under the "List of Publications" division. Volume one covers the years 1954–67, volume 2, 1968 to date.

SECTION E.   PERIODICAL DIGESTS AND ABSTRACTS

1.   Monthly Digest of Tax Articles

This monthly periodical presents significant current tax articles in abridged form. Initially published by Matthew Bender in October, 1950, it was assumed by Newkirk Associates in July, 1952.

2.   Monthly Digest of Legal Articles

Selected legal articles from 200 periodicals are condensed and published monthly, closely following the words and style of the original writers. It began publication in March, 1969, by the Research and Documentation Corp.

3.   Law Review Digest

This bi-monthly digest contains selected, condensed articles from the legal periodical literature. It was started by Kimball-Clark Co. in November, 1950 and was transferred to The Barrister's Press in 1975.

4.   Abstracts on Criminology and Penology

Formerly *Excerpta Criminologica* (Volumes 1–8:1961–68), this is an international abstracting service covering the etiology of crime and juvenile delinquency, the control and treatment of offenders, criminal procedure and the administration of justice. It is prepared by the Criminologica Foundation in cooperation with the University of Leiden, The Hague, Netherlands.

SECTION F.   OTHER SOURCES

References to periodical articles may frequently be found in other reference books. Many state codes and the annotated editions of the

United States Code will cite relevant articles in the notes preceding the annotations. Additionally, many of the digests will, under each topic and key-number, give citations to pertinent law review articles.

1. Shepard's Law Review Citations

Shepard's Law Review Citations lists citations since 1957 to articles in law reviews and legal periodicals. Volumes include citations from all cases reported in the Supreme Court Reporter, the Federal Reporter 2d, the Federal Supplement, and the Federal Rules Decisions. Cases found in any series of state reports or any unit of the National Reporter System are also included in their respective citator volumes. Finally, citations since 1957 appearing in articles in numerous selected law reviews and legal periodicals are shown.

As additional law reviews and legal periodicals are included in *Shepard's Law Review Citations*, a footnote on the page for a particular review or periodical will indicate whenever the citations commence subsequent to 1957. This unit consists of the 1974 bound volume and the paper-covered cumulative supplements. The law reviews and legal periodicals to which citations are shown in this publication are arranged in alphabetical order, and in most instances citations to a particular law review or periodical may be located by reference to the name of the publication which appears at the top of each page of citations.

2. Federal Law Citations in Select Law Reviews

This unit of Shepard's indicates when the United States Supreme Court Reports, Federal Reporter 2d, Federal Supplement, Federal Rules Decisions, the United States Constitution, and the United States Code have been cited in the following law reviews beginning with the volume shown:

61 California Law Review (1973)

73 Columbia Law Review (1973)

58 Cornell Law Review (1973)

61 Georgetown Law Journal (1973)

86 Harvard Law Review (1973)

37 Law and Contemporary Problems (1972)

71 Michigan Law Review (1973)

57 Minnesota Law Review (1973)

48 New York Univ. Law Review (1973)

68 Northwestern Univ. Law Review (1974)

25 Stanford Law Review (1973)

51 Texas Law Review (1973)

20 Univ. Of Calif. at Los Angeles Law Review (1973)

40 Univ. of Chicago Law Review (1973)

1973 Univ. of Illinois Law Forum

121 Univ. of Penna. Law Review (1973)

59 Virginia Law Review (1973)

1973 Wisconsin Law Review

82 Yale Law Journal (1973)

3.   Legal Periodical Citation in Other Units of Shepard's Citations

As indicated in Chapter 15, the state units of *Shepard's Citations* indicate when a case or statute has been cited in a legal periodical published in the state or the twenty law reviews covered by all of the state *Shepard's Citations.*

SECTION G. ILLUSTRATIONS FOR LEGAL PERIODICALS

Problem: Find articles or notes or comments on the constitutionality of having less than twelve person juries.

Illustrations

90. Page from list of subject headings used in the Index to Legal Periodicals.

91. Page from Index to Legal Periodicals—1970–1973.

92. Page from the Michigan Law Review.

93. Page from the Case Western Law Review.

94. Page from Table of Cases—Index to Legal Periodicals—1970–1973.

95. Excerpt from Shepard's Law Review Citations.

96. Excerpt from Shepard's Federal Law Citations in Selected Law Reviews.

97. Page from Index to Legal Periodicals—1970–1973.

[Illustration 90]

PAGE FROM LIST OF SUBJECT HEADINGS USED IN THE INDEX TO LEGAL PERIODICALS—1970–1973

LIST OF SUBJECT HEADINGS　　　　　　　　xxxi

INTERNATIONAL law
　　See also Boundaries; Capitulations; Confiscation; Conflict of laws; Consuls; Diplomatic privileges and immunities; Disarmament; Fishing: international law; Genocide; High seas; International arbitration; International conferences; International courts and tribunals; International labor law; International legal assistance; International organization; International trusteeships; Minorities: international law; Peace; Recognition; Re-

JUDICIAL ethics. See Legal ethics
JUDICIAL notice
JUDICIAL opinions. See Opinions
JUDICIAL process. See Administration of justice
JUDICIAL review
JUDICIAL statistics
JUDICIAL systems. See Administration of justice
➤JURIES
　　See also Grand jury; Instructions to juries; verdicts

> A List of Subject Headings used in the Index to Legal Periodicals will be found at the beginning of each volume.
>
> It should always be consulted first to determine which headings are included.
>
> Note the "See also" references to related topics.

INTERSTATE commerce
　　See also Commerce
INTERVENTION (Civil procedure)
INTERVENTION (International law)
INTOXICATING liquors. See Alcoholic beverages
INTOXICATION. See Drunkenness
INVENTIONS. See Patents
INVESTIGATIONS. See Commissions and committees of inquiry; Criminal investigation; Legislative investigations
INVESTMENT companies
　　See also Holding companies
INVESTMENT trusts
INVESTMENTS
　　See also Bonds; Securities; Stocks
INVITEES and licensees. See Negligence; Trespass
IRRIGATION. See Water and watercourses
ISLAMIC law

JEWISH law
JOINDER of actions
JOINT tenancy
JOINT tortfeasors
JOINT ventures
JUDGES
　　See also Justices of the peace
JUDGMENTS
　　See also Declaratory relief; Enforcement of judgments abroad; Opinions; Precedents; **Recognition** of foreign judgments; Res judicata
JUDICIAL administration. See Administration of justice; Courts
JUDICIAL conferences
JUDICIAL councils

LABOR unions. See Unions
LABORERS' liens. See Mechanics' liens
LACHES
LAND titles. See Title to land
LANDLORD and tenant
　　See also Eviction; Fixtures; Leases; Notice; Possession; Rents and rent control; Repairs
LANDS. See Public lands
LANGUAGE
LARCENY
LAST clear chance
LATIN AMERICA
LATIN AMERICAN free trade association
LAW books. See Bibliography
LAW day
LAW enforcement
　　See also Police
LAW in arts and literature
LAW libraries. See Libraries
LAW office management
LAW reform
LAW reviews. See Periodicals
LAW schools
LAW societies. See Bar associations
LAWYERS. See Attorneys
LEASES
LEGAL aid. See Public legal service
LEGAL drafting
　　See also Briefs
LEGAL education
　　See also Law schools
LEGAL education: continuing
LEGAL education: curricula
LEGAL education: teaching
LEGAL ethics
LEGAL history
　　See also History

[Illustration 91]

PAGE FROM INDEX TO LEGAL PERIODICALS,

1970–1973

SUBJECT AND AUTHOR INDEX   515

JUDICIAL review—*Continued*

     Cases

Breen v. Selective Serv. Local No. 16, 90 Sup
   Ct 661
     W&M L Rev 11:1014 Summer '70
Citizens to Preserve Overton Park, Inc. v.
   Volpe, 91 Sup Ct 814
     Case W Res L Rev 22:804 Je '71
     Suffolk U L Rev 5:1090 Spring '71
General Motors Corp. v. Volpe, 321 F Supp
   1112
     BU L Rev 51:161 Winter '71
Hannam v. Bradford C. C. [1970] 1 W L R 937
     Modern L Rev 34:445 Jl '71
Medical Comm'n for Human Rights v. SEC
   432 F 2d 659
     Am U L Rev 20:190 Ag '70

JUDICIAL statistics

Judicial salaries and retirement plans in the
   United States. Judicature 54:184 D '70
Need for criminal court statistics. J. A. Mc-
   Cafferty. Judicature 55:149 N '71

JUDICIAL systems. See Administration of Justice

JUENGER, Friedrich K.

Conflict of laws: contracts (S)
Conflict of laws: domestic rel (G, R)
Const law—Germany (G)
Jurisdiction (S)
Maritime law (S)
Recognition of foreign judgments (R)

Changes in the criminal jury. Miss L J
   43:214 '72
Communications with a deliberating jury by
   court officers in a Pennsylvania civil case.
   Dick L Rev 76:60 Fall '71
Constitutional law—burden of proof in juror
   discrimination cases in Missouri. Mo L Rev
   38:99 Winter '73
Constitutional law—defendant's right to a
   jury trial—is six enough? Ky L J 59:996
   Summer '71
Constitutional law—jury unanimity no longer
   required in state criminal trials. NC L
   Rev 51:134 N '72
Constitutionality of excluding young people
   from jury service. Wash & Lee L Rev
   29:131 Spring '72
Criminal procedure—change of venue for jury
   prejudice. Duquesne L Rev 10:284 Winter
   '71
Deadlocked juries—the "Allen charge" is de-
   fused. U Richmond L Rev 6:370 Spring '72
Economic discrimination in jury selection.
   L & Soc Order 1970:474 '70
Effect of jury size on the probability of con-
   viction: an evaluation of Williams v. Flor-
   ida (90 Sup Ct 1893) Case W Res L Rev 22:
   529 Ap '71
Empirical study of six- and twelve-member
   jury decision-making processes. U Mich
   J L Ref 6:712 Spring '73
Expediting voir dire: an empirical study. W.
   H. Levit & others. So Calif L Rev 44:916
   Summer '71
Federal jury. J. J. Fisher. St Mary's L J
   5:1 Spring '73
Greeks had a jury for it. M. J. Bertoch. ABA
   J 57:1012 O '71

> Under the Subject Heading, titles of articles are listed al-
> phabetically. Note how each title has to be read to determine
> if it deals with less than 12-person juries. In addition to
> those on this page, there are four more relevant articles on the
> next page (not shown).
>
> Under the Heading "Judicial Review", note how case notes
> are listed. Each one has to be examined to determine which
> aspect of judicial review is involved.
>
> Note how authors are listed. Articles written by F. Juenger
> will be found under the subjects listed below his name. The
> letter (s) in parenthesis is the first letter in the title of the
> article.

Codes and codification (S)
Crim law (C, S)
Crim procedure (S)
Penology (D)

JUNN, Robert S.
United Nations: Security council (A)

JURCO, Olga
Justices of the peace (U)

JURIES
All power to the jury—California's demo-
   cratic evidence code. O. M. Kaus. Loyola
   U L Rev (LA) 4:233 Ap '71
Allen charge: dead law a long time dying.
   U San Francisco L Rev 6:326 Ap '72
. . . and then there were none; the diminu-
   tion of the federal jury. H. Zeisel. U Chi
   L Rev 38:710 Summer '71
Assisting the jury in assessing general
   damages—Gray v. Alanco Developments re-
   visited. G. D. Watson. Can B Rev 48:565 S
   '70
Attorney-conducted voir dire of jurors: a con-
   stitutional right. S. Mac Gutman. Brooklyn
   L Rev 39:290 Fall '72
Case of the rebellious juror. R. F. Maxwell.
   Voir dire has its proper uses. H. E. Youtt.
   ABA J 56:838 S '70; 57:38 Ja '71
Challenging the juror selection system in New
   York. Albany L Rev 36:305 Winter '72

sure a defendant due process under the
   law. St Mary's L J 4:470 Winter '72
Juror selection: the law, a mathematical
   method of analysis, and a case study. D
   Kairys. Am Crim L Rev 10:771 Summer
   '72
Juror selection under the uniform code of
   military justice: fact and fiction. R. R.
   Brookshire. II. Mil L Rev 58:71 Fall '72
Jurors' knowledge of the law: voir dire on
   jury instructions. Idaho L Rev 7:257 Fall
   '70
Jury and the risk of nonpersuasion. R. K.
   Winter, jr. Law & Soc Rev 5:335 F '71
Jury as a political institution. J. M. Van
   Dyke. Catholic Law 16:224 Summer '70
Jury bias in Hudson and Bergen counties: a
   view from the bench. T. I. Botter. Seton
   Hall L Rev 4:1 Fall-Winter '72
Jury composition—the purposeful inclusion of
   American Indians. SD L Rev 16:214 Winter
   '71
Jury discrimination in the south: a remedy?
   Column J L & Soc Prob 8:589 Summer '72
Jury: is it viable? Suffolk U L Rev 6:897
   Summer '72
Jury misconduct in Iowa. Drake L Rev 20:641
   Je '71
Jury nullifcation in conscience cases. W. M.
   Kunstler. Va J Int L 10:71 D '69
Jury nullifcation: the forgotten right. New
   England L Rev 7:105 Fall '71

[Illustration 92]

PAGE FROM THE MICHIGAN LAW REVIEW

UNCOVERING "NONDISCERNIBLE" DIFFERENCES: EMPIRICAL RESEARCH AND THE JURY-SIZE CASES

Richard O. Lempert*

I. REASONS FOR NOT DISCERNING DIFFERENCES

IN *Williams v. Florida*[1] the Supreme Court, relying on a "few experiments" that in the eyes of the majority indicated "no discernible difference" in the results reached by six- and twelve-member juries,[2] held that a decrease in the size of the criminal jury from twelve to six members was not inconsistent with the sixth amendment right to jury trial. In *Colgrove v. Battin*[3] the majority read four recent studies as providing "convincing empirical evidence"[4] confirming the conclusion in *Williams*, and so found a

* Professor of Law, University of Michigan. A.B. 1964, Oberlin College; J.D. 1968, Ph.D. 1971, University of Michigan.—Ed.

I would like to thank Dan Russell, who worked for me as a research assistant. He made particularly valuable contributions in helping me search the social-psychological literature on small groups and in programming the statistical analyses reported in this paper. My ... as stimulated by two excellent se₁ ... 1972 graduate of Yale Law School ... f The University of Michigan Law ... sor Angus Campbell by Stephen ... School. I should also like to not₍ ... reader, the great debt I owe to a ... he University of Chicago Law School. Although this paper in parts builds on a criticism of some of Professor Zeisel's work, my research, like the work of others interested in the American jury and the integrity of the jury system, has been significantly advanced by the many articles published by Professor Zeisel and by his important book, coauthored with Professor Kalven, *The American Jury*. Professor Zeisel was kind enough to read and comment on an earlier version of this paper, as were Professors Francis Allen, Shari Seidman Diamond, Joseph Sanders, and G. Joseph Vining. The paper has been strengthened by their comments.

A typical leading article in a typical law review.

1. 399 U.S. 78 (1970).

2. 399 U.S. at 101. The studies cited were Cronin, *Six-Member Juries in District Courts*, 2 BOSTON B.J. No. 4, at 27 (1958); Phillips, *A Jury of Six in All Cases*, 30 CONN. B.J. 354 (1956); Tamm, *The Five-Man Civil Jury, A Proposed Constitutional Amendment*, 51 GEO. L.J. 120 (1962); Wiehl, *The Six Man Jury*, 4 GONZAGA L. REV. 35 (1968); *New Jersey Experiments with Six-Man Jury*, 9 BULL. OF THE SECTION OF JUD. ADMIN. OF THE ABA (May 1966); *Six-Member Juries Tried in Massachusetts District Court*, 42 J. AM. JUD. SOC. 136 (1958).

3. 413 U.S. 149 (1973).

4. 413 U.S. at 159-60 n.15. The four cited studies were INSTITUTE OF JUDICIAL ADMINISTRATION, A COMPARISON OF SIX- AND TWELVE-MEMBER CIVIL JURIES IN NEW JERSEY SUPERIOR AND COUNTY COURTS (1972); Bermant & Coppock, *Outcomes of Six- and Twelve-Member Jury Trials: An Analysis of 128 Civil Cases in the State of Washington*, 48 WASH. L. REV. 593 (1973); Note, *An Empirical Study of Six- and Twelve-Member Jury Decision-Making Processes*, 6 U. MICH. J. L. REF. 712 (1973); Note,

[Illustration 93]

PAGE FROM THE CASE WESTERN LAW REVIEW

1971]   529

NOTES

The Effect of Jury Size on the Probability of Conviction: An Evaluation of Williams v. Florida

I. INTRODUCTION

M ANY FACTORS are relevant to an analysis of a judicial decision. Some of the more important approaches emphasize: (1) how the new legal rules are related to preexisting law; (2) the personal or psychological reasons for the judge's decision;[1] (3) the institutional context of the court, in an effort to elucidate important strengths and weaknesses in the legal system as a whole;[2] (4) non-scientific appraisals of the practical, social effects of the legal rules

---

[1] There are many problems involved in relating the judge's personality, history, cognitive structure, etc., to the decision he reaches in a particular case. Present models of individual behavior are not sufficiently sophisticated to deal with such broad questions. Even if there were a model that adequately described the judge, there would be enormous problems involved in gathering the personal data necessary to use the model in a given case. The problems that arise in both model-construction and data-gathering are discussed in Lewis, *Systems Theory and Judicial Behavioralism*, 21 CASE W. RES. L. REV. 361 (1970), which focuses particularly on a study of Justice Black.

[2] The institutional context of the court can be analyzed from a number of perspectives. *See generally* L. VON BERTALANFFY, GENERAL SYSTEMS THEORY; FOUNDA-

> A typical law review student note. The purpose of student notes or comments are to provide critical analyses of recent cases or topics of law.
>
> Most notes or comments are from two to twelve pages in length.

---

the law schools. The schools are one of the most important institutions in the legal system, but they provide little education beyond the mere art of manipulating legal rules. Many persons have suggested that they should become more social science oriented to remedy this deficiency. *See, e.g.*, S. FOX, SCIENCE AND JUSTICE (1968); Derham, *Legal Education — A Challenge to the Profession*, 43 AUSTL. L.J. 530 (1969); Traynor, *What Domesday Books for Emerging Law?*, 15 U.C.L.A.L. REV. 1105 (1968). Some law schools have already initiated new courses that depart radically from the narrow, traditional approach. For example, Yale Law School has instituted a program of Law and Modernization whose goal is to combine political, social, and economic developments into a policy of social change through the use of law. *See* Yale University, Bulletin of Yale University: Yale Law School (1970).

[Illustration 94]

PAGE FROM TABLE OF CASES—INDEX TO LEGAL PERIODICALS, 1970–1973

1032   INDEX TO LEGAL PERIODICALS 1970–1973

WILLIAMS v. Brown Mfg. Co (Ill) 261 N E 2d
305
  John Marshall J 4:95 Winter '70
  Loyola U L J (Chicago) 1:388 Summer '70
WILLIAMS v. Eaton, 310 F Supp 1342
  — Kan L Rev 19:316 Winter '71
WILLIAMS v. Florida, 90 Sup Ct 1893
  ABA J 56:995 O '70
  Case W Res L Rev 22:119 N '70
  Case W Res L Rev 22:529 Ap '71
  Harv L Rev 84:165 N '70
  J Urban L 48:519 '71
  Ky L J 59:996 Summer '71
  New England L Rev 6:219 Spring '71
  Suffolk U L Rev 5:278 Fall '70
  Syracuse L Rev 22:814 '71
  U Fla L Rev 23:402 Winter '71
  U Miami L Rev 24:832 Summer '70
  Vill L Rev 16:411, 607 Mr–Ap '71
  Yale L J 81:1342 Je '72
WILLIAMS v. Humble Oil & Refining Co., 432
F 2d 165
  La L Rev 31:527 Ap '71
  La L Rev 32:478 Ap '72
WILLIAMS v. Illinois, 90 Sup Ct 2018
  ABA J 56:1203 D '70
  Ark L Rev 24:545 Winter '71

WINTERS v. Cook, 466 F 2d 1393
  BU L Rev 53:225 Ja '73
  Miss L J 44:293 Ap '73
WINTERS v. Maxey (Tenn) 481 S W 2d 755
  Tenn L Rev 40:259 Winter '73
WINTERS v. Miller, 446 F 2d 65
  Brooklyn L Rev 38:211 Summer '71
  Minn L Rev 56:747 Mr '72
WISCONSIN v. Constantineau, 91 Sup Ct 507
  ABA J 57:368 Ap '71
  J Urban L 49:589 F '72
  Sw L J 25:622 O '71
WISCONSIN v. Yoder, 92 Sup Ct 1526
  ABA J 58:747 Jl '72
  Akron L Rev 6:95 Winter '73
  Albany L Rev 37:329 '73
  Ark L Rev 26:555 Winter '73
  Cumber-Sam L Rev 3:508 Fall '72
  De Paul L Rev 22:539 Winter '72
  Duquesne L Rev 11:433 Spring '73
  Geo L J 61:236 O '72
  J Urban L 50:493 F '73
  Loyola U L J (Chicago) 4:256 Winter '73
  Mercer L Rev 24:479 Winter '73
  NC L Rev 51:302 D '72
  Notre Dame Law 48:741 F '73
  Sw L J 26:912 D '72

> When it is known that a particular case deals with the subject under research, law review citations on the subject can be located in the Table of Cases section of the Index to Legal Periodicals. E.g., if the Williams v. Florida case had already been found, this Table indicates which periodicals have articles or comments on it during 1970–73. Later issues of the I.L.P. should be consulted for later law review citations.

Suffolk U L Rev 6:166 Fall '71
WILLIAMS v. W.M.A. Transit Co. 472 F 2d
1258
  Vill L Rev 18:330 D '72
WILLIAMS v. Weisser, 78 Cal Rptr 542
  NYU L Rev 45:595 My '70
WILLIAMS, In re Marriage of (Iowa) 199 N W
2d 339
  Wake Forest L Rev 9:152 D '72
WILLIAMS & Wilkins Co. v. U.S. 66 Pat.
T.M. & Copyright J 1 (Ct. Cl. Feb 24, 1972)
  Vand L Rev 25:1093 O '72
WILLIAMS & Wilkins Co. v. U.S. No. 73-68
Ct Cl. (Feb. 16, 1972)
  U Cin L Rev 41:511 '72
  W&M L Rev 13:940 Summer '72
WILLIAMS & Wilkins Co. v. U.S. 172 U.S.P.Q.
670
  Tex L Rev 51:137 D '72
WILLIAMSON v. Kelley (Tex) 444 S W 2d 311
  Baylor L Rev 22:409 Summer '70
WILLIAMSON v. Western-Pacific Dredging
Corp. 304 F Supp 509
  San Diego L Rev 7:689 Jl '70
  Wash & Lee L Rev 27:372 Fall '70
WILLIAMSON v. Western Pacific Dredging
Corporation, 441 F 2d 65
  Willamette L J 8:115 Mr '72
WILLIAMSON, In re (Ohio) 246 N E 2d 618
  Ohio S L J 31:607 Summer '70
WILSON v. Flowers (NJ) 277 A 2d 199
  Rutgers L Rev 26:127 Fall '72
WILSON v. State (Ind) 287 N E 2d 875
  Ind L Rev 6:300 D '72
WILSON v. U.S. 322 F Supp 830
  Marq L Rev 54:329 Summer '71
WILSON Appeal (Pa) 264 A 2d 614
  Duquesne L Rev 9:689 Summer '71
WILWORDING v. Swenson, 92 Sup Ct 407
  St Louis U L J 16:384 Spring '72
WINSHIP, In re, 90 Sup Ct 1968
  Albany L Rev 35:338 '71
  Case W Res L Rev 22:115 N '70
  Duquesne L Rev 9:673 Summer '71
  Fordham L Rev 39:121 O '70
  Harv L Rev 84:156 N '70
  J Urban L 48:1008 Je '71
  New England L Rev 6:130 Fall '70
  Notre Dame Law 46:373 Winter '71
  Tulsa L J 7:63 F '71
  Vill L Rev 16:352 D '70
  W&M L Rev 12:132 Fall '70

WOOD v. Ross, 434 F 2d 297
  U Richmond L Rev 5:401 Spring '71
WOODFORK v. Sanders (La) 248 S 2d 419
  La L Rev 32:153 D '71
  Tul L Rev 46:558 F '72
WOODHALL, TCM 1969-279
  J Taxation 37:46 Jl '72
WOODRUFF v. West Virginia Bd of Regents,
328 F Supp 1023
  W Va L Rev 74:430 S '72
WOODS Exploration & Producing Co. v.
Aluminum Co. 438 F 2d 1286
  Tul L Rev 46:526 F '72
WOODWARD v. Comm'r, 90 Sup Ct 1302
  ABA J 56:792 Ag '70
  Baylor L Rev 22:632 Fall '70
  Brooklyn L Rev 37:230 Fall '70
  Mo L Rev 36:263 Spring '71
  NC L Rev 49:375 F '71
  Ohio S L J 32:934 Fall '71
WOOLLERTON and Wilson Ltd. v. Richard
Costain Ltd [1970] 1 W L R 411
  Camb L J 28:201 N '70
  Modern L Rev 33:552 S '70
WORCESTER Works Finance Ltd. v. Cooden
Engineering Co [1971] 3 All E R 708
  Camb L J 30:36 Ap '72
  Modern L Rev 35:186 Mr '72
  NZ U L Rev 5:64 Ap '72
WORDEN v. Mercer County Bd of Elections
(NJ) 294 A 2d 233
  Seton Hall L Rev 4:329 Fall-Winter '72
WORLEY v. State (Fla) 263 S 2d 613
  Tex Tech L Rev 4:420 Spring '73
WORLD Wide SS Co. v. India Supply Mission,
316 F Supp 190
  J Maritime L 2:669 Ap '71
WORTHING v. Rowell and Muston Pty Ltd
(1970) 44 ALJR 230
  M U L R 8:320 Ag '71
  U Queens L J 7:381 D '72
WRIGHT v. City of Brighton, 411 F 2d 447
  Rutgers Camden L J 3:576 Spring '72
  Wayne L Rev 18:1111 My-Je '72
WRIGHT v. Council of the City of Emporia,
92 Sup Ct 2196
  ABA J 58:976 S '72
  Harv L Rev 86:62 N '72
WRIGHT v. Standard Oil Co. 470 F 2d 1280
  Miss L J 44:574 Je '73

[Illustration 95]

EXCERPT FROM SHEPARD'S LAW REVIEW CITATIONS

MISSOURI LAW REVIEW						Vol. 27
Vol. 18	**Vol. 19**	**Vol. 21**	**Vol. 22**	**Vol. 24**	**Vol. 26**	**Vol. 27**
– 1 –	– 214 –	– 105 –	– 14 –	– 137 –	– 1 –	– 1 –
1974LF599	23AU91	2Akr76	Mo	6CnL235	Mo	Mo
		34MdL371	504SW131		512SW459	531SW546
– 215 –	– 372 –			– 281 –		
26FLR654	Mo	– 209 –		Mo		– 354 –
39MoL489	518SW661	214Kan180		514SW600		74WLQ231
		Kan				
– 249 –		519P2d621				– 406 –
31MB333						Mo
						502SW35

This unit of Shepard's provides a means for "Shepardizing" law review articles cited since 1957. Through its use, one can find every time a law review article has been cited by another law review or in a court decision.

– 533 –
Mo
501SW557

[Illustration 96]

EXCERPT FROM SHEPARD'S FEDERAL LAW CITATIONS
IN SELECTED LAW REVIEWS

UNITED STATES SUPREME COURT REPORTS						Vol. 402
– 78 –	**Vol. 400**	83YLJ545	**Vol. 401**	– 395 –	– 437 –	1975LF530
61CaL188				86HLR683	74CR357	73McL242
41ChL219	– 4 –	– 297 –	– 1 –	38LCP568	74CR371	
41ChL282	122PaL336	75CR1473	73CR220	74McL252	75CR376	– 667 –
58CorL199		122PaL304	52TxL1275	68NwL723	62Geo14	59VaL956
61Geo626	– 18 –	52TxL425				
37LCP204	63CaL1503					
39LCP51	21CLA419	– 309 –				
39LCP195	59Cor1050	61CaL101	This Shepard's gives references to articles in 19 selected law reviews which have citations to federal cases.			
1975LF58	62Geo813	42ChL51				
73McL115	72McL332	59Cor852				
73McL492	72McL995	60Cor760	For example, the Williams v. Florida case was reported in 400 U.S. 78. This Shepard's provides an easy way to obtain law review references to articles in which the case was cited.			
73McL644	61VaL22	37LCP194				
74McL236		58MnL444				
57MnL650	– 25 –	59MnL302				
57MnL686	61CaL172	68NwL85	State units of Shepard's also give references to law reviews. See Illustration 75.			
50NYL29	60Cor779	122PaL310				
26StnL61	69NwL687	123PaL126				
27StnL551	50NYL246	27StnL996				
28StnL87	59VaL984	27StnL106				
59VaL993	73WLR508	59VaL981				
	83YLJ539	74WLR320				
– 149 –	84YLJ536	82YLJ947	27StnL542	63Geo140	– 493 –	– 797 –
62Geo146	84YLJ1279		52TxL1282	86HLR1436	1974LF307	60Cor749
72McL756		– 348 –	54TxL57	88HLR1674	70NwL394	58MnL446
73McL77	– 41 –	62Geo170	54TxL209	89HLR350	50NYL580	
74McL211	60Cor206		60VaL16	37LCP45	122PaL1389	– 815 –
50NYL593	122PaL1089	– 379 –	60VaL263	37LCP68	73WLR1047	23CLA437
26StnL1109	53TxL1182	41ChL759	75WLR368	60MnL82	75WLR367	

[Illustration 97]

PAGE FROM INDEX TO LEGAL PERIODICALS—1970–1973

BOOK REVIEW INDEX   1047

FRANCK, Thomas M.
Structure of impartiality. 1968
  T. Ehrlich. Stan L Rev 23:1143 Je '71
—& Weisband, Edward
Word politics: verbal strategy among the
superpowers. 1971
  W. J. Brisk. Cornell L Rev 57:991 Jl '72
  V. P. Nanda. Denver J Int L & Pol 2:111
    Spring '72
  H. J. Berman. Harv L Rev 86:459 D '72
FRANK, John P.
American law, the case for radical reform.
1969
  L. N. Gasaway. Houston L Rev 8:620 Ja
    1969
How L J 16:178 Fall '70
  J. S. Lee. NY L F 16:978 '70
  W. H. Gates jr. Wash L Rev 46:445 '71
FRANKLIN, Marc A.
Injuries and remedies—cases and materials
on tort law and alternatives. 1971
  T. G. Ison. U Ill L F 1971:349 '71
FRASCONA, Joseph L.
C.P.A. law review. 1972
  G. A. Jentz. Am Bus L J 10:314 Winter
    '73
FRATCHER, William F.
Probate can be quick and cheap: trusts and
estates in England. 1968
  R. L. Fletcher. Wash L Rev 46:619 My '71
FREE trade association (Franck, Weisband)
1968

FRIENDLY, Henry J.
Federal jurisdiction: a general view. 1973
  J. P. Frank. ABA J 59:466 My '73
**FRIESEN, Ernest C. jr, Gallas, Edward C. &
Gallas, Hesta M.**
Managing the courts. 1971
  W. A. McRae, jr. Mich L Rev 70:1612
    Ag '72
  B. B. Cook. Wash U L Q 1972:594 Sum-
    mer '72
"Managing the courts" 1972
  M. A. MacPherson. Sask L Rev 37:153
    '72-'73
FULDA, Carl H. & Schwartz Warren F.
Cases and materials on the regulation of in-
ternational trade and investment. 1970
  R. W. Dam. ABA J 57:1018 O '71
  B. S. Fisher. Harv Int L J 13:177 Winter
    '72
  C. Oliver, B. M. Carl. J Legal Ed 25:
    247 '73
  J. P. McMahon. J Maritime L 3:419 Ja
    '72
  D. Wallace, jr. Law & Pol Int'l Bus 3:
    641 '71
  S. Timberg. Mich L Rev 70:780 Mr '72
  P. D. Ehrenhaft. Tex Int L J 7:190 Sum-
    mer '71
  S. D. Metzger. Tex L Rev 49:1152 N '71
  R. E. Hudec. Int L J 12:152 D '71
FULLER, Lon L.
Anatomy of the law. 1968
  C. D. Johnson. Am J Juris 15:186 '70

Each volume or issue of the Index to Legal Periodicals has
a Book Review Section. In it all book reviews published during
the time period of the volume or issue are listed alphabetically
by the author of the book. The names of the reviewers and
citations to the review are listed underneath.

Anatomy of values: problems of personal and
social choice. 1970
  L. Rosen. Colum L Rev 71:1143 Je '71
  F. A. Olafson. Harv L Rev 84:1045 F '71
  S. D. Rose. Vand L Rev 24:871 My '71
FRIEDLAND, Martin L.
Detention before trial: a study of criminal
cases tried in the Toronto magistrates'
courts. 1969
  G. A. Martin. NY L F 17:1172 Spring '72
Double jeopardy. 1969
  B. M. Barker. Alberta L Rev 8:169 '70
  P. J. Levinson. Can B Rev 49:486 S '71
  R. Cross. L Q Rev 87:413 Jl '71
FRIEDMAN, Lawrence M. & Macaulay, Stewart
Law and the behavioral sciences. 1969
  R. I. Nunez. Ad Law Rev 23:96 D '70
  M. S. Yerkes. Fordham L Rev 39:367 D '70
FRIEDMAN, Leon
Wise minority: an argument for draft re-
sistance and civil disobedience. 1971
  H. Zinn. Harv L Rev 85:897 F '72
—& Neuborne, Burt
Unquestioning obedience to the President:
the ACLU case against the legality of the
war in Viet Nam. 1972
  D. Rosenberg. Harv Civil Rights L Rev
    8:223 Ja '73
FRIEDMANN, Wolfgang Gaston
Future of the oceans. 1971
  E. E. Seaton. Colum J Transnat L 11:360
    Spring '72
  K. E. Parker. How L J 17:259 '71
  A. M. Winterhalter. San Diego L Rev
    9:747 My '72
State and the rule of law in a mixed econ-
omy. 1971
  J. A. Farmer. Camb L J 32:168 Ap '73
  E. V. Rostow. Colum L Rev 72:788 Ap '72
—& Beguin, Jean-Pierre
Joint international business ventures in de-
veloping countries. 1971
  L. N. Cutler, J. R. Heller. Law & Pol
    Int'l Bus 4:489 '72
—Lissitzyn, Oliver J. & Pugh, Richard C.
Cases and materials on international law. 1969
  I. Azzam. J Maritime L 2:447 Ja '71
  A. P. Rubin. Harv Int L J 12:382 Spring
    '71

H. J. Liepesny. Am J Comp L 19:381
Spring '71

GADDIS, Thomas E. & Long, James O.
Killer: a journal of murder. 1970
  M. M. Belli. NY L F 17:317 '71
GADSBY, Edward N.
Securities regulations—federal securities ex-
change act of 1934. 3 vols. 1971
  W. H. Riccio. New England L Rev 7:386
    Spring '72
GAJENDRAGADKAR, P. B.
Secularism and the constitution of India. 1971
  N. A. Roberts. Am J Comp L 20:731 Fall
    '72
GAL, Gyula
Space law. 1969
  H. J. Taubenfeld. Am J Comp L 19:599
    Summer '71
  C. Q. Christol. Calif Western Int L J
    1:163 Fall '70
GALBRAITH, John Kenneth
Economics, peace and laughter. 1971
  J. O'Connell. U Ill L F 1971:540 '71
New industrial state, Ed. 2. 1971
  J. O'Connell. U Ill L F 1971:540 '71
GALVIN, Charles O. & Bittker, Boris I.
Income tax: how progressive should it be?
1969
  R. L. Simpson. ABA J 56:1194 D '70
  P. A. Mutino. Ky L J 59:588 '70-'71
  J. C. O'Byrne. Nw U L Rev 65:524 Jl-Ag
    '70
  P. C. Fielder. Sw L J 24:725 O '70
GARBESI, George C.
Consular authority over seamen from the
United States point of view. 1968
  I. Jarett. J Maritime L 1:353 Ja '70
GARBUS, Martin
Ready for the defense. 1971
  B. Rothman. Brooklyn L Rev 38:832
    Winter '72
  T. M. Kerr. Duquesne L Rev 10:148 Fall
    '71
  J. M. MacInnis. U San Francisco L Rev
    6:203 O '71

SECTION H.　INDEX TO LEGAL PERIODICALS
RESEARCH PROCEDURE

1.　Subject Indexes

To locate articles in legal periodicals on a specific subject, consult the Subject Indexes to the *Index to Legal Periodicals*.　For entries since 1961, the combined subject-author section to the *Index* should be consulted.　The subject headings of the *Index* are not subdivided into detailed topics; therefore, broad subject units must be scanned for articles on a particular topic.　For example, articles on promissory estoppel in contract law appear under the heading "Contract."　To locate all the periodical writings on a specific subject from 1926 to date, each three-year cumulative volume must be examined.　For articles published after the last bound cumulation, consult the annual, semi-annual and monthly supplements.

For articles prior to 1926, see *Jones-Chipman's Index*.

2.　Author Indexes

When the author of an article is known and the citation is unknown or to locate articles written by an author, consult the Author Indexes to the *Index to Legal Periodicals* and the combined indexes since 1961.　The Author Indexes refer the user to the subjects under which articles by the author appear in the Subject Index.　Therefore, to find the citation or citations, examine the listings under the noted subject or subjects.　To ascertain all writings of an author, examine the appropriate Author Indexes to the cumulative volumes to 1961 and the combined indexes since 1961.

3.　Book Review Indexes

Citations to book reviews in legal periodicals are listed under the names of the authors of the books in the Book Review Indexes to the *Index to Legal Periodicals*.

For book reviews written by reviewers prior to 1961, consult the Author Indexes to the *Index to Legal Periodicals*.　Check under the reviewer's name and subheading "Book Reviews." The name of the book-author is noted.　Then look under the book-author's name and the book title in the Book Review Index for the complete citation to the book review.　Since 1961, book reviews are not listed under the reviewer's names.

4.　Case Method

The Tables of Cases in the *Index to Legal Periodicals* list cases commented upon in the law reviews.　It does not include cases which are merely cited in articles.　To ascertain whether a discussion on a

case in point has appeared in a journal, consult the pertinent index volume under the Table of Cases. Since the comments appear reasonably soon after the decisions are published, the dates of the case and the discussion are reasonably close together.

———

SECTION I. SUMMARY

1. **Jones-Chipman Index to Legal Periodicals**
   a. Scope.
      (1) Indexes English language legal periodicals published between 1886 and 1937.
      (2) It is not up-to-date but useful to find articles published prior to 1926 (beginning of the cumulative volumes to the *Index to Legal Periodicals*).
   b. Arrangement.
      (1) Author
      (2) Subject

2. **Index to Legal Periodicals**
   a. Scope and Supplementation.
      (1) Indexes numerous American and substantially all British legal periodicals from 1908 to date.
      (2) The three-year cumulative volumes began in 1926.
      (3) Current numbers are published monthly and cumulated semi-annually, annually and for a three-year period.
   b. Arrangement.
      (1) Prior to 1961, the Subject and Author Indexes are separate; since 1961, they are combined.
      (2) Subject entries provide full information, including citations to articles.
      (3) Author entries are brief and cross-reference to the appropriate subject sections for citations to articles.
      (4) Book reviews are separately indexed.
      (5) Tables of cases commented upon in the periodicals.
      (6) Biographies appearing in journals are indexed in the Subject Index prior to 1961 and in the combined indexes since 1961. Biographies appear under the main headings: "Biography: Collective" and "Biography: Individual" and are alphabetically subdivided by the names of the individuals written about.

3. **Index to Periodical Articles Related to Law**
   a. Scope.
      (1) Indexes periodicals in English not covered by the *Index to Legal Periodicals* or the *Index to Foreign Legal Periodicals*.
      (2) Cumulative volumes for 1958–1968 and 1969–1973.
      (3) Current volumes are published quarterly.
   b. Arrangement.
      (1) Subject Index/Index to Articles gives complete information including citations.
      (2) List of Journals Indexed is not cross-referenced.
      (3) Author Index gives page numbers for article citations.

4. **Index to Foreign Legal Periodicals**
   a. Scope.
      (1) Covers legal periodicals of all countries other than the United States, the Britsh Isles and nations of the British Commonwealth since 1960.
      (2) Patterned after the *Index to Legal Periodicals*.
      (3) Published quarterly with annual and triennial cumulations.
   b. Arrangement.
      (1) Subject Index
      (2) Geographical Index
      (3) Book Review Index
      (4) Author Index refers to subject where notations are complete.
      (5) Titles are given in language of publication.

5. **Indexes to Subject Periodicals**

6. **Periodical Digests and Abstracts**

7. **Shepard's Law Review Citations and Federal Law Citations in Selected Law Reviews**

8. **Citation form for legal periodicals may be found in Appendix A, at (I), (B), (2)**

Chapter 18

TREATISES, RESTATEMENTS, MODEL CODES, AND UNIFORM LAWS

SECTION A. TREATISES

The writings of legal scholars have always made significant contributions to the sources of law for all mature legal systems. In the Roman law, great weight was given to the writings of legal experts. The jurisconsults in the classical period of Roman law were unofficial experts who advised the judicial officers on pending cases. The judges were not required to follow these opinions; yet, over the years the preeminence of some jurisconsults was such as to give high favor to their opinions. Under the Emperor Augustus (31 B.C.–14 A.D.) their opinions (responsa) assumed a distinctive authority and were binding on the judges. The jurisconsults wrote legal treatises as well as gave responses, and by the fourth century both the responsa and the treatises became primary authorities. The writings of five preeminent jurists, Papinian, Paulus, Gaius, Ulpian, and Modestinus, were assigned an authoritative position in the Law of Citations (426 A.D.). Emperor Justinian gave statutory authority to his Digest (Pandicts), which consisted mainly of selections from the writings of the jurists. The Digest assumed a preeminent authoritative position in the middle ages, and was favorably received in western Europe during the Renaissance, chiefly through the influence of the legal scholars who had studied its texts.[1] The authoritative influence given to the writings of legal experts by the Roman law was carried over to the civil law countries where legal commentaries still retain much influence.

In English law, the treatise did not hold a position of such eminence. Lord Eldon once commented that a writer who had not held a judicial office should not be cited as an authority.[2] However, it should not be assumed that the treatise has had no influence in England. During the formative period, there was a dearth of judicial precedents; therefore, great weight was given to the writings of the early distinguished scholars. The five great names in early English

---

[1] This summary is derived mainly from the brief discussion in E. PATTERSON, JURISPRUDENCE: MEN AND IDEAS OF THE LAW 218–219 (1953). *See also* J. GRAY, THE NATURE AND SOURCES OF THE LAW §§ 424–434 (1909) and G. PATON, A TEXTBOOK OF JURISPRUDENCE 231–232 (3d ed. 1964).

[2] Johnes v. Johnes, 3 Dow 1, 15 (1814).

literature are: Glanville, Bracton, Littleton, Coke, and Blackstone. Bracton helped lay the foundations of English law, borrowing from Roman law to fill the gaps left by the judicial decisions. Littleton gave to the English case law of real property a basis apart from the Roman law. Coke bridged the systems of medieval and modern law, and later Blackstone organized the diffused principles of case law into a comprehensive, literate statement.

The growth of English law reports, after the time of Coke, meant a decline in the status of the treatise. However, as in modern America, the plethora of cases has meant its return as a guide to "the luxuriant chaos of case law." [3] Paton noted this development when he observed that "In the days of Bracton the text-book was important because there were so few precedents; today it is valued because there are so many." [4]

The development of American law was also similarly influenced by writers of treatises, which were particularly influential from the period of the Revolution until about 1850.[5] By that date, there were sufficient judicial decisions to serve as the sources of American law. In more recent times, the magnitude of reported decisions has placed a new emphasis on treatises, which are now frequently the first sources consulted by a legal researcher.

1. Nature of Treatises

Treatises may be defined as expositions by legal writers on case law and legislation. Generally, treatises are more exhaustive in scope than legal encyclopedias. Treatises may be broadly classified into five types: (1) critical, (2) interpretative, (3) expository, (4) textual (for law students), and (5) educational (for practitioners keeping up in their fields). In most instances, however, treatises do not neatly fall into such a classification, and they frequently may include some features of all five types.

a. *Critical treatises.*

These examine an area of law in depth and constructively criticize, when necessary, rules of law as presently interpreted by the courts. They often include historical analyses in order to show that current rules actually had different meanings or interpretations from those presently given by the courts. The author may include a thought-

---

[3] G. PATON, *supra* note 1, at 229.

[4] *Id.*

[5] R. POUND, THE FORMATIVE ERA OF AMERICAN LAW, ch. IV (1938). *See also* the excellent discussion on the influence of treatises on the development of American law in L. FRIEDMAN, A HISTORY OF AMERICAN LAW 538–546 (1973).

ful examination of the policy reasons for one or more such rules.[6] Critical treatises are not common, but their numbers are increasing.

b.   *Interpretive treatises.*

These provide an analysis and interpretation of the law.   Authors of such works do not attempt to evaluate rules in relation to underlying policy but rather to explain the terminology and meaning of the rules as they exist.   Emphasis is placed upon understanding the law and not upon proposing what the law should be.

c.   *Expository treatises.*

These exist primarily as substitutes for digests and are principally used as case finders.   They consist primarily of essay paragraphs arranged under conventional subject headings with profuse footnote citations.   Usually minimal analysis and synthesis of conflicting cases are the most a researcher can expect to find in them.

A real danger exists if one relies exclusively upon the expository treatise or encyclopedia article without verifying the writer's synopsis of the cases.   As one commentator has noted, "Text-books (expository treatises—ed.) are good for what they are worth; but any lawyer who has had occasion to probe to the root of a subject has learned that it is unsafe to look to the text-book for a final statement of the law on any subject." [7]

d.   *Student textbooks.*

These may also be classified expository because they are elementary treatments and omit the comprehensive, critical, and interpretative features of other works.   Student textbooks are useful case finders; their references are selective and limited to landmark decisions.

e.   *Continuing legal education handbooks.*

In recent years, continuing education for lawyers has become increasingly important.[8]   The American Law Institute—American

---

[6] For example, Professor Richard Powell in his treatise on real property in discussing the interests of a lessor and lessee in a condemnation proceeding criticizes the current rule as follows: *"This is the regrettable position taken by the majority of the jurisdictions* (emphasis ours).   It is a regrettable position because it embodies a rigidly conceptualistic survival of the historical idea that the lessee 'owns the land for his term' * * *.   It would be more businesslike and reasonable to hold * * *."   R. POWELL, 2 POWELL ON REAL PROPERTY ¶ 247[2], at 372.121 (1975).

[7] R. COOLEY, BRIEF MAKING AND THE USE OF LAW BOOK 60 (5th ed. 1926).

[8] For a recent listing of such programs, *see:* AMERICAN LAW INSTITUTE-AMERICAN BAR ASSOCIATION, CATALOG OF CONTINUING LEGAL EDUCATION PROGRAMS IN THE UNITED STATES (vol. 22, 1976).

Bar Association Joint Committee on Continuing Legal Education and the Practising Law Institute hold seminars and symposiums on many current subjects and are all directed toward practicing lawyers to keep them up-to-date on new developments in the law. Many states have their own continuing legal education institutes. It is quite common for such institutes to publish handbooks and texts in connection with their programs. These volumes usually furnish analyses of the law, practical guidance, forms, checklists, and other time-saving aids. Very frequently, these publications deal with such subjects as business transactions, personal injuries, commercial and corporate practice, trial practice, and other subjects of primary interest to practicing attorneys.

2. The Characteristics of Treatises

The fundamental characteristics of treatises are essentially the same. They contain the following elements:

a. Table of Contents

The table of contents shows the topical division of the treatise which is usually arranged by chapters and subdivisions thereof.

b. Table of Cases

The table of cases provides references as to where decisions discussed by the author are cited in the text.

c. Subject Matter

The subject matter of the text is contained in the main body of the publication.

d. Supplementation

The current trend is to provide pocket parts at the back of the volumes to supplement the text and indicate recent statutory and case developments.

Some current treatises are loose-leaf in format, providing for the addition of current material, usually by interfiling.

e. Index

The index, embodying an alphabetical arrangement of the topics, subtopics, fact and descriptive words, and cross references, is the last feature.

SECTION B.   ILLUSTRATIONS: TREATISES

Using treatises to find cases.

Illustrations

[Illustration 98]

PAGE FROM OSBORNE, MORTGAGES, 3rd ed.

DISTINGUISHED FROM ESCROW LOAN

115. The test in distinguishing future advances from an escrow loan is whether the mortgagee has put it out of his power to withhold payments in the future.

In at least one jurisdiction there has been litigation to distinguish between an escrow loan and a mortgage to secure future advances. The problem arises because the full amount of the mortgage loan may be segregated and either placed in the hands of a third person under an escrow or trust agreement ...

tribute ...

mortg... ...

a defi... ...

fact th... ...

money... ...

gage b... ...

loan c... ...

future... ...

mortg... ...

withho... ...

the proceeds are put in the control of an independent third person the courts have no difficulty in finding this to be the case.[90] Even when retained by a financial institution-mortgagee and the loan is either credited on the books of the mortgagee or handed over to the mortgagor and then deposited by him in the lending institution subject to agreements as to withdrawals, it has been held to be a fully present loan.[91] That the same result would be reached in the case of an individual mortgagee seems improbable.[92]

FORMS OF MORTGAGE

116. The mortgage for future advances may assume one of two forms: A total sum stated as a present advance or the total amount left unstated but providing expressly for the advances. The former is a deceptive overstatement of the obligation but is generally upheld. The latter is held sufficiently definite not to invalidate the mortgage.

The mortgage for future advances may be cast into one or the other of two forms. (1) It may name a certain total sum as a present loan although in truth that amount, ... e oral, ... n. Or ... ... ces to ... ... iounts, ... efinite. ... ... re is a ... ... itself, ... nce of ... ... ossible ... ... ard to ... ... over-stated present obligation already mentioned[94] but with two differences. One is that there exists the possibility of increasing the indebtedness up to the amount stated as now owing and doing so in strict accordance with the parties' agreement. The other is that this overstatement ordinarily is deliberate. The second, at least, of these two

---

A typical student treatise. Note use of "Black Letter" law, and the citations in the footnotes to cases and law review articles.

This type of treatise is useful not only for studying a substantive area of law, but as a first step in finding cases.

---

89. See Watkins, Maryland Mortgages for Future Advances, 1940, 4 Md.L.Rev. 111, 127.

90. Neeb v. Atlantic Mill & Lumber Realty Co., 1939, 176 Md. 297, 5 A.2d 283; Manhattan Land Corp. v. New Baltimore Loan & Sav. Ass'n, 1921, 138 Md. ⁵29, 114 A. 469; Western Nat. Bank v. Jenkins, 1917, 131 Md. 239, 252, 101 A. 671, 1 A.L.R. 1577; White Eagle Polish American Bldg. & Loan Ass'n v. Hart Miller Islands Co., 1934, 168 Md. 199, 204, 178 A. 214, 215.

91. Edelhoff v. Horner-Miller Straw-Goods Mfg. Co., 1898, 86 Md. 595, 39 A. 314; New Baltimore Loan & Savings Ass'n v. Tracey, 1923, 142 Md. 211, 120 A. 441; White Eagle Bldg. & Loan Ass'n v. Hart

Miller Islands Co., Co.1934, 168 Md. 199, 204, 178 A. 214, 215.

92. See Groh v. Cohen, 1930, 158 Md. 638, 643, 149 A. 459, 461.

Similarly an elaborate and ingenious attempt to cast a mortgage for future advances under a construction loan into the form of an indemnity mortgage given by a straw man to the mortgagor was balked by the Maryland court. High Grade Brick Co. v. Amos, 1902, 95 Md. 571, 52 A. 582.

93. Tully v. Harloe, 1868, 35 Cal. 302, 95 Am.Dec. 102. See Glenn, Fraudulent Conveyances and References, rev. ed., § 299b. See also note 83, supra.

See also Mortgages for Future Advances: The Need for Legislation in Wisconsin, 1965 Wis.L.Rev. 175, 177; Stealey, The Mortgage for Future Advances in West Virginia, 1954, 56 W.Va.L.Rev. 107, 108, for a résumé of the forms the mortgage for future advances may take.

94. See supra § 108.

[Illustration 99]

PAGE FROM APPLEMAN, INSURANCE LAW AND PRACTICE

§ 573   CAUSES OF LOSS   Pt. 3

thereto attached, on the theory that "riding" a motorcycle implied control or management thereof.[61] Still another court permitted recovery where the motorcycle had a top extending over the driver's seat and a windshield on the theory that it had been converted thereby into a "motor-driven truck" rather than a motorcycle.[62]

A "motor scooter" was held to be a "motorcycle" within an accident policy exception.[62.25]

Where a contract insures against death when struck by a vehicle propelled by electricity, it was held to cover the death of a motorcyclist struck by an electric train.[63]

In one case it was even contended that a bullet was a "vehicle" within an accident policy, but the contention was denied.[63.25]

§ 574. Wrecking or Disablement of Vehicle

In construing clauses referring to wrecking or disablement of a vehicle, the court looks at the entire contract to assist in making

W.Va.—Davis v. Combined Ins. Co. of America, 1952, 70 S.E.2d 814, 137 W.Va. 196.

61. An accident insurance policy providing against liability for "injuries received while riding a motorcycle" held to cover death resulting from an accident arising while deceased was a passenger in a side car attached to motorcycle; to ride,

Ala.App. 435, certiorari denied 71 So.2d 124, 260 Ala. 699; Standifer v. Inter-Ocean Ins. Co., 1954, 69 So. 2d 300, 37 Ala.App. 393.

Contra:

N.C.—Le Croy v. Nationwide Mut. Ins. Co., 1959, 110 S.E.2d 463, 251 N.C. 19 (motor scooter which contained luggage compartment, wind-

---

This set is in 38 volumes and covers the entire subject of the law of insurance. It is directed primarily toward the practicing lawyer and the emphasis is on the current status of the law.

Treatises similar to this one cover subjects in more depth than encyclopedias. Such treatises usually have good indexes and are kept up to date by annual pocket supplements.

So. 357.

62.25 Ala.—Life & Cas. Ins. Co. of Tenn. v. King, 1954, 71 So.2d 121, 37

63.25 La.—Scott v. Life & Casualty Ins. Co. of Tennessee, App.1944, 18 So.2d 58.

[Illustration 100]

PAGE FROM POWELL, LAW OF REAL PROPERTY

372.125   Problems as to Remedies   ¶ 250

¶ 250. Some problems as to remedies.

It is not feasible in a treatise of this type to discuss the multitudinous procedural quirks which arise under the separate laws of fifty states, in effectuating the substantive rights of lessor, of lessee, and of third persons as against lessor and lessee, which have been described in the prior paragraphs of this chapter.[1] Some of these procedural matters are discussed above in the paragraphs dealing with the separate substantive topics. There are, however, three problems as to remedies which have been much in litigation in recent years and which are, therefore, dealt with at this point. They concern (1) the similarities and differences between the modern descendant of ejectment and the modern statutory proceeding designed to restore possession speedily to a complaining lessor;[2] (2) the doctrine of waiver as it operates in the field of lessor-lessee relationships,[3] and (3) the spreading practice of including in a lease a clause authorizing the lessor to claim reimbursement for attorney's fees, the incurring of which has been caused by the lessee's behavior.[4]

The common-law action of ejectment, with statutory modifications, exists in every state as a method for testing the right to land.[5] Traditionally, and even under modern law, it is a

---

[1] See Note, 5 Miami L.Q. 305 (1951), discussing the various remedies landlords may invoke against delinquent tenants; 28 U. Cinc. L. Rev.

lessee, under a lease which terminated the lease on failure to pay rent and thereby entitled lessor to bring the action without a notice to vacate or

---

This 10 volume set is an example of a "critical" treatise. This type is generally written by a law professor and emphasis is placed more on the analysis of an area of law rather than merely offering an explanation of the rules of law.

Sears, Roebuck & Co., 112 Ind. App. 412, 44 N.E.2d 216 (1942), where ejectment was brought against a

ence of a right of redemption in the lessee ousted for failure to pay rent are discussed; Petsch v. Willman, 29

SECTION C. THE RESTATEMENTS OF THE LAW

In the 1920's concern was being shown by prominent American judges, lawyers, and law professors over two main defects in case law —its growing uncertainty and undue complexity. Finally, in 1923, the American Law Institute was founded by a group of these leaders to overcome such weaknesses.[9] The objectives of the Institute were focused on the reduction of the mass of legal publications which had to be consulted by the bench and bar, on the simplification of case law by a clear systematic restatement of it, and on diminishing the flow of judicial decisions. It was feared that the increasing mass of unorganized judicial opinions threatened to break down the system of articulating and developing case law.[10]

To remedy this, the American Law Institute undertook to produce a clear and precise restatement of the existing common law that would have "authority greater than that now accorded to any legal treatise, an authority more nearly on a par with that accorded the decisions of the courts." [11]

Procedurally, this was accomplished by the engagement of eminent legal scholars to be Reporters for the various subjects that were to be restated. Each Reporter prepared tentative drafts which were then submitted to and approved by the members of the Institute.

Between 1923 and 1944, Restatements were adopted for the law of agency, conflict of laws, contracts, judgments, property, restitution, security, torts, and trusts. Since 1952, Restatements, Second Series, have been adopted for agency, conflict of laws, foreign relations law, judgments, property, landlord and tenant, torts (v. 1–3), and trusts.

[9] This discussion on the Restatements is based on the following sources: Lewis, *History of the American Law Institute and the First Restatement of the Law* in AMERICAN LAW INSTITUTE, RESTATEMENT IN THE COURTS (Permanent ed. 1945) ; Goodrich, *The Story of the American Law Institute,* 1951 WASH. U.L.Q. 283 ; H. GOODRICH & P. WOLKIN, THE STORY OF THE AMERICAN LAW INSTITUTE, 1923–1961 (1961) ; THE AMERICAN LAW INSTITUTE 50TH ANNIVERSARY (1973) ; AMERICAN LAW INSTITUTE ANNUAL REPORT (1924– —). *See also,* M. PIMSLEUR, CHECKLISTS OF BASIC AMERICAN LEGAL PUBLICATIONS, AALL PUBLICATIONS SERIES NO. 4, § 5: AMERICAN LAW INSTITUTE, RESTATEMENTS OF THE LAW (1976). This checklist updates all previous checklists and lists all Restatements, preliminary and tentative drafts published through 1975.

[10] Lewis, *supra* note 9, at 1.

[11] *Report of the Committee on the Establishment of a Permanent Organization for the Improvement of the Law Proposing the Establishment of an American Law Institute,* February 23, 1923, THE AMERICAN LAW INSTITUTE 50TH ANNIVERSARY 34 (1973).

There are two aspects of the Restatements which limit their scope and function. First, they lack legislative sanction. It has been recommended that state legislatures be required to approve the Restatements, not as formal legislative enactments, but as aids and guides to the judiciary so that they would feel free to follow the "collective scholarship and knowledge of our profession." [12] But this proposal was not adopted by the Institute. Nevertheless, many courts began to give greater authority to the Restatements than that accorded to treatises and other secondary sources. In many instances, an authority is given to the Restatements nearly equal to that accorded to court decisions.[13]

The First Series of the Restatements reflected the desire of the American Law Institute founders that the Restatements would be admired and adopted by the courts. To this end they deliberately omitted the Reporters' citations and tentative drafts upon which the Restatement rules were based.

With publication of the Second Series of the Restatements, it was decided to abandon the idea of the Restatements serving as a substitute for the codification of the common law. The Second Series will also at times indicate a new trend in the common law and attempt to predict what a new rule will or should be.[14] This change in policy is also reflected in the appearance of citations to court decisions and to the Notes of the Reporters.

Further debate over the value of the Restatements may be left to others.[15] As a legal researcher, however, one must be familiar with the publications of the American Law Institute and their method of use.

1.   The Features of the Restatements

The frequency with which the Restatements are cited by the courts merit their study in legal research. As of April 1, 1975, the Restatements have been cited by the courts 53,681 times.[16] Therefore, they not only provide clear statements of the rules of the common law which are operative in the great majority of the states but

[12] Mason, *Harlan Fiske Stone Assays Social Justice*, 1912–1923, 99 U.PA.L.REV. 887, 915 (1951).

[13] For a discussion of the precedential authority of the Restatements *see* Byrne, *Reevaluation of the Restatement as a Source of Law in Arizona*, 15 ARIZ.L.REV. 1021, 1023–1026 (1973).

[14] *Id.*

[15] An exhaustive list of articles on all aspects of the work of the American Law Institute may be found in each *Annual Report* in a section entitled "The Institute in Legal Literature, A Bibliography." Periodical articles may also be located under the heading "American Law Institute" in the *Index to Legal Periodicals*.

[16] AMERICAN LAW INSTITUTE, ANNUAL REPORT 24 (1975).

also provide very valuable sources for finding cases in point.   Moreover, a comparison of the texts of the Restatements and the case
law of the several states revealed that there were surprisingly few
deviations from the common law as expressed in the Restatements.
It has been suggested, therefore, that there is in fact a common law
which transcends state lines and prevails throughout the nation.[17]
But the legal rules may at times be inaccurately and confusingly stated
by the various courts.   Thus, the objective of the Restatements is
to clear away much of the verbal debris and bring the accepted rules
to the forefront.   To this extent, the Restatements are useful research
aids in the law.

The following features are included in the Restatements, Second
Series:

    a.   Reporters' Notes.

    b.   Citations to the *Restatements* which the courts have
made to the First Series of the *Restatements.*

    c.   Cross references to West's *Key Number System* and
to *American Law Reports Annotated.*

2. Indexes

    a.   *Restatements,* First Series.   A one-volume index to all of the
Restatements has been published.   Each Restatement also has its own
index.

    b.   *Restatements,* Second Series.   Each *Restatement* has its own
index.

3.   Restatements in the Courts

The purpose of this set is to record each time a court cites a section of a Restatement.   Each such case is digested in length under
the appropriate section.   The Permanent Edition covers the years
1932–1944.   There are periodic supplements issued to the Permanent
Edition.

4.   "Shepardizing" the Restatements

Many state editions of Shepard's Citations included in the unbound pamphlet supplements a Part which listed all of the Restatements, and gave citations under each Section to court decisions of the
state which cited each Section.

Starting in 1976, Shepard's Citations has published a new unit
devoted entirely to the *Restatements of the Law.*   This set gives citations to all United States and *Federal Reporters,* all units of the *National Reporter System,* and all state reports which cite a Restate-

---

[17] Goodrich, *Restatement and Codification* in DAVID DUDLEY FIELD CEN-
TENARY ESSAYS 241–250 (1949).

ment Section. It will also include citations which appear in the leading law reviews.

5. State Annotations

Many states have prepared annotations to court citations to the Restatements, *e. g., California Annotations to the Restatement of the Law of Torts* * * *. The card Catalog in local law libraries should be consulted to ascertain if such annotations exist for a particular state.

SECTION D.   ILLUSTRATIONS: RESTATEMENTS
OF THE LAW

Problem: Liability of one who causes emotional damage or distress
by a negligent act, where the act did not involve physical
contact.   (The first step of consulting the General Index
to the Restatements is omitted.)

Illustration

[Illustration 101]

PAGE FROM RESTATEMENT OF THE LAW OF TORTS, 2d

This Section may be located by using the Index to the Restatement of Torts, 2d.

Each Section of a Restatement first states the Rule. It is then followed by the Notes of the Reporter commenting on the Rule.

§ 436 A. **Negligence Resulting in Emotional Disturbance Alone**

If the actor's conduct is negligent as creating an unreasonable risk of causing either bodily harm or emotional disturbance to another, and it results in such emotional disturbance alone, without bodily harm or other compensable damage, the actor is not liable for such emotional disturbance.

See Reporter's Notes.

Comment:

a. The rule stated in this Section stands in contrast to those stated in §§ 46 and 48, as to the intentional infliction of emotional distress. It is also to be contrasted with the rules stated in § 436, under which an actor who has negligently created an unreasonable risk of causing either bodily harm or emotional disturbance to another becomes subject to liability for bodily harm brought about solely by the internal operation of emotional disturbance. Under the rule stated in this Section, the negligent actor is not liable when his conduct results in the emotional disturbance alone, without the bodily harm or other compensable damage. The difference is one between the negligent automobile driver who narrowly misses a woman and frightens her into a miscarriage, and the negligent driver who merely frightens her, without more.

b. The reasons for the distinction, as they usually have been stated by the courts, have been three. One is that emotional disturbance which is not so severe and serious as to have physical consequences is normally in the realm of the trivial, and so falls within the maxim that the law does not concern itself with trifles. It is likely to be so temporary, so evanescent, and so relatively harmless and unimportant, that the task of compensating for it would unduly burden the courts and the defendants. The second is that in the absence of the guarantee of genuineness provided by resulting bodily harm, such emo-

See Appendix for Reporter's Notes, Court Citations, and Cross References

461

[Illustration 101–a]

PAGE FROM RESTATEMENT OF THE LAW OF TORTS, 2d

§ 436 A   TORTS, SECOND   **Ch. 16**

tional disturbance may be too easily feigned, depending, as it must, very largely upon the subjective testimony of the plaintiff; and that to allow recovery for it might open too wide a door for false claimants who have suffered no real harm at all. The third is that where the defendant has been merely negligent, without any element of intent to do harm, his fault is not so great that he should be required to make good a purely mental disturbance.

c. The rule stated in this Section applies to all forms of emotional disturbance, including temporary fright, nervous shock, nausea, grief, rage, and humiliation. The fact that these are

---

After the Comments by the Reporter, Illustrations of the Rule are given.

---

even long continued mental disturbance, as for example in the case of repeated hysterical attacks, or mental aberration, may be classified by the courts as illness, notwithstanding their mental character. This becomes a medical or psychiatric problem, rather than one of law.

→ **Illustration:**

1. A negligently manufactures and places upon the market cottage cheese containing broken glass. B purchases a package of the cheese, and upon eating it finds her mouth full of glass. She is not cut or otherwise physically injured, and she succeeds in removing the glass without bodily harm; but she is frightened at the possibility that she may have swallowed some of the glass. Her fright results in nausea and nervousness lasting for one day, and in inability to sleep that night, but in no other harm. A is not liable to B.

§ 437. **Actor's Subsequent Efforts to Prevent His Negligence From Causing Harm**

If the actor's negligent conduct is a substantial factor in bringing about harm to another, the fact that after the risk has been created by his negligence the actor has exercised reasonable care to prevent it from taking

[Illustration 102]

PAGE FROM APPENDIX VOLUME, RESTATEMENT OF THE LAW OF TORTS, 2d

---

Ch. 16   **APPENDIX**   **§ 436 A**

§ 436 A. Negligence Resulting in Emotional Disturbance Alone.

REPORTER'S NOTES

This Section has been added to the first Restatement.

The general rule is well settled. See for example Tuttle v. Meyer Dairy Products Co., 75 Ohio L. Abs. 587, 138 N.E.2d 429 (App. 1956), from which Illustration 1 is taken. Also Monteleone v. Co-operative Transit Co., 128 W. Va. 340, 36 S.E.2d 475 (1945), headaches and nervousness following broken automobile windshield, where plaintiff received a slight nick "the size of a pimple"; Espinosa v. Beverly Hospital, 114 Cal. App. 2d 232, 249 P.2d 843 (1952), emotional upset at being given the wrong baby by the hospital.

There are, however, some exceptional cases allowing recovery for emotional disturbance alone against a telegraph company which mishandles a message concerning death or illness. Seven states allow such recovery. Western Union Tel. Co. v. Cleveland, 169 Ala. 131, 53 So. 80, Ann. Cas. 1912B, 534 (1910); Mentzer v. Western Union Tel. Co., 93 Iowa 752, 62 N.W. 1, 28 L.R.A. 72, 57 Am. St. Rep. 294 (1895); Cumberland Tel. & Tel. Co. v. Quigley, 129 Ky. 788, 112 S.W. 897, 19 L.R.A. N.S. 575 (1908); Barnes v. Western Union Tel. Co., 27 Nev. 438, 76 P. 931, 65 L.R.A. 666, 103 Am. St. Rep. 776, 1 Ann. Cas. 346 (1903); Russ v. Western Union Tel. Co., 222 N.C. 504, 23 S.E.2d 681 (1943); Western Union Tel. Co. v. Potts, 120 Tenn. 37, 113 S.W. 789, 19 L.R.A. N.S. 479, 127 Am. St. Rep. 991 (1907); Western Union Tel. Co.

v. Lane, 152 S.W.2d 780 (Tex. Civ. 1941).

Four other states have statutes authorizing such recovery. Mac-

> A page from the Appendix volumes to the Restatement of the Law of Torts 2d. Note how the Reporter's notes cite cases upon which his text was based.

181, 58 S.E. 699, 11 L.R.A. N.S. 1149, 121 Am. St. Rep. 210 (1907); Western Union Tel. Co. v. Ferguson, 157 Ind. 64, 60 N.E. 674, 54 L.R.A. 846 (1901); West v. Western Union Tel. Co., 39 Kan. 93, 17 P. 807, 7 Am. St. Rep. 530 (1888); Francis v. Western Union Tel. Co., 58 Minn. 252, 59 N.W. 1078, 25 L.R.A. 406, 49 Am. St. Rep. 507 (1894); Western Union Tel. Co. v. Rogers, 68 Miss. 748, 9 So. 823, 13 L.R.A. 859, 24 Am. St. Rep. 300 (1891); Connell v. Western Union Tel. Co., 116 Mo. 34, 22 S.W. 345, 20 L.R.A. 172, 38 Am. St. Rep. 575 (1893); Morton v. Western Union Tel. Co., 53 Ohio St. 431, 41 N.E. 689, 32 L.R.A. 735, 53 Am. St. Rep. 648 (1895); Western Union Tel. Co. v. Foy, 32 Okla. 801, 124 P. 305, 49 L.R.A. N.S. 343, 3 N.C.C.A. 367 (1912); Connelly v. Western Union Tel. Co., 100 Va. 51, 40 S.E. 618, 56 L.R.A. 663, 93 Am. St. Rep. 919 (1902); Corcoran v.

Cit.—cited; fol.—followed; quot.—quoted; sup.—support.
A complete list of abbreviations faces page 1.

[Illustration 102–a]

PAGE FROM APPENDIX VOLUME, RESTATEMENT OF THE LAW OF TORTS, 2d

§ 436 A   TORTS, SECOND   **Ch. 16**

Postal Telegraph-Cable Co., 80 Wash. 570, 142 P. 29, L.R.A. 1915B, 552 (1914).

The only possible justification for a special rule in the case of telegraph companies appears to be the special responsibility to the public undertaken by the public utility. The federal rule, which controls as to interstate messages, denies recovery for mental suffering without physical consequences. Western Union Tel. Co. v. Speight, 254 U.S. 17, 41 S. Ct. 11, 65 L. Ed. 104 (1920). The majority rule is approved by the Institute, not only because of the weight of authority, but because of the absurdity of making recovery turn upon whether the message crosses a state line.

Cross References to

1. Digest System Key Numbers
Damages ⟜49

2. A.L.R. Annotation
Recovery for emotional disturbance or its physical consequences, in the absence of impact or other actionable wrong. 64 A.L.R.2d 100, 108 et seq.
Recovery by parent for distress caused parent because of personal injuries to child. 32 A.L.R.2d 1060, 1078.
Grief and mental anguish as elements of damages for personal injury resulting in death of infant. 14 A.L.R.2d 485, 495.
Recovery for shock or mental anguish at witnessing injury to, or fear of injury to, another. 18 A.L.R.2d 220.
Recovery by tenant for mental anguish occasioned by wrongful eviction. 17 A.L.R.2d 936.
Anxiety as to future disease, condition, or death therefrom. as element of da, 342.
Recoveryury to or
interf
Mental di Note reference to Key-Numbers and on or ex-
pulsio A.L.R. annotations. Search can be ex-
Humiliatio panded for both additional and later :coverable
by on cases through use of West General Di- ɔnexistent
marri gest or A.L.R. Upkeep Services.
Right to r :equences,
in the A.L.R.2d
100.

§ 437. Actor's Subsequent Efforts to Prevent His Negligence From Causing Harm.

REPORTER'S NOTES

Illustration 1 is based on Haverly v. State Line & S. R. Co., 135 Pa. 50, 19 A. 1013, 20 Am. St. Rep. 848 (1890); Nicholson v. Buffalo, R. & P. R. Co., 302 Pa. 41, 153 A. 128 (1930).

See also cases under division, chapter, topic, title, and subtitle that includes section under examination.

172

[Illustration 103]

PAGE FROM RESTATEMENTS IN THE COURTS, 1970–1971 SUPPLEMENT

TORTS 2d   § **436**

> This set indicates each time a Restatement rule has been cited, and further indicates whether the court supported, or did not support, the rule.
>
> The Restatement in the Courts and its supplements are: 1932–1944, 2 v.; 1954, 4 v.; 1965, 3 v.; 1967, 2 v. Since 1967, supplements are published every two years.

§ 435B. Unintended consequences of intentional invasions

N.J.Super. 1969. Cit. in sup. The plaintiff, a key employee, sued the defendants, his employers and principal stockholders in the company, for damages resulting from a false arrest and criminal charges for a crime the defendants, not the plaintiff, had committed, burning down the company's lumber yard for the insurance. The court held that the requirement of foreseeability should be abandoned in such cases as this, where principles of logic, fairness, and justice dictate that the defendant should be held liable. Seidel v. Greenberg, 108 N.J.Super. 248, 260 A.2d 863, 871, 40 A.L.R.3d 987.

§ 436. Physical harm resulting from emotional disturbance

Hawaii, 1970. Cit. in concurr. and diss. op. This was an action against the state by homeowners seeking damages for the flooding of their house, resulting from failure of a culvert to drain water from a state highway, the culvert having been blocked by beach sand. Plaintiffs alleged that the state had failed to keep the culvert free of such sand. Plaintiffs testified that the flooding of their house had left them "heart-broken" and "shocked." Judgment was for plaintiffs and included an amount for "mental anguish and suffering, inconvenience, disruption of home and family life, past and future, etc." Upon appeal, the court affirmed the judgment, except . . . as to the award for "mental anguish and suffering." In its opinion the court discussed in detail the authorities and cases involving such damages and held that the interest in freedom from negligent infliction of serious mental distress in entitled to independent legal protection, that there is a duty to refrain from the negligent infliction of serious mental distress; that whether or not the defendant is liable to the plaintiff in any particular case will be solved most justly by the application of general tort principles. The court remanded the case to the trial court to decide whether under the facts of the case, serious mental distress to plaintiffs was a reasonably foreseeable consequence of defendant's acts. The concurring and dissenting opinion rejected the position of the majority in this respect. Rodrigues v. State, 472 P.2d 509, 523.

Mich. 1970. Cit. in sup., appendix cit. in ftn. in sup.; subsec. (2) cit. in ftn. in sup., cit but dist. by diss. (and cit in ftn. by diss.) Plaintiffs alleged traumatic neurosis, emotional disturbance, and nervous upset, as well as property damage, from an explosion on their land caused by the defendant. The trial court gave a directed verdict to the defendant, except as to the property damage. The state supreme court reversed and remanded, overruling the impact rule in emotional distress cases. The dissent felt that the Restatement rule was inappropriate. Daley v. La Croix, 384 Mich. 4, 179 N.W.2d 390, 392, 394, 395, 397.

Cit.—cited; com.—comment; fol.—followed; sup.—support.
A complete list of abbreviations precedes page 1.

SECTION E.   UNIFORM LAWS AND MODEL CODES

1.   Uniform Laws

The Restatements, as mentioned, have as their aim the restating of the common law as developed by the courts.   The movement for law reform has also focused on statutory law and the need, in many instances, for similar statutes among the states.   Toward this aim, the American Bar Association passed a resolution recommending that each state and the District of Columbia adopt a law providing for the appointment of Commissioners to confer with Commissioners of other states on the subject of uniformity in legislation on certain subjects. By 1912, all of the states, the District of Columbia, and Puerto Rico passed such a law, and there was formed the National Conference of Commissioners on Uniform State Laws.   Its object is to "promote uniformity in state laws where uniformity is deemed desirable and practicable." [18]

The National Conference meets once a year and considers drafts of proposed uniform laws.   When such a law is approved, it is the duty of the Commissioners to try to convince their state legislatures to adopt it.   The National Conference has approved over two hundred acts.

A complete list of acts approved by the National Conference of Commissioners on Uniform State Laws appears each year in the Appendices in its annual *Handbook*.   These tables also list which states have adopted each uniform law.

a.   Publication of laws approved by the National Conference of Commissioners on Uniform State Laws are published in the following forms.

(1) Separate pamphlet form.

(2) In the annual *Handbook of the National Conference.*

(3) *Uniform Laws Annotated.   Master Edition*, 1969–

This edition, published by the West Publishing Co., replaces all former editions.   To date, thirteen volumes have been published. After each section of a uniform law, pertinent official comment of the Commissioners is given.   This is followed by a list of law review commentaries and then by digests of federal and state court decisions citing the particular section of the uniform law.   It is kept up-to-date by annual pocket supplements.

[18] National Conference of Commissioners on Uniform State Laws.   Handbook. 1974. p. 956.

2. Model Codes

The National Conference of Commissioners on Uniform State Laws has determined that it will designate an act as a "Uniform Act" when it has "a reasonable possibility of ultimate enactment in a substantial number of jurisdictions." [19]   Acts which do not have such possibility are designated as "Model Acts."   As a general rule, "Model Acts" embrace subject areas which do not have substantial interstate implications.

The American Law Institute also occasionally will draft and approve a model act,[20] and will participate jointly with the National Conference of Commissioners on Uniform Laws as it did in the compilation of the *Uniform Commercial Code.*

3. Indexes to Uniform Laws and Model Codes

  a. *Handbook of the National Conference of Commissioners on Uniform State Laws.*   A complete list of acts appears in the annual *Handbook.*   Information is given for all of the Acts and Model Codes promulgated by the National Conference. There are also charts showing which states have adopted specific Acts or Codes, and the date of adoption.

  b. *Directory of Acts and Tables of Adopting Jurisdictions.* This is a pamphlet, frequently reissued, which is published as part of the *Uniform Laws Annotated.*   It lists all Acts in alphabetical order and indicates where they are printed in *Uniform Laws Annotated.*   There is also a table for each state listing all of the Acts adopted.

[19] *Id.* at 990.

[20] *See* AMERICAN LAW INSTITUTE, ANNUAL REPORT (1924–).

[Illustration 104]

PAGE FROM VOLUME I, UNIFORM LAWS ANNOTATED, MASTER EDITION

§ 2—609   UNIFORM COMMERCIAL CODE

I. F [...]
Co[r] [...]
of ga[...]
er to [...]
credi[...]
unsat[...]
later[...]

> Typical Uniform Law adopted by the National Conference of Commissioners on Uniform State Laws.

contract was dependent on failure of buyer to provide cash or satisfactory security; however seller's dissatisfaction with defendant's financial standing must not be false or arbitrary. James B. Berry's Sons Co. v. Monark Gasoline & Oil Co., C.C.A.8, 1929, 32 F.2d 74 (cited in Official Comment, supra).

Where a vendor contracts to deliver goods, and allows a buyer credit for

[...same with-cash ship-ncial omes ques-] tion of the satisfaction of the seller with the buyer's financial responsibility is to be settled by the seller before he parts with the goods; but there must be a real want of satisfaction with the buyer's financial responsibility, and the refusal to ship without payment or security must be based on that reason alone. Corn Products Refining Co. v. Fasola, 1920, 109 A. 505, 94 N.J.Law 181 (cited in Official Comment, supra).

§ 2—610.   Anticipatory Repudiation

When either party repudiates the contract with respect to a performance not yet due the loss of which will substantially impair the value of the contract to the other, the aggrieved party may

    (a) for a commercially reasonable time await performance by the repudiating party; or

    (b) resort to any remedy for breach (Section 2—703 or Section 2—711), even though he has notified the repudiating party that he would await the latter's performance and has urged retraction; and

    (c) in either case suspend his own performance or proceed in accordance with the provisions of this Article on the seller's right to identify goods to the contract notwithstanding breach or to salvage unfinished goods (Section 2—704).

⟶ **Action in Adopting Jurisdictions**

Variations from Official Text:

    Kentucky. In paragraph (b), should refer to 2—703, not to 7—703.

|Official Comment|

Prior Uniform Statutory Provision: See Sections 63(2) and 65, Uniform Sales Act.

For text of prior provision, see Appendix in end volume.

400

[Illustration 104–a]

PAGE FROM VOLUME 1, UNIFORM LAWS ANNOTATED, MASTER EDITION

SALES   **§ 2—610**

Purposes: To make it clear that:

1. With the problem of insecurity taken care of by the preceding section and with provision being made in this Article as to the effect of a defective delivery under an installment contract, anticipatory repudiation centers upon an overt communication of intention or an action which renders performance impossible or demonstrates a clear determination not to continue with performance.

> **After each Section the official comment of the Commissioners explaining the Section is given.**

if he awaits performance beyond a commercially reasonable time he cannot recover resulting damages which he should have avoided.

2. It is not necessary for repudiation that performance be made literally and utterly impossible. Repudiation can result from action which reasonably indicates a rejection of the continuing obligation. And, a repudiation automatically results under the preceding section on insecurity when a party fails to provide adequate assurance of due future performance within thirty days after a justifiable demand therefor has been made. Under the language of this section, a demand by one or both parties for more than the contract calls for

in the way of counter-performance is not in itself a repudiation nor does it invalidate a plain expression of desire for future performance. However, when under a fair reading it amounts to a statement of intention not to perform except on conditions which go beyond the contract, it becomes a repudiation.

3. The test chosen to justify an aggrieved party's action under this section is the same as that in the section on breach in installment contracts—namely the substantial value of the contract. The most useful test of substantial value is to determine whether material inconvenience or injustice will result if the aggrieved party is forced to wait and receive an ultimate tender minus the part or aspect repudiated.

4. After repudiation, the aggrieved party may immediately resort to any remedy he chooses provided he moves in good faith (see Section 1—203). Inaction and silence by the aggrieved party may leave the matter open but it cannot be regarded as misleading the repudiating party. Therefore the aggrieved party is left free to proceed at any time with his options under this section, unless he has taken some positive action which in good faith requires notification to the other party before the remedy is pursued.

Cross References:
Point 1: Sections 2—609 and 2—612.
Point 2: Section 2—609.
Point 3: Section 2—612.
Point 4: Section 1—203.

1 U.L.A. U.C.C.—26   **401**

[Illustration 104–b]

PAGE FROM VOLUME 1, UNIFORM LAWS ANNOTATED, MASTER EDITION

§ 2—610 UNIFORM COMMERCIAL CODE

Definitional Cross References:
"Aggrieved party". Section 1—201.

"Contract". Section 1—201.
"Party". Section 1—201.
"Remedy". Section 1—201.

Cross References

Assurance of performance, see section 2—609.
Good faith, enforcement of contracts, see section 1—203.
Installment contracts, defective delivery, see section 2—612.
Letters of credit
    Anticipatory repudiation for wrongful disposition of, see section 5—115.
    Application of remedies under this section for wrongful repudiation, see
        section 5—115.
Recovery of damages by seller for wrongful repudiation, see section 2—708.

Law Review Commentaries

Anticipatory breach of contract: a comparison of the Texas law and the Uniform Commercial Code. 30 Tex. L.Rev. 744 (1952).

Remedies under law of sales in the proposed Commercial Code. Samuel Williston. 63 Harvard L.Rev. 584 (Feb. 1950).

Remedies under this title. William C. Jones. 30 Mo.L.Rev. 212 (Spring 1965).

Repudiation of a contract under the Code. Arthur Anderson. 14 DePaul L.Rev. 1 (Autumn-Winter 1964).

Sales: "from status to contract". Howard L. Hall. 1952 Wis.L.Rev. 209.

Library References

Sales ☞84, 98, 116, 370, 405.

C.J.S. Sales §§ 79, 98–100, 464, 520.

Notes of Decisions

Construction with other laws 1
Executory contracts, limitation to 2
Insolvency of parties 4
Remedies available on breach 5
Suspension of performance 3
Tender of delivery 6

time of fraud claimed as basis for rescission of contract on ground of anticipatory breach, was executed not executory. Metropolitan Distributors v. Eastern Supply Co., 1959, 21 Pa.D. & C.2d 128, 107 Pitt.L.J. 451.

1. Construction with other laws

This section and sections 2—709, 2—718 and 2—719 relating to anticipatory repudiation of a sales contract, and action for price, liquidation or limitation of damages, and modification or limitation of remedy, must be read and interpreted together, and unconscionable modification or limitation of remedial provisions must be deleted. Denkin v. Sterner, 1956, 10 Pa.D. & C.2d 203, 70 York Leg.Rec. 105.

2. Executory contracts, limitation to

Theory of an anticipatory breach cannot be invoked where contract, at

> At the end of each Section, references to additional research aids are given.
>
> Also, annotations to all court decisions citing the Section are indicated.

refusal to accept performance. Id.

402

[Illustration 105]

PAGE FROM UNIFORM LAWS ANNOTATED—DIRECTORY
OF UNIFORM ACTS

DIRECTORY OF UNIFORM ACTS

List of Uniform Acts or Codes, in alphabetical order, showing where each may be found in Uniform Laws Annotated, Master Edition.

The designation "Pocket Part" under the page column indicates that the particular Act or Code is complete in the Pocket Part. The user should always, of course, consult the Pocket Part, when an Act or Code appears in the main volume, for changes and subsequent material.

Title of Act	Uniform Laws Annotated	
	Volume	Page
Abortion Act (1971 Act)	9	1
Abortion Act, Revised (1974 Act)	9	Pocket Part
Absence as Evidence of Death and Absentees' Property Act	8	1
Acknowledgment Act	12	1
Adoption Act	9	5
Aircraft Financial Responsibility Act	12	21

> This Table lists all Uniform Acts and shows where the text may be found in the Uniform Laws Annotated. Similar information may also be found in the annual Handbook of the National Conference of Commissioners on Uniform State Laws.

Certification of Questions of Law Act	12	49
Child Custody Jurisdiction Act	9	99
Children and minors,		
Abortion Act (1971 Act)	9	1
Abortion Act, Revised (1974 Act)	9	Pocket Part
Adoption Act	9	5
Child Custody Jurisdiction Act	9	99
Civil Liability for Support Act	9	133
Gifts to Minors Act (1966 Act)	8	181
Gifts to Minors Act (1956 Act)	8	225
Juvenile Court Act	9	397
Parentage Act	9	Pocket Part
Paternity Act	9	787
Reciprocal Enforcement of Support Act (1968 Act)	9	805

U.L.A. Table Pamph. '76　　　　**1**

[Illustration 106]

PAGE FROM UNIFORM LAWS ANNOTATED—TABLES OF ADOPTING JURISDICTIONS

JURISDICTIONS AND ACTS ADOPTED

ILLINOIS

Title of Act	Uniform Laws Annotated Volume	Page
Alcoholism and Intoxication Treatment Act	9	41
Anatomical Gift Act	8	15
Arbitration Act	7	1
Attendance of Witnesses From Without the State in Criminal Proceedings, Act to Secure	11	1
Commercial Code	1 to 3	
Common Trust Fund Act	7	37
Controlled Substances Act	9	145
Criminal Extradition Act	11	51
Deceptive Trade Practices Act (1964 Act)	7	347
Declaratory Judgments Act	12	109
Disclaimer of Transfers by Will, Intestacy or		

> This Table lists all of the states alphabetically and then indicates whether uniform acts or codes have been adopted by the individual states.

Federal Tax Lien Registration Act	7	381
Fiduciaries Act	7	393
Foreign Money-Judgments Recognition Act	13	269
Gifts to Minors Act (1966 Act)	8	181
Interstate Compromise of Death Taxes Act	8	271
Limited Partnership Act	6	559
Management of Institutional Funds Act	7	Pocket Part
Partnership Act	6	1
Principal and Income Act (1931 Act)	7	657
Reciprocal Enforcement of Support Act (1968 Act)	9	805
Recognition of Acknowledgments Act	13	503
Rendition of Accused Persons Act	11	541
Rendition of Prisoners as Witnesses in Criminal Proceedings Act	11	547
Simplification of Fiduciary Security Transfers Act	7	797
Simultaneous Death Act	8	605
Single Publication Act	13	517
State Administrative Procedure Act (Model)	13	Pocket Part
Supervision of Trustees for Charitable Purposes Act	7	819
Testamentary Additions to Trusts Act	8	629

20

[Illustration 107]

PAGE FROM THE 1970 HANDBOOK OF THE NATIONAL CONFERENCE OF COMMISSIONERS ON UNIFORM STATE LAWS

UNIFORM LAW COMMISSIONERS' MODEL PUBLIC DEFENDER ACT *

1   SECTION 1 [*Definitions.*] In this Act, the term:

2   (1) "detain" means to have in custody or otherwise deprive

3   of freedom of action;

4   (2) "expenses," when used with reference to representation

5   under this Act, includes the expenses of investigation, other

6   preparation, and trial;

7   (3) "needy person" means a person who at the time his need

> **Model Acts are promulgated for topics where uniformity among the states is not necessary or desirable.**

14   (ii) a misdemeanor or offense any penalty for which in-

15   volves the possibility of confinement for more than 6 months

16   or a fine of more than $500; and

17   (iii) an act that, but for the age of the person involved,

18   would be a serious crime.

COMMENT

The term "detain" is defined in terms, drawn from *Miranda v. Arizona*,[23] that make it clear that the act in this respect is coextensive with the constitutional requirements respecting the kind of situation in which the needy person is entitled to be represented by counsel.

The term "expenses" is given a partial ("includes") rather than an exhaustive ("means") definition, because it is necessary only to make clear that preparation and trial are an integral part of adequate representation.

The term "needy person" is defined to make clear that partial need and supervening need are also included. "Undue hardship," not being susceptible to precise

---

* The National Conference of Commissioners on Uniform State Laws in the promulgation of its Uniform Acts urges, with the endorsement of the American Bar Association, their enactment in each jurisdiction. Where there is a demand for an Act covering the subject matter in a substantial number of the States, but where in the judgment of the National Conference of Commissioners on Uniform State Laws it is not a subject upon which uniformity between the States is necessary or desirable, but where it would be helpful to have legislation which would tend toward uniformity where enacted, Acts on such subjects are promulgated as Model Acts.

[23] 384 U.S. at 477

SECTION G. INTERSTATE COMPACTS

The United States Constitution provides that "No state shall, without the consent of Congress * * * enter into any Agreement or Compact with another state * * *." [21]

In an early interpretation of this clause, the Supreme Court of the United States held that it prohibited all agreement between states unless consented to by Congress.[22] But in a subsequent decision,[23] the Court changed its position and held that Congressional consent was not necessary for agreements or compacts which did not increase the political powers of the states or interfere with the supremacy of the United States. Normally, interstate agreements or compacts are formally enacted by the legislatures of the states involved, and are then submitted to Congress for its consent.[24]

Until about 1900, most interstate compacts dealt with boundary disputes between states. Since then, the compacts have more commonly been used as a means of cooperation for solving problems common to two or more states, such as flood control, control of pollution, or the establishment of a port authority.

1. Publication of Interstate Compacts

As interstate compacts ordinarily do not come into effect until agreed to by the states involved, and with the consent of Congress, the text of agreements or compacts will be found in the session laws of the respective states and in the U. S. Statutes at Large.[25]

A complete listing of compacts through 1970 may be found in Council of State Governments, *Interstate Compacts, 1783–1970 a compilation (1971)*. The index to each volume of the U. S. Statutes at Large also includes a listing of all compacts consented to by the Congress during that session of Congress.

Each biennial edition of the Book of the States has a chapter on current developments in interstate compacts, and a selective listing of the more significant ones.

[21] U.S.CONST. Art. 1, § 10, cl. 3.

[22] Holmes v. Jennison, 14 Pet. (39 U.S.) 540 (1840).

[23] Virginia v. Tennessee, 148 U.S. 503, 518 (1893).

[24] Interstate agreements do not have to be formally enacted. See the annotation to Art. 1, § 10, cl. 3 in THE CONSTITUTION OF THE UNITED STATES OF AMERICA, ANALYSIS AND INTERPRETATION (Lib. of Cong.Ed.) 1973, pp. 419–423, *see also*: F. ZIMMERMAN and M. WENDELL, The Law and Use of Interstate Compacts, 1961; COMMENT, Federal Question Jurisdiction to Interpret Interstate Compacts, 64 Geo.L.J. 87 (1975).

[25] *E.g.* the North Dakota-Minnesota Boundary Agreement is published in 1961 Minn.Sess.Laws, Ch. 236, 1961 North Dakota Sess.Law, Ch. 318 and the Congressional consent as given in P.L. 87–162, 75 Stat. 399.

2. Locating Court Decisions on Interstate Compacts

a. Digests. Cases involving interstate compacts are digested under "States–6" in the Key-Number digests and under States § 52 in the Digest of the U. S. Supreme Court. (L. Coop. Ed.)

b. Annotated Statutes. The practice of including the text of compacts in state codes varies. The indexes to the codes of the states concerned should be checked.

c. Citators. The Statutes section of the appropriate Shepard's Citations may be used to "Shepardize" the state code or session law citation, or the U. S. Statutes at Large citation.

———

SECTION H. TREATISES: RESEARCH PROCEDURE

1. Methods of Research

a. *Case Method*

If the name of a leading decision in point is known, consult the *table of cases* of the treatise to ascertain whether it is discussed in the book. If so, an examination of the cited pages in the text will reveal a discussion of the subject matter with additional cases in point.

b. *Index Method*

Consult the *index* in the back of the book if a case in point is not known. Select an appropriate fact or descriptive word or legal topic to use the index. References will be to the text of the publication.

c. *Topic Method*

The Topic Method can be used through the *table of contents*; however, its effectiveness in locating the pertinent text depends on the researcher's understanding of the structural subdivisions of the subject matter in that table.

d. *Definition Method*

The *index* to the treatise may list words or phrases which are defined and explained in the text.

2. Location of Treatises

a. *Card catalog.*

To locate treatises on a subject, consult the *card catalog* in the law library. The methods of using a *card catalog* are described below.

The card catalog is so made that there are ordinarily three ways of finding a book, namely:

First—Under the AUTHOR'S surname.

Second—Under the TITLE of the book, when it is distinctive.

Third—Under the SUBJECT to which the book relates.

Cards are arranged alphabetically by the first word on the top line, always disregarding "The," "A" and "An." The labels on the outside and the guide cards inside the drawers are to aid in quickly locating the word desired.

To find whether the library has a certain book, consult the catalog as you would a dictionary or telephone directory. In some libraries, the author and subject cards are kept in separate catalogs.

EXAMPLE—To find the books in the library which were written by Oliver Wendel Holmes, look for HOLMES, the surname of the author, in its alphabetical place.

The author of a publication may be an organization, governmental agency or corporation. The main entry in the catalog is under the name of that body.

EXAMPLES:

   American Institute of Accountants

   U. S. Attorney General's Committee on Administrative Procedure

   Bureau of National Affairs

If the publication entitled "The All England Law Reports" is wanted, look for "ALL," the first word of the title not an article.

Again, to find the books on the subject COMMERCIAL LAW, look for those words, where all the cards representing the books on this subject are filed together.

Many large subjects, such as the above, are subdivided to aid in locating specific material.

Cards for books about a person follow the cards representing that person as author.

CALL NUMBER—The number at the upper left hand corner of the card constitutes the "Call Number" and directs you to the book's location on the shelves.

Cross reference cards bear no call numbers but serve to connect related subjects. Examples—Attorneys, see Lawyers. Damages, see also Accident Law, Negligence, Torts.

b. For a comprehensive list of legal treatises, with book review annotations, see:

(1) *New York University, School of Law Library.* *A Catalogue of the Law Collection at* New York University, ed. Julius J. Marke. 1953. 1 vol. This is an excellent source for older treatises.

(2) J. M. Jacobstein & M. G. Pimsleur. *Law Books in Print.* 4 vols. 1976. Supplemented by *Law Books Published,* a quarterly publication with an annual cumulation.

This publication lists legal treatises in English, which were in print as of December 31, 1974. The set is in four volumes. The first and second volumes are by author and title, the third by subject and series, and the fourth by publisher. Complete bibliographic information is furnished for each title.

(3) *Association of American Law Schools.* *Law Books Recommended for Libraries.* 1967– , 6 volumes, and supplements.

This set is a compilation of lists intended to provide carefully selected lists of books for law libraries. It is in six looseleaf volumes with each of the 46 topics in separate pamphlets. No. 47 is an author and subject index to the entire set.

(4) *Harvard Law School Library.* *Annual Legal Bibliography.* July 1, 1960 to date. Vol. 1—.

This is a subject classified list of selected United States and foreign books and periodical articles that are currently acquired by the Harvard Law Library. It covers all fields of law and is subdivided under some 40 jurisdictions. The *Annual* includes (1) an Analytical Table of Contents, subdivided into common law and civil law jurisdictions and private international and public international law, (2) subject indexes in Spanish, German and French, and (3) an Alphabetical Subject Index, covering the topics appearing in the *Annual.*

It is kept up-to-date by a *Current Legal Bibliography* which is published nine times a year, October to June. The material in the *Current* numbers of a year is cumulated into the bound *Annual* volume.

Current Publications in Legal and Related Fields. 1953 to date. Vol. 1—.

This mimeographed bibliography of current legal treatises and related literature is sponsored by the American Association of Law Libraries and is published by Fred B. Rothman & Co. It is issued nine times a year, viz., monthly except June, July and September, with an annual cumulation.

The cumulative issue is divided into two parts.

Each author entry is numbered. The subject index refers to the numbered author entries.

SECTION I. THE RESTATEMENTS: RESEARCH PROCEDURE

1. Index Method

Consult the index to the appropriate Restatement, *e.g., Contracts*. If the precise Restatement covering the problem is not known, refer to the *General Index to the Restatement of the Law*.

For cases which have cited the applicable rules of the Restatement, examine either (1) the *Restatement in the Courts* and its *Supplements* or (2) if the Restatement has been revised, the *Appendix* to the Restatement, Second.

The tentative drafts and the Restatements' Second *Appendix* provide annotated Reporter's notes, with interpretations and citations to leading cases.

To compare the rule in a Restatement with the law of a specific state, consult the *Annotations* to it for that state, if one was published, or consult the *Restatements in the Courts*. A specific section of a Restatement may also be *Shepardized in Shepard's Restatement of the Law Citations*.

2. Topic Method

The table of contents, rather than the index, to a specific Restatement can be examined to locate the appropriate rule.

3. Definition Method

To determine the meaning of words and phrases used in the Restatements, examine the *Glossary of Terms Defined in the Restatement*, which is included in the *Restatement in the Courts*.

SECTION J. SUMMARY

1. Treatises

a. *Scope.*

(1) Expositions, some of which are critical, by legal writers on case law and legislation.

(2) More exhaustive in scope than encyclopedias, but periodical articles are usually more detailed and critical.

(3) Functions.

(a) Views of the writer as to what the law ought to be—critically evaluative.

(b) Interpretation of statutory and case law.

(c) Case finder.

(d) Presents a general view of the principles on a topic.

b.   *Arrangement.*

Treatises usually include these features:

(1) Table of contents.

(2) Table of cases.

(3) Subject matter—text.

(4) Index.

c.   *Supplementation.*

The current practice of publishers is to keep treatises current by cumulative pocket supplements. Some publications are furnished with replacement (revision) volumes.

d.   *Citation.*

The citation form for treatises may be found in Appendix A, at (I), (B), (1).

2.   Restatements

a.   *Scope.*

(1) Simplifies and restates case law on selected subjects.

(2) Weaknesses.

(a) Absence of legislative endorsement and sanction.

(b) Statements treat the subject matter antecedently and not prospectively.

(c) Inconsistency of terminology among Restatements.

b.   *Arrangement and Supplementation.*

(1) Tentative drafts—includes Reporter's notes and case discussion.

(2) Restatements—text.

(3) Revisions—Restatements Second.

(4) *Annotations*—comparison of state case law with Restatement.

(5) *Restatement in the Courts*—digest-reference to cases citing the Restatements.

(6) *Glossary of Terms Defined in the Restatement*—included in the *Restatement in the Courts.*

(7) *Supplements*—amendments and additions to text and supplements to the *Restatement in the Courts.*

   c. *Indexes, First Series.*

   (1) *General Index*—covers the several Restatements.

   (2) Each Restatement also has an individual index.

   d. *Indexes, Second Series.* Each Restatement has its own index.

   e. *Citation.* Citation form for Restatements may be found in Appendix A, at (I), (D), (1).

3. Uniform Laws

   a. *National Conference of Commissioners on Uniform State Laws.*

   (1) Uniform laws adopted by the Conference are published in its annual *Handbook* and in *Uniform Laws Annotated.*

   (2) The annual *Handbook* lists all uniform laws and those states which have adopted them.

   b. *Model Codes.*

   Drafted by National Conference of Commissioners on Uniform State Laws, or the American Law Institute. Some model codes are drafted jointly by both associations.

   Citation form for Model Codes may be found in Appendix A, at (I), (D), (1).

Chapter 19

OTHER RESEARCH AIDS

___

Attorney General Reports, Dictionaries, Directories, Form Books and Briefs and Records on Appeal

This chapter covers sets of law books that are useful in legal research but which fit into none of the categories previously discussed. They are: (1) attorneys general opinions, (2) law dictionaries, (3) directories, (4) briefs and records, (5) form books, and (6) opinions on legal ethics.

___

SECTION A. OPINIONS OF THE ATTORNEYS GENERAL

The opinions of the attorneys general have the characteristics of both primary and secondary authority.[1] As the legal advisor to the executive officials of the government, the attorney general renders requested legal advice to them, generally, in the form of written opinions. Although these opinions are the official statements of an executive officer, issued in accordance with his authority, they are merely advisory statements and are not mandatory orders. Therefore, the inquirers and other officials are not conclusively bound to follow such recommendations and conclusions. However, the opinions are strongly persuasive and are generally followed by executive officers. Also, they have significant influence on the courts in their deliberations.

The opinions, as a general rule, relate to: (1) the interpretations of statutes or (2) general legal problems. Some attorneys general limit their advice and will not render opinions as to the constitutionality of proposed legislation.

[1] For more detailed information on the role of Attorneys General, *see* W. THOMPSON, TRANSMISSION OR RESISTANCE: OPINIONS OF STATE ATTORNEYS GENERAL AND THE IMPACT OF THE SUPREME COURT. 9 VAL.U.L.REV. 55 (1974); *see also* NATIONAL ASSOCIATION OF ATTORNEYS GENERAL. THE OFFICE OF ATTORNEY GENERAL (1974), and FORMER ATTORNEYS GENERAL ANALYZE THE OFFICE (1970). For individual state Attorney General check for articles in *Index to Legal Periodicals* under the heading "Attorney General."

1. Attorney General of the United States

The opinions of the United States Attorney General have been published in 41 volumes, 1789–1960,[2] with an index in each volume. Since 1961, they have been published only as advance sheets. There is a four-volume index to the printed volumes, the first two volumes of which are index digests.

The *United States Code Annotated* and *United States Code Service* include digests of U.S. Attorney General opinions in their annotations. They are also included in the United States and Federal *Shepard's Citations* when cited in a court decision.

2. State Attorneys General Opinions

Nearly every state publishes the opinions of its Attorney General.[3] They are included in the annotations of many state annotated codes and *Shepard's Citations* (state units) indicate when an attorney general's opinion has been cited by a court. From 1937–1969 an annual digest of state attorneys general opinions was published by the Council of States. Since 1970 selected opinions have been published in the *Newsletter and Digest of State Attorneys General Opinions*.[4]

SECTION B. LAW DICTIONARIES

Law dictionaries are useful for locating the definition of words in their legal sense or use. For each word or phrase a short definition is given. Most legal dictionaries also provide a citation to a court decision or other reference tracing the source of the word or phrase. In Chapter 6, Section C, the set entitled *Words and Phrases* was discussed. This set includes digests from all court decisions in which a word or phrase has been interpreted. *Words and Phrases* may also be used as a dictionary, but as it is limited to those words which were involved in litigation, it is not a true dictionary. Moreover, most dictionaries are much more compact and are published in one or two

---

[2] The U. S. Department of Justice plans to continue publishing bound volumes of its opinions and work is in process on Volume 42. Communication from Department of Justice, dated 8/30/76, on file in the Tarlton Law Library, University of Texas, Austin.

[3] A checklist of all published opinions of State Attorneys General may be found in M. PIMSLEUR, CHECKLISTS OF BASIC AMERICAN LEGAL PUBLICATIONS, Section III. 1975.

[4] National Association of Attorneys General, *Newsletter & Digest of Selected Opinions of State Attorneys General*. Published by Iron Works Pike, Lexington, Ky.

volumes. Listed below are some of the more commonly used American and English law dictionaries.[5]

1. American Law Dictionaries

a. Ballentine, *Law Dictionary*, with Pronunciations. 3d Ed. Lawyers Cooperative Publishing Co. 1969. 1429 p.

b. Black, *Law Dictionary*. 4th Ed., West Publishing Co. 1968. 1882 p.

Includes: Guide to Pronounciation of Latin Phrase and a Table of Abbreviations.

c. Bouvier, *Law Dictionary,* (3rd revision) 8th Ed. West Publishing Co. 3 v. 1914.

This edition is now out of date in some respects. It is a particularly scholarly work, however, and many of its definitions are encyclopedic in nature and it still is very useful for many historical terms.

d. Cochran, *Law Lexicon*; Pronouncing Edition. 4th Ed. rev. by W. Gilmore. W. H. Anderson, 1973. 428 p.

2. English Law Dictionaries

a. Jowitt, *The Dictionary of English Law*. Sweet & Maxwell, 1959. 1905 p.

b. Mozley and Whitley, *Law Dictionary*. 8th ed. Butterworths. 1970. 389 p.

3. Special Law Dictionaries

There are also dictionaries devoted to specific subjects, such as labor law or taxation.[6]

SECTION C. LAW DIRECTORIES

Law directories vary in the scope of their coverage. Some attempt to list all lawyers, others are limited to a region, state, municipality, or to a specialty. Law directories are useful in locating information about a particular lawyer and are used by many lawyers when they have to refer a case to a lawyer in another city.

In 1935 the American Bar Association appointed a Special Committee on Law Lists to investigate the law list business. This Committee developed "Rules and Standards as to Law Lists" [7] which were

---

[5] A listing of law dictionaries may be found in J. JACOBSTEIN and M. PIMSLEUR, LAW BOOKS IN PRINT. 1976 ed. vol. 3. p. 144.

[6] A listing may be found under subject in volume 3 of LAW BOOKS IN PRINT, *Id.*

[7] The text may be found in volume Six of *Martindale-Hubbell Law Directory.*

adopted by the American Bar Association in 1937.   The American Bar Association has taken the position that " * * * A law list is conclusively established to be reputable if it is certified by the American Bar Association as being in compliance with its rules and standards." [8]   As a result, nearly all law lists and directories now seek to receive the certification of the American Bar Association.   The importance of the certified lists has been magnified by the restrictions that the Bar Associations have placed on lawyers' ability to advertise. A lifting of these constraints may lead to the emergence of new forms of lawyers' directories.[9]

1.   General Directories

    a.   *Martindale-Hubbell Law Directory.*   This six-volume annual publication is the most comprehensive directory of lawyers. All lawyers admitted to the bar of any jurisdiction are eligible for listing without cost.   The first five volumes are arranged alphabetically by state.   Each of these volumes is in two parts.   The first part consists of two alphabetical lists, one of the cities within each state, and a second of the lawyers within each city.   For each listed attorney, information is given for date of birth, date of admission to the bar, college and law school attended, American Bar Association membership, and specialty.   Confidential ratings [10] are also given which estimate legal ability, recommendations and promptness in paying bills.   The second part is another double alphabetic arrangement, this time done by cities within the state and law firms within each city.   This entry may include the address and telephone number of the firm, names and short biographies of its members, representative clients and areas of practice.   Since this form of advertising carries a charge, the list is selective.

    (1) Special features

        Canadian lawyers are listed in volume 5.   Patent lawyers are separately listed in volumes 1–5.   Lawyers with the United States Government are listed in a separate roster in volume 1.   Information about the American Bar Association is presented in volume 6.   Public Interest Practice Firms and Organizations are listed in volume 6.

    (2) Law Digests

---

[8] AMERICAN BAR ASSOCIATION.   CODE OF PROFESSIONAL RESPONSIBILITY DR 2–102–A–6.

[9] *Goldfarb v. Virginia State Bar*, 421 U.S. 773 (1975) may be a harbinger of such change.

[10] A "Confidential Key" to their ratings is included in the inside covers of volumes 1–5.

In volume 6 there are concise digests of the statutory laws for the fifty states, Canada, and fifty-two of the more important foreign countries. These digests are revised annually by lawyers from each jurisdiction.

b. The Lawyers Directory. *The Lawyers Directory* is an annual publication which lists the following:

Part I, Leading lawyers and law firms in the United States and Canada and a list of foreign lawyers; Part II, Corporate law department counsel roster; Part III, Complete list of foreign embassies and legations in Washington, D.C., and U.S. embassies, legations and consular offices throughout the world.

c. *The American Bar, The Canadian Bar, The International Bar.* This is an annual biographical directory of ranking United States and foreign lawyers. It provides sketches of the North American law offices listed and individual biographical data. The third unit is a professional international directory of "the finest lawyers in the world."

d. Other International Directories. Many other companies publish directories which are to be used to locate a "recommended" attorney in a particular country and city to deal with any general legal questions. Included in this group are *The International List, The International Lawyers,* and *Kime's International Law Directory.*

2. State and Regional Directories

The Legal Directories Publishing Co., Inc.[11] produces 25 directories which are approved by the American Bar Association and list attorneys in specific states or regions. Examples of the state directories are the *Florida Legal Directory,* the *Illinois Legal Directory* and the *Texas Legal Directory.* The regional directories include the *Mountain States Legal Directory,* the *New England Legal Directory,* and the *Virginias, Maryland, Delaware and District of Columbia Legal Directory.* Each of these directories contain sections on:

a. Federal and state officials (including members of the state legislatures);

b. Federal, state and local courts; and

c. Attorneys practicing in the state (arranged by county and city). Also, this section contains some biographical data on law firms and their members.

[11] Legal Directories Publishing Co., Inc., Suite 201, 1314 Westwood Blvd., Los Angeles, California 90024.

3. Specialty Directories

A few directories have been published which contain only the attorneys who practice law in a certain area or specialty. These law lists are helpful to the individual who wishes reference to a lawyer in a specific city on a legal problem common to the specialty. Examples of such directories include *The Probate Counsel*,[12] *American Bank Attorneys*,[13] *International Trial Lawyers*,[14] *Markham's Negligence Counsel*,[15] and *Juvenile Law Litigation Directory*.[16] Other directories are merely membership lists of certain organizations which are concerned with the practice of law in a specialty. They include the *American Patent Law Association*[17] and the *National Association of College and University Attorneys—Directory and Handbook*.[18] Nearly every legal fraternity or professional group also publishes a directory of members which is localized as to state and sometimes city. These directories are of limited usage to the individual wishing referral on a specific legal problem. Finally, a few directories have specialized their listings according to more social categories. An example of one such tool is the *Directory of Women Attorneys in the United States*.[19]

4. Judicial Directories

a. Federal Judges. A few directories give an annual listing of the justices of the Supreme Court, all the federal district and appellate courts, and the special courts. The *Federal Directory*[20] and the *United States Court Directory*[21] are two publications which are

[12] The Probate Counsel, Suite 510-C, 3033 North Central Avenue, Phoenix, Arizona 85012.

[13] *American Bank Attorneys*, Capron Publishing Corp., Wellesley Hills, Mass. 02181.

[14] *International Trial Lawyers*, Directory Publishers, Inc., Galesburg, Ill.

[15] *Markham's Negligence Counsel*, Markham Publishing Corp., 219 Atlantic St., Stamford, Conn. 06901.

[16] *Juvenile Law Litigation Directory*, Institute of Judicial Administration, New York Univ. School of Law, 33 Washington Square West, New York, N.Y. 10011.

[17] *American Patent Law Association*, 2001 Jefferson Davis Hwy., Arlington, Vir. 22202.

[18] *National Association of College and University Attorneys—Directory and Handbook*, Suite 510, One Dupont Circle, N.W., Washington, D.C. 20036.

[19] *Directory of Women Attorneys in the United States*, Ford Associates, Inc., 701 S. Federal Ave., Butler, Ind. 46721.

[20] *The Federal Directory*, Consolidated Directories, Inc., 1133-15th Street, N.W., Washington, D.C. 20005.

[21] *United States Court Directory*, Legal Reporters Associates, c/o DiCesare & Associates, Inc., 1730 K Street, N.W., Washington, D.C. 20006.

annually updated as to membership and mailing addresses. The *Biographical Dictionary of the Federal Judiciary* [22] gives biographical data on the judges of the federal bar, past and present.

b.　State Judges. Some states compile a directory of state and local judge membership in addition to their respective general state directories. *The California Courts and Judges Handbook* [23] is an example of a periodic publication which includes general information and rules of the state's courts, a directory of courts, and a register of individual judges with biographical data.

5.　Academic Directories

Certain directories are compiled to serve the academic world and provide a ready reference to those wishing to make use of the law schools' facilities. *The Directory of Law Teachers* [24] allows one to find bibliographic information on law school faculty as well as indexing by subject or specialty. Law libraries of the United States and Canada are indexed geographically in the *Directory of Law Libraries*.[25] An alphabetical listing of library personnel is also provided in this directory.

SECTION D.　FORM BOOKS

Form books are used as aids in drafting legal documents. Much of a lawyer's time is spent in drafting forms. To assist lawyers in this aspect of their practice, there are available many different types of form books. When using form books it should be kept in mind that they are all general in nature and that before using a form, extreme care should be exercised to make sure that the language is entirely suitable for the purpose for which it is to be used. Books of forms may be classified as follows:

1.　General form books

This type provides forms for all aspects of legal practice and varies from one volume to multi-volume sets. They generally are annotated and each form contains references to cases which have fa-

[22] *Biographical Dictionary of the Federal Judiciary*, Gale Research Co., Book Tower, Detroit, Mich. 48226.

[23] *California Courts and Judges Handbook*, Law Book Service Co., 1001 Franklin St., P.O. Box 14218, San Francisco, California 94114.

[24] *Directory of Law Teachers*, West Publishing Co., 50 West Kellogg Blvd., St. Paul, Minn. 55102.

[25] *Directory of Law Libraries*, Commerce Clearing House, Inc., 420 Lexington Ave., New York, N.Y. 10017.

vorably construed provisions within the form.　Editorial comment is also frequently given.　Examples are: [26]

> *American Jurisprudence*, 2d ed. Legal Forms Annotated.　1971–74.　20 v. with pocket supplements.

> *Modern Legal Forms* (West Pub. Co.).　1950–1972.　17 v. with pocket supplements.

> Nichols, *Cyclopedia of Legal Forms*, Annotated.　1955–1964. 14 v. with pocket supplements.

> Rabkin and Johnson, *Current Legal Forms with Tax Analysis*. 1968.　22 v.　Loose-leaf.

> Warren, *Forms of Agreement*.　1966.　1 v. Loose-leaf.

Most large states also have general form books that are keyed to local practice.　These are published both by commercial publishers and state bar association programs.　They contain the same features as the form books discussed above, but are designed for local use, and hence may be more useful to the practitioner.　Examples are:

> *California Legal Forms, Transaction Guide* (Matthew Bender). 1968.　1 v.

> *Legal Form Manual for Real Estate Transactions* (State Bar of Texas).　1976.　1 v.

2.　Subject Form Books

Many form books are published which are devoted to a special subject.　These are similar in format to the general form books but contain more forms on the aspect of the subject covered than will usually be found in the general ones.　Examples are: [27]

> F. Bailey and H. Rothblatt, *Complete Manual of Criminal Forms*, 2d ed.　Lawyers Cooperative Publishing Co.　1974.　2 v.

> L.　Melville, *Forms and Agreements on Intellectual Property*. Clark Boardman.　1974.　1 v.

> R. Quinn, *Modern Banking Forms*.　Warren, Gorham & Lamont. 1974.　1 v.

3.　Other Sources of Forms

a.　Forms in treatises.　Many multi-volume sets of treatises will have a separate volume of forms.　For example, Volume 4 of K. Davis, *Administrative Law Treatise* consists of forms dealing with the various aspects of administrative law, while W. Fletcher, *Law of Private Corporations* has a multi-volume companion set entitled Corporation Forms Annotated.

---

[26] For a current listing of form books, see LAW BOOKS IN PRINT, *id.* at Footnote 5.

[27] *Id.*

b.   State Codes.   Some state codes include both substantive and procedural forms.   For any particular state code, consult the general index under "Forms."

c.   Procedural Forms.   These were discussed in Chapter 12.

SECTION E.   BRIEFS AND RECORDS ON APPEAL

After a case has been decided at a trial court or an intermediate court of appeal, the case may be appealed to a higher court.   When this happens, the attorneys for each side submit written briefs in which they set forth the reasons why the appellate court should either affirm or reverse the decision below.   Such briefs contain the theories upon which arguments hinge and a discussion and analysis of the law, with citations to the authorities.   Where available, the record of trial court action is submitted with the brief.   This record usually contains forms of the preliminary motions and pleadings in the case;   examination and cross-examination of witnesses;   the instructions to the jury;   the opinion of the lower court, and various other exhibits.

Briefs and records provide an attorney who has a similar case with much of his research and a list of arguments which have or have not impressed an appellate court.

1.   Briefs and Records of the Supreme Court of the United States

A small number of libraries receive copies of the briefs and records which are submitted to the Supreme Court.[28]   Most law school libraries and larger bar association libraries also have these briefs and records available on microform.

2.   Federal Courts of Appeal

Most large law libraries receive the briefs and records for the Federal Court of Appeals for the circuit in which they are located. Others may frequently be obtained from a local law library on interlibrary loan.

SECTION F.   PROFESSIONAL RESPONSIBILITY

The national standard of conduct for lawyers is set forth in the *Code of Professional Responsibility* promulgated by the American Bar Association in 1970.[29]   This Code "is designed to be adopted by

---

[28] *See* Carpentier, *Appellate Records—A Beginning Union List.*   62 LAW LIB.J. 273.   (1969).

[29] CODE OF PROFESSIONAL RESPONSIBILITY AND CODE OF JUDICIAL CONDUCT.   American Bar Association.   1975.   This is published as a separate pamphlet and is reprinted in volume VI of the *Martindale-Hubbell Law Directory.* This Code replaces the ABA Code of Professional Ethics adopted in 1908.

appropriate agencies both as an inspirational guide to the members of the profession and as a basis for disciplinary action when the conduct of a lawyer falls below the required minimum standards stated * * * ".[30] The *Code of Professional Responsibility* consists of three parts: Canons, Ethical Considerations, and Disciplinary Rules.

The American Bar Association, as a voluntary association, has no means for enforcing its Code. Only the state legislatures or the highest court of each state has the power to discipline lawyers. Each state has adopted either its own code or that of the American Bar Association.

1. Discipline of Lawyers

The procedure for the discipline of lawyers varies from state to state. The rules governing discipline may be located by consulting the indexes of the state codes. The common practice is for the highest court of the state to appoint a committee of lawyers who hear complaints and make recommendations to the court.[31]

2. Opinions on Legal Ethics

The American Bar Association and most state bar associations have Committees on Legal Ethics. Lawyers submit to these Committees a situation they are facing and request an opinion as to whether or not their suggested action may be a breach of the *Code of Professional Responsibility*. The Committee on Legal Ethics of the American Bar Association issues its opinions in two series: *Formal Opinions* and *Informal Opinions*. Committees of state bar associations usually publish their opinions in their bar journal or other publications.

SECTION G. CITATION

Citation of special materials is covered in Appendix A, at (I), (D), (1).

[30] *Id.* at 1C.

[31] T. MORGAN AND R. ROTUNDA. PROBLEMS AND MATERIAL ON PROFESSIONAL RESPONSIBILITY. 1976. pp. 143–159.

Chapter 20

INTERNATIONAL LAW

Research in international law is neither esoteric nor limited to the practice of the specialist. American treaties, as primary law, are frequently determinative of the rights and duties of American citizens. To illustrate this point, a Missourian may have a relative in Italy who dies leaving property. A reciprocal treaty with Italy may regulate property and inheritance rights. Therefore, the presence or absence of this treaty would have a significant effect on the rights of inheritance of this Missouri citizen. Another standard example is that of the American citizen who is injured in an airplane accident while traveling over a foreign country. His rights in this case are affected by treaty. These are not isolated illustrations, for they occur more frequently than is generally realized. It is essential, therefore, that the general practitioner have some knowledge of the sources of international law.

International law has been defined as

" * * * [A] body of rules governing the relations between states * * *. Customary, as distinguished from conventional, international law is based upon the common consent of the nations extending over a period of time of sufficient duration to cause it to become crystalized into a rule of conduct. When doubt arises as to the existence or nonexistence of a rule of international law, or as to the application of a rule to a given situation, resort is usually had to such sources as pertinent treaties, pronouncements of foreign offices, statements by writers, and decisions of international tribunals and those of prize courts and other domestic courts purporting to be expressive of the law of nations." [1]

Another international law scholar has defined international law in terms of how it is made.

"When contrasted with national or 'domestic' law, we think of international law as that which is created of two or more states, whether such action is in the form of treaty-making or the formation of international customs." [2]

[1] 1 G. HACKWORTH, DIGEST OF INTERNATIONAL LAW 1 (1940); *see also*: The Paquette Habana, 175 U.S. 677, 700 (1899).

[2] H. KELSEN, PRINCIPLES OF INTERNATIONAL LAW 201 (1952).

International law as so stated is usually known as *public* international law as distinguished from *private* international law, which is defined as:

" * * * [T]hat branch of the law of municipal law which determines before the courts of what nation a particular action or suit should be brought, and by the law of what nation it should be determined." [3]

This chapter will be devoted to that of public international law and specifically to the researching of the conventional international law of the United States as represented in the treaties and other international agreements entered into between the United States and other countries.[4]

SECTION A.   RESEARCH IN INTERNATIONAL LAW IN RELATION TO THE UNITED STATES

1.   Treaties and International Agreements Between the United States and other Countries

Under the Constitution of the United States, the President "shall have the power, by and with the Advice and Consent of the Senate, to make treaties, provided two thirds of the Senate present concur".[5] An international agreement is one that the President may enter into under his constitutional power as President or as authorized by an act of Congress and which does not need the consent of Congress.[6] The actual power of the President to enter into international agreements rather than treaties is not entirely clear and has long been a matter of dispute.[7]   But nevertheless, international agreements are entered into by Presidents much more frequently than treaties.

[3] BLACK'S LAW DICTIONARY, rev. 4th ed. 1968.   In the United States the term "conflict of laws" is generally used rather than private international law.

[4] For additional information on the substantive aspects of international law, *see* the latest edition of J. BRIERLY, THE LAW OF NATIONS, or W. FENWICK, INTERNATIONAL LAW, 4th ed. 1965.   *See also*: W. GOULD, SOCIAL SCIENCE LITERATURE, A BIBLIOGRAPHY OF INTERNATIONAL LAW; I. DOIMI DI DELUPIS, BIBLIOGRAPHY OF INTERNATIONAL LAW. (1975).

[5] U.S.Constitution.   Art. II, Cl. 2.

[6] Restatement of the Law 2d, Foreign Relation Law of the United States § 115a. *See also*: A. GILBERT, EXECUTIVE AGREEMENTS AND TREATIES, 1946–1973 (1973).

[7] J. Murphy, "Treaties and International Agreements other than Treaties: Constitutional Allocation of Power and Responsibility among the President, the House of Representatives, and the Senate."   23 U.KAN.L.REV. 221 (1974/75); P. Fitzgerald, *Executive Agreements and the Intent Behind the Treaty Power*, 2 HAST.CON.L.Q. 757 (1975); *Comment, Executive Agreements, the Treaty-Making Clause, and Strict Constructionism*, 8 LOY. of L.A.L.REV. 587 (1975).

2. Restatement of the Law, Second. Foreign Relations Law of the United States

This *Restatement* was adopted by the American Law Institute in 1965. Its purpose, as stated in the introduction, is to set forth the foreign relations law of the United States, which consist of those rules the United States conceived to be established by international law and those parts of the domestic law which give effect to rules of international law.

SECTION B. SOURCES FOR UNITED STATES TREATIES

1. Current Publications

a.   Since December 27, 1945, all treaties and international agreements are first published in pamphlet form in the *Treaties and Other International Acts Series* (T.I.A.S.).   This Series starts with Treaty Number 1501 as it continues the numbering of two previous publications of treaties and international agreements, i. e. 944 numbers in the *Treaty Series* and 506 numbers in the *Executive Agreement Series*.[8] It contains all treaties which have been proclaimed during the calendar year, to which the United States is a party, and all international agreements other than treaties to which the United States is a party that have been signed, proclaimed, or with reference to which any other final formality has been executed during each calendar year.[9] The documents are literal prints of the originals with marginal notes and footnotes.

b.   Each year all of the pamphlets issued in the *Treaties and Other International Acts Series* are published in bound volumes under the title *United States Treaties and Other International Agreements*

[8] This Series replaces the *Treaty Series*, 1908–45, and the *Executive Agreement Series*, 1929–45. The *Treaty Series* consists of separate treaty prints in pamphlet or slip form, arranged numerically in chronological order of proclamation or publication. The publication of this Series was commenced in January 1908 with Treaty Number 489 by the Department of State. Prior to October 1, 1929 (Treaty Number 813) the *Treaty Series* includes both treaties and executive agreements. From October 1, 1929 (Treaty Number 813) to the end of the publication in December 1945 (Treaty Number 994), however, the *Treaty Series* is limited to treaties and international agreements submitted to the Senate. Another series, called the *Executive Agreement Series*, started its publication on October 1, 1929 and ended on March 16, 1945, also by the Department of State. This Series contains 506 numbers and picks up the executive agreements, exchanges of notes, etc. excluded from the *Treaty Series* for that period. For a fuller explanation of these two series and for the treaties prior to Number 489, see H. MILLER, 1 TREATIES AND OTHER INTERNATIONAL ACTS OF THE UNITED STATES OF AMERICA 35–38, 99–135 (1931).

[9] 1 U.S.C. § 112A (1970 ed.)

(UST). By statute,[10] the treaties contained in the *Statutes at Large* and *United States Treaties and Other International Agreements* are evidence admissible in all federal courts, state courts, and courts of the Territories and insular possessions of the United States.

c. From 1789 to 1950, many treaties were published in the *Statutes at Large*, but until volume 32 (1903) their publication in this set had been irregular. With volume 47, 1931–32,[11] the *Statutes at Large* started to include international agreements as well.

d. In 1968, a new series of *Treaties and Other International Agreements of the United States*, 1776–1949, edited by C. E. Bevans began publication by the Department of State. This Series has completed its publication, with the last volume (Volume 13: General Index) published in February 1976. It includes all treaties and international agreements which were published in the *Statutes at Large* between 1776 and 1949. It includes the English text or in cases where no English text was signed, the official United States Government translations. The first four volumes contain multilateral treaties and agreements, arranged chronologically according to date of signature. The next eight volumes (volumes 5–12) list bilateral treaties and agreements, arranged alphabetically by country. Each volume includes a brief index which is consolidated into volume 13, a cumulative analytical index arranged in one alphabet by country and subject. Although the set is annotated, its essential value rests in its collection of documentary texts. The current status of a treaty or an agreement in this set may be determined by consulting the latest annual volume of *Treaties in Force* and the weekly *Department of State Bulletin*.

e. *Commerce Clearing House, Tax Treaties.* This service provides loose-leaf reporting on income and estate tax treaties between the United States and foreign countries. The Reporter contains interpretative regulations, news on treaties in preparation, significant court decisions and editorial comment. A special section of the publication features *CCH Treaty Charts* which show in graphic style the contents of each treaty relating to some 200 major tax aspects.[12]

2. Collections of United States Treaties

U. S. Treaties have from time to time been published in separate sets. These are:

a. *Malloy's Treaties.* 4 v. (v. 3 often cited as 3 *Redman*; v. 4 as 4 *Trenwith*). This set contains all treaties, etc., between 1776 and

----

[10] *Ibid.*

[11] For a detailed study of the inclusion and exclusion of treaties in the *Statutes at Large, see* Miller, *supra*, Vol. 1, p. 33–35.

[12] A similar service is published by Prentice-Hall.

1937 with some annotations. Volume 4 includes an index to the set and a chronological list of treaties.

b. *Miller's Treaties.* This is a more recent compilation of treaties. However, only 8 volumes covering the years 1776 and 1863 have appeared. It is doubtful if the set will continue. As yet, it has no index.

3. Indexes to U. S. Treaties

a. *Treaties in Force.* This is an annual publication of the U. S. Department of State, listing all treaties and agreements, by country and by subject, that are still in force.

b. I. I. Kavass and M. A. Michael, *United States Treaties and Other International Agreements Cumulative Index*, 1776–1949 (1975).[13] This 4-volume work indexes all treaties and international agreements from 1776–1949 which were published in the *Statutes at Large*, the *Malloy's*, the *Miller's*, the *Bevans'* and other relevant sources. Each volume devotes to a particular type of arrangement: numerical by treaty number, chronological by date of signature, by country and by topic.

c. I. I. Kavass and A. Sprudzs, *UST Cumulative Index*, 1950–1970 (1973).[14] This work has also four volumes and indexes all treaties and international agreements from 1950 to 1970 which were published in the *United States Treaty Series and Other International Agreements* and the *Treaties and International Acts Series*. The arrangements are again numerical, chronological, by country and by topic.

d. U. S. *Statutes at Large*, Vol. 64, pt. 3, p. 1107 et seq. This section lists alphabetically by country all treaties and agreements that were included in volumes 1–64, 1789–1949 except those treaties signed with Indian Tribes.

e. A. Sprudzs, *A Chronological Index to Multilateral Treaties in Force for the United States* (as of Jan. 1, 1972). This is a useful adjunct to *Treaties in Force* which lists multilateral treaties only under subject.

f. *Department of State Bulletin.* This is a weekly publication of the Department of State. Each issue has a section entitled "Treaty Information" which gives current information on treaties. This should be used to supplement *Treaties in Force*. There is a semi-annual index to the *Department of State Bulletin* which may be used to locate current information either by subject or country.

[13] W. S. Hein. Buffalo, N.Y. 1975.

[14] *Id.* 1973.

g. *CCH Congressional Index.* A section of this loose-leaf service has a status table of all treaties that are pending ratification by the United States Senate.

4. Special Subject Indexes

a. American Bar Association, Section of International Law. *Commercial Treaty Index.* This index in loose-leaf format; started in 1973 and is edited by the Committee on Commercial Treaties and indexes certain segments of bilateral commercial treaties between the United States and other countries, mostly of the friendship, commerce and navigation type. It is arranged alphabetically by country.

b. American Indians. A complete checklist and bibliography of Indian treaties appears in *List of Indian Treaties*, U. S. Congress. House Committee on Interior and Insular Affairs. (88th Congr.2d Sess. Committee Print No. 33, 1964). Also, the Uncodified volume of the *United States Code Service*, FCA ed. lists, by year, Indian treaties which have been cited or construed by the courts, with digests of the decisions.

5. Interpretations of Treaties

a. Digests. These are more than case digests and include excerpts from treaties, periodical articles, and court decisions from various countries, and documents of the various international organizations. These digests have been published by the Department of State and the editors have all been distinguished scholars: [15]

(1) Wharton's *Digest of International Law*, 3 v. 1886.

(2) Moore's *Digest of International Law*, 8 v. 1906.

(3) Hackworth's *Digest of International Law.* 8 v. 1940.

(4) Whiteman's *Digest of International Law.* 15 v. 1973. Supplements Hackworth's.

(5) *Digest of United States Practice in International Law.* This is an annual publication which started in 1973.

(6) Contemporary Practice of the United States Relating to International Law. This appears in each quarterly issue of the *American Journal of International Law.* It digests current materials under the same headings as used in the *Digest of United States Practice in International Law.*

6. Citators For Treaties

After the text of a treaty or agreement has been located, steps should be taken to ascertain the interpretations given to them by the

[15] For detailed discussion of these digests see: A. Rovine, *U. S. International Law Digests: Some History and a New Approach*, 67 AMER.J.INTER.LAW 314 (1973).

courts.   The language of treaties, as that of statutes, may not be clear in meaning, or there may be doubt if it was the intent of the treaty to cover certain situations.   Two methods of locating court decisions involving treaties are:

a.   *Shepard's United States Citations*, Statute Volumes.   Treaties entered into before 1950 may be Shepardized in the usual manner in the section for *Statutes at Large (not included in the U.S. Code)*. Treaties entered into after 1950 may be Shepardized in the section for *United States Treaties and Other International Agreements*.

b.   *United States Code Service*, FCA.   The unnumbered volume for uncodified laws and treaties lists treaties by year of ratification and gives annotations to court decisions.

SECTION C. ILLUSTRATIONS: UNITED STATES TREATIES

Problems: Does the United States and France have a treaty on Double Taxation in reference to estate and inheritance tax?

Is the United States a signatory to an International Convention on the Conservation of Seals?

Illustrations

108. Pages from an annual Issue of Treaties in Force.

109. Page from a weekly issue of the Department of State Bulletin.

110. Page from Treaty Status Table—CCH Congressional Index Service.

111. Pages from U. S. Shepard's Citations, Statute volume.

[Illustration 108]

TITLE PAGE FROM ANNUAL ISSUE OF TREATIES IN FORCE

TREATIES IN FORCE

A List of Treaties

and Other International Agreements

of the United States

This publication is reissued each year. It lists treaties and other international agreements of the United States on record in the Department of State on January 1, which had not expired by their terms or which had not been denounced by the parties, replaced or superseded by other agreements, or otherwise definitely terminated.

It is in two sections: Part I lists all countries for which the U.S. has bilateral agreements; Part 2 is arranged alphabetically by subject and lists all multilateral agreements to which the United States is a signatory.

Compiled by the Treaty Affairs Staff,
Office of the Legal Adviser,
Department of State.

[Illustration 108–a]

PAGE FROM ANNUAL ISSUE OF TREATIES IN FORCE

TREATIES IN FORCE   **83**

FRANCE (Cont'd)

> **FINDING BILATERAL TREATIES**
>
> 1. Use Part 1 of latest edition of Treaties in Force. All treaties which the U. S. has entered into with other countries are listed under the name of the other country.
>
> Note citations where text of treaty may be found.

POSTAL MATTERS
Postal money order convention.
Signed at Washington August 19, 1931; operative February 1, 1932.

Convention relative to the exchange of parcel post.
Signed at Paris December 7 and at Washington December 30, 1935; operative August 1, 1935.
49 Stat. 3322; Post Office Department print; 171 LNTS 117.

PUBLICATIONS
Agreement relating to exchange of official publications.
Exchange of notes at Paris August 14, 1945; entered into force January 1, 1946.
60 Stat. 1944; TIAS 1579; 73 UNTS 237.

RELIEF SUPPLIES AND PACKAGES
Agreement for free entry and free inland transportation of relief supplies and packages.
Signed at Paris December 23, 1948; entered into force December 23, 1948.
62 Stat. 3587; TIAS 1873; 67 UNTS 171.

Amendments:
January 31, 1950 (1 UST 224; TIAS 2043; 67 UNTS 171).
August 3, 1950 (1 UST 597; TIAS 2107; 93 UNTS 367).
July 2 and August 5, 1952 (3 UST 5039; TIAS 2684; 181 UNTS 345).

SATELLITES
Agreement on cooperation in intercontinental testing in connection with experimental communications satellites.
Exchange of notes at Paris March 31, 1961; entered into force March 31, 1961.
12 UST 483; TIAS 4738; 409 UNTS 135.

Agreement concerning development of satellite and balloon techniques and instrumentation for the study of meteorological phenomena (Project EOLE).
Exchange of notes at Washington June 16 and 17, 1966; entered into force June 17, 1966.
17 UST 1123; TIAS 6069; 601 UNTS 113.

SMUGGLING
Convention for prevention of smuggling of intoxicating liquors.
Signed at Washington June 30, 1924; entered into force March 12, 1927.
45 Stat. 2403; TS 755; IV Trenwith 4175; 61 LNTS 415.

TAXATION
Agreement relating to relief from double income tax on shipping profits.
Exchange of notes at Washington June 11 and July 8, 1927; entered into force July 8, 1927; operative from January 1, 1921.
47 Stat. 2604; EAS 12; 114 LNTS 413.

Convention for the avoidance of double taxation and the prevention of evasion in the case of taxes on estates and inheritances, and modifying and supplementing the convention relating to income taxation signed July 25, 1939.
Signed at Paris October 18, 1946; entered into force October 17, 1949.
64 Stat. (3) B3; TIAS 1982; 140 UNTS 23.

> Protocol modifying the convention signed October 18, 1946, for the avoidance of double taxation and the prevention of evasion in the case of taxes on <u>estates and inheritances, and modifying and supple</u>menting the convention relating to income taxation signed July 25, 1939.[1]
> Signed at Washington May 17, 1948; entered into force October 17, 1949.
> <u>64 Stat. (3) B28; TIAS 1982; 140 UNTS 50.</u>

Convention supplementing the conventions of July 25, 1939 and October 18, 1946 relating to the avoidance of double taxation, as modified and supplemented by the protocol of May 17, 1948.[1]
Signed at Washington June 22, 1956; entered into force June 13, 1957.
8 UST 843; TIAS 3844; 291 UNTS 101.

Agreement relating to relief from taxation of United States Government expenditures in France in the interests of common defense.
Exchange of notes at Paris June 13, 1952; entered into force June 13, 1952.
3 UST 4828; TIAS 2655; 181 UNTS 3.

---

[1]**Provisions concerning taxes on income, on capital and tax on stock exchange transactions terminated by convention of July 28, 1967 (TIAS 6518).**

[Illustration 108–b]

PAGE FROM PART 2, ANNUAL ISSUE OF TREATIES IN FORCE

SATELLITES (Cont'd)

Ministry of   Syrian Arab

FINDING MULTILATERAL TREATIES.

PROBLEM: Is the United States a signatory to an International Convention on Conservation of Seals.

Check in Part 2 of Treaties in Force under subject: Seals.

Note citations to where text of treaty may be located.

As additional countries become signatories, they are listed in the weekly Department of State Bulletin and then included in the next annual edition of Treaties in Force.

cations
Administration of Posts   Viet-Nam
  and Telecommunications 1
Ministry of Communi-   Yemen Arab
  cations   Republic
Community of the   Yugoslavia
  Yugoslav Posts, Tele-
  graphs and Telephones 1
General Post Office 1   Zambia

SEALS

Interim convention on conservation of North Pacific fur seals.
Signed at Washington February 9, 1957; entered into force for the United States October 14, 1957.
8 UST 2283; TIAS 3948; 314 UNTS 105.
States which are parties:
Canada   Union of Soviet
Japan   Socialist Reps.
                          United States

Protocol amending the interim convention on conservation of North Pacific fur seals.
Done at Washington October 8, 1963; entered into force for the United States April 10, 1964.
15 UST 316; TIAS 5558; 494 UNTS 303.
States which are parties:
Canada   Union of Soviet
Japan   Socialist Reps.
                          United States

Extension:
September 3, 1969 (20 UST 2992; TIAS 6774).

SHIPPING (See MARITIME
        MATTERS; NAVAL VESSELS;
        RULES OF WARFARE)

5 With reservation.

[Illustration 109]

PAGE FROM WEEKLY ISSUE OF THE DEPARTMENT OF STATE BULLETIN

TREATY INFORMATION

Current Actions

MULTILATERAL

Aviation

Convention for the suppression of unlawful acts against the safety of civil aviation. Done at Montreal September 23, 1971.[1]
Accession deposited: Mali, August 24, 1972.

Fisheries

International convention for the Northwest Atlantic fisheries. Done at Washington February 8, 1949. Entered into force July 3, 1950. TIAS 2089;
Protocol to the international convention for the Northwest Atlantic fisheries (TIAS 2089). Done at Washington June 25, 1956. Entered into force January 10, 1959. TIAS 4170;
Declaration of understanding regarding the international convention for the Northwest Atlantic fisheries (TIAS 2089). Done at Washington April 24, 1961. Entered into force June 5, 1963. TIAS 5380;
Protocol to the international convention for the Northwest Atlantic fisheries (TIAS 2089), relating to harp and hood seals. Done at Washington July 15, 1963. Entered into force April 29, 1966. TIAS 6011;
Protocol to the international convention for the Northwest Atlantic fisheries (TIAS 2089), relating to entry into force of proposals adopted by the Commission. Done at Washington November 29, 1965. Entered into force December 19, 1969. TIAS 6840;
Protocol to the international convention for the Northwest Atlantic fisheries (TIAS 2089), relating to measures of control. Done at Washington November 29, 1965. Entered into force December 19, 1969. TIAS 6841;
Protocol to the international convention for the Northwest Atlantic fisheries (TIAS 2089), relating to panel membership and to regulatory measures. Done at Washington October 1, 1969. Entered into force December 15, 1971. TIAS 7432;
Protocol to the international convention for the Northwest Atlantic fisheries (TIAS 2089), relating to amendments to the convention. Done at Washington October 6, 1970.[1]
Adherences deposited: Bulgaria, August 21, 1972.

Judicial Procedures

Convention on the taking of evidence abroad in civil or commercial matters. Done at The Hague March 18, 1970.

---
[1] Not in force.

Ratifications deposited: Norway, August 3, 1972; United States, August 8, 1972.
Enters into force: October 7, 1972.

Satellite Communications System

Agreement relating to the International Telecommunications Satellite Organization (Intelsat), with annexes. Done at Washington August 20, 1971.[1]
Ratification deposited: Chile, August 18, 1972.
Accession deposited: Saudi Arabia, August 24, 1972.
Operating agreement relating to the International Telecommunications Satellite Organization (Intelsat), with annex. Done at Washington August

> The Department of State Bulletin is published weekly. Each issue has a section on Treaty Information which serves as "advance sheets" to Treaties in Force.

June 9, 1967; for the United States November 28, 1968. TIAS 6592.
Ratification deposited: Byelorussian Soviet Socialist Republic, July 11, 1972 (with a reservation and declaration).

White Slave Traffic

Agreement for the suppression of the white slave traffic, as amended by the protocol of May 4, 1949 (TIAS 2332). Signed at Paris May 18, 1904. Entered into force July 18, 1905; for the United States June 6, 1908. 35 Stat. 1979.
Notification that it considers itself bound: Fiji, June 12, 1972.

BILATERAL

Finland

Agreement relating to the deposit by Finland of 10 percent of the value of training services furnished by the United States. Effected by exchange of notes at Helsinki August 17, 1972. Entered into force August 17, 1972; effective February 7, 1972.

Saudi Arabia

Agreement extending the agreement of November 9, 1963, and January 4, 1964, as amended and extended (TIAS 5659, 6071, 6413, 6555, 6998. 7265), relating to the establishment of a television system in Saudi Arabia. Effected by exchange of notes at Jidda April 24 and July 30, 1972. Entered into force July 30, 1972.

Union of Soviet Socialist Republics

Agreement with respect to purchases of grain by the Soviet Union in the United States and credit to be made available by the United States, with exchange of notes. Signed at Washington July 8, 1972. Entered into force July 8, 1972.

[Illustration 110]

PAGE FROM TREATY STATUS TABLE—CCH CONGRESSIONAL INDEX SERVICE

1632   **Treaties**   **78   6-21-72**

signed at Bogota, Colombia, on May 2, 1948, by the plenipotentiaries of the United States and other American republics.

> In Foreign Relations Committee.
> Reported 5/4/71
> Hearing available, May 11, 1971.

Executive O—Crimes—Genocide

Convention on the prevention and punishment of the crime of genocide, adopted unanimously by the General Assembly of the United Nations in Paris on December 9, 1948, and signed on behalf of the United States on December 11, 1948.

> In Foreign Relations Committee.
> Hearing, Jan. 23, 1950.
> Hearing available, May 4, 1950.
> Hearing, March 10, 1971.
> Reported, 5/14/71
> Hearing available, May 11, 1971.

Executive S—Labor—Right to organize

Convention concerning Freedom of Association and Protection of the Right to Organize, adopted by the International Labor Conference at its thirty-first session, held at San Francisco June 17 to July 10, 1948.

> In Foreign Relations Committee.

Eighty-fourth Congress—Second Session

Executive D—Crimes—Plant protection

International plant protection convention, signed on behalf of U. S. and 36 other States at Rome from December 6, 1951, to May 1, 1952.

> Injunction of secrecy removed January 12, 1956.
> In Foreign Relations Committee.
> Reported 6/5/72 (Exec. Rept. 92-22).
> Ratified by S. [Roll Call] June 12, 1972.

Eighty-seventh Congress—Second Session

Executive C—Labor—International Labor Organization—Reports

Convention concerning the partial revision of the conventions adopted by the International Labor Organization to standardize provisions regarding the preparation of reports by its governing body on the working of conventions.

> Injunction of secrecy removed June 1, 1962.
> In Foreign Relations Committee.

Executive   Con   After the President has signed a Treaty, it must   York on
March 3   be ratified by the Senate. This Table lists treaties
     Injun   awaiting ratification by the Senate.
     In Fo   It is arranged by Number of Congress and gives
Executive   information as to the present status of such pending
     Con   treaties. Weekly supplements are issued to this   y Inter-
national   Service.
     Injun
     In Fo

[Illustration 111]

PAGE FROM U.S. SHEPARD'S CITATIONS—STATUTE VOLUME

UNITED STATES STATUTES AT LARGE (Not in United States Code) **1946**

After locating a treaty or other agreement, it may be "Shepardized" to find subsequent amendments, other changes, or court decisions which have cited or interpreted the treaty or agreement.

For treaties or agreements entered into before the publication of the United States Treaties Series, the "Shepardizing" is done under the U.S. Statute at Large citation.

§ 5
70St116

Aug. 13
Ch. 959
60 St. 1049

329US49
91LE29
67SC171
329US684
91LE601
67SC352
329US685
91LE602
67SC364
§ 25
152FS953
70St547

Aug. 13
Ch. 962
60 St. 1057

Rs70A St1
61St798
§§ 1 to 20
Rs70A St1

Aug. 14
Ch. 963
60 St. 1062

§ 1
R74St726
61St214

Aug. 14
Ch. 964
60 St. 1062

68St526
§ 2
Subd. a
¶ 3
61St955
Subd. d
A61St55
61St694
Subd. f
R64St100
§ 3
Subsec. 44
60St1099

Aug. 14
Ch. 966
60 St. 1082

Title 1
§ 11
A61St694

Aug. 14

62St2416
62St2441
62St2862
3UST4177
4UST1921
5UST2493

Aug. 24
Ch. 210
60 St. 121

79St285

Aug. 30
61 St. 1236

64St B33
3UST3922
3UST3927
4UST2058
Protocol
Art. 1
Sg1UST626
62St1654
Art. 2
Sg1UST626
62St1654
3UST3922
3UST3927

Sept. 6
61 St. 4121

2UST460
Art. 8
9UST1468
Schedule 1
Rs9UST
[1468
Schedule 2
Rs9UST
[1468

Sept. 12
61 St. 2688

E13UST
[2266
E14UST359
158FS64
78St1248
13UST408

Art. 1
158FS67

Art. 9
R14UST
[1022
Art. 10
R14UST
[1022
Art. 11
R14UST
[1022
78St1248
Art. 12
R14UST
[1022
78St1248
¶ 1
158FS64
¶ 2
158FS64
Art. 15
¶ 1
A13UST409
A14UST
[1023
Art. 17
A14UST
[1022
78St1248
¶ 2
13UST410
Schedule 1
R14UST
[1022
78St1248
Schedule 2
R14UST
[1022
78St1248
Notes
Rp14UST
[1022

Sept. 13
61 St. 3750

Art. 3
A62St1889

Sept. 23
61 St. 2903

62St3575

Sept. 25

Rs2UST
[1376
Arts. 101 to 116
Rs2UST
[1376

Sept. 25
61 St. 3524

Rs2UST
[1423

Sept. 25
61 St. 3540

Rs2UST
[1458

Sept. 30
61 St. 2495

A6UST6157
Art. 2
A6UST6157
¶ 3
Rn ¶ 4
10UST966
¶ 3
Ad10UST
[966
¶ 4
Rn ¶ 5
10UST966
Art. 4
¶ 2
A10UST969
¶ 3
Rs10UST
[969
¶ 5
A10UST970
¶ 8
A10UST963
¶ 9
Rs10UST
[970
¶ 10
A10UST959
¶ 14
Ad10UST
[961

Art. 5
A6UST6157

Art. 6
A6UST6157
¶ 3
A10UST972
Art. 11
¶ 4
10UST961

Oct. 1
61 St. 1222

62St1659

Oct. 7
61 St. 2398

E3UST351
Sg11UST
[1982
6UST3771
15UST2489
Art. 3
3UST352
Art. 9
6UST3771
Art. 10
6UST3771
Art. 12
11UST1982
Art. 14
11UST1982
Art. 15
11UST1982
Art. 16
11UST1982
Art. 17
11UST1982
Art. 20
11UST1982
Art. 21
11UST1982
Art. 22
11UST1982
Art. 24
11UST1982
Art. 25
11UST1982
Art. 29
11UST1982
Art. 32
11UST1982

Oct. 9

Art. 6
6UST3904
Art. 7
6UST3904
Art. 9
10UST745
Art. 11
10UST745
Art. 12
10UST745
Art. 13
10UST745
Art. 14
10UST745
Art. 15
10UST745
Art. 17
10UST745
Art. 18
10UST745
Art. 19
10UST745
Art. 20
10UST745
Art. 21
10UST745
Art. 25
10UST745

Oct. 18
64 St. B3

Sg8UST843
Art. 7
Subd. a
A8UST847
Art. 17
A8UST848
Protocol
E8UST843
Art. 1
Subd. 3
A8UST845

Oct. 23
61 St. 2876

13UST1918

Oct. 25
61 St. 1044

A61St1073

Oct. 30

5UST2165
12UST846
Art. 2
12UST846
Annex
¶ 2
A12UST847

Nov. 16
61 St. 2479

62St3023
Annex to Air Transport Agreement
§ B
A62St3023

Nov. 20
61 St. 2795

A61St3777

Dec. 2
61 St. 2475

E62St3645
Sg1UST540
109FS343
62St2283
62St3600
63St2630
63St2654
64St B84
¶ 4
A61St3614
¶ 5
A61St3614
¶ 6
Sub ¶ e
Sg1UST541
¶ 8
A61St3614
¶ 12
61St3608

Dec. 2
62 St. 1716

3UST3001

6UST645
8UST69
11UST32
14UST1690
Art. 2
¶ 2
1UST507
¶ 3
A10UST953
Art. 5
1UST507
3UST2999
6UST645
10UST331
11UST33
13UST494
¶ 1
A10UST953
¶ 3
1UST509
7UST658
10UST331
11UST33
13UST494
13UST497
14UST112
14UST1690
Art. 7
8UST70
Art. 11
3UST3003
Schedule
A13UST493
A13UST497
A14UST112
A14UST
[1691
A15UST
[2547
¶ 1
Subd. a
A11UST32
A14UST
[1691
¶ 2
4UST2184
¶ 4
A4UST2181
A6UST647
¶ 4
(6UST645)
Cl. 1
A11UST33
Cl. 2
R7UST657
¶ 5
A4UST2181
Sd7UST657
A8UST2204
A11UST33
A14UST
[1691
¶ 6
A1UST506
A2UST11
A3UST3001
A3UST5094
A4UST2180
A6UST647
¶ 6
(6UST645)
A10UST330
Cl. 1
A13UST498
Continued

See note on page 1219

1645

[Illustration III–a]

PAGE FROM U.S. SHEPARD'S CITATIONS—STATUTES VOLUME

UNITED STATES TREATIES AND OTHER INTERNATIONAL AGREEMENTS							Vol. 8
–597–	**Art. 3**	¶ 7	10UST200	**Art. 14**	**–1421–**	**–1633–**	First
11UST388	12UST1045	Rn¶8	10UST1033	A10UST	8UST869	A13UST	Memo-
–609–	**–721–**	[12UST	10UST1638	[1818	10UST2049	[1482	randum of
13UST288	E8UST1392	[2947	11UST2515	**–1265–**	**–1425–**	**–1725–**	Under-
–617–	**Art. 1**	**–859–**	12UST728	A10UST	10UST2081	Sg12UST	standing
A12UST240	A8UST1392	9UST397	**–1063–**	[1659	**–1427–**	[904	§ 1
¶ 4	**Art. 2**	**–863–**	8UST1069	8UST213	8UST821	**–1741–**	A9UST1355
A12UST240	¶ 1	12UST1195	**–1069–**	8UST1225	8UST866	Sg11UST	E10UST159
–625–	Cl. c	**–866–**	8UST1063	**Art. 6**	**–1431–**	[1405	9UST1003
8UST26	A9UST1167	A8UST1427	**–1073–**	13UST1770	8UST367	**Art. 2**	**–1903–**
8UST77	**–738–**	8UST821	8UST1063	¶ A	9UST237	¶ 7	13UST2645
–637–	A12UST155	**–869–**	8UST1069	A10UST	12UST3176	11UST1406	14UST1424
8UST279	**Art. 4**	10UST2050	**–1093–**	[1659	**–1435–**	¶ 8	**–1937–**
–657–	¶ A	**–890–**	71St454	**Art. 8**	A11UST	11UST1405	10UST2208
8UST680	A12UST155	71St C51	10UST1425	¶ A	[1783	**–1757–**	**–2021–**
22UST508	**Art. 7**	76St1468	14UST1265	A10UST	A13UST	15UST167	A15UST289
13UST2650	A12UST156	77St972	14UST1489	[1660	[1494	**–1767–**	**–2043–**
Art. 1	**–753–**	**–894–**	**Art. 6**	13UST1770	A15UST	77St971	186FS300
A9UST1416	14UST2222	13UST2178	¶ A	¶ B	[2007	10UST272	46ABA24
¶ 1	**–764–**	¶ 3	Cl. 3	A10UST	**–1442–**	13UST2757	**Art. 1**
A9UST1417	E10UST25	13UST2178	A14UST135	[1660	Sg10UST	13UST2823	186FS320
Art. 2	A10UST	Annex A	**Art. 12**	¶ C	[1997	13UST2891	**Art. 5**
A9UST1417	[1383	A9UST1334	10UST87	A10UST	**–1445–**	15UST2590	288F2d375
¶ 1	E11UST	**–899–**	13UST416	[1660	A15UST	¶ I	**Art. 6**
Cl. d	[1455	11UST2165	¶ A	A13UST	[1539	13UST2679	186FS320
A14UST	¶ 6	**Art. 8**	Cl. 1	[1770	**–1457–**	¶ L	**–2205–**
[1066	10UST25	11UST2165	13UST423	**–1289–**	10UST1182	13UST2606	Sg9UST967
Art. 3	**–771–**	**–933–**	14UST1274	A11UST	**–1534–**	¶ N	13UST2068
12UST508	9UST1264	71St C50	¶ C	[1872	8UST1629	13UST2679	**Art. 1**
¶ 1	**–773–**	76St1468	14UST1269	8UST799	9UST1416	¶ R	13UST2070
A9UST1419	R10UST	77St972	**Art. 14**	9UST1	21UST508	13UST2678	¶ 1
¶ 2	[1418	Schedule	¶ D	10UST1049	**–1537–**	¶ W	A9UST305
A9UST1419	**–787–**	¶ 907	71St454	**–1343–**	A13UST	76St1469	

> Treaties and other agreements that are published in the United States Treaties Series may be "Shepardized" under those citations in this section of U.S. Shepard's Citations.

9UST1491	**Art. 3**	[1074	**Art. 12**	**–1363–**	Cl. e	13UST879	A9UST305
9UST1379	¶ 2	**–957–**	¶ C	15UST2209	R13UST	13UST898	9UST968
11UST401	Cl. d	8UST963	15UST1459	**–1367–**	Cl. f	13UST907	9UST1343
–680–	A8UST1289	**Art. 1**	**–1225–**	A13UST	[1878	13UST1037	**–2213–**
8UST657	A11UST	¶ 3	A13UST	[1812	R13UST	13UST1218	9UST1113
–683–	[1872	8UST963	[1486	**Art. 6**	[1878	13UST1818	**–2283–**
Sg11UST	**–821–**	**Art. 5**	8UST213	A13UST	¶ 10	13UST2889	A15UST317
[1982	8UST866	11UST2382	**Art. 4**	[1812	Cl. b	¶ Z	80St1091
–691–	**Art. 1**	**–963–**	¶ 3	**Art. 8**	A13UST	**Art. 35**	**Art. 2**
E10UST22	A8UST866	8UST957	A13UST	A13UST	[1878	11UST1543	¶ 2
E11UST210	A8UST1427	**–965–**	[1486	[1813	Cl. d	**–1862–**	RnCl i
15UST1523	**–832–**	A13UST	**Art. 5**	**Art. 10**	A13UST	Sg11UST	[15UST317
¶ 6	A11UST	[1033	A13UST	¶ B	[1878	[2249	Cl. g
10UST22	[1874	10UST3185	[1487	A13UST	**–1561–**	10UST1730	Ad15UST
–697–	13UST1776	**–970–**	**Art. 11**	[1815	10UST1620	**Art. 1**	[317
A10UST	**–835–**	8UST721	A13UST	**Art. 12**	**–1567–**	A10UST	Cl. h
[1233	A12UST	**–973–**	[1487	A13UST	9UST1379	[1733	Ad15UST
Art. 2	[2947	9UST1444	[1816	**–1593–**	E10UST	**–1869–**	[317
¶ 1	E14UST	**–979–**	**–1245–**	E10UST	[3026	14UST1210	¶ 3
Cl. a	[1178	9UST131	A10UST	**–1391–**	**–1604–**	**–1879–**	A15UST317
A10UST	¶ 4	9UST1073	[1815	8UST721	11UST2337	10UST385	**Art. 3**
[1233	A9UST1547	9UST1075	**Art. 4**	8UST970	**–1626–**	**–1885–**	A15UST318
Cl. b	¶ 6	**–993–**	¶ A	**–1395–**	12UST718	A9UST1003	80St1092
A10UST	Rn¶7	A11UST	A10UST	10UST970	13UST2598	13UST1953	**Art. 5**
[1233	[12UST	[2532	[1815	**–1410–**	**–1629–**	**Art. 1**	80St1093
–715–	[2947	A11UST	**Art. 7**	14UST337	8UST1534	13UST1953	¶ 2
A9UST1025	¶ 6	[2559	A10UST	**–1413–**	9UST1416	**Art. 3**	Cl. e
12UST1044	Ad12UST	9UST1015	[1815	E9UST1146	12UST508	13UST1953	A15UST318
Art. 1	[2947	9UST1474					*Continued*
12UST1045							

SECTION D. SOURCES OF INTERNATIONAL LAW FOR COUNTRIES OTHER THAN THE UNITED STATES

Most countries have collections of their treaties and indexes to them, but their description is beyond the scope of this book.[16] There are, however, more general works published by international organizations which are useful when searching for information on treaties to which the United States is not a signatory. These are briefly discussed below:

1. Multinational Collections of Treaties [17]

a. *The Consolidated Treaties Series, 1648–1918.* This series is a reproduced collection of world treaties in their original languages and existing translations in English or French from the foundation of the modern system of States, 1648, to the date of the commencement of the *League of Nations Treaty Series* (approximately 1918–1920). It is being edited by Clive Parry and is being published by Oceana Publications, Inc., in about 200 volumes. The publisher hopes to complete the series by about 1979. The volumes are arranged chronologically, e. g., 1648–1652, 1653–1655. The final volumes will contain a complete chronological list and cross indices by party and by subject. The annotations will have limited scope, since they will not give the current status of the treaties.

b. *League of Nations Treaty Series.* This set covers the period of 1920 to 1945, and contains treaties of member and nonmember nations registered with the Secretariat.

c. *United Nations Treaty Series,* 1946 to date. This set contains the text of all treaties registered with the Secretariat by its member states, or filed and recorded by nonmember states or international organizations. Each volume also includes a list of notifications of ratifications, accessions, successions, extensions, denunciations, etc., concerning published treaties. The *Series* is published in accordance with Article 102 of the United Nations Charter. The texts are given in their original language with English and French translated editions. Cumulative Indexes to the *United Nations Treaty Series* are published. Each Cumulative Index covers from 50 to 100 volumes and consists

---

[16] For information on other countries, see ROBINSON, INTERNATIONAL LAW AND ORGANIZATIONS: GENERAL SOURCE OF INFORMATION, 1967; and W. BISHOP, INTERNATIONAL LAW, CASES AND MATERIALS. 3d ed. 1971, pp. xliii–xlvi.

[17] A helpful discussion of research techniques for multilateral treaties may be found in A. SPRUDZS, TREATY SOURCES IN LEGAL AND POLITICAL RESEARCH; TOOLS, TECHNIQUES, AND PROBLEMS—THE CONVENTIONAL AND THE NEW, 1971; and A. Sprudzs, *Status of Multilateral Treaties—Researcher's Mystery, Mess, or Muddle?* 66 AM.J. OF INTER.LAW 365 (1972).

of three sections: (1) chronological index of all treaties; (2) chronological index of multilateral treaties; and (3) alphabetical index by country and subject.

d. *United Nations. Office of Legal Affairs. Multilateral Treaties in Respect of which the Secretary-General Performs Depositary Function.* This is an annual publication started in 1968, which covers all multilateral treaties which have been concluded under the auspices of the United Nations and which have been deposited with the Secretary-General.

A loose-leaf volume (Annex) contains final clauses of the treaties deposited. It serves as a reference bank to the annual volumes.

e. *Keesing's Treaties and Alliances of the World.* This single volume publication is designed to present the state of affairs with regard to groupings of States and their important treaties with each other, noting treaties in force as of early 1968. It covers several thousand agreements, mainly bilateral, which deal with trade, economic and technical aid, cultural relations and extradition.

f. *Major Peace Treaties of Modern History, 1648–1967.* This is the first comprehensive collection of peace treaties to appear in English. It consists of four volumes and is edited by Fred L. Israel. The official English translations, prepared by the British Foreign Office, were used whenever available. When such English documents were nonexistent, private translations were used. The first document in the series is the peace treaty of Westphalia, concluded in 1648, and the last document in the set is the peace settlement concluded at Tashkent in 1966 between India and Pakistan through the intercession of the Soviet Union. The treaties are chronologically arranged, with a subject index in volume 4.

g. *Organization of American States Treaty Series* (formerly *Pan American Union Treaty Series*). The General Secretariat of the Organization of American States is responsible not only for the receipt and custody of the instruments of ratification but also for the preparation and publication of the official texts of the Organization.

Since 1957, these texts, in English and Spanish, have been issued by the General Legal Division as part of its Treaty Series. The Series includes Organization treaties and other significant instruments. Treaty Series No. 1 covers the Charter of the Organization of American States, signed at the Ninth International Conference of American States, March 30–May 2, 1948.

No. 5 is a useful chart, revised at regular intervals, showing the Status of Inter-American Treaties and Conventions.

h. *Harvard Law School Library. Index to Multilateral Treaties. 1965.* This is a chronological list of multi-party, international

agreements from the sixteenth century (1596) through 1963, with citations to their text. A subject and regional guide is also provided. The subject analysis does not include specific sections of a treaty; nor is the current status of each treaty given. Supplements were issued for 1966–68.

i. *International Legal Materials: Current Documents.* This bi-monthly publication of American Society of International Law is a collection of current official foreign and United States documents relating to international legal affairs. It began publication in 1962. The documents include: (1) current materials that may not become available in more permanent collections until a later date and (2) recent materials that are not readily accessible in any other form in most law libraries.

j. *World Treaty Index and Treaty Profiles.*[18] The *Index* is a computerized index in five volumes of the *League of Nations Treaty Series*, the *United Nations Treaty Series*, and over 6000 other treaties assembled from forty two national collections from 1920 to 1972 which were not included in these two series. The data base for this index is in machine-readable form and the volumes are printed from it.

Standard information given to each treaty includes: (1) parties; (2) date of signature; (3) topic; (4) citation; and (5) treaty number.

Volume 1   lists entries in treaty number sequence, and gives official citation, signatories, other information about each treaty, and a listing of topical concepts.

Volume 2   lists treaties in sequence by signature data.

Volume 3   lists treaties alphabetically by each country.

Volume 4a lists alphabetically all non-participating international organizations mentioned in the text of the treaties.

Volume 4b lists United Nations Treaty Series alphabetically by UN subject list with alphabetical list of countries under each subject.

Volume 5   lists treaties according to the topical concepts assigned to each treaty in volume 1.

Treaty Profiles is a companion volume based on the same data base, but may be used independently.

About 40 pages in it analyze the significance of recent treaty trends, followed by 208 statistical tables allowing for cross-country comparisons. This set will be kept up-to-date by periodic supplements.

[18] Edited by Peter H. Rohn. American Bibliographical Center-Clio Press, Santa Barbara, CA 1974–76.

SECTION E.   INTERNATIONAL LAW: RESEARCH PROCEDURE

Research methodology relating to treaties can be reduced to these steps: (1) identification of a problem as being within the scope of a treaty and whether a treaty covers the problem, (2) if there is a treaty in point, ascertain its present status and (3) elicit interpretations of the treaty.   The following procedure encompasses these steps.

Some individuals begin their research by checking a status table immediately to determine both the scope and the status of a treaty. Others start with a descriptive publication, such as *Whiteman's Digest*.   Still others commence their research with a treaty collection or an index.   The nature of the problem also influences research procedure.   To facilitate our explanation of methodology, we will follow a conventional procedure.

1.   Determination of the Existence or the Status of an American Treaty

   a.   List of Treaties in Force

Check this publication first for information as to the existence and status of an American treaty.

   b.   Department of State Bulletin

The current issues of the *Bulletin* provide information as to recent developments of important pending treaties.   This supplements the *List of Treaties in Force*.

   c.   Malloy's Treaties and Miller's Treaties

To locate a treaty by subject between the United States and a foreign country refer to *Malloy's Treaties* (1776–1937).   If a treaty is known to exist for the period of 1776 to 1863 and its date is also roughly known, examine *Miller's Treaties*.   The absence of an index makes *Miller's Treaties* a difficult publication to use.   However, its annotations are more inclusive than *Malloy's*.

   d.   Subject Index to the Treaty Series and the Executive Agreement Series, 1931

This subject index, although not up-to-date, is helpful in locating the treaties in these series prior to July, 1931.   An advantage of this guide is that it indexes the content of each article of the treaties rather than the general subject matter of the treaties.

   e.   List of Treaties and Other International Agreements Contained in the United States Statutes at Large (Vol. 64, Pt. 3, Statutes at Large)

This comprehensive list, covering the American treaties prior to 1950, is useful for obtaining the *Statutes at Large* citations which then can be Shepardized. This index is arranged by the names of countries; therefore, the name of a participating country to a treaty must be known to use it.

f. Treaties Signed But Not Yet in Force. Several lists are available for consultation as to treaties which have been signed but are not yet in force. These aids are especially useful for information as to the status of treaties submitted to the Senate for action. They are:

Department of State's Lists of Treaties Submitted to the Senate for 1789–1934 and 1935–1944.

The United States Treaty Developments [19] supplements the above lists for 1944–1950. It contains a list in Appendix I.

More recent information is available in the Treaty Section of the *Commerce Clearing House, Congressional Index* for the current session of Congress.

g. Additional Aids. The *Status of Inter-American Treaties and Conventions* provides information as to the status of the Organization of American States treaties and conventions. This is No. 5 of the *Organization of American States Treaty Series.*

The *Harvard Law School Library. Index to Multilateral Treaties* provides citations to the text of such agreements from 1596 to 1963.

2. Interpretations of Treaties

Judicial and other interpretations of treaties may be located through the following publications:

a. United States Code Service, FCA ed. Uncodified Laws and Treaties Volume.

b. Shepard's United States Citations.

c. Shepard's State Citations.

d. Wharton's Digest.

e. Moore's Digest.

f. Hackworth's Digest.

g. Whiteman's Digest.

h. United States Department of State Bulletin.

---

[19] This is a loose-leaf service of the Department of State that was published from 1944–1950.

i. United States Treaty Developments.

j. U.S. Supreme Court digests.

3. Treaties by Popular Names

When the popular name of a treaty is known, the following publications provide references from that name to the *Statutes at Large* or *Treaties and Other International Agreements* citation:

a. Malloy's Treaties, Index in vol. 4 (Trenwith).

b. Shepard's Federal Acts and Cases by Popular Names.

4. Foreign Treaties

Treaties between foreign countries may be found in a number of publications. The most exhaustive sources for such materials are the *Consolidated Treaty Series*, the *League of Nations Treaty Series* and the *United Nations Treaty Series*. Also, check the *United Nations List of Treaty Collections* for a list of treaty collections since the 18th century.

SECTION F. SUMMARY

1. Treaties Between the United States and Foreign Countries are published in:

a. Prior to 1950, *Statutes at Large*, Part 2 (with some minor variations).

b. Since 1950, *U.S. Treaties and Other International Agreements*.

c. Since 1945, *Treaties and Other International Acts Series* (functions like advance sheets or slip laws).

    (1) Replaced *Treaty Series* and *Executive Agreements Series* since 1945.

2. Consolidated Treaty Series

a. Covers 1648–1918.

b. Chronological listing of treaties in their original languages and existing translations in English or French.

c. Index volumes planned.

3. The League of Nations Treaty Series

a. Covers 1920–1945.

b. Treaties of member and nonmember nations registered with the Secretariat.

4. The United Nations Treaty Series

a. 1946 to date—continues the *League of Nations Treaty Series*.

b. Treaties registered with the United Nations by its members or filed by nonmember states or international organizations.

c. English and French editions.

d. Cumulative Indexes; each covers 50 to 100 volumes of the *Series* and consists of three sections:
    (1) Chronological of all treaties.
    (2) Chronological of multilateral treaties.
    (3) Alphabetical by country and subject.

5. Organization of American States Treaty Series

a. Since 1957.

b. Texts in English and Spanish.

c. Instruments of ratification received by the General Secretariat of the Organization of American States.

d. Official texts of the Organization of American States.

6. Treaty Collections

a. *Statutes at Large.*
    (1) Volume 8, covers 1776–1845.
    (2) Volume 18, Part 2, treaties in force in 1873.
    (3) Volume 7, Indian treaties, 1778–1842.

b. *Malloy's Treaties,* 4 vols.
    (1) Covers 1776–1937.
    (2) Some annotations in volumes 1 and 2.
    (3) General Index in volume 4.
    (4) Chronological list of treaties in volume 4.
    (5) Parallel citations to the *Treaty Series* and the *Statutes at Large.*
    (6) Arranged alphabetically by the names of the participating countries and chronologically thereunder.

c. *Miller's Treaties,* 8 vols.
    (1) Covers 1776–1863.
    (2) No index.
    (3) Arranged chronologically.
    (4) Volume 1 is an introductory outline of the publication and contains a table of documents from 1778 through 1931.

d. C. E. Bevans, *Treaties and Other International Agreements of the United States*, 1776–1949, 13 vols.

(1) Reprints of all treaties and other agreements that were originally published in the *Statutes at Large* between 1776 and 1949.

(2) Vols. 1–4: multilateral treaties, chronological arrangement according to date of signature.

(3) Vols. 5–12: bilateral treaties, alphabetical arrangement by country.

(4) Vol. 13: General Index, alphabetical arrangement by country and topic.

e. *Treaty Series.*

(1) Published by the Department of State in pamphlet form.

(2) Covers 1908–1945, treaty numbers 489–994.

(3) Treaty numbers 489–812 include treaties, international agreements and executive agreements.

(4) Treaty numbers 813–994 include treaties and international agreements submitted to the Senate only.

(5) Numerical arrangement in chronological order of proclamation or publication.

(6) Replaced by *Treaties and Other International Acts Series* since 1945.

f. *Executive Agreement Series.*

(1) Published by the Department of State in pamphlet form.

(2) Covers 1929–1945, agreement number 1–506.

(3) Includes executive agreements, exchanges of notes, etc.

(4) Numerical arrangement in the order of issue from the press.

(5) Replaced by *Treaties and Other International Acts Series* since 1945.

7. Indexes

a. I. I. Kavass and M. A. Michael, *United States Treaties and Other International Agreements Cumulative Index*, 1776–1949, 4 vols.

(1) Indexes treaties published in the *Statutes at Large*, the *Malloy's*, the *Miller's*, the *Bevans'* and other relevant sources between 1776 and 1949.

(2) Arrangements are numerical, chronological, by country and by subject.

b.   I. I. Kavass and A. Sprudzs, *UST Cumulative Index*, 1950–1970, 4 vols.

>   (1) Indexes treaties published in the *United States Treaties Series and Other International Agreements* and the *Treaties and Other International Acts Series.*

>   (2) Arrangements are numerical, chronological, by country and by topic.

c.   Harvard Law School Library, *Index to Multilateral Treaties.* 1965.

>   (1) Chronological list of multi-party international agreements from 1596 to 1963.

>   (2) Contains a subject and regional guide.

>   (3) Annual supplement from 1966 to 1968.

d.   *United Nations List of Treaty Collections.*   1956.

>   (1) List of some 700 treaty collections published since the latter part of the 18th century.

>   (2) Arrangement: (a) general, (b) subject and (c) countries.

e.   *World Treaty Index*, 5 vols., and *Treaty Profiles*, 1 vol.

>   (1) Covers 1920–1972.

>   (2) Indexes the treaties published in the *League of Nations Treaty Series,* and the *United Nations Treaty Series* and 6000 others not included in these two series.

>   (3) Arrangements are numerical, chronological, by country, and by topic.

>   (4) *Treaty Profiles* Volume includes 208 statistical tables allowing for cross-country comparison.

>   (5) Periodic supplements planned.

8.   List of Treaties in Force

a.   Current annual publication of the Department of State.

b.   Lists treaties and other international agreements of the United States which are in force.

>   (1) Part 1 includes bilateral treaties listed by country and subdivided by subject under each country.

>   (2) Part 2 includes multilateral treaties arranged by subject, together with a list of the states which are parties to each agreement.

>   (3) Appendix includes a consolidated tabulation of documents affecting copyright relations of the United States.

9. Digest of United States Practice in International Law

An annual digest which started publication in 1973. Serves as a supplement to Whiteman.

10. United States Department of State Bulletin

a. Weekly publication.

b. Information on the current status of important United States treaties.

11. Status of Inter-American Treaties and Conventions

a. Periodic compilation of the Organization of American States.

b. Provides tabular information as to the status of Inter-American treaties and conventions.

12. Inter-American Treaties and Conventions

a. Information as to signatures, ratifications and deposits (Organization of American States Treaty Series No. 9, Revised 1961).

b. Gives more complete information than the *Status of Inter-American Treaties and Conventions*.

13. Interpretations of Treaties

a. *United States Code Service*, Uncodified Laws and Treaties Volume.

    (1) Multilateral treaties.

    (2) Inter-American treaties, deposited with the Organization of American States.

    (3) Treaties with specific countries.

b. *Shepard's Citations.*

    (1) *United States Citations*, for federal cases construing or mentioning the treaties.

    (2) *State Citations*, for state cases pertaining to treaties.

c. *Wharton's Digest.*
    (1) Not up-to-date.
    (2) Descriptive treatment.

d. *Moore's Digest.*
    (1) Representative of United States policy.
    (2) Descriptive treatment.

e. *Hackworth's Digest.*
    (1) Supplements *Moore's Digest.*
    (2) Supports United States international law position.
    (3) Descriptive treatment.

f. *Whiteman's Digest.*

   (1) Successor to *Hackworth's.*

   (2) Indicates the status of developments in international law.

   (3) Includes official and unofficial materials.

g. *United States Treaty Developments.*

   (1) Published by the Department of State, 1944–1950.

   (2) Interpretations of United States treaties for 1944–1950.

   (3) Status information is obsolete.

   (4) Appendices include a numerical list of the several treaty series and treaty lists by subjects and regions.

h. *International Legal Materials: Current Documents.*

   (1) Collection of current official foreign and United States documents relating to international legal affairs, which are otherwise unavailable.

   (2) 1962 to date; bi-monthly.

i. *CCH Tax Treaties.*

   (1) Loose-leaf reporter on income and estate tax treaties between the United States and foreign countries.

j. *Lists of treaties signed but not yet in force.*

   (1) *Department of State's Lists of Treaties Submitted to the Senate for 1789–1934 and 1935–1944.* The lists are supplemented to 1950 in Appendix I of the *United States Treaty Developments.*

   (2) *CCH Congressional Index*, Treaty Section.

k. *Treaties by popular name.*

   (1) *Malloy's Treaties*, Index in Vol. 4 (Trenwith).

   (2) *Shepard's Federal Acts by Popular Names.*

Chapter 21

ENGLISH LEGAL RESEARCH

SECTION A. INTRODUCTION

The development of American law from that of England was discussed in Chapter One. Even today, English cases are cited as persuasive authority in American courts, and English statutes have served as models for many of our important laws. No book on legal research would be complete without at least an introduction to the methods of finding English primary legal sources. Many American law libraries have English law books in their collections and this chapter will present a brief survey of their organization and use.

1. The English Legal System [1]

The United Kingdom of Great Britain and Northern Ireland does not have a single body of law universally applicable within its boundaries. Although there has been a single Parliament since 1706, Scotland has its own distinctive legal system [2] and Northern Ireland has its own Parliament [3] (as well as being represented in the Parliament at Westminster) and its own courts. While a common court of appeals and common opinions on broad issues have resulted in a common identity, differences in legal procedure and practice exist in Scotland and Northern Ireland. Our discussion will be limited to legal materials of England and Wales.

Perhaps the most fundamental difference between English law and the law of the United States is the lack of a written constitution in England. This difference has been described as follows:

> Since Parliament is the supreme lawmaking body in the United Kingdom, Acts of Parliament are absolutely binding on all courts, taking precedence over all other sources of law; they cannot be *ultra vires* (outside the compe-

[1] Much of this section is based on information obtained from U.K. Central Office of Information, Reference Pamphlet No. 49, The English Legal System (4th ed. 1972).

[2] For a discussion of Scottish law and legal sources, *see* D. Walker, The Scottish Legal System; an Introduction to Scots Law (3d rev. ed. 1969).

[3] For an outline of the legal system of Northern Ireland and its relationship to English law, *see* Preliminary Note to the title *Northern Ireland* in 23 Halsbury's Statutes of England, on 808–821 (3d ed. 1970); but *see also The Northern Ireland* (Temporary Provisions) Act 1972, in 42 Halsbury's Statutes of England, 1404 (3d ed. 1973).

tence of—in this case Parliament) for, although the principles of natural justice (broadly speaking, rules which an ordinary, reasonable person would consider fair) have always occupied an important position in the British constitution, they have never been defined or codified in the form of guaranteed rights. Thus rights, such as the right of personal freedom, the right of freedom of discussion, and the rights of association and public meeting, which are commonly considered more or less inviolate, are not protected against change by Act of Parliament, and the courts could not uphold them if Parliament decreed otherwise. Acts of Parliament are, in fact, formal announcements of rules of conduct to be observed in the future, which remain in force until they are repealed. *The courts are not entitled to question or even discuss their validity*—being required only to interpret them according to the wording used or, if Parliament has failed to make its intentions clear, according to certain canons of interpretation.[4]

2. Sources of English Law

There is no code of English law. Rather, the law is contained in about 3,000 Acts of Parliament, thousands of statutory instruments (administrative regulations, rules, and orders) and over 300,000 reported cases.

SECTION B.   STATUTES

1.   Current Statutes

The Acts of Parliament are classified as either private and local acts, or public and general acts and are published annually in separate sets. The *Public General Acts and Measures* have been published since 1831 by the Public Printer. The same set is also available from a private publisher under the title, *Law Reports, Statutes*. The final volume each year contains an index and other tables listing the acts alphabetically by title and chronologically. Other tables show "derivations and destinations" of the Consolidated Acts and the effect of each statute upon earlier measures.

2.   Codification of Statutes

There has not been in England a general codification of all the enactments of Parliament that is comparable to the *United States Code*. There is, however, a current interest in codifying particular

------

[4] U.K. Central Office of Information, *supra* at Note 1.

branches of the law, such as the criminal law and the law of landlord and tenant. For this purpose, a Law Reform Commission for England and Wales has been created.[5]

a. *Statutes Revised, 3d ed.*

This set is the nearest equivalent to an English statutory codification. It contains all the *Public General Laws* since 1235 which were in force in 1948. The Statute Law Commission charged by Parliament with its publication took each Act that had not been entirely repealed, and reprinted it, incorporating all amendments that added or changed the language of the Act. All of the Acts were then printed in chronological order in thirty-two volumes.

b. *Statutes in Force, Official Revised Edition.*

This is a new set which started in 1972, and when completed in 1980 will supersede the *Statutes Revised, 3d ed.*, which has become cumbersome to use as it lacks a cumulative supplement. This new set is being published in looseleaf volumes with each Act in a separate pamphlet. It will be kept current by the issuance of a new pamphlet to replace repealed or heavily amended sets.

c. *Halsbury's Statutes of England, 3d ed.*

This privately published set is an encyclopedic compilation of English statutes in force, arranged so that all acts on the same subject are brought together under one title. It is kept current by annual continuation volumes, a cumulative supplement, and a looseleaf volume which contains the most recent Acts of Parliament. (See Illustration 113).

3. Early English Statutes

The early English laws were published in many editions. A few sets are:

a. Statutes of the Realm, 12 vols. 1225–1713.

b. Pickering's Statutes at Large, 109 vols. 1225–1869.

c. Chitty's Statutes of Practical Utility, 6th ed., 16 vols. 1235–1910, with supplements to 1948.

4. Acts and Ordinances of the Interregnum, 1642–1640

This is a selected three-volume integration of the laws enacted during the interregnum. Volume 3 includes a Chronological Table of Acts and Ordinances, an Index to Subjects, and an Index of Names, Places, and Things.

[5] U.K. Central Office of Information, *supra* at 36.

SECTION C. ENGLISH ADMINISTRATIVE LAW

The English equivalent to the rules and regulations that are published in the United States in the *Federal Register* and compiled in the *Code of Federal Regulations* is the *Statutory Instruments* (formerly called *Statutory Rules and Orders*). These are orders, rules, and regulations, known as subordinate or delegated legislation, promulgated by a Minister of the Crown under the authority of a statute. By-laws made by local governmental or other authorities exercising power conferred upon them by Parliament are also included.

1. Publication of Statutory Instruments

a. *The Statutory Rules and Orders and Statutory Instruments Revised, 3d ed.*

This set was published in 1949 as the official English administrative code. It contains administrative rules of general applicability and a permanent nature. It is updated by annual volumes of *Statutory Instruments*.

(1) *Guide to Government Orders*. This biennial publication serves as an index to *Statutory Instruments*. It indicates which statutory instruments are still in force. In addition to its subject index, it has a Table of Statutes which refers readers to the appropriate heading in the subject index.

b. *Halsbury's Statutory Instruments*.

This unofficial compilation of statutory instruments arranged by subject, is published as a companion set to *Halsbury's Statutes of England*. It is kept current by the issuance of replacement volumes and a looseleaf cumulative supplement. It is similar in format to the *Code of Federal Regulations*. It also has a separate, frequently replaced index volume.

SECTION D. COURT REPORTING

1. English Court Organization

Modern organization of English courts began with the *Judicature Act of 1873* and continued with subsequent Parliamentary Acts, the latest being the *Courts Act 1971*. The present-day court organization is as follows: [6]

a. House of Lords

This body, in addition to its legislative function, serves as the supreme court of appeal for the United Kingdom in civil cases and

[6] For a more detailed description and history of English courts, *see* R. Walker & M. Walker, The English Legal System 131–137 (2d ed. 1970).

the final court of appeal for criminal cases from England, Wales, and Northern Ireland.

b.   Supreme Court of Judicature

This court is divided into two parts: the Court of Appeals and the High Court of Justice.

(1) Court of Appeals. This court has two divisions: civil and criminal. It hears appeals from the High Court and certain other inferior courts.

(2) High Court. This court [7] now consists of three divisions: the Queen's Bench Division (including the Admiralty Court and Commercial Court), the Chancery Division, and the Family Division. In practice, each division acts as a separate court.

c.   Crown Court

This is a new court created by the *Courts Act 1971*.[8] It is a criminal court with unlimited jurisdiction. It assumes jurisdiction of all criminal cases above the Magistrates' courts and appellate jurisdiction of the Quarter Session courts which have now been abolished.

d.   County Courts

These have limited first instance civil jurisdiction.

e.   Local and Special Courts

These are mainly Magistrates' courts and courts of special jurisdiction such as the Restrictive Trade Practices Court and the Industrial Relations Court.

2.   Development of English Court Reports

The history of court reporting in England is long and confusing.[9] For our purposes, we can divide the reporting of English cases into three periods.

a.   *The Year Books. 1272–1535*

The Year Books are the first available law reports with the original text in "Law French." Their purpose and function are still disputed by legal historians. Other than the fact that they are the sources of modern law reporting, they serve little purpose in most legal research today other than for the study of legal history.

---

[7] Previous to the enactment of the Courts Act 1971, the High Court consisted of (1) Queen's Bench Division, (2) Probate, Divorce, and Admiralty Division, and (3) the Chancery Division. See *Courts Act 1971–I*, 115 Sol.J. 715 (1971).

[8] *Id.*

[9] R. Walker & M. Walker, *supra.*

b.   *Private Names Reporters. 1535–1865*

During this period there was no officially recognized system of court reporting. Any barrister could publish court reports and several hundred different sets were published with many covering the same period of time and the same courts with varying accuracy. It has been customary to refer to these reports by the name of the reporter.

    (1) *English Reports, Full Reprint.* This is a reprint of all English cases from 1220 to 1865. When there were competing sets of the reports, the editors included only the one they deemed most accurate. There are 176 volumes in this set, including a two-volume Table of Cases, and a chart which lists all of the named reports with reference to their location in the *Full Reprint*. Most law libraries have only this set, rather than the original reports.

    (2) *The Revised Reports.* The *Revised Reports* are in 149 volumes and cover the period 1785–1865. Although this set largely duplicates the *English Reports, Full Reprint*, its value lies in the fact that the reports were edited by the distinguished legal historian, Sir Frederick Pollock.

c.   *The Incorporated Council of Law Reporting. 1865–*

In 1865 the Incorporated Council of Law Reporting for England and Wales was formed. While not an official body, it has quasi-official status. In 1865 the Council started publication of the *Law Reports* and this is the preferred set of reports.

3.   Current Court Reports

As previously mentioned, cases reported before 1865 may be found in the *English Reports, Full Reprint* or *The Revised Reports*. Since 1865, the English cases are found in the following sets:

a.   *The Law Reports.*

This set reports decisions since 1865 and is selective in its reporting, covering decisions of permanent significance of the Court of Appeals and High Court. In addition to the opinions of the judges, it also includes the legal argument presented to the court. Although originally published in twelve different series, the *Law Reports* are now published in four series: (1) Appeal Cases (includes both cases from the Court of Appeals and the House of Lords), (2) Queen's Bench, (3) Chancery, and (4) Family Division.

b.   *Weekly Law Reports.*

This set is also published by the Incorporated Council of Law Reporting and includes all cases that will ultimately be published in

the *Law Reports*. It also publishes cases not intended for publication in the *Law Reports*. These appear in the first of the three volumes published each year.

c.   Other Sets of Reports.

Although the Incorporated Council of Law Reporting assumed responsibility for systematizing court reporting, there is no prohibition of private reporting and many such sets were published. Most have now ceased publication.[10] The most important of the private reports is the *All England Law Reports*. This set started in 1936, incorporating the *Law Journal Reports* and the *Times Law Reports*. It includes the decisions of the House of Lords, the Court of Appeals, the High Court, and courts of special jurisdiction. The opinions are released in advance sheets and then in bound volumes.

d.   *All England Law Reports Reprint.*

This set covers selected cases from 1558–1935 and is reprinted from the *Law Journal Reports* in thirty-six volumes plus an index.

SECTION E.   DIGESTS AND ENCYCLOPEDIAS

1.   Digests

a.   *The English and Empire Digest.*

This is a comprehensive digest of English cases reported from the earliest times to date, and is in fifty-six volumes. It also includes cases from the courts of Scotland, Ireland, Canada, and other countries of the British Commonwealth and South Africa. Obsolete cases and cases of only historical interest are excluded from the publication. The *Digest* is arranged topically and has a detailed outline at the beginning of each major subject and an index at the end of each volume. Cases on a particular aspect of a general topic are grouped in chronological order and assigned case numbers.

The English and Empire Digest is an annotated digest "which embodies the citator feature." Each case digest is followed by notes of subsequent cases, if any, showing whether the digested case has been approved, followed, distinguished, overruled or otherwise mentioned. Under each section or subsection of the digest, cross-references and references to pertinent statutes and to *Halsbury's Laws* (an encyclopedia) are given. (See Illustration 114). Volumes 52 through 54 contain a Consolidated Table of Cases, and volumes 55 and 56 comprise a Consolidated Index. The digest is updated with replacement volumes (identifiable by a "green band"), multi-year continuation volumes, and annual cumulative supplements.

---

10 *Id.*

The four methods of research may be used with this digest.   The indexes serve as aids to the Index Method, and the topic outlines in the front of each volume serve the Topic Method.   The table of cases permits use of the digest through the Case Method.   The Consolidated Index lists references to definitions under "Words and Phrases," thus providing for utilization of the Definition Method.

b.   *Mews' Digest of English Case Law*, 2d ed. (1924).

This digest which ceased publication with its 1969 annual supplement, consisted of twenty-four volumes plus ten-year cumulative and annual supplements.   It covered significant early English cases and recent cases through 1969.   It also included some decisions from the courts of Scotland and Ireland.   An Index of Cases Judicially Noticed was contained in volume 23 and served as a citator.   The case citator was kept up to date by tables appearing in the ten-year supplements and annual volumes.   The supplementary volumes also included Tables of Statutes Judicially Considered.   Volume 24 was the Table of Cases.

Ten-year supplements cover the periods 1925–35 and 1936–45.   From 1946 through 1969 annual supplements were published.   The cases are digested and topically arranged in *Mews' Digest*.

2.   Encyclopedias

The standard English encyclopedia for both statutory and case law, is *Halsbury's Laws of England*.   The first volume of the fourth edition was issued in 1972 and until all volumes have been issued it may be necessary to also consult the third edition.   This set should not be confused with *Halsbury's Statutes of England*, a previously described code.

Halsbury's Laws of England is alphabetically arranged by topic. Each topic is subdivided into parts, sections, subsections and paragraphs with appropriate footnote references to cases, statutes, statutory rules and orders or statutory instruments.   *Halsbury's Laws* places great emphasis on statutory law and, unlike its American counterparts, has a Consolidated Table of Cases.   This table contains references to the *English and Empire Digest*, indicating where a case is digested in that set.

There is a two-volume index to the third edition and a temporary index is periodically issued for the completed volumes of the fourth edition.

Both editions are kept current by monthly releases filed in a looseleaf volume.

3. Current Law: Being a Complete Statement of All the Law from Every Source

This set began publication in 1947 and provides a digest of all phases of English law. It is arranged topically and, under each topic, digests cases, statutes, and statutory instruments. It consists of the following:

a. *Current Law.*

A monthly pamphlet advance sheet service.

b. *Current Law Year Book.*

An annual cumulation which includes among other information, a cumulative subject index, table of cases, tables of statutory instruments and instruments affected, and digests of unreported cases.

c. *Master Volume.*

The *Current Law Year Books* were consolidated into a 1947–51 volume; since then, every fifth year, a five-year cumulative Year Book called the *Master Volume* is issued.

d. *Current Law Citators.*

These will be discussed in the section on citators. *Current Law* is also available in Scottish edition.

———

SECTION F. CITATORS

There is no service precisely similar to *Shepard's Citations* for England. There are, however, several methods of obtaining later citations, or, as the British express it, "noting up" cases or statutes.

1. Statutes

Citators for statutes are arranged chronologically. For a particular statute, citations are given for each subsequent statute which amends or repeals the cited statute, and for each case which cites the statute. Citators for statutes are contained in:

a. *Current Law Statute Citator.* (See Illustration 119).

b. *All England Law Reports.* Consolidated Index and Index and Noter-Up volumes.

c. *Halsbury's Statutes of England.*

2. Cases

a. *English and Empire Digest.*

Each case in this set is assigned a case number. After the digest of the case, citations are given to all subsequent decisions which cited

the digested case. After consulting a case in the main volume, later cases citing the digested case can be found by checking the case number in the latest cumulative supplement. (See Illustrations 114 and 115).

b. *All England Law Reports.*

Both the Consolidated Index and the supplementary Index and Noter-Up volume contain a Table of Cases Judicially Considered. All cases reported since 1936 are listed alphabetically. Under each case name, citations are given to all subsequent cases which construed the cited case.

c. *Current Law Citator.*

This soft-bound cumulative volume contains a Case Citator 1947–75 which lists cases alphabetically by name. Subsequent cases citing and statutes affecting the original case appear beneath each case name entry. (See Illustration 120).

3. Authority of English Cases

Until 1966, the House of Lords regarded itself as strictly bound by its earlier decisions. Once the House of Lords had rendered an opinion the rules enunciated in it could only be changed by an Act of Parliament. In 1966 the House of Lords stated that in the future they proposed to depart from their own decisions where it appeared proper to do so.[11]

SECTION G. HOW TO FIND ENGLISH STATUTES AND CASES

1. Statutes

a. *Chronological Table of the Statutes* and *Index to the Statutes in Force.*

This two-volume set is issued annually and serves as the index to the *Statutes Revised, Statutes in Force,* and *The Public General Acts and Measures.* Volume 1 contains a chronological table of all *Public General Acts* since 1235 with references to amendments and repeals. Volume 2 is a subject index to statutes in force. (See Illustration 112).

b. *Halsbury's Statutes of England.*

This set is now in its third edition. It arranges all statutes in force alphabetically by the title of each act. It is kept up to date by

---

[11] [1966] 3 All E.R. 77.

annual supplement volumes and a loose-leaf volume for current statutes. This set is annotated and also contains references to *Halsbury's
Laws of England.* It is comparable to the *United States Code Annotated* or the *United States Code Service.* (See Illustration 113).

2. Cases

a. *English and Empire Digest.*

This is the most comprehensive English case digest. The following steps are involved in its use:

(1) Consult index volumes for topic under investigation.

This will refer to volume and *case number* in main set.

(2) Consult continuation volumes for later cases.

(3) Consult Cumulative Supplement for later citations of
cases found through (1) and (2).

Citations are given to all sets of court reports in which a case
is reported. Frequently, English legal writing gives only one citation for a case. When that set is not available in the law library
being used, check the Consolidated Table of Cases volume in the
English and Empire Digest to locate other citations to the case.

b. *All England Law Reports.*

There is a Consolidated Index including a table of cases, "noter-
up", and subject index for the years 1936–65. Thereafter, Index and
Noter-Up volumes are cumulated periodically. The index section is
a detailed subject index and gives citations to *All England Law Reports* only.

c. *Current Law Year Book.*

Use *Master Year Book* volumes and then subsequent annual
volumes. Citations are given to the location of case digests in the
Year Book.

3. Secondary Sources

It should be mentioned that it is frequently easier in starting
research for English law to commence the search, as described in the
previous chapters on American law, with secondary sources. These
include:

a. *Halsbury's Laws of England.*

b. English treatises.

c. English legal periodicals. The major ones are included in
the *Index to Legal Periodicals.* The *Current Index to Commonwealth Legal Periodicals,* issued monthly, provides subject access to English journals before entries appear in the
Index to Legal Periodicals.

SECTION H.   WORDS AND PHRASES

A number of the English publications include definitions of words and phrases. They are discussed in the preceding sections. In addition, several sources exclusively treat words and phrases.

1.   Stroud's Judicial Dictionary, 4th ed., 1971–1974

This five-volume publication includes not only definitions but also references to cases and statutes from which they are derived. It is kept current by supplementation.

2.   Words and Phrases Legally Defined, 2d ed., 1969–1970

A revision of Burrow's *Words and Phrases Judicially Defined,* this five-volume work has been expanded to include textbook and statutory as well as judicial definitions. A cumulative supplement is published annually.

SECTION I.   ENGLAND AND THE EUROPEAN COMMUNITIES

On January 1, 1973, the United Kingdom became part of the European Communities. As a result, Community law in the form of treaty provisions and secondary legislation became part of English law. Moreover, it became necessary for England to change many aspects of its law to comply with its membership in the European Communities.

Researchers in English law are now faced with the problem of determining when Community law is applicable and of the possible conflict of English law with Community law.[12] To facilitate the location of relevant Community law, *Halsbury's Statutes of England* has published in volume 42A, the *European Continuations, Volume 1, 1952–72,* which includes either full text or digests, with annotations, of all European Communities legislation through 1972 with amendments "noted up" through January 1, 1974. Supplements to this volume will contain later legislation. It is arranged by topic according to the titles used in the main set. By this means it is fairly simple to ascertain which aspects of English law have been affected by Community law.

[12] For a concise explanation of the relationship of English law to the law of the European communities, see L. COLLINS, EUROPEAN COMMUNITY LAW IN THE UNITED KINGDOM. 1975.

SECTION J.   ILLUSTRATIONS

STATUTES

Problem: Which English statute covers the privileges of witnesses in civil proceedings?

Illustrations

112.   Page from Annual Index to Statutes.
113.   Pages from Halsbury's Statutes of England, 3d ed.

CASES

Problem: Find English cases on liability of store keeper for injury to customers.

114.   Page from English and Empire Digest.
115.   Page from Cumulative Supplement, English and Empire Digest.
116.   Page from 1935–56 Index Volume, All England Law Reports.
117.   Page from Index Volume, Halsbury's Laws of England, 3rd ed.
118.   Page from Halsbury's Laws of England, 3rd ed.

CITATORS

119.   Page from Current Law Statute Citator.
120.   Page from Case Section, Current Law Citator.

[Illustration 112]

PAGE FROM ANNUAL INDEX TO STATUTES

INDEX TO THE STATUTES   2127

WITNESS *cont.*

1 General Provisions *cont.*

Before—*cont.*

Patents Act Appeal Tribunal and Comptroller General of Patents *See* PATENTS, 8

Private Legislation Procedure (Scotland) Act Commrs. *See* PROVISIONAL ORDER, S, 2

Probate Ct. *See* SUPREME COURT, E, 6(*a*)

Solicitors Act disciplinary committee *See* SOLICITOR, E, 2(*g*)

Solicitors' Discipline (Scotland) Committee *See* SOLICITOR, S, 4(*a*)

Supreme Ct. *See* 4 *below*

Tithe Act proceedings *See* TITHES, E, 4(*d*)

tribunal of inquiry *See* INQUIRIES, 1

Habeas corpus, bringing up prisoner as witness by *See* HABEAS CORPUS *And see* COUNTY COURT, E, 5(*b*)(iv)

Mode of examination of, in every civil and criminal ct.: E NI (**a**) 1865 c.18 ss.1,3–6,8

1967 c.58 s.10,sch.3,Pt.III

Recognizances to give evidence *See* CORONER, E, 2(*b*): CRIMINAL PROCEDURE, 3(*a*)

FINDING ENGLISH STATUTES.

This volume, issued annually, indexes all English statutes in force. This indicates that privileges of witnesses in civil proceedings is covered in chapter 64 of an Act passed in 1968. This citation could also be found in the sources listed at section B of this chapter.

The next step is to locate the text of this Act.

See next Illustration.

to be binding if administered in form which witness declares binding *See* OATH

declaration or affirmation in lieu of *See* DECLARATION

or affirmation, form if in examination under commn., etc., in Her Majesty's dominions beyond jurisdiction *See* EVIDENCE, 1(*d*)

Perjury, or subornation of perjury *See* PERJURY, E: PERJURY, S

prosecution of witness for, by order of ct.: NI 1851 c.100 s.19

E 1911 c.6 s.9

E 1933 c.36 s.2(2)

1964 c.43 s.5,sch.2

Unsworn evidence *See* EVIDENCE, 3

power of colonial legislatures to make ordinances for admission of: 1843 c.22

(*t*) PROTECTION

Cannot refuse to answer on ground of admitting a debt or subjecting himself to an action:

1806 c.37

Not compellable to answer question tending to criminate himself, save when defendant in a criminal case: E NI 1851 c.99 s.3

E S 1898 c.36 s.1(*e*)(*f*)

Witness compulsorily first disclosing in civil action, destruction, etc., of will, or agent, banker, factor, trustee, or director compulsorily disclosing embezzlement, etc. (*see now* THEFT, E) not liable criminally, except as to bankruptcy: NI 1861,c.96 ss.29,85

E 1914 c.59 s.166

→ Privilege in civil proceedings—

against incrimination of self or spouse: 1968 c.64 ss.14,18

for communications made for patent proceedings: 1968 c.64 ss.15,18

abolition of certain privileges: 1968 c.64 ss.16,18

tribunals, investigations and inquiries: 1968 c.64 s.17

civil proceedings, legal proceedings, court, etc. defined: 1968 c.64 s.18

(**a**) ss.3–6,8 of this Act respectively reproduce ss.22–5 and 27 (now repealed) of the Common Law Procedure Act 1854 c.125

(**b**) For effect to be given to orders of cts. of the Irish Free State (now Republic of Ireland) enforcing attendance of witnesses, etc., *see* SR&O 1923/405: Rev. X, p. 298: 1923, at pp. 402–3

[Illustration 113]

PAGE FROM HALSBURY'S STATUTES OF ENGLAND, 3rd ed.

THE CIVIL EVIDENCE ACT 1968

(1968 c. 64)

ARRANGEMENT OF SECTIONS

PART I

HEARSAY EVIDENCE

> The reference in the previous Illustration was to the Civil Evidence Act, 1968. This is the first page of the text from Vol. 12 of Halsbury's Statutes of England, 3d ed. The same text can also be located in the 1968 volume of The Public General Acts and Measures, but it will not be annotated.

PART II

MISCELLANEOUS AND GENERAL

Convictions, etc. as evidence in civil proceedings

An Act to amend the law of evidence in relation to civil proceedings, and in respect of the privilege against self-incrimination to make corresponding amendments in relation to statutory powers of inspection or investigation

[25th October 1968]

Northern Ireland. This Act does not, in general, apply; see s. 20 (3), *post.*

PART I

HEARSAY EVIDENCE

1. Hearsay evidence to be admissible only by virtue of this Act and other statutory provisions, or by agreement

(1) In any civil proceedings a statement other than one made by a person while giving oral evidence in those proceedings shall be admissible as evidence of any fact stated therein to the extent that it is so admissible by virtue of any provision of this Part of this Act or by virtue of any other statutory provision or by agreement of the parties, but not otherwise.

(2) In this section "statutory provision" means any provision contained in, or in an instrument made under, this or any other Act, including any Act passed after this Act.

[Illustration 113–a]

PAGE FROM HALSBURY'S STATUTES OF ENGLAND, 3rd ed.

CIVIL EVIDENCE ACT 1968, S. 7   917

Supplied to . . . computer. See, further, s. 5 (5) (*a*), *ante.*

Document . . . was produced, etc. See, further, s. 5 (5) (*c*), *ante.*

Sub-s. (4): For the purpose of any enactment, etc. Corroboration is required by statute in actions for breach of promise of marriage under the Evidence Further Amendment Act 1869, s. 2, p. 846, *ante,* and in affiliation proceedings under the Affiliation Proceedings Act 1957, s. 4 (2), Vol. 1, p. 79.

As to corroboration in other cases and the treatment of uncorroborated evidence, see 15 Halsbury's Laws (3rd Edn.) 450.

Sub-s. (4): Maker of the statement. Cf. the note "Statement made by a person" to s. 7, *post.*

Sub-s. (5): Wilfully. This expression, in the words of Lord Russell of Killowen, C.J., in *R.* v. *Senior,* [1899] 1 Q.B. 283, at pp. 290, 291, "means that the act is done deliberately and intentionally, not by accident or inadvertence, but so that the mind of the person who does the act goes with it"; see also, in particular, *R.* v. *Walker* (1934), 24 Cr. App. Rep. 117; *Eaton* v. *Cobb,* [1950] 1 All E.R. 1016; and *Arrowsmith* v. *Jenkins,* [1963] 2 Q.B. 561; [1963] 2 All E.R. 210; but see *Rice* v. *Connolly,* [1966] 2 Q.B. 414; [1966] 2 All E.R. 649.

Material. A statement may be material on the mere ground that it renders more credible something else; cf. *R.* v. *Tyson* (1867), L.R. 1 C.C.R. 107.

Knows. There is authority for saying that, where a person deliberately refrains from making inquiries the results of which he might not care to have, this constitutes in law actual knowledge of the facts in question; see *Knox* v. *Boyd,* 1941 S.C. (J.) 82, at p. 86, and *Taylor's Central Garages (Exeter), Ltd.* v. *Roper* (1951), 115 J.P. 445, at pp. 449, 450, *per* Devlin, J.; and see also, in particular, *Mallon* v. *Allon,* [1964] 1 Q.B. 385; [1963] 3 All E.R. 843, at p. 394 and p. 847, respectively. However, mere neglect to ascertain what would have been found out by making reasonable enquiries is not tantamount to knowledge; see *Taylor's Central Garages (Exeter), Ltd.* v. *Roper, ubi supra, per* Devlin, J.; and cf. *London Computator, Ltd.* v. *Seymour,* [1944] 2 All E.R. 11; but see also *Mallon* v. *Allon, ubi supra*; and cf. *Wallworth* v. *Balmer,* [1965] 3 All E.R. 721.

Indictment. By virtue of the Criminal Law Act 1967, s. 8 (2), Vol. 21, title Magistrates, the offence is triable at quarter sessions.

Fine. There is no specific limit to the amount of the fine which may be imposed. Yet, the fine should be within the offender's capacity to pay; see, in particular, *R.* v. *Churchill (No. 2),* [1967] 1 Q.B. 190; [1966] 2 All E.R. 215 (reversed on other grounds *sub nom. Churchill* v. *Walton,* [1967] A.C. 224; [1967] 1 All E.R. 497); and see also 25 Edw. 1 (Magna Carta) (1297), Vol. 6, p. 401, and the Bill of Rights (1688) (Sess. 2), s. 1, Vol. 6, p. 490.

Hearsay evidence formerly admissible at common law. For provisions as to the admissibility of certain evidence formerly admissible at common law, see s. 9, *post.*

Definitions. For "civil proceedings", see s. 18 (1), *post,* and for "document" and "statement", see s. 10 (1), *post*; and see as to "copy", the latter subsection.

Halsbury's Statutes of England serves as an annotated edition. After each section there are editorial notes, citations to cases interpreting the section, and references to related statutes.

This set is kept up-to-date by a separate loose-leaf volume.

(*b*) evidence tending to prove that, whether before or after he made that statement, that person made (whether orally or in a document or otherwise) another statement inconsistent therewith shall be admissible for the purpose of showing that that person has contradicted himself:

Provided that nothing in this subsection shall enable evidence to be given of any matter of which, if the person in question had been called as a witness and had denied that matter in cross-examination, evidence could not have been adduced by the cross-examining party.

(2) Subsection (1) above shall apply in relation to a statement given in evidence by virtue of section 4 of this Act as it applies in relation to a statement given in evidence by virtue of section 2 of this Act, except that references to

[Illustration 114]

PAGE FROM ENGLISH AND EMPIRE DIGEST

46   Negligence   [Vol. XXXVI

Sect. 1. *In regard to particular persons : Sub-sect.* 1, cont.]

was guilty of a breach of duty towards him in suffering the hole to be unfenced.

FINDING ENGLISH CASES: ENGLISH AND EMPIRE DIGEST.

Step 1 (not shown). Check Index Volume under appropriate headings. This will give citation to volume, page, and case number.

Step 2. Examine volume referred to by Index. The number 246 is not a "key" number but the number assigned to this case in this digest.

Note how the digest of the case is more substantial than those in American digests.

Also note how ctiation is given to all sets where case is reported.

---

the horses met with an accident by stepping upon a board which broke under its weight. Pltf. charged negligence in respect of the rotten condition of the board. There was no evidence that deft. co. placed the board there, or knew or should have known of its presence there :—*Held :* pltf. had failed to prove any negligence of deft. co.—GUERTIN *v.* FASSETT LUMBER CO., [1931] 4 D. L. R. 916 ; O. R. 589.—CAN.

SUB-SECT. 2. DUTY TO INVITEES

A. Who is an Invitee

(a) In General

LAW. *See* HALSBURY'S LAWS (2nd Edn.), Vol. 23, pp. 600 *et seq.*

246. Persons entering premises of owner or occupier—For purposes of business or common interest—On invitation express or implied.]—Upon the premises of deft., a sugar refiner, was a hole or shoot on a level with the floor, used for raising & lowering sugar to & from the different storeys of the building, & usual, necessary, & proper in the way of deft.'s business. Whilst in use, it was necessary & proper that this hole should be unfenced. When not in use, it was sometimes necessary, for the purpose of ventilation, that it should be open. It was not necessary that it should, when not in use, be unfenced ; & it might at such times, without injury to the business, have been fenced by a rail. Whether or not it was usual to fence similar places when not in actual use, did not appear. Pltf., a journeyman gasfitter in the employ of a patentee who had fixed a patent gas regulator upon deft.'s premises, for which he was to be paid provided it effected a certain amount of saving in the consumption of gas, went upon the premises with his employer's agent for the purpose of examining the several burners, so as to test the new apparatus. Whilst thus engaged upon an upper floor of the building, pltf., under circumstances as to which the evidence was conflicting, accidentally, &, as the jury found, without any fault or negligence on his part, fell through the hole, & was injured :—*Held :* inasmuch as pltf. was upon the premises on lawful business, in the course of fulfilling a contract in which he, or his employer & deft. both had an interest, & the hole or shoot was from its nature unreasonably dangerous to persons not usually employed upon the premises, but having a right to go there, deft.

that the customer has come into the shop in pursuance of a tacit invitation given by the shopkeeper, with a view to business which concerns himself. If a customer were, after buying goods, to go back to the shop in order to complain of the quality, or that the change was not right, he would be just as much there upon business which concerned the shopkeeper, & as much entitled to protection during this accessory visit, though it might not be for the shopkeeper's benefit, as during the principal visit, which was. If, instead of going himself, the customer were to send his servant, the servant would be entitled to the same consideration as the master. The class to which the customer belongs includes persons who go not as mere volunteers, or licensees, or guests, or servants or persons whose employment is such that danger may be considered as bargained for, but who go upon business which concerns the occupier, & upon his invitation express or implied (WILLES, J.).—INDERMAUR *v.* DAMES (1866), L. R. 1 C. P. 274 ; Har. & Ruth. 243 ; 35 L. J. C. P. 184 ; 14 L. T. 484 ; 12 Jur. N. S. 432 ; 14 W. R. 586 ; *affd.* (1867), L. R. 2 C. P. 311, Ex. Ch.

Annotations :—**Folld.** Smith *v.* London & St. Katharine Docks Co. (1868), L. R. 3 C. P. 326. **Distd.** Brooks *v.* Courtney (1869), 20 L. T. 440. **Apld.** M. S. & L. Ry. *v.* Woodcock (1871), 25 L. T. 335 ; Smith *v.* Steele (1875), L. R. 10 Q. B. 125 ; Watkins *v.* G. W. Ry. (1877), 46 L. J. Q. B. 817. **Folld.** White *v.* France (1877), 2 C. P. D. 308. **Apld.** Marney *v.* Scott, [1899] 1 Q. B. 986. **Distd.** Cavalier *v.* Pope, [1906] A. C. 428. **Apld.** Lewis *v.* Ronald (1909), 101 L. T. 534. **Distd.** Lucy *v.* Bawden, [1914] 2 K. B. 318. **Consd.** Norman *v.* G. W. Ry., [1915] 1 K. B. 584. **Distd.** Maclenan *v.* Segar, [1917] 2 K. B. 325. **Apld.** Pritchard *v.* Peto, [1917] 2 K. B. 173 ; Anchor Line (Henderson) *v.* Dundee Harbour Trustees, Ellerman Lines *v.* Dundee Harbour Trustees, Thomson, Shepherd *v.* Dundee Harbour Trustees (1922), 38 T. L. R. 299 ; Mercer *v.* S. E. & C. Ry.'s Managing Committee, [1922] 2 K. B. 549. **Consd.** Mersey Docks & Harbour Board *v.* Procter, [1923] A. C. 253. **Folld.** Sutcliffe *v.* Clients Investment Co., [1924] 2 K. B. 746. **Consd.** Forbes, Abbott & Lennard *v.* G. W. Ry. (1927), 138 L. T. 286. **Apld.** Compania Mexicana De Petroleo El Aguila *v.* Essex Transport & Trading Co (1929), 141 L. T. 106. **Consd.** Hillen *v.* I. C. I. (Alkali), Ltd., [1934] 1 K. B. 455 ; Howard *v.* Furness Houlder Argentine Lines, Ltd. & Brown, Ltd., [1936] 2 All E. R. 781 ; Simons *v.* Winslade, [1938] 3 All E. R. 774 ; Canter *v.* Gardner & Co., [1940] 1 All E. R. 325. **Apld.** Horton *v.* London Graving Dock Co., [1949] 2 All E. R. 169. **Consd.** Jacobs *v.* L. C. C., [1949] 1 All E. R. 790 ; Jennings *v.* Cole, [1949] 2 All E. R. 191 ; Denny *v.* Supplies & Transport Co. & Scruttons, Ltd. (1950), 66 (pt. 1) T. L. R. 1168. **Apld.** London Graving Dock Co. *v.* Horton, [1951] 2 All E. R. 1. **Consd.** Hunwick *v.* Essex Rivers Catchment Board, [1952] 1 All E. R. 765. **Refd.**

(partially obscured left column):

was reason...
conditions...
owing to...
questions w...
to give pltf...
& whether...
of defts., w...
not interfe...
(1912), 29...

SCOTTISH

238. *Gene...* upon owners the roof, & n... LAZARUS *v.* T...

239. — of land on w... for damages s... —MARTLE *v...* 3 W. W. R. 2...

240. — MINING CO., B. C. R. 81.—

241. — had a contrac... lumber busin... leading to th...

(partially obscured right column):

best in the who, it was as he finds to wear the is no design cting guests ing servants being there-what is the f a building ereto in the express or a customer only one of is actually' s or not, he of authority reasonable mage from r knows or r left open, ection does tract being r's business upon the fact

[Illustration 115]

PAGE FROM CUMULATIVE SUPPLEMENT, ENGLISH AND EMPIRE DIGEST

539　　　　　Vol. 36—Negligence.　Cases 177—303a: *178a—*261g

SUB-SECT. 1A. OCCUPIER

STATUTE. *See* Occupiers' Liability Act, 1957 (c. 31).

245Aa. *Common law duty of care—Contributory negligence.*]—
ROLES *v.* NATHAN, ROLES *v.* CORNEY (1963). *See*
Continuation Vol. A.

245Ab. —— *"Control"—What amounts to.*]—WHEAT *v.* E.
LACON & CO., LTD. (1966). *See* Continuation Vol. B.
Add. Citation:—[1966] R. A. 193.
Consd. H. & N. Emanuel, Ltd. *v.* Greater London
Council, [1971] 2 All E. R. 835. **Refd.** A. M. F. International, Ltd. *v.* Magnet Bowling, Ltd., [1968] 2
All E. R. 789; Whiting *v.* Hillingdon London B. C.
(1970), 68 L. G. R. 437.

245Ac. —— *Occupier of structure—Structure in occupation of
sub-contractor.*]—KEARNEY *v.* ERIC WALLER, LTD.
(1965). *See* Continuation Vol. B.
Add. Citation:—[1967] 1 Q. B. 29.

245Ad. —— *Position of trespasser.*]—PERISCINOTTI *v.*
BRIGHTON WEST PIER, LTD. (1961). *See* Continuation
Vol. B.

245Ae. —— *Injury to contractor's servant.*]—FISHER *v.* C. H.
T., LTD. (1966). *See* Continuation Vol. B.
Add. Citation:—[1966] 2 Q. B. 475.
Consd. H. & N. Emanuel, Ltd. *v.* Greater London
Council, [1971] 2 All E. R. 835. **Refd.** Wheat *v.* E.
Lacon & Co., Ltd., [1966] 1 All E. R. 582.

245Af. —— *Injury to child.*]—MOLONEY *v.* LAMBETH LONDON
B. C. (1966). *See* Continuation Vol. C.

245Ag. ——.]—WARD *v.* HERTFORDSHIRE C. C. (1970).
See Continuation Vol. C.

245Ah. —— *Injury to visitor—Acceptance of risk.*]—SIMMS
v. LEIGH RUGBY FOOTBALL CLUB, LTD. (1969). *See*
Continuation Vol. C.

245Aj. —— *Pedestrian on railway bridge.*]—GREENHALGH *v.*
BRITI

245Ak. ——
v. CH
tion
As to

245Al. ——
(1970
241Aa. E
RYS.

246. Consd
E. R.
All E
1185;
1 All
E. R.
[1959
v. La
Whe
A. M
[1968
Co., Ltd., [1970] 2 All E. R. 294.

247. *As to* (1) **Refd.** Greenhalgh *v.* British Rys. Board, [1969]
2 All E. R. 114. *Generally,* **Refd.** Hawkins *v.* Coulsdon
& Purley U. D. C., [1954] 1 All E. R. 97.

251. **Refd.** Hawkins *v.* Coulsdon & Purley U. D. C., [1954]
1 All E. R. 97; Scruttons, Ltd. *v.* Midland Silicones,
Ltd., [1962] 1 All E. R. 1; Wheat *v.* E. Lacon & Co.,
Ltd., [1966] 1 All E. R. 582.

255. **Refd.** Hawkins *v.* Coulsdon & Purley U. D. C., [1954]
1 All E. R. 97; Dyer *v.* Ilfracombe U. D. C., [1956] 1
All E. R. 581.

260. **Refd.** Creed *v.* McGeoch & Sons, Ltd., [1955] 3 All
E. R. 123; Scruttons, Ltd. *v.* Midland Silicones, Ltd.,
[1962] 1 All E. R. 1; Wheat *v.* E. Lacon & Co., Ltd.,
[1966] 1 All E. R. 582.

262. *As to* (1) **Consd.** Gough *v.* National Coal Board, [1953]
2 All E. R. 1283; Bates *v.* Stone Parish Council, [1954]
3 All E. R. 38; Dyer *v.* Ilfracombe U. D. C., [1956] 1
All E. R. 581. **Apld.** Perkowski *v.* Wellington Corpn.,
[1958] 3 All E. R. 368. **Refd.** Cuttress *v.* Scaffolding
(Great Britain), Ltd., [1953] 1 All E. R. 165; Slade *v.*
Battersea & Putney Group Hospital Management Committee, [1955] 1 All E. R. 429; Videan *v.* British
Transport Commission, [1963] 2 All E. R. 860. *Generally,* **Consd.** Comr. for Rys. *v.* Quinlan, [1964] 1 All
E. R. 897. **Refd.** Dunster *v.* Abbott, [1953] 2 All E. R.
1573; Hawkins *v.* Coulsdon & Purley U. D. C., [1954]
1 All E. R. 97; Phipps *v.* Rochester Corpn., [1955] 1
All E. R. 129; Herrington *v.* British Rys. Board,
[1971] 1 All E. R. 897.

243a. Occupier acting as guide —Special relationship.]—
HEARD *v.* NEW ZEALAND FOREST PRODUCTS, LTD.
(1960).—N.Z. *See* Continuation Vol. A.

243b. When status changes.]—STEPHENS *v.* CORCORAN (1968).
—CAN. *See* Continuation Vol. C.

275a. *Person on railway premises.*]—BLACKMAN *v.* RAILWAY
EXECUTIVE (1953). *See* Continuation Vol. A.

283. **Refd.** Bates *v.* Parker, [1952] 2 All E. R. 987; Hawkins
v. Coulsdon & Purley U. D. C., [1953] 2 All E. R. 364;
Wheat *v.* E. Lacon & Co., Ltd., [1966] 1 All E. R. 582.

284. **Consd.** Slade *v.* Battersea & Putney Group Hospital
Management Committee, [1955] 1 All E. R. 429.

284a. *Relation visiting patient in state hospital.*]—SLADE *v.*
BATTERSEA & PUTNEY GROUP HOSPITAL MANAGEMENT COMMITTEE (1955). *See* Continuation Vol. A.
Generally, **Refd.** Slater *v.* Clay Cross Co., [1956] 2 All
E. R. 625.

286. **Consd.** The Louis Sheid, [1958] 1 Lloyd's Rep. 606.
Refd. Roe *v.* Ministry of Health, Woolley *v.* Same,
[1954] 2 All E. R. 131; Moore *v.* R. Fox & Sons, [1956]
1 All E. R. 182; Overseas Tankship (U.K.), Ltd. *v.*
Morts Dock & Engineering Co., Ltd., [1961] 1 All
E. R. 404; Wheat *v.* E. Lacon & Co., Ltd., [1966] 1 All
E. R. 582; Swan *v.* Salisbury Construction Co., Ltd.,
[1966] 2 All E. R. 138; Ludgate *v.* Lovett, [1969] 2
All E. R. 1275; S. C. M. (U.K.), Ltd. *v.* W. J.
Whittall & Sons. Ltd., [1970] 2 All E. R. 417; Sir
Robert McAlpine & Sons, Ltd. *v.* Minimax, Ltd.,
Same *v.* Same, [1970] 1 Lloyd's Rep. 397.

287. **Refd.** Green *v.* Fibreglass, Ltd., [1958] 2 All E. R. 521;
Duncan *v.* London Borough of Lambeth, [1968] 1 All
E. R. 84.

290. **Folld.** Hartley *v.* Mayoh, [1953] 2 All E. R. 525.

260a. Swimmer in public pool.]—JAMES *v.* COUNCIL OF
MUNICIPALITY OF KOGARTH (1961).—AUS. *See* Continuation Vol. A.

261a. Customer in steam bath.]—BILINSKI *v.* NEHAJ (1954).

ON *v.* WATT

v. STEVENS

v. DELISLE
61).—CAN.

L AMERICAN
tion Vol. C.

WEALTH OF
ion Vol. C.

ND PRINGLE
ost.

MONWEALTH

768. **Distd.**
E. R. 318;
O'Reilly *v.* Imperial Chemical Industries, Ltd., [1955] 2
All E. R. 567. **Consd.** Wilson *v.* Tyneside Window
Cleaning Co., [1958] 2 All E. R. 265; Roles *v.* Nathan,
Roles *v.* Corney, [1963] 2 All E. R. 908; Bunker *v.*
Charles Brand & Son, Ltd., [1969] 2 All E. R. 59. **Refd.**
Hawkins *v.* Coulsdon & Purley U. D. C., [1954] 1 All
E. R. 97; Wingrove *v.* Prestige & Co., [1954] 1 All
E. R. 576; Cilia *v.* H. M. James & Sons, [1954] 2 All
E. R. 9; Phipps *v.* Rochester Corpn., [1955] 1 All E. R.
129; O'Reilly *v.* I. C. I., Ltd., [1955] 3 All E. R. 382;
Slater *v.* Clay Cross Co., [1956] 2 All E. R. 625; Riden
v. A. C. Billings & Sons, [1956] 3 All E. R. 357; Davie
v. New Merton Board Mills, Ltd., [1958] 1 All E. R. 67;
Smith *v.* Austin Lifts, Ltd., [1959] 1 W. L. R. 100;
Mace *v.* R. & H. Green & Silley Weir, Ltd., [1959] 1
All E. R. 655; McArdle *v.* Andmac Roofing Co., [1967]
1 All E. R. 583; S. C. M. (U.K.), Ltd. *v.* W. J. Whittall
& Son, Ltd., [1970] 2 All E. R. 417.

301. *Duty to exercise reasonable care—To prevent damage
from unusual danger—Which invitor knew or ought to
have known—Danger unknown to invitee.*]—BATES *v.*
PARKER (1953). *See* Continuation Vol. A.
Refd. Smith *v.* Austin Lifts, Ltd., [1959] 1 All E. R.
81; Wigley *v.* British Vinegars, Ltd., [1961] 3 All
E. R. 418.

302. *Generally,* **Refd.** Hawkins *v.* Coulsdon & Purley U. D.
C., [1954] 1 All E. R. 97; Comr. for Rys. *v.* Quinlan,
[1964] 1 All E. R. 897.

303. **Refd.** Braithwaite *v.* South Durham Steel Co., [1958]
3 All E. R. 161.

303a. *Duty to exercise reasonable care—To prevent damage
from unusual danger.*]—SLADE *v.* BATTERSEA & PUTNEY
GROUP HOSPITAL MANAGEMENT COMMITTEE (1955).
See Continuation Vol A (No. 284a).

FINDING ENGLISH CASES: ENGLISH AND EMPIRE DIGEST.

Step 3. After examining cases in main volume, a check should always be made in the Continuation Volumes and the Cumulative Supplement for later cases. This is one method of "Shepardizing" an English case.

* An asterisk indicates a Scottish, Irish or Commonwealth case.

[Illustration 116]

PAGE FROM 1935–56 PERMANENT INDEX, ALL ENGLAND LAW REPORTS

364 **ALL ENGLAND LAW REPORTS**

YEAR VOL. PAGE

INTESTACY
Succession—*Cases subject to special rules—continued.*
Rights of surviving spouse—" Personal chattels "—Herd of

FINDING ENGLISH CASES: ALL ENGLAND LAW RE-PORTS

This set may be used for finding cases reported after 1936. This illustration is from the 1935–56 Permanent Index. The subsequent Index volumes should also be consulted.

This Index only gives citations to the All England Reports.

INVESTMENT
Inducement to invest money. *See* CRIMINAL LAW.
Power to trustees under settlement—*Power to invest " in or upon such
investments as to them may seem fit "* [*Re* HARARI'S SETTLEMENT
TRUSTS] .. .. Ch.D. [1949] 1 430
Unit trust scheme. *See* UNIT TRUST (Scheme).

INVESTMENT CLAUSE
Power to vary investments. *See* TRUST AND TRUSTEE (Investments).
See also SETTLEMENT; WILL.

INVESTMENT COMPANY
Management expenses. *See* INCOME TAX (Repayment—*Management
expenses*).
Surtax. *See* SURTAX.

INVITEE
Bailment of goods with invitor—*Goods on invitor's premises* [TINSLEY
v. DUDLEY] .. .. C.A. [1951] 1 252
Canvasser—*Injury suffered on premises of potential customer—Liability
of occupier* [DUNSTER *v.* ABBOTT] .. .. C.A. [1953] 2 1572
Negligence—*Children injured by scalding tea spilt from an urn being carried
through narrow passage—Whether danger reasonably foreseeable—
Standard of care owed by occupier* [GLASGOW CORPN. *v.* MUIR]
H.L. [1943] 2 44
  *Customer at shop—Defective paving of forecourt to shop—Forecourt
in occupation of landlord of shop* [JACOBS *v.* LONDON COUNTY
COUNCIL] .. .. C.A. [1949] 1 790
H.L. [1950] 1 737
→ *Duty of shopkeeper—Slippery substance on floor* [TURNER *v.*
ARDING & HOBBS, LTD.] .. .. K.B.D. [1949] 2 911
 *Defective ladder removed from building operation—Ladder put back
by unknown person—Onus on invitee to prove invitor's responsibility
for or knowledge of replacement of ladder* [WOODMAN *v.* RICHARDSON
AND CONCRETE, LTD.] .. .. C.A. [1937] 3 866
 *Duty of occupier—Protection against unusual danger—Window
cleaner—Defective window sash—Window safe for ordinary purposes*
[GENERAL CLEANING CONTRACTORS, LTD. *v.* CHRISTMAS] .. C.A. [1952] 1 39
H.L. [1952] 2 1110
  *Protection against unusual danger—Window cleaner—Plywood
panel in window—Occupier's removal of bolts—Failure to
inform cleaner* [BATES *v.* PARKER] .. .. Assizes [1952] 2 987
C.A. [1953] 1 768
  *Workman falling from staging—Workman's knowledge
that staging faulty* [LONDON GRAVING DOCK CO., LTD. *v.*
HORTON] .. .. K.B.D. [1949] 2 169
C.A. [1950] 1 180
H.L. [1951] 2 1
  *Unusual danger—Neighbour entering premises at request of
occupier to tend occupier's bedridden wife—Fall and injury
to leg* [JENNINGS *v.* COLE] .. .. .. K.B.D. [1949] 2 191
   *Person visiting railway station to meet passenger—Oily
patch on platform* [STOWELL *v.* RAILWAY EXECUTIVE]
K.B.D. [1949] 2 193

[Illustration 117]

PAGE FROM INDEX VOLUME, HALSBURY'S LAWS OF ENGLAND

995 **IRELAND, REPUBLIC OF**

INVESTMENT—*contd.*
trustee, by—*contd.*
narrower-range investments—*contd.*
authorised by statute, **38**, 994
two groups of, **38**, 994
personal security, on, **38**, 989
powers, **38**, 993, 994
variation of, **38**, 990, 991
preference stock, in, **38**, 1008
prudence, duty to exercise, **38**, 994n
real securities, in, **38**, 1002, 1003
redeemable securities, in, **38**, 1008
retainer of investment, **38**, 1009
rights offers, **38**, 1007
special cases, **38**, 993
power, **38**, 992
special-range property—
meaning, **38**, 1000

FINDING ENGLISH CASES: HALSBURY'S LAWS OF ENGLAND.

This set is an encyclopedia of English law and should not be confused with Halsbury's Statutes of England.

Step 1. Locate appropriate reference in Index Volume. In this instance, the topic of "invitees" will be found in Vol. 28.

wider-range investments—
meaning, **38**, 993
advice, requirement as to, **38**, 997
authorised by statute, **38**, 997, 998
list of, **38**, 997–998
restrictions on, **38**, 997, 998–1000
trustee savings banks, by, **2**, 160
unauthorised, cestui que trust, by, **2**, 497
See also settled land, *above*
wife, by, in husband's name, **18**, 387

INVESTMENT COMPANY
meaning, **20**, 550
income tax, payment of. *See under* INCOME TAX
surtax liability. *See* INCOME TAX (surtax)

INVITEE
meaning, **28**, 47, 48
carrier of passengers, on premises of, **4**, 180
→ classification of, **28**, 49
common duty of care towards, **28**, 45
duty at common law towards, **28**, 45
licensee, distinguished from, **28**, 41, 48, 49
negligence in relation to, **28**, 41, 45, 47–49
overstaying invitation, **28**, 48
safety of, responsibility for, **28**, 43
theatre, public admitted as, **37**, 3, 4,
trespasser, becoming, **28**, 53n
visitor as, **28**, 47

INVOICE
meaning, **34**, 171
c.i.f. contract; requirement for. *See* C.I.F. [CONTRACT
company—
liquidation, notification on, **6**, 557
name to appear on, **6**, 429
consular, **34**, 171
form of, **34**, 171
prepacked food, for, **17**, 499, 502
provisional, effect of, **34**, 171
warranty, as, **17**, 599

INVOLUNTARY
act or omission, *meaning*, **10**, 272n

IONIAN ISLANDS
registration concerning the individual, **32**, 469, 470

IPSWICH
local court, **9**, 536
navigation rules, **35**, 869
petty court of bailiffs of, **9**, 537
public boxing and wrestling in, **37**, 51n

IRAN
missionary see in, **13**, 19n

IRAQ
exchange control, **27**, 112
independence of, **5**, 546

IRELAND
assurances of land for charitable purposes in, **4**, 264
Bank of. *See* BANK OF IRELAND
banns, publication of, in, **13**, 362

admission as students in England, **3**, 7
call to English Bar, **3**, 9n
Bills of Sale Acts inapplicable, **3**, 257
births, deaths, etc., admissibility of registers in [evidence, **15**, 388, 389
British nationality—
retention by citizens of Eire, **1**, 537, 538, 540, 541
through birth or parentage before 1949, **1**, 537
British subjects before 1949...**1**, 538, 539
chief representative—
distress, privilege from, **12**, 102
income tax exemption, **20**, 97n, 352, 600
privilege, **5**, 433n; **7**, 274, 275
suite, persons in, **7**, 274, 275, 276
citizens of—
citizenship of United Kingdom and Colonies by [registration, **1**, 538–540
claim to remain British subject by, **1**, 540, 541
former naturalised, deprivation of citizenship of [United Kingdom and Colonies, **1**, 562,
limitation on liability for crime, **1**, 531, 532
persons born before 6th December, 1922 in [Northern Ireland held to be, **1**, 539n
registration as citizens of United Kingdom and [Colonies, **1**, 550, 551
renunciation of citizenship of United Kingdom [and Colonies by, **1**, 559
retention of British nationality by, **1**, 538, 540, [541
treated as British subjects, **1**, 498, 531, 541
Commonwealth, secession from, **4**, 458, 459
company formed in, **6**, 833
consular immunities, conferment, **7**, 275
copyright. *See* COPYRIGHT
death duty legislation, not applicable in, **15**, 5
declaration of, **5**, 459
dentists, registration in England, **26**, 86n
diplomatic representatives, **5**, 459n
immunity, **5**, 433n; **7**, 7, 274
double taxation relief—
income tax. *See under* INCOME TAX
estate duty, **15**, 61
legacy duty, **15**, 96
profits tax, **20**, 464, 650
succession duty, **15**, 96
elections, right of citizens to vote, **14**, 10, 11
extradition procedure, **16**, 579n
foreign country, deemed not to be, **1**, 531, 537n, 538

[Illustration 118]

PAGE FROM HALSBURY'S LAWS OF ENGLAND, 3d Ed.

[Pt. 2, Sect. 1]   DUTY OF OCCUPIER   41

has a material interest (*l*); (3) those whom the occupier has licensed to enter the premises for their own purposes (*m*); and (4) persons who trespass upon the premises (*o*).

36. Common law distinction between duty to invitees and duty to licensees. At common law an invitee, using reasonable care on his part for his own safety, was entitled to expect that the occupier would on his part use reasonable care to prevent damage from unusual danger, of which he knew or ought to have known (*p*). The only duty owed by an occupier to a licensee was to warn him of concealed dangers actually known to the occupier but neither known nor obvious to the licensee (*q*). The clarity of this distinction between the duty owed to an invitee and that owed to a licensee had, however, become blurred even before the common law rules were superseded by statute (*r*). If physical facts constituting a concealed danger were known to the occupier and a reasonable man would have appreciated the risks involved, the occupier was treated as having known of the danger so as to render him liable to a licensee, and was not excused by his own failure to appreciate the risk (*s*).

37. The statutory rules. Statutory rules (*t*), in place of those of the common law, regulate the duty which an occupier of premises (*u*) owes to his visitors (*a*) in respect of dangers due to the state of the premises or to things done (*b*) or omitted to be done on them (*c*).

(*l*) Such persons are known as invitees; for the meaning of the term invitee and the distinction between invitees and licensees, see pp. 47 *et seq.*, *post*. For examples of invitees, see p. 49, *post*. There is some conflict of authority, now of little importance, whether the invitee, for his part, must share with the occupier a material interest in the purpose of the visit; see note (*g*), p. 48, *post*.

(*m*) For examples of licensees, see p. 50, *post*.

(*o*) For the limited duty owed to trespassers, see p. 53, *post*.

(*p*) *Indermaur* v. *Dames* (1866), L. R. 1 C. P. 274, at p. 288, *per* WILLES, J.; affirmed (1867), L. R. 2 C. P. 311, Ex. Ch. The word "unusual" is used objectively and means such danger as is not usually found in the circumstances; it is not to be construed subjectively

---

FINDING ENGLISH CASES: HALSBURY'S LAWS OF ENGLAND.

This set gives a textual treatment of the law and footnote citations to cases and statutes.

As it covers both cases and statutes, and has a good index, it is usually best to start the research for English law in this set. A loose-leaf volume keeps the set up-to-date and should always be consulted.

---

at pp. 330, 331; [1954] 1 All E. R. 97, at pp. 102, 103, *per* DENNING, L.J.; *Slade* v. *Battersea and Putney Group Hospital Management Committee*, [1955] 1 All E. R. 429; *Slater* v. *Clay Cross Co., Ltd.*, [1956] 2 Q. B. 264, C. A.; [1956] 2 All E. R. 625; *Perkowski* v. *Wellington Corpn.*, [1959] A. C. 53, P. C., at pp. 60, 61; [1958] 3 All E. R. 368, at p. 371. As to a similar distinction in the case of trespassers, see note (*g*), p. 54, *post*.

(*t*) See the Occupiers' Liability Act, 1957 (5 & 6 Eliz. 2 c. 31), ss. 2, 3.

(*u*) The Occupiers' Liability Act, 1957 (5 & 6 Eliz. 2 c. 31), binds the Crown, except that as regards the Crown's liability in tort that Act does not bind the Crown further than the Crown is made liable in tort by the Crown Proceedings Act, 1947 (10 & 11 Geo. 6 c. 44); the last-mentioned Act and in particular *ibid.*, s. 2 (see titles CONSTITUTIONAL LAW, Vol. 7, p. 251; CROWN PROCEEDINGS, Vol. 11, pp. 4 (note (*s*)), 11), apply in relation to duties under the Occupiers' Liability Act, 1957 (5 & 6 Eliz. 2 c. 31), ss. 2–4, as statutory duties (*ibid.*, s. 6).

(*a*) At common law a reciprocal duty is owed to the occupier by the visitor (*Lomas* v. *M. Jones & Son*, [1944] K. B. 4, C. A.; [1943] 2 All E. R. 548). See also *Sybray* v. *White* (1836), 1 M. & W. 435; *Re Williams* v. *Groucott* (1863), 4 B. & S. 149; *Hawken* v. *Shearer* (1887), 56 L. J. Q. B. 284, criticised in *Hickey* v. *Tipperary County Council*, [1931] I. R. 621.

For notes (*b*), (*c*), see next page.

2*

[Illustration 119]

PAGE FROM CURRENT LAW STATUTE CITATOR

STATUTE CITATOR 1947–71   **1893**

CAP.

56 & 57 Vict.—cont.

22. Appeal (Forma Pauperis) Act, 1893.
repealed: 12–4G.6,c.51,s.17(3)(b).

25. Burgh Police (Scotland) Act, 1893.
applied: 7–8E.2,c.24,s.29(7).
code 49/4801.

26. Prison (Officers' Superannuation) Act, 1893.
repealed: S.L.R. 1950.

27. Land Tax Commissioners Names Act, 1893.
repealed: S.L.R. 1964.

29. Railway Regulation Act, 1893.
repealed: S.L.R. 1960.

31. Rivers Pollution Prevention Act, 1893.

> CITATORS FOR ENGLISH STAT-
> UTES:
>
> This page from the Current Law
> Citator illustrates how citators are
> arranged chronologically and then
> alphabetically by title of Act. Ref-
> erences in this Citator are to the
> Current Law Year Books. For later
> developments be sure to consult the
> Statute Citator Section of the Cumula-
> tive Supplement, Current Law Citator.
> Other citators listed in Section F can
> be used in a similar manner.

s. 64, case 54/1590.
s. 69 (3), amended: 2–3E.2,c.43,s.10(4).
s. 74, regs. 52/1697; 58/1572.
sch. 2, para. 5, amended: 15–6G.6&1
E.2,c.17,s.1(1).

40. Public Works Loans (No. 2) Act, 1893.
repealed: 1964,c.9.sch.3.

52. Burghs Gas Supply (Scotland) Act, 1893.
repealed: 11–2G.6,c.67,sch.4.

53. Trustee Act, 1893.
applied: 6–7E.2,c.55,s.54(5).
s. 5 (4), repealed in part: 6–7E.2.c.11, sch.,II.
s. 21 (1), case 3882.

61. Public Authorities Protection Act, 1893.
case 53/2903.
repealed: 2–3E.2,c.36,s.1,sch.
s. 1, cases 751, 4154, 5759, 7599; 48/4288, 4454–4458; 49/4977, 5036; 50/4983, 5251; 51/3988, 4235, 4376; 52/2922, 4181; 53/4314; 54/3947, 3948; 55/1553, 1554, 3192, 3343; 56/5068, 11454; 63/4191; 64/543, 4395.
s. 3, cases 50/5071; 51/4235; 52/4274.

CAP.

56 & 57 Vict.—cont.

63. Married Women's Property Act, 1893.
article: 215 L.T. 289.
s. 2, repealed: 12–4G.6,c.78,sch.2.

66. Rules Publication Act, 1893.
case 9958.
repealed: 3–4E.2,c.8,sch.

69. Savings Banks Act, 1893.
applied: 12–4G.6,c.13.ss.11(1),13; c.47, s.48(3); 4–5E.2,c.6,s.5(10); 7–8E.2,c.6, s.15(3).
s. 5, sch. 1, repealed: 7–8E.2,c.6,sch.

71. Sale of Goods Act, 1893.
Repeals:
s. 22 (part), repealed: 1967,c.58,sch.3.
applied, restricted, etc.: 8–9E.2,c.65,s.7; 1964,c.53,s.27,sch.1; 1965,c.2,s.22; c. 66,ss.20,54; c.67,s.50.
articles: 14 M.L.R. 173; 1962 S.L.T. (News) 13, 137; 64 L.S.Gaz. 14.
cases 8190: 53/1801, 2979; 54/2991.
s. 1, case 67/1673.
s. 4, cases 9233, 9234, 9235; 52/3149; 53/3283; 54/2998, 2999; repealed: 2–3 E.2,c.34,s.2.
s. 7, case 9196.
s. 11, amended: 1967,c.7,s.4; cases 9244; 50/5328; 55/3656; 64/4422, 4426, 65/3530.
s. 12, article: 24 M.L.R. 690; cases 9239, 9243; 48/4840; 51/4451; 54/3000; 55/2495; 60/3975.
s. 13, cases 9252, 9254: 52/642; 53/3272, 3289; 67/3537.
s. 14, articles: 20 Sol. 87; 22 M.L.R. 484: cases 9189, 9190, 9196, 9244; 48/4844; 49/5123; 50/5328; 52/3131, 4497; 53/3268, 3269, 3272, 4620: 54/2979: 55/1840, 2477: 56/7940, 12882; 57/3205, 4339; 58/3034: 59/92, 4029: 60/2868, 2869; 62/2751, 2753, 3777; 65/3516, 3517; 66/10837: 67/3522.
s. 15, cases 9252: 56/8011: 60/2868.
s. 17, cases 61/626, 11181: 64/3284.
s. 18, cases 9238: 55/2841: 57/3221; 62/2769: 66/710, 2557, 10891.
s. 20, cases 9196, 9221.
s. 21, cases 56/7973; 57/3225; 64/1358.
s. 22, case 9232.
s. 23, case 9239.
s. 24, case 59/3384.
s. 25, cases 52/33; 53/3286; 55/3554; 57/3225; 59/2946, 2953: 65/3529.
s. 25 (2), (3), case 67/4682.
s. 26, case 58/223.
s. 28, cases 9238, 9241.
s. 30, case 62/2766.
s. 32, case 9223.
s. 34, case 53/3266.
s. 35, amended: 1967,c.7,s.4; cases 9184, 9247; 52/3152, 4499: 53/3284; 54/2072; 62/2750; 64/4426.
s. 38, case 58/1455.
s. 39, case 9238.
s. 43, case 57/4343.
s. 47, case 59/2946, 2953.

1181

[Illustration 120]

PAGE FROM CASE SECTION, CURRENT LAW CITATOR

CASE CITATOR 1947–67   **TUR**

Turner, *v.* Derham [1958] Ir.Jur.Rep. 78 .... *Digested,* **59/2284**
—— *v.* Ford Motor Co. [1965] 1 W.L.R. 948; 109 S.J. 354; [1965] 2
   All E.R. 583, C.A. .... *Digested,* **65/2277**
—— *v.* Forwood [1951] W.N. 189; [1951] 1 All E.R. 746; [211 L.T.
   250; 15 Conv. 183], C.A. .... *Digested,* **3744**
—— *v.* Garstang Rural District Council, 109 S.J. 176; 17 P. & C.R. 218;
   [1965] Crim.L.R. 306, D.C. .... *Digested,* 65/**2422**: *Subsequent proceedings,* 66/11740
—— *v.* —— (1965) 64 L.G.R. 28, D.C. .. *Digested,* 66/**11740**: *Previous proceedings,* 65/2422
—— *v.* Goldsmith [1891] 1 Q.B. 544 .... *Applied,* **53/1298**
—— *v.* Hancock (1882) 20 Ch.D. 303 .... *Applied,* **66/9781**
—— *v.* Hatton (Bradford) [1952] 1 T.L.R. 1184; [1952] 1 All E.R. 1286;
   [68 L.Q.R. 445] .... *Digested,* **52/3149**
—— *v.* Jacaranda Clubs [1953] 1 W.L.R. 961; 97 S.J. 491; [1953] 2 All
   E.R. 548 .... *Digested,* **53/2766**
—— *v.* Keiller, 1950 S.L.T. 66 .... *Digested,* **8442**
—— *v.* Last [1965] T.R. 249; 42 T.C. 517; 44 A.T.C. 234 .... *Digested,* **66/6052**
—— *v.* Liverpool Chief Constable [1965] Crim.L.R. 725; 115 L.J. 711 .. *Digested,* **65/1746**
—— *v.* Mason (1845) 14 M. & W. 112 .... *Distinguished,* **59/1168**
—— *v.* Metro-Goldwyn-Mayer Pictures [1950] W.N. 83; 66 T.L.R. (Pt. 1)
   342; 94 S.J. 145; [1950] 1 All E.R. 449; [66 L.Q.R. 145], H.L.;
   reversing (1948) 92 S.J. 541, C.A.; affirming (1947) 91 S.J. 495 ..
   Digested, 5662, 5663, 5664, **5666**, 5667, 5668: *Considered,* 54/1856: 63/1998:
   Applied, 62/1749: *Referred to,* 65/2269: *Dictum not followed,* 66/7036
—— *v.* Meyers (1808) 1 Hag.Con. 414 .... *Applied,* **53/2654**
—— *v.* Midgley [1967] 1 W.L.R. 1247; 111 S.J. 582; [1967] 3 All E.R.
   601, D.C. .... *Digested,* **67/3397**
—— *v.* National Coal Board (1949) 65 T.L.R. 580; [66 L.Q.R. 8], C.A. *Digested,* **6901**
—— *v.* Northern Life Assurance Co. [1953] 1 D.L.R. 427 .... *Digested,* **53/1792**
—— *v.* Stallibrass [1898] 1 Q.B. 56 .... *Applied,* 52/688; 66/567
—— *v.* Tavener, LVC/1757/1964 [1965] J.P.L. 684; [1965] R.V.R. 447;
   11 R.R.C. 209; 195 E.G. 257; [1965] R.A. 277, Lands Tribunal .. *Digested,* **65/3325**
—— *v.* Thorne and Thorne (1959) 21 D.L.R. (2d) 29 .... *Digested,* **60/3257**
—— *v.* Turner [1962] P. 283; [1961] 3 W.L.R. 1269; 105 S.J. 910; [1961]
   3 All E.R. 944, C.A.; affirming 105 S.J. 551; [232 L.T. 241], D.C.
   Digested, 61/**2906**: *Applied,* 63/1053
—— *v.* —— (1964). *See* Slatter's Will Trusts, *Re.*
—— *v.* Underwood [1948] 2 K.B. 284; [1949] L.J.R. 680; 112 J.P. 272;
   92 S.J. 379; [1948] 1 All E.R. 859; 46 L.G.R. 357, D.C. .... *Digested,* **2063**
—— *v.* Waterman (1961) 105 S.J. 1011 .... *Digested,* **61/5840**
—— *v.* Watts (1927) 44 T.L.R. 105 .... *Distinguished,* **54/2866**
—— *v.* —— (1928) 97 L.J.K.B. 403 .... *Applied,* 8895: *Distinguished,* 52/1947
—— *v.* Whitehouse, LVC/540–542/1964 [1965] J.P.L. 248; [1965] R.V.R.
   80; [1965] R.C.N. 50, Lands Tribunal .... *Digested,* **65/3325**
—— *v.* Wilson, 1954 S.C. 296; 1954 S.L.T. 131 .... *Digested,* **54/42**
Turner (G.) & Brothers, *Re, The Times,* February 25, 1959 .... *Reported,* **59/2548**
Turner (G. R.), *Ex p. See* R. *v.* Morleston and Litchurch Commissioners.
Turner & Son *v.* Owen [1956] 1 Q.B. 48; [1955] 3 W.L.R. 700; 120 J.P.
   15; 99 S.J. 799; [1955] 3 All E.R. 565n.; 54 L.G.R. 69, D.C. .... *Digested,* **55/1116**
Turner Bridger
   1959, Lan _____ gested, **60/3133**
Turner's Applic | | gested, **64/3123**
   Lands Tr | CITATORS FOR ENGLISH CASES. |
Turner's and H | | ested, 66/10320
   Lands Tr | Note how cases are listed alpha- | /1515; 61/4269
Turner's Will T | betically rather than by citation as in |
——, *Re*, Bridg | Shepard's Citations. References in this | gested, **59/3005**
   S.J. 545; | Citator are to the Current Law Year | gested, 67/**4069**
——, *Re*, Westn | Book. | rred to, 67/4077
Turney, *Re*, Tu | | gested, 52/**2969**
—— *v.* Hammo | |
Turpin *v.* Midd | Other citators listed in Section F | 7/2962; 58/593
    | may be used in a similar manner. | *ered,* 65/1271:
—— *v.* Turpin | | *lowed,* 65/1271
    |_____|
Turriff Construc
   nom. Cha |
   Industrial Tribunal .... *Digested,* 67/**1447**
Tursi *v.* Tursi [1958] P. 54; [1957] 3 W.L.R. 573; 101 S.J. 680; [1957] 2
   All E.R. 828; [20 M.L.R. 636] .... *Digested,* 57/**518**, 1055: *Followed,* 58/502

SECTION K. SUMMARY

A. Statutes
1. Current

    (a) The Public General Acts and Measures.

    (b) Law Reports, Statutes.

    (c) Current Law, Statutes.

2. Codification

    (a) The Statutes Revised, 3d ed. 1935–1948.

    (b) Statutes in Force, Official Revised Edition, 1972—To be completed in 1980. Looseleaf.

    (c) Halsbury's Statutes of England, 3d ed. Multi-volume collection of statutes in force arranged by topic. Most convenient set to locate English statutes.

B. Administrative Law

English regulations (delegated legislation) published separately as Statutory Instruments. Codified in the Statutory Rules and Orders and Statutory Instruments. Similar to U.S. Code of Federal Regulations. Also privately published in Halsbury's Statutory Instruments.

1. Indexes

    (a) Index to Government Orders. Issued biennially.

    (b) Index volume to Halsbury's Statutory Instruments.

C. Courts
1. Court Organization

Under the Courts Act 1971, English Courts organized as follows:

a. House of Lords

b. Supreme Court of Judicature

    (1) Courts of Appeal

    (2) High Court

        (a) Queen's Bench Division

        (b) Chancery Division

        (c) Family Division

2. Court Reporting

a. Law Reports. Quasi-official, selective in cases reported.

    (1) Law Reports. Appeal Cases. Decisions from House of Lords and Court of Appeals

    (2) Law Reports. Queen's Bench Division

    (3) Law Reports. Family Division

3. All England Law Reports

Privately published comprehensive reporting of English cases, started publication in 1936.

4. English Reports, Full Reprint

Reprint of English cases, 1220–1865.

5. Digests

    a. English and Empire Digest. A comprehensive digest of English cases with selective digests from Scotland, Ireland, Canada, and other countries of the Commonwealth.

    b. Current Law: Being a Complete Statement of All the Law from Every Source. Began publication in 1947.

    c. Halsbury's Laws of England. A comprehensive encyclopedia treatment of English law, cases and statutes.

Method of Citation. See Appendix A, Section II.

Chapter 22

CANADIAN LAW*

SECTION A.   INTRODUCTION

Canada is a federation consisting of ten provinces, and two Territories for which the federal government has direct authority, although power to legislate in certain areas has been delegated to Territorial Councils.   Therefore, in addition to the federal Parliament, there are twelve legislative bodies in Canada, each sovereign within its area of legislative competence.   The division of powers between the federal and the provincial jurisdictions has been laid down primarily by Sections 91 and 92 of the *British North America Act,* and it should be noted that the distribution of legislative power is different from that of the United States.   Criminal law, for example, has been placed under the legislative authority of the federal government.   Residual powers not specifically enumerated are left to the federal authority, not to the state (or province), as is the case in the United States.

In addition, within those areas reserved for exclusive provincial authority, nine provinces adhere strictly to a common law system whereas the tenth, Quebec, has a civil law system based on a civil code in the French tradition in matters concerning personal, family, and property relations.

Although the Imperial statute of 1867 entitled the *British North America Act,*[1] together with its amendments and additions, is of basic importance and is sometimes referred to as the Canadian Constitution, Canada does not have a written constitution embodied in a single document.   The written elements of the constitution are derived from a number of enactments, another example being the *Statute of Westminster, 1931.*[2]   In 1960, the *Canadian Bill of Rights*[3] was passed by the federal Parliament.

---

*This chapter was originally drafted and prepared by F. Diane Teeple, Reference Librarian, York University Law Library of Osgoode Hall Law School, Downsview, Ontario.

[1] 30 & 31 Vict., c. 3 (U.K.)

[2] 22 & 23 Geo.V., c. 4 (U.K.)   This statute provided that Canadian legislation could not be voided by Britain, and that no British law was enforceable in Canada unless by express consent of the federal Parliament; it also provided for the extraterritoriality of Canadian statutes.

[3] S.C.1960, c. 44.

In addition, Canada shares with Britain a tradition of "conventions" or "customs" which form the unwritten elements of the Canadian Constitution and are not included in the documentary sources.

SECTION B.   JUDICIAL REPORTS

1.   Canadian Court Organization

The British North America Act gives the provinces exclusive jurisdiction with respect to "the constitution, maintenance, and organization of provincial courts, both of civil and of criminal jurisdiction". (Section 92(14)). For most purposes, there are no separate federal and provincial courts, but both federal and provincial matters are tried in the same courts. The federal Parliament, however, has been given the power to appoint the judges of the higher courts in the provinces exclusive jurisdiction over criminal law (except the constitution of the courts of criminal jurisdiction, but including procedure in criminal matters) and power to establish a general court of appeal for Canada, as well as any additional courts for the better administration of the laws of Canada. The general court of appeal is the Supreme Court of Canada, and a Federal Court of Canada has also been established.

a.   The Supreme Court of Canada.

The final court of appeal for both civil and criminal cases; no cases begin in the Supreme Court, but are referred to it by the provincial courts of appeal or the Federal Court. On appeals from the provincial courts, the Supreme Court sits as a court of appeal for that province, rather than as a federal court of appeal.

b.   The Federal Court of Canada.

Established in 1970, this court consists of a Trial and an Appeal Division, and has original jurisdiction in those areas formerly within the purview of the Exchequer Court. These are, for example, matters involving claims against the Crown, certain income-tax disputes, industrial property, and admiralty. In addition, it has certain new functions such as the power to hear appeals from the decisions of federal administrative tribunals.

c.   Provincial Courts.

Although the courts differ in name and to a certain extent in jurisdiction from province to province, the basic structure may be characterized as:

(1) a lower tier consisting of the lowest ranking criminal courts (known variously in the provinces as Magistrates' Courts,

Police Courts, or Provincial Courts), and civil courts (known as the Small Claims Courts, Division Courts, Justice's Courts, or Magistrate's Civil Courts) ;

(2) a middle tier comprised of courts with both civil and criminal jurisdiction known as the County or District Courts;

(3) and the highest ranking court in each province, usually known as the Supreme or Superior Court.

2. Canadian Court Reports

Canadian law reports are very selective, even where official reports exist. Both official and unofficial reports are citable in court, and privately-published general series such as the *Dominion Law Reports* or regional reports such as the *Western Weekly Reports* are relied upon exclusively by those provinces which do not publish official reports.

a. Official National Reports

(1) *Canada Supreme Court Reports.* 1876– ——   These cover cases from the Supreme Court, and are issued in monthly paper-bound advance sheets which are replaced by an annual bound volume. Mimeographed slip decisions called "Reasons for Judgment" are also issued by the Supreme Court.

(2) *Canada Exchequer Court Reports.* 1876–1970. This series of reports covered cases involving claims against the Crown, patents, inventions, copyrights and trademarks and admiralty matters, as well as inter-provincial and federal-provincial disputes.

(3) *Canada Federal Court Reports.* 1971–——   Cases from the Federal Court, Trial Division which has original jurisdiction in those areas formerly within the jurisdiction of the Exchequer Court, together with cases of the Appeal Division which has jurisdiction in appeal from every decision in the Trial Division, as well as appeals from federal administrative tribunals, are covered by this series of law reports. Slip decisions are available for the Federal Court as well.

b. Unofficial National Reports

(1) The *Dominion Law Reports*, published from 1912 to the present, contain cases of all jurisdictions, including the highest provincial appellate courts as well as the Supreme and Federal Courts, and is the most comprehensive set. Advance sheets are published weekly.

(2) The *National Reporter* law reports began publication in 1974. Patterned after the National Reporter System, this series contains all the judgments of the Supreme Court of Canada and the Fed-

eral Court, Appeal Division, together with selected decisions of the Trial Division. The reports provide the text of the judgments considerably in advance of their appearance in the official series.

c.   Unofficial Regional Reports

For the Maritime provinces, these include the *Maritime Provinces Reports* which covered the period 1929–1968, and a successor, the *Atlantic Provinces Reports*, which began publication in 1975; for the West, there is the *Western Weekly Reports*, a series which began publication in 1911 and is still published currently.

As in the United States, there are also many special subject reports covering particular legal areas.

d.   Official and Privately Published Provincial Reports

All provinces have had official or quasi-official law reports, but many have ceased publication. The following are currently published:

(1) *Ontario Reports.* 1882–—— These are considered official, although they are published by the Law Society rather than the government. Cases determined in the courts of Ontario which are considered to be of permanent significance are included. A second series began publication in 1974.

(2) *Les Recueils de jurisprudence du Québec, Cour d'appel.* 1970–—— The Queen's Bench Reports (*Les Rapports judiciares du Québec, Cour du banc de la reine*) were the predecessor of these reports, covering the period 1892–1969. Decisions appealed to the highest provincial appeal court are included.

(3) *Les Recueils de jurisprudence du Québec, Cour superior.* 1892–—— Included are reports of decisions of the Superior Court and the Provincial (formerly Magistrates) Court.

In addition, Quebec has a number of unofficial report series such as *Rapports de pratique de Québec/Quebec Practice Reports.* 1898–—— and *La Revue Légale, nouvelle séries,* 1895–——

(4) *New Brunswick Reports, second series,* 1969–—— Decisions of the New Brunswick Supreme Court and occasionally certain other New Brunswick courts, together with selected decisions of the Supreme Court of Canada and Federal Court of Canada originating in New Brunswick are included. The first series covered the period 1825–1928. This series, together with the *Newfoundland and Prince Edward Island Reports,* and the *Nova Scotia Reports, second series, infra,* are published by the Maritime Law Book Company and contain editorial features similar to those of the *National Reporter System.*

(5) *Newfoundland and Prince Edward Island Reports,* 1971–—— This combined series includes decisions of the appeal courts of Newfoundland and Prince Edward Island, certain decisions of other

provincial courts, and Supreme and Federal Court decisions of cases originating in either of the provinces. There was also a series of *Newfoundland Reports* covering the period 1817–1946.

(6) *Nova Scotia Reports, second series.* 1970– —— Included are decisions of the Nova Scotia Court of Appeal and certain other Nova Scotia courts. Two volumes have been published subsequently covering the period 1965–1969. An earlier series covered the years 1834 to 1929.

(7) *P.E.I. Supreme Court Reports*, 1971– —— This recently issued official series has wider coverage of Supreme Court cases, but includes none of the editorial features found in the Maritime Law Book series covering P.E.I. Only one volume has been published to date.

3. Authority of Canadian Cases

a. English Decisions

Prior to 1933 for criminal and 1949 for civil cases, the highest court of appeal for Canada was the Judicial Committee of the Privy Council sitting in London, England. Canadian courts before 1950 were bound to follow decisions of the Privy Council. The colonial appellate courts were considered bound to follow English decisions generally, since uniformity of interpretation was felt desirable. English decisions are now considered persuasive, but not binding.

b. Supreme Court of Canada Decisions

These decisions are binding upon all provincial courts.

c. Provincial Appellate Court Decisions

Decisions of the highest provincial appellate court are binding upon all the lower courts of that jurisdiction. Judgments of courts of co-ordinate jurisdiction are generally followed in the absence of strong reasons to the contrary.

SECTION C. DIGESTS AND ENCYCLOPEDIAS

1. Digests

a. *The Canadian Abridgment*

The most comprehensive digest is the *Canadian Abridgment* which provides subject access to Canadian case law by digesting the cases of all common law jurisdictions under alphabetically-arranged legal topics. Decisions from the courts of Quebec of universal application are included as well. Cases concerned with more than one point of law will be digested under several headings with cross-refer-

ences to the classification where it is treated in length. For each case, an original editorial analysis of the case is included, not a reproduction of the head-notes.

The first edition has now been superseded by the second edition, except for the following volumes still in process of publication at the time of writing: a consolidated Table of Cases, a volume of Words and Phrases, Statutes Judicially Considered, and a General Index.

The second edition currently consists of:

(1) *The Canadian Abridgment*: a digest of reported decisions of the Supreme Court and Exchequer Court of Canada, and of all courts of the Common Law provinces, including appeals to the Privy Council and also decisions from the courts of Quebec of universal application. 2d ed. 38 v. Toronto, Carswell, 1966–74.

—— – ——. *Practice Volumes* 1–3. 1967–70.

—— – ——. *First Permanent Supplement,* covering reports up to December 31, 1974. 3v. (Updates subject titles of the 2d ed. Includes Titles Key for the 2d ed.)

—— – ——. *Cumulative Supplement.* lv. looseleaf. annual. (Updates subject titles of the 2d ed. and First Permanent Supplement. Updated by *Canadian Current Law.*)

—— – ——. *Appendix.* lv. looseleaf. annual. (Includes Cases Judicially Considered from 1974 on and a periodical index with coverage from 1956).

(2) *The Canadian Abridgment. Table of Cases Judicially Considered in Canadian Reports* * * * to December 31, 1973. 4v. 1975–76. (Continued by Cases Judicially Considered in Appendix binder, and in monthly issues of *Canadian Current Law.*)

The Topic Method of Legal Research must be used with this digest, because it does not yet contain a comprehensive table of cases or word index. Each subject title contains a scope note and outline of topical divisions used. (See Illustration 121) The Index Method is permitted to some extent by the word index for each topic contained in the individual volumes of the second edition. To locate the appropriate topic, it is useful to consult the Titles Key found in the First Permanent Supplement, listing those titles which have been used in the second edition and supplement. Once the relevant section has been located in the main volumes, later case summaries are found by checking the same topic and subtopic in the supplement and looseleaf updating services. Subdivision designations are placed in round brackets above each case digest.

b. *Supreme Court of Canada Reports Service*

This set is comprised of three looseleaf volumes which serve as a subject index to all reported decisions of the Supreme Court of

Canada, plus a current service volume.   Although primarily indexing the *Supreme Court Reports*, the service includes certain decisions reported only in other series such as the *Dominion Law Reports*.   The consolidated index covers the period 1876–1969, and presents a synopsis of the subject matter of the cases.   Later material is located in the service issue in volume three.   There is also a case table and a supplemental case table.

The most recent material is included in a fourth volume, the current service, containing full digests of all reasons for judgment released by the Court during the current year.   Issued quarterly, it is intended to include digests of decisions in advance of their publication in the law reports.   Another source for locating recent unreported decisions is *Notes of Recent Judgments in the Supreme Court of Canada*, published in an English and a French language version by the Canadian Law Information Council since 1974.

c.   *Butterworths Ontario Digest, Replacement Edition*

This twelve-volume looseleaf digest of cases provides an index to Ontario case law from 1901.   Cases are classified into titles with each assigned a key (i. e. case) number, with the cases numbering consecutively throughout the volume.

The digest of the case is followed by annotations showing where the digested case has been judicially considered in later cases.   Cross references refer to related titles and subdivisions, as well as indicating where the full treatment is given for related cases.

Volume 12 contains a subject index with references not only to cases since 1901 digested in B.O.D., but also to cases included in the *Digest of Ontario Case Law*, 1823–1900.   Volume 12 provides, in addition, a complete list of titles and subsections included, if the legal analysis approach to the set is being used.   A consolidated Table of Cases is included in Volume 11.   Each volume also contains a Table of Statutes Cited for the topics included in that volume, as well as a Reference Adapter converting digest numbers from the old edition to the current replacement edition.

The B.O.D. is updated annually in each volume by a cumulative Service issue with its own case table, index, and statute citator.   The quarterly Noter-up to Recent Cases refers to more recent case summaries appearing in the *Canadian Weekly Law Sheet* by means of a parallel reference table.

Other currently published Canadian digests include the following:

d.   Beauchamp, Jean Joseph.

Répertoire général de jurisprudence canadienne contenant un résumé, sous forme alphabétique et chronologique, de toutes les

décisions judiciaires rapportées du Conseil privé, de la Cour suprême, de la Cour de l'échiquier, des cours d'amiraute, de la Commission des chemins de fer et des tribunaux de la province de Québec et toute la puissance du Canada dans tout ce qui tombe sous la juridiction du Parlement fédéral, depuis 1770 jusqu'à mai 1913, ainsi qu'une référence aux matières qui se trouvent dans les statuts fédéraux et provinciaux et le texte de ces lois se rapportant au droit civil avec divers appendices.   Montréal, Wilson et Lafleur, 1914–1915.   4v.
_____. Supplément * * * 1913–1925, by J. F. Saint Cyr. 2v.
_____. Supplément * * * 1926–1935, by Maurice Tellier. 2v.
_____. Supplément * * * 1935–1955, by Robert Leveque. 2v.
Continued by *Annuaire de jurisprudence du Quebec* (Montreal, Wilson and Lafleur) since 1955.

This digest includes the decisions of the Quebec courts, with case digests in French or in English if the case was originally published in English.   The subject titles are in French.

e. *Canadian Current Law,* v. 1– 1948–.   Toronto, Carswell, 1948– eleven numbers per year.

This is used primarily as an updating service for the *Canadian Abridgment 2d,* and has contained subject titles identical to those of the *Abridgment* since 1966; and since 1971 the designation of the *Abridgment* subject classification has appeared at the head of the case summaries in round brackets.   Since January, 1973, federal statutes, regulations, and administrative board decisions have been included.   Since January 1974, the designation of the subject classification for the *Canadian Encyclolpedic Digest (Ontario 3d edition)* has also been given, thus making it a monthly noter-up for this legal encyclopedia as well.

f.   Regional and Provincial Digests

Since the beginning of 1975, *Western Weekly Reports* has included digests of additional Western decisions on a weekly basis. All digests have been reproduced in an annual volume, to be issued on a continuing basis.   In 1976, the Maritime Law Book Company issued a digest similar to West's State Key Number Digests covering the first nine volumes of the *New Brunswick Reports,* 2d series.   In addition, individual loose-leaf digests of all decisions of the intermediate and appellate courts have become available for British Columbia (1972–), Alberta, (1974–), Manitoba, (1975–), and Saskatchewan, (1975–), published by Western Legal Publications in Vancouver.   Since 1971, summaries of unreported judgments of the Ontario Court of Appeal have appeared in the paperbound advance sheets of the *Ontario Reports,* with an index published by the Great Library, Law Society of Upper Canada, Department of Continuing Education.

2. Encyclopedias

There are two current Canadian legal encyclopedias, the *Canadian Encyclopedic Digest, Ontario,* which has recently begun publication in a third edition, and the *Canadian Encyclopedic Digest, Western,* which is presently in its second edition. As in American legal research, the encyclopedias provide a starting place for legal research, but their statements of the law applicable to a particular problem are generally regarded as very elementary.

a. *Canadian Encyclopedic Digest (Ont. 2d)*

Since the third edition began publication quite recently, the second edition is still primarily in use. Published in 22 volumes, the set provides a survey of the law of Ontario and the Maritimes, with federal law treated when applicable. It was designed to provide access to the case law, but reference is made to the statutes when required in order to explain the case law.

A Consolidated Analysis, which is a compilation of the tables of contents of all topics included, serves as a general index for the set, but necessitates use of the Topic Method rather than the Index Method, because it is not a word index.

Finally, two citators for the Ontario statutes are included, *Ontario Statutes Judicially Considered, 1859–1950,* and *Ontario Statutes Judicially Considered, 1951–1972.*

b. The looseleaf *Canadian Encyclopedic Digest (Ont. 3d)* promises to remedy many of the deficiencies of C.E.D. (Ont. 2d) with its continuing currency through a looseleaf format, its provision of word indexes for each title (which are to be compiled in one volume upon completion of the set), and its equal emphasis upon the case and the statute law. On the other hand, wider treatment of statute law has been gained at the expense of the coverage of the Maritimes provinces, which are now excluded except in the footnotes. These cover all provinces.

For the Western provinces, the C.E.D. (Western 2d) follows the format of the second edition of the Ontario encyclopedia, with the added feature of a Words and Phrases volume.

Canadian Encyclopedic Digest (Western) being a complete digest on the encyclopedic plan of all reported decisions in Alberta, British Columbia, Manitoba, Saskatchewan and appealed therefrom. 2d ed. Calgary, Burroughs, 1956–1969. 22v.

_____. *First Permanent Supplement,* 1968. Calgary, Burroughs, 1969. 73p. Kept up to date by annual cumulative supplements. Vol. 22, *Index of Words and Phrases Judicially Noticed in Canadian Reports.*

SECTION D. STATUTES

1. Current Statutes

Canadian statutes are published chronologically, in annual volumes arranged by chapter number. Each volume contains the text of the acts passed during a session of the legislature, a Table of Contents listing the acts by short title, a subject index of the acts, usually a Table of Proclamations, and a Table of Public Statutes. The Table of Public Statutes gives the short title of public acts in force, where they can be found, and any amendments to them.

2. Consolidation of Statutes

Since the statutes are published chronologically as passed, it is necessary to provide subject access to those in force. In Canada, this is done by compiling and consolidating every statute in force at certain intervals. Amendments are incorporated into the parent acts and rewritten as necessary, although no new substance is added. Repealed or lapsed legislation is omitted, as well as temporary acts, and acts no longer considered to be of importance, although still in effect.

The consolidation, known as the *Revised Statutes*, is arranged alphabetically by short title of the consolidated acts, and when brought into force it repeals and replaces the previous revision and subsequent sessional volumes. If there is a conflict between the *Revised Statutes* and the original legislation, the version found in the *Revised Statutes* prevails.

Each jurisdiction attempts to revise its statutes on a regular basis, and the Revisions are supplemented by an annual volume of session laws, known as the annual statutes in Canada. Access to the statutes is by means of a subject index included with most Revisions, although these indexes are usually detailed tables of contents listing the statutes by short title, rather than true word indexes. (See Illustration 124)

For new acts or amendments since the current Revision, a Table of Public Statutes is included (usually on coloured pages) which is a statute citator listing all the acts in the Revision and subsequent amendments, as well as any new statutes passed. There is a slip law service for the federal statutes (the *Canada Gazette Part III*), but none for the provinces. Commercial indexing services for the bills are available for some jurisdiction,[4] but not all.

---

[4] *A Current Legislative Digest* is published for federal and Ontario bills which provides a weekly summary of legislative action for government bills. The service is distributed by Richard De Boo Ltd. Two provinces (British Columbia and Saskatchewan) include a "Progress of Bills" table in *Votes and Proceedings*, the daily record of proceedings of the Legislatures.

Most Canadian statutes come into force when they receive Royal Assent. To determine when a statute becomes operative, it is necessary to check the statute to see whether it provides the date that it shall become effective. The provision will usually be in the final sections, and will name a specific date, or state that it comes into force on Royal Assent, or when proclaimed. For statutes which are silent, the Interpretation Act of the jurisdiction will usually state when they are to be considered effective.

3. Revised Statutes of Canada, 1970

The *Revised Statutes of Canada 1970* consists of seven volumes of statutes consolidated to December 31, 1969, two Supplements covering those sessions of Parliament held before the Revision was proclaimed into force on July 15, 1971, an Appendix volume containing constitutional documents and the *Canadian Bill of Rights,* and an Index.

The Supplements were issued because the delay in proclamation meant that certain statutes found in the Revision had been amended before it came into force. Supplement 1, generally speaking, repeals and replaces the annual statute volume for 1969–70. Supplement 2 contains only those statutes for the session 1970–71–72 which amend R.S.C.1970 or Supplement 1, and for new legislation, the 1970–71–72 annual volume is used. The Table of Public Statutes in the *Canada Gazette Part III* will lead the user to the correct volume, however, so that in practice the Revision is less difficult to use than would appear to be the case.

The 2d Supplement contains useful Tables which supersede those found in the Appendix:

(1) Schedule A, a Table showing the acts repealed and replaced by R.S.C.1970, and the extent of the repeal.

(2) A Table showing the History and Disposal of Acts, indicating all statutes in force which have been examined for inclusion in R.S.C.1970, and where they may be located in the Revision.

(3) A Table of Public Statutes to the entire R.S.C.1970, showing the location of acts in the R.S.C. and its Supplements. This Table is updated by that found in the *Canada Gazette Part III.*

(4) A Table of unconsolidated acts, those acts not included in the Revised Statutes (although still in effect) usually because they were temporary, international Agreements, of limited application, or no longer considered to be of importance.[5]

---

[5] The *Canadian Bill of Rights* is an unconsolidated act which is still cited S.C. 1960, c. 44, because it has not been included in the Revision, but is in the Appendix

In addition to these tables, each volume of R.S.C.1970 contains a Table of Contents listing the acts included alphabetically by short title. There is also a one-volume general index.

SECTION E.   CITATORS

As with English legal research, "Shepardizing" is referred to as "noting up" cases and statutes, and there is no comprehensive service analogous to *Shepard's Citations*.   Instead, several services perform partial citator functions, and the careful researcher will check the information found in one service against that given in another before he assumes that his information is complete.[6]   The following outline includes only currently published citators which are of a general rather than a specialized nature in their coverage.

1.   Statutes

a.   Table of Public Statutes.

This Table is the authoritative source for locating amendments to the statutes to the end of the period for which it is available.   The federal Table includes amendments made by regulation which the *Canada Statute Citator, infra*, does not, and it also notes any cases which have declared statutes or portions of statutes to be *ultra vires*.

b.   *The Canada Statute Citator, R.S.C.1970 ed.*, a Complete Annotating Service for R.S.C.1970.   Toronto, Canada Law Book Co., 1971– —— 2v., looseleaf.

This service provides, under the short title of the act, the text of current amendments to the statutes appearing in R.S.C.1970.   New statutes are also noted, but the text is not printed in full.   The date that the amending statute comes into force is shown after the short title, and also the name of the department administering the act. (See Illustration 125)   The primary function of the service is to provide summaries of cases giving judicial interpretation of the statutes, however.

For older cases, the *Canada Statute Annotations*, a collection of cases on the statutes of Canada arranged according to chapter numberings of R.S.C.1970, (but in strict alphabetical sequence by title rather than by subject matter as in the Revision,) presents pertinent

volume with the other constitutional acts and documents. According to the House of Commons *Debates* of April 19th, 1971, at 5021–5023, it was omitted because a technical repeal and replacement would have occurred had it been included, and also because it was widely known by its original form and chapter designation.

6 For a more complete listing of Canadian tools which function as case and statute citators, see E. Boultbee, " 'Noting Up' of Canadian Cases and Statutes," 65 L.Lib.J., 19–32 (1972).

cases back to 1941.   Notes on the history of the acts are also included.   Citators keyed to the earlier Revisions were issued as well.
Source references at the end of each section in R.S.C.1970 indicate the
former citation for that section.

Similar services are available for some provinces, namely Ontario, British Columbia, and Saskatchewan.   Many digests and encyclopedias (*Canadian Abridgment, Butterworth's Ontario Digest,
Replacement Edition.   Canadian Current Law*, and the *Canadian
Encyclopedic Digest (Ont. 2d)*) have statute citator features as well.

2.   Cases

The most comprehensive case citator is published as part of the
*Canadian Abridgment.   Table of Cases Judicially Considered In Cana-
dian Reports*   *   *   *   to December 31, 1973.   4v. 1975–76.   (Continued by Cases Judicially Considered in Appendix binder, and in
monthly issues of *Canadian Current Law*.)

These indexes are not restricted to Canadian cases, but include
Commonwealth cases judicially noticed in Canadian reports.   Separately published case citators are:

> *Dominion Law Reports.   Annotation service.   (second and
> third series)*   Toronto, Canada Law Book, 1970– annual.

This tool is patterned after *Shepard's Citations*, but is limited in
coverage.   Cases reported in the second and third series of the
Dominion Law Reports are listed according to the volume and page
number at which the case appeared, and an indication is given of
whether the case has been appealed, and the nature of any judicial
consideration given to it by later cases.

> *Index Gagnon*.   Edited by Louis-Philippe Gagnon.   Montreal,
> privately published.   1966.   lv., looseleaf; also published 1971, 1974
> and Mise a jeur, 1974.

This case citator lists, under the name of Quebec cases, any subsequent citation to them by later cases.   The main work covers the
period 1923–1965, with supplements providing coverage to 1974.

SECTION F.   CANADIAN ADMINISTRATIVE LAW

In Canada, the Governor-General in Council (in practice, the
Cabinet), is the authority most frequently empowered by statute
to make or approve regulations.   The present decade has brought
considerable growth in the creation of administrative boards, however, and their orders, regulations, and decisions form an increasingly important, although virtually unorganized, part of Canadian legal
bibliography.   Subordinate or delegated legislation is the term used

to describe orders, rules and regulations emanating from the executive or administrative branches of the government, or from an independent regulatory agency. Similarly, "regulations" is a generic term referring to those rules, regulations, by-laws or orders made pursuant to a particular statute.

1. Federal Statutory Regulations

a. *The Canada Gazette.*

Regulations are published in the *Canada Gazette,* a publication similar to the *Federal Register.* Part II, issued biweekly, contains the text of the regulations; the weekly Part I contains all official government notices which are required by statute to be published, such as charters and supplementary letters patent granted to federally incorporated companies, or notices regarding the summoning, opening, prorogation, and dissolution of Parliament. Part III, described earlier, is a slip law service for the federal statutes which began publication in 1975.

b. Publication of Regulations Prior to 1947.

Before 1940, there was no systematic requirement for the publication of federal regulations unless provided for by the statute authorizing the regulation—making power. Those regulations which were published may be located in the *Canada Gazette* which was published in one part prior to 1947, or in a preliminary section of the statute volumes for the period 1875–1939. From 1940–1945, regulations relating to the prosecution of the war were published separately. In 1945, the name changed to *Statutory Orders and Regulations* and publication continued until 1947.

c. Publication of Regulations After 1947.

Since January 1st, 1947, federal subordinate legislation has been published in Part II of the *Canada Gazette,* issued biweekly. In 1950, the *Regulations Act* was first enacted, and this statute set down those regulations to be published and the procedure for publishing them, as well as listing those regulations to be exempted from publication. The *Regulations Act* was replaced by the *Statutory Instruments Act,* S.C. 1970–71–72 c. 38, in force January 1st, 1972, which provides a wider definition of regulations to be published currently, but also wide and vague exemption of large classes of regulations from either publication or scrutiny.

2. Consolidation

Although there is no Canadian equivalent to the *Code of Federal Regulations,* regulations are consolidated from time to time. Regulations currently in force are rewritten to include all amendments, and the version found in the Consolidation then replaces the original

regulation.   There have been two federal Consolidations, one issued in 1949, and a second in 1955.   Since 1955, individual regulations have been consolidated from time to time on an *ad hoc* basis.

The *Statutory Orders and Regulations Consolidation*, 1955, includes the text of the regulations arranged alphabetically by short title of the authorizing act, and a general index to the regulations.

From 1955 to date, the text of the regulations may be located in the *Canada Gazette, Pt. II*.   These are bound annually with the binder's title *Statutory Orders and Regulations*, and are cited S.O.R./65– 106 (referring to number 106 of the *Statutory Orders and Regulations* for 1965) for the period 1947–1972.   In 1973, the name changed to *Statutory Instruments/Textes réglementaires*.   Citation is the same except for those instruments which bear the designation "S.I.", in which case the citation is: SI/73–56.

3.   Search Method

The *Consolidated Index of Statutory Instruments*, issued quarterly with the *Canada Gazette*, lists under the short title of the authorizing act regulations currently in force and where they may be located, whether in the 1955 Consolidation, or in subsequent issues of the *Canada Gazette Pt. II*.   The Table is prepared to show the citation of every regulation and whether it has been amended.   It indicates for each regulation whether it is new, spent, or revises or revokes a previous regulation.   Those few Statutory Orders and Regulations not made pursuant to statutory authority are listed at the end of the Table under a separate heading "Other Than Statutory Authority".

In addition, there is a Table of Regulations Exempt from Publication, (Section III of the *Consolidated Index*) which should be checked to see whether there are relevant regulations that are unpublished, and where they may be inspected.

If the authorizing act is not known, the general index appearing before the Table in the Consolidated Index may be used.   This is an index of the regulations by title, however, rather than a true subject index.   It refers the researcher to the short title of the authorizing act.   The general indexes to the consolidations can also be checked for subject matter, but they are fairly out of date and should be updated by the *Consolidated Index*.

The *Consolidated Index* is bound in each annual volume of the S.O.R.'s, and shows all regulations that were in force at the end of that year.   It is possible to trace back annually through regulations in force to find those regulations in force at a particular point in time.   Even if a regulation were made and revoked during the same year, it would be listed.

The latest issue of the quarterly Consolidated Index for the current year is updated by an index search of subsequent issues of Part II of the *Canada Gazette*. Since no references are given to sections affected by later amendments, it is necessary to examine all amendments listed.

4. Coming Into Force

Unless the regulation or the empowering statute provides otherwise, regulations come into effect when registered. However, s. 11(2) of the *Statutory Instruments Act* provides that no person shall be convicted under an unpublished regulation, unless reasonable steps have been taken to bring it to his attention.

5. Administrative Decisions and Rulings

There is no comprehensive reporting system as yet for the decisions and rulings of Canadian administrative boards, either at the federal or the provincial level. Some boards, in fact, take the view that since their decisions are not binding and each case is dealt with on its own merits, they are not obliged to publish reasons for their decisions. Therefore, decisions in some cases are not published and are not available, or are available only to parties affected by the decision.

Many boards do issue their decisions,[7] however, usually on a selective basis, and usually either in mimeographed form, or as part of the annual report that the board is required to present to Parliament.

In addition, selected decisions of the administrative tribunals are included in many looseleaf services and unofficial topical reports covering particular fields.

SECTION G. CITATORS FOR FEDERAL ADMINISTRATIVE MATERIALS

Although no comprehensive service exists, some tools do perform partial citator function in this area.

a. For Regulations:

    (1) Canada Gazette Part II/Gazette du Canada, partie II, *Consolidated Index of Statutory Instruments/Index codifié des textes réglementaires*. Table II, "Table of Regulations, Statutory Instruments, (other than Regulations), and Other Documents", lists amendments to the regulations since the

---

[7] For a detailed survey of the published decisions of Canadian administrative agencies see A. Janisch, *Publication of Administrative Board Decisions in Canada; a Report*. (London, Ont.: Canadian Association of Law Libraries, 1972).

Consolidation of 1955. Similar tables exist for many of the provinces, indicating any changes since the latest consolidation; others list only amendments for the current year.

(2) Looseleaf services such as the CCH *Canadian Labour Law Reporter.*

b. For Decisions:

(1) Looseleaf services such as *Dominion Tax Cases* list appeals pending from the Tax Review Board, for example. No comprehensive service is available.

c. Provincial Statutory Regulations

Provincial subordinate legislation is published in the official Gazette of the jurisdiction, usually in a separate part two containing only the regulations. Revisions of regulations occur in some, but not all, provinces at regular intervals.

———

SECTION H.   CANADIAN PERIODICAL INDEXES

Index to Canadian Legal Periodical Literature, ed. by
M. Scott.   Montreal, Canadian Association
of Law Libraries, 1961–

This is a bimonthly publication indexing all articles on law found in Canadian periodicals, as well as certain collected essays and audio-visual materials.

A table of periodicals and other materials indexed is given, together with a table of abbreviations used. Patterned after the *Index to Legal Periodicals*, it contains a subject index, a separate author index, a table of cases commented upon, and a book review index. The subject headings used are basically the same as those used by the *Index*, with certain variations where differences in terminology require it, and with wider coverage given to Quebec civil law.

Retrospective indexing of articles prior to 1961 is in progress, but meanwhile the *Index* is used for earlier articles, since it includes the major Canadian legal periodicals. In addition, certain periodicals such as the *Canadian Bar Review* produce individual indexes which cover articles published since the journal's inception.

In addition, the *Appendix Binder* of the *Canadian Abridgment*, 2d ed., includes an index of articles from legal periodicals covering 1956 to date. The articles are arranged by subject, with no reference to authors. The service is updated annually.

SECTION I.   WORDS AND PHRASES

The only Canadian publication treating words and phrases exclusively is:

*Encyclopedia of Words and Phrases, Legal Maxims, Canada,
1825–1962.* Gen. ed., Gerald D. Sanagan. 2nd ed. Toronto,
Richard De Boo, 1963–1965. 5v. Supplement, 1963–1974.

Many of the digests and encyclopedias treat words and phrases
as well. *The Canadian Abridgment* includes a one-volume *Words
and Phrases* published in 1952, with supplementary material covering 1952–1965 included in Binder A and a consolidated volume of
Words and Phrases for the second edition is to be published. Volume 22 of the *Canadian Encyclopedic Digest* (Western 2nd) is a table
of words and phrases. Finally, a table which is cumulative for the
year is included in the monthly issues of *Canadian Current Law.*

Canadian judicial definitions are also included in the English
set entitled *Words and Phrases Legally Defined*, 2d ed., published by
Butterworths.

SECTION J.   HOW TO FIND CANADIAN CASES
AND STATUTES

1.   Cases

a.   *Canadian Abridgment.*

This is the most comprehensive Canadian case digest, although
with the second edition, civil law cases are no longer included.

b.   Research Procedure:

(1) Consult the Titles Key included in the *First Permanent
Supplement* of the second edition; analyze which legal topic
encompasses the problem under research. (See Illustration 121)

(2) Consult the index for the topic which is contained in
the back of the volume, including that topic.

(3) Consult the same topic and subdivisions in the *First
Permanent Supplement* and the looseleaf *Cumulative Supplement* for later cases. The figures in round brackets at the head
of the case summary indicate where cases on the same point of
law have been classed in the main volumes.

(4) Consult the same topic in the monthly *Canadian Current Law* for the latest cases. This includes notations for the
Canadian Abridgement classifications as well.

2.   Statutes

(1) Consult the Index to R.S.C.1970 to find the name of the relevant statute; this Index will also provide a section by section analysis of the contents of each act.   (See Illustration 124)

(2) Consult the most recent Table of Public Statutes in the *Canada Gazette Part III* to find any amendments to the act.

(3) The text of amendments may be located in the *Canada Statute Citator*, 1970 ed.

(4) The status of pending legislation may be located in the *Current Legislative Digest (Canada)*.

3.   Other Methods of Canadian Legal Research

Canadian legal materials are not as well indexed as either the American or the English materials, so that it is usually necessary to begin with the secondary sources.   These include:

  a.   *Canadian Encyclopedic Digest.*

  b.   *Halsbury's Laws of England, Canadian Converter Volumes.*

  c.   Canadian treatises.

  d.   Canadian legal periodical articles.

SECTION K.   CANADIAN LEGAL RESEARCH MANUALS AND BIBLIOGRAPHIES

a.   Banks, Margaret A.   *Using a Law Library; a Guide for Students in the Common Law Provinces of Canada.*   2d ed.   Toronto. Carswell, 1974.   171p.

> Student's guide to the organization of law libraries and the sources and tools of legal research.   Emphasis is placed on Canadian common law sources and English materials most frequently used in Canadian law libraries, especially those which include features useful in Canada.

b.   Boult, Reynald.   *Bibliographie du droit canadien.   A Bibliography of Canadian Law.*   Montréal, Wilson et Lafleur.   1966.   393p.

> A selective bibliography of Canadian legal sources including early law derived from English, French and other sources, right down to January 1, 1965.   The material is arranged under broad subject divisions with a scope note explanatory paragraph outlining that area of law included for many sections.   A subject and an author index are included.

c. Brierly, John E. C. *Bibliographical Guide to Canadian Legal Materials.* 2d ed. Montreal, Faculty of Law, McGill University, 1968. 260p.

> A guide to legal research for the French civil law as well as the common law materials. Bibliographical information as well as an explanation of the uses of both primary and secondary sources is included. Although it is the most comprehensive Canadian legal research manual, it has never been published commercially and is not widely known. Does not contain an index.

d. Christie, Innis M., and John A. Yogis. *Legal Writing and Research Manual.* 2d ed. Toronto, Butterworths, 1974. 136p.

> An introductory work on the sources and techniques of legal research, as well as a basic guide to Canadian legal citation. A teaching book designed for use in the Queen's Faculty of Law for the first year law students, it presents a brief description of the search tools and their use in legal research.

e. Craig, Barbara. *An Outline of Basic Research Materials for Canadian Law Students.* Windsor, Ont., Faculty of Law, University of Windsor, 1971. 67 leaves.

> Designed to assist students in the University of Windsor's legal writing program by providing them with a handbook listing the essential research materials and outlining the features of each.

f. *A Legal Bibliography of the British Commonwealth of Nations.* 2nd ed. London, Sweet & Maxwell, 1955–1964. 7v. Vol. 3, Canadian and British-American colonial law from the earliest times to December 1956. Canada, pp. 1–132.

> A comprehensive, authoritative bibliography which includes the entire legal literature for Canada in general, and for each of the provinces and Territories.

g. Price, Miles Oscar and Harry Bitner. *Effective Legal Research; a Practical Manual of Law Books and Their Use.* New York, A. M. Kelley, Rothman Reprints, 1969, 633p.

> Chapter 29 includes a discussion of Canadian materials (see pp. 295–304). A list of Canadian law reports is included in Appendix II (see pp. 447–450).

SECTION L.   CITATIONS

Citation form for Canadian legal materials may be found in Appendix A, (IV).

SECTION M.   ILLUSTRATIONS

121. Page from Canadian Abridgment (2nd) First Permanent Supplement, Vol. 1.

122. Page from Volume 21, Canadian Abridgment (2nd).

123. Page from Volume 21, Canadian Abridgment (2nd).

124. Page from Revised Statutes of Canada, 1970, Index Volume.

125. Page from the Canada Statute Citator.

126. Page from Volume 3, Cases Judicially Considered, Canadian Abridgment (2nd).

[Illustration 121]

PAGE FROM THE CANADIAN ABRIDGMENT (2ND) FIRST PERMANENT SUPPLEMENT VOL. I, "TITLES KEY"

TITLES KEY

SUBJECT MATTER OR TOPIC	SEE FOLLOWING CAN. ABR. (2nd) TITLES
Conflict of Laws	Volume 6
Conspiracy	Volume 6
Constable	Criminal Law; Public Authorities
Constitutional Law	Volume 7
Constructive Contracts	Contracts
Contagious Diseases	Public Health and Welfare
Contempt of Court	Judges and Courts
Contempt of Parliament	Constitutional Law; Crown; Judges and Courts
Contingent Remedies	Real Property; Wills
Contingent Uses	Real Property; Wills
Contraband	International Law
Contracts	Volume 7
Contribution	Bills of Exchange; Contracts; Damages;

FINDING CANADIAN CASES

Problem: To what extent is an Ontario Provincial Court Judge bound by a decision of a co-ordinate court?

Step 1. Using the Canadian Abridgment.

The Titles Key in this Supplement indicates that the subject "Courts" is found under "Judges and Courts".

Coroners and Inquests	Judges and Courts
Corporations	Volume 8
Corpses	Burial and Cemeteries; Judges and Courts
Costs	Volume P1
Counterfeiting	Criminal Law
→ Courts	Judges and Courts
Courts Martial	Armed Services
Covenants	Actions; Building Contracts; Choses in Action; Contracts; Damages; Easements; Landlord and Tenant; Mortgages; Real Property; Sale of Goods; Sale of Land

cxxxvii

[Illustration 122]

PAGE FROM VOLUME 21, CANADIAN ABRIDGEMENT (2nd)

JUDGES AND COURTS

Step 2. At the beginning of each Title, there is an outline of topical Divisions. For this Topic, it indicates digests of cases on "co-ordinate" decisions will be found on page 664 of the volume of the Canadian Abridgment which contains the Topic "Judges and Courts". See next Illustration.

9

[Illustration 123]

PAGE FROM VOLUME 21, CANADIAN ABRIDGMENT (2nd)

[3839-3846]   Judges and Courts

3839. American and Canadian law not   from accepting as binding on us decisions

> **Step 3.**
> Note digests of cases on co-ordinate jurisdiction. The Permanent Supplements and looseleaf supplement volume should also be checked for later cases. Each volume of the Canadian Abridgment has an index. These cases could also be located by consulting it.
>
> Current cases can also be located by using Canadian Current Law.

upon the Income Tax Appeal Board. Fergusson v. M.N.R. (1952), 52 D.T.C. 319 (App. Bd.).

6. DECISIONS OF COURTS OF CO-ORDINATE JURISDICTION

3841. Decisions of higher courts — Courts of first instance. Per Kinnear Co. Ct. J.: "There appears to be no statute or common law rule by which one court is bound by the decision of another court of co-ordinate jurisdiction. Higher courts so act on grounds of judicial comity. With regard to judges of first instance, the rule might be stated as follows: the second judge ought always to treat former decisions with attention and respect but may decline to follow a previous decision if he thinks the principle of the decision insufficient or inapplicable or wrong in any other way." Norris v. Hamilton, [1943] O.W.N. 566.

3842. Per Hogg J.: "It is hardly necessary to say that the function of the judge is not to make law. That is the function of the legislature, and the trial judge is, of course, bound by the decision in point, of a Court of higher jurisdiction, and also of a Court of co-ordinate jurisdiction except in the most special circumstances. The doctrine of *stare decisis* is one long recognized as a principle of our law." R. v. Morris, [1942] O.W.N. 447.

3843. Decision of courts of another province on statute adopted therefrom — Effect. Per Harvey C.J.A.: "This division had held more than once that a judicial interpretation [in another province] of a statutory provision made prior to its being adopted by our Legislature should be accepted as the guide for determining our Legislature's intention but that is, of course, quite different

to develop. . . . In a criminal case he is permitted greater latitude, and if after giving great weight to the decision of a brother judge he still feels that on full consideration of the relevant authorities he is fully convinced that the former decision is wrong, he should follow his own opinion. . . . The Judicature Act does not apply . . . and even if it did s. 31 would be impractical." R. v. Nor. Elec. Co., 21 C.R. 45, [1955] O.R. 431, 111 C.C.C. 241, [1955] 3 D.L.R. 449, 24 C.P.R. 1.

3845. Per Robertson J.: "As the Courts of Appeal for criminal cases are now constituted, the decision of the Judges of one court is not binding on the Judges sitting in another court of the same jurisdiction. In this respect the law is different as regards civil actions. There is a statutory provision in the Ontario Judicature Act which makes the decision of a court of co-ordinate jurisdiction in civil cases binding, but no such provision exists as regards the Courts of Criminal Appeal. The party, therefore, appealing, has the right to the opinion of the particular court appealed to, as of first instance; that court would, as a matter of course, give all due weight to the opinion expressed by another court of co-ordinate jurisdiction, and would hesitate before deciding contrary to that opinion, although competent to do so". R. v. Hammond, (1898) 29 O.R. 211, 1 C.C.C. 373 (C.A.).

3846. Prior decision in another province on Criminal Code or other federal Act — Reasons for and desirability of uniformity — Limitation of application of principle. Per Martin J.A.: "The practice of this Court of Criminal Appeal . . . has been to follow the decisions of other like Courts of Canada on Federal statutes, particularly criminal, with the intention of harmonizing the decisions and securing uniformity of

[Illustration 124]
PAGE FROM REVISED STATUTES OF CANADA 1970, INDEX

Revised Statutes Index

(References are to sections)

COOPERATIVE CREDIT ASSOCIATIONS
ACT, R.S., c. C-29—(cont'd)
loan or investment, penalty re, waiver
78(3)
purchase or sale of business by association, approval re 10
report to Governor in Council 63(2)
Municipal securities
defined 43

School securities
defined 43
Secretary
bookkeeping 29(1)
Share
by-laws re 22(3)
forfeiture 28
lien of an association on 67

COPYRIGHT
See Canada Corporations Act, R.S., c. C-32,
s.121(1)(k)(iv); Copyright Act, R.S., c. C-
30; National Film Act, R.S., c. N-7,
s.10(1)(f)

COPYRIGHT ACT, R.S., c. C-30
Acting Commissioner
appointment and duties 30
Additional Protocol
application 4, 16(8), 28, 47
Annual statement 48(2)
Architectural work of art
defined 2
injunction re 23
Artistic work
defined 2
Assignment of copyright
conditions and form 12(4)
limitation 12(5)
ownership 12(6)
Author
defined 42(4)
reputation, prejudice to, rights re 12(7)
residence 3(6)
term of protection 8(2)
Book
defined 2
endorsement on 14(10)
importation, notice of intention 28
later edition 14(13)
licence of publication 14
serial publication 15
stamp for payment of royalties 16(7)
Canada Gazette
publication in 4, 42, 49, 50(8)
Certificate of registration
evidence of copyright 36(3)
grant of interest in copyright, of 40(2)
Chairman of the Board
qualifications 50(2)
Cinematograph
defined 2
Collective work
defined 2
separate rights in, protection 20(5)
Commissioner of Patents
control of business 35
powers 30, 32, 33
Consolidated Revenue Fund
payments out of 41(5)
Contrivance
alterations necessary to adaptation 19(2)
copyright, enforcement 19(10)
exception 19(3)
making 19(1)
consent of owner of copyright to
19(7)
manuscript arrangement for 19(4)
provisions re musical works already
published 19(9)
royalties
apportionment 19(6)
rates 19(5)

FINDING CANADIAN STATUTES

Problem: Which Canadian statute covers the granting
of copyright in Canada?

Step 1. Consult index volume to R.S.C., 1970. This indicates that Copyright is covered in C. 30.

After reading the text, it must be determined if any
of the sections of the act have been amended or repealed.
This is done by checking in the Table of Public Statutes,
Part III of the Canada Gazette.

---

quorum 12(2)
replacement 13(5)
tenure of office 12(1)
Parliament
declaration of eligibility of organization,
repeal 83
member of association, eligibility, declaration re 80(1)(b)
membership in association, eligibility to,
powers re 4(1)
President of the board of directors
absence at meetings 15
duties re meetings 15
election 14(1)
vacancy 16(1)
Procedure
actions 36
call of money, enforcement re 34
service of process or notice 35
winding up 37
Promissory note
issue by association 66
Province
organization incorporated by, exercise of
powers 82, 84(2)
Real estate
valuation 59
Report to Minister
allowable assets 60(1)
assets insufficient 63(1)
inquiries by Superintendent 58
real estate, valuation 59
Superintendent, by 57
statement, correction 60(2)
statement of assets and liabilities,
amendment 62
Reserve fund
establishment, powers of board re 50(2)

assessment of association 65
auditor, nomination 56(4)
by-law, certified copy 25
by-law re borrowing and deposit, recommendation 47(2)
defined 2
examination under oath 56(3)
expenses of special audit, approval 56(5)
inquiry, report re 58(1)
inspection by 56(1)
liability 64
notice of membership registration 29(3)
report to Minister 56(1), 57, 58(2), 59,
60, 62, 63(1)
request of information by 86
statement of assets and liabilities,
amendment 62
valuation
bonds 51(3)
debentures 51(3)
real estate 59
securities 51(3)
Trading by association
prohibition 49
Vice-president of the board of directors
absence at meetings 15
duties re meetings 15
election 14(1)
vacancy 16(1)
Violation of Act 76
Vote
member, payment in arrears 31

COOPERATIVE FARM ASSOCIATION
See Farm Syndicates Credit Act, R.S., c.
F-4

[Illustration 125]

PAGE FROM THE CANADA STATUTE CITATOR, R.S.C. 1970 ED.

46—24 THE CANADA STATUTE CITATOR

COPYRIGHT ACT—*Continued*

> Another method of determining if a statute has been amended is by using The Canada Statute Citator. Although this is more convenient and current than the Table of Statutes, it is not authoritative.
>
> Note how this Citator indicates an amendment to Sec. 17 of the Copyright Act.
>
> Also note how it cites cases under each statutory Section.

Section 16

Subsec. (3) repealed and the following substituted by R.S.C. 1970, c. 10 (2nd Supp.), s. 65:

(3) The owner of the copyright, in addition to any other remedy in respect to such licence as a contract, is entitled, in case of default by the licensee in observing the terms of such licence, on application to the Federal Court of Canada, to have such licence cancelled.

Section 17

For cases 1941 to 1971, see *Canada Statute Annotations,* R.S.C. 1970 edition.

Subsec. (2) amended by 1974-75, c. 50, s. 47 (to come into force on proclamation).

Subsec. (4) *Godfrey, MacSkimming & Bacque Ltd. et al. v. Coles Book Stores Ltd.* (1973), 1 O.R. (2d) 362, 40 D.L.R. (3d) 346, 13 C.P.R. (2d) 89 (Ont. H.C.J.).

Copyright is infringed under this section when the American editions of published works, printed in Canada, are brought into Canada by a person when that person knows that such importation is without the consent of the holder of the copyright.

Section 19

For cases 1941 to 1971, see *Canada Statute Annotations,* R.S.C. 1970 edition.

Section 20

For cases 1941 to 1971, see *Canada Statute Annotations,* R.S.C. 1970 edition.

White Rose Nurseries v. Ashton-Potter Ltd. (1972), 9 C.P.R. (2d) 112n, [1972] F.C. 1442 (C.A.), revg 7 C.P.R. (2d) 29, [1972] F.C. 689.

A plaintiff claiming an interest in a copyright by licence must plead in his statement of claim facts upon which the rights of the licensors are based.

[Illustration 126]

PAGE FROM THE CANADIAN ABRIDGMENT, 3rd ED., CASES JUDICIALLY CONSIDERED, VOL. 3

CASES JUDICIALLY CONSIDERED

Manitoulin Quartzite Ltd., 13 C.B.R. 404.
Aff. [1933] 4 D.L.R. 132.

Mankin v. Scala Theodrome Co., [1947] K.B. 257.
Consd. Bermann v. Occhipinti, [1953] O.R. 1035.

Manley v. Burns, [1916] 2 K.B. 121.
Apld. McGillivray v. Dom. Coal Co., 35 D.L.R. (2d) 345.

Manley v. Collom, 8 B.C.R. 153; 32 S.C.R. 371.

Dist. Chersinoff v. Allstate Ins. Co., 67 W.W.R. 750.
Dist. Boulianne v. Flynn, [1970] 3 O.R. 84.

Mann v. Balaban, [1970] S.C.R. 74.
Dist. Hellenius v. Lees, 20 D.L.R. (3d) 369.

Mann v. Brodie, 10 App. Cas. 378.
Apld. Rowland v. Edmonton, 50 S.C.R. 520.

Mann v. Crittenden, 11 O.L.R. 46.
Apld. Re Avery, [1952] O.W.N. 475.

> **Noting Up Canadian Cases**
>   Problem: Has Mann v. R., 1966 S.C.R. 238, been accepted as precedent by later cases?
>
>   This can be determined by using the volumes of Cases Judicially Considered of the Canadian Abridgment (2nd). Note all the citations to it.
>
>   After checking this volume, the Appendix Binder should be consulted.
>
>   For the most current information, check the Table of Cases Judicially Considered in the latest monthly issues of Canadian Current Law.

W.W.R. 655.

Manley v. St. Helens Canal, 27 L.J. Ex. 159.
Folld. McCrimmon v. B.C. Elec. Ry., 7 W.W.R. 137.

Manley v. Scott, 1 Siderfin 109.
Consd. Thompson v. Findlay, [1938] O.W.N. 490.

Manly, Re, 3 Sw. & Tr. 56.
Apld. Re Williamson, [1940] 3 W.W.R. 120.

Mann, Re, [1942] P. 146.
Apld. Re Mather, [1943] 1 W.W.R. 310.
Apld. Re Tachibana, 63 W.W.R. 99.

Mann, Re, [1972] 5 W.W.R. 23.
Aff. [1973] 4 W.W.R. 223.

Mann v. Amer. Auto Ins. Co., 52 B.C.R. 460.
Folld. Chersinoff v. Allstate Ins. Co., 69 D.L.R. (2d) 653.

Mann v. R., [1966] S.C.R. 238. ←
Folld. McIver v. R., 48 C.R. 4.
Dist. R. v. Morrison, 59 W.W.R. 120.
Apld. La Caisse Populaire Notre Dame Ltee v. Moyen, 59 W.W.R. 129.
Apld. R. v. Miller, 9 Cr. L.Q. 505.
Apld. Binus v. R., 2 C.R.N.S. 118.
Apld. Ryan v. R., [1968] 1 C.C.C. 78.
Consd. A.G. Alta. v. Hatfield, 4 C.R.N.S. 348.
Dist. Peda v. R., 7 C.R.N.S. 243.
Consd. R. v. Prince, 73 W.W.R. 328.
Apld. R. v. Paul, 12 C.C.C. (2d) 497.
Consd. Ross v. Registrar of Motor Vehicles, 23 C.R.N.S. 319.

Mann v. Rudolph, 36 Que. S.C. 57.
Rev. 37 Que. S.C. 299.

Mann v. Saulnier, 19 D.L.R. (2d) 130.
Consd. Phillips v. California Standard Co., 31 W.W.R. 331.
Apld. Zien v. Field, 43 W.W.R. 577.
Consd. Grosvenor Park Shopping Centre Ltd. v. Waloshin, 49 W.W.R. 237.

Chapter 23

COMPUTERS AND MICROFORMS IN LEGAL RESEARCH

The purpose of this chapter * is to describe the application of advanced information technology in the field of law, giving descriptions of the various computerized word-search systems and resources currently available for retrieval of law information. The first section deals with the principles and techniques of accessing computerized word-search systems and concludes with a description of systems providing access to machine-readable files in law and legislation as well as a selection of systems and data bases in other disciplines in order to point out not only the computerized law retrieval systems,[1] but those non-law data files of possible application to legal research. Section F describes the role of microforms in legal research.

———

SECTION A. DATA BASES FOR COMPUTERS

The foregoing chapters of this text have described the various printed indexes, digests, citators, abstracts and services used in manually searching for the law. In most instances, these search tools provide effective approaches for the retrieval of legal information, yet there are times and occasions when the computerized word-search systems, now a reality in many areas of legal research, provide an attractive alternative or a valuable supplement to these traditional approaches.

The capacity of the computer to store and search rapidly through its stored documents for specified patterns of words, phrases, numbers or combinations of them makes it an effective tool to use: 1) when the inquiry is multi-dimensional, requiring the coordination of two or more concepts, one or each of which may have a number of synonymous and related terms; 2) when the inquiry covers a span of years and no single cumulated index exists; or 3) when traditional indexes have been unproductive and one's budget permits an exhaustive, in-depth search. Provided the documents which have been

* This chapter was originally drafted by Signe M. Larson, U. S. Department of the Interior, Natural Resources Library, Law Branch, Washington, D.C., and modified by the authors.

[1] For a more detailed description of the use of computers as an aid in legal research, see: J. SPROWL, A MANUAL FOR COMPUTER-ASSISTED LEGAL RESEARCH, 1976.

stored in the computer's memory contain the information, the computer can search for and assemble quickly, for example: 1) statutes or judicial opinions containing specific phrases, word pairs or words; 2) the documents concerning specific factual situations; 3) the decisions rendered by a particular judge, or by a particular court over a specified period, or the decisions in which a particular attorney is named as counsel; or, 4) the judicial decisions citing a particular decision or statute. Any computerized search is limited, it should be noted, to the material actually in machine-readable form and made accessible through the services of a vendor if not via an in-house computer facility.

1. Machine-Readable Data Bases—Creation and Growth

Since the early seventies, an ever-increasing number and variety of machine-readable data bases [2] have become available for online interactive searching.[3] Most of these data bases have been in disciplines other than law; however, in recent years, computerized systems for legal research have experienced a significant growth in number, variety and depth of coverage.

Many of the computer-based information resources are marketed to subscribers by private sector timesharing [4] companies. The subscriber to the data base services may interrogate a machine-readable data base of documents or document representations offered by the vendor through a terminal connected to the host computer by some communication channel, most often a regular telephone line. Basically, there are three different types of data bases:

(a) Textual or bibliographic data bases

(b) Numerical or computational data bases

(c) Graphic, image, or picture processing data bases.

Our concern for the most part will be with the first type of data base: the textual or bibliographic data base which, it should be added, may be further characterized according to:

(1) The extent of the record input into the system—ranging from a bibliographic citation or document representation to the entire text of the document, or to

---

[2] A data base is defined as an organized collection of information or data recorded in machine-readable form.

[3] Online interactive searching permits the user via a computer to interrogate a machine-readable data base directly in a conversational mode, with the searcher and the system program taking turns in the dialogue. An interactive search gives the user the ability to view the results of his search at various stages and to revise his request to conform to what he discovers about the data base online.

[4] Timesharing in the operation of a computer system permits many users to operate the system simultaneously in such a way that each is unaware that the system is being used by others.

(2) The indexing scheme employed—ranging from data bases which assign index terms from a controlled vocabulary (a thesaurus or hierarchical index) to those which provide no subject indexing at all but rely on natural or free text access in selecting index terms from words appearing in the document and/or abstract itself.

Many of the data bases which are now available for online searching are the by-products of a publishing activity, created originally not for information retrieval per se, but created to facilitate electronic photocomposition in the publishing of catalogs or indexing and abstracting services. Indeed, whenever computerized photocomposition is used in publishing, the potential for a machine-searchable file exists. Once in machine-readable form, these files can be reorganized or reformatted by the processor to meet various users' needs or specifications for the retrieval of information.

A few data bases, such as certain of the full text systems used in the retrieval of law information, however, are created not as the by-products of a publishing activity but are created by keyboarding and storing in the computer's memory the entire text of the already-published source documents: cases, statutes, rules, regulations, slip opinions, briefs, etc. The materials so stored are not pre-indexed, digested or abstracted. Instead, each word contained in the stored documents (except certain non-substantive or connecting words such as *of, by, and, the, in,* and so on) is computer indexed by the system and thus made searchable and retrievable. One full text system described below, it should be noted, (See FLITE, p. 468) is not an online system, but operates in a batch processing mode.[5]

2. Searching Machine-Readable Data Bases Online

Machine-readable data bases are made available by system vendors or suppliers who have developed online computer retrieval programs capable of searching the data bases in response to queries. The subscriber to these services can search the data bases online through a terminal linked by a communications system to the vendor's computer. The language used at the terminal keyboard to communicate with the retrieval system and to instruct and interact with it is known as a command language. Each system has its own command language which must be mastered by the user if he is to make effective use of the system's capabilities.

In addition to being thoroughly familiar with the system's command language, the user must be knowledgeable about the nature and

---

[5] In a batch processing system, multiple searches are "batched" together and run at the same time against a serially or sequentially arranged file. When fast response is not a primary requirement, batch processing can provide a useful service.

structure of the data bases the system services: their content, coverage and searchable elements. Some data bases, it should be noted, are common to several systems, but the user should be aware of the depth of the file and how each system has processed it. Thirdly, the online searcher should be able to operate the online terminal with ease and be familiar as well with the other equipment associated with online searching: the coupler or data set and the printer.

SECTION B. FORMULATED SEARCH STRATEGIES AND LOGIC

The following section outlines briefly some of the general guidelines to follow in planning an online search. It is not the purpose of the section to give explicit details in searching individual systems, but merely to identify the basic principles of computerized searching and the particular features common to most online systems.

Although variations exist among systems, typically an online retrieval search will proceed through a series of separate steps including:

LOG IN (Establishing communication with the system and identifying the data base to be interrogated)

SEARCH (Entering terms for searching by the system)

COMBINE (Linking concepts logically)

BROWSE and/or **PRINT** (Trying out aspects of the request or the whole request; revising; and/or printing the results)

LOG OFF (Terminating the session)

To make online searches effective and thorough, it is advisable to formulate search strategies "offline," before beginning a terminal session. The starting point of any successful online search is a clearly defined search objective or query. The query should be carefully analyzed by the researcher and separated into the logical and distinct concepts which comprise it. For each concept, a family of synonymous words, word phrases or other related terms is identified and listed. The terms so identified can range from slight variations in spelling to semantic relatives. How successful a searcher will be at the terminal is dependent upon the knowledge of the vocabulary of the data base, be it full text or pre-indexed.

The searcher of a full text, natural language data base, such as LEXIS, formulates a strategy by listing the words, word pairs or phrases he believes are likely to be in the documents he wishes to retrieve. Since full text systems receive no prior indexing, the searcher is dependent upon anticipating the word usage in the documents

themselves. The searcher of a pre-indexed data base, on the other hand, such as WESTLAW or CIS, must take care to select terms represented in the data base vocabulary or those he believes to be in the headnote summaries or abstracts.

Although various retrieval aids (thesauri and word frequency lists) have been developed for searching machine-readable data bases in the scientific, technical and social science fields, such aids have not been extensively developed for searching data bases containing law information. Researchers, may, however, turn to the printed indexes, digests and legal texts for assistance in developing the appropriate terminology to use in searching. In addition, the online alphabetic displays of terms which are available in some online systems may be useful in recalling terms the user may otherwise forget to include. It should be noted that several systems allow the user to specify word proximity—that words be either adjacent to or within a specified distance of each other as well as in a certain portion of the record or document. Most systems also allow searches to be conducted on word truncation, where the requestor enters an incomplete term or word root to retrieve the basic term as well as any terms that contain the root and one or more suffixes.

Having separated the query into its distinct concepts, the searcher next focuses upon linking or combining the terms in such a way that the desired result is achieved. At the present time, there are two principal methods of linking terms: Boolean algebra and weighting. The first is more widely used currently. Boolean logic [6] is a technique of using the most basic forms of expression to represent any logical possibility: that is, a thing either exists or it does not, it is either present or absent, and so on. Strictly speaking, Boolean logic provides two conditions to express the relationships between elements of data. This is extended in practice to three by the use of negative logic. The three conditions are AND, OR, and NOT. The Boolean operator AND linking two terms is a restrictive condition and narrows the scope of the search to only those records which satisfy both conditions. The Boolean operator OR linking two terms, on the other hand, broadens the scope of the search to include all those records satisfying either condition. The OR is used more often in linking synonyms together while AND is used for intersecting distinct concepts. NOT, which is the logical opposite of AND, is sometimes written as AND NOT. (See Venn diagrams, p. 462)

Weighting of a search request consists of assigning a numerical value to the search terms according to their degree of importance. While some searchers find the technique easier to apply than the use

---

[6] Developed and codified by the English mathematician, George Boole (1815–1864).

of Boolean expressions, others do not.   The technique has the advantage of being able to rank documents according to the degree to which they match the search strategy.

Having formulated the strategy offline, the searcher next keys in his terms and instructions to the system at the terminal.   In browsing the data base online, the searcher has the opportunity to view the results of his request and to revise his strategy, if need be.   Success at this point may depend upon the searcher's ability to diagnose why certain results were or were not achieved and his ability to think of alternate approaches.   Satisfied that he can do no better, the searcher may request that the final results be printed either online or offline and mailed.   Most systems allow the format to be specified by the user: i. e., in the form of citations or keyword-in-context (KWIC) or full text.

VENN DIAGRAMS

Venn * diagrams are often helpful to sort out the Boolean relationships, as illustrated below:

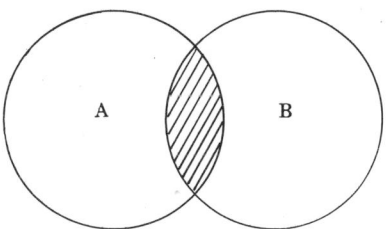
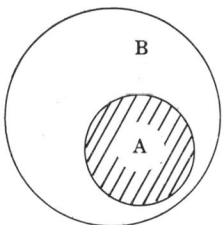

AND is restrictive

A AND B must be present, i. e., Jurisdiction AND Standing to sue

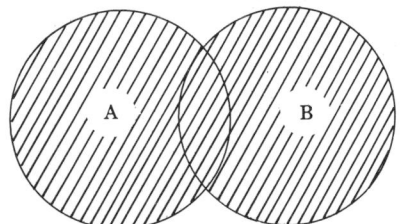
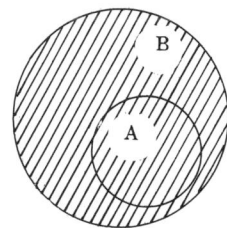

OR is expansive

Either A OR B may be present, i. e., Marijuana OR Marihuana

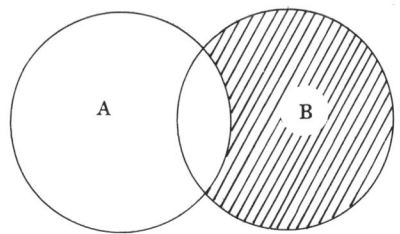
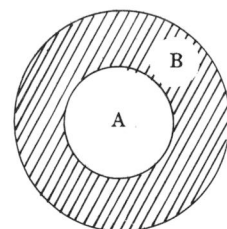

NOT negates

B must be present but NOT A, i. e., Information but NOT Freedom

* Named after the English logician John Venn (1834–1923).

SECTION C. SELECTED LEGAL DATA BASES
AND THEIR USE

The section that follows presents a series of descriptive profiles of selected data base systems currently available for the retrieval of law or law-related information. Since new developments in online systems can occur frequently and rapidly, portions of this text will become outdated rather quickly. The reader is urged to consult system representatives to obtain the latest information on data base content, coverage and charges as well as further information on system features.

It will be seen that the systems and the data bases differ in many ways, and that each has special features the others lack. The researcher is advised, therefore, to learn as much about them as he can to recognize those situations where their use may be advantageous.

1. LEXIS

This is a full text, interactive legal information retrieval system which is commercially available through Mead Data Central of Dayton, Ohio. Many of the state data bases were developed with the sponsorship of the state bar associations. It is the ultimate objective of the Mead Data Corporation for LEXIS to contain data bases for all federal statutes and court decisions as well as those of the fifty states. LEXIS also contains special subject data bases. With the LEXIS system, each data base must be searched separately.

a. Data Base Content and Coverage

(1) Federal Library. United States Code. Court decisions of the Supreme Court, 1938 to date. Courts of Appeal, 1959 to date. District Courts, 1970 to date.

(2) State Data Bases.

California.	Supreme Court, 1961 to date. Appellate Courts, 1961 to date.
Illinois.	Supreme Court, 1962 to date. Appellate Court, 1962 to date.
Kansas.	Kansas Statutes. Supreme Court, 1963 to date.
Missouri.	Missouri Revised Codes. Supreme Court, 1945 to date. Court of Appeals, 1945 to date.
Massachusetts.	Supreme Judicial Court, 1950 to date. Appeals Court, 1973 to date.
Pennsylvania.	Supreme Court, 1955 to date. Superior Court, 1955 to date. Commonwealth Courts, 1970 to date.

Texas. Supreme Court, 1955 to date. Court of Criminal Appeals, 1965 to date. Court of Civil Appeal, 1955 to date.

(3) Special Data Bases.

Delaware Corporations Library. Decisions of Delaware Courts construing Delaware corporation law, reported decisions, 1898 to date; unreported, 1970 to date. Federal court decisions construing Delaware corporation law, 1930 to date.

Federal Tax Library. Internal Revenue Code, Regulations, and Cumulative Bulletin. Tax Court decisions. Board of Tax Appeal opinions. Federal court decisions on taxation. Legislative histories of 1954 Act and all amendments.

Securities Law. U.S. Code, Title 15, § 77a–80b. S.E.C. Rules and Regulations. S.E.C. Interpretive Releases. Federal court decisions on securities, 1933 to date. Selected S.E.C. decisions, 1933 to date. Legislative histories of 1933 and 1934 Acts and amendments thereto. No-Action letters, 1971 to date.

b. Searchable Elements and Special Features

Inverted files are created by LEXIS for every word occurring in an input document except for certain syntactic and other nonsubstantive words. The system, thus, can search for documents containing any word, word pair or phrase. All Boolean searching is possible and word positional indicators may be used. In addition, word truncation is possible. Searchers may be restricted to individual segments of a document, such as: name of the case; citation; majority opinion; dissenting opinion; author of either majority or dissenting opinion; date, and so on. Output can be in citation form or in keyword-in-context (KWIC) or in full-text form.

c. Searching Aids

The *LEXIS Deskbook* is a user's manual which covers the use of the LEXIS retrieval program, instructions in the use of the various libraries, as well as instructions in the operation of the terminal. LEXIS also has an abbreviated guide for users, *LEXIS, A Primer*.

d. Access and Hours of Availability

LEXIS is made available on a subscription basis with charges made up of three elements: (1) Equipment and communication charges which cover all costs including maintenance for a LEXIS terminal (a video display unit), an associated hardcopy printer, and communication equipment and all communications costs between the

terminal and MDC's computer center in Dayton, Ohio; (2) Use charges; and (3) Installation and training charges. For further information, contact:

Mead Data Central
200 Park Avenue
New York, New York 10017

2. WESTLAW (West Computer Law Retrieval System)

WESTLAW is a commercially available, online, interactive system which is based upon West's *Digest and Key Number System*. In contrast to other computerized law retrieval systems, WESTLAW does not contain the full text of judicial decisions, but includes, rather, the headnotes, Key Numbers, and topic headings of West's *National Reporter System*.

a.   Data Base Content and Coverage

The data base contains the key-numbered headnotes or case summaries prepared by West lawyer-editors to represent the points of law in all reported decisions of:

U. S. Supreme Court, 1961 to present.

U. S. Court of Appeals, 1961 to present.

U. S. District Courts, 1961 to present.

All reported decisions of State courts, 1967 to present.

The data base is national in scope, reflecting the coverage of case law as reported in the National Reporter System. Majority opinions only are headnoted and thus retrievable. The data base is updated on a daily basis and since decisions are input into the system as soon as the West editorial staff has assigned key number topics and headnoted the cases, information is available online often before advance sheets have been received.

b.   Searching Methods

Searches may be entered using natural language, either in a series of single words, or, in narrative form such as would be used to state the problem orally or in writing. The system searches for all documents containing one or more of the words entered, eliminating any common words such as articles, pronouns and other "stop" words having no search value. The searchable words are automatically ORed by the system which also ranks the retrieved documents and displays them in the order of their relevance to the search.

Other Boolean searching is possible and a search may be restricted by the Boolean operators AND or NOT by entering the appropriate symbols. The ampersand (&) entered between words requires

---

* In mid-1977, West announced that on or before Jan. 1, 1978, the *full text* of federal opinions (1961–) and state appellate opinions (1978–) would also be available in WESTLAW'S data bank.

that one or more of the words appearing on either side of the symbols appear in the retrieved documents' key-numbered headnotes. The percent symbol (%) entered between words insures that documents which contain any of the words following the (%) symbol in their key-numbered headnotes will not be retrieved.

c.   Searchable Elements

(1) Key or descriptive words: Key or descriptive words, their synonyms and/or antonyms may be entered.

(2) Phrase: A single phrase, enclosed in quotation marks, may be searched for separately or may be linked with AND (&) or NOT (%). A phrase using quotation marks may not be incorporated within a natural language search, however, where terms are ORed.

(3) Topics and Key Numbers: Topics and Key numbers into which the documents have been classified are searchable by using the topic and Key number or the name of any topic in the West Digest System and a Keyline.

(4) Name of Case or Citation: The full name of the case may be entered, if known, or the name of a party, if only one name is known, or the citation.

(5) Particular State: A search of decisions rendered in a particular state may be made by linking the state to the search terms desired.

(6) Particular Circuit: A search to cases from a particular circuit of the U.S. Court of Appeals may be made by linking the circuit to the search terms desired.

(7) Particular Federal District Court: A search to decisions rendered in a particular Federal district court may be made by linking search terms to the district court.

(8) Year of Decision: The year of decision may be specified, but may not be specified to a certain date within that year.

(9) Additional: The search may be limited to the specific part or parts of the key-numbered headnotes: Topic and Key Number; Topic; Keyline; Courtyear; Headnote; Title; Citation.

d.   Special Features

Truncation: The asterisk (*) attached to the stem of any word or set of letters or numbers enables retrieval of all words or numbers having the specified letters or numbers as a root. Truncation searching is helpful in searching standard plurals, possessives or adverbial forms of a word or a series of numbers.

Dictionary of Terms: An alphabetic listing of terms used in headnotes may be displayed online showing the number of postings assigned to each.

e.   Searching Aids

The *WESTLAW User's Manual* provides details on system usage and the various West Digests with scope notes and indexes provide assistance in choice of terms.   Further information about WESTLAW may be obtained from:

West Publishing Company
50 Kellogg Blvd.
P.O. Box 3526
St. Paul, Minnesota   55165

3.   AUTO-CITE (Automated Citation Testing Service)

Developed by the Lawyers Co-operative Publishing Company, AUTO-CITE is a commercially available online, interactive system which enables the researcher to verify reported federal and state case citations and determine their current status.   The system queried on a case reference will respond with the appellate history with official and unofficial references to all higher court opinions affecting the validity of that case.

a.   Data Base Content and Coverage

The data base includes more than 3,000,000 reported decisions from more than 238 published reporters, beginning with the earliest cases in American law and progressing to present-day cases.   Updated daily, approximately 50,000 new cases are added annually to the date base.   Virtually all federal and state jurisdictions are represented from the appeal level up.   Limited to American case law only, AUTO-CITE does not include statutes or administrative law.   Cases which merely cite the original case in question without affecting its validity are excluded.   Some specialized reporters are not yet available in the data base: SEC, NLRB, Court of Military Appeals, *Federal Cases*, and *Tax Court Memorandums* (Tax Court decisions, however, are included).   In addition, some early lower appeal level cases in Ohio (1816–1934) and Pennsylvania (Pa. D & C 1st & 2nd series, County Reports) are excluded.

b.   Searchable Elements

Standard Case Citation: The data base is searchable *only* by standard case citation: volume number, reporter name, page number. The request can be either the official or any valid parallel.   The system responds with: the title of the case; the year of decision; citation references giving the official first (if one exists) followed by unofficial sources for the same opinion; history designation which, in an abbreviated word or phrase, defines subsequent court action having an official and direct effect upon the status of the case; and, history references which provide citation to where later opinions are reported, the official followed by parallels.

c. Searching Aids

The AUTO–CITE *User's Manual* provides detailed instructions on system usage. Further information about AUTO–CITE may be obtained from:

> The Lawyers Co-operative Publishing Co.
> 50 Broad Street
> Rochester, New York   14614

4. FLITE and JURIS

These two systems, developed by the U.S. Department of Defense and the U.S. Department of Justice, have access limited to those connected with these departments and other federal lawyers.

a. FLITE (Federal Legal Information through Electronics)

FLITE is a computerized legal research service of the Department of Defense, operated by the Office of the Judge Advocate General, U.S. Air Force. It is a full-text information retrieval system designed primarily to process statutory and regulatory material plus decisional material pertaining to legal and judicial interpretations and the receipt and disbursement of public funds.

Batch processing is the primary base of system operation. FLITE, however, plans to progress toward adding interactive capability.

Basically, FLITE is a professional service center activity. The user, upon contacting FLITE, is referred to an attorney who analyzes the inquiry for the legal issues involved and frames the search strategy for interrogating the system. A search report is provided within 24 hours to the FLITE attorney-analyst who reviews the report prior to its transmittal to the user. For further information contact:

> FLITE (HQ USAF/JAESL)
> Denver, Colorado   80279

b. JURIS

JURIS, developed by the U.S. Department of Justice for the use of its attorneys, is a computerized legal research system which makes the full text of documents used in legal research available in an online, interactive mode.

Data Base Content and Coverage: Basically, JURIS contains three different kinds of data: case law materials; statutory materials; and "work product" materials, or documents written by attorneys in the various divisions and offices in the Department of Justice:

briefs, memoranda, policy directives, and procedural manuals.   Further information about JURIS can be obtained from:

> Legal Information Systems Group
> Department of Justice
> Washington, D.C.   20530

SECTION D.   SELECTED NON–LEGAL DATA BASES

1.   CIS INDEX (Congressional Information Service Index)

The CIS INDEX is a data base made available by the System Development Corporation of Santa Monica, California, and corresponds to the printed *CIS INDEX,* an indexing and abstracting service published by the Congressional Information Service of Washington, D.C.

a.   Data Base Content and Coverage

The data base covers the following Congressional publications: Hearings; Committee Prints; House and Senate Reports; House and Senate Documents; and Senate Executive Documents.   The years of coverage are from 1970 to date and the file, which currently holds more than 60,000 records, is updated monthly with an average of 1,000 new records.   Fully-indexed legislative histories for Public Laws are included and this portion of the data base is updated on an annual basis.   Excluded from coverage are: the *Congressional Record*; reports and hearings on private bills; publications which are ceremonial in nature; reports concerning internal housekeeping matters; reports on land conveyances; and reprints of documents previously made available in departmental editions.   The data base provides full bibliographic information and abstracts for the documents included.   Microfiche copies of the full text of the documents are available from CIS and may be ordered online.

b.   Indexing

CIS assigns subject index terms from a controlled vocabulary and indexes to specific rather than to general terms.   The CIS-assigned index terms may be either single or multiple word subject terms.   The "Index to Subject and Names" in the *CIS/Annual* provides the guide to the terms used in the controlled vocabulary.   Additional subject access is provided in the free term field which is computer-created by SDC.   These free-text terms are single word terms derived by SDC from the titles or abstracts of the CIS record.

c.   Searchable Elements

The following elements are searchable directly:

Index Terms: Index terms from the CIS-controlled vocabulary or single-word, free-text terms computer-created by SDC are searchable directly.

Names: Organization names; government agencies; federal programs; names and affiliations of witnesses; official and popular names of laws, reports, and bills; and subcommittee names are searchable directly. House, Senate, and Joint Committees are searchable via assigned committee codes.

Accession Numbers: The complete accession number of the document is searchable, or parts of it are searchable separately, enabling retrieval by: type of document, such as committee print, hearing, report, or document; by source, such as Senate, House, or Joint; by Committee code: or by entry year.

Specific Publication Numbers: Specific publication numbers are searchable: Report numbers; Document numbers; Public Bill or Public Law numbers; and Superintendent of Documents item numbers.

Publication Type or Source: The search may specify that specific types of documents, i. e., hearings, reports, committee prints, be included or excluded from the search or that retrieval include or exclude publications of a particular body, i. e., House, Senate, Joint, or specific committee or committees.

Date or Congress: The year of a publication's entry into the CIS INDEX data base is searchable as is the Congress and session.

d.   Special Features

Word-proximity Searching: Elements not searchable directly may be accessed through the serial-searching capabilities of "string searching" or "set-searching" which enables multiple-word proximity searching on previously retrieved sets.

Online Ordering of Documents: Microfiche copies of the full text of the documents are available from CIS and may be ordered online.

Format Specification: Printouts may be tailored to a format to suit the user's specifications.

Further information about the SDC/CIS INDEX data base may be obtained from:

System Development Corporation
2500 Colorado Avenue
Santa Monica, California   90406

Congressional Information Service, Inc.
7101 Wisconsin Avenue
Washington, D. C.   20014

2. SOCIAL SCISEARCH

SOCIAL SCISEARCH is a data base corresponding to the printed *Social Sciences Citation Index*, an indexing service published by the Institute for Scientific Information (ISI) of Philadelphia, Pennsylvania. The data base is made available online by Lockheed Information Systems of Palo Alto, California.

a.   Data Base Content and Coverage

ISI indexes every article and significant editorial item from every issue of more than 1,400 social science journals plus social science articles in more than 1,200 natural and physical sciences journals. One hundred twenty law reviews are covered as well as an equal number of journals in the fields of political science and international relations. The years of coverage are from 1972 to date and the file, which currently holds more than 370,000 records is updated monthly with an average of 7,500 new records. The data base provides full bibliographic information for the citations included. The full text of articles which appear in the journals covered by the data base may be obtained from ISI through its Original Article Tear Sheet (OATS) Service.

b.   Indexing

The basic index is a natural language index made up of all meaningful single-word terms taken from the title, corporate source, or author affiliation fields of the articles included in the data base—no additional indexing supplements the subject information found in the titles of the citations included. In addition to retrieval by source searching (by title words or phrases, corporate sources, source authors or journal names), the SOCIAL SCISEARCH data base permits citation searching, or searching by way of the author's cited references. "Landmark" papers in a given subject area can be used to retrieve more recent papers that have cited these works.

c.   Searchable Elements

Title or Corporate Source: Single-word terms taken from the title or corporate source fields provide subject access. The user may specify that the search be conducted on the title

field only (to avoid false drops of subject-type words occurring in the corporate source field), or from the corporate source field to retrieve, for example, citations emanating from a particular organization.

Source Author: The names of up to ten source authors of a particular publication are searchable.

Cited Reference: The references listed in each article included in the data base are indexed under the first author of the cited reference. In the absence of a personal author, the title of the publication is used.

Document Type: The type of source articles to be retrieved may be specified, such as: abstracts, editorials, bibliographies, reviews, letters, meeting proceedings, brief articles, discussions, tributes or corrections.

Source Journal: A journal title may be entered to retrieve all articles indexed from that journal or to limit retrieval of a particular search to articles from that journal.

Language Code: Articles written in a particular language may be retrieved directly and then combined with a subject.

Update Code: The search results can be restricted to a given update of the data base to obtain the latest information on a given subject.

d. Special Features:

Full-text Searching: DIALOG's full-text searching capability enables the specification of the desired proximity and order or words, their occurrence in either title or corporate source fields, or any combination of these.

Limit Specification: Searches may be limited to years; to English language only; to foreign language only; to journal articles only; to non-journal articles only; or to certain combinations of these.

Format Specification: Formats for the retrieved citations may be specified to any of four different formats varying from the short accession number to the full record format.

Further information about SOCIAL SCISEARCH may be obtained from:

Lockheed Information Systems
3251 Hanover Street
Palo Alto, California   94306

Institute for Scientific Information
325 Chestnut Street
Philadelphia, Pennsylvania   19106

3. THE INFORMATION BANK

THE INFORMATION BANK is a data base consisting of abstracts of news and editorial matter published in the *New York Times* and selected material taken from approximately sixty other newspapers and periodicals. The data base is made available online by THE INFORMATION BANK of Parsippany, New Jersey, a subsidiary of the New York Times Company.

a.   Data Base Content and Coverage

The data base, which is updated daily, currently holds more than 1,180,000 abstracts of:

(1) Nearly all news stores, editorials, articles, surveys and other material published in the final *Late City Edition* of the *New York Times*, including the Sunday *Times* feature sections, and the daily and Sunday regional material not distributed within New York City, and

(2) Material selected from over sixty other newspapers and periodicals.

Coverage of the *New York Times* extends from January 1, 1969, to the present time while coverage of non-*Times* material generally dates from 1972. New publications are added to the data base from time to time while others are dropped as user interest dictates. The system is not purged, however, of the publications no longer covered. Approximately 20,000 abstracts are added to the file each month.

The *Times* material is abstracted and placed online for retrieval generally within forty-eight hours of the publication of the original article. Abstracts of material selected from the more-than-ten other newspapers and more than fifty different periodicals now included in the data base are entered into the system at varying rates according to established priorities, with top priority given to *Business Week,* the *Los Angeles Times*, the *Wall Street Journal* and the *Washington Post*. Non-*Times* material is abstracted and included in the data base if it deals with subjects not covered by the *Times*, if it provides more detail, treats subjects from different points of view, covers regional issues of national importance, or provides items of substantial research value. THE INFORMATION BANK generally excludes such items as paid personal notices, advice and gossip columns and the classified sections of the publications indexed. Public interest or paid political ads that relate to current issues are included in the BANK, however. Each abstract is fully edited and assigned one or more index terms from a controlled vocabulary, and all personal names, geographic terms or organizational names appearing in the article are also represented. Nearly 80 percent of all search terms appearing in THE INFORMATION BANK are personal names. The

citation appended to each abstract identifies all the bibliographic information needed to locate the original article; the journal, date of publication, page, column, and, for the *Times* material, the microfiche number.

The full text of the articles, including any published illustration, is available in microfiche format under a separate subscription service for all the *New York Times* material. Otherwise, the full text is retrievable from the hardcopy editions or the roll microfilm editions of the *Times*. For many inquiries, however, the abstracts provide all the information needed. The microfiche service, it should be noted, does not extend to publications other than the *Times*.

b.   Indexing

Guided by the terms included in the *New York Times Thesaurus of Descriptors,* the abstractors assign one or more index terms to each abstract to characterize its subject content. All personal names, organization names and geographic terms are represented also. The indexing and abstracting is reviewed and corrected by senior indexers before input to the system. The *Thesaurus* is open-ended in that new terms are added to the system when needed if they can be integrated properly into the basic vocabulary. A listing of these new subject terms can be viewed online by keying the request, "New Search Terms."

c.   Searchable Elements

The searchable elements include:

(1) Descriptors or index terms taken from a controlled vocabulary

(2) Personal or organizational names, or geographic terms, and

(3) Personal name modifiers or bibliographic modifiers.

If the term as entered by the user matches a term in the file precisely, that term only will be displayed. If, however, the entered term matches two or more terms in the file, all will be displayed in alphabetical order and numbered, and the user is requested to select one or more of the displayed terms. The search terms, once selected, may be modified in a number of ways. Information retrieved on a personal name may be limited to retrieval of either brief or detailed biographical material. The search results may be limited also to retrieval by certain bibliographic modifiers, such as: date, journal, source, type of material, illustration, section, page, or column.

d.   Special Features

Limit Specifications: The searcher may specify certain limitations to his search, e.g., that, for retrieval, a search term be limited to one of four categories: person, subject, organiza-

tion or geographic area, or that search terms, as entered, be modified by personal name or by bibliographic modifiers.

Sorting: The system can sort up to 112 abstracts chronologically.

Business News Update: This feature provides an online alternative service to the contents of various current business publications.

Automatic Cross References: The system automatically switches to a term used by the BANK from synonyms of the term.

Further information about THE INFORMATION BANK may be obtained from:

The Information Bank
1719–A Mt. Pleasant Office Park
Route 10
Parsippany, New Jersey   07054

SECTION E. DATA COMMUNICATION COMPONENTS

The following section describes the data communication components necessary to access online retrieval systems.

The subscriber to online services establishes and carries out communication with the host computer through communication components comprising:

a communications terminal

a communications line

a communications line interface

1. Terminals

The computerized word-search systems described in this chapter can be accessed by one or, in some cases, both of two types of interactive [7] terminals: the cathode ray tube (CRT) display terminal (sometimes called a video terminal) and the typewriter terminal (or hard copy terminal). The use of a specific terminal in interrogating a system's data base is dependent upon a number of factors, most important of which is system compatibility. The terminal and the system must be compatible in terms of speed (the rate at which data can be transmitted) and in terms of the communication code used to transmit and receive data. The speed for transmitting and receiving data for the systems described may range from 10 to 960 characters per second. The two common communication codes are the American Standard Code for Information Interchange (ASCII) and the Extended Binary Coded Decimal Interchange Code (EBCDIC). Most American terminal manufacturers have adopted the ASCII code. In

---

[7] Interactive terminals are those which can transmit and receive data as opposed to passive terminals which can only receive data.

general, CRT's are more expensive than typewriter terminals and since they do not provide hard copy, an added expense is incurred if hard copy is desired.   Typewriter terminals, on the other hand, provide hard copy and are less expensive but their transmission speed is restricted by the speed of the operator or the user and their receiving speed is restricted by the speed of their printing function.

2.   Communications Lines

Data is transmitted from the terminal's keyboard to the computer via voice-grade telephone lines, generally, in either dial-up or dedicated mode.   In some cases, online systems may be accessed by a local call service while in others a long distance toll call is required. Users in outlying areas from the computer facility may utilize also the services of communication networks, such as Tymnet or Telenet which are designed to permit access to the systems through a local telephone number, precluding the need for a long distance telephone call to the computer facility.   Tymshare's Tymnet service exists in approximately seventy-five major cities of the United States while the Telenet network may be accessed in some twenty-six major U. S. cities from coast to coast.   In addition, WATS or FTS lines may be utilized for data communication.

3.   Communication Line Interfaces-Modems and Acoustic Couplers

Interface devices for data communication, e.g., modems or acoustic couplers, are required to convert the digital signals emitted by the computer and the terminal to the frequency signals carried on telephone lines.   The modem (or data set or dataphone) is a direct physical connection between the terminal and communication line or the computer and communication line.   In addition to converting digital signals to frequency signals and vice versa, modems control the transmission rate of data over communication lines.   The acoustic coupler, on the other hand, is a type of modem that accommodates portable terminals and no permanent connection to the terminal is required.   Many terminals are supplied with built-in acoustic couplers, but others may be attached to the coupler by a cable.   The connection to the telephone voice circuit is made by placing the telephone handset in the cradle of the acoustic coupler.

SECTION F.   MICROFORMS

A microform is a unit of information, i. e., a page of text or a drawing, photographically reproduced in a form too small to be read without magnification.   Though microform technology has been developing for more than thirty-five years, only recently has it begun to have a significant impact on law libraries.

Librarians acquire microforms for a number of reasons: to obtain materials not otherwise available because they are out-of-print, rare, or prohibitively expensive; to replace items which are deteriorating; to replace large or bulky materials, such as backfiles of newspapers and periodicals; to conserve stack space; to store older materials that have little probability of use. Perhaps the greatest advantage to the researcher offered by a microform collection is that of file integrity. That is, once a series or collection of documents is converted to microform, there is less danger that a particular item will disappear or be misplaced. Every page of a publication remains intact as originally published. Microforms may be reproduced and converted into hard copy quickly and inexpensively if that format is desired.

Current standards of the Association of American Law Schools (AALS) permit microforms to be counted for up to 20% of the core collection required for law library accreditation.[8] The expansion of materials available in microform, however, coupled with the advantages outlined above may soon lead to an increase in the formula to 30% or even 40% of the core collection.

Since the researcher will have occasion to consult texts in microform, he should have a basic understanding of this media. The sections that follow describe the characteristics of microforms and offer lists of titles of interest to the legal scholar.

1. MICROFORM FORMATS AND CHARACTERISTICS.

There are many distinctive features of microforms which can vary. The following section illustrates the most important of these.

a. Common Features of Microforms

(1) Reduction Ratio.

The reduction ratio is a measure of the number of times a given linear dimension of an object is reduced when photographed, and is expressed as 16X, 24X, etc. Although microforms are available at reduction ratios below 15X and higher than 90X, the most common reduction ratios are 18X, 20X, and 24X.

(2) Polarity.

Film polarity refers to the change or retention of the dark to light relationship of an image in the filming process. Positive film retains the original material's tonal values so that the light areas of the original are recorded on the film as light, and the dark areas as dark. Negative film reverses the original tonal values, thus light areas are recorded

[8] NEW YORK UNIVERSITY, PROCEEDINGS, CONFERENCE AND SEMINAR: EXPANDING USE OF MICROFORMS IN LAW LIBRARIES. 12 (1973).

as dark and dark areas are recorded as light. Many microforms are available in either positive or negative format, and libraries choose the type which best serves the needs of their patrons. Positive film preserves the quality of illustrations and half tones, and is, therefore, the format chosen for publications with many illustrations. Negative film produces better hardcopy and is chosen for publications which will be photocopied frequently. Either type of film can be easily read on the standard microform readers.

b. Formats

(1) Microfilm.

Microfilm, still the most common microform, is a roll of film packaged in either reels, cartridges, or cassettes. Typically, it is the format chosen for storing serial publications such as newspapers and journals. It is available in many widths, from 8mm. to 105mm., but at the present time the standard microfilm is either 16mm. or 35mm. Microfilm in cartridges or cassettes is not usually purchased by libraries, since such storage units are not interchangeable among different models of readers. Also, microfilm on reels is less expensive.

The newest development in the microfilm area is COM (computer output microfilm). It is produced directly from information stored on computer tapes, and may become a viable substitute for library card catalogs in the future.

(2) Microfiche.*

Basically, microfiche is a sheet of microfilm which may vary in size from 3 x 5 inches to 6 x 9 inches. The standard microfiche, as approved by the National Microfilm Association, is 4 x 6 inches in size and has microimages arranged on it in a grid pattern. The standard reduction ratio on microfiche is 24X, allowing for a maximum of 98 pages to appear on a sheet, but microfiche of other reduction ratios are available. In addition to making hardcopy photocopies of pages appearing on a microfiche, it is now possible to reproduce copies of sheets of microfiche quickly on the printer-processor.

(3) Ultrafiche.

Ultrafiche is a type of microfiche with much higher reduction ratios. It contains microimages in a reduction range of more than 90X which permits many thousands of images

---

* "Fiche" is French for "card", so that the literal meaning of "microfiche" is "little card."

to be stored on a single fiche. For example, the West ultra-fiche edition of the *National Reporter System, First Series,* permits 1,450 pages to be displayed on a single sheet. Commerce Clearing House has produced a *CCH Ultrafiche Tax Library* with up to 1,700 pages on a single ultrafiche sheet, reducing a 351 volume library to just 10 inches of shelf space.

(4) Micro-opaques.

Micro-opaques are similar to microfiche in format, but the microimages are all positive in polarity and are arranged on opaque paper stock rather than on transparent film. This enables separate sets of images to be printed on both sides of the card, doubling data storage capacity. The cards vary in size from 3 x 5 inches to 6 x 9 inches.[9] These are the least popular microform. They are more difficult to read than the other varieties and cannot be as efficiently duplicated.

c. Microform Equipment [10]

The legal scholar may have negative feelings about using microforms from past experience with bulky, inefficient old-model microform readers. However, microform equipment technology has made rapid advances in recent times. Researchers can now obtain efficient portable readers with high resolution viewing screens which make reading microforms almost as easy and comfortable as reading from a book.

Microform equipment is available in many price ranges. Portable readers are now available at between $60 and $150. These are small, light-weight machines (under 15 lbs.) designed to be moved from place to place by the user. There are portable readers for use with microfilm and microfiche. Desk model readers which are ¾ the size of the standard stationary readers are also produced for use with both formats. They range in price from about $150 to $300. The stationary microfiche and microfilm readers range in price from $125 to $1500. Whereas most microfiche readers are usable with a number of different reduction ratios, a special reader with an expensive lens must be purchased for use with the highly reduced images of ultrafiche.

Reader-printers which produce hard copy printouts of microform images are available for either microfiche or microfilm. They range in price from $1,350 to more than $9,000. There are also

[9] The micro-opaque sizes vary by their trade names: "Microcard" in 3 x 5 inches and 4 x 6 inches; "Microprint" measuring 6 x 9 inches; "Microlex" in 6½ x 8½ inches; "Mini-Print" in 6 x 9 inches.

[10] See "Selected List of Microform Equipment Dealers" on p. 486.

microfiche printer-processors available which reproduce copies of individual sheets of microfiche. Costs start as low as $785.

2. COMMON LEGAL MATERIALS IN MICROFORM.[11]

The following is a selected list of law materials frequently found in microform research collections. It illustrates the wide range and variety of law materials and formats available.

a. Primary Sources

(1) Case Reports.

(a) *National Reporter System, First Series*

The West Publishing Company has reproduced all nine units of the *National Reporter System, First Series,* in ultrafiche. The 75x reduction permits 1,450 pages to be displayed on a single fiche with each fiche corresponding to one large physical volume.

(b) *State reports prior to the National Reporter System*

Trans-Media Publishing Company offers all the state court decisions prior to the National Reporter System covering more than 4,000 volumes, on 35mm. microfilm. The set also includes reports of the territories and many collateral state reports not included in the state reports or the National Reporter System.

(c) *U. S. Reports*

Lawyers Microfilm Company offers this case series on 32x microfiche.

(2) Statutes.

(a) *U. S. Statutes at Large*

Several micropublishers have issued the statutes on 16mm. or 35mm. microfilm. The Library of Congress has reproduced the statutes from vol. 1 through vol. 76A (1789–1962) on 35mm. microfilm. Information Handling Services (formerly Microcard Editions) has produced the statutes from 1789 through 1972 on microfiche.

(b) *State Session Laws*

The session laws of American states and territorial legislatures from 1776 through 1969 have been produced on microfiche by Xerox University Microfilms. Information Handling Services offers session laws covering the period 1970–1974 for all fifty states, the Virgin

[11] See "Selected List of Micropublishers of Law-Related Materials" on p. 486.

Islands, Puerto Rico, Guam, American Samoa, and the Pacific Island territories on microfiche.   Both companies are planning to issue session laws up to the current date.

(3) Treaties.

(a) *United Nations Treaty Series*

United Nations Publications offers the *United Nations Treaty Series,* vols. 1–750 (1947–1970) on microfiche. The series is also published on 35mm. microfilm by Trans-Media.

(b) *League of Nations Treaty Series*

The *League of Nations Treaty Series,* vols. 1–205 (1920–1946), has been produced on 35mm. microfilm by Datamatics.

(4) Administrative Regulations.

(a) *Federal Register*

A number of micropublishers have produced the *Federal Register* on 16mm. and 35mm. microfilm.   In addition, Information Handling Services offers the *Federal Register* on microfiche.

(b) *Code of Federal Regulations*

Trans-Media Publishing Company offers the *Code of Federal Regulations* on 35mm. microfilm, covering the period 1939–1971.   The U. S. Government Printing Office has conducted a pilot project of filming and distributing microfiche copies of the current CFR to a selected number of government depository libraries to test the feasibility of supplying it and certain other publications in microform.   However, it is not possible to order the CFR from the Government Printing Office in microform at this time.

(5) Congressional Materials.

(a) Proceedings of the U. S. Congress

The records of the debates in the United States Congress appearing in the *Annals of Congress* (1789–1824), the *Register of Debates* (1824–1837), the *Congressional Globe* (1833–1873), and the *Congressional Record* (1873 to date) are available in several formats (16mm. and 35mm. microfilm and microfiche) from a number of micropublishers.   In addition, one service offers microfiche copies of the daily edition of the *Record* by monthly subscription.

(b) Congressional Bills

The Library of Congress has filmed the House and Senate Bills from the 1st through the 72nd Congress (1789–1933) and the 92nd Congress (1971–1972) on 35mm. microfilm. Congressional Information Service, CIS, offers the Congressional bills, resolutions and public laws on microfiche from the 90th Congress (1967–1968) through the 94th Congress (1975–1976), and will continue the series. Beginning with the 93rd Congress, CIS has filmed all versions of a bill consecutively, followed by the public or private law, if enacted. Readex Microprint Publications has also issued the House and Senate bills from 1957 through 1965 on micro-opaques.

(c) Legislative Histories

From 1970 to date Congressional Information Service has published the *CIS/Microfiche Library*, which contains the complete text of the following Congressional publications: all Committee Hearings, Committee Prints, House and Senate Reports, House and Senate Special Publications, Senate Executive Reports, and Senate Executive Documents. The collection does not include the *Congressional Record*, reports and hearings on private bills, ceremonial publications, reports on internal housekeeping matters, reports on land conveyances, and reprints of documents previously made available in departmental editions. The *CIS/Index* provides access to the items included. It should be noted that the publications included in the *CIS/Microfiche Library* can be searched on-line through the SDC ORBIT system, and that the documents may be ordered either on-line for delivery to the requestor or may be ordered from CIS directly via its regular on-demand service program.

Greenwood Press, a subsidiary of CIS, offers an extensive microfiche collection of U. S. Congressional hearings from the 25th Congress (1839) through the 91st Congress, First session (1969). A *Witness Index* to the hearings from the 25th to the 89th Congress (1839–1966) has been issued by Greenwood on microfiche.

Readex Microprint Publications has produced a micro-opaque edition of Congressional hearings and prints covering the 84th Congress, 2nd session (1956) through the 92nd Congress (1971–1972).

Information Handling Services publishes the legislative histories of important laws dating from the 82nd Congress (1951) to date on microfiche. The histories are selected by a committee of the American Association of Law Libraries and are compiled by law librarians. The collection is arranged by public law number and is fully indexed.

(d) *U. S. Serial Set.*[12]

Congressional Information Service has begun publishing the entire *U. S. Serial Set* (1789–1969) on microfiche. The microfiche are being published in groups, and by the end of 1976 will cover the period from 1924–1969. The collection is scheduled for completion in 1979.

Another microfiche edition of the *U. S. Serial Set* is published by Information Handling Services which covers the 15th through the 61st Congress (1817–1913). A micro-opaque edition has also been produced which covers the 15th through the 61st Congress (1817–1911).

b.   Secondary Sources

(1) *The United States Supreme Court Records and Briefs.*

This valuable collection of the written arguments of counsel in U. S. Supreme Court cases dating from 1832 to date is immense. Information Handling Services offers historic documentation on Full-Opinion, Per Curiam and Certiorari Denied cases from 1832 to 1896 on 35mm. microfilm. The documentation on microfiche is available from 1897 to the present. Per Curiam and Certiorari Denied Case Records and Briefs are available on microfiche from 1950 to the present. Both the historic and the current Records and Briefs are comprehensively indexed in hard copy.

Scholarly Resources Inc. publishes the Records and Briefs from 1832–1929 on 35mm. microfilm. A hardcopy Guide-Index is published for use with the collection.

Law Reprints Inc. issues the Records and Briefs from 1974 to the present on microfiche. The collection is arranged by docket number, and a hardcopy cumulative index accompanies the set.

(2) Periodicals and Newspapers.

Library researchers have become accustomed to finding back issues of periodicals and newspapers in microform rather

---

[12] The *U. S. Serial Set* is the collected edition of publications compiled by direction of Congress, including House and Senate documents and reports, executive branch publications, and certain reports by non-governmental organizations.

than in bound volumes.   Most of the leading law reviews are available in either 16mm. or 35mm. microfilm.   Rothman Reprints, Inc. publishes an extensive collection of legal periodicals in two series: one series covering leading current law reviews, and the other covering periodicals in English from the earliest period up to the 20th century which have ceased publication.   A newspaper of particular interest to the legal researcher, *New York Law Journal,* is available from 1888 to the present on 35 mm. microfilm from the Godfrey Memorial Library of Middletown, Connecticut.

(3) Treatises.

Increasingly, microform is the format chosen by publishers for reprinting rare or out-of-print books.   For example, University Publications of America publishes Joseph Chitty's classic 19th century treatises on procedure, criminal law, and commercial law in 35mm. microfilm.

Dissertations relating to legal topics by United States scholars are published by Xerox University Microfilms on 35mm. microfilm.   Rothman Reprints Inc. publishes microfiche editions of treatises in the public domain which are listed in the Association of American Law Schools' series, *Law Books Recommended for Libraries.*

(4) Trials.

Several microform collections of trials have been issued by micropublishers.   Information Handling Services publishes a microfiche series of the 102 most famous British and American 18th and 19th century trials.   The collection includes public records and documents, scholarly treatises, newspaper accounts, and personal narratives.   Compilations of materials relating to current-interest trials have appeared in microform.   For example, Microfilming Corporation of America issues the official court transcript of the Watergate trial on both 35mm. microfilm and microfiche.

3.   GUIDES TO MICROFORM COLLECTIONS.

It is often difficult for the researcher to identify which publications are available in microform.   The following section lists guides to legal microform materials and general microform sourcebooks.

In order to convey more detailed bibliographic information, the citations included do not follow strict citation form as outlined in Appendix A.

a.   Law-Related Guides

(1) *Legal Materials in Microform; a Bibliography*, comp. G. Sell. 3d ed., Provo, Utah: J. Reuben Clark Law Library, 1976.

The third edition of this comprehensive bibliography lists legal microform materials and includes a glossary, table of symbols, and an extensive index.

(2) Tseng, H. *Complete Guide to Legal Materials in Microform*. Arlington: University Publications of America, 1976.

The treatise lists by author and title law and law-related microforms, both domestic and international, in English and foreign languages which were in print or in the process of completion as of November 2, 1975. Also included are a glossary of microform terms and a directory of microform publishers.

b.   General Guides

(1) *Guide to Microforms in Print*. Weston, Conn.: Microform Review Inc., annual.

This guide lists in alphabetical order all materials available on microfilm, microfiche and micro-opaques from publishers within the United States and around the world.

(2) *Microform Review*. Weston, Conn.: Microform Review Inc., issued six times per year.

This journal presents timely articles on micropublishing in addition to reviews by microform specialists of all current microform publications.

(3) *Micrographics Equipment Review*. Weston, Conn.: Microform Review Inc., quarterly.

This service publishes approximately 24 reviews per year on equipment that is most likely to be used in library and business applications.

(4) *Microlist*. Weston, Conn.: Microform Review Inc., issued ten times per year.

This bibliographic service lists new microform titles from publishers in the United States and around the world.

(5) *Micropublishers' Trade List Annual (MTLA)*. Weston, Conn.: Microform Review Inc., annual.

The MTLA contains the current catalogs on microfiche of over 200 micropublishers from the U. S. and aboard. A printed hard copy index provides direct access to the catalogs.

(6) *National Register of Microform Masters.* Washington, D. C.: Library of Congress, annual.

The *Register* is the most comprehensive listing of microforms available. It records masters that are retained solely for the purpose of making other copies. Included are foreign and domestic books, serials, and foreign doctoral dissertations available from publishers in the U. S. and abroad.

(7) *Subject Guide to Microforms in Print.* Weston, Conn.: Microform Review Inc., annual.

This companion volume to the *Guide to Microforms in Print* lists microform publications under 135 subject headings.

SELECTED LIST OF MICROFORM EQUIPMENT DEALERS

Bell and Howell
Microimagery Group
6800 McCormick Road
Chicago, Ill. 60645

Blue-Ray, Inc.
4469 Westbrook Road
Essex, Conn. 06426

Bruning Division, A–M Corp.
1834 Walden Office Square
Schaumberg, Ill. 60172

Eastman Kodak Company Business
Systems Markets Division
343 State St.
Rochester, N. Y. 14650

Library Microfilms & Materials Co.
5709 Mesmer Ave.
Culver City, Calif. 90230

Luxor Corporation
104 Lake View Ave.
Waukegan, Ill. 60085

Micobra Corporation
176 King St.
P. O. Box 1187
Hanover, Mass. 02339

Micrographix Systems
1056 Spring St., N. W.
Atlanta, Ga. 30309

Northwest Microfilm, Inc.
6840 Shingle Creek Parkway
Minneapolis, Minn. 55430

3M Company
3M Center
St. Paul, Minn. 55101

Xerox-University Microfilms
Equipment Customer Service
300 North Zeeb Rd.
Ann Arbor, Michigan 48106

SELECTED LIST OF MICROPUBLISHERS OF
LAW–RELATED MATERIALS

Congressional Information Service
600 Montgomery Bldg.
Washington, D. C. 20014

Rothman Reprints, Inc.
57 Leuning St.
So. Hackensack, N. J. 07606

Information Handling Services
22498 Statler Blvd.
St. Clair Shores, Michigan 48081

Scholarly Resources, Inc.
1508 Pennsylvania Ave.
Wilmington, Del. 19806

Law Reprints, Inc.
37 W. 20th St.
New York, N. Y. 10011

Trans-Media Publishing Co.
75 Main St.
Dobbs Ferry, N. Y. 10522

Lawyers Microfilm
P. O. Box 533
319 W. Poplar
Rogers, Arkansas 72756

University Publications of
    America, Inc.
2523 Wilson Blvd.
Arlington, Virginia 22201

Microfilming Corp. of America
21 Harristown Rd.
Glen Rock, N. J. 07452

West Publishing Company
50 W. Kellogg Blvd.
St. Paul, Minnesota 55102

Readex Microprint Corp.
101 Fifth Ave.
New York, N. Y. 10003

Xerox-University Microfilms
300 N. Zeeb Rd.
Ann Arbor, Michigan 48106

FURTHER READINGS

Amundson, *Law Office Memos; From Carrier Pigeons to Law Books*,
    59 A.B.A.J. 1048 (1973).

HOW TO SELECT A MICROFORM READER OR READER–
    PRINTER.   Silver Springs, Md.: National Microfilm Assoc.,
    1974.

INTRODUCTION TO MICROGRAPHICS.   Silver Springs, Md.: Na-
    tional Microfilm Assoc., 1973.

MICROFORMS IN LIBRARIES; A READER, ed. A. DIAZ. Weston,
    Conn.: Microform Review Inc., 1975.

NMA STANDARD GLOSSARY OF MICROGRAPHICS, ed. D. AVE-
    DON.   Silver Springs, Md.: National Microfilm Assoc., 1973.

NEW YORK UNIVERSITY.   PROCEEDINGS, CONFERENCE
    AND SEMINAR: EXPANDING USE OF MICROFORM IN
    LAW LIBRARIES.   Dobbs Ferry, N. Y.: Trans-Media, 1973.

F. SPIGAI.   THE INVISIBLE MEDIUM: THE STATE OF THE
    ART OF MICROFORM AND A GUIDE TO THE LITERA-
    TURE.   Stanford: ERIC Clearinghouse on Media and Tech-
    nology, March, 1973.

USER EQUIPMENT, ed. H. BALLOU.   6th ed., Silver Springs, Md.:
    National Microfilm Assoc., 1975.

Chapter 24

A GENERAL SUMMARY OF RESEARCH
PROCEDURE

No system of legal research yet constructed can replace the professional judgment of a trained legal mind. Legal research is as much an art as it is a science. There are as many approaches to legal research as there are problems to be solved and persons who assume the task.

We have studied each of the various types of research tools available for the resolution of legal problems. The final step in our study is to develop a systematic approach to problem solving using these research tools. The approaches to legal research discussed in this chapter are simply suggestions and nothing more. In the end, we must develop a system which suits our own individual needs.

The approach one adopts as a novice must be systematic in order to minimize the possibility of error. As we gain expertise, this approach can and should be refined, eliminating steps which can be accomplished mentally and decreasing the time required to execute the task.

No matter how sophisticated we become in any particular field of law, there will always be problems calling for research into areas of the law with which we are utterly unfamiliar. It is at these moments when the basic approach developed as novices becomes the artful technique of a trained professional.

Any worthwhile system of legal research can be broken down into five basic steps. These are:

STEP 1.   Identify the operative facts.

STEP 2.   Frame the legal issues to be researched.

STEP 3.   Identify the relevant sources of law.

STEP 4.   Research the issues presented.

STEP 5.   Communicate the solution of the problem.

Our discussion will focus on each of these steps individually; however, it is to be remembered that each step is closely interrelated to all the others and that while we are in the actual process of executing any one of the steps we will simultaneously be refining the work which has been done under all of the previous steps.

Step 1.   Identify the Operative Facts

The first task of the researcher is to isolate and identify the facts surrounding the particular problem to be solved. Some of the facts are operative; that is, they have legal significance. Others are inoperative, having no legal significance. We begin the task of legal research by compiling a descriptive statement of operative facts. This task is closely related to the second step in the problem solving process —that of framing the legal issues raised by the facts. As we gain expertise in a particular field of law, we become more skilled in the process of isolating operative facts having legal significance. On the other hand, it is often quite difficult for a novice to identify the operative facts and to discard insignificant facts. Consequently, if we are researching a problem of uncertain legal dimensions it is always best to err on the side of over-inclusion rather on the side of exclusion.

We must also keep in mind that the words used to describe a particular problem, the words used to characterize the fact complex to be researched, can both assist and retard the research process. Most of the research tools available are indexed by a set of descriptive words. Failure to describe the fact complex with sufficient detail can sometimes cause us to completely overlook important legal issues because we fail to find descriptive words in the legal indices which correspond to the words used in our statement of facts. For example, using a person's name rather than a person's legal status in the statement of facts can result in overlooking relevant legal authority dealing with the person's legal status. If, after completing our legal research, it is determined that the person's legal status is irrelevant to the problem, the facts can always be rewritten so as to exclude this inoperative fact.

There are at least two alternative ways to write a description of the facts. These are in narrative and in numbered outline form. Both of these forms can be arranged in a number of patterns. For example, the facts can be stated chronologically or they can be grouped according to the legal issues involved. This latter technique is more adapted to research in familiar fields of law.

Step 2.   Frame the Legal Issues to be Researched

Writing a clear, concise statement of each legal issue raised by the operative facts is undoubtedly the most important and often the most difficult task associated with legal research. Attorneys spend three years in law school learning how to isolate legal issues from a set of given facts. The process of developing this still continues throughout one's career.

Failure to frame all the issues raised by a particular set of facts can and often will result in reaching an erroneous solution. For this

reason, we must exercise our legal imagination to its fullest capacity when we frame our issues to be researched. This process should be done in an unhurried, methodical way.

It is best for the novice to err on the side of too many issues. Insignificant issues can always be discarded after they have been thoroughly investigated. In addition, overlapping issues can be consolidated if we discover that they are simply restatements of the same legal question.

The framing of legal issues is a continuing process which is carried on at every step of the research process. As we research a particular issue we often discover that it is overly broad and are forced to narrow our statement of the issue, eliminating in significant matters. We may also be forced to split the original issue into two or more questions or to divide the original issue into a main issue containing two or more sub-issues. Sometimes we find that our original statement of an issue is too narrow and, consequently, is not leading us to relevant authority in point. At this time we are forced to increase the breadth of our statement of the issue in order to gain access to relevant legal authority. During our research we often discover issues we had not thought of initially. For these reasons, the task of framing legal issues is never truly completed until we have finished the research project.

When we encounter an unfamiliar field of law, it will probably be necessary to conduct a preliminary investigation of legal authority in the field for the purpose of isolating the legal issues deserving of meticulous research. As we noted in Chapter 15, secondary expository publications, such as encyclopedias, treatises, periodical articles and annotations can be of significant value in identifying and explaining general principles in unfamiliar fields of law.

Once we have drafted a preliminary statement of each legal issue which we think is fairly raised by the operative facts, we must arrange them in some logical pattern which provides continuity and preserves the integrity of our thought process as we conduct our legal research. Logically related issues can often be combined as sub-issues under a broader main issue. Issues which depend upon the outcome of other threshold issues should be ordered accordingly.

When we are arranging our issues we should keep in mind that it is usually best to exhaust all the relevant legal authority on one issue before going on to research another issue. This technique is more methodical than is an approach which exhausts a given legal authority on all the issues raised by the facts before moving on to the next source of law.

The technique of exhausting all the relevant authorities on a particular issue before going on to the next issue also serves other prac-

tical purposes. It allows us to focus our sometimes short attention span on a fairly narrow area of the law, thus avoiding the temptation to stray into interesting but irrelevant areas. It permits us to perform work unrelated to our legal research project without unnecessarily disturbing the research process. And, it allows us to quickly gain some knowledge of the time required to complete the project so that we can accurately schedule each step of the process, ensuring that it will be completed on time.

For these reasons, it is always advisable to frame the issues so that they can be independently researched and to arrange these issues and sub-issues into a logically progressive pattern.

Step 3. Identify the Relevant Sources of Law

The preceding Chapters of this book have given us a preliminary overview of the contents of every important source of legal authority. The problem at this point in your legal research is to decide, for each issue to be investigated, which sources to use, which sources not to use, and the order in which these sources should be examined.

This is probably the easiest step of the research process and, for that reason, it is often omitted. By failing to give some conscious thought to the precise sources we intend to use before we begin to research a particular issue, we run the risk of omitting a vital source of law and, more importantly, we may start our research from the wrong end, unnecessarily increasing the difficulty of the task. For these reasons, the novice should always prepare a list of sources arranged in the order they will be used for each issue to be researched.

For convenience in selecting our sources of authority, we classify general legal problems into four categories: (1) constitutional law, (2) statutory law, (3) case law (common law) and (4) administrative law. In this connection, we do not concern ourselves with international law, which we studied in Chapter 20, for the solutions of its problems are not found in the systematic use of general legal publications.

Each of these categories is generally subdivided into federal, state and local law. As you will observe in your practice many legal issues cross over categories, relate to more than one area and concurrently may refer to federal, state or local laws within a single category. To illustrate, a controversy may pertain to the interpretation of a state statute and its constitutionality, thus fitting into categories one and two, above. Also, the constitutional issue may have both federal and state ramifications. It follows that legal issues cannot be compartmentalized. This is one reason why it is usually advisable to thoroughly research each issue separately and completely before turning to the next issue.

Notwithstanding this interrelationship of legal issues, we will endeavor to list the relevant sources of legal authority as separate, independent units. Thus, for example, a suggested list of authoritative sources is presented for a constitutional law problem. The constitutional law authorities are listed in a suggested order of use which will minimize the time required to solve a constitutional law problem. It must be remembered that if a particular issue overlaps more than one category, we must prepare a list of sources containing authorities drawn from all the applicable categories. In addition to simply listing the sources in their order of intended use, we must give some thought as to how we intend to coordinate our use of the relevant sources in obtaining a rapid, accurate solution of the issue being researched.

The following is a suggested list of sources which should be consulted in solving problems in each of the four basic categories we developed above. Each list is broken down into subcategories, reflecting the divisions between federal, state and local laws. Finally, each list contains explanatory notes designed to assist in coordinating our use of the relevant sources to obtain rapid, accurate answers to our legal problems. Following the list of sources is a "Chart on Legal Procedure" which summarizes the information previously presented in narrative form.

SECTION A.　CONSTITUTIONAL LAW PROBLEM

1.　Federal Constitution

a.　General Background

For a general discussion of a federal constitutional law question, consult a general legal encyclopedia (*Corpus Juris Secundum* or *American Jurisprudence 2d*). More critical and detailed studies may be found in the periodical literature by examining the *Index to Legal Periodicals*. A recent treatise may be consulted to explore the area. Several other interpretative sources are given in Chapter 8.

Examine the *American Law Reports* and the *United States Supreme Court Reports* (L.Ed.) for possible annotations.

b.　Text and Interpretation

If the matter is a recognizable federal constitutional problem, consult the following sources:

For the text of the Constitution and its interpretation see:

United States Code Annotated.
United States Code Service.
Constitution of the United States (Library of Congress ed. 1972).

c. *Shepard's Citations*

Shepardize: (1) several important cases and (2) the applicable provision of the Constitution in *Shepard's United States Citations* and the provision in the appropriate *Shepard's State Citations*.   Use *Shepard's Federal Reporter Citations* when given an intermediate or lower court decision.   Numerous case citations under a provision of the Constitution in *Shepard's United States Citations* may make the Constitution section in *Shepard's* unwieldly and unusable.

d. Additional Cases

Check a United States Supreme Court digest, the *Federal Practice Digest 2d* (and its earlier editions), or the *American Digest System* for additional judicial interpretations.

e. Intent

In the absence of adequate judicial interpretation or to re-examine the meaning given to the Constitution by its framers, the following historical source materials should be studied.

The Madison Papers.

Elliott's Debates.

The Federalist.

The Documentary History of the Constitution, 1786–1870.

Documents Illustrative of the Formation of the Union of the American States.

2. State Constitution

a. General Background

For a discussion of a state constitution, consult a local encyclopedia, if one is published for the state, e. g., *Texas Jurisprudence 2d* and *Illinois Law and Practice*.   In the absence of a local encyclopedia, a general encyclopedia (C.J.S. or Am.Jur.2d) may provide a helpful general discussion of the question.   An *American Law Reports* annotation or a periodical article also may treat the constitutional issue.

b. Text and Interpretation

The text and case interpretations of a state constitution are included in the appropriate annotated state code.

Additional cases may be located through the state digest.

c. *Shepard's Citations*

Shepardize: (1) several leading cases and (2) the provision of the state constitution in the appropriate *Shepard's State Citations*.

d. Additional Cases

For cases of other states, consult the *American Digest System*.

The *Index Digest of State Constitutions*, 2d edition, cites comparative state constitutions. Through these references, the annotated constitutions of other states may be examined, evaluated and compared. This procedure is useful in citing persuasive decisions from another state whose provision was copied or where the provision, situation and setting are comparable or where there is a dearth of judicial interpretation of the provision by your state courts.

Comparative constitutional study also may be engaged by Shepardizing cases under their *Reporter* citations in the appropriate *Shepard's Reporter Citations*.

e. Intent

Examine the proceedings, reports and other documents relating to state constitutional conventions for the meaning given the provision by its draftsmen.

SECTION B. STATUTORY PROBLEM

1. Federal Statute

a. General Background

Treatises are available for a number of federal statutory laws, e. g., *Callman, Law of Unfair Competition, Trademarks and Monopolies*, 3rd ed. 1969, 5 vols. They provide not only background but also detailed subject information. Thus they are valuable not only for their informational content but also as case finders.

Annotations in the *American Law Reports* and the *United States Supreme Court Reports* (L.Ed.) and periodical literature are additional useful secondary aids.

b. Text and Interpretation

For the text and interpretation of a federal statute which is in force, use the *United States Code Annotated* or the *United States Code Service*. The amendatory history of the act is included in these annotated codes.

For the legislative history (intent of the draftsmen) of the act, consult the Congressional bills, reports, hearings and debates. See Chapter 10.

c. *Shepard's Citations*

Shepardize: (1) the provision (*United States Code* or *Statutes at Large*) for the history and the treatment of the act and (2) several significant cases in *Shepard's United States Citations*. Consult *Shepard's Federal Reporter Citations* to Shepardize intermediate and lower federal court cases.

State court decisions which cite federal statutes are listed in *Shepard's State Citations*.

d.   Additional Cases

When there are meager case interpretations, examine the United States Supreme Court digests, the *Federal Practice Digest 2d* (and its earlier editions, the *Modern Federal Practice Digest* and the *Federal Digest*), or the *American Digest System*.

2.   State Statute

a.   General Background

The local encyclopedia is helpful in providing information and interpretations to a state statute. Local treatises and periodical articles, having more detailed bearing on the act, are equally useful references.

Where there is no local encyclopedia, Am.Jur.2d and C.J.S. may give general information on some topics.

Annotations in the *American Law Reports* cover statutory law of the several states.

b.   Text and Interpretation

Unannotated state codes provide the text of the statutes.

Annotated state codes give both the text of the statutes and case interpretations.

The codes provide the amendatory history of the state acts. For legislative histories, consult the official and unofficial sources (see Chapter 1).

c.   *Shepard's Citations*

Shepardize: (1) the provision of the state statute and (2) several important cases in the applicable *Shepard's State Citations*.

d.   Additional Cases

For additional cases interpreting the statute, examine the state digest.

If there is a dearth of statutory interpretation in the state, consult the annotated codes of other states for other states' interpretations. Such interpretation can be very persuasive. Some codes list comparative legislation of representative and neighboring states.

3.   Local Ordinances and Codes

a.   Text and Interpretation

The text of city ordinances are included in city codes. Generally, city codes are not annotated.

The appropriate state digest is useful in providing interpretations to the city ordinance, but the problem must be approached by subject or topic.

In the absence of a current city code, check the ordinances in the office of the city counsel, city clerk or other local official whose duties include the maintenance of a current file of city laws.

b. *Shepard's Citations*

Shepardize: (1) the provision of the city code and (2) several significant cases, if existing, in the applicable *Shepard's State Citations*.

SECTION C. CASE LAW PROBLEM

1. General Background

When the problem is not covered by a constitution or a statute, then the answer must be sought in the judicial decisions of a state.

As noted in Section A2, above, the local encyclopedia is a good source for a discussion of the topic. In the absence of a local encyclopedia, *American Jurisprudence 2d* or *Corpus Juris Secundum* may be consulted for an exposition on the case law.

American Jurisprudence 2d may give specific references to *American Law Reports* annotations, eliminating the use of A.L.R. indexes or regional digests.

In some fields of the law, the researcher might begin with a local treatise or periodical article.

2. Interpretation

References to state court cases may be found in the appropriate state digest.

3. *Shepard's Citations*

You are to *Shepardize* several of the significant cases in *Shepard's State Citations*.

4. Additional Cases

Other state digests, the regional digests and the *American Digest System* provide judicial decisions of other states on the point of law.

Shepard's Reporter Citations gives additional references to cases from other states which have cited an applicable state case.

SECTION D.   ADMINISTRATIVE LAW PROBLEM

1.   Federal Administrative Law

a.   General Background

Corpus Juris Secundum or *American Jurisprudence 2d* discuss federal administrative law. *Pike and Fischer, Administrative Law*, treatises (e. g., *Davis, Administrative Law*) and periodical literature provide more detailed studies of administrative law.

Annotations on the subject are included in the *American Law Reports* and the *United States Supreme Court Reports* (L.Ed.).

b.   Text and Interpretation

The text of federal administrative regulations are contained in: (1) loose-leaf services and (2) the *Code of Federal Regulations* and the *Federal Register*.

The decisions of federal administrative agencies are included in: (1) loose-leaf services and (2) agency reports.

Interpretative sources of federal administrative law are: (1) loose-leaf services, (2) U.S. Supreme Court digests and (3) the *Modern Federal Practice Digest* and the *Federal Digest*.

c.   *Shepard's Citations*

Cases of certain agencies may be *Shepardized* in *Shepard's United States Administrative Citations*.

Court cases on federal administrative law are *Shepardized* in *Shepard's United States Citations* and *Shepard's Federal Reporter Citations*.

2.   State Administrative Law

a.   General Background

Refer to a local encyclopedia for a discussion of state administrative law.

Other secondary aids, such as local treatises, periodical articles and *American Law Reports* annotations, also are helpful sources.

b.   Text and Interpretation

If a state has a current administrative code, check it for state regulatory material.   In the absence of an administrative code, inquiry should be directed to the appropriate agency for its regulations.

If a loose-leaf service covers the state law, it can be consulted for agency rules and decisions.

The accessibility of agency decisions should be determined by inquiry.

Interpretative cases are covered by the state digest.

c. *Shepard's Citations*

Shepardize applicable court cases in *Shepard's State Citations.*

d. Additional Cases

Court decisions of other states relating to a comparable administrative law problem may be located in (1) other state digests, (2) regional digests, and (3) the *American Digest System.*

Shepard's Reporter Citations also provides citations to cases of other states which cited a state court decision in point.

3. Local Administrative Law

a. Text and Interpretation

If available, city administrative regulations generally are published separately as pamphlets for each body. Information regarding these rules, such as regulatory and licensing provisions, should be obtained directly from the local administrative department.

Cases pertaining to local administrative law are included in the state digest.

b. *Shepard's Citations*

Shepardize cases on the problem by using *Shepard's State Citations.*

SECTION E.   CHART ON LEGAL RESEARCH PROCEDURE

The outline of research procedure, presented in the preceding sections, is summarized graphically in the following chart:

CHART ON LEGAL RESEARCH PROCEDURE

RESEARCH PROBLEM	GENERAL BACKGROUND	MORE CRITICAL & DETAILED STUDIES	ANNOTATIONS	TEXT OF LAW	LEGISLATIVE HISTORY	INTERPRETATION	SHEPARDIZING	ADDITIONAL CASES
CONSTITUTIONAL LAW 1. Federal	1. C.J.S. 2. Am. Jur.2d	1. Treatises 2. Periodicals: Index Leg. P.	A.L.R. L.Ed.	1. U.S.C.A. 2. F.C.A. 3. L.C. Const.	Citations: U.S.C.A., F.C.A., Shep.U.S., U.S.C., Stat. at L. Intent: Mad. Papers, Federalist, etc.	1. U.S.C.A. 2. F.C.A.	1. Provisions: U.S., State / Cases: U.S., Fed., State 2. Cases: U.S. Fed., State	1. U.S.Sup.Ct.digs. 2. Mod. Fed. P. Dig. & Fed. Dig. 3. Am. Dig.
2. State	1. Local Ency. 2. C.J.S. or Am. Jur.2d	1. Periodicals: Index Leg. P.	A.L.R.	State Code	State Const. Conv. 1. Proceedings 2. Reports, etc.	1. Annot. State Code 2. State Dig.	1. Provisions: State Cit. 2. Cases: State Cit.	1. Am. Dig. 2. Index Dig. of State Const. 2d ed. 3. Shepard's Reporter Clts.
STATUTORY LAW 1. Federal	(C.J.S. or Am. Jur.2d)	1. Treatises 2. Periodicals	A.L.R. L.Ed.	1. U.S.C.A. 2. F.C.A.	Citations: U.S.C.A., F.C.A., Shep.U.S. Intent: Cong. Bills, Reps., Hear., Debates	1. U.S.C.A. 2. F.C.A.	Prov. & Cases: U.S. Cases: Fed. Prov.: State	1. U.S.Sup.Ct.Digs. 2. Mod.Fed.Prac.Dig. & Fed.Dig.
2. State	Loc. Ency. (C.J.S. or Am. Jur.2d)	1. Treatises 2. Periodicals	A.L.R.	State Code	Citations: State Code Intent: Official & Unofficial Sources	Annot. State Code	Prov. & Cases: State Cit.	1. State Dig. 2. Comparative Leg. In State Code.
3. Local				Mun. Code		State Dig.	Prov. & Cases: State Cit.	

CHART ON
LEGAL RESEARCH PROCEDURE
(Continued)

RESEARCH PROBLEM	GENERAL BACKGROUND	MORE CRITICAL & DETAILED STUDIES	ANNOTATIONS	TEXT OF LAW	LEGISLATIVE HISTORY	INTERPRETATION	SHEPARDIZING	ADDITIONAL CASES
CASE LAW: STATE	1. Loc. Ency. 2. C.J.S. or Am. Jur.2d	1. Treatises 2. Periodicals	A.L.R.			State Dig.	State Cit.	1. Am. Dig. 2. Other state digs. 3. Shepard's Reporter Cits.
ADMINISTRATIVE LAW 1. Federal	C.J.S. or Am.Jur.2d	1. Pike & Fischer 2. Treatises 3. Periodicals	A.L.R. L.Ed.	1. Loose-Leaf Serv.: Rules & Decs. 2. C.F.R. & Fed. Reg.: Rules 3. Agency Reps.: Decs.		1. Loose-Leaf Services 2. U.S.Sup.Ct. digs. 3. Mod.Fed.P. Dig. & Fed. Dig.	Loose-Leaf Agency Services Cases: U.S.Admin. U.S.Sup.Ct. Cit. Court Cases: U.S. and Fed. Cases: Fed.	
2. State	Loc.Ency.	1. Treatises 2. Periodicals	A.L.R.	1. Ad. Code, if pub. 2. Loose-Leaf Serv.: Rules & Decs. 3. Agency: Rules & Decs.		State Dig.	Cases: State Cit.	1. Am. Dig. 2. Other state digs. 3. Shepard's Reporter Cits.
3. Local				1. Local Adm. Dept. 2. Pamph.		State Dig.	**Cases: State Cit.**	

Step 4.   Research the Issues Presented

Once we have framed our issues and listed our sources of legal authority in the order we intend to use them, it is time to begin researching the first issue. Remember, we will complete our research of the first issue, exhausting all relevant authorities in point, before progressing to the second issue.

We begin by entering the first source on our list through its index, using the descriptive words developed by applying the TARP method discussed in Chapter 2. We thoroughly exhaust the contents of the first source, compiling a list of the statutes, cases and other relevant authorities cited thereby and taking notes from the text. If our first source is analyzed by *Shepard's Citations*, we *Shepardize* the source. We completely exhaust the first source for all materials in point so that there will be no need to return to this source again during our research of the first issue.

The next step is to read all the authorities cited by our first source. These authorities should be consulted in the following order: (1) constitutions, (2) statutes and local ordinances, (3) cases, (4) administrative materials, and finally (5) secondary authorities. As we read each of these cited authorities, we continue to compile a list of authorities which they cite (checking to eliminate duplicative citations previously noted from other sources) and we continue to take notes from text. Each cited source is thoroughly *Shepardized* before moving on to the next cited source. This entire process is continued until all the authorities cited in the first source on our list are completely exhausted. We then go to the second source on our original list and repeat the process. This pattern is repeated until all sources on our original list and the authorities they cite are fully researched.

At this point it is worth noting that as we move down our original list of sources the frequency of repetitive citations begins to increase rapidly. This informs us that we are beginning to exhaust the available sources in point. Near the end of our list of sources we will usually find that all of the citations are repetitive, indicating that our research is both thorough and complete. Of course, it is imperative that we organize our list of citations in a manner which allows us to quickly check for duplicative citations. This can be done by placing our citations on note cards organized according to the type of source involved. Failure to maintain an accurate list of citations will result in much wasted time and may cause us to completely overlook crucial sources of authority.

The following is a quick example of the process just described. Suppose that we are presented with a state law problem. The first source on our list is the local encyclopedia (or a general encyclopedia

if a state encyclopedia is not available). We enter through the index using the TARP method, read the text, and develop a list of citations which, for example, contains citations to the state annotated statutes and to several cases.

Since an encyclopedia cannot be *Shepardized*, we now begin to read our cited authorities, starting with the annotated statutes. We *do not* use the index of the statutes, but simply read the relevant statutory provisions cited by the encyclopedia, taking notes and compiling a list of citations from the annotations of the statutes. We then Shepardize the annotated statutes, continuing to add to our list of citations.

The next step is to read and *Shepardize* all of the cases cited by the encyclopedia, the annotated statutes we have just read, and by *Shepard's Citations*. Again, we take notes and compile a list of citations contained in the cases. We then *Shepardize* the cases. All the citations remaining on our list are investigated and we continue to *Shepardize* the sources referenced until we have systematically traced down every lead obtained from our reading of the local encyclopedia.

The next step is to go back to our original list of sources and to exhaust the second source contained on the list. The second source on that list will probably be the state annotated statutes. We have investigated this source before, but this time we enter through the index using the TARP method. At this point we usually discover that, in exhausting the citations emanating from an encyclopedia, we have read all or most all of the statutory provisions now located by using the index to the statutes. We now begin to develop a sense that we have exhausted the statutory authority in point.

Once we have completely exhausted all the citations obtained from our second look at the annotated statutes (in most cases this will be a short task) we move to our third source on the original list of sources. Suppose that this is the state digest. We enter through the descriptive word index. Again, we will discover that we have previously read all or virtually all of the relevant cases cited by the digest when we traced the cases cited by the local encyclopedia. Once we exhaust the state digest and the cases it cites we move on to the next source on our original list. The process is continued until the original list of authorities is completed. At this point our research of the first issue is complete and we can now proceed to begin our research of the second issue.

As we gain increased expertise in the process of executing legal research, we begin to develop certain shortcuts which increase our speed without sacrificing accuracy. For example, we begin to use a host of abbreviations such as those used by *Shepard's Citations*.

Skilled researchers can rapidly evaluate the potential value of a case without reading the entire reported decision. One such technique is as follows: (1) read the headnotes, selecting those which bear on the issue being researched; (2) read that portion of the text relating to the headnotes selected; (3) read the facts of the case and as much of the opinion as is necessary to understand the point of law involved; (4) jot down the headnote numbers for Shepardizing if the textual material is in point; (5) jot down every important citation to authority made by the textual material in point; (6) then, read the entire case *only if* it is a vital link in the chain of case law authority in point. Of course, if the skilled researcher discovers at any point in the above process that the case adds nothing to the point of law being researched or that it is of little value for some other reason, the researcher will discard the case and mark it off the list of cases.

Skilled researchers also develop insight into knowing when they can safely terminate their research without exhausting every source on their list of authorities. There is no uniform rule which tells one how extensive the research should be in solving a legal problem. The extensiveness of research is often influenced by extraneous factors such as limitations of time, compensation, etc.; the nature of the problems; the legal measures being adopted; and the research habits and attitudes of the researcher.

The preceding discussion in this chapter describes an exhaustive system of legal research; however, such complete procedures are not always necessary. Carrying a problem through all the sources can be needless, unwarranted or repetitious. Common sense and professional insight, therefore, play a significant role in research procedure.

Obviously, there is no pat answer to the question which we, as researchers, ask every time we investigate a legal problem: "Can I safely stop here?" It has been suggested that if our research uncovers several cases, all in point, and no opposing decisions, with at least one recent and one state Supreme Court case, that might be adequate.[1] The novice should apply rules such as this with great caution.

In the last analysis, the skills of sophisticated researchers are measured as much for the knowledge of what can be omitted as for what and how research materials are used to solve legal problems. In some instances, a skilled researcher merely spot-checks a *single* publication, e. g., a general encyclopedia. A skilled researcher usually does not consult duplicative sources of the same type, i. e., Am.Jur. 2d and C.J.S. The researcher's stock in trade is *time*; a skilled researcher knows how to wisely use it. On the other hand, the research-

---

[1] Emery, A Streamlined Briefing Technique 30 (1955).

er must always solve the problem accurately. For this reason, the novice is cautioned to always err on the side of over-inclusion, duplication and excessive time; because, the work product expected of the novice is no different from that expected of the skilled professional—an accurate solution of the problem.

Step 5. Communicate the Solution of the Problem

The final step of the research process is somewhat outside the scope of this work, being reserved for individualized instruction at the classroom level. Nevertheless, the true test of our capacity to research legal issues is found in our capacity to communicate the results to other persons.

The notes which we prepared during Step 4, above, should be in a form which can easily be organized and presented orally or in written form. If the research is to be reduced to written form, usually a memorandum of law, there are several techniques which can be used to ensure that the written words accurately convey the results of our research. The most important rule to follow is that the words we select must be objective in nature, avoiding an adversary approach. We must always evaluate the merits of both sides of each legal issue.

The key elements of a well drafted memorandum of law are: (1) a title identifying the nature of the writing; (2) a statement of the issues presented in the order they are to be discussed; (3) a brief answer of all the issues presented; (4) a statement of the operative facts; (5) a discussion of each issue presented; and (6) a conclusion (optional). We note that in executing Steps 1 and 2 of our research process, above, we completed the second and fourth elements of a memorandum of law.

We should begin writing the memorandum by refining our statement of the issues and by reducing our statement of facts so as to eliminate all irrelevancies. Our next step is to outline and then carefully write the discussion section. The brief answer section is then prepared, stating, in as few words as possible, the conclusions drawn in the discussion section of the memorandum. A conclusion section should only be used in complex memoranda when the reader requires a more detailed summary of the problem than is provided by the conclusory statements contained in the brief answer. The entire memorandum should then be given a short, highly descriptive title, and edited for citation errors, literary style, and most important, for brevity.

The discussion section is the heart of the memorandum and deserves a bit more explanation. It should be organized issue-by-issue. Each issue and sub-issue should be completely discussed before pro-

gressing to the next issue. The most widely accepted method of discussing an issue of law employs the following format: (1) state the issue; (2) state the law which applies to the issue; (3) apply the law to the relevant operative facts; and (4) draw a conclusion. This format can be repeated for each issue and sub-issue in the memorandum.

Finally, there are a few common errors which must be avoided if a memorandum is to be a professional document. Backtracking or excessive interplay of issues is to be avoided. Each issue and sub-issue should be distinct and logically complete. Excessive overlapping of thought in the discussion section usually indicates that the issues have not been drafted with sufficient precision.

When an authority is cited it must stand for the proposition asserted. If a citation is to dictum in a case, it must be so identified. One must avoid excessive citation to authority. String citations are rarely appropriate. Try to cite only the leading authority or authorities in point. Do not use quotations as a substitute for analysis and use quotations only where they add to, rather than supplement the body of the memorandum.

Never give the appearance of avoiding resolution of a problem by pleading the need for additional facts. On the other hand, a memorandum should deal with potentially variant outcomes by assuming the existence of any facts which are clearly within the ambit of and which have not been negated by the given fact complex.

The greatest temptation of the novice is to include information which the researcher has spent many hours developing but which were later discovered to be wholly irrelevant to a proper analysis of the issues presented. A novice should expect to investigate a host of irrelevant leads during the research process. Avoid the burning temptation to include this information in the memorandum as it detracts from and often masks the legal analysis which is directly in point.

It must always be remembered that a memorandum is objective in nature. It is not intended to be an adversary document. The presentation of analysis in adversary form casts grave doubt in the mind of the reader as to the objective validity of the memorandum. Your task is to explore both the strengths and the weaknesses of each conclusion drawn. The task of the writer is to evaluate, not to persuade.

We have now completed our first exposure to the mechanics of executing a legal research project from its beginning to its end. The system we have discussed is one of many possible approaches. The ultimate objective of the researcher is to develop the capacity to rapidly and accurately solve legal problems. That capacity can only be developed by constructing a basic, systematic approach to legal research. Therefore, it is now the task of the reader to synthesize the

materials contained in this chapter and to fashion a system of legal research which is commensurate with the reader's existing professional skills and which assures the reader of a professional work product each and every time the system is utilized.

Appendix A *

CITATION FORM FOR TYPEWRITTEN WORK

I. UNITED STATES CITATIONS

Citation Locator

INTRODUCTION

The following material embodies an attempt to furnish the reader with the basic citation forms to be used in typewritten work by legal practitioners and students in the United States. This material may also be used effectively as a citation guide by those outside the legal profession. Most of the rules recited herein are similar to the rules prescribed in A UNIFORM SYSTEM OF CITATION (12th ed. 1976) [hereinafter BLUE BOOK], for printed work. Some rules, however, were intentionally changed. No attempt has been made to

---

* This Appendix was prepared with the assistance of the University of Texas School of Law Legal Research Board under the direction of Josh R. Morriss and Thomas Ray Guy.

compete with the BLUE BOOK but rather to offer an alternative approach.

For better understanding of the rules of proper citation, the authors have emphasized examples illustrating application of the rules. Please note that the examples are merely illustrative and many are fictitious in their particulars. The treatment herein is far from exhaustive; whenever additional help is needed, the reader should refer to the BLUE BOOK for a more exhaustive treatment.

Citation form is important primarily because readers should be furnished with sufficient information to find references easily and to determine their relative authority and secondarily because of the pleasing effect of consistency. When in doubt about the form to use, a writer should endeavor to include all information necessary for easy location and assessment and to be internally consistent.

SECTION A. PRIMARY AUTHORITY

1. Constitutions

The citation form for the federal constitution and for state constitutions is relatively simple. As a general rule, constitutions are divided into articles and sections. When citing a constitution, either federal or state, three elements must always be included: the jurisdiction, the article number, and the section number. If the citation is to a portion of the constitution that is still in effect, it is not necessary to include the date of the constitution.

U.S. CONST. art. II, § 2 cl. 1.

TEX. CONST. art. II, § 2.

If the constitutional provision cited to has been significantly amended, or if it is no longer in effect, it is necessary to include the provision's date of adoption as part of the citation.

N.J. CONST. art. III, § 4 (1902).

When citing to a constitutional amendment, the amendment number should be included in lieu of the article number.

U.S. CONST. amend. V, § 1.

Proper citation form for constitutions always involves the use of all capital letters for the abbreviations for the jurisdiction and the word "constitution."

2. Statutes

a. Federal Statutes. These may be classified as either public laws or private laws. Public laws are those of general applicability, whereas private laws are laws which only apply to those specifically designated in the law. Private laws are not codified in the

same manner as public laws, but are only incorporated into the *Statutes at Large* (Stat.). Private laws thus are cited to the *Statutes at Large* only. Necessary information includes the Private Law Number, the chapter, volume and page numbers, and the date:

Priv. L. No. 406, ch. 298, 52 Stat. 602 (1939).

The balance of the discussion of federal statute citation form concerns public laws only.

Federal public laws are codified under 50 subject headings or titles. The publication of these titles, however, lags behind the actual adoption of the statutes by the Congress and their signing by the President. A statute may have been signed into law by the President and thus be currently in force, but not yet be available in codified form. In such instances, the statute should be cited to either the *United States Code Congressional and Administrative News* or the advance sheet service of the United States Code Service, Lawyers Edition according to three elements: its Public Law Number, the appropriate section number, and the exact date of its passage.

Pub. L. No. 89–429 (May 24, 1966). U.S. CODE CONG. & ADM. NEWS 1478 (1966).

If the statute does not yet appear in the above source, cite it to the applicable Public Law Number.

Pub. L. No. 89–531 (Aug. 11, 1966).

Shortly after enactment, a federal statute will be published in the official codification, the *United States Code*, and in the two privately published, annotated codifications, the *United States Code Annotated* and the *United States Code Service*. When a statute appears in codified form, it should be cited to one of these sources rather than to the *Statutes at Large*.

The official codification of federal statutes is the *United States Code* (U.S.C.). A new edition of the U.S.C. is published every six years, with bound cumulative annual supplements published during the intervening years. If a particular statute appears in the U.S.C. main volumes or a supplement thereto, the citation should be to the U.S.C. Three elements must always be included in a citation to U.S.C.: the title number, the section number, and the date of the code volume. If the cited section appears in a supplement to the U.S.C., such should also be indicated.

12 U.S.C. § 94 (1970).

7 U.S.C. § 2651 (Supp. III, 1973).

When citing to the U.S.C. main volumes, the date in parentheses is the date of the most recent edition. This date appears on the title page of each volume. When citing to a U.S.C. Supplement volume,

the date used is the date of the Supplement, which also appears on the title page of the supplement. If no such date appears, use the copyright date of the supplement.

The two privately-published, annotated editions of the codified federal statutes are West's *United States Code Annotated* (U.S.C.A.) and Lawyer's Co-operative/Bancroft-Whitney's *United States Code Service* (U.S.C.S.).[1] The titles and sections of both are identical with the arrangement of the U.S.C. The general rule is to cite to U.S.C. if it is available, but often an unofficial service must be cited because the library does not have U.S.C. or because the supplementation of the U.S.C. lags behind that of the unofficial services. Both U.S.C.A. and U.S.C.S. are supplemented annually with pocket supplements and several times each year by pamphlet supplements. Recent statutes and amendments are thus more likely to appear in the unofficial services than in U.S.C. Citation to U.S.C.A. or U.S.C.S. involves the identical three elements as citation to U.S.C.—title number, section number and date (with appropriate indication if the section appears in a supplement to the volume).

28 U.S.C.S. § 18c (1970).

18 U.S.C.A. § 711a (Supp. 1974).

When citing to the U.S.C.A. or U.S.C.S. main volumes, the appropriate date to use is the date conspicuously appearing on the title page of the volume, unless the volume is a replacement of an earlier codification. If it is a replacement volume, the date cited is the copyright date of the volume. If the citation is to the pocket part supplements, the date used should be the date of the supplement. This date appears on the title page of the supplement. If no such date appears, use the copyright date of the supplement.

Cite to the current Internal Revenue Code separately, without the use of a parenthetical date.

INT. REV. CODE OF 1954, § 2053.

The name of a federal statute may be provided as part of the citation if it will aid in the reader's identification of the statute. Any official name given in the statute should be used. If the official name is used, the citation should also include a reference to the sec-

---

1 Lawyer's Co-operative Publishing Company (based in Rochester, New York) is the parent organization of Bancroft-Whitney (based in San Francisco, California). Works of national or broad jurisdiction, such as U.S.C.S., are issued jointly under both names. For works of local jurisdiction, the United States is divided by a line made up of the western boundaries of Minnesota, Iowa, Missouri, Arkansas, and Louisiana, and in most cases, Lawyer's Co-op issues law books dealing with areas to the east and Bancroft-Whitney to the west of this demarcation.

tion number in the original enactment. A popular name may be used if an official name is not available.

Securities Exchange Act § 10b, 15 U.S.C. § 78j (1971).[2]

Mann Act, 18 U.S.C. § 2421 (1970).

Federal statutes not currently in force are cited to the *Statutes at Large* (Stat.). Citation is also to the *Statutes at Large* if the language is materially different from that in the codifications. Elements in this citation are the exact date, the chapter (pre-1959) or Public Law Number (post-1959), and the section, volume and page numbers:

Act of April 11, 1963, Pub. L. No. 89–12, § 43, 75 Stat. 98.

Occasionally it may be necessary to discuss the legislative history of a federal statute. One major source of such information is the various committee reports issued during each session. Citation to these reports should contain the following information: the report number, an identification of the legislative session, the page number, and the date:

H.R. Rep. No. 248, 87th Cong., 1st Sess. 17 (1961).

S. Rep. No. 204, 87th Cong., 1st Sess. 8 (1961).

Another convenient source is the records of congressional debate which appear in the *Congressional Record*. As the pagination in the bound volume is different from that of the daily editions, cite to the bound volumes of the *Congressional Record* whenever possible, providing the volume, page numbers, and the date. If the particular issue is not yet bound, cite to the daily publication. Citation to the daily issues should include the exact date of the issue:

98 CONG. REC. 8669 (1952).

113 CONG. REC. 12,791 (daily ed. April 10, 1967).

The hearings of a Senate or House Committee should be cited as follows:

Hearings on S. 3149 Before the Subcomm. on Labor of the Senate Comm. on Labor and Public Welfare, 90th Cong., 2d Sess. 35 (1968).

The bills introduced in Congress are cited:

H.R. 3030, 87th Cong., 1st Sess.

S. 1126, 87th Cong., 1st Sess.

b. State Statutes. It is difficult to generalize concerning proper citation form for state statutes. Every state has a form peculiar to itself, dictated by the method of compilation or codification of the laws. Certain rules of citation may, however, be identified. More specific citation problems are not within the scope of this chapter.

---

[2] Typewritten citations customarily substitute underlining for italics, since italicization is impossible on most typewriters.

State statutes are generally compiled similarly to federal statutes. The statutes are arranged in a logical order, generally by subject matter classifications, with amendments incorporated into the text and repealed statutes eliminated. The codification process lags behind the actual passage of the laws by the state legislative bodies. However, all states publish the laws enacted by each legislature in bound volumes generally referred to as "session laws." If the statute appears only in the session law publication, citation must be to that volume. A complete citation identifies the state, the year of the session, the organizational units of the law (e. g., chapter or section), and the page number. Important information may be added in parentheses after the page number:

Tex. Laws 1965, ch. 679, § 7, at 1563.

Ill. Laws 1935, ch. 14, § 12, at 117 (4th Spec. Sess.).

Citation to a state compilation always includes three elements: the name of the compilation, the statute number, and the date of the compilation.[3] The nomenclature applied to a state compilation differs from state to state, ranging from "Code" to "Revised Statutes" to "Annotated Statutes," among others. Reference should be made to the particular compilation for the correct terminology. In addition, for some states it is necessary to include the name of the publisher of the volume in the date parenthetical.

CONN. GEN. STAT. ANN. § 19–17 (1969).

TEX. REV. CIV. STAT. ANN. art. 5526 (1958).

OHIO REV. CODE ANN. § 4107.47 (Page 1973).

State compilations are generally updated by use of pocketpart supplements or periodic paperback supplements. If the citation is to a supplement to the main volumes, this should also be indicated.

TEX. REV. CIV. STAT. ANN. art. 6701b (Supp.1974).

Special rules apply to New York laws and California codes. Citations to these statutes should include the name of the particular law or code and the name of the publisher.

CAL. CIVIL CODE § 501 (West 1954).

N.Y. BANK LAW § 101 (McKinney 1954).

The uncodified laws of these two states are cited to the particular organizational unit.

CAL. GEN. LAWS ANN. Act 7003, § 12 (Deering 1960).

N.Y. UNCONSOL. LAWS § 81 (McKinney 1969).

---

[3] Before the current edition of the Blue Book was published, it was necessary when citing state statutes to refer to an annual publication of the Harvard Law Review Association, *State Statutory Citations*. The Twelfth Edition of the Blue Book, however, includes a thorough section of specific citations, which adequately covers state statutory material as well as state case citations. BLUE BOOK 104–42.

The date to use in a statute citation may present some problems. The general rule is to cite the date appearing conspicuously on the title page of the main volume or supplement. If the volume is a replacement of an earlier volume, however, the date used should be the copyright date of the replacement. An easy way to determine if the volume being cited is a replacement volume is to compare the copyright date with the date appearing on the title page. If the two dates differ by more than two years, the volume most probably is a replacement volume. If no date appears conspicuously on the title page, the copyright date of the volume should be used.

The name of a state statute may be given as part of the citation if it will aid the reader in identification. The official name should be used, if one is available. Otherwise, the popular name of the statute may be used. When using the official name, the section number in the original enactment should also be included.

Blue Sky Law § 2, N.Y. GEN. BUS. LAW § 353 (McKinney 1962).

Guest Statute, TEX. REV. CIV. STAT. ANN. art. 6701b (Supp. 1974).

If the statute or the particular language being cited to is no longer in force, the citation should be to the session laws. The session law cited to should be fully identified, including the session law number, the date of passage, the organization unit, and the page number, if available.

Ark. Acts 1922, No. 198, at 106 (expired 1940).

Tex. Laws 1929, ch. 234, § 6, at 294.

c. Special Statutory Citation Problems. Generally, uniform laws are cited to the section number, without the use of a date. If the statutory language has been modified or repealed, however, the date of the act being cited should be included in parentheses. Likewise, if the citation is to be an official comment associated with the act, this should be indicated:

UNIFORM COMMERCIAL CODE § 2–207.

UNIFORM PROBATE CODE § 203 (1957).

UNIFORM COMMERCIAL CODE § 1–102, Comment 3.

If a state has adopted a uniform act, it should be cited as a statute of that state.

TEX. BUS. & COMM. CODE ANN. § 2.403 (Tex. UCC 1968).

If a citation is to consecutive articles, sections, or subsections of a statute, give only the first and the last numbers separated by a dash.

The word "to" may be used in lieu of a dash in order to avoid possible confusion.

> 18 U.S.C. §§ 103–07 (1970).
>
> UNIFORM COMMERCIAL CODE §§ 2–201 to –206.
>
> TEX. REV. CIV. STAT. ANN. arts. 5069–1.06 to –1.09 (1974).

If the citation is to non-consecutive sections, separate them with commas.

> 12 U.S.C. §§ 94, 96 (1971).
>
> WIS. STAT. §§ 2.20, .23–.25 (1963).

It may be relevant to indicate that a statute has been amended in some manner. When the statute has been amended so that the former version is completely superseded or repealed, the former version is cited to the statutes at large or the session laws, while the present version is cited to the appropriate code or compilation. The version being discussed should appear first, followed by the other version. The notation "*as amended*" or "*formerly*" should also be included.

> Securities Exchange Act § 10b, ch. 25, § 17, 57 Stat. 420 (1934), *as amended*, 15 U.S.C. § 78j (1971).
>
> Securities Exchange Act § 10b, 15 U.S.C. § 78j (1971), *formerly* ch. 35, § 17, 57 Stat. 420 (1934).

If the subsequent version only makes additions to the former, without repealing it, cite both versions to the appropriate compilation or codification. Again, the version being discussed should appear first:

> Guest Statute, TEX. REV. CIV. STAT. ANN. art. 6701b (Supp. 1974), *amending* TEX. REV. CIV. STAT. ANN. art. 6701b (1969).
>
> Guest Statute, TEX. REV. CIV. STAT. ANN. art. 6701b (1969), *as amended*, TEX. REV. CIV. STAT. ANN. art. 6701b (Supp. 1974).

When citing to the more recent version, the citation to the former version should be included only when the repeal or modification is relevant to the discussion. When citing to the former version, the subsequent version should always be cited.

d. Ordinances. The same general rules that apply to statutory citations also apply to the citation of city and county ordinances. The citation should always include the name of the municipal unit and the state. Codified ordinances are cited to the code, the organizational unit, and to the date of passage.

> NASHVILLE, TENN., CODE § 181 (1968).

Uncodified ordinances are cited to the number or name and to the exact date of passage.

> Conway, Ark., Ordinance 411, April 2, 1969.

  e. Regulations, Executive Orders, and Rules. Federal regulations, rulings promulgated by administrative agencies and executive departments are initially published in the *Federal Register* and later codified in the *Code of Federal Regulations* (C.F.R.). If the regulation does not yet appear in the C.F.R., cite to the *Federal Register*; otherwise, cite to the C.F.R. The elements of a C.F.R. citation are the volume number, the section, and the date of the volume. A *Federal Register* citation includes the page number in lieu of a section number.

> 12 C.F.R. § 326.10 (1975).
>
> 9 Fed. Reg. 8103 (1963).

  Internal Revenue Regulations are cited without source if the section cited has not been amended. The year of promulgation should be indicated. Proposed regulations are cited to the *Federal Register*. Revenue Rulings are cited to the *Cumulative Bulletin*:

> Treas. Reg. § 1.163–1 (1966).
>
> Proposed Treas. Reg. § 20.213–1, 24 Fed. Reg. 5431 (1966).
>
> Rev. Rul. 146, 1954–1 CUM. BULL. 98.

  Executive orders are cited to title 3 in the *Code of Federal Regulations*. A parallel citation to the U.S.C. should also be given if the order is printed therein.

> Exec. Order No. 12,087, 3 C.F.R. § 260 (Supp. 1970), 12
>   U.S.C. § 412 (Supp. 1970).

  Current rules of court procedure, both civil and criminal, are cited to their respective codifications without reference to a date. Rules no longer in force are cited to the last official source in which they appear, with a date reference.

> FED. R. CRIM. P. 26.
>
> TEX. R. CIV. P. 193 (1967).

A case reported in *Federal Rules Decisions* is cited:

> *Petrikin v. Chicago, R. I. & P. R.*, 15 F.R.D. 346 (W.D. Mo.
>   1954).

3. Cases

A case citation consists of the name of the case,[4] the reporter segment, the date or court-date parenthetical, and the history.

> *Jones v. Smith*, 386 S.W.2d 100 (Tex.1970), *cert. denied,*
> (Name)　　　　　(Reporter Segment)　　(Court-date)
> 351 U.S. 1 (1971).
> (History)

> *Smith v. Jones*, 126 Mass. 111, 93 N.E.2d 236 (1943), *aff'd,*
> (Name)　　　　　(Reporter Segment)　　　　　(Court-date)
> 133 U.S. 907 (1945).
> (History)

The correct case citation for most situations can be obtained by using the following instructions as a guide.

a.　Name.　Cite the name of the case as it appears at the beginning of the opinion in the official report, unless one of the following rules applies.

If the case includes more than one action, cite only the action listed first.

> *Jones v. Smith*, 499 S.W.2d 102 (Mo. Ct. App. 1973).
> not *Jones v. Smith, Davis v. Ames*, 499 S.W.2d 102 (Mo. Ct.
> App. 1973).

Include only the first party on each side.

> *Jones v. Smith*, 499 S.W.2d 102 (Mo. Ct. App. 1973).
> not *Jones, Williams, and Brown v. Smith, Green, and Black,*
> 499 S.W.2d 102 (Mo.Ct.App.1973).

Omit multiple party designations such as "et al." and "et ux."

> *Jones v. Smith*, 499 S.W.2d 102 (Mo.Ct.App.1973).

> not *Jones, et al. v. Smith, ex ux.*, 499 S.W.2d 102 (Mo.Ct.App.
> 1973).

Include the first relator listed and all of a partnership or firm name.

> *Jones ex rel. Ames v. J. V. Smith & Co.*, 158 Tex. 23, 301 S.W.
> 2d 101 (1957).

> not *Jones v. Smith*, 158 Tex. 23, 301 S.W.2d 101 (1957).

Except in administrative actions or when adversary parties are named, include the first listed procedural phrase such as "In re" and "Ex parte." Exclude non-procedural phrases such as "Estate of" and "Will of."

> *In re Jones*, 39 Neb. 545, 58 N.W. 202 (1894).

> not *In the Matter of the Estate of Jones*, 39 Neb. 545, 58 N.
> W. 202 (1894).

---

[4] For typewritten work underline, rather than italicize, case names and procedural histories. See note 2, *supra*.

In administrative actions, omit all procedural terms and cite by the full name of the first party or by the official subject-matter title:

Estate of John D. Jones, 40 T.C. 215 (1962).

Dallas-Ft. Worth Area Case, 12 C.A.B. 642 (1967).

In arbitrations, treat as a regular case if adversary parties are named and as an administrative action if not:

Jones v. Smith, 14 Lab. Arb. 130 (1949) (Jerre, Arbitrator).

John D. Jones, 23 Lab. Arb. 219 (1951) (Williams, Arbitrator).

Except in administrative actions, include only the surnames of individuals. For corporations, partnerships, or business firms, include the full name unless the name includes words such as "Co.," "Bros.," or "Assoc." followed by words such as "Inc." and "Ltd." In that case, include only the first designation:

Jones v. J. V. Smith & Co., 522 F.2d 717 (D.C. Cir. 1975).

not *J. Jones v. J. V. Smith & Co., Inc.,* 522 F.2d 717 (D.C. Cir. 1975).

Include all parts of a completely Chinese name:

White Cloud v. Mao Ng Chiong, 366 F. Supp. 1350 (N.D. Cal. 1973).

not *Johnny White Cloud v. Charles Ying,* 290 F.2d 111 (1960).

Include the surname and all names following if the party's name is of Spanish or Portuguese derivation:

Gomez y Ortega v. Feliciano Santiago, 390 U.S. 414 (1968).

not *Gomez v. Santiago,* 390 U.S. 414 (1968).

Omit "the" if it is the first word of a party's name other than "The King" or "The Queen" or where it is part of the name of an object in an *in rem* action.

For federal cases in which a state is a party, omit "State of." In state court, use the designation "State" and omit the name of the state:

Federal Court:

Texas v. Smith, 470 F.2d 919 (1st Cir. 1971).

not *State of Texas v. Smith,* 470 F.2d 919 (1st Cir. 1971).

State Court:

State v. Smith, 171 Tex. Crim. 203, 350 S.W.2d 100 (1961).

not *State of Texas v. Smith,* 171 Tex. Crim. 202, 350 S.W.2d 100 (1961).

Omit location designations of less than national scope unless only one word would remain in the name:

> *Bank of Texas v. First National Bank*, 516 S.W.2d 200 (Tex. 1975).

> not *Bank v. First National Bank of Dallas*, 516 S.W.2d 200 (Tex. 1975).

Omit "of America" following "United States" and "of Internal Revenue" following "Commissioner":

> *United States v. Aluminum Co. of Am.*, 148 F.2d 416 (2d Cir. 1945).

> not *United States of America v. Aluminum Co.*, 148 F.2d 416 (2d Cir. 1945).

> *Commissioner v. Smith*, 150 F.2d 11 (1st Cir. 1946).

> not *Commissioner of Internal Revenue v. Smith*, 150 F.2d 11 (1st Cir. 1946).

"United States" is not abbreviated in the name of the case in the following example:

> *Miami Transportation Co. v. United States*, 350 U.S. 27 (1945).

> not *Miami Transportation Co. v. U. S.*, 350 U.S. 27 (1945).

Omit parenthetical descriptions of parties:

> *Jones v. Smith*, 499 S.W.2d 102 (Mo. Ct. App. 1973).

> not *Jones, Trustee v. Smith*, 499 S.W.2d 102 (Mo.Ct.App. 1973).

If a party's name is commonly recognized by its initials, cite it in that manner:

> *NLRB v. Smith*, 107 F. Supp. 600 (S.D.N.Y. 1952).

> not *National Labor Relations Board v. Smith*, 107 F. Supp. 600 (S.D.N.Y. 1952).

If a party is a Railroad, abbreviate "Railroad" to "R.R." and "Railway" to "Ry." Omit the use of "Co." even if cited as "R. Co." in the official report, unless the full name cited is simply "Railroad Co." Abbreviate geographical words, other than the first word of a party's name, to the initial letter or a recognized abbreviation, unless they complete a name begun by the first word:

> *Pennsylvania Cent. R. R. v. Northern Pac. Ry.*, 250 F.2d 880 (2d Cir. 1957).

> not *Penn. C. R. Co. v. Northern P. Railway*, 250 F.2d 880 (2d Cir. 1957).

> *Railroad Co. v. Kansas City Ry.*, 324 U.S. 291 (1945).

> not *R. R. v. Kansas C. Railway*, 324 U.S. 291 (1945).

If a party is a labor union, omit everything except the first word indicating a craft or industry (or the commonly recognized abbreviation of the union's name), and use the local designation, shortened to the form "Local 104." If there is no local designation, use the term "Union" or other appropriate term:

Local 104, UAW v. Smith, 197 F. Supp. 207 (N.D. Cal. 1961).

not *Local Union No. 104, United Automobile, Aircraft, and Agricultural Implement Workers of America, CIO v. Smith,* 197 F. Supp. 207 (N.D. Cal. 1961).

For parties other than Railroads, Unions and those commonly referred to by their initials, do not abbreviate words in the case name except for "Co.," "Corp.," "Inc.," "Ltd." and "&."

Southeastern Corp. v. Smith & Jones, Inc., 512 S.W.2d 617 (Ark. 1975).

not *S. E. Corporation v. Smith and Jones, Inc.,* 512 S.W.2d 617 (Ark. 1975).

b. Reporter Segment

(1) Federal Court Cases: U. S. Supreme Court decisions should be cited to the official reports, the *United States Reports,* when possible and convenient. Since the two unofficial reporters—West's *Supreme Court Reporter* and Lawyer's Co-operative/Bancroft-Whitney's *Lawyers Edition, United States Supreme Court Reports*—contain, in their bound volumes, cross-pagination to the *United States Reports,* the writer can cite to the official reports without actually consulting them. On the other hand, the pamphlet supplements or advance sheets to the unofficial reporters do not contain cross-pagination; thus, if a recent case is reported only in such a pamphlet supplement it becomes necessary to cite directly to one of the unofficial reporters. Very recent cases, unavailable even in the pamphlet supplements, should be cited to *United States Law Week:*

Adams v. Jefferson, 346 U.S. 219 (1952).

Adams v. Jefferson, —— U.S. ——, 98 S. Ct. 301 (1974).

Adams v. Jefferson, 43 U.S.L.W. 3962 (U.S. Dec. 15, 1969).

The first 90 volumes of the *United States Reports* require a parenthetical notation of the name of the reporter.

Jones v. Gray, 81 U.S. (14 Wall.) 607 (1871).

For Courts of Appeals and District Courts, cite only to the West Reports: *Federal Reporter, Federal Supplement, Federal Rules Decisions,* or *Federal Cases.*

Grant v. Lee, 411 F.2d 913 (2d Cir. 1971).

Patton v. Rommel, 204 F. Supp. 37 (E.D. Tenn. 1961).

Black v. Decker, 128 F.R.D. 137 (1954).

Massena v. Junot, 13 F. Cas. 22 (No. 6999) (C.C.N.D. Ill.
     1875).

Cite decisions in the *Federal Cases* (covering federal judicial opinions prior to 1880) as follows:

Dike v. Kuhns, 7 F. Cas. 696, No. 3907 (C.C.W.D. Pa. 1857).

The old circuit courts, abolished on January 1, 1912, are cited by reference to the district:

Thayer v. Hart, 24 F. 588 (C.C.S.D.N.Y.1885).

If the same decision is in both F. Supp. and F.R.D., cite to F. Supp. Specialized courts, such as the Court of Claims and the Court of Customs and Patent Appeals, are cited to F.2d or F. Supp. if their cases are reported therein and otherwise to the respective official reports. Cases reported in loose-leaf reporters or services are cited:

Sinkfield v. Flemming, CCH Unemp. Ins. Rep. ¶ 12,427.50
     (E.D. Mich. 1960).

(2) State Court Cases: Cite to all official and West reports in the following order: official, West regional, and West local reporter. California and New York cases are cited to all three sources.

Ames v. Paschal, 60 Cal. 2d 208, 359 P.2d 35, 50 Cal. Rptr.
     47 (1965).

Rawles v. Gray, 4 N.Y.2d 117, 143 N.E.2d 131, 176 N.Y.S.2d
     502 (1960).

For cases of other states, where only the official report and one West reporter exist, cite the official report first.

West v. Omar, 217 Ala. 679, 232 S.E.2d 988 (1957).

In many states, official reports are no longer published. However, cases decided in the period of official reports should include the official report in the citation.

Williams v. Oregon, 157 Tex. 109, 300 S.W.2d 643 (1957).

If there is no official report, cite the West report:

Curry v. Guy, 482 S.W.2d 964 (Tex. 1973).

If the official report has not yet been published, cite the unofficial report, such as the *National Reporter System,* and indicate the jurisdiction and date:

Corsair v. Dempsey, 218 A.2d 478 (R.I. 1966).

Administrative Cases: In administrative cases, cite to the official report if it is available:

Chitwood v. Gray, 26 T.C. 225 (1961).

If the official report is not yet bound, cite by the case number and include the full date:

> *Tuthill v. Tatum,* 29 T.C. No. 106 (Feb. 7, 1962).

If the official report is unavailable, cite to an official release and include the full date:

> *Alletag v. Jones,* SEC Securities Act Release No. 11,421 (June 2, 1961).

If there are no official sources available, cite to an unofficial report:

> *Thompson v. Griffin,* 15 CCH Tax. Ct. Mem. 1093 (1953).

Parallel citation is permissible if it would aid the reader.

    c.   Court-Date Parenthetical

    (1) Federal Court Cases: When the court is apparent from the name of the report, no parenthetical court designation is necessary. The date used is the year of the decision (never use the date of rehearing), unless the cite is to *United States Law Week.* In that situation, give the court and exact date:

> *Lucas v. Strickland,* 40 U.S.L.W. 307 (U.S. May 9, 1973).

For circuit and district courts give the court name and date. Do not indicate the division in district courts:

> *Suleiman v. Epstein,* 505 F.2d 33 (5th Cir. 1975).
>
> not *Suleiman v. Epstein,* 505 F.2d 33 (C.C.A. 5th 1975).
>
> *Botts v. Elkins,* 330 F.2d 404 (D.C. Cir. 1963).
>
> not *Botts v. Elkins,* 330 F.2d 404 (C.C.A.D.C.1963).
>
> *Friedman v. Irwin,* 328 F. Supp. 1091 (S.D. Tex. 1971).
>
> not *Friedman v. Irwin,* 328 F. Supp. 1091 (S.D. Tex. N.D. 1971).
>
> *Ragsdale v. Gibbons,* 320 F. Supp. 813 (D.D.C. 1953).
>
> not *Ragsdale v. Gibbons,* 320 F. Supp. 813 (Dist. D.C. 1953).

For other federal courts and agencies, use the abbreviations in BLUE BOOK rule 10:4, at 42–44 and the year of decision.

> (Ct. Cl. 1974) not (Ct. Claims 1974).
>
> (T.C. 1969) not (Tax Ct. 1969).

    (2) State Court Cases: When there is an official report with the same name as that of the jurisdiction, it is assumed the court is the highest court in that jurisdiction:

> *Johnson v. Muldoon,* 126 Mass. 111, 93 N.E.2d 236 (1943).
>
> not *Johnson v. Muldoon,* 126 Mass. 111, 93 N.E.2d 236 (Mass. 1943).

If the court is not the highest court in the jurisdiction or if the name of the report does not supply the court and jurisdiction, give this information parenthetically.

> *Odom v. Taylor*, 121 Misc. 91, 37 N.Y.S.2d 313 (Sup. Ct. 1931).

> *Lucas v. Kaine*, 518 S.W.2d 442 (Mo. Ct. App. 1975).

If the name of the report does not give the jurisdiction and court and the court is the highest court in the jurisdiction, include only the jurisdiction:

> *Sutton v. Barbee*, 231 P.2d 963 (Okla. 1971).

> not *Sutton v. Barbee*, 231 P.2d 963 (Okla. Sup. Ct. 1971).

d. History

Normally, cite only the opinion of the highest court that has considered the case. If the language of a lower court is cited, give the subsequent history:

> *Robinson v. Allen*, 394 F.2d 913, 916 (5th Cir. 1969), *rev'd*, 398 U.S. 130 (1970).

Give the subsequent history when a court of last resort has refused to hear a case from a lower court, or when it has agreed to hear the case but has not yet done so.

> *Dwight v. Phiffer*, 375 F.2d 611 (9th Cir. 1965), *cert. denied*, 398 U.S. 96 (1966); *Davis v. Peters*, 401 F.2d 103 (2d Cir.), *cert. granted*, 411 U.S. 455 (1974).

The history on remand and any denial of rehearing are omitted unless significant to the point for which the case is cited.

When several decisions have occurred in the same year, the date is included only once—with the last cited decision:

> *Watson v. Knobloch*, 421 F.2d 993 (3d Cir.), *aff'd*, 396 U.S. 138 (1968).

When the parties' names are different on appeal, use *"sub nom.,"* unless the names are only reversed or the subsequent history is a denial of certiorari or an administrative action in which the name of the private party remains the same:

> *Smith v. Jones*, 210 F.2d 843 (5th Cir. 1951), *aff'd sub nom.*

> *Brown v. Smith*, 196 U.S. 898 (1952).

SECTION B.   SECONDARY AUTHORITY

1. Books and Pamphlets

Generally, the form for citing a book or pamphlet in a legal memorandum sets out the essential identification clues in the follow-

ing sequence: volume number, author's name, title, page, edition, and date. The qualifications to this simple formula are set forth below:

a. Volume. If there is more than one volume, begin with the volume number:

2 L. LOSS, SECURITIES REGULATION 863 (2d ed. 1961).

b. Author's Name. Use last name and first initial only, unless more is necessary for identification, with uniform capitals:

K. DECROW, SEXIST JUSTICE 123 (1974).

c. Title. Use the full title whenever possible. The title may be shortened when necessary at a major mark of punctuation, but never at the expense of clear identification. When the work will be cited repeatedly, use of the "hereinafter" rule is proper. The "hereinafter" rule is set out under Shortened Forms for Repeated Citations, *infra*. The title should be in uniform capitals:

W. SHIRER, THE RISE AND FALL OF THE THIRD REICH: A HISTORY OF NAZI GERMANY 924 (1960) [hereinafter RISE AND FALL].

d. Page. If the work is being cited generally, no page number is used. If a work is clearly organized by paragraphs or sections, the paragraph or section number is used, followed by "at" and the page number; otherwise, simply use the page number.

J. WHITE & R. SUMMERS, HANDBOOK OF THE LAW UNDER THE UNIFORM COMMERCIAL CODE § 3– 9, at 109 (1972).

e. Edition and Date

Use an edition designation if there has been more than the original edition. Some books will have provisions for updating material. When cited material is contained in a pocket part or supplement, "Supp." and the date of the supplement are used. For the date, use that of publication:

J. CHOMMIE, THE LAW OF FEDERAL INCOME TAXA- TION § 57, at 147 (2d ed. 1973).

C. WRIGHT, HANDBOOK OF THE LAW OF FEDERAL COURTS § 50, at 22 (Supp. 1972).

4. Legal Periodicals

Generally, the sequence in citation to articles in legal periodicals is the author's last name, the title of the article, volume number, name of publication, page numbers and the date.

a. Author's Name. Use the author's name only when the material being cited is an article, and then use only the last name. The

author's name is never used when a student work in a law review is being cited. Citation to such a work is instead opened with the publisher's designation for the work, such as Comment, Book Note, or Case Note.

> McClintock, *Skyjacking: Its Domestic, Civil and Criminal Ramifications,* 39 J. AIR L. & COMM. 29 *passim* (1973).

> Note, 52 TEXAS L. REV. 806, 814 (1974). [a short student work]

> Recent Development, 74 COL. L. REV. 528 (1974). [a short student work]

b. Title. Use the title when citing either an article or a long student work. The title is omitted from citations of short student works such as Case Notes, unless it will be of particular assistance to the reader. Titles of short student works are typically descriptive and very long. If inclusion of the title of such work is desirable, shortening the title as described with some reservation under "Title" of the books and pamphlets section above is especially appropriate:

> Reis, *The Proposed Court of Administrative Appeals,* 1938 WIS. L. REV. 281, 285.

> Comment, *Accumulated Earnings Tax: An Appeal for Flexibility,* 52 N.C.L. REV. 1179, 1210 (1974). [a long student work]

> Comment, 26 BAYLOR L. REV. 71 (1974). [a short student work]

Note that publisher's designations such as Comment or Note may not be reliable indicators of proper classification as long or short student work. For purposes of citation form, "long work" refers to one containing analysis and "short work" is limited in scope to commentary or reporting. The length of a typical short student work is under twelve pages.

c. Volume Number. Most legal periodicals are published in volumes numbered in sequence from Volume 1 in the first year of publication. Several periodicals, however, are numbered by year, date or have no volume number at all. If the volumes are not numbered, use the year of publication in place of the volume number. Citations to those periodicals which require a year date preceding the name of the publication (instead of a volume number) omit the date at the end of the citation:

> Reis, *The Proposed Court of Administrative Appeals,* 1938 WIS. L. REV. 281, 285.

> Comment, 26 BAYLOR L. REV. 71 (1974). [a short student work]

d. Name of Publication. Proper citation form requires that names of periodicals be abbreviated, but in a recognizable and uniform manner:

HARV. L. REV.

TEMP. L.Q.

A.B.A.J.

The BLUE BOOK is the authority for these abbreviations and a set of guidelines, as well as some specific abbreviations, appears in BLUE BOOK rule 17:2, at 87–93. If the particular periodical to be cited is not in that list, refer to Appendix A or B. If the correct abbreviation cannot be found in either of these sources, the abbreviation for the name of any periodical may be constructed from the list of geographical abbreviations inside the back cover of the BLUE BOOK and the list of abbreviations of other words appearing on page 44.

e. Page Numbers. When citing a work generally, use the number of the first page of the article. When citing specific information within a work, the initial page number should be followed by a comma and the number of the page containing such information. If the particular proposition for which the source is cited is repeated throughout the source, indicate this by omitting specific page numbers and inserting *"passim"* after the initial page number.

Note, *SEC Rules 144 and 146: Private Placements for the Few*, 59 VA. L. REV. 886, 889 (1973). [a long student work]

McClintock, *Skyjacking: Its Domestic, Civil and Criminal Ramifications*, 39 J. AIR L. & COMM. 29 *passim* (1973).

f. Date. Use the year only and enclose in parentheses. The date is omitted here if included as a volume number. See *Volume Number* above.

SECTION C. ORDER OF CITATIONS

Since the objective of citations is to persuade and inform the reader, the most important authority should be cited first, followed by the less important in descending order. Thus, primary authority is cited before secondary materials. Within the framework of pri-

mary authority, statutes should precede judicial interpretations. Cases should be cited in this order:

1.　United States Supreme Court cases.

2.　United States Court of Appeals cases.

3.　United States District Court cases.

4.　State court cases in the alphabetical order of states.

5.　English and other foreign cases.

Within each of the above divisions, the citations should be in reverse chronological order, first giving the most recent cases.

In the absence of circumstances suggesting an arrangement determined by the intrinsic worth of the writings or the reputation of authors, secondary authorities should be listed in the following order:

1.　Treatises, arranged alphabetically by names of the authors.

2.　Leading articles, arranged alphabetically by names of the authors.

3.　Comments and notes, arranged alphabetically by names of the journals.　Some law reviews cite their own journal first, followed by the others in alphabetical order.

SECTION D.　SPECIAL CITATION FORMS

1.　General

Some works which are commonly cited do not conform in all respects to the general form above.　Below are examples of types of such works which may be used as guides for citation of similar authorities:

BLACK'S LAW DICTIONARY 439 (4th ed. rev. 1968).

ABA–ALI MODEL BUS. CORP. ACT § 9 (1953).

Annot., 82 A.L.R.2d 1099 (1962).　[Note that the title of the annotation is not to be included.]

96 C.J.S. *Wills* § 891 (1957).

74 AM. JUR. 2d *Tender* § 5 (1974).

RESTATEMENT (SECOND) OF TORTS § 285, comment *n* at 20 (1965).

RESTATEMENT (SECOND) OF TORTS § 746A (Tent. Draft No. 8, 1963).

ABA COMM. ON PROFESSIONAL ETHICS, OPINIONS, No. 293 (1967).

1 WILLISTON, CONTRACTS § 86 (3d ed. 1957).

23 OPS. ATTY. GEN. IND. 191.

2. Looseleaf Services and Reports

The commercial services are extremely helpful and will be often cited in some areas of research. Cite bound service material using the form shown for cases under Reporter Segment, *supra*. The material is usually published, however, in looseleaf form for easy updating. The sequence of citation for looseleaf services is case name, volume number, publisher, name, title, subtitle, paragraph or topic, page number and date.

a. Case Name. Follow the Rules set forth under Cases, *Name, supra*.

b. Volume Number. Not all looseleaf services number volumes; some distinguish volumes by subtitle only. If the material cited is in a volume both numbered and subtitled, the volume number may be omitted if the source is unambiguously identified by the subtitle. If there is any doubt, include both volume number and subtitle.

c. Publisher Name. Developments in some areas of law, taxation, for example, are reported by more than one commercial service. If more than one service has the same title, the publisher's name is included in abbreviated form.

d. Title and Subtitle. Use an abbreviated form of the title containing the reference. The list contained in BLUE BOOK rule 19:2, at 95–99 contains the abbreviations for most of the services.

Subtitles are included for clear identification of the reference source. For example, if the service volumes are divided by state names, the subtitle (name of the state) may be a clearer and more appropriate identification than the volume number. A state division with two or more volumes would require the volume number and subtitle for an unambiguous citation.

e. Paragraph or Topic. Typically the services are organized by paragraph or topic numbers. Always use a paragraph or topic number when one is provided. Note that a paragraph number may be denoted by "¶" or "para."

f. Page Number. Use the page number when citing material not organized by topic or paragraph. To cite material within a long paragraph or topic, follow the paragraph or topic number with "at" and the page number.

g. Date. If the year is included in the title or subtitle, the date is not repeated; otherwise, enclose the year of promulgation in parentheses to close the citation.

Jackson v. Grant, 2 AV. L. REP. ¶ 16,023 (1972).

Brennan v. Goose Creek School Dist., 11 LAB. REL. REP., Fair Employment Practice Cases 313 (1975).

Tony Lama Co., [1974–1975 Transfer Binder] CCH FED. SEC. L. REP. para. 79,901 (1975).

3. Shortened Forms for Repeated Citations

A source of authority will often be cited in a memorandum more than once. A few devices are commonly used to avoid full citation at each reference, specifically, *hereinafter, id., supra, op. cit. supra,* and *infra.* These devices are usually inapplicable to brief writing and in that connection their use is not recommended. However, to understand their application in treatises, law reviews, memoranda and footnoted briefs, these terms are described below.

a. *Hereinafter.* A particular authority may be central to the discussion in a memorandum and, therefore, require repeated reference. To shorten repeated citations, choose a shortened form (the author's name, or the name of one of the parties in a case, or a word or words from the title) which will clearly identify the source throughout. Immediately after the first full citation of such an authority, enclose in brackets the chosen shortened form. Thereafter, such shortened form should be used consistently throughout the text. If citing to particular material within the authority, indicate the page, paragraph or section number.

Black & White Taxicab & Transfer Co. v. Brown & Yellow Taxicab & Transfer Co., 276 U.S. 518 (1928) [hereinafter *Taxicab.*]

Taxicab at 521.

Wright § 236.

b. *Id.* Used alone, *Id.* refers the reader back to the immediately preceding citation. If the reference is precisely the same, *Id.* is sufficient alone. If the reference is to the same authority, but to a different page, section, or paragraph number within it, indicate the changes. Parallel citations require an indication of the specific change in both sources:

Id., at 623.

Id. § 1431.

Id. para. 127(b)(ii).

Id. at 623, 167 S.W.2d at 223.

Where the publication, such as *Williston on Contracts,* contains more than one volume, repeat the volume number:

2 *Id.* § 1095.

c. *Supra.* Like *Id., supra* refers the reader back to an authority already fully cited. *Supra,* however, is never used to cite the immediately preceding authority since *Id.* is appropriate in that situa-

tion. *Supra* is seldom helpful in memoranda for three reasons. First, its use is proper only when the full citation to the authority to which it refers appears on the same page of the final copy. Second, its use is improper in citation of statutory or quasi-statutory materials. Finally, the source of a previously fully-cited authority can often be made clear within the text of the memo by the use of an underlined party name or a shortened citation following the "hereinafter" rule. When *supra* is used to cite a case having parallel reporters, indicate the specific change in both sources:

Prosser, supra.

Prosser, supra § 321, at 491. [long section]

WHITE & SUMMERS, *supra,* § 7–4. [short section]

If the case or other publication has been previously cited in the same footnote, a dictum or another reference may be indicated as follows:

Attorney General v. Taggart, supra at 369, 29 Atl. at 1031.

Henning, supra at 310.

Reference to a complete footnote is made as follows:

See note 5, *supra.*

d. *Op. cit. supra.*

To avoid repeating titles of books and periodical articles, the following abbreviations are suggested:

If a text has been cited previously within reasonable footnote range, use *op. cit. supra,* preceded by the author's name and followed by the previous footnote reference and the page number.

Finletter, *op. cit. supra* note 12, at 535.

5 Fletcher, *op. cit. supra* note 9 § 2169.

Where reference is to a section number, the word "at" is omitted as shown in the second example above.

Op. cit. supra should be used only when the omission of the title effects some saving in space and when the second reference is not too far removed from the first.

Periodical articles, previously cited, may be referred to as illustrated below.

Seavey, *supra* note 4, at 384.

e. *Infra.* This should not be used as a shortened citation form in a memorandum because all authorities should be fully cited at their first appearance. *Infra* may be used, however, to refer the reader to a general discussion which appears later in the memo: "as is discussed at issue III, *infra.*"

4. Signals

To conserve space and save time, a system of standardized signals, identifying the distinctions and gradations of authorities and arguments, has been developed. This scheme of using symbols to indicate supporting, contrary and other positions relating to propositions is particularly popular in law review writing. However, the usage of the symbols has too frequently been indiscriminate and careless, with resulting misunderstanding and confusion as to their meanings. An explanation of the designations may help clarify these discrepancies and at the same time be informative.

Unless the authority cited is the source of a quotation or direct support for a statement, introductory signals are required to indicate the purpose of the citation. Always underline signals.

The following are the most commonly used signals in memo and brief writing:

a.   [No signal]   If a holding is squarely in point or a statute directly supports the proposition, a signal is not used. The reference is a standard citation without a symbol.

> *Westlake Mercantile Finance Corp. v. Merritt*, 204 Cal. 673,
>   269 P. 620 (1928).

b.   *Accord*.   *Accord* is used to indicate substantial support of a proposition although the holding, facts or jurisdiction may be distinguishable in some respects.

> *Workman v. Wright*, 33 Ohio St. 405 (1878); *accord, Shinew*
>   *v. First National Bank*, 84 Ohio St. 297, 95 N.E. 881
>   (1911).

> *Accord, Justice v. Stonecipher*, 267 Ill. 448, 108 N.E. 722
>   (1915).

c.   *Alternative Holding*.   *Alternative Holding* is used to identify a case decided on two or more independent principles either of which can be interpreted as a holding.

> *Schechter Poultry Corp. v. United States*, 295 U.S. 495
>   (1935) (alternative holding).

d.   *Contra*.   *Contra* indicates a direct contradiction to the statement made.

> *Westlake Mercantile Finance Corp. v. Merritt*, 204 Cal. 673,
>   269 P. 620 (1928). *Contra, Heller v. Cuddy*, 172 Minn.
>   126, 214 N.W. 924 (1927).

> *Contra, Johnson v. Bradstreet Co.*, 77 Ga. 172, 4 Am. St. Rep.
>   77 (1886).

e. *Cf.* Support for this statement may be drawn from an analogous conclusion drawn from materially different facts.

> *Fonseca v. Cunard S. S. Co.*, 153 Mass. 553, 27 N.E. 665 (1891); *cf. Murray v. Cunard S. S. Co.*, 235 N.Y. 162, 139 N.E. 226 (1923).

> *Cf. Wisconsin v. Minnesota Mining & Mfg. Co.*, 311 U.S. 452 (1940).

f. *See.* *See* (in italics) is support for the conclusion or opinion which comes from perusal of the cited authority.

> *See Shattuck v. Shattuck*, 67 Ariz. 122, 130, 192 P.2d 229, 234 (1948).

g. "See". "See" (in Roman type) is used in a non-signal sense to introduce secondary authority which supports the proposition.

> See Scott, *Collateral Estoppel by Judgment*, 56 HARV. L. REV. 1, 15 (1942).

h. *But See.* *But See* (in italics) indicates a dictum which is opposed to the proposition. Dicta pages should be cited.

> *But see United States v. Wong Kim Ark*, 169 U.S. 649, 703 (1898).

i. "But see". "But see" (in Roman type) is used in a non-signal sense to introduce secondary authority which opposes the proposition. Specific pages should be cited.

> But see Slocombe, *The Psychology of Safety*, 20 PERSONNEL J. 42, 105 (1941).

j. *But cf.* *But cf.* is used to indicate a contrary holding in a case with substantially different facts.

> *But cf. Easton v. Medema*, 246 Mich. 130, 224 N.W. 636 (1929).

k. *Semble.* If the holding of a case is not clear, use *semble* following the citation.

> *Rushmore v. Manhattan Screw and Stamping Works*, 163 Fed. 939 (2d Cir. 1908) (semble).

l. Dissenting or Concurring Opinion.

To cite a dissenting or a concurring opinion, introduce the citation with *see* and follow with a parenthetical explanation.

> *See Winters v. New York*, 333 U.S. 507, 520 (1947) (dissenting opinion).

m. *Compare* . . . *with* . . .

Some cases, taken together, lend authority to the statement.

Compare McPhee v. People, 108 Colo. 530, 120 P.2d 814
    (1941), *with Stewart v. United States,* 300 F. 769
    (8th Cir. 1924).

n. *e. g.* The support of a proposition by numerous holdings or dicta may be illustrated by a selected citation of one or a few cases preceded by *e. g.,* always followed by a comma. Another signal may precede it to indicate a distinction with an example where there are many cases in point.

E. g., Eichten v. Central Minn. Cooperative Power Ass'n,
    224 Minn. 180, 28 N.W.2d 862 (1947).

See, e. g., Toledo Newspaper Co. v. United States, 247 U.S.
    402 (1918).

o. *Accord, see* and *cf.* The rules do not require that these signals, which support the proposition, be set off by new sentences. They are generally preceded by a semi-colon when used with a string of citations.

Kasanovich v. George, 348 Pa. 199, 34 A.2d 523 (1943);
    cf. Potter v. Gillmore, 282 Mass. 49, 184 N.E. 373
    (1933).

p. *Contra, but see* and *but cf.* These signals, indicating opposition to the proposition, are always introduced by new sentences.

Westlake Mercantile Finance Corp. v. Merritt, 204 Cal. 673,
    269 P. 620 (1928). *Contra, Heller v. Cuddy,* 172
    Minn. 126, 214 N.W. 924 (1927).

Other introductory signals are treated in BLUE BOOK rule 2.3, at 6–8.

5. Parentheticals

A citation to material in a case other than a nonalternative holding of a majority of the court should include a parenthetical explanation preceding the subsequent history:

Davis v. Alaska, 415 U.S. 308 (1974) (dissenting opinion).

Granite City Steel Co. v. Environmental Protection Agency,
    501 F.2d 925, 928 (7th Cir. 1974) (dictum), *cert denied,*
    414 U.S. 561 (1975).

Morris v. Hoerster, 368 S.W.2d 639 (Tex. Civ. App.—Dallas)
    (per curiam), *aff'd,* 370 S.W.2d 451 (Tex. 1963).

Further commentary may be included in parentheses following the subsequent history.

6. Capitalization

Rules of capitalization and quotations are substantially standardized throughout formal writing. Unless a word is part of a proper name, it is probably not capitalized. "Court" is capitalized only when naming a court in full or when referring to the Supreme Court of the United States. Except when used as a part of a proper name such as "Rule Against Perpetuities," the word "rule" should not be capitalized. The word "constitution" should be capitalized only when naming a constitution in full or when referring to the United States Constitution. Parts of a constitution should not be capitalized except when referring to them by a popular name like "Equal Rights Amendment."

7. Quotations

When the exact language of a source is quoted, the language should be enclosed in quotation marks. The quoted language should otherwise be presented as found in the source, except for desired additions, designations of omissions, and disclaimers of errors in usage. Words or short phrases, in brackets, may be inserted into or substituted for quoted language if it aids the reader's understanding and does not change the meaning of the language in context. An omission from the beginning of a sentence is designated by capitalizing the first letter and enclosing it in brackets; an omission from the middle, by three periods; and an omission from the end, by four periods. When quoted language contains an obvious error in usage, the error should be quoted as it appears, followed immediately by "[sic]" to show that the error was contained in the original.

Original: But the jury erred, finding him innocent. He were guilty. He did it.

"[T]he jury erred . . .. He were [sic] guilty."

"[T]he jury . . . [found] him innocent. . . . He did it."

Quoted material exceeding four typewritten lines in the final memorandum should be indented, single spaced, and presented without quotations marks. The citation to the source is not included in the indented material. It follows the quotation, but at the original margin to distinguish it from any concluding citation which may be part of the quotation. For example:

Because the validity of the order is of obvious importance, we granted the petition for a writ of certiorari filed by the Commission in No. 72–1490 and by the estate of Mrs. James R. Dougherty, an intervenor in the Court of Appeals, in No. 72–1491. 414 U.S. 817 (1973).

Federal Power Commission v. Texaco, 417 U.S. 380, 383 (1974).

II. ENGLISH CITATIONS

SECTION A

Prior to 1962, English statutes were cited by name, regnal year (the year of the sovereign's reign in which statute was passed) and chapter. E. g., *National Services Act, 11 & 12 Geo. 6, c. 64.* This method of citation made it necessary to consult a Table to determine the year of passage. As all legal writing on English prior to 1962 cited to regnal year, a Table of Regnal Years is set forth for convenience.

TABLE OF REGNAL YEARS

Sovereign	Reign Began	Sovereign	Reign Began
William I	Oct. 14, 1066	Mary	July 6, 1553
William II	Sept. 26, 1087	Jane	July 6, 1553
Henry I	Aug. 5, 1100	Philip & Mary	July 25, 1554
Stephen	Dec. 26, 1135	Elizabeth I	Nov. 17, 1558
Henry II	Dec. 19, 1154	James I	Mar. 24, 1603
Richard I	Sept. 3, 1189	Charles I	Mar. 27, 1625
John	May 27, 1199	Charles II	Jan. 30, 1649
Henry III	Oct. 28, 1216	James II	Feb. 6, 1685
Edward I	Nov. 20, 1272	William & Mary	Feb. 13, 1689
Edward II	July 8, 1307	Anne	Mar. 8, 1702
Edward III	Jan. 25, 1327	George I	Aug. 1, 1714
Richard II	June 22, 1377	George II	June 11, 1727
Henry IV	Sept. 30, 1399	George III	Oct. 25, 1760
Henry V	Mar. 21, 1413	George IV	Jan. 29, 1820
Henry VI	Sept. 1, 1422	William IV	June 26, 1830
Edward IV	Mar. 4, 1461	Victoria	June 20, 1837
Edward V	Apr. 9, 1483	Edward VII	Jan. 22, 1901
Richard III	June 26, 1483	George V	May 6, 1910
Henry VII	Aug. 22, 1485	Edward VIII	Jan. 20, 1936
Henry VIII	Apr. 22, 1509	George VI	Dec. 11, 1936
Edward VI	Jan. 28, 1547	Elizabeth II	Feb. 6, 1952

This method of citation was changed by the Acts of Parliament Numbering and Citation Act, 1962. Under it, citation is to the name of the Act and calendar year. Since 1898, each Act of Parliament has a section indicating the title of the Act under which it is to be cited. E. g., Section 87 of *Highways Acts of 1971* is entitled *Short Titles, Citations, and Commencement and Extent.*

SECTION B. CASES

1. Prior to 1865

The favored citation to English cases prior to 1865 is to give the original report and the parallel reference in the *English Reports, Full Reprint*.

How v. Lacy, 1 Taunt. 119, 127 Eng.Rep. 777 (C.P.1808).

2. 1865 to date

The *Law Reports* citation is given if the case appears therein.

Blackpool Corp. v. Locker, [1948] 1 K.B. 349.

Galloway v. Galloway, [1954] P. 312 (C.A.).

A case in the *All England Law Reports* is cited:

Harding v. Price, [1948] 1 All E.R. 284 (K.B.).

SECTION C. ADMINISTRATIVE REGULATIONS

Statutory Rules and Orders (Revised 1948) are cited to the annual volume which preceded the revision:

(1919) Stat.Rules & Orders 53 (No. 1517) or S.R. & O.1919 (No. 1517) 53.

Since 1948, the series is identified as *Statutory Instruments*. Cite by year, number, volume and page.

(1950) 2 Stat.Instr. 478 (No. 1556) or
S.I.1950 (No. 1556) 2, p. 478.

III. CANADIAN CITATIONS

1. Citation Manuals

There is no standard citation manual which has gained the acceptance enjoyed by *A Uniform System of Citation* (the Harvard White book). Citation manuals are:

Caparros, Ernest. *La Documentation juridique;* référence et abbréviations par Ernest Caparros et Jean Goulet. Québec, Les presses de l'université Laval, 1973. 182p.

Samuels, Joseph W. *Legal Citation for Canadian Lawyers*. Toronto, Butterworths, 1968. 34p.

Christie's *Legal Writing and Research Manual, infra,* also serves as a basic guide to Canadian legal citation. In addition, most law reviews and groups engaged in legal research have prepared unpublished style manuals for the use of their contributors, reflecting their own preferred mode of citation. Nevertheless, certain general conventions are found in all current practice.

a. Cases

(1) Both official and unofficial reports are citable in Canadian courts. The official version, if available, is preferred however.

(2) If parallel cites are given, the recommended order is the official series of reports first, followed by the unofficial reports in order of size of geographical area covered.

(3) The date is enclosed in square brackets if it is essential in order to find the case cited. For example, the *Dominion Law Reports* began publication in 1912 and volumes 1 to 70 were published, covering 1912 to 1922. In 1923, the volume numbering ceased, and only the year of the volume appears on the spine. Since there were four volumes published in 1923, the volumes are marked 1923 volume 1, and so on. Citation is therefore:

(1912), 1 D.L.R. 311 (Man.C.A.) for the first 70 vols.

[1923] 1 D.L.R. 821 (Sask.C.A.) for the vols. issued from 1923 to 1955.

In 1955, a second series began, with volumes numbered consecutively from v. 1, 1955, to v. 70, 1968.

Citation is:

(1956), 1 D.L.R. (2d) 225 (Alta.S.C.)

In 1969, a third series began, with volumes numbered consecutively from v. 1, 1969 on. Citation is:

(1969), 1 D.L.R. (3d) 305 (S.C.C.)

The date put in round brackets is more properly the date that the decision was rendered, if it is not the same as the date which appears on the spine.

b. Statutes

The short title of the statute is cited exactly as provided by that statute, including capitalization, punctuation, and whether or not "the" and a date are to be included.

A statute in the latest federal Revision, amended by the 2nd Supplement, would be cited:

Electricity Inspection Act, R.S.C.1970, c. E–4, as amended by R.S.C.1970 c. 6 (2nd Supp.)

New legislation in a later Annual would be cited:

Federal-Provincial Fiscal Arrangements Act, 1972, S.C.1972 c. 8.

c. Administrative Regulations

Regulations in the Consolidation are cited:

Fair Wages Policy Order, S.O.R. Cons./55, Vol. 2, 1251.

(The last number given is a page, since the regulations are not numbered in the Consolidation).

Regulations made since the Consolidation are cited:

Pension Benefits Standards Regulations, S.O.R. /71–76 (referring to number 76 of the Statutory Orders and Regulations for 1971.)

Appendix B *

SELECTIVE LEGAL MATERIALS AND THEIR
ABBREVIATIONS

Legal research is never so frustrating as when the question inevitably arises, "What is the correct abbreviation for this legal periodical or that set of court reports?" Many beginning law students soon learn that Rule 11 of *A Uniform System of Citation* does not cover every possible journal title or that Rule 1:2 does not include all reports of opinions. At the opposite end of the spectrum, even the legal scholar may encounter an abbreviation whose complete title is difficult to identify. He or she may have to consult, for example, as specialized a treatise as William H. Bryson's *Dictionary of Sigla and Abbreviations to and in Law Books before 1607* (Charlottesville: University Press of Virginia, 1975).

As primary and secondary legal materials continue to proliferate each year, it is virtually impossible to include in one place all their titles and abbreviations. Appendices B and C are restricted primarily to the English language periodicals, court reports, and looseleaf services which one could expect to find in a large, American, law school library as of April 1, 1976. B is arranged alphabetically by title and C by abbreviation, but the two lists are not mirror images of one another. B is a selective list of major legal titles and their abbreviations; C includes every title in B under its appropriate abbreviation but also contains many esoteric and historical citations which would have been impractical to duplicate in B.

In most cases abbreviations conform to *A Uniform System of Citation*, the most widely used guide among legal writers in the United States. Occasionally, however, abbreviations have been constructed on the basis of analogy and common sense when the rules do not apply or are unclear. Appendices B and C are not presumed to be authoritative in an official sense but to reflect acceptable usage by most members of the legal community. Superseded titles have been retained because they are never out-of-date as possible citations.

Bibliographic information on legal periodicals may be found in Eugene M. Wypyski's *Legal Periodicals in English* (Dobbs Ferry, N. Y.: Glanville, 1976), a looseleaf service which is still in the process of being completed. The Harvard Law Review Association periodically issues a mimeographed list of abbreviations of state codes, *State Statutory Codifications*, which are not included in the following Appendices.

A/E Legal Newsletter --------------------------- A/E Legal Newsl.
AELE Legal Liability Reporter -------------------- AELE Legal Liab.
                                                            Rep.
ALI–ABA CLE Review ------------------------- ALI–ABA CLE Rev.
APLA Quarterly Journal ---------------------- APLA Q.J.

* Prepared with the assistance of Ronald E. Day, Reference Librarian, Biddle Law Library, University of Pennsylvania.

Abbott's Appeal Decisions `------------------------` Abb.App.Dec.
Abbott's New Cases `-------------------------------` Abb.N.Cas.
Abbott's Practice Reports `------------------------` Abb.Pr.
Abogada Internacional `--------------------------` Abogada Int'l
Abstracts on Criminology and Penology `------------` Abstr.Crim. & Pen.
Academy of Political Science Proceedings `----------` Acad.Pol.Sci.Proc.
Acta Criminologica `-----------------------------` Acta Crim.
Acta Juridica `----------------------------------` Acta Jur.
Adelaide Law Review `---------------------------` Adelaide L.Rev.
Administrative Court Digest `----------------------` Ad.Ct.Dig.
Administrative Law `-----------------------------` Ad.L.
Administrative Law Bulletin `---------------------` Ad.L.Bull.
Administrative Law News `------------------------` Ad.L.News
Administrative Law Newsletter `-------------------` Ad.L.Newsl.
Administrative Law, Second Series `----------------` Ad.L.2d
Administrative Law Review `------------------------` Ad.L.Rev.
Advance California Appellate Reports `-------------` A.C.A.
Advance California Reports `----------------------` A.C.
Advocate, The `----------------------------------` Advocate
African Law Digest `-----------------------------` Afr.L.Dig.
African Law Reports `---------------------------` Afr.L.R.
African Law Reports, Malawi Series `--------------` Afr.L.R., Mal.Ser.
African Law Reports, Sierre Leone Series `----------` Afr.L.R., Sierre L.
Ser.
African Law Studies `---------------------------` Afr.L.Stud.
Agriculture Decisions `--------------------------` Agr.Dec.
Air Force Law Review `--------------------------` Air Force L.Rev.
Air Law `----------------------------------------` Air Law
Air Law Review `---------------------------------` Air L.Rev.
Akron Law Review `--------------------------------` Akron L.Rev.
Alabama Appellate Court Reports `-----------------` Ala.App.
Alabama Court of Appeals Reports `----------------` Ala.App.
Alabama Law Journal `---------------------------` Ala.L.J.
Alabama Law Review `----------------------------` Ala.L.Rev.
Alabama Lawyer, The `---------------------------` Ala.Law
Alabama Reports `-------------------------------` Ala.
Alabama State Bar Foundation Bulletin `-----------` Ala.St.B.Found.Bull.
Alaska Bar Brief `-------------------------------` Alaska B.Brief
Alaska Bar Journal `-----------------------------` Alaska B.J.
Alaska Law Journal `-----------------------------` Alaska L.J.
Alaska Reports `---------------------------------` Alaska
Albany Law Journal `-----------------------------` Alb.L.J.
Albany Law Review `------------------------------` Albany L.Rev.
Alberta Law Quarterly `--------------------------` Alta.L.Q.
Alberta Law Reports `---------------------------` Alta.
Alberta Law Review `----------------------------` Alta.L.Rev.
Albuquerque Bar Journal `------------------------` Albuquerque B.J.
All England Law Reports `------------------------` All E.R.
All India Criminal Decisions `--------------------` All India Crim.Dec.

All India Reporter ------------------------------------- All India Rptr.
All Nigeria Law Reports ------------------------------ All N.L.R.
All Pakistan Legal Decisions ---------------------- All Pak.Leg.Dec.
Allen ---- --- Allen
Alternatives --- Alternatives
American Academy of Matrimonial Lawyers
    Journal -- Am.Acad.Matri.Law.
    J.
American and English Annotated Cases ----------- Am. & Eng.Ann.Cas.
American Bankruptcy Law Journal ---------------- Am.Bankr.L.J.
American Bankruptcy Reports --------------------- Am.Bankr.R.
American Bankruptcy Reports, New Series --------- Am.Bankr.R. (N.S.)
American Bankruptcy Review --------------------- Am.Bankr.Rev.
American Bar Association Journal ---------------- A.B.A.J.
American Bar Association Reports ---------------- A.B.A.Rep.
American Bar Association Section of Insurance,
    Negligence and Compensation Law Proceedings -- A.B.A. Sect.Ins.N. &
    C.L.Proc.
American Bar Foundation Research Journal -------- A.B.F.Res.J.
American Bar News ---------------------------------- Am.B.News
American Business Law Journal -------------------- Am.Bus.L.J.
American Criminal Law Quarterly --------------- Am.Crim.L.Q.
American Criminal Law Review ------------------- Am.Crim.L.Rev.
American Decisions -------------------------------- Am.Dec.
American Federal Tax Reports --------------------- Am.Fed.Tax R.
American Federal Tax Reports, Second Series ------ Am.Fed.Tax R.2d
American Foreign Law Association Newsletter ---- Am.For.L.Ass'n
    Newsl.
American Indian Journal --------------------------- Am.Ind.J.
American Indian Law Newsletter ------------------ Am.Ind.L.Newsl.
American Indian Law Review ---------------------- Am.Ind.L.Rev.
American International Law Cases, 1783–1968 ------ A.I.L.C.
American Journal of Comparative Law ------------- Am.J.Comp.L.
American Journal of Criminal Law --------------- Am.J.Crim.L.
American Journal of International Law ----------- Am.J.Int'l L.
American Journal of Jurisprudence --------------- Am.J.Jurisprud.
American Journal of Law and Medicine ----------- Am.J.L. & Med.
American Journal of Police Science --------------- Am.J.Police Sci.
American Journal of Legal History ---------------- Am.J.Legal Hist.
American Jurisprudence ---------------------------- Am.Jur.
American Jurisprudence, Second Series ----------- Am.Jur.2d
American Labor Arbitration Awards (P–H) -------- P–H Am.Lab.Arb.
    Awards
American Labor Cases (P–H) ---------------------- P–H Am.Lab.Cas.
American Labor Legislation Review --------------- Am.Lab.Leg.Rev.
American Law Journal ------------------------------ Am.L.J.
American Law Magazine --------------------------- Am.L.Mag.
American Law Register ----------------------------- Am.L.Reg.
American Law Register, New Series --------------- Am.L.Reg., (N.S.)

American Law Register, Old Series ---------------- Am.L.Reg., (O.S.)
American Law Reports --------------------------- A.L.R.
American Law Reports, Second Series ------------- A.L.R.2d
American Law Reports, Third Series -------------- A.L.R.3d
American Law Reports Federal ------------------- A.L.R.Fed.
American Law Review --------------------------- Am.L.Rev.
American Law School Review -------------------- Am.L.Sch.Rev.
American Lawyer ------------------------------- Am.Law.
American Maritime Cases ----------------------- A.M.C.
American Notary ------------------------------- Am.Notary
American Political Science Review -------------- Am.Pol.Sci.Rev.
American Reports ------------------------------ Am.R.
American Society of International Law Proceed-
    ings -- Am.Soc'y Int'l L.
                                                                   Proc.
American State Reports ------------------------- Am.St.R.
American Trial Lawyers Journal ---------------- Am.Trial Law J.
American Trial Lawyers Law Journal ----------- Am.Trial Law.L.J.
American University Law Review --------------- Am.U.L.Rev.
Amicus (South Bend, Ind.) --------------------- Amicus
Amicus (Thousand Oaks, Cal.) ----------------- Amicus
Anglo-American Law Review ------------------- Anglo-Am.L.Rev.
Annals of the American Academy of Political and
    Social Science ------------------------------- Annals
Annotated Legal Forms Magazine --------------- Ann.Leg.Forms Mag.
Annotated Tax Cases -------------------------- Ann.Tax.Cas.
Annual Digest and Reports of International Law
    Cases --------------------------------------- Ann.Dig.
Annual Law Register of the United States --------- Ann.L.Reg.U.S.
Annual Review of International Affairs ----------- Ann.Rev.Int'l Aff.
Annual Survey of African Law ------------------ Ann.Survey Afr.L.
Annual Survey of American Law ---------------- Ann.Survey Am.L.
Annual Survey of Commonwealth Law ----------- Ann.Survey Com-
                                                                    monw.L.
Annual Survey of Indian Law ------------------- Ann.Survey Ind.L.
Annual Survey of South African Law ------------ Ann.Survey S.Afr.L.
Antitrust Bulletin ----------------------------- Antitrust Bull.
Antitrust Law and Economics Review ----------- Antitrust L. & Econ.
                                                                    Rev.
Antitrust Law Journal ------------------------- Antitrust L.J.
Antitrust Law Symposium ---------------------- Antitrust L.Sym.
Appeals Cases, District of Columbia ------------ App.D.C.
Appellate Division Reports, N. Y. Supreme Court --- App.Div.
Appellate Division Reports, N. Y. Supreme Court,
    Second Series -------------------------------- App.Div.2d
Arbitration Journal, New Series ---------------- Arb.J. (N.S.)
Arbitration Journal, Old Series ----------------- Arb.J. (O.S.)
Arbitration Law; A Digest of Court Decisions ----- Arb.L.Dig.
Arizona Appeals Reports ----------------------- Ariz.App.

Arizona Bar Journal -- Ariz.B.J.
Arizona Law Review -------------------------------------- Ariz.L.Rev.
Arizona Reports --- Ariz.
Arizona State Law Journal ------------------------ Ariz.St.L.J.
Arkansas Law Review ------------------------------------ Ark.L.Rev.
Arkansas Lawyer, The ----------------------------------- Ark.Law
Arkansas Reports -- Ark.
Army Lawyer -- Army Law.
Art and the Law -- Art & L.
Asian Comparative Law Review -------------------- Asian Comp.L.Rev.
Association of Trial Lawyers of America News-   Ass'n Trial Law.Am.
  letter --- Newsl.
Ateneo Law Journal ------------------------ ---------- Ateneo L.J.
Atlantic Reporter -- A.
Atlantic Reporter, Second Series -------------------- A.2d
Atomic Energy Law Journal ---------------------- Atomic Energy L.J.
Atomic Energy Law Reporter (CCH) ------------- CCH Atom.En.L.Rep.
Attorney General -- Att'y Gen.
Attorney General's Opinions, United States -------- Op.Att'y Gen.
Attorney General's Reports, United States ---------- Att'y Gen.Rep.
Auckland University Law Review ------------------- Auck.U.L.Rev.
Australian and New Zealand Journal of Criminology- Austl. & N.Z.J.Crim.
Australian Argus Law Reports -------------------- Austl.Argus L.R.
Australian Bankruptcy Cases --------------------- Aust.Bankr.Cas.
Australian Business Law Review ------------------- Austl.Bus.L.Rev.
Australian Commercial Journal -------------------- Austl.Com.J.
Australian Conveyancer and Solicitors Journal ----- Austl.Convey. & Sol.
                                                    J.

Australian Current Law Review ------------------- Austl.Current L.Rev.
Australian Journal of Forensic Sciences ----------- Austl.J.For.Sci.
Australian Jurist ----------------------------------- Austl.Jur.
Australian Law Journal ---------------------------- Austl.L.J.
Australian Law Journal Reports -------------------- Austl.L.J.Rep.
Australian Law Times ------------------------------- Austl.L.Times
Australian Lawyer ------------------------------------ Austl.Law.
Australian Tax Decisions -------------------------- Austl.Tax
Australian Yearbook of International Law ---------- Austl.Y.B.Int'l L.
Automobile Cases ----------------------------------- Auto.Cas.
Automobile Cases, Second Series -------------------- Auto.Cas.2d
Automobile Law Reporter (CCH) -------------------- Auto.L.Rep.
Aviation Cases -------------------------------------- Av.Cas.
Aviation Law Reporter (CCH) --------------------- Av.L.Rep.
B. Monroe --- B.Mon.
Balance of Payments Reports (CCH) --------------- Bal.Pay't Rep.
Banking Law Journal -------------------------------- Banking L.J.
Bankruptcy Bar Bulletin --------------------------- Bankr.B.Bull.
Bankruptcy Law Reporter (CCH) ------------------ Bankr.L.Rep.
Bar Bulletin -- B.Bull.
Bar Examination Journal --------------------------- B.Exam.J.

Bar Examiner ----------------------------------- B.Exam.
Bar Leader ------------------------------------- B.Leader
Barbour's Supreme Court Reports ---------------- Barb.
Barrister (Chicago) ---------------------------- Barrister
Barrister (Coral Gables, Fla.) ----------------- Barrister
Barrister (Davis, Cal.) ------------------------ Barrister
Barrister (Toronto) ---------------------------- Barrister
Baylor Law Review ------------------------------ Baylor L.Rev.
Belgian Review of International Law ------------- Belg.Rev.Int'l L.
Bill of Rights Journal -------------------------- Bill of Rights J.
Bill of Rights Review --------------------------- Bill Rights Rev.
Binney --- Binn.
Black -- Black
Black Law Journal ------------------------------ Black L.J.
Blue Sky Law Reporter (CCH) -------------------- Blue Sky L.Rep.
Board of Review (Army) ------------------------- B.R. (Army)
Board of Review and Judicial Council of the Army -- B.R.-J.C. (Army)
Board of Tax Appeals Report -------------------- B.T.A.
Bombay Law Journal ---------------------------- Bombay L.J.
Boston Bar Journal ----------------------------- Boston B.J.
Boston College Industrial and Commercial Law
   Review ----------------------------------- B.C.Ind. & Com.L.
      Rev.

Boston University Law Review ------------------- B.U.L.Rev.
Boyce -- Boyce
Brief, The ------------------------------------- Brief
Briefcase -------------------------------------- Briefcase
Brigham Young University Law Review ----------- Brigham Young U.L.
      Rev.

British Columbia Law Notes --------------------- B.C.L. Notes
British Columbia Law Reports ------------------- B.C.
British Institute of International and Comparative
   Law Newsletter ------------------------------ B.I.C.I.L.Newsl.

British International Law Cases ----------------- B.I.L.C.
British Journal of Administrative Law ----------- Brit.J.Ad.L.
British Journal of Criminology ----------------- Brit.J.Criminol.
British Journal of Law and Society -------------- Brit.J.Law & Soc'y
British Practice in International Law ------------ Brit.Prac.Int'l L.
British Shipping Laws (Stevens) ---------------- Brit.Ship.L.
British Tax Review ----------------------------- Brit.Tax Rev.
British Year Book of International Law ---------- Brit.Y.B.Int'l L.
Brooklyn Barrister ----------------------------- Brooklyn Barrister
Brooklyn Journal of International Law ----------- Brooklyn J. Int'l L.
Brooklyn Law Review --------------------------- Brooklyn L.Rev.
Buffalo Law Review ----------------------------- Buffalo L.Rev.
Bulletin for International Fiscal Documentation --- Bull.Int'l Fiscal Doc.
Bulletin of Canadian Welfare Law --------------- Bull.Can.Welfare L.
Bulletin of Czechoslovak Law ------------------- Bull.Czech.L.

Bulletin of Law, Science and Technology ---------- Bull.L.Science & Tech.

Bulletin of Legal Developments -------------------- Bull.Legal Devel.

Bulletin of the American Academy of Psychiatry and the Law -- Bull.Am.Acad.Psych. & L.

Bulletin of the Copyright Society of the U. S. A. --- Bull.Copyright Soc'y

Bulletin of the United States Trademark Association, New Series ----------------------------------- Trademark Bull. (N. S.)

Bulletin, Waseda University Institute of Comparative Law -------------------------------------- Bull.Waseda U.Inst. Comp.L.

Bureau of National Affairs ---------------------- B.N.A.

Bush --- Bush

Business and Law ----------------------------- Bus. & L.

Business Law Review (England) ------------------ Bus.L.Rev.

Business Law Review (United States) ------------- Bus.L.Rev.

Business Lawyer, The ------------------------- Bus.Law.

Business Regulation Law Report ------------------ Bus.Reg.L.Rep.

CLU Journal ---------------------------------- CLU J.

Cahiers de Droit, Les ------------------------- Cahiers de Droit

Caines' Cases ------------------------------- Cai.Cas.

Caines' Reports ----------------------------- Cai.R.

Calcutta Weekly Notes ------------------------ Calcutta W.N.

California Appellate Reports --------------------- Cal.App.

California Appellate Reports, Second Series -------- Cal.App.2d

California Appellate Reports, Third Series --------- Cal.App.3d

California Jurisprudence ------------------------ Cal.Jur.

California Jurisprudence, Second Edition --------- Cal.Jur.2d

California Law Review ------------------------- Calif.L.Rev.

California Reporter --------------------------- Cal.Rptr.

California Reports --------------------------- Cal.

California Reports, Second Series ----------------- Cal.2d

California Reports, Third Series ------------------ Cal.3d

California State Bar Journal -------------------- Cal.St.B.J.

California Trial Lawyers Journal ----------------- C.T.L.J.

California Western International Law Journal ----- Calif.W.Int'l L.J.

California Western Law Review ------------------- Calif.W.L.Rev.

Call --- Call

Cambrian Law Review ------------------------- Cambrian L.Rev.

Cambridge Law Journal ------------------------ Camb.L.J.

Cameron's Privy Council Decisions ---------------- Cam.

Cameron's Supreme Court Cases ----------------- Cameron

Campaign Law Reporter ------------------------ Campaign L.Rep.

Canada Exchequer Court Reports ----------------- Can.Exch.

Canada Law Journal -------------------------- Can.L.J.

Canada Law Reports, Exchequer ----------------- Can.Exch.

Canada Law Reports, Supreme Court -------------- Can.S.Ct.

Canada Supreme Court Reports ------------------- Can.S.Ct.
Canada Tax Appeal Board Cases ------------------- Can.Tax App.Bd.
Canada Tax Cases ---------------------------------- (   ) C.T.C.
Canada Tax Cases Annotated --------------------- Can.Tax Cas.Ann.
Canadian Bankruptcy Reports Annotated ---------- Can.Bankr.Ann.
Canadian Bankruptcy Reports Annotated, New
  Series -- Can.Bankr.Ann. (N.
                                                          S.)

Canadian Bar Association, British Columbia
  Branch Meeting Program Reports --------------- B.C.Branch Lect.
Canadian Bar Association Journal ----------------- Can.B.A.J.
Canadian Bar Association: Yearbook ------------- Can.B. Ass'n Y.B.
Canadian Bar Journal ---------------------------- Can.B.J.
Canadian Bar Review ---------------------------- Can.B.Rev.
Canadian Commercial Law Reports ---------------- Can.Com.R.
Canadian Communications Law Review ----------- Can.Com.L.Rev.
Canadian Criminal Cases Annotated --------------- Can.Crim.Cas.Ann.
Canadian Criminal Cases, New Series ------------- Can.Crim.Cas. (N.S.)
Canadian Environmental Law News --------------- Can.Env.L.News
Canadian Green Bag ----------------------------- Can.Green Bag
Canadian Journal of Criminology and Corrections -- Can.J.Crim. & Corr.
Canadian Labor Law Reports --------------------- C.L.L.R.
Canadian Labour --------------------------------- Can.Lab.
Canadian Labour Law Cases ---------------------- C.L.L.C.
Canadian Law Review ---------------------------- Can.L.Rev.
Canadian Law Times ----------------------------- Can.L.Times
Canadian Legal Studies -------------------------- Can.Legal Stud.
Canadian Municipal Journal --------------------- Can.Mun.J.
Canadian Oil and Gas (Butterworths) ------------- Can.Oil & Gas
Canadian Patent Reporter ----------------------- C.P.R.
Canadian Public Administration ------------------- Can.Pub.Ad.
Canadian Railway and Transport Cases ----------- Can.Ry. & T.Cas.
Canadian Railway Cases ------------------------- Can.Ry.Cas.
Canadian Reports, Appeal Cases ------------------ Can.App.
Canadian Tax Foundation Report of Proceedings of
  the Tax Conference --------------------------- Can.Tax Found.Rep.
                                                          Proc.Tax Conf.

Canadian Tax Journal --------------------------- Can.Tax J.
Canadian Tax News ----------------------------- Can.Tax News
Canadian Welfare -------------------------------- Can.Wel.
Canadian Yearbook of International Law ---------- Can.Yearbook Int'l
                                                          L.

Capital University Law Review ------------------- Capital U.L.Rev.
Carolina Law Journal ---------------------------- Carolina L.J.
Carolina Law Repository ------------------------- Carolina L.Repos.
Carribean Law Journal --------------------------- Carribean L.J.
Cartwright's Constitutional Cases (Can.) ---------- Cart.B.N.A.
Case & Comment --------------------------------- Case & Com.

Case Western Reserve Journal of International Law	Case W.Res.J.Int'l L.
Case Western Reserve Law Review	Case W.Res.L.Rev.
Cassels' Practice Cases (Can.)	Cass.Prac.Cas.
Cassels' Supreme Court Decisions	Cass.S.C.
Catholic Lawyer, The	Catholic Law.
Catholic University of America Law Review	Catholic U.L.Rev.
Censorship Today	Censorship Today
Central Law Journal	Cent.L.J.
Ceylon Law Review	Ceylon L.Rev.
Chicago Bar Record	Chi.B.Record
Chicago-Kent Law Review	Chi.-Kent L.Rev.
Chicago Law Journal	Chicago L.J.
Chicano Law Review	Chicano L.Rev.
China Law Review	China L.Rev.
Chinese Law and Government	Chin.L. & Gov't
Chitty's Law Journal	Chitty's L.
Cincinnati Bar Association Journal	Cin.B.Ass'n J.
Cincinnati Law Review	Cin.L.Rev.
City-Hall Reporter	City-Hall Rep.
City of London Law Review	London L.Rev.
Civil Aeronautics Authority Reports	C.A.A.
Civil Aeronautics Board Reports	C.A.B.
Civil and Military Law Journal	Civ. & Mil.L.J.
Civil Liberties Docket	Civ.Lib.Dock.
Civil Liberties Reporter	Civ.Lib.Rptr.
Civil Liberties Review	Civ.Lib.Rev.
Civil Liberty	Civ.Lib.
Civil Rights Digest	Civ.Rights Dig.
Clarke and Scully's Drainage Cases (Ont.)	C. & S.
Class Action Reports	Class Act.Rep.
Clearinghouse Review	Clearinghouse Rev.
Cleveland Bar Association Journal	Clev.Bar Ass'n J.
Cleveland State Law Review	Clev.St.L.Rev.
Cleveland-Marshall Law Review	Clev.-Mar.L.Rev.
Code of Federal Regulations	C.F.R.
Code Reporter	Code Rep.
Coldwell	Cold.
Coleman & Caines' Cases	Cole. & Cai.Cas.
Coleman's Cases	Cole.Cas.
College Law Bulletin	Coll.L.Bull.
College Law Digest	Coll.L.Dig.
Colloque International de Droit Compare	Col.Int'l Dr.Comp.
Colombo Law Review (Ceylon)	Colombo L.Rev.
Colorado Court of Appeals Reports	Colo.App.
Colorado Law Reporter	Colo.L.Rep.
Colorado Lawyer	Colo.Law.
Colorado Reports	Colo.
Columbia Human Rights Law Review	Colum.Human Rights L.Rev.

Connecticut Supplement	Conn.Supp.
Consolidated Treaty Series	C.T.S.
Constitution	Const.
Constitutional Review	Const.Rev.
Constitutions and Laws of the American Indian Tribes (Scholarly Resources)	C.L.A.I.T.
Constitutions of African States (Oceana)	Const.Afr.States
Constitutions of Dependencies and Special Sovereignties	Const.Dep. & Sp.Sov.
Constitutions of Nations (Nijhoff)	Const.Nations
Constitutions of the Countries of the World (Oceana)	Const.World
Consumer Product Safety Guide (CCH)	Consumer Prod.Saf'y Guide
Contemporary Drug Problems	Contemp.Drug Prob.
Conveyancer	Convey.
Conveyancer & Property Lawyer (New Series)	Convey. (N.S.)
Copp's Land Owner	Copp's Land Owner
Copyright	Copy.
Copyright Bulletin	Copy.Bull.
Copyright Law Symposium (ASCAP)	Copy.L.Sym. (ASCAP)
Cornell International Law Journal	Cornell Int'l L.J.
Cornell Law Forum	Cornell L.F.
Cornell Law Journal	Cornell L.J.
Cornell Law Quarterly	Cornell L.Q.
Cornell Law Review	Cornell L.Rev.
Corporate Practice Commentator	Corp.Pract.Comment.
Corporate Practice Review	Corp.Pract.Review
Corporate Reorganizations	Corp.Reorg.
Corporation (P–H)	P–H Corp.
Corporation Journal	Corp.J.
Corpus Juris	C.J.
Corpus Juris Secundum	C.J.S.
Council of Europe Consultative Assembly, Official Report of Debates	Eur.Consult.Ass.Deb.
Court of Appeals for District of Columbia	D.C.Cir.
Court of Claims	Ct.Cl.
Court of Customs and Patents Appeals Reports	C.C.P.A.
Court of Customs Appeals Reports	Ct.Cust.App.
Court of Military Appeals (U. S.)	U.S.C.M.A.
Court Review	Ct.Rev.
Court Martial Reports	C.M.R.
Court-Martial Reports of the Judge Advocate General of the Air Force	C.M.R. (Air Force)
Coutlea's Supreme Court Cases	Coutlea
Cowen	Cow.
Cox's Criminal Cases	Cox Crim.Cas.
Cranch	Cranch

Creighton Law Review ------------------------------- Creighton L.Rev.
Crime and Delinquency ----------------------------- Crime & Delin'cy
Crime and Delinquency Abstracts ------------------- Crime & Delin'cy
Abstr.
Crime and Delinquency Literature ---------------- Crime & Delin'cy
Lit.
Crime and Social Justice ------------------------- Crime & Soc.Just.
Criminal Appeal Reports ------------------------- Crim.App.
Criminal Case and Comment --------------------- Crim.Case & Com.
Criminal Defense ------------------------------- Crim.Def.
Criminal Justice ------------------------------- Crim.Just.
Criminal Justice and Behavior ----------------- Crim.Just. & Behav.
Criminal Justice Newsletter -------------------- Crim.Just.Newsl.
Criminal Justice Quarterly --------------------- Crim.Just.Q.
Criminal Justice Review ------------------------ Crim.Just.Rev.
Criminal Law Audio Series ---------------------- C.L.A.S.
Criminal Law Bulletin -------------------------- Crim.L.Bull.
Criminal Law Journal --------------------------- Crim.L.J.
Criminal Law Magazine and Reporter ------------- Crim.L.Mag. & Rep.
Criminal Law Quarterly ------------------------- Crim.L.Q.
Criminal Law Reporter -------------------------- Crim.L.Rptr.
Criminal Reports (Canada) ---------------------- Can.Crim.
Criminal Reports, New Series ------------------- Crim.Rep. (N.S.)
Criminal Law Review (England) ------------------ Crim.L.Rev. (Engl.)
Criminal Law Review (Manhattan) ---------------- Crim.L.Rev.
Criminologica --------------------------------- Criminologica
Criminologie ---------------------------------- Criminologie
Criminologist --------------------------------- Criminologist
Criminology ----------------------------------- Criminology
Cumberland Law Review ------------------------- Cumb.L.Rev.
Cumberland-Samford Law Review ----------------- Cum.-Sam.L.Rev.
Cumulative Bulletin --------------------------- Cu.Bull.
Current Comment and Legal Miscellany ----------- Current Com. & Leg.
Mis.
Current Law ------------------------------------ Current L.
Current Law and Social Problems ---------------- Current L. & Soc.
Prob.
Current Law Yearbook -------------------------- Current L.Y.B.
Current Legal Problems ------------------------- Current Legal Prob.
Current Legal Thought -------------------------- Current Legal
Thought
Current Medicine for Attorneys ----------------- Current Med.
Cushing --------------------------------------- Cush.
Customs Court Reports ------------------------- Cust.Ct.
Cyprus Law Reports --------------------------- C.L.R.
Czechoslovak Journal of International Law ------- Czech.J.Int'l L.
Czechoslovak Yearbook of International Law ------ Czech.Y.B.Int'l L.
Dakota Law Review --------------------------- Dak.L.Rev.
Dakota Reports (Territorial) -------------------- Dak.

Dalhousie Law Journal	Dalhousie L.J.
Dallas	Dall.
Daly	Daly
Debates of the European Parliament	Eur.Parl.Deb.
Decalogue Journal	Decalogue J.
Decisiones de Puerto Rico	D.P.R.
Defense Law Journal	Defense L.J.
Delaware Chancery Reports	Del.Ch.
Delaware County Reports	Del.County
Delaware Journal of Corporate Law	Del.J.Corp.L.
Delaware Reports	Del.
Demarest's Surrogate Courts Reports	Dem.
Denio	Denio
Denver Journal of International Law and Policy	Denver J.Int'l L. & Policy
Denver Law Journal	Denver L.J.
Department of State Bulletin, United States	Dep't State Bull.
DePaul Law Review	DePaul L.Rev.
Detroit College Law Review	Det.Coll.L.Rev.
Detroit Law Journal	Det.L.J.
Detroit Law Review	Det.L.Rev.
Dickinson Law Review	Dick.L.Rev.
Dicta	Dicta
Digest of Commercial Laws of the World (Oceana)	Dig.C.L.W.
Digest of International Law (Hackworth)	D.I.L. (Hack.)
Digest of International Law (Moore)	D.I.L. (Moore)
Digest of International Law (White)	D.I.L. (White)
Dine Israel	Dine Israel
District Court, District of Columbia	D.D.C.
District of Columbia Bar Journal	D.C.B.J.
District of Columbia, Court of Appeals Cases	D.C.Cir.
Docket (Lebanon, Pa.)	Docket
Docket (St. Paul, Minn.)	Docket
Docket Call	Docket Call
Dominion Law Reports	D.L.R.
Dominion Law Reports, 1912–1922	D.L.R.
Dominion Law Reports, 1923–1955	[ ] D.L.R.
Dominion Law Reports, Second Series	D.L.R.2d
Dominion Law Reports (Third Series), 1969–Present	D.L.R.3d
Dominion Tax Cases	D.T.C.
Doshisha Law Review	Doshisha L.Rev.
Drake Law Review	Drake L.Rev.
Draper (Ont.)	Draper
Drug Abuse Law Review	Drug Abuse L.Rev.
Dublin University Law Review	Dublin U.L.Rev.
Duke Bar Association Journal	Duke B.Ass'n J.
Duke Law Journal	Duke L.J.
Duquesne Law Review	Duquesne L.Rev.
Duquesne University Law Review	Duquesne U.L.Rev.

Duvall	Duv.
Earth Law Journal	Earth L.J.
East Africa Law Reports	E.Afr.L.R.
East African Law Journal	E.Afr.L.J.
Eastern Africa Law Review	E.Afr.L.Rev.
Eastern Journal of International Law	E.J.Int'l L.
Eastern Law Reporter	E.L.R.
Eastern School Law Review	E.School L.Rev.
Eastern United States Business Law Review	E.U.S.Bus.L.Rev.
Ecology Law Quarterly	Ecology L.Q.
Employee Relations Law Journal	Empl.Rel.L.J.
Emory Law Journal	Emory L.J.
Employment Practices Decisions (CCH)	E.P.D.
Employment Safety and Health Guide (CCH)	Empl.Saf'y & Health Guide
Encyclopedia of European Community Law	E.E.C.L.
Energy Controls (P–H)	Energy Controls
Energy Users Report (BNA)	Energy Users Rep.
English Historical Review	Engl.Hist.Rev.
English Reports—Full Reprint	Eng.Rep.
Environment Law Review	Env.L.Rev.
Environment Reporter (B.N.A.)	Env.Rptr.
Environmental Affairs	Env.Affairs
Environmental Law	Env.L.
Environmental Law Reporter (E.L.I.)	Env.L.Rptr.
Environmental Policy and Law	Env.Pol'y & L.
Environmental Reporter Cases	ERC
Equal Employment Opportunity Commission Compliance Manual (CCH)	E.E.O.C. Compliance Manual
Estate Planning (P–H)	P–H Est.Plan.
Estate Planning Review	Est.Plan.Rev.
Estates and Trusts Quarterly	Estates & Trusts Q.
Eurolaw Commercial Intelligence	Eurolaw Com.Intel.
European Law Digest	Eur.L.Dig.
European Law Newsletter	Eur.L.Newsl.
European Law Review	Eur.L.Rev.
European Parliament Working Documents	Eur.Parl.Docs.
European Taxation	Eur.Tax.
European Transport Law	Eur.Trans.L.
European Treaty Series	Europ.T.S.
European Yearbook	Eur.Y.B.
Examiner (New York)	Examiner
Examiner (Quebec)	Examiner
Excerpta Criminologica	Excerpta Crim.
Exchequer Court Reports (Canada) 1923–present	( ) Ex.C.R.
Exchequer Reports of Canada	Can.Exch.
Executive Agreement Series, United States	E.A.S.
Executive Order	Exec.Order

FDA Consumer --- FDA Consumer
F.O.I. Digest --- F.O.I.Dig.
Faculty of Law Review (Toronto) ----------------- Fac.L.Rev.
Fair Employment Practice Cases (BNA) ----------- F.E.P.Cas.
Family Law Commentator ---------------------------- Family L.Commtr.
Family Law Newsletter ------------------------------ Family L.Newsl.
Family Law Quarterly ------------------------------- Family L.Q.
Family Law Reporter (BNA) ----------------------- Family L.Rep.
Federal Banking Law Reporter (CCH) ------------ CCH Fed.Banking L.
                                                                                    Rep.
Federal Bar Journal --------------------------------- Fed.B.J.
Federal Bar News ------------------------------------ Fed.B.News
Federal Carriers Cases (CCH) --------------------- F.Carr.Cas.
Federal Carriers Reporter (CCH) ------------------ Fed.Carr.Rep.
Federal Cases --- Fed.Cas.
Federal Communications Bar Journal ------------- Fed.Com.B.J.
Federal Communications Commission Reports ------ F.C.C.
Federal Communications Commission Reports,
    Second Series ------------------------------------ F.C.C.2d
Federal Estate and Gift Tax Reporter (CCH) ------ Fed.Est. & Gift Tax
                                                                                    Rep.
Federal Law Reports --------------------------------- Fed.L.Rep.
Federal Law Review --------------------------------- Fed.L.Rev.
Federal Maritime Commission Reports ------------ F.M.C.
Federal Power Commission Reports ---------------- F.P.C.
Federal Probation ----------------------------------- Fed.Prob.
Federal Register -------------------------------------- Fed.Reg.
Federal Reporter ------------------------------------- F.
Federal Reporter, Second Series ------------------- F.2d
Federal Rules Decisions ---------------------------- F.R.D.
Federal Rules Service -------------------------------- Fed.Rules Serv.
Federal Rules Service, Second Series -------------- Fed.Rules Serv.2d
Federal Securities Law Reporter (CCH) ----------- CCH Fed.Sec.L.Rep.
Federal Supplement --------------------------------- F.Supp.
Federal Taxes (P–H) --------------------------------- P–H Fed.Taxes
Federal Trade Commission Decisions -------------- F.T.C.
Federal Wage and Hour (P–H) --------------------- P–H Fed.Wage &
                                                                                    Hour
Federation of Insurance Counsel Quarterly -------- Fed'n Ins.Counsel Q.
Finance Taxation and Company Law (Pakistan) --- Fin.Tax. & Comp.L.
Fire and Casualty Cases (CCH) -------------------- Fire & Casualty Cas.
Florida Bar Journal --------------------------------- Fla.B.J.
Florida Law Journal --------------------------------- Fla.L.J.
Florida Reports -------------------------------------- Fla.
Florida State University Law Review -------------- Fla.St.U.L.Rev.
Florida Supplement --------------------------------- Fla.Supp.
Food Drug Cosmetic Law Journal ------------------ Food Drug Cosm.L.J.
Food Drug Cosmetic Law Reporter (CCH) --------- F.D.Cosm.L.Rep.
Fordham Law Review -------------------------------- Ford.L.Rev.

Fordham Urban Law Journal ---------------------- Ford.Urban L.J.
Foreign Tax Law Bi-Weekly Bulletin ------------- For.Tax Bull.
Forensic Science ------------------------------- For.Sci.
Fortnightly Law Journal ------------------------ Fort.L.J.
Forum, The ------------------------------------- Forum
Forum Law Journal (U. of Baltimore) ------------ F.L.J.
Foundation Law Review -------------------------- Found.L.Rev.
Fox's Patent, Trade Mark, Design and Copyright
   Cases ------------------------------------- Fox Pat.C.
Francisco College Law Journal ------------------ Fran.Coll.L.J.
Freedom of Information Center Reports ----------- F.O.I.C.R.
Gazette -- Gaz.
Gazette Law Reports ---------------------------- Gaz.L.R.
Gazette of Bankruptcy -------------------------- Gaz.Bankr.
George Washington Law Review ------------------- Geo.Wash.L.Rev.
Georgetown Law Journal ------------------------- Geo.L.J.
Georgia Appeals Reports ------------------------ Ga.App.
Georgia Business Lawyer ------------------------ Ga.Bus.Law.
Georgia Journal of International & Comparative
   Law ------------------------------------- Ga.J.Int'l & Comp.L.
Georgia Law Review ----------------------------- Ga.L.Rev.
Georgia Reports -------------------------------- Ga.
Georgia State Bar Journal ---------------------- Ga.St.B.J.
Gilmer --- Gilm.
Glendale Law Review ---------------------------- Glendale L.Rev.
Golden Gate University Law Review -------------- Golden Gate U.L.Rev.
Gonzaga Law Review ----------------------------- Gonzaga L.Rev.
Government Contracts Reporter (CCH) ------------ Gov't Cont.Rep.
Grattan -- Gratt.
Gray --- Gray
Graya -- Graya
Green Bag -------------------------------------- Green Bag
Greene --- Greene
Group Legal Review ----------------------------- Group Legal Rev.
Guild Notes ------------------------------------ Guild Notes
Guild Practitioner ----------------------------- Guild Prac.
Harrington ------------------------------------- Harr.
Harrington, W. W. ------------------------------ W.W.Harr.
Harrison & Hodgins' Municipal Reports (Ont.) ---- Harr. & Hodg.
Harvard Business Review ------------------------ Harv.Bus.Rev.
Harvard Civil Rights—Civil Liberties Law Review -- Harv.Civ.Rights–
   Civ.Lib.L.Rev.
Harvard International Law Journal --------------- Harv.Int'l L.J.
Harvard Journal on Legislation ----------------- Harv.J.Legis.
Harvard Law Review ----------------------------- Harv.L.Rev.
Harvard Law School Bulletin -------------------- Harv.L.S.Bull.
Harvard World Tax Series (CCH) ----------------- Harv.W.Tax Serv.
Hastings Constitutional Law Quarterly ----------- Hastings Const.L.Q.
Hastings Law Journal --------------------------- Hastings L.J.

Hazzard & Warburton's Reports (P.E.I.) ----------- P.E.I.
Hawaii Bar Journal ------------------------------ Hawaii B.J.
Hawaii Reports --------------------------------- Hawaii
Haywood --------------------------------------- Hay.
Head -- Head
Health Care Labor Manual ----------------------- H.C.L.M.
Health Lawyers News Report --------------------- H.L.N.R.
Heiskell --------------------------------------- Heisk.
Hempstead's Circuit Court Reports -------------- Hemp.
Hening and Munford --------------------------- Hen. & M.
Hennepin Lawyer ------------------------------ Henn.Law.
Hill -- Hill
Hitotsubashi Journal of Law and Politics ----------- Hitotsubashi J.L. &
　　　　　　　　　　　　　　　　　　　　　　　　　　　Pol.

Hofstra Law Review ----------------------------- Hofstra L.Rev.
Hong Kong Law Journal ------------------------- Hong Kong L.J.
Housing and Development Reporter (BNA) --------- Housing & Devel.
　　　　　　　　　　　　　　　　　　　　　　　　　　　Rep.

Houston --------------------------------------- Houst.
Houston Law Review --------------------------- Houst.L.Rev.
Houston Lawyer ------------------------------- Houston Law.
Howard --------------------------------------- How.
Howard Law Journal --------------------------- How.L.J.
Howard's Practice ----------------------------- How.Pr.
Howard's Practice, New Series ------------------ How.Pr. (N.S.)
Human Rights --------------------------------- Human Rights
Human Rights in U.S.S.R. ---------------------- Human Rights
　　　　　　　　　　　　　　　　　　　　　　　　　　　U.S.S.R.

Human Rights Journal -------------------------- Human Rights J.
Humphrey ------------------------------------- Humph.
Hun -- Hun
Hungarian Law Review ------------------------- Hung.L.Rev.
Hunters Torrens Cases ------------------------- Hunt.Torrens
I.C.C. Practitioners' Journal -------------------- I.C.C.Prac.J.
ISL Law Review ------------------------------- ISL L.Rev.
Idaho Law Journal ----------------------------- Idaho L.J.
Idaho Law Review ----------------------------- Idaho L.Rev.
Idaho Reports --------------------------------- Idaho
Idea -- Idea
Illinois Appellate Court Reports ---------------- Ill.App.
Illinois Appellate Court Reports, Second Series ----- Ill.App.2d
Illinois Appellate Court Reports, Third Series ------ Ill.App.3d
Illinois Bar Journal --------------------------- Ill.B.J.
Illinois Circuit Court -------------------------- Ill.Cir.
Illinois Continuing Legal Education -------------- Ill.Cont.Legal Ed.
Illinois Court of Claims Reports ---------------- Ill.Ct.Cl.
Illinois Law Review --------------------------- Ill.L.Rev.
Illinois Reports ------------------------------- Ill.
Illinois Reports, Second Series ----------------- Ill.2d

Immigration and Nationality Decisions ------------ I. & N.Dec.
Immigration Bar Bulletin ------------------------- Immig.B.Bull.
India Supreme Court Reports --------------------- India S.Ct.
Indian Advocate ---------------------------------- Ind.Advocate
Indian Cases ------------------------------------- Indian Cas.
Indian Claims Commission Decisions -------------- Ind.Cl.Comm.
Indian Journal of International Law -------------- Ind.J.Int'l L.
Indian Jurist ------------------------------------ Indian Jurist
Indian Law Journal ------------------------------ Indian L.J.
Indian Law Quarterly Review --------------------- Ind.L.Q.Rev.
Indian Law Reports, (e. g) ---------------------- Indian L.R. (e. g.)
　　Allahabad Series ----------------------------- Allahabad Ser.
Indian Law Review ------------------------------- Ind.L.Rev.
Indian Rulings ---------------------------------- Indian Rul.
Indian Territory Reports ------------------------ Indian Terr.
Indian Yearbook of International Affairs --------- Ind.Y.B.Int'l Aff.
Indiana Appellate Reports ----------------------- Ind.App.
Indiana Law Journal ----------------------------- Ind.L.J.
Indiana Law Review ------------------------------ Ind.L.Rev.
Indiana Law Student ----------------------------- Ind.L.Stud.
Indiana Legal Forum ----------------------------- Ind.Legal F.
Indiana Reports --------------------------------- Ind.
Individual Rights and Responsibilities Newsletter -- I.R.R.Newsl.
Industrial and Intellectual Property in Australia -- Ind. & Intell.Prop.
　　　　　　　　　　　　　　　　　　　　　　　　　　　　　　Austl.
Industrial and Labor Relations Review ------------ Ind. & Lab.Rel.Rev.
Industrial Law Journal --------------------------- Indus.L.J.
Industrial Law Review --------------------------- Indus.L.Rev.
Industrial Property ------------------------------ Ind.Prop.
Industrial Property Quarterly -------------------- Ind.Prop.Q.
Industrial Relations, American Labor Arbitration
　　(P–H) -- P–H Ind.Rel., Lab.
　　　　　　　　　　　　　　　　　　　　　　　　　　　　　　Arb.
Industrial Relations:　Journal of Economy and
　　Society --------------------------------------- Ind.Rel.J.Econ. &
　　　　　　　　　　　　　　　　　　　　　　　　　　　　　　Soc.
Industrial Relations, Union Contracts and Collec-
　　tive Bargaining (P–H) ------------------------ P–H Ind.Rel., Union
　　　　　　　　　　　　　　　　　　　　　　　　　　　　　　Conts.
Inequality in Education -------------------------- Inequal.Ed.
Inheritance, Estate, and Gift Tax Reporter (CCH) -- CCH Inh.Est. & Gift
　　　　　　　　　　　　　　　　　　　　　　　　　　　　　　Tax Rep.
Institute of Advanced Legal Studies Annual Re-
　　port -- Inst.Ad.Legal Stud.
　　　　　　　　　　　　　　　　　　　　　　　　　　　　　　Ann.R.
Institute on Mineral Law (La.S.U.) --------------- Inst.Min.L.
Institute on Planning and Zoning ---------------- Inst.Plan. & Zoning
Institute on Planning, Zoning and Eminent Domain　Inst.Plan., Zoning &
　　　　　　　　　　　　　　　　　　　　　　　　　　　　　　E.D.

Institute on Securities Regulation	Inst.Sec.Reg.
Insurance Counsel Journal	Ins.Counsel J.
Insurance Law Journal	Ins.L.J.
Insurance Law Reporter (CCH)	Ins.L.Rep.
Insurance Law Reporter (Can.)	I.L.R.
Inter Alia	Inter Alia
Inter-American Law Review	Inter-Am.L.Rev.
Interior Department Decisions	Interior Dec.
Interior Department Decisions, Second Series	I.D.2d
Internal Revenue Bulletin	Int.Rev.Bull.
Internal Revenue Code of 1954	Int.Rev.Code of 1954
International Affairs	Int'l Aff.
International and Comparative Law Bulletin	Int'l & Comp.L.Bull.
International and Comparative Law Quarterly	Int'l & Comp.L.Q.
International Arbitration Journal	Int'l Arb.J.
International Bar Journal	Int'l B.J.
International Business Lawyer	Int'l Bus.Lawyer
International Business Series (Ernst & Ernst)	Int'l Bus.Ser.
International Conciliation	Int'l Concil.
International Court of Justice Reports	I.C.J.
International Court of Justice Yearbook	I.C.J.Y.B.
International Criminal Police Review	Int'l Crim.Pol.Rev.
International Digest of Health Legislation	Int'l Dig.Health Leg.
International Encyclopedia of Comparative Law	Int'l Encycl.Comp.L.
International Journal	Int'l J.
International Journal of Criminology and Penology	Int'l J.Crim. & Pen.
International Journal of Law Libraries	Int'l J.L.Lib.
International Journal of Legal Research	Int'l J.Legal Res.
International Journal of Offender Therapy and Comparative Criminology	Int'l J.Off.Ther. & Comp.Crim.
International Journal of Politics	Int'l J.Pol.
International Juridical Association Monthly Bulletin	Int'l Jurid.Ass'n Bull.
International Labour Review	Int'l Lab.Rev.
International Law Documents	Int'l L.Doc.
International Law News	Int'l L.News
International Law Perspective	Int'l L.Persp.
International Law Quarterly	Int'l L.Q.
International Law Reports	I.L.R.
International Law Studies	Int'l L.Stud.
International Lawyer, The	Int'l Law.
International Legal Center Newsletter	I.L.C. Newsl.
International Legal Education Newsletter	Int'l Legal Ed.Newsl.
International Legal Materials	Int'l Legal Materials
International Review of Administrative Sciences	Int'l Rev.Ad.Sci.
International Review of Criminal Policy	Int'l Rev.Crim.Policy

Journal of Church and State ------ -------------- J.Church & St.
Journal of Collective Negotiations in the Public
  Sector -- J.C.N.P.S.
Journal of College and University Law ------------ J.Coll. & U.L.
Journal of Common Market Studies --------------- J.Comm.Mkt.Stud.
Journal of Comparative Legislation and Interna-
  tional Law, Third Series --------------------- J.Comp.Leg. & Int'l
                                              L.3d
Journal of Conflict Resolution --------------------- J.Confl.Res.
Journal of Constitutional and Parliamentary
  Studies -- J.Const. & Parl.Stud.
Journal of Consumer Affairs ------------- -------- J.Cons.Affairs
Journal of Contemporary Law --------------------- J.Contemp.L.
Journal of Contemporary Roman-Dutch Law ------- J.Contemp.R.D.L.
Journal of Corporate Taxation -------------------- J.Corp.Tax.
Journal of Corporation Law ---------------------- J.Corp.L.
Journal of Criminal Justice ---------------------- J.Crim.Just.
Journal of Criminal Law (England) -------------- J.Crim.L. (Eng.)

Journal of Criminal Law and Criminology
  (U.S.) --- J.Crim.L. (U.S.)
Journal of Criminal Law, Criminology and Police
  Science -- J.Crim.L.C. & P.S.
Journal of Criminal Science ---------------------- J.Crim.Sci.
Journal of Energy and Development -------------- J.Energy & Devel.
Journal of Ethiopian Law ------------------------ J.Eth.L.
Journal of Family Law -------------------------- J.Fam.L.
Journal of Forensic Medicine -------------------- J.For.Med.
Journal of Forensic Sciences -------------------- J.For.Sci.
Journal of International Affairs ------------------ J.Int'l Aff.
Journal of International Law and Diplomacy ------ J.Int'l L. & Dipl.
Journal of International Law and Economics ------ J.Int'l L. & Econ.
Journal of International Law and Politics --------- J.Int'l L. & Pol.
Journal of Islamic and Comparative Law --------- J.Islam. & Comp.L.
Journal of Jurisprudence ------------------------ J.Juris.
Journal of Land & Public Utility Economics ------- J.Land & P.U.Econ.
Journal of Law -------------------------------- J.L.
Journal of Law and Economic Development ------- J.Law & Econ.Dev.
Journal of Law and Economics ------------------ J.Law & Econ.
Journal of Law and Education -------------------- J.L. & Ed.
Journal of Law and Politics --------------------- J.L. & Pol.
Journal of Law Reform -------------------------- J.Law Reform
Journal of Legal Education ---------------------- J.Legal Ed.
Journal of Legal Medicine ---------------------- J.Legal Med.
Journal of Legal Studies ------------------------ J.Legal Studies
Journal of Maritime Law & Commerce ------------ J.Mar.Law & Com.
Journal of Planning and Environment Law ------- J.Plan. & Env.L.
Journal of Planning and Property Law ----------- J.Plan. & Prop.L.
Journal of Police Science and Administration ----- J.Pol.Sci. & Admin.
Journal of Psychiatry and Law ------------------ J.Psych. & L.

Journal of Public Law ------------------------------ J.Pub.L.

Journal of Radio Law ------------------------------ J.Radio L.

Journal of Real Estate Taxation ------------------ J.Real Est.Tax.

Journal of Reprints for Antitrust Law and Eco-
    nomics -- J.Reprints Antitrust
                                                      L. & Econ.

Journal of Space Law ------------------------------ J.Space L.

Journal of Taxation ------------------------------- J.Tax.

Journal of the American Judicature Society ------- J.Am.Jud.Soc'y

Journal of the American Medical Association ------ J.A.M.A.

Journal of the American Society of Chartered Life
    Underwriters ----------------------------------- J.Am.Soc'y C.L.U.

Journal of the Association of Law Teachers ------- J.Ass'n L. Teachers

Journal of the Association of Trial Lawyers of
    America -- ATLA L.J.

Journal of the Bar Association of the State of
    Kansas -- J.B.Ass'n St.Kan.

Journal of the Beverly Hills Bar Association ------ J.Beverly Hills B.
                                                       Ass'n

Journal of the Canadian Bar Association ---------- J.Can.B.Ass'n

Journal of the Denning Law Society -------------- J.Denning L.Soc'y

Journal of the Forensic Science Society ---------- J.For.Sci.Soc'y

Journal of the Indian Law Institute -------------- J.Ind.L.Inst.

Journal of the International Commission of Jurists-- J.Int'l Comm.Jur.

Journal of the Kansas Bar Association ------------ J.Kan.B.Ass'n

Journal of the Law Society of Scotland ----------- J.L.Soc'y

Journal of the Missouri Bar --------------------- J.Mo.Bar

Journal of the National Association of Referees in
    Bankruptcy (Referees' Journal) ---------------- Ref.J.

Journal of the Patent Office Society -------------- J.Pat.Off.Soc'y

Journal of the Society of Comparative Legislation -- J.Soc'y Comp.Leg.

Journal of the Society of Public Teachers of Law -- J.Soc'y Pub.Teachers
                                                       L.

Journal of the State Bar of California ------------ J.St.Bar Calif.

Journal of Urban Law ----------------------------- J.Urban L.

Journal of World Trade Law ---------------------- J.World Trade L.

Judge Advocate Journal, The --------------------- Judge Advoc.J.

Judges' Journal ---------------------------------- Judges' J.

Judicature --------------------------------------- Judicature

Juridical Review --------------------------------- Jurid.Rev.

Jurimetrics Journal ------------------------------- Jurimetrics J.

Juris Doctor ------------------------------------- J.D.

Jurisprudence ------------------------------------ Juris.

Jurist (Eng.) ------------------------------------ Jurist

Jurist (Wash., D.C.) ----------------------------- Jurist

Justice of the Peace ----------------------------- J.P.

Justice of the Peace and Local Government Review --- Just.P.

Justice System Journal --------------------------- Just.Syst.J.

Justiciary Cases --------------------------------- Just.Cas.

Justinian --- Justinian
Juvenile Court Journal ---------------------------- Juv.Ct.J.
Juvenile Court Judges Journal -------------------- Juv.Ct.Judges J.
Juvenile Justice ----------------------------------- Juv.Just.
KY Bench and Bar --------------------------------- KY Bench & B.
Kansas Bar Association Journal ------------------ Kan.B.Ass'n J.
Kansas Law Journal ------------------------------- Kan.L.J.
Kansas Reports ------------------------------------ Kan.
Karachi Law Journal (Pakistan) ------------------ Karachi L.J.
Kentucky Commentator ---------------------------- Ky.Comment'r
Kentucky Law Journal ----------------------------- Ky.L.J.
Kentucky Law Reporter ---------------------------- Ky.L.Rptr.
Kentucky Reports ---------------------------------- Ky.
Kentucky State Bar Journal ---------------------- Ky.St.B.J.
Kenya Law Reports -------------------------------- Kenya L.R.
Kerala Law Journal ------------------------------- Kerala L.J.
Kernan --- Kern.
King's Counsel ------------------------------------ K.Counsel
Kingston Law Review ----------------------------- Kingston L.Rev.
Knapp, Privy Council ---------------------------- Kn.P.C.
Knight's Industrial Reports --------------------- Knight's Ind.
Kobe University Law Review --------------------- Kobe U.L.Rev.
Korea Law Review -------------------------------- Korea L.Rev.
Korean Journal of Comparative Law ------------- Korean J.Comp.L.
Korean Journal of International Law ------------- Korean J.Int'l L.
Korean Law -- Korean L.
Kwansei Gaknin Law Review -------------------- Kwansei Gak.L.Rev.
Kyoto Law Review --------------------------------- Kyoto L.Rev.
L.A.G. Bulletin ------------------------------------ L.A.G.Bull.
Labor and Automation Bulletin ------------------ Lab. & Auto.Bull.
Labor Arbitration Awards (CCH) ----------------- CCH Lab.Arb.Awards
Labor Arbitration Reports (BNA) ---------------- Lab.Arb.
Labor Cases (CCH) -------------------------------- CCH Lab.Cas.
Labor Law Journal --------------------------------- Lab.L.J.
Labor Law Reporter (CCH) ----------------------- CCH Lab.L.Rep.
Labor Relations Law Letter --------------------- Lab.Rel.L.Letter
Labor Relations Reference Manual (BNA) -------- L.R.R.M.
Labor Relations Reporter (BNA) ----------------- Lab.Rel.Rep.
Labour Arbitration Cases ------------------------ L.A.C.
Lackawana Bar ------------------------------------ Lackawana B.
Land and Water Law Review --------------------- Land & Water L.Rev.
Land Development Law Reporter ------------------ L.D.L.R.
Lansing's Supreme Court ------------------------- Lans.
Latin American Journal of Politics, Economics and
  Law -- L.A.J.P.E.L.
Law -- Law
Law Advertiser ----------------------------------- L.Advertiser
Law and Computer Technology ------------------- L. & Computer Tech.
Law and Contemporary Problems ---------------- Law & Contemp.Prob.

Law and Justice ----- L. & Just.
Law and Legislation in the German Democratic Republic ----- L. & Leg.GDR
Law and Liberty ----- L. & Lib.
Law and Order ----- L. & Order
Law and Policy in International Business ----- Law & Pol'y Int'l Bus.
Law and Psychology Review ----- L. & Psych.Rev.
Law and Society Review ----- Law & Soc'y Rev.
Law and the Social Order Arizona State Law Journal ----- Law & Soc.Ord.
Law Book Adviser ----- L.Book Adviser
Law Chronicle ----- L.Chron.
Law Chronical and Law Students' Magazine ----- L.Chron. & L.Stud. Mag.
Law Chronicle and Law Students' Magazine, New Series ----- L.Chron. & L.Stud. Mag., (N.S.)
Law Coach ----- L.Coach
Law Commentary ----- L.Comment'y
Law Gazette ----- L.Gaz.
Law Guardian ----- L.Guard.
Law in American Society ----- L.Am.Soc'y
Law in Eastern Europe ----- L.East.Eur.
Law in Japan ----- L.Japan
Law in Society ----- L. in Soc'y
Law in Transition Quarterly ----- L.Trans.Q.
Law Institute Journal ----- L.Inst.J.
Law Institute Journal of Victoria ----- L.Inst.J.Vict.
Law Journal New Series Chancery ----- L.J.Ch.
Law Journal New Series Common Law, Magistrates Cases (discontinued) ----- L.J.Mag.
Law Journal New Series Exchequer ----- L.J.Ex.
Law Journal New Series House of Lords ----- L.J.H.L.
Law Journal New Series Privy Council ----- L.J.P.C.
Law Journal New Series Queen's Bench (or King's Bench) ----- L.J.Q.B. or L.J.K.B.
Law Journal Old Series (1822–1830) ----- L.J.O.S.
Law Journal Reports, (e. g.) King's Bench, New Series ----- (e. g.) L.J.K.B. (N. S.)
Law Librarian ----- L.Lib.
Law Library Journal ----- L.Lib.J.
Law Magazine and Review ----- L.Mag. & Rev.
Law Notes ----- Law Notes
Law Notes for the General Practitioner ----- L.Notes Gen.Prac.
Law Office Economics and Management ----- L.Off.Econ. & Mgt.
Law Quarterly ----- L.Q.
Law Quarterly Review ----- L.Q.Rev.
Law Recorder ----- L.Record.
Law Reports ----- L.R.

Law Reports Appeal Cases, Second Series ----------- App.Cas.
Law Reports Appeal Cases, Third Series ------------ A.C.
Law Reports Chancery ------------------------------- L.R.Ch.
Law Reports Chancery Division, Second Series ------ Ch.D.
Law Reports Chancery Division, Third Series -------- Ch.
Law Reports Common Pleas --------------------------- L.R.C.P.
Law Reports Common Pleas Division to 1880 --------- C.P.D.
Law Reports Equity --------------------------------- L.R.Eq.
Laws Reports Exchequer ---------------------------- L.R.Ex.
Law Reports Exchequer Division to 1880 ----------- Ex.D.
Law Reports House of Lords ----------------------- L.R.H.L.
Law Reports, Indian Appeals ---------------------- L.R.Indian App.
Law Reports, Ireland ----------------------------- L.R.Ir.
Law Reports King's Bench, Third Series ----------- K.B.
Law Reports Probate and Divorce ------------------ L.R.P. & D.
Law Reports Probate, Divorce & Admiralty Division,
    Second Series -------------------------------- P.D.
Law Reports Probate, Divorce & Admiralty Division,
    Third Series --------------------------------- P.
Law Reports Queen's Bench ------------------------ L.R.Q.B.
Law Reports Queen's Bench Division, Second Series -- Q.B.D.
Law Reports Queen's Bench, Third Series ----------- Q.B.
Law Reports Weekly Law Reports ------------------- W.L.R.
Law Review Digest -------------------------------- L.Rev.Dig.
Law Society Gazette (Toronto) -------------------- Law Soc'y Gaz.
Law Society Journal (Boston) --------------------- Law Soc'y J.
Law Society Journal (New South Wales) ----------- Law Soc'y J.
Law Society's Gazette (London) ------------------- Law Soc'y Gaz.
Law Student's Helper ----------------------------- L.Stud.Helper
Law Students' Journal ---------------------------- L.Stud.J.
Law Teacher ------------------------------------- L.Teacher
Law Times (Pa.) --------------------------------- L.T.
Law Times, New Series (Eng.) --------------------- L.T. (N.S.)
Law Times, Old Series (Eng.) --------------------- L.T. (O.S.)
Law Times Reports, New Series -------------------- L.T.R. (N.S.)
Lawasia --- Lawasia
Lawyer -- Law.
Lawyer and Banker and Central Law Journal ------- Lawyer & Banker
Lawyer of the Americas -------------------------- Law.Am.
Lawyer's and Magistrate's Magazine -------------- Law. & Magis.Mag.
Lawyers' Edition, U. S. Supreme Court Reports ---- L.Ed.
Lawyers' Edition, U. S. Supreme Court Reports,
    Second Series -------------------------------- L.Ed.2d
Lawyers' Medical Journal ------------------------- Lawyers' Med.J.
Lawyers Reports Annotated ------------------------ L.R.A.
Lawyers Reports Annotated, 1915a–1918F --------- (e. g.) 1917E L.R.A.
                                                        405
Lawyers Reports, Annotated, New Series ---------- L.R.A. (N.S.)
Lawyers' Title Guaranty Funds Newsletter -------- L.T.G.F.Newsl.

League of Nations Official Journal --------------- League of Nations Off.J.

League of Nations Treaty Series ------------------ L.N.T.S.

Learning and the Law ---------------------------- Learn. & L.

Lefroy and Cassels' Practice Cases (Ont.) --------- L. & C.

Legal and Insurance Reporter (Pa.) -------------- Legal & Ins.

Legal Bibliography ---------------------------- Legal Bibl.

Legal Economics ------------------------------ Legal Econ.

Legal Examiner ------------------------------- Legal Exam.

Legal Issues of European Integration ------------ Legal Iss.Eur.Integr.

Legal Literature ----------------------------- Legal Lit.

Legal News --------------------------------- Legal News

Legal Observer ------------------------------ Legal Obser.

Legal Reporter (Tenn.) ----------------------- Leg.Rep.

Leigh -------------------------------------- Leigh

Lex et Scientia ------------------------------ Lex & Sci.

Liaison ------------------------------------ Liaison

Liberian Law Journal ------------------------- Liberian L.J.

Liberian Law Reports ------------------------- Liber.L.R.

Life (Health & Accident) Cases (CCH) ----------- Life Cas.

Life (Health & Accident) Cases, Second Series
  (CCH) ---------------------------------- Life Cas.2d

Lincoln Law Review --------------------------- Lincoln L.Rev.

Litigation ---------------------------------- Litigation

Livingston's Monthly Law Magazine -------------- Livingston's M.L. Mag.

Lloyd's List Law Reports ---------------------- L.L.Rep.

Lloyd's List Law Reports Admiralty -------------- Lloyd's Rep.

Lloyd's Maritime and Commercial Law Quarterly ---- L.M.C.L.Q.

Local Courts and Municipal Gazette -------------- Local Ct. & Mun.Gaz.

Local Government and Magisterial Reports -------- Local Gov't

Local Government Reports of Australia ----------- Local Gov't R.Austl.

Lois Recentes du Canada ---------------------- Lois Rec.

Long Beach Bar Bulletin ----------------------- Long Beach B.Bull.

Los Angeles Bar Journal ----------------------- L.A.B.J.

Louisiana Annual Reports ---------------------- La.Ann.

Louisiana Bar Journal ------------------------- La.B.J.

Louisiana Courts of Appeal Reports -------------- La.App.

Louisiana Law Journal ------------------------ La.L.J.

Louisiana Law Review ------------------------ La.L.Rev.

Louisiana Supreme Court Reports --------------- La.

Louisville Lawyer ---------------------------- Louisville Law.

Lower Canada Jurist -------------------------- Low.Can.Jurist

Lower Canada Law Journal --------------------- Low.Can.L.J.

Lower Canadian Reports ----------------------- Low.Can.R.

Loyola Consumer Protection Journal
  (Los Angeles) --------------------------- Loyola Cons.Prot.J.

Loyola Digest -------------------------------- Loyola Dig.

Loyola Law Review --------------------------- Loyola L.Rev.

Loyola Lawyer ----------------------------------- Loyola Law.
Loyola of Los Angeles Law Review ---------------- Loyola L.A.L.Rev.
Loyola University Law Journal (Chicago) --------- Loyola U.L.J.
Luzerne Legal Observer -------------------------- Luz.Leg.Obs.
MacArthur --------------------------------------- MacArth.
MacArthur and Mackey ---------------------------- MacArth. & M.
McCahon --- McCahon
McGill Law Journal ------------------------------ McGill L.J.
Mackey -- Mackey
Madras Law Journal ------------------------------ Madras L.J.
Madras Law Journal Criminal --------------------- Madras L.J.Crim.
Magisterial Cases ------------------------------- Mag.Cas.
Magistrate and Constable ------------------------ Mag. & Const.
Magistrate and Municipal and Parochial Lawyer ---- Mag.Mun.Par.Law.
Maine Law Review -------------------------------- Maine L.Rev.
Maine Reports ----------------------------------- Me.
Major Peace Treaties of Modern History
   1648–1967 -------------------------------------- M.P.T.M.H.
Malaya Law Review ------------------------------- Mal.L.Rev.
Malayan Law Journal ----------------------------- Mal.L.J.
Manitoba Bar News ------------------------------- Man.B.News
Manitoba Law Journal ---------------------------- Man.L.J.
Manitoba Law Reports ---------------------------- Man.
Manning's Unreported Cases ---------------------- Mann.Unrep.Cas.
Marijuana Review, The --------------------------- Marijuana Rev.
Maritime Law Cases, New Series ------------------ Mar.L.Cas. (N.S.)
Maritime Notes and Queries ---------------------- M.N. & Q.
Maritime Provinces Reports ---------------------- Mar.Prov.
Marquette Law Review ---------------------------- Marq.L.Rev.
Martin Mining Cases ----------------------------- Martin Mining
Marvel -- Marv.
Maryland Appellate Reports ---------------------- Md.App.
Maryland Bar Journal ---------------------------- Md.B.J.
Maryland Law Forum ------------------------------ Md.L.F.
Maryland Law Review ----------------------------- Md.L.Rev.
Maryland Reports -------------------------------- Md.
Massachusetts Appeals Court Reports ------------- Mass.App.Rep.
Massachusetts Appellate Decisions (1941–47) ----- Mass.App.Dec.
Massachusetts Appellate Division Reports (1936–50) -- Mass.App.Div.
Massachusetts Law Quarterly --------------------- Mass.L.Q.
Massachusetts Reports --------------------------- Mass.
Medical Trial Technique Quarterly --------------- Med.Trial Tech.Q.
Medicine, Law and Public Policy ----------------- Med.L. & Pub.Pol.
Medicine, Science and the Law ------------------- Med.Sci. & L.
Medico-Legal and Criminological Review ---------- Med.-Legal Crim.Rev.
Medico-Legal Journal ---------------------------- Med.-Legal J.
Medico-Legal Society Transactions --------------- Med.-Legal Soc'y
                                                                    Trans.
Melanesian Law Journal (Papua and New Guinea) -- Melanesian L.J.

Melbourne University Law Review ----------------- Melb.U.L.Rev.
Memphis Law Journal (Tenn.) ---------------------- Memp.L.J.
Memphis State University Law Review ------------ Memphis St.U.L.Rev.
Mercantile Adjuster and the Lawyer
  and Credit Man --------------------------------- M.A.L.C.M.
Mercer Beasley Law Review ----------------------- Mercer Beasley
                                                   L.Rev.
Mercer Law Review ----------------------------- Mercer L.Rev.
Metcalf --- Met.
Miami Law Quarterly ---------------------------- Miami L.Q.
Michigan Court of Appeals Reports --------------- Mich.App.
Michigan Law Review --------------------------- Mich.L.Rev.
Michigan Reports ------------------------------- Mich.
Michigan State Bar Journal --------------------- Mich.St.B.J.
Middle East Law Review ------------------------ Mid.East L.Rev.
Military Law Reporter -------------------------- M.L.R.
Military Law Review --------------------------- Mil.L.Rev.
Mills -- Mills
Minnesota Continuing Legal Education ---------- Minn.Cont.Legal Ed.
Minnesota Law Review ------------------------- Minn.L.Rev.
Minnesota Reports ----------------------------- Minn.
Mississippi Law Journal ------------------------ Miss.L.J.
Mississippi Reports ---------------------------- Miss.
Missouri Appeal Reports ------------------------ Mo.App.
Missouri Bar Journal -------------------------- Mo.B.J.
Missouri Law Review --------------------------- Mo.L.Rev.
Missouri Reports ------------------------------ Mo.
Mitchell's Maritime Register -------------------- Mitchell's Mar.Reg.
Modern Federal Practice Digest ----------------- M.F.P.D.
Modern Law and Society ----------------------- Mod.L. & Soc'y
Modern Law Review --------------------------- Mod.L.Rev.
Modern Practice Commentator ------------------ Mod.Pract.Comm.
Monash University Law Review ----------------- Monash Univ.L.Rev.
Monroe, B. ----------------------------------- B.Mon.
Monroe, T. B. -------------------------------- T.B.Mon.
Montana Law Review -------------------------- Mont.L.Rev.
Montana Reports ------------------------------ Mont.
Monthly Digest of Tax Articles ----------------- Month.Dig.Tax
                                                   Articles
Monthly Law Reporter (Boston) ----------------- Month.L.Rep.
Montreal Law Reports (Queen's Bench) ---------- M.L.R. (Q.B.)
Montreal Law Reports (Superior Court) --------- M.L.R. (S.C.)
Moore, New Series, Privy Council --------------- Moo.P.C. (N.S.)
Moore, Privy Council -------------------------- Moo.P.C.
Motor Carrier Cases, Interstate Commerce
  Commission --------------------------------- M.C.C.
Munford --------------------------------------- Munf.
Municipal Attorney ---------------------------- Mun.Att'y
Municipal Law Court Decisions ----------------- Mun.L.Ct.Dec.

Municipal Law Journal .... Mun.L.J.
Municipal Ordinance Review .... Mun.Ord.Rev.
Mysore Law Journal .... Mysore L.J.
NACCA Law Journal .... NACCA L.J.
N.D. Journal of Legislation .... N.D.J.Legis.
N.I.M.L.O. Municipal Law Review .... N.I.M.L.O.Mun.L.
               Rev.
N.L.A.D.A. Briefcase .... NLADA Brief.
Narcotics Control Digest .... Narcotics Control
               Dig.
Narcotics Law Bulletin .... Narcotics L.Bull.
National Civic Review .... Nat'l Civic Rev.
National Income Tax Magazine .... Nat'l Income Tax
               Mag.
National Journal cf Criminal Defense .... Nat'l J.Crim.Defense
National Labor Relations Board Decisions .... N.L.R.B.
National Legal Magazine .... Nat'l Legal Mag.
National Municipal Review .... Nat'l Mun.Rev.
National Railroad Adjustment Board Awards .. [e. g.] N.R.A.B. (4th
               Div.)
National School Law Reporter .... Nat'l School L.Rptr.
National Taiwan University Law Journal ..... Nat'l Taiwan U.L.
               Rev.
National Tax Journal .... Nat'l Tax J.
Natural Law Forum .... Natural L.F.
Natural Resources Journal .... Natural Resources J.
Natural Resources Law Newsletter .... Natural Resources
               L.Newsl.
Natural Resources Lawyer .... Natural Resources
               Law.
Nebraska Law Review .... Neb.L.Rev.
Nebraska Reports .... Neb.
Nebraska State Bar Journal .... Neb.St.B.J.
Negligence & Compensation Cases Annotated .. Negl. & Comp.Cas.
               Ann.
Negligence & Compensation Cases Annotated, New
 Series .... Negl. & Comp.Cas.
               Ann. (N.S.)
Negligence & Compensation Cases Annotated, Third
 Series .... Negl. & Comp.Cas.
               Ann.3d
Negligence Cases (CCH) .... Negl.Cas.
Negligence Cases, Second Series (CCH) Negl.Cas.2d
Netherlands International Law Review .... Neth.Int'l L.Rev.
Netherlands Yearbook of International Law ... Neth.Y.B.Int'l Law
New Brunswick Equity Reports .... N.B.Eq.
New Brunswick Reports .... N.B.
New England Journal on Prison Law .... N.Eng.J.Prison L.
New England Law Review .... N.Eng.L.Rev.

New Hampshire Bar Journal --------------------- N.H.B.J.
New Hampshire Reports ----------------------- N.H.
New Jersey Equity Reports ---------------------- N.J.Eq.
New Jersey Law ------------------------------ N.J.L.
New Jersey Law Journal ------------------------ N.J.L.J.
New Jersey Law Reports ------------------------ N.J.Law
New Jersey Law Review ------------------------ N.J.L.Rev.
New Jersey Miscellaneous Reports ------------------ N.J.Misc.
New Jersey Reports -------------------------- N.J.
New Jersey State Bar Journal -------------------- N.J.St.B.J.

New Jersey Superior Court and County Courts
    Reports ------------------------------------ N.J.Super.

New Jersey Superior Court Reports ---------------- N.J.Super.
New Jersey Supreme Court Reports---------------- N.J.
New Law Journal ------------------------------ New L.J.
New Mexico Law Review ----------------------- N.Mex.L.Rev.
New Mexico Reports --------------------------- N.M.
New South Wales State Reports ------------------- N.S.W.
New York Civil Procedure --------------------- N.Y.Civ.Proc.
New York Civil Procedure, New Series ------------ N.Y.Civ.Proc. (N.S.)
New York Continuing Legal Education ------------ N.Y.Cont.Legal Ed.

New York County Lawyers Association Bar
    Bulletin ------------------------------------- N.Y. County Law.
                                                   Ass'n B.Bull.

New York Court of Appeals Reports ---------------- N.Y.
New York Court of Appeals Reports, Second Series -- N.Y.2d
New York Criminal Reports --------------------- N.Y.Crim.
New York Department Reports -------------------- N.Y.Dep't R.
New York Judicial Repository -------------------- N.Y.Jud.Repos.
New York Jurisprudence ----------------------- N.Y.Jur.
New York Law Forum -------------------------- N.Y.L.F.
New York Law Journal ------------------------- N.Y.L.J.
New York Law Review -------------------------- N.Y.L.Rev.
New York Miscellaneous Reports ------------------- N.Y.Misc.
New York Miscellaneous, Second Series ----------- N.Y.Misc.2d

New York Monthly Law Bulletin ------------------ N.Y.Month.L.Bull.
New York Monthly Law Record -------------------- N.Y.Month.L.Rec.
New York State Bar Journal --------------------- N.Y.St.B.J.
New York Supplement -------------------------- N.Y.S.
New York Supplement, Second Series -------------- N.Y.S.2d
New York Supreme Court, Appellate Division Re-
    ports -- App.Div.
New York Supreme Court, Appellate Division Reports,
    Second Series ------------------------------ App.Div.2d
New York University Conference on Charitable Foun-
    dations Proceedings ------------------------- N.Y.U.Conf.Chari-
                                                   table
New York University Conference on Labor --------- N.Y.U.Conf.Lab.

New York University Institute on Federal Taxation -- (e. g.) N.Y.U.7th Inst. on Fed.Tax.

New York University Intramural Law Review -------- N.Y.U.Intra.L.Rev.

New York University Journal of International Law
    and Politics -- N.Y.U.J.Int'l Law & Pol.

New York University Law Center Bulletin ----------- N.Y.U.L.Cent.Bull.

New York University Law Quarterly Review -------- N.Y.U.L.Q.Rev.

New York University Law Review ------------------- N.Y.U.L.Rev.

New York University Review of Law and Social
    Change --- N.Y.U.Rev.Law & Soc.C.

New Yugoslav Law ----------------------------------- New Yugo.L.

New Zealand Law Journal --------------------------- N.Z.L.J.

New Zealand Law Reports --------------------------- N.Z.L.R.

New Zealand Universities Law Review -------------- N.Z.U.L.Rev.

Nevada Reports ------------------------------------- Nev.

Nevada State Bar Journal --------------------------- Nev.St.B.J.

Newfoundland Reports ------------------------------ Nfld.R.

Newfoundland Supreme Court Decisions ------------ Newf.S.Ct.

Nigeria Law Reports -------------------------------- Nigeria L.R.

Nigerian Monthly Law Reports --------------------- N.M.L.R.

Noise Regulation Reporter (BNA) ------------------ Noise Reg.Rep.

NOLPE Notes --------------------------------------- NOLPE Notes

NOLPE School Law Journal ------------------------- NOLPE School L.J.

North Atlantic Regional Business Law Rev. --------- N.Atlantic Reg.Bus. L.Rev.

North Carolina Central Law Journal ---------------- N.C.Cent.L.J.

North Carolina Court of Appeals Reports ----------- N.C.App.

North Carolina Law Review ------------------------- N.C.L.Rev.

North Carolina Reports ----------------------------- N.C.

North Central School Law Review ------------------- N.Cent.School L.Rev.

North Dakota Law Review --------------------------- N.D.L.Rev.

North Dakota Reports ------------------------------- N.D.

North Eastern Reporter ----------------------------- N.E.

North Eastern Reporter, Second Series ------------- N.E.2d

North West Territories Law Reports ---------------- N.W.T.L.R.

North Western Reporter ---------------------------- N.W.

North Western Reporter, Second Series ------------- N.W.2d

Northern Ireland Law Reports ---------------------- N.Ir.L.R.

Northern Ireland Legal Quarterly ------------------- N.Ir.L.Q.

Northern Kentucky State Law Forum ---------------- N.Ky.St.L.F.

Northumberland Legal Journal ---------------------- Northumb.Legal J.

Northwest Territories Supreme Court Reports ------- N.W.Terr.

Northwestern University Law Review --------------- Nw.U.L.Rev.

Notre Dame Lawyer --------------------------------- Notre Dame Law.

Nova Scotia Reports -------------------------------- N.S.R.

Nuclear Law Bulletin ------------------------------- Nuclear L.Bull.

Nuclear Regulation Reporter ----------------------- Nuclear Reg.Rep.

Obiter Dictum	Obiter Dictum
Occupational, Safety, and Health Decisions (CCH)	O.S.H.Dec.
Occupational, Safety, and Health Reporter (BNA)	O.S.H.Rep.
Ocean Development and International Law	Ocean Devel. & Int'l L.
Office of Contract Settlement Decisions	O.C.S.
Official Gazette. United States Patent Office	O.G.Pat.Off.
Official Journal of the European Communities	E.E.C.J.O.
Ohio Appellate Reports	Ohio App.
Ohio Appellate Reports, Second Series	Ohio App.2d
Ohio Circuit Court Reports	Ohio C.C.R.
Ohio Circuit Court Reports, New Series	Ohio C.C.R. (N.S.)
Ohio Circuit Decisions	Ohio C.Dec.
Ohio Courts of Appeals Reports	Ohio Ct.App.
Ohio Decisions	Ohio Dec.
Ohio Decisions, Reprint	Ohio Dec.Reprint
Ohio Jurisprudence	Ohio Jur.
Ohio Jurisprudence, Second Series	Ohio Jur.2d
Ohio Law Abstract	Ohio L.Abs.
Ohio Law Bulletin	Oh.L.Bull.
Ohio Law Journal	Oh.L.J.
Ohio Miscellaneous Reports	Ohio Misc.
Ohio Nisi Prius Reports	Ohio N.P.
Ohio Nisi Prius Reports, New Series	Ohio N.P. (N.S.)
Ohio Northern University Law Review	Ohio North.U.L.Rev.
Ohio Opinions	Ohio Op.
Ohio Opinions, Second Series	Ohio Op.2d
Ohio Reports	Ohio
Ohio State Law Journal	Ohio St.L.J.
Ohio State Reports	Ohio St.
Ohio State Reports, Second Series	Ohio St.2d
Ohio Supplement	Ohio Supp.
Oil & Gas Compact Bulletin	Oil & Gas Compact Bull.
Oil and Gas Institute	Oil & Gas Inst.
Oil and Gas Journal	Oil & Gas J.
Oil & Gas Law & Taxation Institute (Southwestern Legal Foundation)	Oil & Gas L. & Tax. Inst. (Sw.Legal Fdn.)
Oil and Gas Reporter	Oil & Gas Rptr.
Oil and Gas Tax Quarterly	Oil & Gas Tax Q.
Oklahoma Bar Association Journal	Okla.B.Ass'n J.
Oklahoma Criminal Reports	Okla.Crim.
Oklahoma Law Journal	Okla.L.J.
Oklahoma Law Review	Okla.L.Rev.
Oklahoma Reports	Okla.
Ontario Appeal Reports	O.A.R.
Ontario Election Cases	Ont.Elec.

Ontario Labour Relations Board Monthly Report ---- [ ] November
                                                        Monthly Report (O.
                                                        L.R.B.)

Ontario Law Reports, 1901–1930 ------------------- O.L.R.
Ontario Reports, 1882–1900 ----------------------- O.R.
Ontario Reports, 1931 to present ----------------- [ ] O.R.
Ontario Weekly Notes, 1909–1932 ----------------- O.W.N.
Ontario Weekly Notes, 1933–1962 ----------------- [ ] O.W.N.
Ontario Weekly Reporter -------------------------- O.W.R.
Opinions of the Attorney General, United States ----- Op.Att'y Gen.
Orange County Bar Journal ----------------------- Orange County B.J.
Oregon Court of Appeals Reports --- ------------- Ore.App.
Oregon Law Review ------------------------------ Ore.L.Rev.
Oregon Reports --------------------------------- Ore.
Oregon State Bar Bulletin ----------------------- Ore.St.B.Bull.
Oregon Tax Court Reports ------------------------ Ore.Tax Ct.
Osaka University Law Review --------------------- Osaka U.L.Rev.
Osgoode Hall Law Journal ------------------------ Osgoode Hall L.J.
Otago Law Review ------------------------------- Otago L.Rev.
Ottawa Law Review ------------------------------ Ottawa L.Rev.
Oxford Lawyer ---------------------------------- Oxford Law.
Pacific Coast Law Journal ------------------------ P.Coast L.J.
Pacific Law Journal ----------------------------- Pacific L.J.
Pacific Law Magazine --------------------------- P.L.Mag.
Pacific Law Reporter --------------------------- P.L.Rep.
Pacific Reporter -------------------------------- P.
Pacific Reporter, Second Series ------------------- P.2d
Pakistan Criminal Law Journal ------------------- Pak.Crim.L.J.
Pakistan Law Reports, (e. g.) Lahore Series -------- [e. g.] Pak.L.R.La-
                                                        hore Ser.

Pan-American Treaty Series --------------------- Pan-Am.T.S.
Papua and New Guinea Law Reports -------------- Papua & N.G.
Patent and Trade Mark Review ------------------- Pat. & T.M.Rev.
Patent Law Review ----------------------------- Pat.L.Rev.
Patent, Trademark & Copyright Journal ----------- Pat.T.M. & Copy.J.
Patents, Decisions of Commissioner and of U. S.
    Courts ------------------------------------- Dec.Com.Pat.
Pennewill -------------------------------------- Penne.
Pennsylvania Bar Association Quarterly ----------- Pa.B.Ass'n Q.
Pennsylvania Bar Brief -------------------------- Pa.B.Brief
Pennsylvania County Court Reports --------------- Pa.County Ct.
Pennsylvania District and County Reports --------- Pa.D. & C.
Pennsylvania District and County Reports, Second
    Series ------------------------------------- Pa.D. & C.2d
Pennsylvania District Reports -------------------- Pa.Dist.
Pennsylvania Fiduciary Reporter ----------------- Pa.Fid.
Pennsylvania Law Journal ----------------------- Pa.L.J.
Pennsylvania Law Record ------------------------ Pa.L.Rec.
Pennsylvania Miscellaneous Reports --------------- Pa.Misc.

Pennsylvania State Reports --------------------- Pa.
Pennsylvania Superior Court Reports --------------- Pa.Super.
Penrose and Watts ------------------------------ Pen. & W.
Pension and Profit-Sharing Tax Journal ----------- P.P.S.T.J.
Pension Reporter -------------------------------- Pension Rep.
Pepperdine Law Review --------------------------- Pepperdine L.Rev.
Performing Arts Review --------------------------- Performing Arts Rev.
Permanent Court of International Justice Advisory
   Opinions, Cases, Judgments, Pronouncements ----- P.C.I.J.
Permanent Court of International Justice Annual Re-
   ports --- P.C.I.J.Ann.R.
Personal Finance Law Quarterly Report ------------ Pers.Finance L.Q.
Personal Injury Commentator --------------------- Pers.Inj.Comment'r
Peters --- Pet.
Philanthropist ------------------------------------- Philanthrop.
Philippine International Law Journal --------------- Phil.Int'l L.J.
Philippine Law Journal --------------------------- Phil.L.J.
Pickering --- Pick.
Pike & Fischer Radio Regulation ----------------- R.R.
Pike & Fischer Radio Regulation, Second Series ------ R.R.2d
Pinney --- Pin.
Pittsburgh Legal Journal ------------------------- Pitt.L.J.
Planning and Compensation Reports ---------------- Plan. & Comp.
Planning, Zoning & Eminent Domain Institute ------- Plan., Zoning & E.D.
                                           Inst.
Police Journal ------------------------------------- Police J.
Police Law Quarterly ----------------------------- Police L.Q.
Polish Yearbook of International Law -------------- Pol.Y.B.Int'l L.
Political Science Quarterly ----------------------- Pol.Sci.Q.
Pollution Abstracts ------------------------------- Pollution Abs.
Pollution Control Guide (CCH) -------------------- Poll.Contr.Guide
Poor Law and Local Government Magazine ---------- Poor L. & Local Gov't
                                           Mag.
Portia Law Journal ------------------------------- Portia L.J.
Portland University Law Review ------------------- Portland U.L.Rev.
Practical Lawyer --------------------------------- Prac.Law.
Practice Reports (Ont.) --------------------------- P.R.
Prentice-Hall ------------------------------------- P-H
Preview of United States Supreme Court Cases ---- Preview
Price's Mining Commissioner's Cases (Ont.) ------- Price
Prince Edward Island ---------------------------- Pr.Edw.Isl.
Prison Law Reporter ----------------------------- Prison L.Rptr.
Probate and Property ----------------------------- Prob. & Prop.
Probate Lawyer ---------------------------------- Prob.Law.
Product Safety and Liability Reporter (BNA) ------ Prod.Safety & Liab.
                                           Rep.
Property and Compensation Reports --------------- Prop. & Comp.
Property Lawyer --------------------------------- Prop.Law.
Prosecutor --------------------------------------- Prosecutor

Public Administration Review ---------------------- Pub.Ad.Rev.
Public Contract Law Journal ---------------------- Pub.Contract L.J.
Public Contract Newsletter ---------------------- Pub.Contract Newsl.
Public Em.loyee Relations Reports ---------------- Pub.Employee Rel.
    Rep.
Public International Law ------------------------- Pub.Int'l L.
Public Land and Resources Law Digest ----------- Pub.Land & Res.L.
    Dig.
Public Law ------------------------------------- Pub.L.
Public Utilities Fortnightly ----------------------- Pub.Util.Fort.
Public Utilities Reports -------------------------- P.U.R.
Public Utilities Reports, New Series --------------- P.U.R. (N.S.)
Public Utilities Reports, Third Series ------------- P.U.R.3d
Publications of the Pipe Roll Society -------------- Pipe Roll Soc'y
Publications of the Pipe Roll Society, New Series --- Pipe Roll Soc'y, N.S.
Publishing, Entertainment, Advertising and Allied
    Fields Law Quarterly -------------------------- PEAL
Puerto Rico, Decisiones de ---------------------- D.P.R.
Puerto Rico Federal Reports ---------------------- P.R.F.
Puerto Rico Reports ----------------------------- P.R.R.
Pyke's Reports, King's Bench (Que.) --------------- Pyke
Quarterly Law Review ---------------------------- Q.L.Rev.
Quarterly Newsletter—Special Committee on Environ-
    mental Law ---------------------------------- Q.Newsl.–Spec.
    Comm.Env.L.
Quebec Law Reports ----------------------------- Que.L.R.
Quebec Official Reports (King's Bench or Queen's
    Bench) 1941 to present ------------------------ [　] Que.K.B. or
    [　] Que.Q.B.
Quebec Official Reports (Queen's Bench or King's
    Bench) 1892–1941 ---------------------------- Que.Q.B. or Que.K.
    B.
Quebec Official Reports (Superior Court) 1892–
    1941 -- Que.S.C.
Quebec Official Reports (Superior Court) 1942–
    present ------------------------------------- [　] Que.S.C.
Quebec Practice Reports ------------------------- Que.Prac.
Quebec Rapports Judiciares Officiels (Banc de la
    Reine); Cour supérieure ---------------------- Que.B.R.; Que.C.S.
Quebec Revised Reports -------------------------- R.J.R.O.
Queens Bar Bulletin ----------------------------- Queens B.Bull.
Queen's Bench, Manitoba temp. Wood, by Armour -- Armour
Queen's Intramural Law Journal ------------------- Q.Intramural L.J.
Queen's Law Journal ----------------------------- Q.L.J.
Queensland Justice of the Peace Reports ----------- Queensl.J.P.Rep.
Queensland Law Society Journal ------------------- Queensl.L.Soc'y J.
Queensland Lawyer ------------------------------ Queens.Law.
Queensland Reports ----------------------------- Queensl.
Queensland State Reports ------------------------ Queensl.St.Rep.
Quis Custodiet? -------------------------------- Quis Cust.

Race -- Race
Race Relations Law Reporter ------------------------ Race Rel.L.Rep.
Race Relations Law Survey ------------------------- Race Rel.L.Survey
Radio Regulation Reporter ------------------------- P & F Radio Reg.
Ramsay's Appeal Cases (Que.) --------------------- R.A.C.
Randolph -- Rand.
Rawle -- Rawle
Real Estate Law Journal -------------------------- Real Est.L.J.
Real Estate Law Report --------------------------- Real Est.L.Rep.
Real Estate Review ------------------------------- Real Est.Rev.
Real Property, Probate and Trust Journal --------- Real Prop.Prob. &
                                                                 Trust J.
Recent Law -- Rec.L.
Recent Laws in Canada ---------------------------- Rec.Laws
Record of the Association of the Bar of the City of
   New York --- Record of N.Y.C.B.A.
Recueil des Cours --------------------------------- Recueil des Cours
Referees' Journal (Journal of National Association
   of Referees in Bankruptcy) --------------------- Ref.J.
Religion and the Public Order --------------------- Rel. & Pub.Order
Reports of Cases before the Court of Justice of
   the European Communities --------------------- E.C.R.
Reports of Family Law ---------------------------- Rep.Fam.L.
Reports of International Arbitral Awards ---------- Int'l Arb.Awards
Reports of Patent Cases -------------------------- R.P.C.
Reports of Patent, Design and Trade Mark Cases --- Pat.Cas.
Reports of Restrictive Practices Cases ------------ Restric.Prac.
Reports of Tax Cases ----------------------------- Tax Cas.
Res Ipsa Loquitur -------------------------------- Res Ipsa
Res Judicatae ------------------------------------ Res Judicatae
Revenue, Judicial, and Police Journal ------------ Rev., Jud., & Police
                                                                 J.
Review of Contemporary Law --------------------- Rev.Contemp.L.
Review of Ghana Law ----------------------------- Rev.Ghana L.
Review of Law and Social Change ----------------- Rev.L. & Soc.Change
Review of Polish Law ----------------------------- Rev.Pol.L.
Review of Securities Regulation, The ------------- Rev.Sec.Reg.
Review of Selected Code Legislation -------------- Rev.Sel.Code Leg.
Review of Socialist Law -------------------------- Rev.Soc.L.
Review of the International Commission of Jurists -- Rev.Int'l Comm.Jur.
Revised Reports ---------------------------------- Rev.R.
Revised Statutes --------------------------------- Rev.Stat.
Revista de Derecho del Colegio de Abogados de
   Puerto Rico -------------------------------------- Rev.C.Abo.P.R.
Revista de Derecho Puertorriqueño ---------------- Rev.D.P.R.
Revista Juridica de la Universidad de Puerto Rico -- Rev.Jur.U.P.R.
Revue de Droit Universite de Sherbrooke ---------- Rev.D.U.S.
Revue de Notariat -------------------------------- Rev.Not.
Revue du Barreau -------------------------------- Rev.Bar.

Revue Generale de Droit ------------------------------- Rev.Gen.D.
Revue Juridique Themis, La --------------------- Themis
Revue Legale --- Rev.Legale
Rhode Island Bar Journal ------------------------ R.I.B.J.
Rhode Island Reports ------------------------------ R.I.
Rhodesia and Nyasaland Law Reports ------------- R. & N.L.R.
Rhodesian Law Journal ---------------------------- Rhodesian L.J.
Rights --- Rights
Robinson -- Rob.
Rocky Mountain Law Review --------------------- Rocky Mt.L.Rev.
Rocky Mountain Mineral Law Institute ------------ Rocky Mt.Min.L.Inst.
Rocky Mountain Mineral Law Newsletter ---------- Rocky Mt.Min.L.
                                                                            Newsl.
Rocky Mountain Mineral Law Review ------------- Rocky Mt.Mineral L.
                                                                            Rev.
Russell's Election Cases (Nova Scotia) ------------ Rus.
Russell's Equity Decisions (Nova Scotia) ---------- R.E.D.
Rutgers Journal of Computers and the Law -------- Rutgers J.Computers
                                                                            & Law
Rutgers Law Review -------------------------------- Rutgers L.Rev.
Rutgers-Camden Law Journal --------------------- Rutgers-Camden L.J.
SALT News --- SALT News
St. John's Law Review ----------------------------- St. John's L.Rev.
St. Louis Law Review ------------------------------ St. Louis L.Rev.
Saint Louis University Law Journal --------------- St. Louis U.L.J.
St. Mary's Law Journal --------------------------- St. Mary's L.J.
Samoan Pacific Law Journal --------------------- Samoan P.L.J.
San Diego Law Review ----------------------------- San Diego L.Rev.
San Francisco Law Journal ---------------------- S.F.L.J.
Santa Clara Law Review -------------------------- Santa Clara L.Rev.
Santa Clara Lawyer -------------------------------- Santa Clara Law.
Saskatchewan Bar Review ------------------------- Sask.B.Rev.
Saskatchewan Law Reports ----------------------- Sask.
Saskatchewan Law Review ------------------------ Sask.L.Rev.
Scandinavian Studies in Criminology ------------- Sc.St.Crim.
Scandinavian Studies in Law --------------------- Sc.St.L.
Scottish Court of Session Cases ------------------- Sess.Cas.
Scottish Law Journal and Sheriff Court Record ---- Scot.L.J.
Scottish Law Magazine and Sheriff Court Re-
    porter -- Scot.L.Mag.
Scottish Law Review and Sheriff Court Reports ---- Scot.L.Rev.
Scots Law Times Reports -------------------------- Scots.L.T.R.
Scrivener --- Scrivener
Search and Seizure Bulletin ---------------------- Search & Seizure
Securities and Exchange Commission Decisions and
    Reports -- S.E.C.
Securities Law Review ----------------------------- Sec.L.Rev.
Securities Regulation & Law Report --------------- BNA Sec.Reg.
Securities Regulation and Transfer Report -------- Sec.Reg. & Trans.

Selden's Notes --- Seld.
Selected Judgments of the West African Court
   of Appeal --- W.A.C.A.
Selective Service Law Reporter -------------------- S.S.L.R.
Seoul Law Journal ----------------------------------- Seoul L.J.
Sergeant and Rawle ---------------------------------- S. & R.
Session Laws --- Sess.Laws
Seton Hall Law Review ----------------------------- Seton Hall L.Rev.
Seton Hall Legislative Journal -------------------- Seton Hall Leg.J.
Sex Problems Court Digest, The -------------------- Sex.Prob.Ct.Dig.
Sexual Law Reporter --------------------------------- Sex.L.Rep.
Shingle --- Shingle
Singapore Law Review ------------------------------- Singapore L.Rev.
Smedes and Marshall -------------------------------- S. & M.
Sneed --- Sneed
Social Action and the Law ------------------------- Soc.Action & L.
Social and Labour Bulletin ------------------------ Soc. & Lab.Bull.
Social Security Bulletin ---------------------------- Soc.Sec.Bull.
Social Security Taxes (P–H) ----------------------- P–H Soc.Sec.Taxes
Solicitor --- Sol.
Solicitor Quarterly --------------------------------- Sol.Q.
Solicitors' Journal --------------------------------- Sol.J.
Somerset Legal Journal ----------------------------- Som.L.J.
South African Law Journal ------------------------- S.Afr.L.J.
South African Law Reports ------------------------- S.Afr.L.R.
South African Law Reports Appellate ------------- S.Afr.L.R.App.
South African Law Review -------------------------- S.Afr.L.Rev.
South African Law Times ---------------------------- S.Afr.L.T.
South African Tax Cases ---------------------------- S.Afr.Tax Cas.
South Australia State Reports --------------------- S.Austl.
South Australian Law Reports --------------------- S.Austl.L.R.
South Carolina Law Quarterly --------------------- S.C.L.Q.
South Carolina Law Review ------------------------- S.C.L.Rev.
South Carolina Reports ----------------------------- S.C.
South Dakota Law Review ---------------------------- S.D.L.Rev.
South Dakota Reports -------------------------------- S.D.
South Dakota State Bar Journal ------------------- S.D.St.B.J.
South Eastern Reporter ----------------------------- S.E.
South Eastern Reporter, Second Series ----------- S.E.2d
South Pacific Law Review --------------------------- S.Pac.L.Rev.
South Texas Law Journal ---------------------------- S.Tex.L.J.
South Western Reporter ----------------------------- S.W.
South Western Reporter, Second Series ----------- S.W.2d
Southern California Law Review ------------------- S.Cal.L.Rev.
Southern Law Journal (Nashville) ----------------- So.L.J.
Southern Law Review (Nashville) ------------------ So.L.Rev.
Southern Law Review (St. Louis) ------------------ So.L.Rev.
Southern Reporter ----------------------------------- So.
Southern Reporter, Second Series ----------------- So.2d

Southern University Law Review ------------------ So.U.L.Rev.
Southwestern Law Journal ---------------------- Sw.L.J.
Southwestern University Law Review ------------ Sw.U.L.Rev.
Soviet Law and Government -------------------- Soviet L. & Gov't
Soviet Statutes and Decisions -------------------- Soviet Stat. & Dec.
Soviet Year-Book of International Law ------------ Soviet Y.B. Int'l L.
Special Lectures of the Law Society of Upper Can-
    ada --- Lect.L.S.U.C.
Standard Federal Tax Reporter (CCH) ----------- CCH Stand.Fed.Tax
    Rep.
Stanford Journal of International Studies --------- Stan.J.Int'l Stud.
Stanford Law Review ---------------------------- Stan.L.Rev.
State and Local Taxes (P–H) ----- ------------------ P–H State & Local
    Taxes
State Government ------------------------------- State Gov't
State Tax Cases Reporter (CCH) ------------------ CCH State Tax Cas.
    Rep.
State Tax Review (CCH) ------------------------- CCH State Tax Rev.
Statutes at Large ------------------------------- Stat.
Statutory Rules & Orders and Statutory Instru-
    ments Revised ------------------------------------ S.R. & O. and S.I.
    Rev.
Stewart's Vice-Admiralty Reports (N.S.) ---------- Stewart
Stockton's Vice-Admiralty Reports (N.B.) --------- Stockton
Storey --- Storey
Straits Law Journal and Reporter ----------------- Straits L.J. & Rep.
Student Lawyer --------------------------------- Student Law.
Student Lawyer Journal ------------------------- Student Law.J.
Studia Canonica -------------------------------- Studia Canonica
Studies in Law and Economic Development --------- Stud.L. & Econ.Dev.
Studies on International Fiscal Law -------------- Stud.Int'l Fiscal L.
Sudan Law Journal and Reports ------------------ S.L.J.R.
Suffolk University Law Review ------------------- Suffolk U.L.Rev.
Supreme Court Historical Society Yearbook -------- Sup.Ct.Hist.Soc'y
    Y.B.
Supreme Court Reporter ------------------------- S.Ct.
Supreme Court Reports (Canada) 1876–1922 ------- S.C.R.
Supreme Court Reports (Canada) 1923–present ----- [ ] S.C.R.
Supreme Court Review -------------------------- S.Ct.Rev.
Sydney Law Review ----------------------------- Sydney L.Rev.
Symposium l'Association de jeune Barreau de Mon-
    treal -- Symposium Jun.B.
Syracuse Journal of International Law and Com-
    merce -- Syracuse J.Int'l L. &
    Com.
Syracuse Law Review --------------------------- Syracuse L.Rev.
T. B. Monroe ---------------------------------- T.B.Mon.
Tasmania University Law Review ----------------- Tasm.U.L.Rev.
Tasmanian Law Reports ------------------------- Tasm.L.R.

Tasmanian State Reports --- Tasm.
Tax Administrators News --- Tax Adm'rs News
Tax Adviser, The --- Tax Adviser
Tax Appeal Board Cases --- Tax A.B.C.
Tax Cases --- Tax Cas.
Tax Counselor's Quarterly --- Tax Counselor's Q.
Tax Court Memorandum Decisions (CCH) --- CCH Tax Ct.Mem.
Tax Court Memorandum Decisions (P–H) --- P–H Tax Ct.Mem.
Tax Court of the United States Reports --- T.C.
Tax Court Reporter (CCH) --- CCH Tax Ct.Rep.
Tax Court Reports and Memorandum Decisions
   (P–H) --- P–H Tax Ct.Rep. &
   Mem.Dec.

Tax Law Review --- Tax L.Rev.
Tax Lawyer, The --- Tax Law.
Tax Magazine --- Tax Mag.
Tax Management Memorandum (BNA) --- TMM
Tax Practitioners Forum --- Tax Pract.Forum
Taxation for Lawyers --- Tax. for Law.
Taxation Reports --- Tax.R.
Taxes, the Tax Magazine --- Taxes
Tel-Aviv University Studies in Law --- Tel-Aviv U.Stud.L.
Temple Law Quarterly --- Temp.L.Q.
Tennessee Appeals Reports --- Tenn.App.
Tennessee Appellate Bulletin --- Tenn.App.Bull.

Tennessee Bar Journal --- Tenn.B.J.
Tennessee Chancery Reports --- Tenn.Ch.
Tennessee Criminal Appeals Reports --- Tenn.Crim.App.
Tennessee Law Review --- Tenn.L.Rev.
Tennessee Reports --- Tenn.
Territories Law Reports (N.W.T.) --- Terr.L.R.
Terry --- Terry
Texas Bar Journal --- Tex.B.J.
Texas Civil Appeals Reports --- Tex.Civ.App.
Texas Court of Appeals Reports --- Tex.Ct.App.R.
Texas Criminal Reports --- Tex.Crim.
Texas International Law Forum --- Tex.Int'l L.F.
Texas International Law Journal --- Tex.Int'l L.J.
Texas Jurisprudence --- Tex.Jur.
Texas Jurisprudence, Second Series --- Tex.Jur.2d
Texas Law Review --- Texas L.Rev.
Texas Lawman --- Tex.Law.
Texas Reports --- Tex.
Texas Southern University Law Review --- Tex.So.U.L.Rev.
Texas Supreme Court Reporter --- Tex.S.Ct.
Texas Tech Law Review --- Tex.Tech L.Rev.
Timber Tax Journal --- Timber Tax J.
Times Law Reports --- T.L.R.
Title News --- Title News

Trade Cases (CCH) --- Trade Cas.
Trade Regulation Reporter (CCH) ----------------- Trade Reg.Rep.
Trade-Mark Bulletin ------------------------------- Trademark Bull.
Trade-Mark Bulletin, New Series ----------------- Trademark Bull
         (n.s.)

Trade-Mark Reporter ------------------------------ Trademark Rptr.
Transportation Law Journal ----------------------- Transp.L.J.
Transvaal and Witswatersrand Reports ------------ Trans. & Wit.
Trauma --- Trauma
Treasury Decisions -------------------------------- T.D.
Treaties and Other International Act Series, United
    States --- T.I.A.S.
Treaties and Other International Agreements of
    the United States of America 1776–1949 ---------- T.I.Agree.
Treaties in Force --------------------------------- T.I.F.
Treaty Series, United States --------------------- T.S.
Trial --- Trial
Trial Lawyers Forum ------------------------------ Trial Law.Forum
Trial Lawyers' Guide ------------------------------ Trial Law.Guide
Trial Lawyers' Quarterly --------------------------- Trial Law.Q.
Trueman's Equity Cases (New Brunswick) --------- Trueman Eq.
Trust Bulletin ------------------------------------ Trust Bull.
Trust Territory Reports --------------------------- Trust Terr.
Trusts and Estates -------------------------------- Trusts & Estates

Tucker and Clephane ------------------------------ Tuck. & Cl.
Tulane Law Review -------------------------------- Tul.L.Rev.
Tulane Tax Institute ------------------------------ Tul.Tax Inst.
Tulsa Law Journal -------------------------------- Tulsa L.J.
U.C.L.A. Intramural Law Review ----------------- U.C.L.A.Intra.L.Rev.
U.C.L.A. Law Review ------------------------------ U.C.L.A.L.Rev.
U.C.L.A.-Alaska Law Review ---------------------- U.C.L.A.-Alaska L.
         Rev.

UMKC Law Review -------------------------------- UMKC L.Rev.
Uganda Law Focus ------------------------------- Uganda L.Foc.
Unauthorized Practice News ---------------------- Un.Prac.News
Unemployment Insurance Reporter (CCH) --------- Unempl.Ins.Rep.
Unification of Law Yearbook ---------------------- Unific.L.Y.B.
Uniform Commercial Code Law Journal ----------- U.C.C.L.J.
Uniform Commercial Code Law Letter ------------ U.C.C.Law Letter
Uniform Commercial Code Reporting Service ------ U.C.C.Rep.Serv.
Uniform Law Conference of Canada --------------- Unif.L.Conf.Can.
Uniform Law Review ------------------------------- Uniform L.Rev.
United Nations Commission on International
    Trade Law Yearbook ----------------------------- U.N.Comm.Int'l
         Trade L.Y.B.
United Nations Documents ------------------------ U.N.Doc.
United Nations Economic and Social Council
    Records --------------------------------------- U.N.ECOSOC
United Nations General Assembly Official Records-- U.N.GAOR

United Nations Juridical Yearbook .... U.N.Jur.Y.B.
United Nations Law Reports .... U.N.
United Nations Multilateral Treaties .... U.N.M.T.
United Nations Reports of International Arbitral
  Awards .... U.N.R.I.A.A.
United Nations Resolutions, Series I .... U.N.Res., Ser.I.
United Nations Security Council Official Records .. U.N.SCOR
United Nations Treaty Series .... U.N.T.S.
United States Air Force JAG Law Review .... JAG L.Rev.
United States and Canadian Aviation Reports ...... U.S. & Can.Av.
United States Attorneys General's Opinions .... Op.Att'y Gen.
United States Attorneys General's Reports .... Att'y Gen.Rep.
United States Aviation Reports .... U.S.Av.
United States Civil Aeronautics Board Reports .... C.A.B.
United States Code .... U.S.C.
United States Code Annotated .... U.S.C.A.
United States Code Congressional and Administra-
  tive News .... U.S.Code Cong. &
                                                  Adm.News
United States Code Service .... U.S.C.S.
United States Code, Supplement .... U.S.C. (Supp.)
United States Comptroller General Decisions .... Comp.Gen.
United States Comptroller of Treasury Decisions ... Comp.Dec.
United States Court of Customs Appeals Reports ... Ct.Cust.App.
United States Court of Military Appeals .... U.S.C.M.A.
United States Department of State Bulletin .... Dep't State Bull.
United States Federal Communications Commission
  Reports .... F.C.C.
United States Federal Power Commission Reports .. F.P.C.
United States Federal Trade Commission Decisions . F.T.C.
United States Interior Department Decisions ...... Interior Dec.
United States Internal Revenue Bulletin .... Int.Rev.Bull.
United States Internal Revenue Code of 1954 .... Int.Rev.Code of 1954
United States Internal Revenue Cumulative Bulletin. Cum.Bull.
United States Interstate Commerce Commission,
  Motor Carrier Cases .... M.C.C.
United States Interstate Commerce Commission
  Reports .... I.C.C.
United States Interstate Commerce Commission
  Valuation Reports .... Val.R. (I.C.C.)
United States Law Review .... U.S.L.Rev.
United States Law Week (B.N.A.) .... U.S.L.W.
United States Monthly Law Magazine .... U.S.M.L.Mag.
United States National Labor Relations Board
  Decisions .... N.L.R.B.
United States Office of Contract Settlement De-
  cisions .... O.C.S.
United States Patent Quarterly .... U.S.P.Q.
United States Securities and Exchange Commission.. S.E.C.

United States Supreme Court Reporter (West) _____ S.Ct.
United States Supreme Court Reports _____ U.S.
United States Supreme Court Reports (Lawyers'
    Edition) _____ L.Ed.
United States Supreme Court Reports (Lawyers'
    Edition Second Series) _____ L.Ed.2d
United States Tax Cases (CCH) _____ U.S.Tax Cas.
United States Tax Court Reports _____ T.C.
United States Treasury Decisions _____ T.D.
United States Treaties and Other International
    Agreements _____ U.S.T.
United States Treaty Developments _____ U.S.T.D.
United States Treaty Series _____ T.S.
University of Baltimore Law Review _____ U.Balt.L.Rev.

University of British Columbia Law Review _____ U.B.C.L.Rev.
University of British Columbia Legal Notes _____ U.B.C.Notes
University of California at Davis Law Review _____ U.C.D.L.Rev.
University of Chicago Law Review _____ U.Chi.L.Rev.
University of Chicago Law School Record _____ U.Chi.L.Rec.
University of Cincinnati Law Review _____ U.Cin.L.Rev.
University of Colorado Law Review _____ U.Colo.L.Rev.
University of Detroit Law Journal _____ U.Det.L.J.
University of Florida Law Review _____ U.Fla.L.Rev.
University of Ghana Law Journal _____ U.Ghana L.J.
University of IFE Law Reports (Nigeria) _____ U.I.L.R.
University of Illinois Law Forum _____ U.Ill.L.F.
University of Kansas City Law Review _____ U.Kan.City L.Rev.
University of Kansas Law Review _____ Kan.L.Rev.

University of Miami Law Review _____ U.Miami L.Rev.
University of Michigan Journal of Law Reform _____ U.Mich.J.Law
                                                            Reform
University of Missouri at Kansas City Law Review __ U.Mo.K.C.L.Rev.
University of Missouri Bulletin Law Series _____ U.Mo.Bull.L.Ser.
University of New Brunswick Law Journal _____ U.N.B.L.J.
University of Newark Law Review _____ U.Newark L.Rev.
University of Osaka Prefecture Bulletin _____ Osaka Pref.Bull.
University of Pennsylvania Law Review _____ U.Pa.L.Rev.
University of Pittsburgh Law Review _____ U.Pitt.L.Rev.
University of Queensland Law Journal _____ U.Queens.L.J.
University of Richmond Law Review _____ U.Rich.L.Rev.
University of San Fernando Valley Law Review _____ U.San Fernando V.L.
                                                           Rev.
University of San Francisco Law Review _____ U.San Fran.L.Rev.
University of Santo Tomas Law Review _____ Santo Tomas L.Rev.
University of South Carolina Governmental Review__ U.S.C.Govt'l Rev.
University of Southern California Tax Institute ____ [e. g.] U.So.Cal.1955
                                                           Tax Inst.

University of Tasmania Law Review (or Tasmania
    University Law Review) _____ U.Tasm.L.Rev.

University of the East Law Journal	U.East L.J.
University of Toledo Law Review	U.Toledo L.Rev.
University of Toronto Faculty of Law Review	U.Tor.Fac.L.Rev.
University of Toronto Law Journal	U.Toronto L.J.
University of Washington Law Review	U.Wash.L.Rev.
University of West Los Angeles Law Review	U.W.L.A.L.Rev.
University of Western Australia Law Review	U.W.Austl.L.Rev.
University of Windsor Law Review	U.Windsor L.Rev.
Upper Canada Chambers Reports	Ch.R.
Upper Canada Chancery Chambers Reports	Chy.Chrs.
Upper Canada Chancery Reports, by Grant	Gr.
Upper Canada Common Pleas	U.C.C.P.
Upper Canada Error & Appeal Reports, by Grant	E. & A.
Upper Canada King's Bench Reports, by Taylor	Taylor
Upper Canada Law Journal	Up.Can.L.J.
Upper Canada Queen's Bench, Old Series	U.C.Q.B. (O.S.)
Upper Canada, Queen's Bench Reports	U.C.Q.B.
Urban Affairs Reporter (CCH)	Urban Affairs Rep.
Urban Law Annual	Urban Law Ann.
Urban Law Review	Urban L.Rev.
Urban Lawyer, The	Urban Law.
Utah Law Review	Utah L.Rev.
Utah Reports	Utah
Utah Reports, 2d Series	Utah 2d
Utilities Law Reporter (CCH)	Util.L.Rep.
Utility Section Newsletter	Util.Sect.Newsl.
Valparaiso University Law Review	Val.U.L.Rev.
Valuation Reports, Interstate Commerce Commission	Val.R. (ICC)
Vanderbilt Journal of Transnational Law	Vand.J.Transnat'l L.
Vanderbilt Law Review	Vand.L.Rev.
Vermont Reports	Vt.
Victoria University Law Review	Vict.U.L.Rev.
Victoria University of Wellington Law Review	Vict.U.Well.L.Rev.
Victorian Law Reports	Vict.L.R.
Victorian Reports	Vict.
Villanova Law Review	Vill.L.Rev.
Virgin Islands Bar Journal	V.I.B.J.
Virgin Islands Reports	V.I.
Virginia Bar News	Va.Bar News
Virginia Cases (criminal)	Va.Cas.
Virginia Journal of International Law	Va.J.Int'l L.
Virginia Law Register, New Series	Va.L.Reg. (N.S.)
Virginia Law Review	Va.L.Rev.
Virginia Reports	Va.
W.C.J. Meredith Memorial Lectures	Meredith Lect.
W. W. Harrington	W.W.Harr.
Wage and Hour Cases (BNA)	Wage & Hour Cas.

Wage-Price Law and Economics Review ----------- Wage-Price L. & Econ.Rev.

Wake Forest Intramural Law Review ------------ Wake For.Intra.L. Rev.

Wake Forest Law Review ----------------------- Wake For.L.Rev.

Wallace ------------------------------------- Wall.

Washburn Law Journal -------------------------- Washburn L.J.

Washington and Lee Law Review ---------------- Wash. & Lee L.Rev.

Washington Appellate Reports -------------------- Wash.App.

Washington Law Review ------------------------ Wash.L.Rev.

Washington Reports -------------------------- Wash.

Washington Reports, Second Series -------------- Wash.2d

Washington Territory Reports ------------------ Wash.Terr.

Washington University Law Quarterly ----------- Wash.U.L.Q.

Watts -------------------------------------- Watts

Watts and Sargeant -------------------------- W. & S.

Wayne Law Review --------------------------- Wayne L.Rev.

Weekly Law Bulletin (Ohio) -------------------- W.L.Bull.

Weekly Law Reports -------------------------- W.L.R.

Weekly Notes -------------------------------- W.N.

Weekly Reports ------------------------------ W.R.

Welfare Law Bulletin ------------------------- Welfare L.Bull.

Welfare Law News ---------------------------- Welfare L.News

Wendell ----------------------------------- Wend.

West African Court of Appeal Reports ------------ W.Afr.App.

West Coast Reporter -------------------------- W.Coast Rptr.

West Virginia Criminal Justice Review ----------- W.Va.Crim.Just.Rev.

West Virginia Law Review --------------------- W.Va.L.Rev.

West Virginia Reports ------------------------- W.Va.

Western Australia Industrial Gazette ------------- W.Austl.Ind.Gaz.

Western Australia Justice of the Peace ----------- W.Austl.J.P.

Western Australia Law Reports ------------------ W.Austl.L.R.

Western Australian Reports -------------------- West.Austl.

Western Law Reporter ------------------------- West.L.R.

Western Law Review --------------------------- West.L.Rev.

Western Law Times and Reports ----------------- W.L.T.

Western Legal Observer ------------------------ West.Legal Obser.

Western Ontario Law Review -------------------- W.Ont.L.Rev.

Western Reserve Law Review -------------------- W.Res.L.Rev.

Western School Law Review --------------------- West. School L.Rev.

Western State University Law Review ----------- West.St.U.L.Rev.

Western Weekly Reports ----------------------- W.W.R.

Western Weekly Reports, New Series 1951–1955 ---- W.W.R. (N.S.)

Westmoreland County Law Journal --------------- Wes.C.L.J.

West's Federal Practice Digest, Second Series ------ W.F.P.D.2d

Wharton ----------------------------------- Whart.

Wheaton ----------------------------------- Wheat.

Willamette Law Journal ------------------------------ Willamette L.J.
William & Mary Law Review ------------------------ Wm. & Mary L.Rev.
William and Mary Review of Virginia Law -------- Wm. & Mary Rev.
                              Va.L.
Wisconsin Bar Bulletin ------------------------------ Wis.B.Bull.
Wisconsin Board of Tax Appeals Reports --------- Wis.B.T.A.
Wisconsin Law Review ------------------------------ Wis.L.Rev.
Wisconsin Reports ------------------------------------ Wis.
Wisconsin Reports, Second Series ----------------- Wis.2d
Wisconsin Student Bar Journal -------------------- Wisc.Stud.B.J.
Wisconsin Tax Appeals Commission Reports -------- Wis.Tax App.C.
Woman Offender Report ---------------------------- Woman Offend.Rep.
Women Law Reporter -------------------------------- W.L.R.
Women Lawyer's Journal --------------------------- Women Law.J.
Women's Rights Law Reporter -------------------- Women's Rights L.
                              Rptr.
Workmen's Compensation Law Review ------------- Workmen's Comp.L.
                              Rev.
World Jurist -- World Jurist
World Polity --- World Pol.
Wyoming Law Journal ------------------------------- Wyo.L.J.
Wyoming Reports -------------------------------------- Wyo.
Yale Law Journal ------------------------------------- Yale L.J.
Yale Review of Law and Social Action ------------- Yale Rev.Law & Soc.
                              Act'n
Yale Studies in World Public Order --------------- Yale Stud.World
                              Pub.Order
Yearbook of Air and Space Law -------------------- Y.B.A.S.L.
Yearbook of International Organizations ----------- Y.B. Int'l Org.
Yearbook of the Association of Attenders and
   Alumni of the Hague Academy of Internation-
   al Law -- Y.B.A.A.A.
Yearbook of the European Convention on Human
   Rights --- Y.B.Eur.Conv. on
                              Human Rights
Yearbook of the International Court of Justice ----- I.C.J.Y.B.
Yearbook of the International Law Commission ---- Y.B.Int'l L.Comm'n
Yearbook of the League of Nations ---------------- Y.B.League
Yearbook of the United Nations ------------------- Y.B.U.N.
Yearbook of World Polity -------------------------- Y.B.World Pol.
Yearbook on Human Rights ------------------------ Y.B.Human Rights
Yeates -- Yeates
Young's Admiralty Decisions (Nova Scotia) -------- Y.A.D.
Yugoslav Law -- Yugo.L.
Zambia Law Journal ---------------------------------- Zambia L.J.

Appendix C

TABLE OF LEGAL ABBREVIATIONS

A

A.	Atlantic Reporter
A.2d	Atlantic Reporter, Second Series
A. & E.	Adolphus & Ellis Queen's Bench (Eng.)
A. & E.Ann. Cas.	American & English Annotated Cases
A. & E.Anno.	Same
A. & E.Cas.	Same
A. & E.Corp. Cas.	American & English Corporation Cases
A. & E.Corp. Cas.(N.S.)	Same, New Series
A. & E.Enc. L. & Pr.	American & English Encyclopedia of Law and Practice
A. & E.Ency.	American & English Encyclopedia of Law
A. & E.Ency. Law	Same
A. & E.P. & P.	American & English Pleading and Practice
A. & E.R.Cas.	American & English Railroad Cases
A. & E.R.Cas. (N.S.)	Same, New Series
A. & E.R.R. Cas.	American & English Railroad Cases
A. & E.R.R. Cas. (N.S.)	Same, New Series
A.B.	Anonymous Reports at end of Benloe, or Bendloe (1661) (Eng.)
A.B.A.J.	American Bar Association Journal
A.B.A.Jour.	Same
A.B.A.Rep.	American Bar Association Reports
A.B.A.Sect. Ins.N. & C.L. Proc.	American Bar Association Section of Insurance, Negligence and Compensation Law Proceedings
A.B.C.Newsl.	International Association of Accident Boards and Commissions Newsletter
A.B.F.Res.J.	American Bar Foundation Research Journal
A.B.F. Research Reptr.	American Bar Foundation Research Reporter

A.C.	Law Reports Appeal Cases (Eng.)
	Law Reports Appeal Cases (Eng.) Third Series
	Appeal Cases (Can.)
	Advance California Reports
A.C.A.	Advance California Appellate Reports
A.C.L.U.Leg. Action Bull.	American Civil Liberties Union Legislative Action Bulletin
A.C.R.	American Criminal Reports
A.D.	American Decisions
A/E Legal Newsl.	A/E Legal Newsletter
AELE Legal Liab. Rep.	AELE Legal Liability Reporter
AFTR	American Federal Tax Reports
A.I.D.	Accident/Injury/Damages
A.I.L.C.	American International Law Cases 1783–1968
A.K.Marsh.	A.K. Marshall (Ky.)
A.L.I.	American Law Institute
ALI–ABA CLE Rev.	ALI–ABA CLE Review
A.L.R.	American Law Reports
A.L.R.2d	Same, Second Series
A.L.R.3d	Same, Third Series
A.L.R.Fed.	American Law Reports Federal
A.L.Rec.	American Law Record
A.L.Reg. (N.S.)	American Law Register, New Series
A.L.Reg. (O.S.)	American Law Register, Old Series
A.M. & O.	Armstrong, Macartney & Ogle Nisi Prius (Ir.)
A.M.C.	American Maritime Cases
A.O.C.Newsl.	Administrative Office of the Courts Newsletter
APLA Q.J.	APLA Quarterly Journal
A.R.C.	American Ruling Cases
A.R.M.	Appeals & Review Memorandum Committee (I.R.Bull.)
A.R.R.	Appeals & Review Recommendation (I.R.Bull.)
A.S.A.Newsl.	Association for the Study of Abortion Newsletter

584

A.S.R.	American State Reports		Add.Rep.	Same
A.T.	Alcohol Tax Unit (I.R.Bull.)		Adelaide L.Rev.	Adelaide Law Review
A.T.L.A.J.	American Trial Lawyers Association Journal		Adm. & Ecc.	Admiralty & Ecclesiastical (Eng.)
ATLA L.J.	Journal of the Association of Trial Lawyers of America		Advocate	The Advocate
			Afr.L.Dig.	African Law Digest
			Afr.L.R.	African Law Reports
Ab.N.	Abstracts, Treasury Decisions, New Series		Afr.L.R., Mal.Ser.	African Law Reports, Malawi Series
			Afr.L.R., Sierre L.Ser.	African Law Reports, Sierre Leone Series
Abb.	Abbott (U.S.)		Afr.L.Stud.	African Law Studies
Abb.Adm.	Abbott's Admiralty (U.S.)		Agri.Dec.	Agriculture Decisions
Abb.App.Dec.	Abbott's Appeal Decisions (N.Y.)		Aik.	Aikens (Vt.)
Abb.Dec.	Abbott's Decisions (N.Y.)		Air Force L.Rev.	Air Force Law Review
Abb.Dict.	Abbott's Dictionary		Air L.Rev.	Air Law Review
Abb.N.Cas.	Abbott's New Cases (N.Y.)		Air Law	Air Law
			Akron L.Rev.	Akron Law Review
Abb.Prac.	Abbott's Practice (N.Y.)		Ala.	Alabama
Abb.Prac.N.S.	Same, New Series		Ala.App.	Alabama Court of Appeals
Abb.R.P.S.	Abbott's Real Property Statutes (Wn.)		Ala.L.J.	Alabama Law Journal
			Ala.L.Rev.	Alabama Law Review
A'Beck.Res. Judgm.	A'Beckett's Reserved Judgments (Victoria)		Ala.Law.	The Alabama Lawyer
			Ala.Sel.Cas.	Alabama Select Cases
Abogada Int'l Abs.	Abogada Internacional Abstracts, Treasury Decisions		Ala.St.B. Found.Bull.	Alabama State Bar Foundation Bulletin
			Alaska	Alaska Reports
	Ohio Law Abstract		Alaska B.Brief	Alaska Bar Brief
Abstr.Crim & Pen.	Abstracts on Criminology and Penology		Alaska B.J.	Alaska Bar Journal
			Alaska L.J.	Alaska Law Journal
Acad.Pol. Sci.Proc.	Academy of Political Science Proceedings		Alb.L.J.	Albany Law Journal
Act.	Acton Prize Cases Privy Council (Eng.)		Alb.L.Q.	Alberta Law Quarterly
			Alb.L.R.	Alberta Law Reports
			Alb.L.Rev.	Albany Law Review
Acta Cancelariae	English Chancery Reports		Albany L.Rev.	Same
			Albuquerque B.J.	Albuquerque Bar Journal
Acta Crim.	Acta Criminologica			
Acta Jur.	Acta Juridica		Alc. & N.	Alcock & Napier King's Bench (Ir.)
Acton	Acton Prize Cases Privy Council (Eng.)		Alc.Reg.Cas.	Alcock Registry Cases (Ir.)
Ad. & El.	Adolphus & Ellis Queen's Bench (Eng.)		Ald.	Alden's Condensed Reports (Pa.)
Ad. & El. (N.S.)	Same, New Series		Aleyn	Aleyn, King's Bench (Eng.)
Ad.Ct.Dig.	Administrative Court Digest		Alison Pr.	Alison Practice (Sc.)
Ad.L.	Administrative Law		All E.R.	All England Law Reports
Ad.L.2d	Same, Second Series			
Ad.L.Bull.	Administrative Law Bulletin		All India Crim.Dec.	All India Criminal Decisions
Ad.L.News	Administrative Law News		All India Rptr.	All India Reporter
Ad.L.Newsl.	Administrative Law Newsletter		All N.L.R.	All Nigeria Law Reports
Ad.L.Rev.	Administrative Law Review		All Pak. Leg.Dec.	All Pakistan Legal Decisions
Adams	Adams (Me.) Adams (N.H.)		Allen	Allen (Mass.)
Add.	Addison (Pa.)		Allen N.B.	Allen, New Brunswick
Add.Eccl.Rep.	Addams' Ecclesiastical Reports (Eng.)		Allinson	Allinson, Pa.Superior District Courts
Add.Penn.	Addison (Pa.)			

Alta.	Alberta Law Reports
Alta.L.	Alberta Law
Alta.L.Q.	Alberta Law Quarterly
Alta.L.Rev.	Alberta Law Review
Alternatives	Alternatives
Am. & E.Corp. Cas.	American & English Corporation Cases
Am. & E.Corp. Cas. (N.S.)	Same, New Series
Am. & E.R. Cas.	American & English Railroad Cases
Am. & E.R. Cas. (N.S.)	Same, New Series
Am. & Eng. Ann.Cas.	American & English Annotated Cases
Am. & Eng. Eq.D.	American & English Decisions in Equity
Am. & Eng. Pat.Cas.	American & English Patent Cases
Am.Acad. Matri.Law. J.	American Academy of Matrimonial Lawyers Journal
Am.B.News	American Bar News
Am.B.R. (N.S.)	American Bankruptcy Reports, New Series
Am.Bankr.L.J.	American Bankruptcy Law Journal
Am.Bankr. Reg.	American Bankruptcy Register (U.S.)
Am.Bankr. Rep.	American Bankruptcy Reports
Am.Bankr. Rev.	American Bankruptcy Review
Am.Bus.L.J.	American Business Law Journal
Am.Corp.Cas.	American Corporation Cases
Am.Cr.	American Criminal Reports
Am.Crim.L.Q.	American Criminal Law Quarterly
Am.Crim. L.Rev.	American Criminal Law Review
Am.Dec.	American Decisions
Am.Elect.Cas.	American Electrical Cases
Am.Fed. Tax R.	American Federal Tax Reports
Am.Fed. Tax R.2d	Same, Second Series
Am.For.L. Ass'n Newsl.	American Foreign Law Association Newsletter
Am.Hist.Rev.	American Historical Review
Am.Ind.J.	American Indian Journal
Am.Ind.L. Newsl.	American Indian Law Newsletter
Am.Ind.L.Rev.	American Indian Law Review
Am.Insolv. Rep.	American Insolvency Reports
Am.J.Comp.L.	American Journal of Comparative Law

Am.J.Crim.L.	American Journal of Criminal Law
Am.J.Int.L.	American Journal of International Law
Am.J. Jurisprud.	American Journal of Jurisprudence
Am.J.L. & Med.	American Journal of Law and Medicine
Am.J.Legal Hist.	American Journal of Legal History
Am.J.Police Sci.	American Journal of Police Science
Am.Jur.	American Jurisprudence American Jurist
Am.Jur.2d	American Jurisprudence, Second Series
Am.L.Ins.	American Law Institute
Am.L.J.	American Law Journal (Pa.)
Am.L.J. (N.S.)	Same, New Series
Am.L.Mag.	American Law Magazine
Am.L.Rec.	American Law Record (Ohio)
Am.L.Reg.	American Law Register
Am.L.Reg. (N.S.)	Same, New Series
Am.L.Reg. (O.S.)	Same, Old Series
Am.L.Rev.	American Law Review
Am.L.Sch. Rev.	American Law School Review
Am.L.T. Bankr.	American Law Times Bankruptcy Reports
Am.Lab.Leg. Rev.	American Labor Legislation Review
Am.Law.	American Lawyer
Am.Law Rec.	American Law Record
Am.Law Reg.	American Law Register
Am.Negl.Cas.	American Negligence Cases
Am.Negl.Rep.	American Negligence Reports
Am.Notary	American Notary
Am.Pol.Sci. Rev.	American Political Science Review
Am.Pr.Rep.	American Practice Reports (D.C.)
Am.Prob.	American Probate Reports
Am.Prob. (N.S.)	Same, New Series
Am.R.	American Reports
Am.R. & Corp.	American Railroad Corporation
Am.R.Rep.	American Railway Reports
Am.Railw.Cas.	American Railway Cases (Smith & Bates)
Am.Rep.	American Reports

Am.Ry.Rep.	American Railway Reports
Am.Soc'y Int'l L.Proc.	American Society of International Law Proceedings
Am.St.R.	American State Reports
Am.St.R.D.	American Street Railway Decisions
Am.St.Rep.	American State Reports
Am.Tr.M.Cas.	American Trademark Cases (Cox)
Am.Trial Law.J.	American Trial Lawyers Journal
Am.Trial Law.L.J.	American Trial Lawyers Law Journal
Am.U.Intra.L. Rev.	American University Intramural Law Review
Am.U.L. Rev.	American University Law Review
Amb.	Ambler, Chancery (Eng.)
Ames	Ames (R.I.) Ames (Minn.)
Ames K. & B.	Ames, Knowles & Bradley (R.I.)
Amicus	Amicus (South Bend, Ind.) Amicus (Thousand Oaks, CA)
An.B.	Anonymous Reports at end of Benloe, or Bendloe (1661) (Eng.)
And.	Anderson Common Pleas (Eng.)
Andr.	Andrews King's Bench (Eng.)
Ang.	Angell (R.I.)
Ang. & Dur.	Angell & Durfee (R.I.)
Anglo-Am. L.Rev.	Anglo-American Law Review
Ann.	Annaly's Hardwicke King's Bench (Eng.)
Ann.Cas.	American Annotated Cases
Ann.Dig.	Annual Digest and Reports of International Law Cases
Ann.L.Reg. U.S.	Annual Law Register of the United States
Ann.Leg. Forms Mag.	Annotated Legal Forms Magazine
Ann.Rev. Int'l Aff.	Annual Review of International Affairs
Ann.Survey Afr.L.	Annual Survey of African Law
Ann.Survey Am.L.	Annual Survey of American Law
Ann.Survey Commonw. L.	Annual Survey of Commonwealth Law
Ann.Survey Ind.L.	Annual Survey of Indian Law
Ann.Survey S.Afr.L.	Annual Survey of South African Law
Ann.Tax Cas.	Annotated Tax Cases

Annals	Annals of the American Academy of Political and Social Science
Annaly	Annaly's Hardwicke King's Bench (Eng.)
Anst.	Ansthruther, Exchequer (Eng.)
Anth.N.P.	Anthon's Nisi Prius (N.Y.)
Antitrust Bull.	Antitrust Bulletin
Antitrust L. & Econ. Rev.	Antitrust Law and Economics Review
Antitrust L.J.	Antitrust Law Journal
Antitrust L.Sym.	Antitrust Law Symposium
App.	Appleton (Me.)
App.Cas.	Law Reports Appeal Cases (Eng.)
App.Cas.2d	Same, Second Series
App.D.C.	Appeal Cases (D.C.)
App.Div.	Appellate Division (N.Y.)
App.Div.2d	Same, Second Series
App.N.Z.	Appeal Reports (New Zealand)
App.R.N.Z.	Same, Second Series
App.Rep.Ont.	Ontario Appeal Reports
Arb.J.	Arbitration Journal
Arb.J. (N.S.)	Same, New Series
Arb.J. (O.S.)	Same, Old Series
Arb.L.Dig.	Arbitration Law; A Digest of Court Decisions
Archer	Archer (Fla.)
Archer & H.	Archer & Hogue (Fla.)
Argus L.R.	Argus Law Reports (Aust.)
Ariz.	Arizona
Ariz.App.	Arizona Appeals Reports
Ariz.B.J.	Arizona Bar Journal
Ariz.L.Rev.	Arizona Law Review
Ariz.St.L.J.	Arizona State Law Journal
Ark.	Arkansas
Ark.Just.	Arkley's Justiciary (Sc.)
Ark.L.J.	Arkansas Law Journal
Ark.L.Rev.	Arkansas Law Review
Ark.Law.	The Arkansas Lawyer
Armour	Queen's Bench, Manitoba Temp. Wood, by Armour
Arms.Con. Elec.	Armstrong's Contested Elections (N.Y.)
Army Law.	Army Lawyer
Arn.	Arnold Common Pleas (Eng.)
Arn. & H.	Arnold & Hodges Queen's Bench (Eng.)
Arnold	Arnold Common Pleas (Eng.)
Art & L.	Art and the Law
Ashm.	Ashmead (Pa.)

Asian Comp. L.Rev.	Asian Comparative Law Review	Austl.Bankr. Cas.	Australian Bankruptcy Cases
Aspin.	Aspinall's Maritime Cases (Eng.)	Austl.Bus. L.Rev.	Australian Business Law Review
Ass'n Trial Law.Am. Newsl.	Association of Trial Lawyers of American Newsletter	Austl.Com.J.	Australian Commercial Journal
		Austl.Convey. & Sol.J.	Australian Conveyancer and Solicitors Journal
Ateneo L.J.	Ateneo Law Journal	Austl.Current L.Rev.	Australian Current Law Review
Atk.	Atkyns Chancery (Eng.)		
Atl.	Atlantic Reporter	Austl.J. For.Sci.	Australian Journal of Forensic Sciences
Atomic Energy L.J.	Atomic Energy Law Journal	Austl.Jur.	Australian Jurist
Att'y Gen.	Attorney General	Austl.L.J.	Australian Law Journal
Att'y Gen.Rep.	United States Attorneys General's Reports	Austl.L.J. Rep.	Australian Law Journal Reports
		Austl.L.Times	Australian Law Times
Atty.Gen.	Attorney General	Austl.Law.	Australian Lawyer
Atwater	Atwater (Minn.)	Austl.Tax	Australian Tax Decisions
Auck.U.L.Rev.	Auckland University Law Review	Austl.Y.B. Int'l L.	Australian Yearbook of International Law
		Austr.C.L.R.	Commonwealth Law Reports, Australia
Aust.Jur.	Australian Jurist		
Aust.L.T.	Australian Law Times	Auto.Cas.	Automobile Cases
Austl. & N.Z. J.Crim.	Australian and New Zealand Journal of Criminology	Auto. Cas.2d	Same, Second Series
		Auto.L.Rep.	Automobile Law Reporter (CCH)
Austl.Argus L.R.	Australian Argus Law Reports	Av.Cas.	Aviation Cases
		Av.L.Rep.	Aviation Law Reporter (CCH)

B

B.	Weekly Law Bulletin	B. & Macn.	Brown & Macnamara Railway Cases (Eng.)
B. & A.	Barnewall & Alderson, King's Bench (Eng.)		
B. & Ad.	Barnewall & Adolphus King's Bench (Eng.)	B. & P.	Bosanquet & Puller, Common Pleas (Eng.)
B. & Ald.	Barnewall & Alderson, King's Bench (Eng.)	B. & P.N.R.	Bosanquet & Puller's New Reports (Eng.)
B. & Arn.	Barron & Arnold Election Cases (Eng.)	B. & S.	Best & Smith, Queen's Bench (Eng.)
B. & Aust.	Barron & Austin Election Cases (Eng.)	B.Bull.	Bar Bulletin
B. & B.	Ball & Beatty's Chancery (Ir.)	B.C.	British Columbia
	Broderip & Bingham Common Pleas (Eng.)	B.C.Branch Lec.	Canadian Bar Association, British Columbia Branch Meeting Program Reports
B. & C.	Barnewall & Cresswell's King's Bench (Eng.)	B.C.C.	Bail Court Cases (Eng.)
B. & C.R.	Reports of Bankruptcy & Companies Winding up Cases (Eng.)	B.C.Ind. & Com.L.Rev.	Boston College Industrial and Commercial Law Review
B. & D.	Benloe & Dalison Common Pleas (Eng.)	B.C.L.Notes	British Columbia Law Notes
		B.C.C.	Bail Court Cases (Eng.)
B. & F.	Broderip & Freemantle's Ecclesiastical (Eng.)	B.D. & O.	Blackham, Dundas & Osborne, Nisi Prius (Ir.)
		B.Exam.	Bar Examiner
B. & H.Cr. Cas.	Bennet & Heard's Criminal Cases (Eng.)	B.Exam.J.	Bar Examination Journal
		B.I.C.I.L. Newsl.	British Institute of International and Comparative Law Newsletter
B. & H.Crim. Cas.	Same	B.I.L.C.	British International Law Cases

B.Leader	Bar Leader
B.Mon.	B. Monroe (Ky.)
BNA	Bureau of National Affairs
BNA Sec.Reg.	Securities Regulation & Law Report
B.R. (Army)	Board of Review (Army)
B.R.C.	British Ruling Cases
B.R.–J.C. (Army)	Board of Review and Judicial Council of the Army
B.T.A.	Board of Tax Appeals Reports
B.U.L.Rev.	Boston University Law Review
B.W.C.C.	Butterworth's Workmen's Compensation Cases (Eng.)
Bac.Abr.	Bacon's Abridgment (Eng.)
Bag. & Har.	Bagley & Harman (Cal.)
Bagl.	Bagley (Cal.)
Bagl. & H.	Bagley & Harman (Cal.)
Bail Ct.Cas.	Bail Court Cases (Lowndes & Maxwell) (Eng.)
Bail.Eq.	Bailey's Equity (S.C.)
Baild.	Baildon's Select Cases in Chancery (Eng.)
Bailey	Bailey's Law (S.C.)
Bal.Ann. Codes	Ballinger's Annotated Codes & Statutes (Wash.)
Bal.Pay't Rep.	Balance of Payments Reports (CCH)
Baldw.	Baldwin (U.S.)
Balf.Pr.	Balfour's Practice (Sc.)
Ball & B.	Ball & Beatty Chancery (Ir.)
Balt.L.T.	Baltimore Law Transcript
Ban. & A.	Banning & Arden Patent Cases (U.S.)
Bank. & Ins.R.	Bankruptcy & Insolvency Reports (Eng.)
Bank.Cas.	Banking Cases
Bank.Ct.Rep.	Bankrupt Court Reports
Bank.L.J.	Banking Law Journal
Banking L.J.	Same
Bankr.B. Bull.	Bankruptcy Bar Bulletin
Bankr.L.Rep.	Bankruptcy Law Reporter (CCH)
Bankr.Reg.	National Bankruptcy Register (N.Y.)
Banks	Banks (Kan.)
Bann.	Bannister's Common Pleas (Eng.)
Bann. & A.	Banning & Arden, Patent Cases (U.S.)

Bann. & Ard.	Same
Bar. & Arn.	Barron & Arnold, Election Cases (Eng.)
Bar. & Aust.	Barron & Austin, Election Cases (Eng.)
Barb.	Barber (Ark.) Barbour (N.Y.)
Barb.Ch.	Barbour's Chancery (N.Y.)
Barber	Barber (N.Y.)
Barn.	Barnardiston, King's Bench (Eng.)
Barn. & Ad.	Barnewall & Adolphus, King's Bench (Eng.)
Barn. & Ald.	Barnewall & Alderson, King's Bench (Eng.)
Barn. & C.	Barnewall & Cresswell, King's Bench (Eng.)
Barn. & Cress.	Same
Barn.Ch.	Barnardiston Chancery (Eng.)
Barnes	Barnes Practice Cases (Eng.)
Barnes' Notes	Barnes' Notes (Eng.)
Barnet	Barnet's Reports, Common Pleas (Eng.)
Barr	Barr (Pa.)
Barr.Ch.Pr.	Barroll Chancery Practice (Md.)
Barr.MSS.	Barradall Manuscript Reports (Va.)
Barrister	Barrister (Chicago)
Barrister	Barrister (Coral Gables, Fla.)
Barrister	Barrister (Davis, Cal.)
Barrister	Barrister (Toronto)
Bart.Elec. Cas.	Bartlett's Election Cases
Bates Ch.	Bates Chancery (Del.)
Batty	Batty, King's Bench (Ir.)
Baxt.	Baxter (Tenn.)
Bay	Bay (Mo.) Bay (S.C.)
Baylor L. Rev.	Baylor Law Review
Beasl.	Beasley (N.J.)
Beav.	Beavan Rolls Court (Eng.)
Beav. & W. Ry.Cas.	Beavan & Walford's Railway & Canal Cases (Eng.)
Beav.R. & C. Cas.	Beavan, Railway & Canal Cases (Eng.)
Beaw.Lex Mer.	Beawes Lex Mercatoria (Eng.)
Bee	Bee's Admiralty U.S. District Court (S.C.)

Bee Adm.	Bee's (U.S.)	Bick.	Bicknell (Nev.)
Bee C.C.R.	Bee's Crown Cases Reserved (Eng.)	Bick. & H.	Bickness & Hawley (Nev.)
Belg.Rev. Int'l L.	Belgian Review of International Law	Big.Ov.Cas.	Bigelow's Overruled Cases
Bell.	Bellewe, King's Bench (Eng.)	Bill of Rights J.	Bill of Rights Journal
Bell App.Cas.	Bell's Appeal Cases, House of Lords (Sc.)	Bill Rights Rev.	Bill of Rights Review
Bell C.C.	Bell's Crown Cases Reserved (Eng.)	Bing.	Bingham New Cases Common Pleas (Eng.)
Bell Cas.	Bell's Cases (Sc.)	Binn.	Binney (Pa.)
Bell.Cas.t.H. VIII	Bellewe, King's Bench, temp. Henry VIII (Eng.)	Biss.	Bissell (U.S.)
		Bitt.Rep. in Ch.	Bittleson's Reports, Queen's Bench (Eng.)
Bell.Cas.t.R.II	Same, temp. Richard II (Eng.)	Bitt.W. & P.	Bittleson, Wise & Parnell Practice Cases (Eng.)
Bell Comm.	Bell's Commentaries (Eng.)	Bk.	Black (U.S.)
Bell Cr.C.	Bell's Crown Cases Reserved (Eng.)	Bl.	William Blackstone's King's Bench (Eng.)
Bell H.L.	Bell's Appeal Cases, House of Lords (Sc.)	Bl.H.	Henry Blackstone's Common Pleas (Eng.)
Bell P.C.	Bell's Parliament Cases (Sc.)	Bl.W.	William Blackstone's King's Bench (Eng.)
Bell Sc.Cas.	Bell's Scotch Court of Sessions Cases	Bla.	Same
Bell Ses.Cas.	Same	Bla.H.	Henry Blackstone's Common Pleas (Eng.)
Bellewe	Bellewe, King's Bench (Eng.)	Bla.W.	William Blackstone's King's Bench (Eng.)
Ben.	Benedict (U.S. District Court)	Black	Black (Ind.)
Ben. & H.L.C.	Bennett & Heard Leading Criminal Cases (Eng.)		Black (U.S.)
Bendl.	Bendloe's English Common Pleas	Black L.J.	Black Law Journal
Bened.	Benedict (U.S. District Court)	Black.	William Blackstone's King's Bench (Eng.)
Benl.	Benloe's Common Pleas (Eng.)	Black.Cond.	Blackwell's Condensed Reports (Ill.)
	Benloe's King's Bench (Eng.)	Black.Cond. Rep.	Same
Benl. & D.	Benloe & Dalison Common Pleas (Eng.)	Black.D. & O.	Blackham, Dundas & Osborne Nisi Prius (Ir.)
Benl. & Dal.	Benloe & Dalison Common Pleas (Eng.)	Black.H.	Henry Blackstone's Common Pleas (Eng.)
Benl.K.B.	Benloe's King's Bench (Eng.)	Black.Jus.	Blackerby's Justices' Cases (Eng.)
Benl.Old	Benloe Old English Common Pleas	Blackf.	Blackford (Ind.)
Benn.	Bennett (Cal.)	Blackst.R.	William Blackstone's King's Bench (Eng.)
	Bennett (Dakota)		
	Bennett (Mo.)	Blackw.Cond.	Blackwell's Condensed Reports (Ill.)
Bent.	Bentley's Chancery (Ir.)	Blair Co.	Blair County (Pa.).
Berry	Berry (Mo.)	Blake	Blake (Mont.)
Bibb	Bibb (Ky.)	Blake & H.	Blake & Hedge (Mont.)
Bibl.Cott.	Cotton MSS.		

Bland	Bland's Chancery (Md.)
Blatchf.	Blatchford (U.S.)
Blatchf. & H.	Blatchford & Howland (U.S. District Court)
Blatchf.Prize Cas.	Blatchford's Prize Cases (U.S.)
Bleckley	Bleckley (Ga.)
Bli.	Bligh House of Lords (Eng.)
Bli. (N.S.)	Same, New Series
Bligh	Same
Bligh (N.S.)	Same, New Series
Bliss	Bliss Delaware County (Pa.)
Blue Sky L.Rep.	Blue Sky Law Reporter (CCH)
Bluett	Bluett's Isle of Man Cases
Bombay L.J.	Bombay Law Journal
Bond	Bond (U.S.)
Book of Judg.	Book of Judgments (Eng.)
Boor.	Booraem (Calif.)
Bos.	Bosworth, Superior Court (N.Y.)
Bos. & P.	Bosanquet & Puller, Common Pleas (Eng.)
Bos. & P.N.R.	Bosanquet & Puller's New Reports Common Pleas (Eng.)
Bos. & Pul.	Bosanquet & Puller, Common Pleas (Eng.)
Bos.Pol.Rep.	Boston Police Reports
Bost.L.R.	Boston Law Reporter
Boston B.J.	Boston Bar Journal
Bosw.	Bosworth, Superior Court (N.Y.)
	Boswell (Sc.)
Bott Poor Law Cas.	Bott's Poor Laws Settlement Cases (Eng.)
Bott's Set. Cas.	Same
Bould.	Bouldin (Ala.)
Bouv.	Bouvier Law Dictionary
Bov.Pat.Cas.	Bovill's Patent Cases
Boyce	Boyce (Del.)
Br. & B.	Broderip & Bingham, Common Pleas (Eng.)
Br. & Col.	British & Colonial Prize Cases
Br. & F.Ecc.	Broderick & Freemantle's Ecclesiastical Cases (Eng.)
Br. & Gold.	Brownlow & Goldesborough's Common Pleas (Eng.)
Br. & L.	Brownlow & Lushington's Admiralty Cases (Eng.)
Br. & Lush.	Same
Br.N.C.	Brooks New Cases, King's Bench (Eng.)
Br.N.Cas.	Same
Bract.	Bracton De Legibus et consuetudinibus Angliae (Eng.)
Bradf.	Bradford (Iowa)
Bradf.Surr.	Bradford's Surrogate Court (N.Y.)
Bradl.	Bradley (R.I.)
Bradw.	Bradwell (Ill.)
Brame	Brame (Miss.)
Branch	Branch (Fla.)
Brantly	Brantly (Md.)
Brayt.	Brayton (Vt.)
Breese	Breese (Ill.)
Brev.	Brevard (S.C.)
Brew.	Brewer (Md.)
	Brewster (Pa.)
Brews.	Brewster (Pa.)
Bridg.	J. Bridgmore, Common Pleas (Eng.)
Bridg.J.	Sir J. Bridgman, Common Pleas (Eng.)
Bridg.O.	Sir Orlando Bridgman, Common Pleas (Eng.)
Brief	The Brief
Briefcase	Briefcase
Brigham Young U.L.Rev.	Brigham Young University Law Review
Brightly	Brightly (Pa.)
Brightly El. Cas.	Brightly's Leading Election Cases (Pa.)
Brisb.	Brisbin (Minn.)
Brit.J. Criminol.	British Journal of Criminology
Brit.Cr.Cas.	British Crown Cases
Brit.J.Ad.L.	British Journal of Administrative Law
Brit.J.Law & Soc'y	British Journal of Law and Society
Brit.Prac. Int'l L.	British Practice in International Law
Brit.Ship.L.	British Shipping Laws (Stevens)
Brit.Tax Rev.	British Tax Review
Brit.Y.B. Int'l L.	British Year Book of International Law
Bro. & F.	Broderick & Freemantle's Ecclesiastical (Eng.)
Bro. & Fr.	Same
Bro. & Lush.	Browning & Lushington's Admiralty (Eng.)
Br.Eccl.	Brown's Ecclesiastical (Eng.)
Bro.Just.	Brown's Justiciary (Sc.)
Brock.	Brockenbrough (U.S.)
Brock. & Hol. Cas.	Brockenbrough & Holmes Cases (Va.)

Brock.Cas.	Brockenbrough's Cases (Va.)	Buck.	Bucknill's Cooke's Cases of Practice Common Pleas (Eng.)
Brod. & F.Ecc. Cas.	Broderick & Freemantle's Ecclesiastical Cases (Eng.)	Buck.Dec.	Buckner's Decisions (Freeman's Chancery) (Miss.)
Brod. & Fr. Ecc.Cas.	Same	Buffalo L.Rev.	Buffalo Law Review
Brodix Am. & El.Pat.Cas.	Brodix American & English Patent Cases	Bull.	Weekly Law Bulletin
Brook Abr.	Brook's Abridgment (Eng.)	Bull.Am.Acad. Psych. & L.	Bulletin of the American Academy of Psychiatry and the Law
Brooklyn Barrister	Brooklyn Barrister	Bull.Can.Welfare L.	Bulletin of Canadian Welfare Law
Brooklyn J. Int'l L.	Brooklyn Journal of International Law	Bull. Copyright Soc'y	Bulletin of the Copyright Society of the U.S.A.
Brooklyn L.Rev.	Brooklyn Law Review	Bull.Czech.L.	Bulletin of Czechoslovak Law
Brook N.Cas.	Brook's New Cases, King's Bench (Eng.)	Bull.Int'l Fiscal Doc.	Bulletin for International Fiscal Documentation
Brooks	Brooks (Mich.)	Bull.L.Science & Tech.	Bulletin of Law, Science and Technology
Brown	Brown (Miss.)	Bull.Legal Devel.	Bulletin of Legal Developments
	Brown (Mo.)	Bull.Waseda U. Inst.Comp.L.	Bulletin, Waseda University Institute of Comparative Law
	Brown (Neb.)		
Brown & MacN.	Brown & MacNamara, Railway Cases (Eng.)	Buller N.P.	Buller's Nisi Prius (Eng.)
Brown & R.	Brown & Rader (Mo.)	Bulstr.	Bulstrode (London) King's Bench (Eng.)
Brown A. & R.	Brown's United States District Court Admiralty & Revenue Cases	Bunb.	Bunbury Exchequer (Eng.)
Brown Adm.	Brown's Admiralty (U.S.)	Burf.	Burford (Okla.)
Brown Ch.	Brown's Chancery (Eng.)	Burgess	Burgess (Ohio)
Brown Dict.	Brown's Law Dictionary	Burk	Burk (Va.)
Brown Ecc.	Brown's Ecclesiastical (Eng.)	Burlesque Rep.	Skillman's New York Police Reports
Brown N.P.	Brown's Nisi Prius (Mich.)	Burnett	Burnett (Ore.)
Brown Parl. Cas.	Brown's House of Lords Cases (Eng.)		Burnett (Wis.)
Brown P.C.	Same	Burr.	Burrow, King's Bench (Eng.)
Brown. & L.	Browning & Lushington, Admiralty (Eng.)	Burr.S.Cases	Burrow's Settlement Cases (Eng.)
Browne	Browne (Mass.)	Burr.t.M.	Burrow's Reports, temp. Mansfield (Eng.)
	Browne Common Pleas (Pa.)	Bus. & L.	Business and Law
Browne & G.	Browne & Gray (Mass.)	Bus.L.Rev.	Business Law Review (England)
Browne & H.	Browne & Hemingway (Miss.)	Bus.L.Rev.	Business Law Review (United States)
Browne Bank Cas.	Browne's National Bank Cases	Bus.Law	The Business Lawyer
Brownl. & G.	Brownlow & Goldesborough, Common Pleas (Eng.)	Bus.Reg.L. Rep.	Business Regulation Law Report
Bruce	Bruce (Sc.)	Busb.Eq.	Busby Equity (N.C.)
Brunn.Coll. Cas.	Brunner's Collected Cases (U.S.)	Busb.L.	Busbee Law (N.C.)
Bt.	Benedicts (U.S.)	Bush	Bush (Ky.)
Buck	Buck Bankrupt Cases (Eng.)	Buxton	Buxton (N.C.)
	Buck (Mont.)		

C

C.	Cowen (N.Y.)
C. & A.	Cooke & Alcock King's Bench and Exchequer (Ir.)
C. & C.	Case and Comment
	Colemand & Caines Cases (N.Y.)
C. & D.	Corbett & Daniel's Election Cases (Eng.)
	Crawford & Dix's Abridged Cases (Ir.)
C. & D.A.C.	Crawford & Dix's Abridged Cases (Ir.)
C. & D.C.C.	Crawford & Dix's Circuit Cases (Ir.)
	Crawford & Dix's Criminal Cases (Ir.)
C. & E.	Cababe & Ellis Queen's Bench (Eng.)
C. & F.	Clark & Finnelly House of Lords (Eng.)
C. & J.	Crompton & Jervis Exchequer (Eng.)
C. & K.	Carrington & Kirwan Nisi Prius (Eng.)
C. & L.	Connor & Lawson's Chancery (Ir.)
C. & L.C.C.	Caines & Leigh Crown Cases (Eng.)
C. & M.	Carrington & Marshman's Nisi Prius (Eng.)
	Crompton & Meeson's Exchequer (Eng.)
C. & Marsh.	Carrington & Marshman's Nisi Prius (Eng.)
C. & N.	Cameron & Norwood's North Carolina Conference
C. & P.	Carrington & Payne's Nisi Prius (Eng.)
	Craig & Phillips Chancery (Eng.)
C. & R.	Cockburn & Rowe's Election Cases
C. & S.	Clarke & Scully's Drainage Cases (Ont.)
C.A.A.	Civil Aeronautics Authority Reports
C.A.B.	Civil Aeronautics Board Reports

C.A.D.	Customs Appeals Decisions
C.B.	Cumulative Bulletin (Internal Revenue)
	Common Bench (Manning, Granger & Scott) (Eng.)
C.B. (N.S.)	Common Bench (Manning, Granger & Scott), New Series (Eng.)
C.B.R.	Canadian Bankruptcy Reports
C.C.	Ohio Circuit Court Reports
C.C. (N.S.)	Ohio Circuit Court Reports, New Series
C.C.A.	Circuit Court of Appeals (U.S.)
C.C.C.	Canadian Criminal Cases, 1893–1962
[ ] C.C.C.	Canadian Criminal Cases, 1963–
CCF	Federal Contract Cases, CCH
CCH	Commerce Clearing House
CCH Atom. En.L.Rep.	Atomic Energy Law Reporter (CCH)
CCH Comm. Mkt.Rep.	Common Market Reporter (CCH)
CCH Fed. Banking L. Rep.	Federal Banking Law Reporter (CCH)
CCH Fed.Sec. L.Rep.	Federal Securities Law Reporter (CCH)
CCH Inh.Est. & Gift Tax Rep.	Inheritance, Estate, and Gift Tax Reporter (CCH)
CCH Lab.Arb. Awards	Labor Arbitration Awards (CCH)
CCH Lab.Cas.	Labor Cases (CCH)
CCH Lab.L. Rep.	Labor Law Reporter (CCH)
CCH Stand. Fed.Tax Rep.	Standard Federal Tax Reporter (CCH)
CCH State Tax Cas. Rep.	State Tax Cases Reporter (CCH)
CCH State Tax Rev.	State Tax Review (CCH)
CCH Tax Ct.Mem.	Tax Court Memorandum Decisions (CCH)
CCH Tax Ct.Rep.	Tax Court Reporter (CCH)
C.C.P.A.	Court of Customs & Patent Appeals (U.S.)
	Court of Customs & Patent Appeals Reports

C.C.Supp.	City Court Reports Supplement (N.Y.)	C.R.T.C.	Canadian Railway & Transport Cases
C.D.	U. S. Customs Court Decisions	C.Rob.	Christopher Robinson's Admiralty (Eng.)
	Commissioner of Patents	C.S.C.R.	Cincinnati Superior Court Reporter
	Ohio Circuit Decisions		
C.E.Gr.	C. E. Greene's Equity (N.J.)	C.S.T.	Capital Stock Tax Division (I.R.Bull.)
C.E.Greene	Same	C.T.	Carriers Taxing Ruling (I.R.Bull.)
C.F.R.	Code of Federal Regulations	[ ] C.T.C.	Canada Tax Cases
C.I.L.C.	Commonwealth International Law Cases	C.T.L.J.	California Trial Lawyers Journal
C.I.L.J.S.A.	Comparative and International Law Journal of Southern Africa	C.T.S.	Consolidated Treaty Series
		C.W.Dud.	C. W. Dudley's Law or Equity (S.C.)
C.J.	Corpus Juris	C.W.Dudl.Eq.	C. W. Dudley's Equity (S.C.)
C.J.Ann.	Corpus Juris Annotations		
C.J.S.	Corpus Juris Secundum	Cab. & E.	Cababe & Ellis Queen's Bench (Eng.)
C.L.A.I.T.	Constitutions and Laws of the American Indian Tribes (Scholarly Resources)	Cahiers	Les Cahiers de Droit
		Cai.	Caines (N.Y.)
C.L.A.S.	Criminal Law Audio Series	Cai.Cas.	Caines' Cases
C.L.Chambers	Chambers' Common Law (Upper Can.)	Cai.R.	Caines' Reports
		Cal.	California
C.L.L.C.	Canadian Labour Law Cases	Cal.2d	California, Second Series
C.L.L.R.	Canadian Labor Law Reports (CCH)	Cal.3d	California Reports, Third Series
C.L.R.	Common Law Reports (Eng.)	Cal.App.	California Appellate
	Common Law Reports (Aust.)	Cal.App.2d	California Appellate, Second Series
	Cyprus Law Reports	Cal.App.3d	California Appellate Reports, Third Series
C.L.Rec.	Cleveland Law Record	Cal.App.Dec.	California Appellate Decisions
C.L.Reg.	Cleveland Law Register		
C.L.Rep.	Cleveland Law Reporter	Cal.Dec.	California Decisions
C.L.S.R.	Computer Law Service Reporter	Cal.Ind.Acci. Dec.	California Industrial Accidents Decision
CLU J.	CLU Journal	Cal.Jur.	California Jurisprudence
C.L.W.	Commercial Laws of the World (Oceana)	Cal.Jur.2d	California Jurisprudence, Second Edition
C.M. & R.	Crompton, Meeson & Roscoe Exchequer (Eng.)	Cal.Leg.Rec.	California Legal Record
		Cal.Prac.	California Practice
C.M.R.	Court-Martial Reports	Cal.Rptr.	California Reporter (West)
C.M.R. (Air Force)	Court-Martial Reports of the Judge Advocate General of the Air Force	Cal.S.B.J.	California State Bar Journal
		Cal.St.B.J.	California State Bar Journal
C.P.Coop.	C. P. Cooper Chancery (Eng.)	Cal.Unrep. Cas.	California Unreported Cases
C.P.D.	Law Reports Common Pleas Division (Eng.) (1865–1880)	Calcutta W.N.	Calcutta Weekly Notes
		Cald.	Caldecott's Magistrate's and Settlement Cases (Eng.)
C.P.R.	Canadian Patent Reporter		
C.P.Rep.	Common Pleas Reporter (Pa.)		Caldwell (W.Va.)
C.R.	Criminal Reports (Canada)	Cald.J.P.	Caldecott's Magistrate's and Settlement Cases (Eng.)
C.R.A.C.	Canadian Reports, Appeal Cases	Cald.M.Cas.	Same
C.R.C.	Canadian Railway Cases	Cald.Mag.Cas.	Same

Cald.S.C.	Same
Cald.Sett.Cas.	Same
Calif.L.Rev.	California Law Review
Calif.W.Int'l L.J.	California Western International Law Journal
Calif.Western L.Rev.	California Western Law Review
Call	Call (Va.)
Calthr.	Calthrop (Eng.)
Cam.	Cameron's Privy Council Decisions
Cam. & N.	Cameron & Norwood's Conference (N.C.)
Cam.Cas.	Cameron's Cases (Can.)
Camb.L.J.	Cambridge Law Journal
Cambrian L. Rev.	Cambrian Law Review
Cameron	Cameron's Supreme Court Cases
Cameron Pr.	Cameron's Practice (Can.)
Camp	Camp (N.D.)
Campaign L. Rep.	Campaign Law Reporter
Campb.	Campbell (Neb.)
	Campbell's Nisi Prius (Eng.)
Campb.L.G.	Campbell's Legal Gazette (Pa.)
Can.App.Cas.	Canadian Appeal Cases
Can.B.A.J.	Canadian Bar Association Journal
Can.B.Ass'n Y.B.	Canadian Bar Association: Year Book
Can.B.J.	Canadian Bar Journal
Can.B.R.	Canadian Bar Review
Can.B.Rev.	Same
Can.Bankr. Ann.	Canadian Bankruptcy Reports Annotated
Can.Bankr. Ann. (N.S.)	Same, New Series
Can.Com.L. Rev.	Canadian Communications Law Review
Can.Com.R.	Canadian Commercial Law Reports
Can.Cr.Cas.	Canadian Criminal Cases
Can.Crim.	Criminal Reports (Can.)
Can.Crim. Cas. (N.S.)	Canadian Criminal Cases, New Series
Can.Crim. Cas.Ann.	Canadian Crimnial Cases Annotated
Can.Env.L. News	Canadian Environmental Law News
Can.Exch.	Canadian Exchequer
Can.Green Bag	Canadian Green Bag
Can.J.Correction	Canadian Journal of Correction
Can.J. Crim & Corr.	Canadian Journal of Criminology and Corrections
Can.L.J.	Canada Law Journal

Can.L.J. (N.S.)	Same, New Series
Can.L.Rev.	Canadian Law Review
Can.L.T. Occ.N.	Canadian Law Times Occasional Notes
Can.L.Times	Canadian Law Times
Can.Lab.	Canadian Labour
Can.Legal Stud.	Canadian Legal Studies
Can.Mun.J.	Canadian Municipal Journal
Can.Oil & Gas	Canadian Oil and Gas (Butterworths)
Can.Pub.Ad.	Canadian Public Administration
Can.R.Cas.	Canadian Railway Cases
Can.Ry.Cas.	Same
Can.S.C.	Canada Supreme Court
Can.S.Ct.	Canada Supreme Court Reports
Can.Tax App.Bd.	Canada Tax Appeal Board Cases
Cas.Tax Cas.Ann.	Canada Tax Cases Annotated
Can.Tax Found.Rep. Proc.Tax Conf.	Canadian Tax Foundation Report of Proceedings of the Tax Conference
Can.Tax.J.	Canadian Tax Journal
Can.Tax News	Canadian Tax News
Can.Wel.	Canadian Welfare
Can.Yearbook Int'l L.	Canadian Yearbook of International Law
Cane & L.	Cane & Leigh's Crown Cases Reserved (Eng.)
Capital U.L. Rev.	Capital University Law Review
Car. & K.	Carrington & Kirwan, Nisi Prius (Eng.)
Car. & P.	Carrington & Payne, Nisi Prius (Eng.)
Car.H. & A.	Carrow, Hamerton & Allen (Eng.)
Carolina L.J.	Carolina Law Journal
Carolina L. Repos.	Carolina Law Repository
Carp.	Carpenter (Cal.)
Carp.P.C.	Carpmael Patent Cases (Eng.)
Carribean L.J.	Carribean Law Journal
Cart.B.N.A.	Cartwright's Constitutional Cases (Can.)
Carter	Carter (Ind.)
	Carter Common Pleas (Eng.)
Carth.	Carthew King's Bench (Eng.)
Cartwr.Cas.	Cartwright's Cases (Can.)
Cary	Cary Chancery (Eng.)
Cas.C.L.	Cases in Crown Law (Eng.)
Cas.t.Hardw.	Cases temp. Hardwicke King's Bench (Eng.)

Cas.t.Holt	Cases temp. Holt, King's Bench (Eng.)	Chamb.Rep.	Chancery Chambers (Ont.)
Cas.t.King	Cases temp. King, Chancery (Eng.)	Chandl.	Chandler (N.H.) Chandler (Wis.)
Cas.t.Northington	Cases temp. Northington, Chancery Reports (Eng.)	Chaney	Chaney (Mich.)
		Charley Pr. Cas.	Charley's Practice Cases (Eng.)
Cas.t.Talb.	Cases temp. Talbot, Chancery (Eng.)	Charlt.	Charlton, R.M. (Ga.) Charlton, T.U.P. (Ga.)
Cas.t.Wm. III	Cases temp. William III (Eng.)	Chase	Chase (U.S.)
Cas.Tak. & Adj.	Cases Taken and Adjudged (Reports in Chancery, First Edition) (Eng.)	Chest.Co.	Chester County (Pa.)
		Chev.Ch.	Cheve's Chancery (S.C.)
		Chev.Eq.	Same
Case & Com.	Case & Comment	Cheves	Cheves Law (S.C.)
Case W.Res.J. Int'l L.	Case Western Reserve Journal of International Law	Chi.B. Record	Chicago Bar Record
		Chi.-Kent L.Rev.	Chicago-Kent Law Review
Case W.Res. L.Rev.	Case Western Reserve Law Review	Chi.Leg.N.	Chicago Legal News (Ill.)
Casey	Casey (Pa.)	Chic.L.T.	Chicago Law Times
Cass.Prac. Cas.	Cassels' Practice Cases (Can.)	Chicago L.B.	Chicago Law Bulletin
		Chicago L.J.	Chicago Law Journal
Cass.S.C.	Cassels' Supreme Court Decisions	Chicago L.Rec.	Chicago Law Record
		Chicano L.Rev.	Chicano Law Review
Cates	Cates (Tenn.)	Chin.L. & Gov't	Chinese Law and Government
Catholic Law.	The Catholic Lawyer	China L.Rev.	China Law Review
Catholic U.L. Rev.	Catholic University of America Law Review	Chip.	Chipman (N.Bruns.) Chipman (Vt.)
Censorship Today	Censorship Today	Chit.	Chitty's Bail Court (Eng.)
		Chit.B.C.	Same
Cent.Dig.	Century Digest	Chitt.	Same
Centr.L.J.	Central Law Journal	Chitty's L.J.	Chitty's Law Journal
Ceylon L.Rev.	Ceylon Law Review	Choyce Cas.Ch.	Choyce's Cases in Chancery (Eng.)
Ch.	Law Reports, Chancery (Eng.) Law Reports Chancery Division, Third Series	Chr.Rep.	Chamber Reports (Upper Can.)
		Chr.Rob.	Christopher Robinson's Admiralty (Eng.)
Ch.Cal.	Calendar of Proceedings in Chancery (Eng.)	Chy.Chrs.	Upper Canada Chancery Chambers Reports
Ch.Cas.	Cases in Chancery (Eng.)	Cin.B. Ass'n J.	Cincinnati Bar Association Journal
Ch.Chamb.	Chancery Chambers (Upper Can.)	Cin.L.Rev.	Cincinnati Law Review
Ch.Col.Op.	Chalmer's Colonial Opinions	Cin.Law Bull.	Weekly Law Bulletin (Ohio)
Ch.D.	Law Reports, Chancery Division (Eng.)	Cin.Mun.Dec.	Cincinnati Municipal Decisions
Ch.D.2d	Same, Second Series	Cin.R.	Cincinnati Superior Court Reporter
Ch.Prec.	Precedents in Chancery		
Ch.R.	Upper Canada Chambers Reports	Cin.S.C.R.	Same
		Cin.S.C.Rep.	Same
		Cinc.L.Bul.	Same
Ch.R.M.	R. M. Charlton (Ga.)	Cinc.Sup.Ct. Rep.	Same
Ch.Rep.	Chancery Reports (Eng.) Chancery Reports (Ir.)	Cincinnati Law Bull.	Weekly Law Bulletin (Ohio)
Ch.Sent.	Chancery Sentinel (N.Y.)	Cir.Ct.Dec.	Ohio Circuit Court Decisions
Ch.T.U.P.	T.U.P. Charlton (Ga.)		
Cha.App.	Chancery Appeal Cases English Law Reports	City Ct.R.	City Court Reports (N.Y.)

City Ct.R. Supp.	City Court Reports Supplements (N.Y.)	Clif.South.El. Cas.	Clifford, Southwick Election Cases
City Hall Rec.	City Hall Recorder (N.Y.)	Clk's Mag.	Clerk's Magazine (London)
City Hall Rep.	City Hall Reporter, Lomas (N.Y.)		Clerk's Magazine (R.I.)
Civ. & Mil. L.J.	Civil and Military Law Journal		Clerk's Magazine (Upper Can.)
Civ.Lib.	Civil Liberty	Co.Ct.Cas.	County Court Cases (Eng.)
Civ.Lib.Dock.	Civil Liberties Docket		
Civ.Lib.Rev.	Civil Liberties Review	Co.Ct.Ch.	County Court Chronicle (Eng.)
Civ.Lib.Rptr.	Civil Liberties Reporter		
Civ.Proc.R.	Civil Procedure Reports (N.Y.)	Co.Ct.Rep.	Pennsylvania County Court Reports
Civ.Rights Dig.	Civil Rights Digest	Co.Inst.	Coke's Institutes (Eng.)
		Co.Litt.	Coke on Littleton (Eng.)
Cl. & F.	Clark & Finnelly, House of Lords (Eng.)	Co.Mass.Pr.	Colby Mass. Practice
		Co.P.C.	Coke Pleas of the Crown (Eng.)
Clark	Clark (Ala.)		
	Clark (Pa.)	Cobb	Cobb (Ala.)
Clark & F.	Clark & Finnelly, House of Lords (Eng.)		Cobb (Ga.)
		Cochr.	Cochran (Nova Scotia)
Clark & F. (N.S.)	Same, New Series		Cochrane (N.D.)
		Cockb. & R.	Cockburn & Rowe's Election Cases (Eng.)
Clark App.	Clark Appeal Cases House of Lords (Eng.)		
		Cocke	Cocke (Ala.)
			Cocke (Fla.)
Clark Col.Law	Clark Colonial Law	Code Rep.	Code Reporter (N.Y.)
Clarke	Clarke (Iowa)	Code Rep. (N.S.)	Code Reporter, New Series (N.Y.)
	Clarke (Mich.)		
Clarke & S. Dr.Cas.	Clarke & Scully's Drainage Cases (Ont.)	Coff.Prob.	Coffey's Probate (Cal.)
		Coke	Coke King's Bench (Eng.)
Clarke Ch.	Clarke Chancery (N.Y.)	Col.	Coleman (Ala.)
Class Act.Rep.	Class Action Reports	Col. & C.Cas.	Coleman & Caine's Cases (N.Y.)
Clayt.	Clayton's Reports York Assizes (Eng.)	Col.Cas.	Coleman's Cases (N.Y.)
Clearinghouse Rev.	Clearinghouse Review	Col.Int'l Dr. Comp.	Colloque International de Droit Comparé
Clemens	Clemens (Kan.)	Col.L.Rev.	Columbia Law Review
		Cold.	Coldwell
Clev.Bar Ass'n J.	Cleveland Bar Association Journal	Coldw.	Coldwell (Tenn.)
		Cole	Cole (Ala.)
Clev.St. L.Rev	Cleveland State Law Review		Cole (Iowa)
		Cole. & Cai. Cas.	Coleman & Caines' Cases
Cleve.L.Rec.	Cleveland Law Record (Ohio)	Cole.Cas.	Coleman's Cases
Cleve.L.Reg.	Cleveland Law Register (Ohio)	Coll.	Collyer's Chancery (Eng.)
Cleve.L.Rep.	Cleveland Law Reporter (Ohio)	Coll. & E. Bank.	Collier's & Eaton's American Bankruptcy Reports
Cleve.Law R.	Cleveland Law Reporter (Ohio)	Coll.L.Bull.	College Law Bulletin
		Coll.L.Dig.	College Law Digest
Cleve.Law Rec.	Cleveland Law Record (Ohio)	Colles.	Colles Cases in Parliament (Eng.)
Cleve.Law Reg.	Cleveland Law Register (Ohio)	Colo.	Colorado
		Colo.App.	Colorado Appeals
Clev.-Mar.L. Rev.	Cleveland-Marshall Law Review	Colo.Law Rep.	Colorado Law Reporter
		Colo.Law.	Colorado Lawyer
Cliff.	Clifford (U.S.)	Colombo L.Rev.	Colombo Law Review (Ceylon)

Coltm.   Coltman Registration
                Appeal Cases
                (Eng.)

Colq.   Colquit (Modern) (Eng.)

Colum.   Columbia Human Rights
Human   Law Review
Rights
L.Rev.

Colum.J.   Columbia Journal of Envi-
Env.L.   ronmental Law

Colum.J.Int'l   Columbia Journal of Inter-
Aff.   national Affairs

Colum.J.   Columbia Journal of
Transnat'l   Transnational Law
Law

Colum.L.Rev.   Columbia Law Review

Colum.Soc'y   Columbia Society of Inter-
Int'l L.Bull.   national Law Bulletin

Colum.   Columbia Survey of Hu-
Survey   man Rights Law
Human
Rights L.

Com. & Mun.   Commercial & Municipal
L.Rep.   Law Reporter

Com.B.   Common Bench (Manning,
                Granger & Scott)
                (Eng.)

Com.Cas.   Commercial Cases
                Since 1895 (Eng.)

Com.Dec.   Commissioners' Decisions
                (Patent)

Com.L.   Commercial Law (Can.)

Com.L.J.   Commercial Law Journal

Com.P.Reptr.   Common Pleas Reporter
                (Scranton)

Comb.   Comberbach, King's
                Bench (Eng.)

Comb.B. (N.S.) Common Bench (Manning,
                Granger & Scott)
                (Eng.)

Comm.Cause   Common Cause
Comm.Mkt.   Common Market Law Re-
L.R.   ports
Comm.Mkt.   Common Market Law Re-
L.Rev.   view
Commodity   Commodity Futures Law
Futures   Reporter (CCH)
L.Rep.
Community   Community Property Jour-
Prop.J.   nal
Commw.Arb.   Commonwealth Arbitra-
                tion Reports
Commw.L.R.   Commonwealth Law
                Reports
Comp.Dec.   U. S. Comptroller of
                Treasury Decisions
Comp.Gen.   U. S. Comptroller
                General Decisions
Comp.   Comparative Juridical
Jurid.Rev.   Review
Comp.L.J.   Company Law Journal
Comparisons   Comparisons in Law and
in L. &   Monetary Comments
Monet.Com.

Comptr.Treas.   U. S. Comptroller of Treas-
Dec.   ury Decisions
Computer L. &   Computer Law and Tax
Tax   Report
Computers &   Computers and Law
L.
Comst.   Comstock Appeals (N.Y.)
Comyns   Comyns King's Bench and
                Common Pleas (Eng.)
Comyns Dig.   Comyns Digest (Eng.)
Con.B.J.   Connecticut Bar Journal
Condit.   Conditional Sale-Chattel
Sale-Chat.   Mortgage (CCH)
Mort.Rep.
Conf.   Conference Reports
                (N.C.)
Conf.Teach.   Conference of Teachers of
Int'l L.   International Law
Cong.Dig.   Congressional Digest
Cong.Rec.   Congressional Record
                (U.S.)
Conn.   Connecticut
Conn.B.J.   Connecticut Bar Journal
Conn.Cir.Ct.   Connecticut Circuit Court
                Reports
Conn.L.Rev.   Connecticut Law Review
Conn.Supp.   Connecticut Supplement
Conn.Surr.   Connolly's Surrogate
                (N.Y.)
Conov.   Conover (Wis.)
Const.   Constitution
Const.Afr.   Constitutions of African
States   States (Oceana)
Const.Dep. &   Constitutions of Dependen-
Sp.Sov.   cies and Special Sover-
                eignties
Const.Nations   Constitutions of Nations
                (Nijhoff)
Const.Rep.   Constitutional Reports
                (S.C.)
Const.Rev.   Constitutional Review
Const.World   Constitutions of the Coun-
                tries of the World
                (Oceana)
Consumer   Consumer Product Safety
Prod.Saf'y   Guide (CCH)
Guide
Contemp.   Contemporary Drug Prob-
Drug Prob.   lems
Convey.   Conveyancer
Convey.   Conveyancer & Property
(N.S.)   Lawyer, New Series
Cook Vice-   Cook's Vice-Admiralty
Adm.   (Lower Can.)
Cooke   Cooke Cases of Practice,
                Common Pleas (Eng.)
                Cooke (Tenn.)
Cooke & A.   Cooke & Alcock
                King's Bench (Ir.)
Cooley   Cooley (Mich.)

Coop.	Cooper (Fla.)
	Cooper's Chancery (Eng.)
	Cooper's Chancery (Tenn.)
Coop.C. & P. R.	Cooper's Chancery Practice Reporter (U.S.)
Coop.Pr.Cas.	Cooper's Practice Cases (Eng.)
Coop.t.Brough.	Cooper's Cases temp. Brougham Chancery (Eng.)
Coop.t.Cott.	Cooper's Cases temp. Cottenham Chancery (Eng.)
Coop.t.Eldon	Cooper's Reports temp. Eldon Chancery (Eng.)
Cope	Cope (Cal.)
Copp Min.Dec.	Copp's Mining Decisions (U.S.)
Copp's Land Owner	Copp's Land Owner
Copy.	Copyright
Copy.Bull.	Copyright Bulletin
Copyright L. Sym.	Copyright Law Symposium (ASCAP)
Corb. & D.	Corbett & Daniels Election Cases (Eng.)
Cornell Int'l L.J.	Cornell International Law Journal
Cornell L.F.	Cornell Law Forum
Cornell L.J.	Cornell Law Journal
Cornell L.Q.	Cornell Law Quarterly
Cornell L.Rev.	Cornell Law Review
Corp.J.	Corporation Journal
Corp.Pract. Comment.	Corporate Practice Commentator
Corp.Pract. Rev.	Corporate Practice Review
Corp.Reorg.	Corporate Reorganizations
Corp.Reorg. & Am.Bank. Rev.	Corporate Reorganization & American Bankruptcy Review
Coup.	Couper's Justiciary (Sc.)
Court. & MacL.	Courtenay & MacLean (Sc.)
Coutlea	Coutlea's Supreme Court Cases
Cow.	Cowen (N.Y.)
Cow.Cr.	Cowen's Criminal (N.Y.)
Cowp.	Cowper King's Bench (Eng.)
Cowp.Cas.	Cowper's Cases (Chancery) (Eng.)
Cox	Cox (Ark.)
Cox & Atk.	Cox & Atkinson Registration Appeals (Eng.)
Cox Am.T. Cas.	Cox's American Trademark Cases
Cox C.C.	Cox's Criminal Cases (Eng.)
Cox Ch.	Cox's Chancery (Eng.)
Cox Crim.Cas.	Cox's Criminal Cases

Cox Eq.	Cox's Equity
Cox J.S.Cas.	Cox's Joint Stock Cases (Eng.)
Coxe	Coxe (N.J.)
Cr. & M.	Crompton & Meeson, Exchequer (Eng.)
Cr. & Ph.	Craig & Phillips Chancery (Eng.)
Cr.App.	Criminal Appeals (Eng.)
Cr.Cas.Res.	Crown Cases Reserved, Law Reports (Eng.)
Crabbe	Crabbe (U.S.)
Craig & Ph.	Craig & Phillips Chancery (Eng.)
Cranch	Cranch (U.S.)
Cranch C.C.	Cranch's Circuit Court (U.S.)
Cranch Pat. Dec.	Cranch's Patent Decisions (U.S.)
Crane	Crane (Mont.)
Craw.	Crawford (Ark.)
Crawf. & D. Abr.Cas.	Crawford & Dix's Abridged Cases (Ir.)
Crawf. & Dix	Crawford & Dix Circuit Cases (Ir.)
	Crawford & Dix Criminal Cases (Ir.)
Creighton L.Rev.	Creighton Law Review
Crim.	Criminologie
Crim. & Soc. Just.	Crime and Social Justice
Crim.App.	Criminal Appeal Reports
Crim.App. Rep.	Cohen's Criminal Appeals Reports (Eng.)
Crim.Case & Com.	Criminal Case and Comment
Crim.Def.	Criminal Defense
Crim.Just.	Criminal Justice
Crim.Just. & Behav.	Criminal Justice and Behavior
Crim.Just. Newsl.	Criminal Justice Newsletter
Crim.Just.Q.	Criminal Justice Quarterly
Crim.Just.Rev.	Criminal Justice Review
Crim.L.Bull.	Criminal Law Bulletin
Crim.L.Mag.	Criminal Law Magazine (N.J.)
Crim.L.Mag. & Rep.	Criminal Law Magazine and Reporter
Crim.L.Q.	Criminal Law Quarterly
Crim.L.Rec.	Criminal Law Recorder
Crim.L.Rep.	Criminal Law Reporter
Crim.L.Rev.	Criminal Law Review (Manhattan)
Crim.L.Rev. (Eng.)	Criminal Law Review (Eng.)
Crim.L.Rptr.	Criminal Law Reporter

Crim.Rep. (N.S.)	Criminal Reports, New Series	Ct.Cust.App.	Court of Customs Appeals (U.S.)
Crime & Delin'cy	Crime & Delinquency	Ct.Rev.	Court Review
Crime & Delin'cy Abst.	Crime and Delinquency Abstracts	Cum.Bull.	Cumulative Bulletin
		Cum.-San. L.Rev.	Cumberland-Sanford Law Review
Crime & Delin'cy Lit.	Crime and Delinquency Literature	Cumb.L.Rev.	Cumberland Law Review
Criminologica	Criminologica	Cummins	Cummins (Idaho)
Criminologist	Criminologist	Cunn.	Cunningham King's Bench (Eng.)
Criminology	Criminology	Cur.Leg. Thought	Current Legal Thought
	Croke's King's Bench	Current Com. & Leg.Mis.	Current Comment and Legal Miscellany
Cripp Ch.Cas.	Cripp's Church & Clergy Cases	Current L.	Current Law
Critch.	Critchfield (Ohio St.)	Current L. & Soc.Prob.	Current Law and Social Problems
Cro.	Croke's King's Bench (Eng.)	Current L.Y.B.	Current Law Yearbook
Cro.Car.	Croke temp. Charles I (Eng.)	Current Legal Prob.	Current Legal Problems
Cro.Eliz.	Croke temp. Elizabeth (Eng.)	Current Legal Thought	Current Legal Thought
Cro.Jac.	Croke temp. James I King's Bench (Eng.)	Current Med.	Current Medicine for Attorneys
Cromp.	Star Chamber Cases (Eng.)	Curry	Curry (La.)
Cromp. & J.	Crompton & Jervis Exchequer (Eng.)	Curt.	Curtis Circuit Court (U.S.)
Cromp. & M.	Crompton & Meeson Exchequer (Eng.)	Curt.Eccl.	Curtis Ecclesiastical (Eng.)
Cromp.M. & R.	Crompton, Meeson & Roscoe, Exchequer (Eng.)	Cush.	Cushing (Mass.)
		Cust.App.	United States Customs Appeals
Crosw.Pat. Cas.	Croswell's Collection of Patent Cases (U.S.)	Cust.Ct.	Custom Court Reports (U.S.)
Crounse	Crounse (Neb.)	Cyc.	Cyclopedia of Law & Procedure
Crumrine	Crumrine (Pa.)	Czech.J. Int'l L.	Czechoslovak Journal of International Law
Ct.Cl.	Court of Claims (U.S.)	Czech.Y.B. Int'l L.	Czechoslovak Yearbook of International Law
Ct.Cust. & Pat.App.	Court of Customs & Patent Appeals		

D

D.	Disney (Ohio) Ohio Decisions	D. & J.B.	De Gex & Jones Bankruptcy (Eng.)
D. & B.	Dearsley & Bell's Crown Cases (Eng.)	D. & L.	Dowling & Lowndes Bail Court (Eng.)
D. & B.C.C.	Same	D. & M.	Davison & Merivale's Queen's Bench (Eng.)
D. & C.	Dow & Clark's Parliamentary Cases (Eng.) Deacon & Chitty's Bankruptcy Cases (Eng.)	D. & P.	Denison & Pearce's Crown Cases (Eng.)
D. & Ch.	Same	D. & R.	Dowling & Ryland's King's Bench (Eng.)
D. & Chit.	Same	D. & R.M.C.	Dowling & Ryland's Magistrates' Cases (Eng.)
D. & E.	Dwinford & East's King's Bench Term Reports (Eng.)	D. & R.Mag. Cas.	Same
D. & J.	De Gex & Jones' Chancery (Eng.)	D. & R.N.P.	Dowling & Ryland's Nisi Prius Cases (Eng.)

D. & R.N.P.C.	Same
D. & S.	Drewry & Smale's Chancery (Eng.)
	Deane & Swabey's Ecclesiastical (Eng.)
D. & Sm.	Drewry & Smale's Chancery (Eng.)
D. & Sw.	Deane & Swabey Ecclesiastical (Eng.)
D. & W.	Drewry & Walsh's Chancery (Ir.)
	Drewry & Warren's Chancery (Ir.)
D. & War.	Drewry & Warren's Chancery (Ir.)
D.B.	Domesday Book
D.B. & M.	Dunlop, Bell & Murray (Sc.)
D.C.	Treasury Department Circular (I.R.Bull.)
	District of Columbia
D.C.A.	Dorion's Queen's Bench (Can.)
D.C.App.	District of Columbia Appeals
D.C.B.J.	District of Columbia Bar Journal
D.C.Cir.	District of Columbia Court of Appeals Cases
D.Chip.	D. Chipman (Vt.)
D.Chipm.	Same
D.D.C.	District Court, District of Columbia
D.Dec.	Dix's School Decisions (N.Y.)
D.I.L. (Hack.)	Digest of International Law (Hackworth)
D.I.L. (Moore)	Digest of International Law (Moore)
D.I.L. (White.)	Digest of International Law (Whiteman)
D.L.R.	Dominion Law Reports (Can.) 1912–1922
[ ] D.L.R.	Same, 1923–1955
D.L.R.2d	Same, Second Series
D.L.R.3d	Same, Third Series, 1969–present
D.P.R.	Decisiones de Puerto Rico
D.Rep.	Ohio Decisions Reprint
D.Repr.	Same
D.T.C.	Dominion Tax Cases
Dak.	Dakota
Dak.L.Rev.	Dakota Law Review
Dal.C.P.	Dalison's Common Pleas (Eng.)
Dale	Dale (Okla.)
Dale Ecc.	Dale's Ecclesiastical (Eng.)
Dale Eccl.	Same
Dale Leg.Rit.	Dale's Legal Ritual (Eng.)

Dalhousie L.J.	Dalhousie Law Journal
Dall.	Dallam's Decisions
	Dallas (Pa.)
	Dallas (U.S.)
Dall. in Keil.	Dallison in Keilway's King's Bench (Eng.)
Dalr.	Dalrymple's Decisions (Sc.)
Daly	Daly (N.Y.)
Dan.	Daniell's Exchequer & Equity (Eng.)
Dana	Dana (Ky.)
Dane Abr.	Dane's Abridgment (Eng.)
Dann	Dann (Ariz.)
	Dann (Cal.)
Dann.	Danner (Ala.)
Dans. & L.	Danson & Lloyd's Mercantile Cases (Eng.)
Dans. & Lld.	Same
D'Anv.Abr.	D'Anver's Abridgment (Eng.)
Dass.Ed.	Dassler's Edition, Kansas Reports
Dauph.Co.	Dauphin County (Pa.)
Dav. & M.	Davison & Merivale Queen's Bench (Eng.)
Dav. & Mer.	Same
Daveis	Daveis (Ware) (U.S.)
Davies or Davis	Davis King's Bench (Ir.)
Davis	Daveis (Ware) (U.S.)
	Davis (Hawaii)
	Davis King's Bench (Ir.)
Davys	Davys King's Bench
Day	Day (Conn.)
Dayton	3 Ohio Miscellaneous Decisions
Dayton T.R.	Same
Dayton Term Rep.	Iddings' Term Reports (Ohio)
Dea.	Deady, U. S. Circuit & District Courts (Cal. & Ore.)
Dea. & Chit.	Same
Dea. & Sw.	Deane & Swabey's Ecclesiastical (Eng.)
	Deane & Swabey's Probate & Divorce (Eng.)
Deac.	Deacon, Bankruptcy (Eng.)
Deac. & C.	Deacon & Chitty, Bankruptcy (Eng.)
Deac. & Chit.	Same
Deacon & C.	Same
Deacon, Bankr.Cas.	Deacon, Bankruptcy (Eng.)
Deady	Deady, U. S. Circuit and District Courts (Cal. & Ore.)

Deane	Deane (Vt.)	Denis	Denis (La.)
	Deane (& Swabey's) Probate & Divorce (Eng.)	Denver J. Int'l L. & Policy	Denver Journal of International Law and Policy
Deane & S. Eccl.Rep.	Deane & Swabey's Ecclesiastical (Eng.)	Denver L.J.	Denver Law Journal
Deane & Sw.	Same	De Paul L. Rev.	De Paul Law Review
Deane Ecc.	Same		
Deane Ecc. Rep.	Same	Dept.State Bull.	Department of State Bulletin, United States
Dears.	Dearsley & Bell Crown Cases (Eng.)	Des.	Dessaussure's Equity (S. C.)
Dears. & B.	Same	Desaus.Eq.	Same
Dears. & B. C.C.	Same	Dess.	Same
		Dessaus.	Same
Dears.C.C.	Same	Det.Coll.L. Rev.	Detroit College of Law Review
Deas & A.	Deas & Anderson (Sc.)		
Deas & And.	Same	Det.L.J.	Detroit Law Journal
Dec.Com.Pat.	Decisions of Commissioner of Patents	Det.L.Rev.	Detroit Law Review
		Det.Leg.N.	Detroit Legal News
Dec.Dig.	Decennial Digest	Detroit L.Rev.	Detroit Law Review
Dec.Rep.	Ohio Decisions Reprint	Dev.	Devereux's Equity (N.C.)
Dec.U.S. Compt.Gen.	Decisions of U. S. Comptroller General		Devereux's Law (N.C.)
			Devereux's U. S. Court of Claims
Decalogue	Decalogue Journal		
Defense L.J.	Defense Law Journal	Dev. & B.	Devereux & Battle's Equity (N.C.)
De G. & J.	De Gex & Jones, Chancery (Eng.)		Devereux & Battle's Law (N.C.)
De G. & Sm.	De Gex & Smale, Chancery (Eng.)	Dev.Ct.Cl.	Devereux's Court of Claims (U.S.)
De G.F. & J.	De Gex, Fisher & Jones, Chancery (Eng.)	Dew.	Dewey (Kan.)
		De Witt	De Witt (Ohio)
De G.J. & S.	De Gex, Jones & Smith, Chancery (Eng.)	Di.	Dyer's King's Bench (Eng.)
De G.M. & G.	De Gex, Macnaughten & Gordon, Chancery (Eng.)	Dice	Dice (Ind.)
		Dick.	Dickens' Chancery (Eng.)
De Gex	De Gex Bankruptcy (Eng.)		Dickinson's Equity (N.J.)
Del.	Delaware	Dick.L.Rev.	Dickinson Law Review
Del.Ch.	Delaware Chancery	Dicta	Dicta of Denver Bar Association
Del.Co.	Delaware County (Pa.)		
Del.County	Delaware County Reports	Dig.C.L.W.	Digest of Commercial Laws of the World (Oceana)
Del.Cr.Cas.	Delaware Criminal Cases	Dill.	Dillon, Circuit Court (U.S.)
Del.J.Corp.L.	Delaware Journal of Corporate Law	Dine Israel	Dine Israel
Dem.	Demarest's Surrogate (N. Y.)	Dirl.Dec.	Direlton's Decisions (Sc.)
		Disn.	Disney (Ohio)
Dem.Surr.	Same	Disney	Same
Den.	Denio (N.Y.)	Docket	Docket (Lebanon, Pa.)
	Denis (La.)		Docket (St. Paul, Minn.)
Den. & P.	Denison & Pearce's Crown Cases (Eng.)	Docket Call	Docket Call
Den. & P.C.C.	Same	Dod.	Dodson's Admiralty (Eng.)
Den.C.C.	Denison's Crown Cases (Eng.)	Dod.Adm.	Same
		Dods.	Same
Den.L.J.	Denver Law Journal	Dom.L.R.	Dominion Law Reports (Can.)
Den.L.N.	Denver Legal News		
Denio	Denio (N.Y.)	Donaker	Donaker (Ind.)

Donn.	Donnelly's Chancery (Eng.)
	Donnelly's Irish Land Cases
Donnelly	Same
Dorion	Dorion (Lower Can.)
Doshisha L. Rev.	Doshisha Law Review
Doug.	Douglas (Mich.)
	Douglas' King's Bench (Eng.)
Dougl.	Douglas (Mich.)
Dougl.El.Cas.	Douglas Election Cases (Eng.)
Dougl.K.B.	Douglas' King's Bench (Eng.)
Dow	Dow's House of Lords (Parliamentary) Cases (Eng.)
Dow.	Dowling's Practice Cases (Eng.)
Dow & Cl.	Dow & Clark's House of Lords Cases (Eng.)
Dow. & L.	Dowling & Lowndes' Bail Court (Eng.)
Dowl. & Lownd.	Dowling & Lowndes' Practice Cases (Eng.)
Dowl. & R.	Dowling & Ryland's King's Bench (Eng.)
	Dowling & Ryland's Queen's Bench & Magistrates' Cases (Eng.)
Dowl.P.C. (N.S.)	Dowling Practice Cases, New Series (Eng.)
Dowl.Pr.Cas.	Dowling Practice Cases (Eng.)
Down. & Lud.	Downton & Luder's Election Cases (Eng.)
Drake L.Rev.	Drake Law Review
Draper	Draper (Upper Can.)
Drew	Drew (Fla.)
Drew.	Drewry's Chancery (Eng.)
Drew. & S.	Drewry & Smale's Chancery (Eng.)

Drinkw.	Drinkwater Common Pleas (Eng.)
Drug Abuse L.Rev.	Drug Abuse Law Review
Drury	Drury's Chancery (Ir.)
Dublin U.L. Rev.	Dublin University Law Review
Dudl.	Dudley (Ga.)
	Dudley's Equity (S.C.)
	Dudley's Law (S.C.)
Duer	Duer's Superior Court (N. Y.)
Duke B. Ass'n J.	Duke Bar Association Journal
Duke L.J.	Duke Law Journal
Duke's Charitable Uses	Duke's Charitable Uses (Eng.)
Dunc.Ent.Cas.	Duncan Entail Cases (Sc.)
Dunc.N.P.	Duncombe Nisi Prius
Dunl.	Dunlop, Bell & Murray (Sc.)
Dunl.B. & M.	Same
Dunlop	Dunlop (Sc.)
Dunn.	Dunning's King's Bench (Eng.)
Duquesne L.Rev.	Duquesne Law Review
Duquesne U.L.Rev.	Duquesne University Law Review
Durf.	Durfee (R.I.)
Durfee	Same
Durie	Durie (Sc.)
Durn. & E.	Durnford & East's King's Bench (Term Reports) (Eng.)
Dutch.	Dutcher's Law (N.J.)
Duv.	Duval's Supreme Court (Can.)
	Duval's Reports (Can.)
Dy.	Dyer's King's Bench (Eng.)
Dyer	Same

E

E.	East's King's Bench (Eng.)
E. & A.	Spink's Ecclesiastical & Admiralty (Eng.)
	Upper Canada Error & Appeal Reports, Grant
E. & B.	Ellis & Blackburn's Queen's Bench (Eng.)
E. & E.	Ellis & Ellis' Queen's Bench (Eng.)
E. & I.	English & Irish Appeals, House of Lords (Eng.)
E.A.S.	Executive Agreement Series, United States

E.Afr.L.J.	East African Law Journal
E.Afr.L.R.	East Africa Law Reports
E.Afr.L.Rev.	Eastern Africa Law Review
E.B. & E.	Ellis, Blackburn & Ellis' Queen's Bench (Eng.)
E.B. & S.	Ellis, Best & Smith's Queen's Bench (Eng.)
E.C.	English Chancery
E.C.L.	English Common Law
E.C.R.	Reports of Cases before the Court of Justice of the European Communities
E.D.S.	E. D. Smith (N.Y.)

E.D.Smith	Same	Edw.Abr.	Edward's Abridgment Privy Council
E.E.	English Exchequer		
E.E.C.J.O.	Official Journal of the European Communities		Edward's Abridgment Prerogative Court Cases
E.E.C.L.	Encyclopedia of European Community Law (Bender)	Edw.Adm.	Edward's Admiralty (Eng.)
E.E.O.C.Compliance Manual	Equal Employment Opportunity Commission Compliance Manual (CCH)	Edw.Ch.	Edward's Chancery (N.Y.)
		Edw.Lead.Dec.	Edward's Leading Decisions in Admiralty
E.E.R.	English Ecclesiastical Reports	Edw.Pr.Cas.	Edward's Prize Cases (Eng.Admiralty)
E.G.L.	Encyclopedia of Georgia Law	Edw.Pr.Ct. Cas.	Edward's Prerogative Court Cases
E.L. & Eq.	English Law & Equity Reports	Efird	Efird (S.C.)
E.L.R.	Eastern Law Reporter (Can.)	El.	Elchie's Decisions (Sc.)
E.P.D.	Employment Practices Decisions (CCH)	El. & B.	Ellis & Blackburn's Queen's Bench (Eng.)
E.R.	East's King's Bench (Eng.)	El. & Bl.	Same
E.R.C.	English Ruling Cases	El. & El.	Ellis & Ellis, Queen's Bench (Eng.)
	Environmental Reporter Cases	El.B. & E.	Ellis, Blackburn & Ellis' Queen's Bench (Eng.)
E.School L.Rev.	Eastern School Law Review	El.B. & El.	Same
E.T.	Estate Tax Division (I.R. Bull.)	El.B. & S.	Ellis, Best & Smith's Queen's Bench (Eng.)
Ea.	East's King's Bench (Eng.)	El.Bl. & El.	Ellis, Blackburn & Ellis' Queen's Bench (Eng.)
Eag. & Y.	Eagle & Young's Tithe Cases (Eng.)	El.Cas.	Election Cases
		Elchies'	Elchies' Decisions (Sc.)
Eag.T.	Eagle's Commutation of Tithes (Eng.)	Elect.Cas. (N.Y.)	Election Cases, Armstrong, New York
Earth L.J.	Earth Law Journal	Elect.Rep.	Election Reports, Ontario
East	East's King's Bench (Eng.) Eastern Reporter (U.S.)	Ell. & Bl.	Ellis & Blackburn's Queen's Bench (Eng.)
East P.C.	East's Pleas of the Crown (Eng.)	Ell.Bl. & Ell.	Ellis, Blackburn & Ellis' Queen's Bench (Eng.)
East.J.Int'l L.	Eastern Journal of International Law	Els.W.Bl.	Elsley's Edition of Wm. Blackstone's King's Bench (Eng.)
East.L.R.	Eastern Law Reporter (Can.)		
East.Rep.	Eastern Reporter (U.S.)	Em.App.	Emergency Court of Appeals (U.S.)
East.T.	Eastern Term (Eng.)	Emory L.J.	Emory Law Journal
East.U.S.Bus. L.Rev.	Eastern United States Business Law Review	Empl.Rel.L.J.	Employee Relations Law Journal
Ebersole	Ebersole (Iowa)	Empl.Saf'y & Health Guide	Employment Safety and Health Guide (CCH)
Eccl. & Adm.	Spink's Ecclesiastical & Admiralty (Upper Can.)		
Eccl.R.	Ecclesiastical Reports (Eng.)	Enc.Pl. & Pr.	Encyclopedia of Pleading & Practice
Eccl.Rep.	Same	Enc.U.S.Sup. Ct.Rep.	Encyclopedia of United States Supreme Court Reports
Ecology L.Q.	Ecology Law Quarterly		
Ed.	Eden's Chancery (Eng.)	Energy Controls	Energy Controls (P–H)
Ed.Ch.	Edward's Chancery (N.Y.)		
Eden	Eden's Chancery (Eng.)	Energy Users Rep.	Energy Users Report (BNA)
Edg.	Edgar (Sc.)		
Edinb.L.J.	Edinburgh Law Journal	Eng.	English (Ark.)
Edm.Sel.Cas.	Edmond's Select Cases (N. Y.)	Eng.Adm.	English Admiralty
		Eng.Adm.R.	Same
Edw.	Edwards (Mo.)	Eng.C.C.	English Crown Cases
	Edward's Chancery (N.Y.)		

Eng.C.L.	English Common-Law Reports		Esp.N.P.	Same
Eng.Ch.	English Chancery Condensed English Chancery		Est.Plan.Rev.	Estate Planning Review (CCH)
Eng.Com.L.R.	English Common-Law Reports		Estates & Trusts Q.	Estates and Trusts Quarterly
Eng.Cr.Cas.	English Crown Cases		Euer	Euer Doctrina Placitandi (Eng.)
Eng.Ecc.R.	English Ecclesiastical Reports		Eur.Consult. Ass.Deb.	Council of Europe Consultative Assembly, Official Report of Debates
Eng.Eccl.	Same			
Eng.Exch.	English Exchequer		Eur.L.Dig.	European Law Digest
Eng.Hist.Rev.	English Historical Review		Eur.L.Newsl.	European Law Newsletter
Eng.Ir.App.	Law Reports English & Irish Appeals		Eur.L.Rev.·	European Law Review
Eng.Judg.	English Judges (Sc.)		Eur.Parl.Deb.	Debates of the European Parliament
Eng.L. & Eq.	English Law & Equity Reports		Eur.Parl.Docs.	European Parliament Working Documents
Eng.L. & Eq.R.	Same		Eur.Tax.	European Taxation
Eng.Rep.	English Reports, Full Reprint		Eur.Trans.L.	European Transport Law
			Eur.Y.B.	European Yearbook
Eng.Rep.R.	Same		Eurolaw Com. Intel.	Eurolaw Commercial Intelligence
Eng.Ry. & C. Cas.	English Railway and Canal Cases		Europ.T.S.	European Treaty Series
Eng.Sc.Ecc.	·English & Scotch Ecclesiastical Reports		Evans	Evans, Washington Territory Reports
Env.Affairs	Environmental Affairs		Ex.	Exchequer Reports (Eng.)
Env.L.	Environmental Law		Ex.C.R.	Exchequer Court Reports (Can.) (1923–present)
Env.L.Rev.	Environmental Law Review			
Env.L.Rptr.	Environmental Law Reporter		Ex.D.	Law Reports Exchequer Division (Eng.) (To 1880)
Env.Pol'y & L.	Environmental Policy and Law			
Env.Rptr.	Environment Reporter (B.N.A.)		Ex.Div.	Same
			Examiner	Examiner (New York) Examiner (Quebec)
Eq.Cas.Abr.	Equity Cases Abridged (Eng.)		Excerpta Crim.	Excerpta Criminologica
Eq.Rep.	Harper's Equity (S.C.)		Exch.	Exchequer (Welsby, Hurlstone & Gordon) (Eng.)
Equity Rep.	Equity Reports (Gilbert) (Eng.)			Exchequer (Sc.)
	Harper's Equity (S.C.) English Chancery Appeals		Exch.Can.	Exchequer Reports (Can.)
Err. & App.	Error & Appeals (Upper Can.)		Exch.Cas.	Exchequer Cases (Sc.)
Ersk.	Erskine (U.S.C.C. in 35 Ga.)		Exch.Rep.	Exchequer Reports
			Exec.Order	Executive Order
Esp.	Espinasse's Nisi Prius (Eng.)		Eyre	Eyre's King's Bench (Eng.)

F

F.	Federal Reporter (U.S.)		F.C.	Faculty Collection of Decisions (Sc.)
F.2d	Same, Second Series			
F. & F.	Foster & Finlanson Nisi Prius (Eng.)		F.C.A.	Federal Code Annotated
F.A.D.	Federal Anti-Trust Decisions		F.C.C.	Federal Communication Commission Reports
F.B.C.	Fonblanque's Bankruptcy Cases (Eng.)		F.Carr.Cas.	Federal Carriers Cases (CCH)
FBILEB	F.B.I. Law Enforcement Bull.		F. (Ct.Sess.)	Fraser's Court of Sessions Cases (Sc.)

F.D.Cosm.L. Rep.	Food, Drug, Cosmetic Law Reporter (CCH)	Ferg.Cons.	Fergusson's Consistory (Divorce) (Sc.)
F.E.P.Cas.	Fair Employment Practice Cases	Fergusson	Fergusson (of Kilkeran) (Sc.)
F.H.L.	Fraser, House of Lords (Sc.)	Fin.Tax. & Comp.L.	Finance Taxation and Company Law (Pakistan)
F.L.J.	Forum Law Journal (U. of Baltimore)	Finch	Finch's Chancery (Eng.)
F.L.P.	Florida Law and Practice	Fire &	Fire and Casualty Cases
F.M.C.	Federal Maritime Commission Reports	Casualty Cas.	(CCH)
F.O.I.Dig.	F.O.I. Digest	Fish.Pat.Cas.	Fisher's Patent Cases (U.S.)
F.O.I.C.R.	Freedom of Information Center Reports	Fish.Pat.R.	Fisher's Patent Reports (U.S.)
F.P.C.	Federal Power Commission Decisions	Fish.Prize Cas.	Fisher's Prize Cases (U.S.)
FR	Federal Register		
F.R.D.	Federal Rules Decisions	Fitzh.	Fitzherbert's Abridgment (Eng.)
F.Supp.	Federal Supplement		
F.T.C.	Federal Trade Commission Decisions	Fitzh.N.Br.	Fitzherbert's Natura Brevium (Eng.)
Fac.L.Rev.	Faculty of Law Review (Toronto)	Fla.	Florida
Fairf.	Fairfield (Me.)	Fla. & K.	Flanagan & Kelly, Rolls (Ir.)
Falc.	Falconer's Court of Sessions Cases (Sc.)	Fla.B.J.	Florida Bar Journal
Falc. & F.	Falconer & Fitzherbert's Election Cases (Eng.)	Fla.Jur.	Florida Jurisprudence
Family L. Commtr.	Family Law Commentator	Fla.L.J.	Florida Law Journal
Family L. Newsl.	Family Law Newsletter	Fla.St.U.L. Rev.	Florida State University Law Review
Family L.Q.	Family Law Quarterly	Fla.Supp.	Florida Supplement
Family L.Rep.	Family Law Reporter (BNA)	Flan. & Kel.	Flanagan & Kelly, Rolls (Ir.)
Far.	Farresley's King's Bench (Eng.)	Flipp.	Flippin (U.S.)
		Fogg	Fogg (N.H.)
Far East. L.Rev.	Far Eastern Law Review	Fonbl.	Fonblanque's Bankruptcy (Eng.)
Fed.	Federal Reporter (U.S.)		
Fed.B.A.J.	Federal Bar Association Journal	Food Drug Cosm.L.J.	Food, Drug, Cosmetic Law Journal
Fed.B.J.	Federal Bar Journal	For.Sci.	Forensic Science
Fed.B.News	Federal Bar News	For.Tax Bull.	Foreign Tax Law Bi-Weekly Bulletin
Fed.Carr.Rep.	Federal Carriers Reporter (CCH)	Ford.L.Rev.	Fordham Law Review
Fed.Cas.	Federal Cases (U.S.)		
Fed.Comm.B.J.	Federal Communications Bar Journal	Ford.Urban L.J.	Fordham Urban Law Journal
Fed.Est. & Gift Tax Rep.	Federal Estate and Gift Tax Reporter (CCH)	Fordham L.Rev.	Fordham Law Review
Fed.Juror	Federal Juror	Form.	Forman (Ill.)
Fed.L.Rep.	Federal Law Reports	Forr.	Forrest's Exchequer (Eng.)
Fed.L.Rev.	Federal Law Review	Forrester	Forrester's Chancery Cases temp. Talbot (Eng.)
Fed.Prob.	Federal Probation		
Fed.Reg.	Federal Register		
Fed.Rules Serv.	Federal Rules Service	Fort.L.J.	Fortnightly Law Journal
Fed.Rules Serv.2d	Same, Second Series	Fortesc.	Fortescue's King's Bench (Eng.)
Fed'n Ins. Counsel Q.	Federation of Insurance Counsel Quarterly	Forum	The Forum

Fost.	Foster's Crown Cases (Eng.)
	Foster (Hawaii)
	Foster's Legal Chronicle Reports (Pa.)
	Foster (N.H.)
Found.L.Rev.	Foundation Law Review
Fount.Dec.	Fountainhall's Decisions (Sc.)
Fox	Fox's Registration Cases (Eng.)
	Fox's Decisions (Me.)
Fox & S.	Fox & Smith's King's Bench (Ir.)

Fox Pat.C.	Fox's Patent, Trade Mark, Design and Copyright Cases
Fran.Coll.L.J.	Franciso College Law Journal
France	France (Colo.)
Fraser	Fraser, Court of Session Cases (Sc.)
Freem.	Freeman (Ill.)
Freem.Ch.	Freeman's Chancery (Miss.)
Freem.K.B.	Freeman's King's Bench (Eng.)
French	French (N.H.)
Fuller	Fuller (Mich.)

G

G. & D.	Gale & Davison's Queen's Bench (Eng.)
G. & G.	Goldsmith & Guthrie (Mo.)
G. & J.	Gill & Johnson (Md.)
	Glyn & Jameson's Bankruptcy (Eng.)
G. & R.	Geldert & Russell (N.S.)
GA	Decisions of General Appraisers (U.S.)
G.C.M.	General Counsel's Memorandum (I.R.Bull.)
G.Coop.	G. Cooper's Chancery (Eng.)
G.S.R.	Gongwer's State Reports (Ohio)
Ga.	Georgia
Ga.App.	Georgia Appeals
Ga.B.J.	Georgia Bar Journal
Ga.Bus.Law.	Georgia Business Lawyer
Ga.Dec.	Georgia Decisions
Ga.J.Int'l & Comp.L.	Georgia Journal of International & Comparative Law
Ga.L.J.	Georgia Law Journal
Ga.L.Rep.	Georgia Law Reports
Ga.L.Rev.	Georgia Law Review
Ga.St.B.J.	Georgia State Bar Journal
Ga.Supp.	Georgia Supplement (Lester)
Galb.	Galbraith (Fla.)
Galb. & M.	Galbraith & Meek (Fla.)
Gale	Gale's Exchequer (Eng.)
Gale & D.	Gale & Davison's Queen's Bench (Eng.)
Gale & Dav.	Same
Gall.	Gallison (U.S. Circuit Court)

Gard.N.Y. Reptr.	Gardenier's New York Reporter
Garden.	Gardenhire (Mo.)
Gaz.	Weekly Law Gazette (U.S.)
	Gazette
Gaz.Bankr.	Gazette of Bankruptcy
Gaz.L.R.	Gazette Law Reports
Geld. & M.	Geldart & Maddock's Chancery (Eng.)
Geld. & O.	Geldert & Oxley (N.S.)
Geo.L.J.	Georgetown Law Journal
Geo.Wash.L. Rev.	George Washington Law Review
George	George (Miss.)
Gibb.Surr.	Gibbon's Surrogate (N.Y.)
Gibbs	Gibbs (Mich.)
Giff.	Giffard's Chancery (Eng.)
Giff. & H.	Giffard & Hemming's Chancery (Eng.)
Gil.	Gilman (Ill.)
Gilb.	Gilbert's Chancery (Eng.)
Gilb.C.P.	Gilbert's Common Pleas (Eng.)
Gilb.Cas.	Gilbert's Cases, Law & Equity (Eng.)
Gilb.Exch.	Gilbert's Exchequer (Eng.)
Gildr.	Gildersleeve (N.Mex.)
Gilf.	Gilfillan (Minn.)
Gill	Gill (Md.)
Gill & J.	Gill & Johnson (Md.)
Gill & Johns.	Same
Gilm.	Gilmer (Va.)
Gilm. & Falc.	Gilmour & Falconer (Sc.)
Gilp.	Gilpin (U.S.)
Gl. & J.	Glyn & Jameson's Bankruptcy Cases (Eng.)

Glanv.	Glanville De Legibus et Consuetudinibus Angliae (Eng.)	Grant	Grant's Cases (Pa.)
Glanv.El.Cas.	Glanville's Election Cases (Eng.)	Grant Err. & App.	Grant's Error & Appeal (Upper Can.)
Glasc.	Glascock (Ir.)	Gratt.	Grattan (Va.)
Glendale L. Rev.	Glendale Law Review	Gray	Gray (Mass.) Gray (N.C.)
Glenn	Glenn (Louisiana Annual)	Graya	Graya
Glyn & J.	Glyn & Jameson's Bankruptcy Cases (Eng.)	Green	Green Equity (N.J.) Green Law (N.J.) Green (Okla.) Green (R.I.)
Glyn & Jam.	Same	Green Bag	Green Bag
Godb.	Godbolt's King's Bench (Eng.)	Green Cr.	Green's Criminal Law (Eng.)
Goebel	Goebel's Probate (Ohio)	Greene	Greene (Iowa)
Gold. & G.	Goldsmith & Guthrie (Mo.)		Greene's Annotated Cases (N.Y.)
Golden Gate L.Rev.	Golden Gate Law Review	Greenl.	Greenleaf (Me.)
Golden Gate U.L.Rev.	Golden Gate University Law Review	Greenl.Ov.Cas.	Greenleaf's Overruled Cases
Gonzaga L.Rev.	Gonzaga Law Review	Grein.Pr.	Greiner Louisiana Practice
		Griffith	Griffith (Ind.)
Gottschall	Gottschall (Ohio)	Gris.	Griswold (Ohio)
Gouldsb.	Gouldsborough's King's Bench (Eng.)	Griswold	Same
		Group Legal Rev.	Group Legal Review
Gov't Cont. Rep.	Government Contracts Reporter (CCH)	Guild Notes	Guild Notes
Gow	Gow's Nisi Prius (Eng.)	Guild Prac.	Guild Practitioner
Gr.	Grant, Upper Canada Chancery Reports	Guthrie	Guthrie (Mo.)
Granger	Granger (Ohio)	Gwill.T.Cas.	Gwillim's Tithe Cases (Eng.)

H

H.	Handy (Ohio)	H. & N.	Hurlstone & Norman's Exchequer (Eng.)
H. & B.	Hudson & Brooke's King's Bench (Ir.)	H. & R.	Harrison & Rutherford's Common Pleas (Eng.)
H. & C.	Hurlstone & Coltman's Exchequer (Eng.)	H. & S.	Harris & Simrall (Miss.)
H. & D.	Hill & Denio, Lalor's Supplement (N.Y.)	H. & T.	Hall & Twell's Chancery (Eng.)
H. & G.	Harris & Gill (Md.) Hurlstone & Gordon's Exchequer (Eng.)	H. & W.	Harrison & Wollaston's King's Bench (Eng.) Hurlstone & Walmsley's Exchequer (Eng.)
H. & H.	Harrison & Hodgin's Municipal Reports (Upper Can.) Horn & Hurlstone's Exchequer (Eng.)	H.Bl.	Henry Blackstone's Common Pleas (Eng.)
H. & J.	Harris & Johnson (Md.) Hayes & Jones' Exchequer (Ir.)	H.C.L.M.	Health Care Labor Manual
		H.L.Cas.	House of Lords Cases (Eng.)
H. & J.Ir.	Same	H.L.N.R.	Health Lawyers News Report
H. & M.	Hening & Munford (Va.) Hemming & Miller's Vice-Chancery (Eng.)	H.W.Gr.	H. W. Green's Equity (N.J.)
H. & M.Ch.	Hemming & Miller's Vice-Chancery (Eng.)	Ha.	Hare's Vice-Chancery (Eng.)
		Ha. & Tw.	Hall & Twell's Chancery (Eng.)
H. & McH.	Harris & McHenry (Md.)	Had.	Hadley (N.H.)

Hadd.	Haddington MSS Reports (Sc.)
Hadl.	Hadley (N.H.)
Hagan	Hagan (Utah)
Hagans	Hagans (W.Va.)
Hagg.Adm.	Haggard's Admiralty (Eng.)
Hagn. & M.	Hagner & Miller (Md.)
Hailes Dec.	Haile's Decisions (Sc.)
Hale	Hale (Cal.)
	Hale's Common Law (Eng.)
Hale P.C.	Hale's Pleas of the Crown (Eng.)
Hall	Hall (N.H.)
	Hall's Superior Court (N.Y.)
Hall & Tw.	Hall & Twell's Chancery (Eng.)
Hall.	Hallett (Colo.)
Halst.	Halsted's Equity (N.J.)
	Halsted's Law (N.J.)
Ham.	Hammond (Ga.)
	Hammond (Ohio)
Ham. & J.	Hammond & Jackson (Ga.)
Ham.A. & O.	Hamerton, Allen & Otter, New Session Cases (Eng.)
Hamlin	Hamlin (Me.)
Hammond	Hammond (Ohio)
Han.	Handy (Ohio)
Han.N.B.	Hannay's Reports (New Brunswick)
Hand	Hand (N.Y.)
Handy	Handy (Ohio)
Hans.	Hansbrough (Va.)
Har.	Harrington (Del.)
	Harrington's Chancery (Mich.)
	Harrison (La.)
	Harrison's Chancery (Mich.)
Harc.	Harcarse, Decisions (Sc.)
Hard.	Hardesty Term Reports (Del.)
Hardes.	Same
Hardin	Hardin (Ky.)
Hardres	Hardres' Exchequer (Eng.)
Hare	Hare's Vice-Chancery (Eng.)
Hare & W.	American Leading Cases, Hare & Wallace
Harg.	Hargrove (N.C.)
Harp.	Harper's Equity (S.C.)
	Harper's Law (S.C.)
Harper	Harper's Conspiracy Cases (Md.)
Harr.	Harrington

Harr.	Harrison (Ind.)
	Harrison (N.J.)
Harr. & H.	Harrison & Hodgins' Municipal Reports (Upper Can.)
Harr. & Hodg.	Same
Harr. & J.	Harris & Johnson (Md.)
Harr. & M.	Harris & McHenry (Md.)
Harr. & R.	Harrison & Rutherford's Common Pleas (Eng.)
Harr. & W.	Harrison & Wollaston's King's Bench (Eng.)
Harr.Ch.	Harrison's Chancery (Eng.)
Harris	Harris (Pa.)
Harris & G.	Harris & Gill (Md.)
Harris & S.	Harris & Simrall (Miss.)
Hart.	Hartley (Tex.)
Hart. & H.	Hartley & Hartley (Tex.)
Harv.Bus.Rev.	Harvard Business Review
Harv.Civ. Rights–Civ. Lib.L.Rev.	Harvard Civil Rights– Civil Liberties Law Review
Harv.Int'l L.J.	Harvard International Law Journal
Harv.J.Legis.	Harvard Journal on Legislation
Harv.L.Rev.	Harvard Law Review
Harv.L.S.Bull.	Harvard Law School Bulletin
Harv.W.Tax Ser.	Harvard World Tax Series (CCH)
Hasb.	Hasbrouck (Idaho)
Hask.	Haskell (U.S. Mine) (Fox's Decisions)
Hast.	Hastings (Me.)
Hastings Const.L.Q.	Hastings Constitutional Law Quarterly
Hastings L.J.	Hastings Law Journal
Havil.	Haviland (Prince Edward Island)
Hawaii	Hawaii Reports
Hawaii B.J.	Hawaii Bar Journal
Hawk.	Hawkins' Louisiana Annual
Hawk.P.C.	Hawkins' Pleas of the Crown
Hawks	Hawks (N.C.)
Hawl.	Hawley (Nev.)
Hay & H.	Hay & Hazelton (U.S.)
Hay & M.	Hay & Marriott's Admiralty (Eng.)
Hay.	Haywood
Hayes	Hayes' Exchequer (Ir.)
	Hayes (Sc.)
Hayes & J.	Hayes & Jones' Exchequer (Ir.)
Hayw.	Haywood (N.C.)
	Haywood (Tenn.)

Haz.Reg.	Hazard's Register (Pa.)	Home	Home MSS. Decisions, Court of Sessions (Sc.)
Head	Head (Tenn.)		
Heath	Heath (Me.)	Hong Kong L.J.	Hong Kong Law Journal
Hedges	Hedges (Mont.)		
Heisk.	Heiskell (Tenn.)	Hook.	Hooker (Conn.)
Helm	Helm (Nev.)	Hope Dec.	Hope's Decisions (Sc.)
Hem. & M.	Heming & Miller's Vice-Chancery (Eng.)	Hopk.	Hopkins' Chancery (N.Y.)
		Hopk.Dec.	Hopkinson's Admiralty Decisions (Pa.)
Heming.	Hemingway (Miss.)	Hopw. & C.	Hopwood & Coltman's Registration Appeal Cases (Eng.)
Hemp.	Hempstead's Circuit Court Reports		
Hempst.	Hempstead (U.S.)	Hopw. & P.	Hopwood & Philbrick's Registration Appeal Cases (Eng.)
Hen. & M.	Hening & Munford (Va.)		
Henn.Law.	Hennepin Lawyer	Horner	Horner (S.D.)
Hepb.	Hepburn (Colo.)	Horw.Y.B.	(Horwood) Year Book of Edward I
Het.	Hetley's Common Pleas (Eng.)		
Hibb.	Hibbard (N.H.)	Hosea	Hosea (Ohio)
Hight	Hight (Iowa)	Hoskins	Hoskins (N.D.)
Hil.T.	Hilary Term (Eng.)	Houghton	Houghton (Ala.)
Hill	Hill (Ill.)	Housing & Devel.Rep.	Housing and Development Reporter (BNA)
	Hill (N.Y.)	Houst.	Houston (Del.)
	Hill's Equity (S.C.)	Houst.Cr.	Houston Criminal Cases (Del.)
	Hill's Law (S.C.)		
Hill & D.	Hill & Denio (N.Y.)	Houst.L.Rev.	Houston Law Review
Hillyer	Hillyer (Cal.)	Houston Law.	Houston Lawyer
Hilt.	Hilton (N.Y.)	Hov.	Hovenden's Supplement, Vesey's Chancery (Eng.)
Hines	Hines (Ky.)		
Hitotsubashi J.L. & Pol.	Hitotsubashi Journal of Law and Politics	How.	Howard (Miss.)
Hob.	Hobart's Common Pleas & Chancery (Eng.)		Howard (U.S. Supreme Court)
Hobart	Hobart's King's Bench (Eng.)		Howell (Nev.)
		How. & Beat.	Howell & Beatty (Nev.)
Hod.	Hodges' Common Pleas (Eng.)	How. & N.	Howell & Norcross (Nev.)
		How.A.Cas.	Howard's Appeal Cases (N.Y.)
Hodg.El.	Hodgin's Election (Upper Can.)		
		How.Ch.	Howard's Chancery (Ir.)
Hodges	Hodges' Common Pleas (Eng.)	How.L.J.	Howard Law Journal
		How.N.P.	Howell's Nisi Prius (Mich.)
Hoffm.	Hoffman's Chancery (N.Y.)		
	Hoffman's Land Cases (U.S.)	How.Pr.	Howard's Practice (N.Y.)
		How.Pr. (N.S.)	Same, New Series
Hofstra L. Rev.	Hofstra Law Review	How.St.Tr.	Howell's State Trials (Eng.)
Hog.	Hogan's Rolls Court (Ir.)		
Hogue	Hogue (Fla.)	Howard L.J.	Howard Law Journal
Holl.	Hollingshead (Minn.)	Hubb.	Hubbard (Me.)
Holmes	Holmes (Ore.)	Hud. & B.	Hudson & Brooke's King's Bench (Ir.)
	Holmes (U.S.)		
Holt Adm.	Holt's Admiralty Cases (Eng.)	Hughes	Hughes (Ky.)
			Hughes (U.S.)
Holt Eq.	Holt's Equity Vice-Chancery (Eng.)	Human Rights	Human Rights
		Human Rights J.	Human Rights Journal
Holt K.B.	Holt's King's Bench (Eng.)		
Holt N.P.	Holt's Nisi Prius (Eng.)	Human Rights U.S.S.R.	Human Rights in U.S.S.R.

Hume	Hume's Decisions (Sc.)	Hurl. & G.	Hurlstone & Gordon's Exchequer (Eng.)
Humph.	Humphrey		
Humphr.	Humphrey's (Tenn.)	Hurl. & W.	Hurlstone & Walmsley's Exchequer (Eng.)
Hun	Hun (N.Y.)	Hutch.	Hutcheson (Ala.)
Hung.L.Rev.	Hungarian Law Review	Hutt.	Hutton's Common Pleas (Eng.)
Hunt.Torrens	Hunter's Torrens Cases		

I

I. & N.Dec.	Immigration and Nationality Decisions	Ill.Cir.	Illinois Circuit Court
ICC	Interstate Commerce Commission	Ill.Cont.L.Ed.	Illinois Continuing Legal Education
I.C.C.Pract.J.	Interstate Commerce Commission Practitioners' Journal	Ill.Cont. Legal Ed.	Same
		Ill.Ct.Cl.	Illinois Court of Claims Reports
I.C.J.	International Court of Justice Reports	Ill.L.B.	Illinois Law Bulletin
I.C.J.Y.B.	Yearbook of the International Court of Justice	Ill.L.Q.	Illinois Law Quarterly
		Ill.L.Rev.	Illinois Law Review
I.D.	Interior Department Decisions, Public Land (Since v. 53)	Immig.B.Bull.	Immigration Bar Bulletin
		Ind.	Indiana
IIC	International Review of Industrial Property and Copyright Law	Ind. & Intell. Prop.Austl.	Industrial and Intellectual Property in Australia
		Ind. & Lab. Rel.Rev.	Industrial and Labor Relations Review
I.L.C.Newsl.	International Legal Center Newsletter	Ind.Advocate	Indian Advocate
I.L.E.	Indiana Law Encyclopedia	Ind.App.	Indiana Appellate Court Reports
I.L.P.	Illinois Law and Practice	Ind.Cl.Comm.	Indian Claims Commission Decisions
I.L.R.	Insurance Law Reporter (Can.)	Ind.J. Int'l L.	Indian Journal of International Law
	International Law Reports	Ind.L.J.	Indiana Law Journal
		Ind.L.Q.Rev.	Indian Law Quarterly Review
I.L.W.	Investment Laws of the World (Oceana)	Ind.L.Rev.	Indiana Law Review Indian Law Review
I.O.C.C.Bull.	Interstate Oil Compact Commission Bulletin	Ind.L.Stud.	Indiana Law Student
		Ind.Legal F.	Indiana Legal Forum
I.R.	Internal Revenue Decisions	Ind.Prop.	Industrial Property
		Ind.Prop.Q.	Industrial Property Quarterly
I.R.B.	Internal Revenue Bulletin	Ind.Rel.J. Econ. & Soc.	Industrial Relations: Journal of Economy and Society
I.R.C.	Internal Revenue Code		
I.R.R.Newsl.	Individual Rights and Responsibilities Newsletter	Ind.S.C.	Indiana Superior Court
ISL L.Rev.	ISL Law Review	Ind.Y.B.Int'l Aff.	Indian Yearbook of International Affairs
IT	Internal Revenue Bulletin	India Crim. L.J.R.	India Criminal Law Journal Reports
I.T.R.	Irish Term Reports (Ridgeway)	India S.Ct.	India Supreme Court Reports
Idaho	Idaho Reports	Indian Cas.	Indian Cases
Idaho L.J.	Idaho Law Journal	Indian Jurist	Indian Jurist
Idaho L.Rev.	Idaho Law Review	Indian L.J.	Indian Law Journal
Idd.T.R.	Idding's Term Reports (Dayton, Ohio)	Indian L.R. [e.g.] Allahabad Ser.	Indian Law Reports [e.g.] Allahabad Series
Idding	Same		
Iddings T.R. D.	Same	Indian Rul.	Indian Rulings
Idea	Idea	Indian Terr.	Indian Territory Reports
Ill.	Illinois Reports	Indus.L.J.	Industrial Law Journal
Ill.2d	Same, Second Series	Indus.L.Rev.	Industrial Law Review
Ill.App.	Illinois Appellate Court	Inequal.Ed.	Inequality in Education
Ill.App.2d	Same, Second Series		
Ill.App.3d	Same, Third Series		
Ill.B.J.	Illinois Bar Journal		

Ins.Counsel J.	Insurance Counsel Journal	Int'l Jurid. Ass'n Bull.	International Juridical Association Monthly Bulletin
Ins.L.J.	Insurance Law Journal (Pa.)	Int'l L.Doc.	International Law Documents
Ins.L.Rep.	Insurance Law Reporter (CCH)	Int'l L.News	International Law News
Inst.Ad.Legal Stud.Ann.	Institute of Advanced Legal Studies Annual	Int'l L.Persp.	International Law Perspective
Inst.Est.Plan.	Institute on Estate Planning (U. of Miami)	Int'l L.Q.	International Law Quarterly
Inst.Lab.Rel. Bull.	Institute for Labor Relations Bulletin	Int'l L.Stud.	International Law Studies
Inst.Min.L.	Institute on Mineral Law (La.S.U.)	Int'l Lab.Rev.	International Labour Review
Inst.Plan. & Zoning	Institute on Planning and Zoning	Int'l Law.	The International Lawyer
Inst.Plan., Zoning & E.D.	Institute on Planning, Zoning and Eminent Domain	Int'l Legal Ed.Newsl.	International Legal Education Newsletter
		Int'l Legal Materials	International Legal Materials
Inst.Sec.Reg.	Institute on Securities Regulation (PLI)	Int'l Rev.Ad. Sci.	International Review of Administrative Sciences
Int.Arb.J.	International Arbitration Journal	Int'l Rev.Crim. Policy	International Review of Criminal Policy
Int.Jurid. Assn.Bull.	International Juridical Association Bulletin	Int'l Soc'y of Barr.Q.	International Society of Barristers Quarterly
Int.Rev.Bull.	Internal Revenue Bulletin	Int'l Survey L.D.L.L.	International Survey of Legal Decisions on Labour Laws
Int.Rev. Code	Internal Revenue Code		
Int.Rev.Code of 1954	Internal Revenue Code of 1954	Int'l Sym. Comp.L.	International Symposium on Comparative Law
Int.Rev.Rec.	Internal Revenue Record	Int'l Tax J.	International Tax Journal
Inter Alia	Inter Alia	Int'l Trade L.J.	International Trade Law Journal
Inter-Am.L. Rev.	Inter-American Law Review	Int'l Woman Law.	International Woman Lawyer
Interior Dec.	United States Interior Department Decisions	Intramural L.J.	Intramural Law Journal
Int'l & Comp. L.Bull.	International and Comparative Law Bulletin	Intramural L.Rev.	Intramural Law Review
Int'l & Comp. L.Q.	International and Comparative Law Quarterly	Iowa	Iowa Reports
Int'l Aff.	International Affairs	Iowa L.B.	Iowa Law Bulletin
Int'l Arb. Awards	Reports of International Arbitral Awards	Iowa L.Rev.	Iowa Law Review
		Ir.	Law Reports (Ir.)
Int'l Arb.J.	International Arbitration Journal	Ir.C.L.	Irish Common Law
Int'l B.J.	International Bar Journal	Ir.Ch.	Irish Chancery
Int'l Bus. Lawyer	International Business Lawyer	Ir.Cir.	Irish Circuit Reports
Int'l Bus.Ser.	International Business Series (Ernst & Ernst)	Ir.Eccl.	Irish Ecclesiastical Reports
Int'l Concil.	International Conciliation	Ir.Eq.	Irish Equity
Int'l Crim. Pol.Rev.	International Criminal Police Review	Ir.Jur.	Irish Jurist
Int'l Dig. Health Leg.	International Digest of Health Legislation	Ir.L. & Eq.	Irish Law & Equity
		Ir.L.T.R.	Irish Law Times Reports
Int'l Encycl. Comp.L.	International Encyclopedia of Comparative Law	Ir.R.	Irish Reports
Int'l J.	International Journal	Ir.R.C.L.	Irish Reports Common Law
Int'l J.Crim. & Pen.	International Journal of Criminology and Penology	Ir.R.Eq.	Irish Reports Equity
		Ired.	Iredell's Law (N.C.)
Int'l J.L.Lib.	International Journal of Law Libraries	Ired.Eq.	Iredell's Equity (N.C.)
		Irv.Just.	Irvine's Justiciary (Sc.)
Int'l J.Legal Res.	International Journal of Legal Research	Israel L.Rev.	Israel Law Review
Int'l J.Off. Ther. & Comp.Crim.	International Journal of Offender Therapy and Comparative Criminology	Israel Y.B. Human Rights	Israel Yearbook on Human Rights
Int'l J.Pol.	International Journal of Politics	Issues Crim.	Issues in Criminology
		Iustitia	Iustitia

J

J. & C.	Jones & Cary's Exchequer (Ir.)	J.Comp.Leg. & Int'l L.3d	Journal of Comparative Legislation and International Law, Third Series
J. & H.	Johnson & Hemming's Chancery (Eng.)	J.Confl.Res.	Journal of Conflict Resolution
J. & L.	Jones & La Touche's Chancery (Ir.)	J.Cons.Affairs	Journal of Consumer Affairs
J. & La T.	Same	J.Const. & Parl.Stud.	Journal of Constitutional and Parliamentary Studies
J. & S.	Jones & Spencer's Superior Court (N.Y.)	J.Contemp.L.	Journal of Contemporary Law
J. & W.	Jacob & Walker's Chancery (Eng.)	J.Contemp. R.D.L.	Journal of Contemporary Roman-Dutch Law
JAG Bull.	JAG Bulletin (USAF)	J.Corp.L.	Journal of Corporation Law
JAG J.	JAG Journal		
JAG L.Rev.	United States Air Force JAG Law Review	J.Corp.Tax.	Journal of Corporate Taxation
J.A.M.A.	Journal of the American Medical Association	J.Crim.Just.	Journal of Criminal Justice
J.Accountancy	Journal of Accountancy	J.Crim.L. (Eng.)	Journal of Criminal Law (Eng.)
J.Afr.L.	Journal of African Law	J.Crim.L. (U.S.)	Journal of Criminal Law and Criminology (U.S.)
J.Air L. & Com.	Journal of Air Law and Commerce	J.Crim.L. & Criminology	Journal of Criminal Law and Criminology
J.Am.Jud. Soc'y	Journal of the American Judicature Society	J.Crim.L., C. & P.S.	Journal of Criminal Law, Criminology and Police Science
J.Am.Soc'y C.L.U.	Journal of the American Society of Chartered Life Underwriters	J.Crim.Sci.	Journal of Criminal Science
J.Ass'n L. Teachers	Journal of the Association of Law Teachers	J.D.	Juris Doctor
		J.Denning L.Soc'y	Journal of the Denning Law Society
J.B.Ass'n D.C.	Journal Bar Association of the District of Columbia	J.Energy & Devel.	Journal of Energy and Development
J.B.Ass'n St.Kan.	Journal of the Bar Association of the State of Kansas	J.Eth.L.	Journal of Ethiopian Law
		J.Fam.L.	Journal of Family Law
J.B.Moore	J. B. Moore's Common Pleas (Eng.)	J.For.Med.	Journal of Forensic Medicine
J.Beverly Hills B.Ass'n	Journal of the Beverly Hills Bar Association	J.For.Sci.	Journal of Forensic Sciences
J.Bridg.	Sir John Bridgman's Common Pleas (Eng.)	J.For.Sci. Soc'y	Journal of the Forensic Science Society
		J.Ind.L.Inst.	Journal of the Indian Law Institute
J.Bridgm.	Same	J.Int'l Aff.	Journal of International Affairs
J.Bus.L.	Journal of Business Law		
J.C.	Johnson's Cases (N.Y.)	J.Int'l Comm.Jur.	Journal of the International Commission of Jurists
J.C.N.P.S.	Journal of Collective Negotiations in the Public Sector	J.Int'l L. & Dipl.	Journal of International Law and Diplomacy
J.C.R.	Johnson's Chancery (N.Y.)	J.Int'l L. & Econ.	Journal of International Law and Economics
J.Can.B.Ass'n	Journal of the Canadian Bar Association	J.Int'l L. & Pol.	Journal of International Law and Politics
	Johnson's Chancery (N.Y.)	J.Islam. & Comp.L.	Journal of Islamic and Comparative Law
J.Ceylon L.	Journal of Ceylon Law	J.J.Mar.	J. J. Marshall (Ky.)
J.Ch.	Johnson's Chancery (N.Y.)	J.J.Marsh. (Ky.)	Same
J.Church & St.	Journal of Church and State		
J.Coll. & U.L.	Journal of College and University Law	J.Juris.	Journal of Jurisprudence
J.Comm.Mkt. Stud.	Journal of Common Market Studies	J.Kan.B.Ass'n	Journal of the Kansas Bar Association

J.L.	Journal of Law
J.L. & Ed.	Journal of Law and Education
J.L. & Pol.	Journal of Law and Politics
J.L.Soc'y	Journal of the Law Society of Scotland
J.Land & P.U.Econ.	Journal of Land and Public Utility Economics
J.Law & Econ.	Journal of Law and Economics
J.Law & Econ,Dev.	Journal of Law and Economic Development
J.Law Reform	Journal of Law Reform
J.Legal Ed.	Journal of Legal Education
J.Legal Educ.	Journal of Legal Education
J.Legal Med.	Journal of Legal Medicine
J.Legal Studies	Journal of Legal Studies
J.Mar.Law & Com.	Journal of Maritime Law and Commerce
J.Mo.Bar	Journal of the Missouri Bar
J.P.	Justice of the Peace (Eng.)
J.P.Sm.	J. P. Smith's King's Bench (Eng.)
J.Pat.Off. Soc'y	Journal of the Patent Office Society
J.Plan. & Env.L.	Journal of Planning and Environment Law
J.Pol.Sci. & Admin.	Journal of Police Science and Administration
J.Psych. & L.	Journal of Psychiatry and Law
J.Pub.L.	Journal of Public Law
J.R.	Johnson (N.Y.)
J.Radio L.	Journal of Radio Law
J.Real Est. Tax.	Journal of Real Estate Taxation
J.Reprints Antitrust L. & Econ.	Journal of Reprints for Antitrust Law and Economics
J.S.Gr.(N.J.)	J. S. Green (N.J.)
J.Soc'y Comp. Leg.	Journal of the Society of Comparative Legislation
J.Space L.	Journal of Space Law
Jac.	Jacob's Chancery (Eng.)
Jac. & W.	Jacob & Walker's Chancery (Eng.)
Jac. & Walk.	Same
Jac.L.Dict.	Jacob's Law Dictionary
Jack.	Jackson (Ga.)
Jack. & L.	Jackson & Lumpkin (Ga.)
Jack.Tex.App.	Jackson's Texas Appeals
James	James' Reports (Nova Scotia)
James. & Mont.	Jameson & Montagu's Bankruptcy (Eng.)

Jap.Ann.Int'l L.	Japanese Annual of International Law
Japan Ann.L. & Pol.	Japan Annual of Law and Politics
Jebb	Jebb's Crown Cases (Ir.)
Jebb & B.	Jebb & Bourke's Queen's Bench (Ir.)
Jebb & S.	Jebb & Symes' Queen's Bench (Ir.)
Jebb & Sym.	Same
Jebb C.C.	Jebb's Crown Cases (Ir.)
Jeff.	Jefferson (Va.)
Jenk.	Jenkins' Exchequer (Eng.)
Jenk.Cent.	Same
Jenks	Jenks' (N.H.)
Jenn.	Jennison (Mich.)
Jew.Y.B. Int'l L.	Jewish Yearbook of International Law
Jo. & La T.	Jones & La Touche's Chancery (Ir.)
John.	Johnson (N.Y.)
	Johnson's Vice-Chancery (Eng.)
John Mar.J. Prac. & Proc.	John Marshall Journal of Practice and Procedure
John Marsh. L.J.	John Marshall Law Journal
John Marsh. L.Q.	John Marshall Law Quarterly
Johns.	Johnson (N.Y.)
	Johnson's Vice-Chancery (Eng.)
Johns. & H.	Johnson & Hemming's Chancery (Eng.)
Johns. & Hem.	Same
Johns.Cas.	Johnson's Cases (N.Y.)
Johns.Ch.	Johnson's Chancery Decisions (Md.)
	Johnson's Chancery (N.Y.)
Johns.Ct.Err.	Johnson's Court of Errors (N.Y.)
Johns.Dec.	Johnson's Chancery Decisions (Md.)
Johns.N.Z.	Johnson's New Zealand Reports
Johns.U.S.	Johnson's U. S. Circuit Court Decisions
Jon. & L.	Jones & La Touche's Chancery (Ir.)
Jon. & La T.	Same
Jones	Jones (Ala.) (Mo.) (Pa.)
	Jones' Exchequer (Ir.)
	Jones' Law or Equity
	Jones, T., King's Bench (Eng.)
	Jones' Reports (Upper Can.)
	Jones, W., King's Bench (Eng.)

Jones & C.	Jones & Cary's Exchequer (Ir.)
Jones & L.	Jones & La Touche's Chancery (Ir.)
Jones & La T.	Same
Jones & McM. (Pa.)	Jones & McMurtrie (Pa.)
Jones & S.	Jones & Spencer's Superior Court (N.Y.)
Jones & Spen.	Same
Jones, B. & W. (Mo.)	Jones, Barclay & Whittelsey (Mo.)
Josephs	Josephs (Mo.)
Jud.Rep.	Judicial Repository (N.Y.)
Jud.Repos.	Same
Judd	Judd (Hawaii)
Judge Advoc. J.	The Judge Advocate Journal

Judges' J.	Judges' Journal
Judge's J.	Judge's Journal
Judicature	Journal of the American Judicature Society
	Judicature
Jur.	Jurist (Eng.)
Jur. (N.S.)	Jurist, New Series
Jurid.Rev.	Juridical Review
Jurimetrics J.	Jurimetrics Journal
Juris.	Jurisprudence
Jurist	Jurist (Wash., D. C.)
Just.Cas.	Justiciary Cases
Just.L.R.	Justice's Law Reporter (Pa.)
Just.P.	Justice of the Peace and Local Government Review
Just.Syst.J.	Justice System Journal
Justinian	Justinian
Juv.Ct.J.	Juvenile Court Journal
Juv.Ct. Judges J.	Juvenile Court Judges Journal
Juv.Just.	Juvenile Justice

K

K. & G.	Keane & Grant's Registration Appeal Cases (Eng.)
K. & Gr.	Same
K. & G.R.C.	Same
K.B.	Law Reports King's Bench (Eng.)
K.Counsel	King's Counsel
Kames Dec.	Kames' Decisions (Sc.)
Kames Elucid.	Kames' Elucidation (Sc.)
Kames Rem. Dec.	Kames' Remarkable Decisions (Sc.)
Kames Sel. Dec.	Kames' Select Decisions (Sc.)
Kan.	Kansas
Kan.App.	Kansas Appeals
Kan.B.Ass'n J.	Kansas Bar Association Journal
Kan.C.L.Rep.	Kansas City Law Reporter
Kan.City L.Rev.	Kansas City Law Review
Kan.L.J.	Kansas Law Journal
Kan.L.Rev.	University of Kansas Law Review
Kan.St.L.J.	Kansas State Law Journal
Karachi L.J.	Karachi Law Journal (Pakistan)
Kay	Kay's Vice-Chancery (Eng.)
Kay & J.	Kay & Johnson's Chancery (Eng.)
Ke.	Keen's Rolls Court (Eng.)
Keane & G. R.C.	Keane & Grant's Registration Appeal Cases (Eng.)
Keane & Gr.	Same

Keb.	Keble's King's Bench (Eng.)
Keen	Keen's Rolls Court (Eng.)
Keil.	Keilway's King's Bench (Eng.)
Kel.C.C.	Kelyng's Crown Cases (Eng.)
Kel.W.	Kelyng's Chancery (Eng.)
Kellen	Kellen (Mass.)
Kelly	Kelly (Ga.)
Kelly & C.	Kelly & Cobb (Ga.)
Kenan	Kenan (N.C.)
Keny.	Kenyon (Lord) King's Bench (Eng.)
	Kenyon, Notes (Hammer)
Keny.Ch.	Kenyon's Chancery (Eng.)
Kenya L.R.	Kenya Law Reports
Kerala L.J.	Kerala Law Journal
Kern	Kern (Md.)
Kern.	Kernan (N.Y.)
Kerr	Kerr (Ind.)
	Kerr (N.B.)
	Kerr's Civil Procedure (N.Y.)
Keyes	Keyes (N.Y.)
Kilk.	Kilkerran's Decisions (Sc.)
Kilkerran	Same
King	King's Civil Practice Cases (Colo.)
	King's Louisiana Annual
Kingston L.Rev.	Kingston Law Review
Kirby	Kirby (Conn.)
Kn.P.C.	Knapp's Privy Council (Eng.)

Knapp	Knapp's Privy Council (Eng.)	Korean L.	Korean Law
Knapp & O.	Knapp & Ombler's Election Cases (Eng.)	Kreider	Kreider (Wash.)
		Kress	Kress (Pa.)
		Kulp	Kulp (Pa.)
Knight's Ind.	Knight's Industrial Reports	Kwansei Gak. L.Rev.	Kwansei Gaknin Law Review
Knowles	Knowles (R.I.)	Ky.Bench & B.	Ky Bench and Bar
Knox	Knox (N.S.W.)	Ky.	Kentucky
Knox & F.	Knox & Fitzhardinge (N.S.W.)	Ky.Comment'r	Kentucky Commentator
		Ky.Dec.	Kentucky Decisions
Kobe U.L.Rev.	Kobe University Law Review	Ky.L.J.	Kentucky Law Journal
		Ky.L.R.	Kentucky Law Reporter
		Ky.L.Rptr.	Same
Korea L.Rev.	Korea Law Review	Ky.Op.	Kentucky Opinions
Korean J. Comp.L.	Korean Journal of Comparative Law	Ky.St.B.J.	Kentucky State Bar Journal
Korean J. Int'l L.	Korean Journal of International Law	Kyoto L.Rev.	Kyoto Law Review

L

L. & B.Bull.	Weekly Law and Bank Bulletin (Ohio)	L.Chron. & L. Stud.Mag., (N.S.)	Law Chronicle and Law Students' Magazine, New Series
L. & C.	Leigh & Cave's Crown Cases Reserved (Eng.)	L.Coach	Law Coach
		L.Comment'y	Law Commentary
L. & C.	Lefroy and Cassels' Practice Cases (Ont.)	L.D.	Land Office Decisions (U.S.)
L. & Computer Tech.	Law and Computer Technology	L.D.L.R.	Land Development Law Reporter
L. & E.	English Law & Equity Reports (Boston)	L.East.Eur.	Law in Eastern Europe
L. & E.Rep.	Law & Equity Reporter (N.Y.)	L.Ed.	Lawyers' Edition, U. S. Supreme Court Reports
L. & Just.	Law and Justice	L.Ed.2d	Same, Second Series
L. & Leg. GDR	Law and Legislation in the German Democratic Republic	L.G.	Law Glossary
		L.Gaz.	Law Gazette
		L.Guard.	Law Guardian
L. & Lib.	Law and Liberty	L. in Soc'y	Law in Society
L. & M.	Lowndes & Maxwell, Bail Cases (Eng.)	L. in Trans.Q.	Law in Transition Quarterly
L. & Order	Law and Order	L.Inst.J.	Law Institute Journal
L. & Psych. Rev.	Law and Psychology Review	L.Inst.J. Vict.	Law Institute Journal of Victoria
L.A.B.J.	Los Angeles Bar Journal	L.J.Adm.	Law Journal Admiralty (Eng.)
L.A.C.	Labour Arbitration Cases		
L.A.G.Bull.	L.A.G. Bulletin	L.J.Bankr.	Law Journal Bankruptcy (Eng.)
L.A.J.P.E.L.	Latin American Journal of Politics, Economics and Law	L.J.C.P.	Law Journal Common Pleas, Old Series (Eng.)
L.Advertiser	Law Advertiser		
L.Am.Soc'y	Law in American Society	L.J.C.P. (O.S.)	Law Journal Common Pleas Old Series (Eng.)
L.Book Adviser	Law Book Adviser	L.J.Ch.	Law Journal Chancery, New Series (Eng.)
L.C.	Lower Canada		
L.C.D.	Ohio Decisions (Ohio Lower Decisions)	L.J.Ch. (O.S.)	Law Journal Chancery, Old Series (Eng.)
L.C.Jur.	Lower Canada Jurist	L.J.Eccl.	Law Journal Ecclesiastical (Eng.)
L.C.L.J.	Lower Canada Law Journal	L.J.Exch.	Law Journal Exchequer, New Series (Eng.)
L.C.Rep.S.Qu.	Lower Canada Reports Seignorial Questions	L.J.Exch. (O.S.)	Law Journal Exchequer, Old Series (Eng.)
L.Chron.	Law Chronicle	L.J.H.L.	Law Journal House of Lords, New Series
L.Chron. & L. Stud.Mag.	Law Chronicle and Law Students' Magazine		

L.J.K.B.	Law Journal King's Bench, New Series (Eng.)
L.J.K.B. (O.S.)	Law Journal King's Bench, Old Series (Eng.)
L.J.M.C.	Law Journal Magistrate Cases, New Series (Eng.)
L.J.M.C. (O.S.)	Law Journal Magistrate Cases, Old Series (Eng.)
L.J.Mag.	Law Journal New Series Common Law, Magistrates Cases (discontinued)
L.J.N.C.	Law Journal Notes of Cases (Eng.)
L.J.O.S.	Law Journal, Old Series (1822–1830)
L.J.P. & M.	Law Journal Probate & Matrimonial (Eng.)
L.J.P.C.	Law Journal Privy Council (Eng.)
L.J.P.C. (N.S.)	Same, New Series
L.J.P.D. & Adm.	Law Journal Probate, Divorce & Admiralty (Eng.)
L.J.Q.B.	Law Journal Queen's Bench, New Series (Eng.)
L.Japan	Law in Japan
L.L.J.	Law Library Journal
L.Lib.	Law Librarian
L.Lib.J.	Law Library Journal
L.M. & P.	Lowndes, Maxwell & Pollock's Bail Cases (Eng.)
L.M.C.L.Q.	Lloyd's Maritime and Commercial Law Quarterly
L.Mag. & Rev.	Law Magazine and Review
L.N.T.S.	League of Nations Treaty Series
L.Notes Gen. Pract.	Law Notes for the General Practitioner
L.Off.Econ. & Mgt.	Law Office Economics and Management
L.Q.	Law Quarterly
L.Q.Rev.	Law Quarterly Review
L.R.	Law Recorder (Ir.)
	Law Reports (Eng.)
	Ohio Law Reporter
L.R.A.	Lawyers' Reports Annotated (U.S.)
L.R.A. & E.	Law Reports Admiralty & Ecclesiastical (Eng.)
L.R.A. (N.S.)	Lawyers' Reports Annotated, New Series
L.R.App.Cas.	Law Reports House of Lords Appeal Cases (Eng.)
L.R.C.C.	Law Reports Crown Cases (Eng.)
L.R.C.C.R.	Law Reports Crown Cases Reserved (Eng.)
L.R.C.P.	Law Reports Common Pleas Cases (Eng.)
L.R.C.P.D.	Law Reports Common Pleas Division (Eng.)
L.R.Ch.	Law Reports Chancery Appeal Cases (Eng.)
L.R.Ch.D.	Law Reports Chancery Division (Eng.)
L.R.Eq.	Law Reports Equity Cases (Eng.)
L.R.Exch.	Law Reports Exchequer Cases (Eng.)
L.R.Exch.D.	Law Reports Exchequer Division (Eng.)
L.R.H.L.	Law Reports House of Lords (English & Irish Appeal Cases)
L.R.H.L.Sc.	Law Reports, House of Lords (Scotch Appeal Cases)
L.R.Indian App.	Law Reports, Indian Appeals (Eng.)
L.R.Ir.	Law Reports (Ir.)
L.R. (N.S.)	Irish Law Recorder, New Series
L.R.N.S.W.	Law Reports New South Wales
L.R.P.C.	Law Reports Privy Council (Eng.)
L.R.P. & D.	Law Reports Probate & Divorce (Eng.)
L.R.Q.B.	Law Reports, Queen's Bench (Eng.)
L.R.Q.B.Div.	Law Reports, Queen's Bench Division (Eng.)
L.R.R.	Labor Relations Reporter
L.R.R.M.	Labor Relations Reference Manual (BNA)
L.R.S.A.	Law Reports, South Australia
L.Record.	Law Recorder
L.Rev.Dig.	Law Review Digest
L.S.G.	Law Society Gazette (Eng.)
L.Stud.Helper	Law Student's Helper
L.Stud.J.	Law Students' Journal
L.T.	Law Times (Pa.)
L.T. (N.S.)	Law Times, New Series (Eng.)
L.T. (O.S.)	Law Times, Old Series (Eng.)
L.T.G.F. Newsl.	Lawyers' Title Guaranty Funds Newsletter
L.T.R. (N.S.)	Law Times Reports, New Series (Eng.)
L.T.Rep.N.S.	Law Times, Reports, New Series (Eng.)
L.Teacher	Law Teacher

L.Trans.Q.	Law in Transition Quarterly	Law Lib.J.	Law Library Journal
La.	Louisiana	Law Notes	Law Notes
La.Ann.	Louisiana Annual	Law Rep.	Law Reports (Eng.) (1865–1875)
La.App.	Louisiana Appeals		Law Reporter (Mass.)
La.App. (Orleans)	Court of Appeal, Parish of Orleans	Law Rep. (N.S.)	Law Reports, New Series (N.Y.)
La.B.J.	Louisiana Bar Journal	Law Soc'y Gaz.	Law Society's Gazette (London)
La.L.J.	Louisiana Law Journal		Law Society Gazette (Toronto)
La.L.Rev.	Louisiana Law Review	Law Soc'y J.	Law Society Journal (Boston)
La.T.R.	Martin's Louisiana Term Reports		Law Society Journal (New South Wales)
Lab.	Labatt's District Court (Cal.)	Law.	Lawyer
Lab. & Auto. Bull.	Labor and Automation Bulletin	Law. & Magis. Mag.	Lawyer's and Magistrate's Magazine
Lab.Arb.	Labor Arbitration Reports (BNA)	Law.Am.	Lawyer of the Americas
Lab.L.J.	Labor Law Journal	Lawasia	Lawasia
Lab.Rel.L. Letter	Labor Relations Law Letter	Lawr.	Lawrence (Ohio)
		Lawrence	Same
Lab.Rel.Rep.	Labor Relations Reporter	Lawyer & Banker	Lawyer and Banker and Central Law Journal
Lack.Jur.	Lackawanna Jurist (Pa.)	Lawyer's Med.J.	Lawyers' Medical Journal
Lack.Leg.N.	Lackawanna Legal News (Pa.)	Ld.Raym.	Lord Raymond's King's Bench (Eng).
Lack.Leg.Rec.	Lackawanna Legal Record (Pa.)	Lea	Lea (Tenn.)
Lackawanna B.	Lackawanna Bar	Leach C.C.	Leach's Crown Cases, King's Bench (Eng.)
Ladd	Ladd (N.H.)		
Lalor	Lalor's Supplement to Hill & Denio (N.Y.)	League of Nations Off.J.	League of Nations Official Journal
Lamar	Lamar (Fla.)	Learn. & L.	Learning and the Law
Lamb	Lamb (Wis.)	Lect.L.S.U.C.	Special Lectures of the Law Society of Upper Canada
Lanc.Bar	Lancaster Bar (Pa.)		
Lanc.L.Rev.	Lancaster Law Review (Pa.)	Lee	Lee (Calif.)
Land & Water L. Rev.	Land and Water Law Review	Lee Eccl.	Lee's Ecclesiastical (Eng.)
		Lee t.Hardw.	Lee temp. Hardwicke, King's Bench (Eng.)
Land Dec.	Land Decisions (U.S.)		
Lane	Lane's Exchequer (Eng.)	Leese	Leese (Neb.)
Lans.	Lansing (Mich.)	Leg. & Ins.R.	Legal & Insurance Reporter (Pa.)
Latch	Latch's King's Bench (Eng.)		
		Leg.Chron.	Legal Chronicle (Pa.)
Lath.	Lathrop (Mass.)	Leg.Gaz.	Legal Gazette Reports (Pa.)
Law	Law		
Law & Bk. Bull.	Weekly Law and Bank Bulletin (Ohio)	Leg.Int.	Legal Intelligencer (Pa.)
Law & Contemp.Prob.	Law and Contemporary Problems	Leg.Op.	Legal Opinions (Pa.)
		Leg.Rec.	Legal Record (Pa.)
Law & Pol'y Int'l Bus.	Law and Policy in International Business	Leg.Rep.	Legal Reporter (Tenn.)
Law & Soc. Ord.	Law and the Social Order Arizona State Law Journal	Leg.Rev.	Legal Review (Eng.)
		Legal Bibl.	Legal Bibliography
		Legal Econ.	Legal Economics
Law & Soc'y Rev.	Law and Society Review	Legal Exam.	Legal Examiner
		Legal Iss. Eur.Integr.	Legal Issues of European Integration
Law Cases	Law Cases, Wm. I to Rich. I (Eng.) (Placita Anglo-Normannica)	Legal Lit.	Legal Literature
		Legal News	Legal News

Legal Obser.	Legal Observer		Lock.Rev.Cas.	Lockwood's Reversed Cases (N.Y.)
Lehigh Co. L.J.	Lehigh County Law Journal (Pa.)		Lofft	Lofft's King's Bench (Eng.)
Lehigh Val. L.R.	Lehigh Valley Law Reporter (Pa.)		Lois Rec.	Lois Recentes du Canada
Leigh	Leigh (Pa.)		London L.Rev.	City of London Law Review
Leigh & C.	Leigh & Cave's Crown Cases (Eng.)		Long & R.	Long & Russell's Election Cases (Mass.)
Leigh & C. C.C.	Same		Long Beach B.Bull.	Long Beach Bar Bulletin
Leo.	Leonard, King's Bench, Common Pleas, Exchequer (Eng.)		Longf. & T.	Longfield & Townsend's Exchequer (Ir.)
Leon.	Same		Louisville Law.	Louisville Lawyer
Lester	Lester (Ga.)		Low.Can. Jurist	Lower Canada Jurist
Lester & B.	Lester & Butler's Supplement (Ga.)		Low.Can.L.J.	Lower Canada Law Journal
Lev.	Leving, King's Bench, Common Pleas (Eng.)		Low.Can.R.	Lower Canadian Reports
Lew.C.C.	Lewin's Crown Cases (Eng.)		Lowell	Lowell (U.S.)
Lewis	Lewis (Mo.) (Nev.)		Lower Ct.Dec.	Lower Court Decisions (Ohio)
	Lewis' Kentucky Law Reporter		Loyola Cons. Prot.J.	Loyola Consumer Protection Journal (Los Angeles)
Lex & Sci.	Lex et Scientia		Loyola Dig.	Loyola Digest
Ley	Ley King's Bench, Common Pleas, Exchequer, Court of Wards and Court of Star Chamber (Eng.)		Loyola L.A.L.Rev.	Loyola of Los Angeles Law Review
			Loyola L.Rev.	Loyola Law Review (New Orleans)
Liaison	Liaison		Loyola Law.	Loyola Lawyer
Liberian L.J.	Liberian Law Journal		Loyola U.L.J.	Loyola University Law Journal (Chicago)
Life Cas.	Life (Health & Accident) Cases (CCH)		Ludd.	Ludden (Me.)
Life Cas.2d	Same, Second Series		Lump.	Lumpkin (Ga.)
Lincoln L.Rev.	Lincoln Law Review		Lush.	Lushington's Admiralty (Eng.)
Litigation	Litigation			
Livingston's M.L.Mag.	Livingston's Monthly Law Magazine		Lutw.	Lutwyche's Common Pleas (Eng.)
Ll. & G.t.Pl.	Lloyd & Goold temp. Plunkett, Chancery (Ir.)		Lutw.Reg.Cas.	Lutwyche's Registration Cases (Eng.)
Ll. & G.t.S.	Lloyd & Goold temp. Sugden, Chancery (Ir.)		Luz.L.J.	Luzerne Law Journal (Pa.)
Ll. & W.	Lloyd & Welsby Mercantile Cases (Eng.)		Luz.L.T.	Luzerne Law Times (Pa.)
Ll.L.Rep.	Lloyd's List Reports (Eng.)		Luz.Leg.Obs.	Luzerne Legal Observer (Pa.)
Lloyd's Rep.	Lloyd's List Law Reports Admiralty		Luz.Leg.Reg.	Luzerne Legal Register (Pa.)
Local Ct. & Mun.Gaz.	Local Courts and Municipal Gazette		Lynd.	Lyndwoode, Provinciale (Eng.)
Local Gov't	Local Government and Magisterial Reports		Lyne	Lyne's Chancery (Ir.)
Local Gov't R.Austl.	Local Government Reports of Australia			

M

M. & A.	Montague & Ayrton's Bankruptcy (Eng.)		M. & C.	Montague & Chitty's Bankruptcy (Eng.)
M. & Ayr.	Same			
M. & B.	Montague & Bligh's Bankruptcy (Eng.)			Mylne & Craig's Chancery (Eng.)

M. & Cht. Bankr.	Montague & Chitty's Bankruptcy (Eng.)	M.L.P.	Michigan Law and Practice
M. & G.	Maddock & Geldhart's Chancery (Eng.)	M.L.R.	Military Law Reporter
	Manning & Granger's Common Pleas (Eng.)	M.L.R. (Q.B.)	Montreal Law Reports (Queen's Bench)
		M.L.R. (S.C.)	Montreal Law Reports (Superior Court)
M. & Gel.	Maddock & Geldhart's Chancery (Eng.)	M.P.R.	Maritime Province Reports
M. & Gord.	Macnaghten & Gordon's Chancery (Eng.)	M.P.T.M.H.	Major Peace Treaties of Modern History 1648– 1967
M. & H.	Murphy & Hurlstone's Exchequer (Eng.)	Mac.	Macnaghten's Chancery (Eng.)
M. & K.	Mylne & Keen's Chancery (Eng.)	Mac. & G.	Macnaghten & Gordon's Chancery (Eng.)
M. & M.	Moody & Malkin's Nisi Prius (Eng.)	Mac. & Rob.	Maclean & Robinson's Appeals, House of Lords (Sc.)
M. & McA.	Montague & McArthur's Bankruptcy (Eng.)	McAll.	MacAllister (U.S.)
M. & P.	Moore & Payne's Common Pleas & Exchequer (Eng.)	MacAr.	McArthur's District of Columbia
M. & R.	Maclean & Robinson's Appeal Cases (Sc.)		MacArthur's Patent Cases
		MacAr. & M.	MacArthur & Mackey's District of Columbia Supreme Court
	Manning & Ryland's King's Bench (Eng.)		
	Moody & Robinson's Nisi Prius (Eng.)	MacAr. & Mackey	Same
M. & R.M.C.	Manning & Ryland's Magistrates' Cases, King's Bench (Eng.)	MacAr.Pat. Cas.	MacArthur's Patent Cases (D.C.)
		MacArth.	MacArthur (D.C.)
M. & Rob.	Moody & Robinson's Nisi Prius (Eng.)		MacArthur's Patent Cases (D.C.)
M. & S.	Manning & Scott's Common Pleas (Eng.)	MacArth. & M.	MacArthur & Mackey (D.C.)
	Maule & Selwyn's King's Bench (Eng.)	McBride	McBride (Mo.)
		McC.	McCahon (Kan.)
	Moore & Scott's Common Pleas (Eng.)	McCah.	Same
		McCarter	McCarter's Chancery (N.J.)
M. & Scott	Same	McCartney	McCartney's Civil Procedure (N.Y.)
M. & W.	Meeson & Welsby's Exchequer (Eng.)	McClell.	McClelland's Exchequer (Eng.)
M. & W.Cas.	Mining & Water Cases (Annotated)	McClell. & Y.	McClelland & Younge's Exchequer (Eng.)
M. & Y.	Martin & Yerger (Tenn.)	McCook	McCook (Ohio)
		McCord	McCord's Chancery (S.C.)
M.A.L.C.M.	Mercantile Adjuster and the Lawyer and Credit Man	McCork.	McCorkle (N.C.)
		McCrary	McCrary (U.S.)
		MacFarl.	MacFarlane, Jury Court (Sc.)
M.C.C.	Mixed Claims Commission		
	Motor Carriers' Cases (I.C.C.)	McG.	McGloin (La.)
		McGill L.J.	McGill Law Journal
M.C.J.	Michigan Civil Jurisprudence	Mackey	Mackey
		MacL.	MacLean, U. S. Circuit Court
M.D.	Master's Decisions (Patents)		
M.F.P.D.	Modern Federal Practice Digest	MacL. & R.	Maclean & Robinson's House of Lords (Eng.)
M.L.E.	Maryland Law Encyclopedia	McLean	McLean (U.S.)

McMul.	McMullan's Chancery (S.C.)	Mar.L.Cas. (N.S.)	Maritime Law Cases, New Series
	McMullan's Law (S.C.)	Mar.N. & Q.	Maritime Notes and Queries
Macn. & G.	Macnaghten & Gordon's Chancery (Eng.)	Mar.Prov.	Maritime Provinces Reports
Macph.	Macpherson, Court of Sessions (Sc.)	March	March's King's Bench (Eng.)
Macph.L. & B.	Macpherson, Lee & Bell (Sc.)	Marijuana Rev.	The Marijuana Review
Macph.S. & L.	Macpherson, Shireff & Lee (Sc.)	Mark's & Sayre's	Mark's & Sayre's (Ala.)
Macq.	Macqueen's Scotch Appeal Cases	Marq.L.Rev.	Marquette Law Review
Macr.	Macrory's Patent Cases (Eng.)	Mars.Adm.	Marsden's Admiralty (Eng.)
		Marsh.	Marshall, A. K. (Ky.)
McWillie	McWillie (Miss.)		Marshall, J. J. (Ky.)
Madd.	Maddock (Mont.)		Marshall (U.S.)
	Maddock's Chancery (Eng.)		Marshall (Utah)
			Marshall's Common Pleas (Eng.)
Madd. & B.	Maddock & Back (Mont.)	Mart. & Y.	Martin & Yerger (Tenn.)
Madd.Ch.Pr.	Maddock's Chancery Practice (Eng.)	Martin	Martin (Ga.) (Ind.) (La.) (U.S.)
Madras L.J.	Madras Law Journal		Martin's Decisions (Law) (N.C.)
Madras L.J. Crim.	Madras Law Journal Criminal	Martin Mining	Martin Mining Cases
Mag.	Magruder (Md.)		Martin's New Series (La.)
Mag. & Const.	Magistrate and Constable	Marv.	Marvel (Del.)
Mag.Cas.	Magisterial Cases	Mason	Mason (U.S.)
Mag.Mun. Par.Law.	Magistrate and Municipal and Parochial Lawyer	Mass.	Massachusetts
Maine L.Rev.	Maine Law Review	Mass.App.Dec.	Massachusetts Appellate Decisions
Mal.L.J.	Malayan Law Journal	Mass.App.Div.	Massachusetts Appellate Division Reports
Mal.L.Rev.	Malaya Law Review		
Malloy	Malloy's Chancery (Ir.)	Mass.App.Rep.	Massachusetts Appeals Court Reports
Malone	Malone's Heiskell (Tenn.)		
Man.	Manitoba Law	Mass.L.Q.	Massachusetts Law Quarterly
	Manning (Mich.)		
Man. & G.	Manning & Granger's Common Pleas (Eng.)	Mathews	Mathews (W.Va.)
Man. & Ry. Mag.	Manning & Ryland's Magistrates' Cases (Eng.)	Matson	Matson (Conn.)
		Md.	Maryland
Man. & S.	Manning & Scott's Common Bench (Old Series) (Eng.)	Md.App.	Maryland Appellate Reports
		Md.B.J.	Maryland Bar Journal
Man.B.News	Manitoba Bar News	Md.Ch.	Maryland Chancery
Man.G. & S.	Manning, Granger & Scott's Common Bench (Eng.)	Md.L.F.	Maryland Law Forum
		Md.L.Rec.	Maryland Law Record
Man.Gr. & S.	Same	Md.L.Rep.	Maryland Law Reporter
Man.L.J.	Manitoba Law Journal	Md.L.Rev.	Maryland Law Review
Man.t.Wood	Manitoba temp. Wood	Me.	Maine
Man.Unrep. Cas.	Manning's Unreported Cases (La.)	Means	Means (Kan.)
		Med.L. & Pub. Pol.	Medicine, Law and Public Policy
Mann.	Manning (Mich.)		
Mann. & G.	Manning & Granger's Common Pleas (Eng.)	Med.-Legal Crim.Rev.	Medico-Legal and Criminological Review
		Med.-Legal J.	Medico-Legal Journal
Mansf.	Mansfield (Ark.)	Med.-Legal Soc'y Trans.	Medico-Legal Society Transactions
Manson	Manson's Bankruptcy (Eng.)	Med.Sci. & L.	Medicine, Science and the Law

Med.Trial Tech.Q.	Medical Trial Technique Quarterly	Misc.Dec.	3 Ohio Miscellaneous Decisions
Medd.	Meddaugh (Mich.)	Miss.	Mississippi
Meg.	Megone Company Cases (Eng.)	Miss.Dec.	Mississippi Decisions (Jackson)
Meigs	Meigs (Tenn.)	Miss.L.J.	Mississippi Law Journal
Melanesian L.J.	Melanesian Law Journal (Papua and New Guinea)	Miss.St.Cas.	Mississippi State Cases
		Mister	Mister (Mo.)
Melb.U.L. Rev.	Melbourne University Law Review	Mitchell's Mar.Reg.	Mitchell's Maritime Register
Memp.L.J.	Memphis Law Journal (Tenn.)	Mo.	Missouri
		Mo.A.R.	Missouri Appellate Reporter
Memphis St. U.L.Rev.	Memphis State University Law Review	Mo.App.	Missouri Appeals
Menken	Menken's Civil Procedure (N.Y.)	Mo.B.J.	Missouri Bar Journal
		Mo.Dec.	Missouri Decisions
Mercer Beasley L.Rev.	Mercer Beasley Law Review	Mo.L.Rev.	Missouri Law Review
		Moak	Moak (Eng.)
Mercer Law Rev.	Mercer Law Review	Mod.	Modern (Eng.)
		Mod.L. & Soc'y	Modern Law and Society
Meredith Lect.	W. C. J. Meredith Memorial Lectures	Mod.L.Rev.	Modern Law Review
		Mod.Pract. Comm.	Modern Practice Commentator
Meriv.	Merivale's Chancery (Eng.)	Moll.	Molloy's Chancery (Ir.)
Met.	Metcalf	Mon.	Monroe, B. or T. B. (Ky.)
Metc.	Metcalf (Mass.) (R.I.) (Ky.)	Monash Univ. L.Rev.	Monash University Law Review
Miami L.Q.	Miami Law Quarterly	Mont.	Montana Reports
Mich.	Michigan	Mont. & Ayr.	Montagu & Ayrton's Bankruptcy (Eng.)
Mich.App.	Michigan Court of Appeals Reports	Mont. & M.	Montagu & McArthur's Bankruptcy (Eng.)
Mich.L.Rev.	Michigan Law Review	Mont.L.Rev.	Montana Law Review
Mich.N.P.	Michigan Nisi Prius	Mont.Super.	Montreal Law Reports (Superior Court)
Mich.St.B.J.	Michigan State Bar Journal	Month.Dig. Tax Articles	Monthly Digest of Tax Articles
Mich.T.	Michaelmas Term (Eng.)	Month.L.J.	Monthly Journal of Law (Wash.)
Michie's Jur.	Michie's Jurisprudence of Va. and W Va.	Month.L.Mag.	Monthly Law Magazine (London)
Mid.East L. Rev.	Middle East Law Review	Month.L.Rep.	Monthly Law Reporter (Boston)
Mil.L.Rev.	Military Law Review		Monthly Law Reports (Can.)
Miles	Miles (Pa.) Miles' Philadelphia District Court	Month.L.Rev.	Monthly Law Review
Mill.	Miller (Law) (Md.)	Month.Leg. Exam.	Monthly Legal Examiner (N.Y.)
Mill Const.	Mill's Constitutional Reports (S.C.)	Month.West. Jur.	Monthly Western Journal (Bloomington)
Mill.Dec.	Miller's Decisions (U.S.)	Montr.Cond. Rep.	Montreal Condensed Reports
Mills	Mills (N.Y. Surrogate)	Montr.Leg.N.	Montreal Legal News
Milw.	Milward's Ecclesiastical (Ir.)	Montr.Q.B.	Montreal Law Reports Queen's Bench
Min.	Minor (Ala.)	Moo.C.C.	Moody's Crown Cases Reserved (Eng.)
Minn.	Minnesota	Moo.P.C.	Moore, Privy Council
Minn.Cont. L.Ed.	Minnesota Continuing Legal Education	Moo.P.C. (N.S.)	Moore, New Series, Privy Council
Minn.Cont. Legal Ed.	Same		
Minn.L.Rev.	Minnesota Law Review	Mood. & Mack.	Moody & Mackin's Nisi Prius (Eng.)
Misc.	Miscellaneous (N.Y.)		

Mood. & Malk.	Moody & Malkin's Nisi Prius (Eng.)	Mun.Att'y	Municipal Attorney
		Mun.Corp.Cas.	Municipal Corporation Cases
Mood. & Rob.	Moody & Robinson's Nisi Prius (Eng.)	Mun.L.Ct.Dec.	Municipal Law Court Decisions
Moody Cr.C.	Moody's Crown Cases Reserved (Eng.)	Mun.L.J.	Municipal Law Journal
Moon	Moon (Ind.)	Mun.Ord.Rev.	Municipal Ordinance Review
Moore	Moore (Ala.) (Ark.) (Tex.)	Mun.Rep.	Municipal Reports, Canada
Moore & S.	Moore & Scott's Common Pleas (Eng.)	Munf.	Munford (Va.)
		Munic. & P.L.	Municipal & Parish Law Cases (Eng.)
Moore & W.	Moore & Walker (Tex.)	Mur.	Murray's New South Wales Reports
Moore C.P.	Moore's Common Pleas (Eng.)		
Moore Indian App.	Moore's Indian Appeals (Eng.)		Murray's Scotch Jury Court Reports
Moore K.B.	Moore's King's Bench (Eng.)	Mur. & H.	Murphy & Hurlstone's Exchequer (Eng.)
Moore P.C.C.	Moore's Privy Council Cases (Eng.)	Mur. & Hurl.	Same
Morg.	Morgan's Chancery Acts & Orders (Eng.)	Murph.	Murphy (N.C.)
		Murph. & H.	Murphy & Hurlstone's Exchequer (Eng.)
Morr.	Morrill's Bankruptcy Cases (Eng.) Morris (Cal.) (Iowa) (Miss.)	Murr.	Murray's Scotch Jury Court Reports
Morr.St.Cas.	Morris State Cases (Miss.)	Murr.Over. Cas.	Murray's Overruled Cases
Morr.Trans.	Morrison's Transcript U. S. Supreme Court Decisions	Myer Fed.Dec.	Myer's Federal Decisions
		Myl. & C.	Mylne & Craig's Chancery (Eng.)
Morris.	Morrissett's (Ala.)	Myl. & Cr.	Same
Morrow	Morrow (Ore.)	Myl. & K.	Mylne & Keen's Chancery (Eng.)
Morse Exch. Rep.	Morse's Exchequer Reports (Can.)	Mylne & K.	Same
Mosely	Mosely's Chancery (Eng.)	Myr.	Myrick's Probate (Cal.)
Moult.Ch.	Moulton's Chancery Practice (N.Y.)	Myr.Prob.	Same
		Myrick (Cal.)	Same
Mun.	Munford (Va.)	Mysore L.J.	Mysore Law Journal

N

NACCA L.J.	NACCA Law Journal	N. & P.	Nevile & Perry's King's Bench (Eng.)
NLADA Brief.	NLADA Briefcase		
NOLPE Notes	NOLPE Notes	N.Atlantic Reg.Bus. L.Rev.	North Atlantic Regional Business Law Review
NOLPE School L.J.	NOLPE School Law Journal		
NOLPE School L.Rep.	NOLPE School Law Reporter	N.B.	New Brunswick
		N.B.Eq.	New Brunswick Equity
N. & H.	Nott & Huntington's U. S. Court of Claims	N.B.Rep.	New Brunswick Reports
		N.Benl.	New Benloe, King's Bench (Eng.)
N. & M.	Neville & Manning's King's Bench (Eng.)	N.C.	North Carolina
		N.C.App.	North Carolina Court of Appeals Reports
N. & Mc.	Nott & McCord (S.C.)		
N. & McC.	Same	N.C.C.	New Chancery Cases (Eng.)
N. & Macn.	Nevile & Macnamara Railway & Canal Cases (Eng.)	N.C.C.A.	Negligence & Compensation Cases Annotated

N.C.Cent. L.J.	North Carolina Central Law Journal	N.S.	Nova Scotia
N.C.Conf.	North Carolina Conference Reports	N.S.Dec.	Nova Scotia Decisions
		N.S.R.	Nova Scotia Reports
N.C.L.Rev.	North Carolina Law Review	N.S.W.	New South Wales State Reports
N.C.T.Rep.	North Carolina Term Reports	N.S.W.St.R.	New South Wales State Reports
N.Cent. School L.Rev.	North Central School Law Review	N.S.Wales	New South Wales
		N.S.Wales L.	New South Wales Law
N.Chipm.	North Chipman (Vt.)	N.S.Wales L.R.Eq.	New South Wales Law Reports Equity
N.D.	North Dakota	N.W.	Northwestern Reporter
N.D.J.Legis.	N.D. Journal of Legislation	N.W.2d	Same, Second Series
N.D.L.Rev.	North Dakota Law Review	N.W.T.L.R.	North West Territories Law Reports
N.E.	Northeastern Reporter		
N.E.2d	Northeastern Reporter, Second Series	N.W.Terr.	Northwest Territories Supreme Court Reports
N.Eng.J. Prison L.	New England Journal on Prison Law	N.Y.	New York
N.Eng.L.Rev.	New England Law Review	N.Y.2d	New York Court of Appeals Reports, Second Series
N.H.	New Hampshire		
N.H.B.J.	New Hampshire Bar Journal	N.Y.Anno.Cas.	New York Annotated Cases
N.I.M.L.O. Mun.L.Rev.	N.I.M.L.O. Municipal Law Review	N.Y.Anno.Dig.	New York Annotated Digest
N.Ir.L.Q.	Northern Ireland Legal Quarterly	N.Y.App.Div.	New York Supreme Court Appellate Division Reports
N.Ir.L.R.	Northern Ireland Law Reports	N.Y.Cas.Err.	New York Cases in Error (Claim Cases)
N.J.	New Jersey	N.Y.Ch.Sent.	Chancery Sentinel (N.Y.)
	New Jersey Reports	N.Y.City Ct.	New York City Court
N.J.Eq.	New Jersey Equity	N.Y.City Ct. Supp.	New York City Court Supplement
N.J.L.	New Jersey Law		
N.J.L.J.	New Jersey Law Journal	N.Y.City H. Rec.	New York City Hall Recorder
N.J.L.Rev.	New Jersey Law Review	N.Y.Civ.Pro.	New York Civil Procedure
N.J.Law	New Jersey Law Reports		
N.J.Misc.	New Jersey Miscellaneous Reports	N.Y.Civ.Pro. R. (N.S.)	Same, New Series
N.J.St.B.J.	New Jersey State Bar Journal	N.Y.Civ.Proc.	New York Civil Procedure
N.J.Super.	New Jersey Superior Court and County Court Reports	N.Y.Civ.Proc. (N.S.)	Same, New Series
		N.Y. Code Rep.	New York Code Reporter
N.Ky.St.L.F.	Northern Kentucky State Law Forum	N.Y.Code Rep. (N.S.)	New York Code Reports, New Series
N.L.R.B.	National Labor Relations Board Reports		
N.M.	New Mexico	N.Y.Cond.	New York Condensed Reports
N.M.L.R.	Nigerian Monthly Law Reports	N.Y.Cont. L.Ed.	New York Continuing Legal Education
N.Mex.L.Rev.	New Mexico Law Review		
N.P.	Ohio Nisi Prius Reports	N.Y.Cont. Legal Ed.	Same
N.P. (N.S.)	Ohio Nisi Prius Reports, New Series	N.Y.County Law.Ass'n B.Bull.	New York County Lawyers Association Bar Bulletin
N.P. & G.T. Rep.	Nisi Prius & General Term Reports (Ohio)		
[e.g.] N.R.A.B. (4th Div.)	National Railroad Adjustment Board Awards	N.Y.Cr.	New York Criminal
		N.Y.Crim.	New York Criminal Reports

N.Y.Daily L.Gaz.	New York Daily Law Gazette	N.Y.U.Rev. Law & Soc. C.	New York University Review of Law and Social Change
N.Y.Daily L.Reg.	New York Daily Law Register	N.Y.Wkly.Dig.	New York Weekly Digest
N.Y.Dep't R.	New York Department Reports	N.Z.L.J.	New Zealand Law Journal
		N.Z.L.R.	New Zealand Law Reports
N.Y.Elec.Cas.	New York Election Cases	N.Z.U.L.Rev.	New Zealand Universities Law Review
N.Y.Jud. Repos.	New York Judicial Repository	Napt.	Napton (Mo.)
		Napton	Same
N.Y.Jur.	New York Jurisprudence New York Jurist	Narcotics Control Dig.	Narcotics Control Digest
N.Y.L.Cas.	New York Leading Cases	Narcotics L.Bull.	Narcotics Law Bulletin
N.Y.L.F.	New York Law Forum	Nat.Bankr. Reg.	National Bankruptcy Register (U.S.)
N.Y.L.J.	New York Law Journal	Nat.Corp.Rep.	National Corporation Reporter
N.Y.L.Rec.	New York Law Record		
N.Y.L.Rev.	New York Law Review	Nat.L.Rep.	National Law Reporter
N.Y.Leg.N.	New York Legal News	Nat.Munic. Rev.	National Municipal Review
N.L.Leg. Obs.	New York Legal Observer	Nat.Reg.	National Register (By Mead)
N.Y.Misc.	New York Miscellaneous Reports	Nat'l Civic Rev.	National Civic Review
N.Y.Misc.2d	Same, Second Series	Nat'l Income Tax Mag.	National Income Tax Magazine
N.Y.Month.L. Bull.	New York Monthly Law Bulletin	Nat'l J.Crim. Defense	National Journal of Criminal Defense
N.Y.Month.L. Rep.	New York Monthly Law Reports	Nat'l Legal Mag.	National Legal Magazine
N.Y.Mun.Gaz.	New York Municipal Gazette	Nat'l Mun.Rev.	National Municipal Review
		Nat'l School L.Rptr.	National School Law Reporter
N.Y.P.R.	New York Practice Reports	Nat'l Taiwan U.L.Rev.	National Taiwan University Law Journal
N.Y.Pr.Rep.	Same		
N.Y.Rec.	New York Record	Nat'l Tax J.	National Tax Journal
N.Y.S.	New York Supplement	Nat'l L.F.	Natural Law Forum
N.Y.S.2d	Same, Second Series	Natural Resources J.	Natural Resources Journal
N.Y.St.	New York State Reporter		
N.Y.St.B.J.	New York State Bar Journal	Natural Resources L.Newsl.	Natural Resources Law Newsletter
N.Y.Super.	New York Superior Court		
N.Y.Supp.	New York Supplement	Natural Resources Law.	Natural Resources Lawyer
N.Y.U.Conf. Charitable	New York University Conference on Charitable Foundations Proceedings	Neb.	Nebraska
		Neb. (Unoff.)	Nebraska Unofficial Reports
N.Y.U.Conf. Lab.	New York University Conference on Labor	Neb.L.Bul.	Nebraska Law Bulletin
[e.g.] N.Y.U. Inst.on Fed.Tax.	New York University Institute on Federal Taxation	Neb.L.Rev.	Nebraska Law Review
		Neb.St.B.J.	Nebraska State Bar Journal
N.Y.U.Intra.L. Rev.	New York Intramural Law Review	Negl. & Comp.Cas. Ann.	Negligence & Compensation Cases Annotated
N.Y.U.J.Int'l Law & Pol.	New York University Journal of International Law and Politics	Negl. & Comp.Cas. Ann. (N.S.)	Same, New Series
N.Y.U.L. Center Bull.	New York University Law Center Bulletin	Negl. & Comp.Cas. Ann.3d	Same, Third Series
N.Y.U.L.Q. Rev.	New York University Law Quarterly Review		
N.Y.U.L.Rev.	New York University Law Review	Negl.Cas.	Negligence Cases (CCII)
		Negl.Cas.2d	Same, Second Series

Negro.Cas.	Bloomfield's Manumission (N.J.)
Nels.	Nelson's Chancery (Eng.)
Nels.Abr.	Nelson's Abridgment (Eng.)
Neth.Int'l L.Rev.	Netherlands International Law Review
Neth.Y.B. Int'l Law	Netherlands Yearbook of International Law
Nev.	Nevada
Nev. & P.	Neville & Perry's King's Bench (Eng.)
Nev.St.Bar J.	Nevada State Bar Journal
New L.J.	New Law Journal
New Rep.	New Reports in All Courts (Eng.)
New Sess.Cas.	New Session Cases (Eng.)
New Yugo.L.	New Yugoslav Law
New Zeal.L.	New Zealand Law
New.	Newell (Ill.)
Newb.Adm.	Newberry's Admiralty (U.S.)
Newf.S.Ct.	Newfoundland Supreme Court Decisions
Newfoundl.	Newfoundland
Nfld.R.	Newfoundland Reports
Nigeria L.R.	Nigeria Law Reports

Nigerian L.J.	Nigerian Law Journal
Noise Reg.Rep.	Noise Regulation Reporter (BNA)
Nolan	Nolan, Magistrates' Cases (Eng.)
Norc.	Norcross (Nev.)
Norris	Norris (Pa.)
North	North (Ill.)
North & G.	North & Guthrie (Mo.)
North.	Northington's Chancery (Eng.)
North.Co.	Northampton County Legal News (Pa.)
Northumb.Co. Leg.News	Northumberland County Legal News (Pa.)
Northumb. Legal J.	Northumberland Legal Journal
Notes of Cas.	Notes of Cases (Eng.)
Notre Dame Law.	Notre Dame Lawyer
Noy	Noy, King's Bench (Eng.)
Nuclear L.Bull.	Nuclear Law Bulletin
Nuclear Reg. Rep.	Nuclear Regulation Reporter (CCH)
Nw.U.L.Rev.	Northwestern University Law Review

O

O.	Ohio, Oklahoma, Oregon
O.A.	Ohio Appellate
O.A.R.	Same
	Ontario Appeal Reports
O.App.	Ohio Appellate
O.B. & F.N.Z.	Olliver, Bell & Fitzgerald's New Zealand Reports
O.Ben.	Old Benloe, Common Pleas (Eng.)
O.Benl.	Same
O.Bridgm.	Orlando Bridgman, Common Pleas (Eng.)
O.C.A.	Ohio Courts of Appeals Reports
O.C.C.	Ohio Circuit Court Decisions
	Ohio Circuit Court Reports
O.C.C. (N.S.)	Ohio Circuit Court Reports, New Series
O.C.D.	Ohio Circuit Decisions
O.C.S.	Office of Contract Settlement Decisions
O.D.	Office Decisions (I.R. Bull.)
	Ohio Decisions
O.D.C.C.	Ohio Circuit Decisions

O.D.N.P.	Ohio Decisions
O.Dec.Rep.	Ohio Decisions Reprint
O.E.M.	Office of Emergency Management
O.F.D.	Ohio Federal Decisions
O.G.	Official Gazette (U.S.) Patent Office
O.G.Pat.Off.	Same
O.L.A.	Ohio Law Abstract
O.L.B.	Weekly Law Bulletin (Ohio)
O.L.D.	Ohio (Lower) Decisions
O.L.J.	Ohio Law Journal
O.L.Jour.	Same
O.L.N.	Ohio Legal News
O.L.R.	Ohio Law Reporter
	Ontario Law Reports, 1901–1930
O.L.R.B.	Ontario Labour Relations Board Monthly Report
O.L.Rep.	Ohio Law Reporter
O.Legal News	Ohio Legal News
O.Lower D.	Ohio (Lower) Decisions
O.N.P.	Ohio Nisi Prius
O.N.P. (N.S.)	Same, New Series
O.O.	Ohio Opinions

O.R.	Ontario Reports, 1882–1900	Ohio App.2d	Same, Second Series
[ ] O.R.	Same, 1931 to present	Ohio Bar	Ohio State Bar Association Reports
O.S.	Ohio State Reports	Ohio C.A.	Ohio Courts of Appeals Reports
O.S.C.D.	Ohio Supreme Court Decisions (Unreported Cases)	Ohio C.C.	Ohio Circuit Court Reports
O.S.H.Dec.	Occupational, Safety, and Health Decisions (CCH)	Ohio C.C.R.	Same
O.S.H.Rep.	Occupational, Safety, and Health Reporter (BNA)	Ohio C.C.R. (N.S.)	Same, New Series
O.S.L.J.	Ohio State Law Journal	Ohio C.Dec.	Ohio Circuit Decisions
O.S.U.	Ohio Supreme Court Decisions (Unreported Cases)	Ohio Cir.Ct.	Ohio Circuit Court Decisions
O.St.	Ohio State Reports	Ohio Cir.Ct. (N.S.)	Ohio Circuit Court Reports, New Series
O.Su.	Ohio Supplement	Ohio Cir.Ct.R.	Ohio Circuit Court Reports
O.W.N.	Ontario Weekly Notes, 1909–1932	Ohio Cir.Ct.R. (N.S.)	Same, New Series
[ ] O.W.N.	Same, 1933–1962		
O.W.R.	Ontario Weekly Reporter	Ohio Ct.App.	Ohio Courts of Appeals Reports
Obiter Dictum	Obiter Dictum	Ohio Dec.	Ohio Decisions
Ocean Devel. & Int'l L.	Ocean Development and International Law	Ohio Dec. Repr.	Ohio Decisions Reprint
Odeneal	Odeneal (Ore.)	Ohio F.Dec.	Ohio Federal Decisions
Off.Brev.	Officina Brevium	Ohio Fed.Dec.	Same
Off.Gaz.	Official Gazette (U.S.) Patent Office	Ohio Jur.	Ohio Jurisprudence
		Ohio Jur.2d	Same, Second Edition
Officer	Officer (Minn.)	Ohio L.Abs.	Ohio Law Abstract
Ogd.	Ogden (La.)	Ohio L.B.	Weekly Law Bulletin (Ohio)
Oh.	Ohio Reports (1821–1852)		
Oh.A.	Ohio Court of Appeals	Ohio L.J.	Ohio Law Journal
Oh.Cir.Ct.	Ohio Circuit Court	Ohio L.R.	Ohio Law Reporter
Oh.Cir.Ct. (N.S.)	Same, New Series	Ohio Law Abst.	Ohio Law Abstract
Oh.Cir.Dec.	Ohio Circuit Decisions	Ohio Law Bull.	Weekly Law Bulletin (Ohio)
Oh.Dec.	Ohio Decisions		
Oh.Dec. (Reprint)	Ohio Decisions (Reprint)	Ohio Law J.	Ohio Law Journal
Oh.F.Dec.	Ohio Federal Decisions	Ohio Law R.	Ohio Law Reporter
Oh.Jur.	Ohio Jurisprudence	Ohio Leg.N.	Ohio Legal News
Oh.L.Bull.	Ohio Law Bulletin	Ohio Legal N.	Same
Oh.L.Ct.D.	Ohio Lower Court Decisions	Ohio Lower Dec.	Ohio (Lower) Decisions
Oh.L.J.	Ohio Law Journal	Ohio Misc.	Ohio Miscellaneous Reports
Oh.L.Rep.	Ohio Law Reporter		
Oh.Leg.N.	Ohio Legal News	Ohio Misc.Dec.	3 Ohio Miscellaneous Decisions
Oh.N.P.	Ohio Nisi Prius		
Oh.N.P. (N.S.)	Same, New Series	Ohio N.P.	Ohio Nisi Prius Reports
Oh.Prob.	Ohio Probate	Ohio N.P. (N.S.)	Same, New Series
Oh.S. & C.P.	Ohio Superior & Common Pleas Decisions	Ohio (N.S.)	Ohio Reports, Annotated
		Ohio North U.L.	Ohio Northern University Law Review
Oh.S.C.D.	Ohio Supreme Court Decisions (Unreported Cases)	Ohio Op.	Ohio Opinions
		Ohio Op.2d	Same, Second Series
Oh.St.	Ohio State Reports	Ohio Prob.	Goebel's Ohio Probate Reports
Ohio	Ohio Reports (1821–1852)		
Ohio App.	Ohio Appellate Reports	Ohio R.Cond.	Ohio Reports Condensed

Ohio S. & C.P. Dec.	Ohio Decisions	Ont.Elec.	Same
		Ont.L.	Ontario Law
Ohio S.U.	Ohio Supreme Court Decisions (Unreported Cases)	Ont.L.J.	Ontario Law Journal
		Ont.L.J. (N.S.)	Same, New Series
Ohio St.	Ohio State Reports	Ont.L.R.	Ontario Law Reports
Ohio St.2d	Same, Second Series	Ont.Pr.	Ontario Practice
Ohio St.L.J.	Ohio State Law Journal	Ont.W.N.	Ontario Weekly Notes
Ohio St. (N.S.)	Ohio State Reports, Annotated	Ont.W.R.	Ontario Weekly Reporter
Ohio Sup. & C.P.Dec.	Ohio Decisions	Op.	Opinions of Attorneys General (U.S.)
Ohio Supp.	Ohio Supplement	Op.Att'y Gen.	Opinions of the Attorney General, United States
Ohio Unrep. Jud.Dec.	Pollack's Ohio Unreported Judicial Decisions Prior to 1823	Op.Sol.Dept.	Opinions of the Solicitor, U. S. Department of Labor
Ohio Unrept. Cas.	Ohio Supreme Court Decisions (Unreported Cases)	Ops.Atty.Gen.	Opinions of Attorneys General (U.S.)
		Or.	Oregon
Oil & Gas Compact Bull.	Oil and Gas Compact Bulletin	Orange County B.J.	Orange County Bar Journal.
		Ore.	Oregon Reports
Oil & Gas Inst.	Oil and Gas Institute	Ore.App.	Oregon Court of Appeals Reports
Oil & Gas J.	Oil and Gas Journal	Ore.L.Rev.	Oregon Law Review
Oil & Gas L. & Tax.Inst. (Sw.Legal Fdn.)	Oil & Gas Law & Taxation Institute (Southwestern Legal Foundation)	Ore.St.B.Bull.	Oregon State Bar Bulletin
		Ore.Tax Ct.	Oregon Tax Court Reports
		Orleans' App.	Orleans' Appeals (La.)
Oil & Gas Rptr.	Oil and Gas Reporter	Orleans Tr.	Orleans Term Reports (La.)
Oil & Gas Tax Q.	Oil and Gas Tax Quarterly	Ormond	Ormond (Ala.)
		Osaka Pref. Bull.	University of Osaka Prefecture Bulletin
Okla.	Oklahoma		
Okla.B. Ass'n J.	Oklahoma Bar Association Journal	Osaka U.L. Rev.	Osaka University Law Review
Okla.Cr.	Oklahoma Criminal	Osgoode Hall L.J.	Osgoode Hall Law Journal
Okla.Crim.	Oklahoma Criminal Reports		
		Otago L.Rev.	Otago Law Review
Okla.L.J.	Oklahoma Law Journal	Ottawa L.Rev.	Ottawa Law Review
Okla.L.Rev.	Oklahoma Law Review	Otto	Otto (U.S.)
Okla.S.B.J.	Oklahoma State Bar Journal	Out.	Outerbridge (Pa.)
		Outerbridge	Same
Olcott	Olcott (U.S.)	Over.	Overton (Tenn.)
Oliv.B. & L.	Oliver, Beavan & Lefroy (Eng. Ry. & Canal Cases)	Overt.	Same
		Overton	Same
Olliv.B. & F.	Olliver, Bell & Fitzgerald (New Zealand)	Ow.	Owen's King's Bench & Common Pleas (Eng.)
O'M. & H.El. Cas.	O'Malley & Hardcastle, Election Cases (Eng.)	Owen	Same
		Oxford Law.	Oxford Lawyer
Ont.	Ontario Reports	Oxley	Young's Vice Admiralty Decisions (Nova Scotia) (By Oxley)
Ont.A.	Ontario Appeals		
Ont.El.Cas.	Ontario Election Cases		

P

P.	Pacific Reporter	P.2d	Pacific Reporter, Second Series
	Pickering (Mass.)		
	Probate	P. & B.	Pugsley & Burbridge's Reports, New Brunswick
	Law Reports Probate, Divorce & Admiralty Division, Third Series	P. & C.	Prideaux & Cole's New Sessions Cases (Eng.)

P. & D.	Perry & Davison's Queen's Bench (Eng.)
P. & F. Radio Reg.	Radio Regulation Reporter
P. & H.	Patton & Heath (Va.)
P. & K.	Perry & Knapp Election Cases (Eng.)
P. & W.	Penrose & Watts (Pa.)
P.C.	Price Control Cases (CCH)
P.C.I.J.	Permanent Court of International Justice Advisory Opinions, Cases, Judgments, Pronouncements
P.C.I.J.Ann.R.	Permanent Court of International Justice Annual Reports
P.Coast L.J.	Pacific Coast Law Journal
P.D.	Law Reports Probate, Divorce & Admiralty Division, Second Series Division
	Pension and Bounty (U.S. Dept. of Interior)
P.Div.	Law Reports, Probate Division (Eng.)
PEAL	Publishing, Entertainment, Advertising and Allied Fields Law Quarterly
P.E.I.	Haszard & Warburton's Reports (P.E.I.)
P.F.Smith	P. F. Smith (Pa.)
P–H	Prentice-Hall
P–H Am.Lab. Arb.Awards	American Labor Arbitration Awards (P–H)
P–H Am.Lab. Cas.	American Labor Cases (P–H)
P–H Corp.	Corporation (P–H)
P–H Est.Plan.	Estate Planning (P–H)
P–H Fed. Taxes	Federal Taxes (P–H)
P–H Fed.Wage & Hour	Federal Wage and Hour (P–H)
P–H Ind.Rel., Lab.Arb.	Industrial Relations, American Labor Arbitration (P–H)
P–H Ind.Rel., Union Conts.	Industrial Relations, Union Contracts and Collective Bargaining (P–H)
P–H Soc.Sec. Taxes	Social Security Taxes (P–H)
P–H State & Local Taxes	State and Local Taxes (P–H)
P–H Tax Ct.Mem.	Tax Court Memorandum Decisions (P–H)
P–H Tax Ct.Rep. & Mem.Dec.	Tax Court Reported and Memorandum Decisions (P–H)
P.L.Mag.	Pacific Law Magazine
P.L.E.	Pennsylvania Law Encyclopedia
P.L.Rep.	Pacific Law Reporter
P.Jr. & H.	Patton, Jr., & Heath (Va.)
P.R.	Parliamentary Reports
	Probate Reports
	Practice Reports (Ont.)
	Puerto Rico Supreme Court Reports
P.R. & D.El. Cas.	Power, Rodwell & Dew's Election Cases (Eng.)
P.R.F.	Puerto Rico Federal Reports
P.R.R.	Puerto Rico Reports
P.T.	Processing Tax Division (I.R.Bull.)
P.U.Fort.	Public Utilities Fortnightly
P.U.R.	Public Utilities Reports
P.U.R. (N.S.)	Same, New Series
P.U.R.3d	Same, Third Series
P.Wms.	Peere-Williams Chancery (Eng.)
Pa.	Pennsylvania
Pa.B.Ass'n Q.	Pennsylvania Bar Association Quarterly
Pa.B.Brief	Pennsylvania Bar Brief
Pa.C.P.	Common Pleas Reporter
Pa.C.Pl.	Penn. Common Pleas
Pa.Cas.	Penn. Supreme Court Cases (Sadler)
Pa.Co.Ct.	Penn. County Court
Pa.D. & C.	Penn. District & County Reporter
Pa.D. & C.2d	Same, Second Series
Pa.Dist.	Penn. District Reporter
Pa.Fid.	Pennsylvania Fiduciary Reporter
Pa.L.J.	Pennsylvania Law Journal
Pa.L.J.R.	Clark's Penn. Law Journal Reports
Pa.L.Rec.	Pennsylvania Law Record
Pa.Misc.	Pennsylvania Miscellaneous Reports
Pa.State	Penn. State Reports
Pa.Super.	Penn. Superior Court Reporter
Pac.	Pacific Reporter
Pacific L.J.	Pacific Law Journal
Paige	Paige's Chancery (N.Y.)
Paine	Paine (U.S.)
Pak.Crim.L.J.	Pakistan Criminal Law Journal
[e.g.] Pak.L. R.Lahore Ser.	Pakistan Law Reports, [e.g.] Lahore Series
Palm.	Palmer (N.H.) (Vt.)
	Palmer, King's Bench & Common Pleas (Eng.)
Pan-Am.T.S.	Pan-American Treaty Series

Papua & N.G.	Papua and New Guinea Law Reports	Pension Rep.	Pension Reporter (BNA)
Papy	Papy (Fla.)	Pepperdine L.Rev.	Pepperdine Law Review
Park.	Parker's Exchequer (Eng.)	Perry & K.	Perry & Knapp's Election Cases (Eng.)
Park.Cr.	Parker's Criminal Reports (N.Y.)	Pers.Finance L.Q.	Personal Finance Law Quarterly Report
Park.Cr.Cas.	Same	Pers.Inj. Comment'r	Personal Injury Commentator
Park.Ins.	Parker's Insurance	Pet.	Peters
Parker	Parker (N.H.)	Pet.Ab.	Petersdorf's Abridgment
Parker Cr. Cas.	Parker's Criminal Reports (N.Y.)	Pet.Adm.	Peters' Admiralty (U.S.)
Pars.Dec.	Parson's Decisions (Mass.)	Pet.Br.	Petit (Or Little) Brook (Brooke) New Cases King's Bench (Eng.)
Pars.Eq.Cas.	Parsons' Select Equity Cases (Pa.)	Pet.C.C.	Peters' Circuit Court (U.S.)
Pasch.	Paschal (Tex.)		
Pat. & T.M. Rev.	Patent & Trade Mark Review	Peters	Peters (U.S.)
Pat. & Tr.Mk. Rev.	Same	Pheney Rep.	Pheney's New Term Reports. See Harrison & Wollaston (Eng.)
Pat.Cas.	Reports of Patent, Design and Trade Mark Cases	Phil.	Phillips' (Ill.)
Pat.L.Rev.	Patent Law Review		Phillips' Chancery (Eng.)
Pat.Off.Rep.	Patent Office Reports		Phillips' Equity (N.C.)
Pat.T.M. & Copy.J.	Patent, Trademark & Copyright Journal		Phillips' Law (N.C.)
Pater.Ap.Cas.	Paterson's Appeal Cases (Sc.)	Phil.El.Cas.	Phillips Election Cases (Eng.)
Paton App. Cas.	Paton's Appeal Cases (Can.)	Phil.Int'l L.J.	Philippine International Law Journal
Patt. & H.	Patton & Heath (Va.)	Phil.L.J.	Philippine Law Journal
Peab.L.Rev.	Peabody Law Review	Phila.	Philadelphia (Pa.)
Peake N.P.	Peake's Nisi Prius (Eng.)	Philanthrop.	Philanthropist
Peake N.P. Add.Cas.	Peake, Additional Cases Nisi Prius (Eng.)	Phillim.	Phillimore Ecclesiastical (Eng.)
Pearce C.C.	Pearce's (Dearsley's) Crown Cases (Eng.)	Pick.	Pickering (Mass.)
		Pickle	Pickle (Tenn.)
Pearson	Pearson, Common Pleas (Pa.)	Pig. & R.	Pigott & Rodwell's Registration Cases (Eng.)
Peck	Peck (Ill.)	Pike	Pike (Ark.)
	Peck (Tenn.)	Pin.	Pinney (Wis.)
Peck.El.Cas.	Peckwell's Election Cases (Eng.)	Pinn.	Pinney (Wis.)
		Pipe Roll Soc'y	Publications of the Pipe Roll Society
Peeples	Peeples (Ga.)	Pipe Roll Soc'y (N.S.)	Publications of the Pipe Roll Society, New Series
Peeples & Stevens	Peeples & Stevens (Ga.)	Pitblado Lect.	Isaac Pitblado Lectures on Continuing Legal Education
Peere Williams	Peere Williams' Chancery (Eng.)		
Peere Wms.	Same	Pitts.L.J.	Pittsburgh Legal Journal
Pen.	Pennington's Law (N.J.)	Pitts.Leg.J. (N.S.)	Pittsburgh Legal Journal, New Series (Pa.)
Pen. & W.	Penrose and Watts		
Penn.B.A.Q.	Penn.Bar Association (Quarterly)	Pitts.Rep.	Pittsburgh Reports (Pa.)
		Pittsb.	Pittsburgh (Pa.)
Penn.Del.	Pennewill (Del.)	Pittsb.Leg.J.	Pittsburgh Legal Journal (Pa.)
Pennyp.	Pennypacker (Pa.)		
Pennyp.Col. Cas.	Pennypacker's Colonial Cases	Pittsb.R. (Pa.)	Pittsburgh Reporter (Pa.)
Penr. & W.	Penrose & Watts (Pa.)	Pl.Ang.-Norm.	Placita Anglo-Normannica Cases (Bigelow)

Plan. & Comp.	Planning and Compensation Reports	Pract.Law.	Practical Lawyer
Plan., Zoning & E.D.Inst.	Planning, Zoning & Eminent Domain Institute	Prec.Ch.	Precedents in Chancery (Eng.)
		Preview	Preview of United States Supreme Court Cases
Plowd.	Plowden, King's Bench (Eng.)	Price	Price (Exchequer) (Eng.)
Pol.	Pollack's Ohio Unreported Judicial Decisions Prior to 1823		Price's Mining Commissioner's Cases (Ont.)
		Price Pr.Cas.	Price's Notes of Practice Cases (Eng.)
	Pollexfen, King's Bench (Eng.)	Prick.	Prickett (Idaho)
Pollexf.	Same	Prin.Dec.	Printed Decisions (Sneed's) (Ky.)
Pol.Sci.Q.	Political Science Quarterly	Prison L. Rptr.	Prison Law Reporter
Pol.Y.B. Int'l L.	Polish Yearbook of International Law		
Police J.	Police Journal	Prob. & Prop.	Probate and Property
Police L.Q.	Police Law Quarterly	Prob.Law.	Probate Lawyer
Poll.Contr. Guide	Pollution Control Guide (CCH)	Prob.Rep.	Probate Reports (Ohio)
		Prod.Safety & Liab.Rep.	Product Safety and Liability Reporter (BNA)
Pollution Abs.	Pollution Abstracts		
Pomeroy	Pomeroy (Cal.)	Prop. & Comp.	Property and Compensation Reports
Poor L. & Local Gov't Mag.	Poor Law and Local Government Magazine	Prop.Law.	Property Lawyer
		Prosecutor	Prosecutor
Poph.	Popham, King's Bench & Common Pleas & Chancery (Eng.)	Prouty	Prouty (Vt.)
		Pub.Ad.Rev.	Public Administration Review
Port.	Porter (Ala.) (Ind.)	Pub.Contract L.J.	Public Contract Law Journal
Portia L.J.	Portia Law Journal	Pub.Contract Newsl.	Public Contract Newsletter
Portland U.L. Rev.	Portland University Law Review		
		Pub.Employee Rel.Rep.	Public Employee Relations Reports
Porto Rico Fed.	Porto Rico Federal	Pub.Int'l L.	Public International Law
Posey	Posey (Tex.)	Pub.L.	Public Law
Posey Unrep. Cas.	Posey's Unreported Commissioner Cases (Texas)	Pub.Land & Res.L.Dig.	Public Land and Resources Law Digest
Post	Post (Mich.) (Mo.)	Pub.Util.Fort.	Public Utilities Fortnightly
Potter	Potter (Wyo.)		
Pow.Surr.	Power's Surrogate (N.Y.)	Pugs.	Pugsley (New Brunswick)
Pr.	Price (Exchequer) (Eng.)	Pugs. & B.	Pugsley & Burbridge (New Brunswick)
Pr.Edw.Isl.	Prince Edward Island		
Pr.Reg.B.C.	Practical Register, Bail Court (Eng.)	Pugs. & T.	Pugsley & Trueman (New Brunswick)
Pr.Reg.C.P.	Practical Register Common Pleas (Eng.)	Puls.	Pulsifer (Me.)
Pr.Reg.Ch.	Practical Register Chancery (Eng.)	Pulsifer	Same
Pr.Rep.	Practice Reports (Eng.)	Pyke	Pyke (Lower Can.)
	Practice Reports (Upper Can.)		Pyke's Reports, King's Bench (Que.)

Q

Q.B.	Law Reports, Queen's Bench, Third Series	Q.B.U.C.	Queen's Bench (Upper Canada)
Q.B.D.	Law Reports, Queen's Bench Division, Second Series	Q.Intramural L.J.	Queen's Intramural Law Journal
		Q.L.	Quebec Law
Q.B.L.C.	Queen's Bench (Lower Canada)	Q.L.J.	Queen's Law Journal
		Q.L.R.	Quebec Law Reports

Q.L.Rev.	Quarterly Law Review
Q.Newsl.-Spec. Comm.Env.L.	Quarterly Newsletter-Special Committee on Environmental Law
Que.B.R.; Que.C.S.	Quebec Rapports Judicaires Officiels (Banc de la Reine; Cour supérieure)
[ ] Que.K.B. or [ ] Que. Q.B.	Quebec Official Reports (King's Bench or Queen's Bench) 1941 to present
Que.L.	Quebec Law
Que.L.R.	Quebec Law Reports
Que.Pr.	Quebec Practice
Que.Prac.	Quebec Practice Reports
Que.Q.B. or Que.K.B.	Quebec Official Reports (Queen's Bench or King's Bench) 1892–1941
Que.Rev.Jud.	Quebec Revised Judicial
Que.S.C.	Quebec Official Reports (Superior Court) 1892–1941

[ ] Que.S.C.	Same, 1942 to present
Que.Super.	Quebec Reports Superior Court
Queens B.Bull.	Queens Bar Bulletin
Queensl.	Queensland Reports
Queensl.J.P.	Queensland Justice of the Peace
Queensl.J.P. Rep.	Queensland Justice of the Peace Reports
Queensl.L.	Queensland Law
Queensl.L.J.	Queensland Law Journal
Queensl.L. Soc'y J.	Queensland Law Society Journal
Queensl.Law.	Queensland Lawyer
Queensl.S.C.R.	Queensland Supreme Court Reports
Queensl.St. Rep.	Queensland State Reports
Queensl.W.N.	Queensland Weekly Notes
Quincy	Quincy (Mass.)
Quis Cust.	Quis Custodiet?

R

R.	Rawle (Pa.) The Reports, Coke's King's Bench (Eng.)
R. & C.	Russell & Chesley (Nova Scotia)
R. & Can.Cas.	Railway & Canal Cases (Eng.)
R. & Can.Tr. Cas.	Railway & Canal Traffic Cases (Eng.)
R. & M.	Russell & Mylne's Chancery (Eng.)
R. & M.C.C.	Ryan & Moody's Crown Cases (Eng.)
R. & N.L.R.	Rhodesia and Nyasaland Law Reports
R. & R.	Russell & Ryan Crown Cases (Eng.)
R. 1 Cro.	Croke, Elizabeth
R. 2 Cro.	Croke, James I.
R. 3 Cro.	Croke, Charles I.
R.A.C.	Ramsay's Appeal Cases (Que.)
R.C.L.	Ruling Case Law
R.E.D.	Russell's Equity Decisions (Nova Scotia)
R.I.	Rhode Island
R.I.B.J.	Rhode Island Bar Journal
R.J.R.Q.	Quebec Revised Reports
R.L. & S.	Ridgeway, Lapp & Schoales, King's Bench (Ir.)
R.L. & W.	Robert, Leaming & Wallis County Court (Eng.)
R.L.B.	U. S. Railroad Labor Board Decisions

R.M.C.C.	Ryan & Moody's Crown Cases (Eng.)
R.M.C.C.R.	Same
R.M.Charlt.	R. M. Charlton (Ga.)
R.P.C.	Reports of Patent Cases
R.P. & W.	(Rawle) Penrose & Watt (Pa.)
R.P.W.	Same
R.R.	Pike & Fischer Radio Regulation Revised Reports (Eng.)
R.R.2d	Pike & Fischer Radio Regulation, Second Series
Race	Race
Race Rel.L. Rep.	Race Relations Law Reporter
Race Rel.L. Survey	Race Relations Law Survey
Rader	Rader (Mo.)
Rand	Rand (Ohio)
Rand.	Randolph (Kan.) (Va.) Randall (Ohio)
Rand.Ann.	Randolph Annual (La.)
Raney	Raney (Fla.)
Rawle	Rawle (Pa.)
Raym.	Raymond (Iowa)
Real Est.L.J.	Real Estate Law Journal
Real Est. L.Rep.	Real Estate Law Report
Real Est.Rev.	Real Estate Review
Real Prop. Prob. & Trust J.	Real Property, Probate and Trust Journal

Reap.Dec.	U. S. Customs Court Reappraisement Dec. (From Treas. Dec. & C.D.)	Rev.Int'l Comm.Jur.	Review of the International Commission of Jurists
Rec.L.	Recent Law	Rev., Jud., & Police J.	Revenue, Judicial, and Police Journal
Rec.Laws	Recent Laws in Canada	Rev.Jur. U.P.R.	Revista Juridica de la Universidad de Puerto Rico
Record of N.Y.C.B.A.	Record of the Association of the Bar of the City of New York	Rev.L. & Soc. Change	Review of Law and Social Change
Recueil des Cours	Recueil des Cours	Rev.Leg.	Revue Legale (Can.)
Redf. & B.	Redfield & Bigelow's Leading Cases (Eng.)	Rev.Leg. (N.S.)	Same, New Series
Redf.Surr.	Redfield's Surrogate (N.Y.)	Rev.Leg. (O.S.)	Same, Old Series
Reding.	Redington (Me.)	Rev.Legale	Revue Legale
Reese	Reese, Heiskell's (Tenn.)	Rev.Not.	Revue de Notariat Revue du Notariat
Reeve Eng.L.	Reeve's English Law	Rev.Pol.L.	Review of Polish Law
Ref.J.	Referees' Journal (Journal of National Association of Referees in Bankruptcy)	Rev.R.	Revised Reports (Eng.)
		Rev.Rep.	Revised Reports (Eng.)
		Rev.Sec.Reg.	Review of Securities Regulation
Rel. & Pub. Order	Religion and the Public Order	Rev.Sel. Code Leg.	Review of Selected Code Legislation
Remy	Remy (Ind.)	Rev.Soc.L.	Review of Socialist Law
Rep.Atty.Gen.	Attorneys General's Reports (U.S.)	Rev.Stat.	Revised Statutes
		Revised Rep.	Revised Reports (Eng.)
Rep.Pat.Cas.	Reports of Patent Cases (Eng.)	Reyn.	Reynolds (Miss.)
Rep.Pat.Des. & Tr.Cas.	Reports of Patents Designs & Trademark Cases	Rhodesian L.J.	Rhodesian Law Journal
		Rice	Rice's Equity (S.C.) Rice's Law (S.C.)
Reports	Reports Coke's King's Bench (Eng.)	Rich.	Richardson (N.H.) Richardson's Equity (S.C.) Richardson's Law (S.C.)
Reprint	English Reports, Full Reprint	Rich. & H.	Richardson & Hook's Street Railway Decisions
Rept.t.Finch	Cases temp. Finch (Chancery) (Eng.)	Rich. & W.	Richardson & Woodbury (N.H.)
Rept.t.Holt	Cases temp. Holt (King's Bench) (Eng.)	Rich.C.P.	Richardson's Practice, Common Pleas (Eng.)
Res Ipsa	Res Ipsa Loquitur	Rich.Ct.Cl.	Richardson's Court of Claims
Res Judic.	Res Judicatae		
Res. & Eq. Judgm.	Reserved & Equity Judgments (N.S.Wales)	Ridg.Ap.	Ridgeway's Appeals Parliament Cases (Ir.)
Restric. Prac.	Reports of Restrictive Practices Cases	Ridg.App.	Same
Rettie	Rettie, Crawford & Melville's Session Cases (Sc.)	Ridg.L. & S.	Ridgeway, Lapp & Schoales' King's Bench (Ir.)
Rev.Bar.	Revue du Barreau	Ridg.P.C.	Ridgeway's Parliamentary Cases (Ir.)
Rev.C.Abo.Pr.	Revista de Derecho del Colegio de Abogados de Puerto Rico	Ridg.t.Hardw.	Ridgeway temp. Hardwicke, Chancery, King's Bench
Rev.Contemp.L.	Review of Contemporary Law		
Rev.Crit.	Revue Critique (Can.)	Ried.	Riedell (N.H.)
Rev.D.P.R.	Revista de Derecho Puertorriqueno	Rights	Rights
Rev.D.U.S.	Revue de Droit Université de Sherbrooke	Riley	Riley (W.Va.) Riley's Equity (S.C.) Riley's Law (S.C.)
Rev. de Legis.	Revue de Legislation (Can.)		
Rev.Gen.D.	Revue Générale de Droit		
Rev.Ghana L.	Review of Ghana Law	Ritchie	Ritchie's Equity (Can.)

Rob.	Robard (Mo.)
	Robard Conscript Cases (Tex.)
	Robert's Louisiana Annual
	Robertson (Hawaii)
	Robertson's Marine Court (N.Y.)
	Robertson's Superior Court (N.Y.)
	Robinson (Calif.) (Colo.) (La.) (Nev.) (Upper Can.) (Va.)
	Robinson's (La.) Annual
Rob. & J.	Robard & Jackson (Tex.)
	Robertson & Jacob's Marine Court (N.Y.)
Rob.Adm.	Robinson, Admiralty (Eng.)
Rob.Eccl.	Robertson's Ecclesiastical (Eng.)
Rob.L. & W.	Robert, Leaming & Wallis' County Court (Eng.)
Robb Pat.Cas.	Robb's Patent Cases (U.S.)
Robert.App. Cas.	Robertson's Appeal Cases (Sc.)
Robin.App.Cas.	Robinson's Appeal Cases (House of Lords) (Sc.)
Rocky Mt.L. Rev.	Rocky Mountain Law Review
Rocky Mt.Min. L.Inst.	Rocky Mountain Mineral Law Institute
Rocky Mt.Min. L.Newsl.	Rocky Mountain Mineral Law Newsletter
Rocky Mt. Miner.L.Rev.	Rocky Mountain Mineral Law Review
Rodm.	Rodman (Ky.)
Rogers	Rogers (La.) Annual
Roll.	Rolle (King's Bench) (Eng.)
Rolle	Same
Rolle Abr.	Rolle's Abridgment (Eng.)
Rom.Cas.	Romilly's Notes of Cases (Eng.)
Root	Root (Conn.)
Rose	Rose Bankruptcy (Eng.)
Rose's Notes (U.S.)	Rose's Notes on U. S. Reports
Ross Lead.Cas.	Ross Leading Cases (Eng.)
Rot.Chart.	Rotulus Chartarum (The Charter Roll)

Rot.Claus.	Rotuli Clause (The Close Roll)
Rot.Parl.	Rotulae Parliamentarum
Rot.Pat.	Rotuli Patenes
Rot.Plac.	Rotuli Placitorum
Rotuli Curiae Reg.	Rotuli Curiae Regis (Eng.)
Rowe	Rowe, Parliament & Military Cases (Eng.)
Rowell	Rowell (Vt.)
Rowell El.Cas.	Rowell Election Cases (U.S.)
Rucker	Rucker (W.Va.)
Ruff. & H.	Ruffin & Hawks (N.C.)
Runn.	Runnell (Iowa)
Rus.	Russell's Election Cases (Nova Scotia)
Rus. & C.Eq. Cas.	Russell & Chesley's Equity Cases (N.S.)
Russ. & Geld.	Russell & Geldert (N.S.)
Russ. & M.	Russell & Mylne Chancery (Eng.)
Russ. & Ry.	Russell & Ryan Crown Cases (Eng.)
Russ.El.Cas.	Russell's Election Reports (Can.)
	Russell's Election Cases (Mass.)
Russ.Eq.Cas.	Russell's Equity Cases (N.S.)
Russ.t.Eld.	Russell's Chancery temp. Eldon (Eng.)
Russell	Russell's Chancery (Eng.)
Rutgers J. Computers & Law	Rutgers Journal of Computers and the Law
Rutgers L.Rev.	Rutgers Law Review
Rutgers U.L. Rev.	Rutgers University Law Review
Rutgers-Camden L.J.	Rutgers-Camden Law Journal
Ry. & M.	Ryan & Moody's Nisi Prius (Eng.)
Ry.M.C.C.	Ryan & Moody Crown Cases (Eng.)
Ryan & M.	Ryan & Moody's Nisi Prius (Eng.)
Ryde	Ryde's Rating Appeals (Eng.)

S

S.	Shaw, Dunlop & Bell (Sc.)
	Shaw's Appeal Cases, House of Lords (Sc.)
	Southern Reporter
SALT News	SALT News

S. & B.	Smith & Batty's King's Bench (Ir.)
S. & C.	Saunders & Cole's Bail Court (Eng.)
S. & C.P.Dec.	Ohio Decisions

S. & D.	Shaw, Dunlop & Bell's 1st Series (Sc.)	S.Ct.Rev.	Supreme Court Review
		S.D.	South Dakota
S. & L.	Schoales & Lefroy's Chancery (Ir.)	S.D.L.Rev.	South Dakota Law Review
		S.D.St.B.J.	South Dakota State Bar Journal
S. & M.	Smedes & Maclean's Appeal Cases, House of Lords (Sc.)	S.E.	South Eastern Reporter
		S.E.2d	Same, Second Series
	Smedes & Marshall (Miss.)	S.E.C.	U. S. Security and Exchange Commission Decisions
S. & M.Ch.	Smedes & Marshall's Chancery (Miss.)		
S. & Mar.	Smedes & Marshall (Miss.)	S.F.L.J	San Francisco Law Journal
		S.L.C.	Stuart's Appeal Cases (Lower Can.)
S. & Mar.Ch.	Smedes & Marshall's Chancery (Miss.)	S.L.J.R.	Sudan Law Journal and Reports
S. & R.	Sergeant & Rawle (Pa.)		
S. & S.	Sausse & Scully's Rolls Court (Ir.)	S.M.	Solicitor's Memorandum (Treasury) (I.R.Bull.)
	Simons & Stuart's Vice-Chancery (Eng.)	S.Pac.L.Rev.	South Pacific Law Review
		S.R.	Solicitor's Recommendation (I.R.Bull.)
S. & Sc.	Sausse & Scully's Rolls Court (Ir.)	S.R. & O. and S.I.Rev.	Statutory Rules & Orders and Statutory Instruments Revised
S. & Sm.	Searle & Smith's Probate & Divorce Cases (Eng.)		
		S.S.L.R.	Selective Service Law Reporter
S. & T.	Swabey & Tristram's Probate & Divorce Cases (Eng.)	S.S.T.	Social Security Tax Ruling (I.R.Bull.)
S.Afr.L.J.	South African Law Journal	S.T.	Sales Tax Division (I.R. Bull.)
S.Afr.L.R.	South African Law Reports	S.Tex.L.J.	South Texas Law Journal
		S.W.	South Western Reporter
S.Afr.L.R. App.	South African Law Reports Appellate	S.W.2d	Same, Second Series
		S.W.L.J.	South Western Law Journal (Nashville)
S.Afr.L.Rev.	South African Law Review		
S.Afr.L.T.	South African Law Times	Sadler	Sadler's Cases (Pa.)
S.Afr.Tax Cas.	South African Tax Cases	St. John's L.Rev.	St. John's Law Review
S.Aust.L.	South Australian Law	St. Louis L.Rev.	St. Louis Law Review
S.Austl.	South Australia State Reports	St. Louis U.L.J.	St. Louis University Law Journal
S.Austl.L.R.	South Australian Law Reports	St. Mary's L.J.	St. Mary's Law Journal
S.B.J.	State Bar Journal (Cal.)	Sal.	Salinger (Iowa)
S.C.	Court of Session Cases (Sc.)	Salk.	Salkeld King's Bench Common Pleas & Exchequer (Eng.)
	South Carolina		
S.C.Cas.	Supreme Court Cases (Cameron's) (Can.)	Samoan P.L.J.	Samoan Pacific Law Journal
S.C.Eq.	South Carolina Equity	San Diego L. Rev.	San Diego Law Review
S.C.L.Q.	South Carolina Law Quarterly		
		San Fran.L.J.	San Francisco Law Journal
S.C.L.Rev.	South Carolina Law Review	Sand.I.Rep.	Sandwich Islands Reports (See Robertson's Reports) (Hawaii)
S.C.R.	Supreme Court Reports (Canada) 1876–1922		
[ ]S.C.R.	Same, 1923 to present	Sandf.	Sandford's Superior Court (N.Y.)
S.Cal.L.Rev.	Southern California Law Review	Sandf.Ch.	Sandford Chancery (N.Y.)
S.Calif.Law Rev.	Southern California Law Review	Sanf.	Sanford (Ala.)
S.Ct.	Supreme Court Reporter (U.S.)	Santa Clara L. Rev.	Santa Clara Law Review

Santa Clara Law.	Santa Clara Lawyer	Sec.Reg.L.J.	Securities Regulation Law Journal
Santo Tomas L.Rev.	University of Santo Tomas Law Review	Sel.Cas.	Yates' Select Cases (N.Y.)
Sar.Ch.Sen.	Saratoga Chancery Sentinel	Sel.Cas.Ch.	Select Cases in Chancery (Eng.)
Sask.	Saskatchewan Law Reports	Sel.Serv.L. Rptr.	Selective Service Law Reporter
Sask.B.Rev.	Saskatchewan Bar Review	Seld.	Selden's Notes (N.Y.)
Sask.L.	Saskatchewan Law	Selden	Selden's N. Y. Court of Appeals
Sask.L.Rev.	Saskatchewan Law Review	Selw.N.P.	Selwyn's Nisi Prius (Eng.)
Sau. & Sc.	Sausee & Scully, Rolls Court (Ir.)	Seoul L.J.	Seoul Law Journal
		Serg. & R.	Sergeant & Rawle (Pa.)
Sauls.	Saulsbury (Del.)	Sess.Ca.	Sessions Cases King's Bench (Eng.)
Saund.	Saunders King's Bench (Eng.)		
Saund. & Cole	Saunders & Cole, Bail Court (Eng.)	Sess.Cas.	Court of Sessions Cases (Sc.)
Sav.	Savile, Common Pleas & Exchequer (Eng.)		Sessions Cases King's Bench (Eng.)
Sawy.	Sawyer Circuit Court (U.S.)	Sess.Laws	Session Laws
		Seton Hall L. Rev.	Seton Hall Law Review
Sax.	Saxton's Chancery (N.J.)	Seton Hall Leg.J.	Seton Hall Legislative Journal
Say.	Sayer, King's Bench (Eng.)	Sex.L.Rep.	Sexual Law Reporter
Sc.Sess.Cas.	Scotch Court of Sessions Cases	Sex Prob.Ct. Dig.	Sex Problems Court Digest
Sc.St.Crim.	Scandinavian Studies in Criminology	Shad.	Shadford's Victoria Reports
Sc.St.L.	Scandinavian Studies in Law	Shan.	Shannon (Tenn.)
Scam.	Scammon (Ill.)	Shand	Shand (S.C.)
Sch. & Lef.	Schoales & Lefroy, Equity (Ir.)	Shand Pr.	Shand, Practice, Court of Sessions (Sc.)
Scher.	Scherer's Miscellaneous Reports (N.Y.)	Shaw	Shaw (Vt.)
			Shaw Appeal Cases, English House of Lords From Scotland
Schm.L.J.	Schmidt's Law Journal (New Orleans)		Shaw, Scotch Justiciary Cases
Schuyl.L.Rec.	Schuylkill Legal Record (Pa.)		Shaw, Scotch Teind Reports, Court of Sessions
Scot.Jur.	Scottish Jurist	Shaw & D.	Shaw & Dunlop (Sc.)
Scot.L.J.	Scottish Law Journal and Sheriff Court Record	Shaw & Dunl.	Same
Scot.L.Mag.	Scottish Law Magazine and Sheriff Court Reporter	Shaw & M.	Shaw & McLean Appeals, House of Lords (Sc.)
Scot.L.Rep.	Scottish Law Reporter	Shaw & Macl.	Same
Scot.L.Rev.	Scottish Law Review and Sheriff Court Reports	Shaw App.	Shaw Appeal Cases (Sc.)
Scot.L.T.	Scottish Law Times	Shaw Crim. Cas.	Shaw's Criminal Cases, Justiciary Court (Sc.)
Scots L.T.R.	Scots Law Times Reports		
Scott	Scott Common Pleas (Eng.)	Singapore L. Rev.	Singapore Law Review
Scott N.R.	Scott's New Reports, Common Pleas (Eng.)	Shaw, D. & B.	Shaw, Dunlop & Bell's Court of Sessions (1st Series) (Sc.)
Scr.L.T.	Scranton Law Times (Pa.)		
Scrivener	Scrivener		Shaw, Dunlop & Bell's Session Cases (Sc.)
Search and Seizure	Search and Seizure Bulletin		
Sec.L.Rev.	Securities Law Review	Shaw, D. & B. Supp.	Shaw, Dunlop, & Bell's Supplement, House of Lords Decisions (Sc.)
Sec.Reg. & Trans.	Securities Regulation and Transfer Report		

Shaw Dec.	Shaw's Decisions in Scotch Court of Sessions (1st Series)
Shaw, Dunl. & B.	Shaw, Dunlop & Bell's Sessions Cases (Sc.)
Shaw, W. & C.	Shaw, Wilson & Courtnay, House of Lords
Shep.	Shepherd (Ala.) Shepley (Me.)
Shep.Abr.	Sheppard's Abridgment
Shep.Sel.Cas.	Shepherd's Select Cases (Ala.)
Sher.Ct.Rep.	Sheriff Court Reports (Sc.)
Shingle	Shingle
Shipp	Shipp (N.C.)
Shirl.	Shirley (N.H.)
Shirl.L.C.	Shirley's Leading Crown Cases (Eng.)
Show.	Shower King's Bench (Eng.)
Show.P.C.	Shower's Parliamentary Cases (Eng.)
Sick.	Sickel's Court of Appeals (Eng.)
Sid.	Siderfin King's Bench (Eng.)
Sil.	Silver Tax Division (I.R. Bull.)
Silv.A.	Silvernail's Appeals (N.Y.)
Silv.Sup.	Silvernail's Supreme Court (N.Y.)
Silv.Unrep.	Silvernail's Unreported Cases (N.Y.)
Sim.	Simmon's (Wis.) Simon's Vice-Chancery (Eng.)
Sim. (N.S.)	Simon's Vice-Chancery, New Series (Eng.)
Sim. & C.	Simmons & Conover (Wis.)
Sim. & St.	Simons & Stuart's Vice-Chancery (Eng.)
Skill.Pol.Rep.	Skillman's N. Y. Police Reports
Skin.	Skinner (King's Bench) (Eng.)
Skink.	Skinker (Mo.)
Sm. & M.	Smedes & Marshall (Miss.)
Sm. & M.Ch.	Smedes & Marshall, Chancery (Miss.)
Smale & G.	Smale & Gifford's Vice-Chancery (Eng.)
Smith	Smith (Calif.) (Dak.) (Eng.) (Ind.) (Me.) (Mo.) (N.H.) (Wis.)
	Smith, E. B. (Ill.)
	Smith, E. D. Common Pleas (N.Y.)
	Smith, E. H. Court of Appeals (N.Y.)
	Smith, E. P. Court of Appeals (N.Y.)
	Smith. P. F. (Pa.)
Smith & B.	Smith & Batty, King's Bench (Ir.)
Smith & B.R.C.	Smith & Bates, American Railway Cases
Smith & G.	Smith & Guthrie (Mo.)
Smith & H.	Smith & Heiskell (Tenn.)
Smith C.C.M.	Smith Circuit Courts-Martial (Me.)
Smith Cond.	Smith's Condensed Alabama Reports
Smith K.B.	Smith's King's Bench (Eng.)
Smith L.J.	Smith's Law Journal
Smith Lead. Cas.	Smith's Leading Cases (Eng.)
Smith Reg. Cas.	Smith's Registration Cases (Eng.)
Smy.	Smythe Common Pleas (Ir.)
Smythe	Same
Sneed	Sneed (Tenn.) Sneed's Decisions (Ky.)
Sneed Dec.	Sneed's Kentucky Decisions
Sneedy Ky.	Same
Snow	Snow (Utah)
So.	Southern Reporter
So.2d	Same, Second Series
So.Calif.L. Rev.	Southern California Law Review
So.Car.Const.	South Carolina Constitutional Reports
So.Car.L.J.	South Carolina Law Journal
So.L.J.	Southern Law Journal (Nashville)
So.L.Q.	Southern Law Quarterly
So.L.Rev.	Southern Law Review (Nashville)
	Southern Law Review (St. Louis)
So.L.Rev. (N.S.)	Southern Law Review, New Series (St. Louis)
So.Law T.	Southern Law Times
So.Tex.L.J.	South Texas Law Journal
So.U.L.Rev.	Southern University Law Review
Soc. & Lab. Bull.	Social and Labour Bulletin
Soc.Action & L.	Social Action and the Law
Soc.Sec.Bull.	Social Security Bulletin
Sol.	Solicitor
Sol.J.	Solicitor's Journal (Eng.)

Sol.Op.	Solicitor's Opinions (I.R. Bull.)	Stev. & G.	Stevens & Graham (Ga.)
Sol.Q.	Solicitor Quarterly	Stew.	Stewart (Ala.) (S.D.)
Somerset L.J.	Somerset Legal Journal		Stewart's Reports (N.S.)
Southard	Southard (N.J.)	Stew. & P.	Stewart & Porter (Ala.)
Southwestern L.J.	Southwestern Law Journal	Stew.Admr.	Stewart's Admiralty (N.S.)
Soviet L. & Gov't	Soviet Law and Government	Stew.Eq.	Stewart's Equity (N.J.)
Soviet Stat. & Dec.	Soviet Statutes and Decisions	Stewart	Stewart's Vice-Admiralty Reports (N.S.)
Soviet Y.B. Int'l L.	Soviet Year-Book of International Law	Stiles	Stiles (Iowa)
		Still.Eccl.Cas.	Stillingfleet's Ecclesiastical Cases (Eng.)
Spaulding	Spaulding (Me.)	Stiness	Stiness (R.I.)
Spear	Spear's Law (S.C.)	Stockett	Stockett (Md.)
Spear Ch.	Spear's (or Speer) Chancery (S.C.)	Stockt.	Stockton's Equity (N.J.)
Spear Eq.	Spear's Equity (S.C.)	Stockt.Vice-Adm.	Stockton's Vice-Admiralty (N.B.)
Speer	See Spear	Stockton	Same
Spenc.	Spencer (Minn.)	Storey	Storey
	Spencer Law (N.J.)	Story	Story (U.S.)
Spencer	Spencer Law (N.J.)	Story Eq.Jur.	Story on Equity Jurisprudence
Spinks	Spinks Ecclesiastical and Admiralty (Eng.)	Str.	Strange's King's Bench (Eng.)
Spinks Eccl. & Adm.	**Same**	Stra.	Same
Spoon.	Spooner (Wis.)	Strahan	Strahan (Ore.)
Spooner	Same	Straits L.J. & Rep.	Straits Law Journal and Reporter
Spott.	Spottiswoode (Sc.)	Stratton	Stratton (Ore.)
Spott.C.L. Rep.	Spottiswoode's Common Law	Stringf.	Stringfellow (Mo.)
Spottis.	Spottiswoode (Sc.)	Strob.	Strobhart's Law (S.C.)
Spottis.C.L. & Eq.Rep.	Common Law & Equity Reports published by Spottiswoode	Strob.Eq.	Strobhart's Equity (S.C.)
		Stu.M. & P.	Stuart, Milne & Peddie (Sc.)
Spottis.Eq.	Spottiswoode's Equity (Sc.)	Stu.Mil. & Ped.	Same
Sprague	Sprague (U. S. District Court Admiralty)	Stuart	Stuart's King's Bench (Lower Can.)
St.Rep.	State Reporter	Stuart Vice-Adm.	Stuart's Vice-Admiralty (Lower Can.)
St.Rep.N.S.W.	State Reports (New South Wales)	Stud.Int'l Fiscal L.	Studies on International Fiscal Law
Stafford	Stafford (Vt.)	Stud.L. & Econ.Dev.	Studies in Law and Economic Development
Stair	Stair (Sc.)	Student Law.	Student Lawyer
Stan.J.Int'l Stud.	Stanford Journal of International Studies	Student Law. J.	Student Lawyer Journal
Stan.L.Rev.	Stanford Law Review	Studia Canonica	Studia Canonica
Stan.Pa.Prac.	Standard Pennsylvania Practice	Style	Style, King's Bench, Rolle & Glyn's Decisions (Eng.)
Stant.	Stanton (Ohio)		
Stanton	Same	Suffolk U.L. Rev.	Suffolk University Law Review
Star Ch.Cas.	Star Chamber Cases (Eng.)	Summerfield	Summerfield (Nev.)
Stark.	Starkie's Nisi Prius (Eng.)	Sumn.	Sumner Circuit Court (U.S.)
Stat.	Statutes at Large (U.S.)	Sup. & C.P. Dec.	Ohio Decisions
Stat. at L.	Same		
State Gov't	State Government	Sup.Ct.	Superior Court (Pa.)
State Tr.	State Trials (Eng.)	Sup.Ct.Hist. Soc'y Y.B.	Supreme Court Historical Society Yearbook
Stath.Abr.	Statham's Abridgment		

Sup.Ct.Rep.	Supreme Court Reporter (U.S.)	Swin.	Swinton's Registration Appeal Cases (Sc.)
Susq.Leg. Chron.	Susquehanna Legal Chronical (Pa.)	Sydney L. Rev.	Sydney Law Review
Sw.L.J.	Southwestern Law Journal	Syme	Syme's Justiciary Cases (Sc.)
Sw.U.L.Rev.	Southwestern University Law Review	Symposium Jun.B.	Symposium ı Association de jeune Barreau de Montreal
Swab.	Swabey's Admiralty (Eng.)	Syn.Ser.	Synopsis Series of Treasury Decisions (U.S.)
Swab. & Tr.	Swabey & Tristram, Probate & Divorce (Eng.)	Syracuse J. Int'l L. & Com.	Syracuse Journal of International Law and Commerce
Swan	Swan (Tenn.)		
Swanst.	Swanston Chancery (Eng.)	Syracuse L. Rev.	Syracuse Law Review
Sween.	Sweeney's Superior Court (N.Y.)		

T

T.	Tappan's Reports (Ohio)	T.M.Bull.	Trade Mark Bulletin (U.S.)
	Tobacco Division (I.R.Bull.)	T.M.Bull. (N.S.)	Same, New Series
T. & C.	Thompson & Cook N. Y. Supreme Court Reports	T.M.M.	Tax Management Memorandum (BNA)
T. & G.	Tyrwhitt & Granger's Exchequer (Eng.)	T.M.Rep.	Trade Mark Reporter
T. & M.	Temple & Mew's Crown Cases (Eng.)	T.N.E.C.	Temporary National Economic Committee
T. & P.	Turner & Phillips' Chancery (Eng.)	T.R.	Term Reports, King's Bench (Durnford & East) (Eng.)
T. & R.	Turner & Russell's Chancery (Eng.)	T.Raym.	Thomas Raymond, King's Bench (Eng.)
T.B. & M.	Tracewell, Bowers & Mitchell, Comptroller's Decisions (U.S.)	T.S.	Treaty Series (U.S.)
		T.U.P.Charlt.	T. U. P. Charlton (Ga.)
T.B.M.	Tax Board Memorandum (I.R.Bull.)	Tait	Tait's Manuscript Decisions (Sc.)
T.B.Mon.	T. B. Monroe (Ky.)	Tal.	Cases temp. Talbot, Chancery (Eng.)
T.B.R.	Advisory Tax Board Recommendation (I.R.Bull.)	Talb.	Same
		Tam.	Tamlyn (Rolls Court) (Eng.)
T.C.	Tax Court of the United States Reports	Taml.	Same
		Tamlyn	Tamlyn's Chancery (Eng.)
T.D.	Treasury Decisions	Tamlyn Ch.	Same
t.Holt	Same as Modern Cases (Eng.)	Taney	Taney, Circuit Court (U.S.)
T.I.A.S.	Treaties and Other International Acts Series (U.S.)	Tann.	Tanner (Ind.)
		Tanner	Same
T.I.Agree.	Treaties and Other International Agreements of the United States of America 1776–1949	Tapp.	Tappan's Reports (Ohio)
		Tappan	Same
T.I.F.	Treaties in Force	Tasm.	Tasmanian State Reports
T.Jones	Thomas Jones, King's Bench and Common Pleas (Eng.)	Tasm.L.R.	Tasmania Law Reports
		Tasm.U.L. Rev.	Tasmania University Law Review
T.L.R.	Times Law Reports (Eng.)	Taun.	Taunton, Common Pleas (Eng.)
		Taunt.	Same

Tax A.B.C.	Canada Tax Appeal Board Cases
Tax Adm'rs News	Tax Administrators News
Tax Advisor	The Tax Advisor
Tax Cas.	Tax Cases (Eng.)
Tax Counselor's Q.	Tax Counselor's Quarterly
Tax L.Rep.	Tax Law Reporter
Tax L.Rev.	Tax Law Review
Tax Law.	The Tax Lawyer
Tax Mag.	Tax Magazine
Tax Pract. Forum	Tax Practitioners Forum
Tax. for Law.	Taxation for Lawyers
Tax.R.	Taxation Reports
Taxes	Taxes, The Tax Magazine
Tay.	Taylor's Carolina Reports (N.C.)
	Taylor's King's Bench (Can.)
	Taylor's Term Reports (N.C.)
Taylor	Same
Taylor, U.C.	Taylor, King's Bench (Ont.)
Tel-Aviv U. Stud.L	Tel-Aviv University Studies in Law
Temp. & M.	Temple & Mew Crown Cases (Eng.)
Temp.Geo.II	Cases in Chancery temp. Geo. II. (Eng.)
Temp.L.Q.	Temple Law Quarterly
Temp.Wood	Manitoba Reports temp. Wood (Can.)
Temple & M.	Temple & Mew Crown Cases (Eng.)
Temple L.Q.	Temple Law Quarterly
Tenn.	Tennessee
Tenn.App.	Tennessee Appeals
Tenn.App. Bull.	Tennessee Appellate Bulletin
Tenn.B.J.	Tennessee Bar Journal
Tenn.C.C.A.	Tennessee Court of Civil Appeals
Tenn.Cas.	Shannon's Tennessee Cases
Tenn.Ch.	Tennessee Chancery, Cooper
Tenn.Ch.App.	Tennessee Chancery Appeals
Tenn.Civ.App.	Tennessee Court of Civil Appeals
Tenn.Crim. App.	Tennessee Criminal Appeals Reports
Tenn.L.Rev.	Tennessee Law Review
Tenn.Leg.Rep.	Tennessee Legal Reporter
Term	Term Reports, King's Bench (See Durnford & East) (Eng.)
Term N.C.	Term Reports, North Carolina (Taylor)
Term R.	Term Reports, King's Bench (See Durnford and East) (Eng.)
Term Rep.	Same
Terr.	Terrell (Tex.)
Terr. & Wal.	Terrell & Walker (Tex.)
Terr.L.R.	Territories' Law Reports N. W.
Terrv	Terry
Tex.	Texas
Tex.A.Civ. Cas.	White & Wilson's Civil Cases (Tex.)
Tex.A.Civ. Cas. (Wilson)	Texas Court of Appeal Civil Cases
Tex.App.	Texas Civil Appeals Cases
	Texas Court of Appeals Cases
Tex.B.J.	Texas Bar Journal
Tex.Civ.App.	Texas Civil Appeals
Tex.Civ.Rep.	Same
Tex.Com.App.	Texas Commission Appeals
Tex.Cr.App.	Texas Criminal Appeals
Tex.Cr.R.	Same
Tex.Crim.	Texas Criminal Reports
Tex.Ct.App. R.	Texas Court of Appeals Reports
Tex.Dec.	Texas Decisions
Tex.Int.L. Forum	Texas International Law Forum
Tex.Int'l L.F.	Same
Tex.Int'l L.J.	Texas International Law
Tex.Jur.	Texas Jurisprudence
Tex.Jur.2d	Same, Second Series
Tex.L.J.	Texas Law Journal
Tex.L.Rev.	Texas Law Review
Tex.Law.	Texas Lawman
Tex.S.Ct.	Texas Supreme Court Reporter
Tex.So.U.L. Rev.	Texas Southern University Law Review
Tex.Supp.	Texas Supplement
Tex.Tech L. Rev.	Texas Tech Law Review
Tex.Unrep. Cas.	(Posey's) Unreported Cases (Tex.)
Texas L.Rev.	Texas Law Review
Th. & C.	Thompson & Cook's N. Y. Supreme Court
Thatcher Cr.	Thatcher's Criminal Cases (Mass.)
Thayer	Thayer (Ore.)
Themis	La Revue Juridique Themis
Thom.	Thomson's Reports (Nova Scotia)

Thomas & Fr.	Thomas & Franklin Chancery (Md.)	Trial Law. Guide	Trial Lawyer's Guide
Thomp.	Thompson (Cal.)	Trial Law.Q.	Trial Lawyers' Quarterly
Thomp.Tenn. Cas.	Thompson's Unreported Tennessee Cases	Trin.T.	Trinity Term (Eng.)
Thompson & C.	Thompson & Cook New York Supreme Court	Tripp	Tripp (Dak.Terr.)
		Tru.	Trueman's Equity Cases (N.B.)
Thomson	Thomson's Reports (Nova Scotia)	Tru.Railw. Rep.	Truman, American Railway Reports
Thor.	Thorington (Ala.)		
Thorpe	Thorpe's Louisiana Annual	Truem.Eq. Cas.	Trueman's Equity Cases (N.B.)
Tiff.	Tiffany Court Appeals (N.Y.)	Trust Bull.	Trust Bulletin
		Trust Terr.	Trust Territory Reports
Tiffany	Same	Trusts & Estates	Trusts and Estates
Till.	Tillman (Ala.)		
Tillman	Same	Tuck.	Tucker (Mass.)
Timber Tax J.	Timber Tax Journal	Tuck. & C.	Tucker & Clephane (D.C.)
		Tuck.Dist. of Col.	Tucker's Appeals (D.C.)
Tinw.	Tinwald (Sc.)		
Title News	Title News	Tuck.Sel.Cas.	Tucker's Select Cases (Newf.)
Tobey	Tobey (R.I.)		
Toth.	Tothill's Chancery (Eng.)	Tuck.Surr.	Tucker's Surrogate (N.Y.)
Tr. & H.Pr.	Troubat & Haly's Practice (Pa.)	Tul.L.Rev.	Tulane Law Review
		Tul.Tax Inst.	Tulane Tax Institute
Trace. & M.	Tracefell & Mitchell (Comptroller's Decisions) (U.S.)	Tulane L.Rev.	Tulane Law Review
		Tulsa L.J.	Tulsa Law Journal
Trade Cas.	Trade Cases (CCH)	Tupp.App.	Tupper's Appeal Reports (Ont.)
Trade Reg. Rep.	Trade Regulation Reporter (CCH)	Turn.	Turner (Ark.)
			Turner (Ky.)
Trade Reg. Rev.	Trade Regulation Review		Turner & Russell's Chancery (Eng.)
Trademark Bull.	Trade-Mark Bulletin	Turn. & P.	Turner & Phillips' Chancery (Eng.)
Trademark Bull.(N.S.)	Same, New Series	Turn. & Ph.	Same
Trademark Rptr.	Trade-Mark Reporter	Turn. & R.	Turner & Russell's Chancery (Eng.)
Trans. & Wit.	Transvaal & Witswatersrand Reports	Turn. & Rus.	Same
		Turn. & Russ.	Same
Transc.A.	Transcript Appeals (N.Y.)	Tutt.	Tuttle (Cal.)
Transp.L.J.	Transportation Law Journal	Tutt. & C.	Tuttle & Carpenter (Cal.)
Trauma	Trauma	Tutt. & Carp.	Same
Tread.Const.	Treadway's Constitutional Rep. (S.C.)	Tyler	Tyler (Vt.)
		Tyng	Tyng (Mass.)
Treas.Dec.	Treasury Decisions (U.S.)	Tyrw.	Tyrwhitt Exchequer (Eng.)
Trem.P.C.	Tremaine, Pleas of Crown		
Trial	Trial		
Trial Law. Forum	Trial Lawyers Forum	Tyrw. & G.	Tyrwhitt & Granger Exchequer (Eng.)

U

UMKC L.Rev.	UMKC Law Review	U.C.	Upper Canada
U.B.C.L.Rev.	University of British Columbia Law Review	U.C. (O.S.)	Upper Canada Queen's Bench Reports, Old Series
U.B.C.Notes	University of British Columbia Legal Notes		
U.Balt.L.Rev.	University of Baltimore Law Review	U.C.App.	Upper Canada Appeal Reports

U.C.App. Rep.	Same	U.C.R.	Upper Canada Queen's Bench Reports
U.C.C.L.J.	Uniform Commercial Code Law Journal	U.C.Rep.	Upper Canada Reports
U.C.C.Law Letter	Uniform Commercial Code Law Letter	U.Chi.L.Rec.	University of Chicago Law School Record
U.C.C.P.	Upper Canada Common Pleas Reports	U.Chi.L.Rev.	University of Chicago Law Review
U.C.C.P.D.	Upper Canada Common Pleas Division Reports (Ont.)	U.Cin.L.Rev.	University of Cincinnati Law Review
U.C.C.Rep. Serv.	Uniform Commercial Code Reporting Service	U.Colo.L. Rev.	University of Colorado Law Review
U.C.Ch.	Upper Canada Chancery Reports	U.Det.L.J.	University of Detroit Law Journal
U.C.Ch. Rep.	Same	U.East. L.J.	University of the East Law Journal
U.C.Cham.	Upper Canada Chamber Reports	U.Fla.L.Rev.	University of Florida Law Review
U.C.Chamb. Rep.	Same	U.Ghana L.J.	University of Ghana Law Journal
U.C.Chan.	Upper Canada Chancery Reports	U.I.L.R.	University of IFE Law Reports (Nigeria)
U.C.D.L.Rev.	University of California at Davis Law Review	U.Ill.L.F.	University of Illinois Law Forum
U.C.E. & A.	Upper Canada Error & Appeals Reports	U.Ill.L.Forum	University of Illinois Law Forum
U.C.Err. & App.	Same	U.Kan.City L.Rev.	University of Kansas City Law Review
U.C.I.S.	Benefit Series, Unemployment Compensation Interpretation Service	U.Miami L. Rev.	University of Miami Law Review
		U.Mich.J.Law Reform	University of Michigan Journal of Law Reform
	Federal Series, Unemployment Compensation Interpretation Service	U.Mo.Bull.L. Ser.	University of Missouri Bulletin Law Series
		U.Mo.K.C. L.Rev.	University of Missouri at Kansas City Law Review
	State Series, Unemployment Compensation Interpretation Service	U.N.	United Nations Law Reports
U.C.Jur.	Upper Canada Jurist	U.N.B.L.J.	University of New Brunswick Law Journal
U.C.K.B.	Upper Canada King's Bench Reports, Old Series	U.N.Comm. Int'l Trade L.Y.B.	United Nations Commission on International Trade Law Yearbook
U.C.L.A. Intra.L.Rev.	U.C.L.A. Intramural Law Review	U.N.Doc.	United Nations Documents
U.C.L.A. L.Rev.	U.C.L.A. Law Review	U.N. ECOSOC	United Nations Economic and Social Council Records
U.C.L.A.— Alaska L. Rev.	U.C.L.A.—Alaska Law Review	U.N. GAOR	United Nations General Assembly Official Records
U.C.L.J.	Upper Canada Law Journal	U.N.Jur.Y.B.	United Nations Juridical Yearbook
U.C.L.J. (N.S.)	Same, New Series	U.N.M.T.	United Nations Multilateral Treaties
U.C.P.R.	Upper Canada Practice Reports	U.N.R.I.A.A.	United Nations Reports of International Arbitral Awards
U.C.Pr.	Same	U.N.Res., Ser. I	United Nations Resolutions, Series I
U.C.Q.B.	Upper Canada Queen's Bench Reports	U.N. SCOR	United Nations Security Council Official Records
U.C.Q.B. (O.S.)	Same, Old Series	U.N.T.S.	United Nations Treaty Series
		U.Newark L.Rev.	University of Newark Law Review

U.Pa.L.Rev.	University of Pennsylvania Law Review	U.S.T.	United States Treaties and Other International Agreements
U.Pitt.L.Rev.	University of Pittsburgh Law Review	U.S.T.D.	United States Treaty Development
U.Queens.L.J.	University of Queensland Law Journal	U.S.Tax Cas.	United States Tax Cases (CCH)
U.Rich.L.Rev.	University of Richmond Law Review	U.S.V.A.A.D.	U. S. Veterans Administration Administrator's Decisions
U.S.	United States Reports		
U.S. & Can. Av.	United States and Canadian Aviation Reports	U.S.V.B.D.D.	U. S. Veterans Bureau Directors Decisions
U.S.App.	United States Appeals	U.San.Fernando V.L.Rev.	University of San Fernando Valley Law Review
U.S.Av.R.	Aviation Reports (U.S.)		
U.S.Aviation	Same	U.San.Fran. L.Rev.	University of San Francisco Law Review
U.S.C.	United States Code		
U.S.C. (Supp.)	United States Code, Supplement	[e.g.] U.So.Cal. 1955 Tax Inst.	University of Southern California Tax Institute
U.S.C.A.	U. S. Code Annotated		
U.S.C.Govt'l Rev.	University of South Carolina Governmental Review	U.Tasm.L. Rev.	University of Tasmania Law Review (or Tasmania University Law Review)
U.S.C.M.A.	United States Court of Military Appeals	U.Toledo L. Rev.	University of Toledo Law Review
U.S.C.S.	United States Code Service	U.Tor.Fac.L. Rev.	University of Toronto Faculty of Law Review
U.S.Code Cong. & Ad.News	United States Code Congressional & Administrative News	U.Tor.L.Rev.	University of Toronto School of Law Review
U.S.Ct.Cl.	United States Court of Claims Reports	U.Toronto L.J.	University of Toronto Law Journal
U.S.D.C.	United States District Court	U.W.Austl.L. Rev.	University of Western Australia Law Review
U.S.I.C.C.V.R.	U. S. Interstate Commerce Commission Valuation Reports	U.W.L.A.L. Rev.	University of West Los Angeles Law Review
U.S.Jur.	United States Jurist (D.C.)	U.Wash.L. Rev.	University of Washington Law Review
U.S.L.Ed.	United States Supreme Court Reports, Lawyers' Edition	U.Windsor L.Rev.	University of Windsor Law Review
		Udal	Fiji Law Reports (Fiji)
U.S.L.J.	United States Law Journal	Uganda L.Foc.	Uganda Law Focus
		Un.Prac.News	Unauthorized Practice News
U.S.L.Mag.	United States Law Magazine	Unempl.Ins. Rep.	Unemployment Insurance Reporter (CCH)
U.S.L.Rev.	United States Law Review	Unif.L.Conf. Can.	Uniform Law Conference of Canada
U.S.L.Week	United States Law Week		
U.S.Law.Ed.	United States Supreme Court Reports, Lawyers' Edition	Unific.L.Y.B.	Unification of Law Yearbook
		Uniform L.Rev.	Uniform Law Review
U.S.M.C.	U. S. Maritime Commission	Unof.	Unofficial Reports
U.S.M.L.Mag.	United States Monthly Law Magazine	Up.Can.L.J.	Upper Canada Law Journal
U.S.P.Q.	United States Patent Quarterly	Urban Affairs Rep.	Urban Affairs Reporter (CCH)
U.S.S.B.	U. S. Shipping Board	Urban Law Ann.	Urban Law Annual
U.S.S.C.Rep.	United States Supreme Court Reports	Urban L.Rev.	Urban Law Review
		Urban Law.	Urban Lawyer
		Utah	Utah
U.S.Sup.Ct. Rep.	United States Supreme Court Reporter (West)	Utah 2d	Same, Second Series
		Utah L.Rev.	Utah Law Review

Util.L.Rep.	Utilities Law Reporter (CCH)	Util.Sect. Newsl.	Utility Section Newsletter

V

V.C.Rep.	Vice Chancellor's Reports (Eng.)	Ventr.	Ventris King's Bench (Eng.)
V.I.	Virgin Islands Reports	Ver.	Vermont
V.I.B.J.	Virgin Islands Bar Journal	Vern.	Vernon's Cases (Eng.)
V.R.	Valuation Reports, Interstate Commerce Commission	Vern. & S.	Vernor & Scriven, King's Bench (Ir.)
Va.	Virginia	Vern. & Sc.	Same
		Vern. & Scr.	Same
Va.Bar News	Virginia Bar News	Vern. & Scriv.	Same
Va.Cas.	Virginia Cases	Vern.Ch.	Vernon's Chancery (Eng.)
Va.Ch.Dec.	Chancery Decisions (Va.)	Ves.	Vesey Chancery Reports (Eng.)
Va.Dec.	Virginia Decisions		
Va.J.Int'l L.	Virginia Journal of International Law		Vesey, Senior, Chancery (Eng.)
Va.L.J.	Virginia Law Journal		
Va.L.Reg.	Virginia Law Register	Ves. & B.	Vesey & Beames' (Eng.)
Va.L.Reg. (N.S.)	Same, New Series	Ves. & Bea.	Same
		Ves. & Beam.	Same
Va.L.Rev.	Virginia Law Review	Ves.Jr.	Vesey, Junior, Chancery (Eng.)
Va.R.	Virginia Reports (Gilmer)		
		Ves.Jun.	Same
Val.R. (I.C.C.)	Interstate Commerce Commission Valuation Reports	Ves.Jun.Supp.	Vesey, Junior, Supplement, Chancery (Eng.)
		Ves.Sen.	Vesey, Senior, Chancery (Eng.)
Val.U.L.Rev.	Valparaiso University Law Review		
		Ves.Sr.	Same
Van K.	Van Koughnett's Common Pleas (Upper Can.)	Ves.Supp.	Vesey, Senior, Supplement, Chancery (Eng.)
		Vez.	Vezey, Same as Vesey
Van Ness Prize Cas.	Van Ness Prize Cases (U.S.)	Vict.	Victoria
		Vict.Admr.	Victorian Admiralty
Vand.J. Transnat'l L.	Vanderbilt Journal of Transnational Law	Vict.Eq.	Victorian Equity
		Vict.L.	Victorian Law
Vand.L.Rev.	Vanderbilt Law Review	Vict.L.R.	Victorian Law Reports
Vaug.	Vaughan Common Pleas (Eng.)	Vict.L.R.Min.	Victorian Law Mining Reports
Vaugh.	Same	Vict.L.T.	Victorian Law Times
Vaughan	Same	Vict.Rev.	Victorian Review
Vaux	Vaux Decisions (Pa.)	Vict.St.Tr.	Victorian State Trials
	Vaux Recorder's Decisions (Pa.)	Vict.U.L.Rev.	Victoria University Law Review
Ve.	Vesey Chancery Reports (Eng.)	Vict.U.Well. L.Rev.	Victoria University of Wellington Law Review
	Vesey, Senior, Chancery (Eng.)	Vil. & Br.	Vilas & Bryant's Ed. Reports (Wis.)
Ve. & B.	Vesey & Beames Chancery (Eng.)	Vilas	Vilas' N. Y. Criminal Reports
Veaz.	Veazey (Vt.)	Vill.L.Rev.	Villanova Law Review
Veazey	Same	Vin.Abr.	Viner's Abridgment (Eng.)
Vent.	Ventris King's Bench (Eng.)	Vin.Supp.	Viner's Abridgment Supplement (Eng.)
	Ventris Common Pleas (Eng.)	Vir.	Virgin (Me.)

Virgin	Same	Vroom	Vroom, G. D. W.
Virgin Is.	Virgin Islands	(G.D.W.)	(N.J.)
Vr.	Vroom's Law Reports (N.J.)	Vroom (P.D.)	Vroom, P. D. (N.J.)
Vroom	Same	Vt.	Vermont

W

W.	Watts (Pa.)	W.Jo.	William Jones King's Bench, Common Pleas, House of Lords and Exchequer (Eng.)
	Wandell (N.Y.)		
	Wheaton's Supreme Court (U.S.)		
	Wright (Ohio)	W.Jones	Same
W.A'B. & W.	Webb, A'Beckett & Williams (Victoria)	W.Kel.	William Kellynge, King's Bench & Chancery (Eng.)
W.A.C.A.	Selected Judgments of the West African Court of Appeals	W.L.Bull.	Weekly Law Bulletin
		W.L.G.	Weekly Law Gazette (Ohio)
W. & C.	Wilson & Courtenay's Appeal Cases	W.L.Gaz.	Same
W. & M.	Woodbury & Minot Circuit Court (U.S.)	W.L.J.	Western Law Journal
		W.L.Jour.	Weekly Law Journal
		W.L.M.	Western Law Monthly (Ohio)
W. & S.	Watts & Sergeant (Pa.)	W.L.R.	Weekly Law Reports (Eng.)
	Wilson & Shaw's Appeal Cases (Sc.)		Western Law Reporter
W. & W.	White & Webb's Victorian Reports		Women Law Reporter
W. & W.Vict.	Wyatt & Webb's Victorian Reports	W.L.T.	Western Law Times and Reports
W.Afr.App.	West African Court of Appeal Reports	W.N.	Weekly Notes (Eng.)
W.Austl.Ind. Gaz.	Western Australia Industrial Gazette	W.Ont.L.Rev.	Western Ontario Law Review
W.Austl.J.P.	Western Australia Justice of the Peace	W.R.	Weekly Reports
		W.Res.L. Rev.	Western Reserve Law Review
W.Austl.L.R.	Western Australia Law Reports	W.Rob.	William Robinson's Admiralty (Eng.)
W.Bl.	Sir William Blackstone's King's Bench & Common Pleas (Eng.)	W.Va.	West Virginia
		W.Va.Crim. Just.Rev.	West Virginia Criminal Justice Review
W.Bla.	Same	W.Va.L.Q.	West Virginia Law Quarterly
W.C.C.	Washington's Circuit Court (U.S.)	W.Va.L.Rev.	West Virginia Law Review
	Workmen's Compensation Cases	W.W. & D.	Willmore, Wollaston & Davison, Queen's Bench (Eng.)
W.C.Ins.Rep.	Workmen's Compensation & Insurance Reports	W.W. & H.	Willmore, Wollaston & Hodges' Queen's Bench (Eng.)
W.C.Rep.	Workmen's Compensation Reports	W.W.Harr.	W. W. Harrington (Del.)
W.Coast Rep.	West Coast Reporter	W.W.R.	Western Weekly Report (Can.)
W.F.P.D.2d	West's Federal Practice Digest, Second Series	W.W.R. (N.S.)	Same, New Series, 1951–1955
W.H. & G.	Welsby, Hurlstone & Gordon's Exchequer (Eng.)	Wa.	Watts (Pa.)
			Wage and Hour Reporter
W.H.Cases	Wage & Hour Cases	Wage & Hour Cas.	Wage and Hour Cases (BNA)
W.H.Man.	Wages & Hours Manual	Wage & Hour Rep.	Wage & Hour Reporter
W.H.R.	Wage & Hour Reporter		

Wage-Price L. & Econ. Rev.	Wage-Price Law and Economics Review	Washb.	Washburn (Vt.)
Wake For. L.Rev.	Wake Forest Law Review	Washburn L.J.	Washburn Law Journal
Wake Forest Intra.L.Rev.	Wake Forest Intramural Law Review	Watts	Watts (Pa.) (W.Va.)
Wal.By L.	Wallis, Irish Chancery (By Lyne)	Watts & S.	Watts & Sergeant (Pa.)
		Watts & Ser.	Same
Wal.Jr.	Wallace Junior (U.S.)	Watts & Serg.	Same
Walk.	Walker (Ala.) (Miss.) (Pa.) (Tex.)	Wayne L.Rev.	Wayne Law Review
		Webb	Webb (Kans.) (Tex.)
			Webb's Civil Appeals (Tex.)
Walk.Ch.	Walker's Chancery (Mich.)	Webb & D.	Webb & Duval (Tex.)
Walk.Ch.Cas.	Same	Webb & Duval	Same
Wall.	Wallace (U.S.) (Philadelphia)	Webb, A'B. & W.	Webb, A'Beckett & Williams Reports (Aust.)
Wall.C.C.	Wallace Circuit Court (U.S.)	Webs.Pat.Cas.	Webster's Patent Cases (Eng.)
Wall.Jr.	Wallace Junior (U.S.)	Week.Cin.L.B.	Weekly Law Bulletin (Ohio)
Wall.Rep.	Wallace's Supreme Court Reports (U.S.) Wallace, The Reporters	Week.Dig.	Weekly Digest (N.Y.)
		Week.Jur.	Weekly Jurist (Ill.)
		Week.L.Gaz.	Weekly Law Gazette (Ohio)
Wall.Sr.	Wallace Senior (U.S.)	Week.L.Rec.	Weekly Law Record
Wallis	Wallis' Chancery (Ir.)	Week.Law Bull.	Weekly Law Bulletin (Ohio)
Wallis by L.	Wallis, Irish Chancery (By Lyne)		
		Week.Law Gaz.	Weekly Law Gazette (Ohio)
Walsh	Walsh's Registry Cases (Ir.)	Week.Notes Cas.	Weekly Notes of Cases (London)
Ward.	Warden (Ohio)		Weekly Notes of Cases (Pa.)
Ward. & Sm.	Warden & Smith (Ohio)	Week.Rep.	Weekly Reporter (Eng.)
Warden's Law & Bk.Bull.	Weekly Law & Bank Bulletin (Ohio)	Week.Trans. Rep.	Weekly Transcript Reports (N.Y.)
Ware	Ware, District Court (U.S.)	Weekly L.R.	Weekly Law Reports (Eng.)
Wash.	Washington Washington Reports (Va.)	Welfare L. Bull.	Welfare Law Bulletin
Wash.2d	Washington Reports, Second Series	Welfare L. News	Welfare Law News
Wash.App.	Washington Appellate Reports	Welsb.H. & G.	Welsby, Hurlstone & Gordon's Exchequer (Eng.)
Wash. & Haz. P.E.I.	Washburton & Hazard's Reports (Prince Edward Island)	Welsby H. & G.	Same
Wash. & Lee L.Rev.	Washington & Lee Law Review	Welsh	Welsh's Registry Cases (Ir.)
Wash.C.C.	Washington Circuit Court (U.S.)	Wend.	Wendell (N.Y.)
		Wenz.	Wenzell (Minn.)
Wash.L.Rep.	Washington Law Reporter (D.C.)	Wes.C.L.J.	Westmoreland County Law Journal
Wash.L.Rev.	Washington Law Review	West	West's Chancery (Eng.)
Wash.Terr.	Washington Territory	West Ch.	West's Chancery (Eng.)
Wash.Terr. (N.S.)	Same, New Series	West Va.	West Virginia
Wash.Ty.	Washington Territory	West.	Weston (Vt.)
Wash.U.L.Q.	Washington University Law Quarterly	West.Austl.	Western Australian Reports

West.Jur.	Western Jurist (Des Moines)	Wight.	Wightwick, Exchequer (Eng.)
West.L.Gaz.	Western Law Gazette (Ohio)	Wightw.	Wightwick, Exchequer (Eng.)
West.L.J.	Western Law Journal	Wilc.	Wilcox (Ohio)
West.L.M.	Western Law Monthly (Ohio)	Wilc.Cond.	Wilcox Condensed Ohio Reports
West.L.Mo.	Same	Wilcox	Wilcox (Ohio)
West.L.Month.	Same		Wilcox (Pa.)
West.L.R.	Western Law Reporter (Can.)	Wilcox Cond.	Wilcox Condensed Ohio Reports
West.L.Rev.	Western Law Review	Wilk.	Wilkinson (Aust.)
West.Law J.	Western Law Journal		Wilkinson Court of
West.Law M.	Western Law Monthly (Ohio)		Appeals and Civil Appeals (Tex.)
West.Legal Obser.	Western Legal Observer	Will.	Williams (Mass.)
West.R.	Western Reporter		Willson (Tex.)
West.School L.Rev.	Western School Law Review	Will.L.J.	Willamette Law Journal
West.St.U.L. Rev.	Western State University Law Review	Will. Woll. & Dav.	Willmore, Wollaston & Davison Queen's Bench (Eng.)
West t.Hardw.	West temp. Hardwicke, Chancery (Eng.)	Will.Woll. & H.	Willmore, Wollaston & Hodges' Queen's Bench (Eng.)
West.Week. Rep.	Western Weekly Reports (Can.)	Will.Woll. & Hodg.	Same
West.Wkly.	Western Weekly (Can.)	Willes	Willes, King's Bench & Common Pleas (Eng.)
Western Res. L.Rev.	Western Reserve Law Review		
Westm.	Statute of Westminster (Eng.)	Williams	Williams (Mass.) (Utah) (Vt.)
Westm.L.J.	Westmoreland Law Journal (Pa.)		Peere-Williams' English Chancery Reports
Wethey	Wethey's Queen's Bench (Upper Can.)	Williams & Bruce Ad.Pr.	Williams & Bruce's Admiralty Practice
Whart.	Wharton (Pa.)	Williams P.	Peere-Williams' English Chancery Reports
Whart.Law Dict.	Wharton's Law Lexicon	Williams-Peere	Same
Whart.St.Tr.	Wharton's State Trials (U.S.)	Willm.W. & D.	Willmore, Wollaston & Davison's Queen's Bench (Eng.)
Wheat.	Wheaton (U.S.)		
Wheel.	Wheeler's Criminal Cases (N.Y.)	Willm.W. & H.	Willmore, Wollaston & Hodges' Queen's Bench (Eng.)
	Wheelock (Tex.)		
Wheeler Abr.	Wheeler's Abridgment	Willson	Willson Civil Cases (Tex.)
Wheeler C.C.	Wheeler's Criminal Cases (N.Y.)	Willson, Civ. Cas.Ct.App.	Same
Wnit.Pat.Cas.	Whitman's Patent Cases (U.S.)	Wilm.	Wilmot's Notes (Eng.)
White	White (W.Va.) (Tex.)	Wils.	Wilson (Cal.) (Minn.) (Ore.)
	White's Justiciary Cases (Sc.)		Wilson (Superior Court) (Ind.)
White & T. Lead. Cas.Eq.	White & Tudor's Leading Cases in Equity (Eng.)		Wilson's King's Bench & Common Pleas (Eng.)
White & W.	White & Wilson (Tex.)	Wils. & S.	Wilson & Shaw (House of Lords) (Sc.)
Whitm.Lib. Cas.	Whitman's Libel Cases (Mass.)		
Whitt.	Whittlesey (Mo.)		
Wight	Wight's Election Cases (Sc.)		

Wils.Ch.	Wilson's Chancery (Eng.)	Wol.	Wolcott's Chancery (Del.)
Wils.C.P.	Wilson's Common Pleas (Eng.)		Wollaston's English Bail Court Reports (Eng.)
Wils.Exch.	Wilson's Exchequer (Eng.)	Wolf. & B.	Wolferstan & Bristow's Election Cases (Eng.)
Wils.K.B.	Wilson's King's Bench (Eng.)	Wolf. & D.	Wolferstan & Dew's Election Cases (Eng.)
Wils.P.C.	Wilson's Privy Council (Eng.)	Woll.	Wollaston's English Bail Court Reports
Winch	Winch, Common Pleas (Eng.)	Woll.P.C.	Same
Winst.	Winston (N.C.)	Woman Of-fend.Rep.	Woman Offender Report
Wis.	Wisconsin	Women Law. J.	Women Lawyer's Journal
Wis.2d	Wisconsin Reports, Second Series	Women Lawyer's J.	Same
Wis.B.Bull.	Wisconsin Bar Bulletin	Women's Rights L. Rptr.	Women's Rights Law Reporter
Wis.B.T.A.	Wisconsin Board of Tax Appeals Reports	Wood.	Woodbury & Minot, Circuit Court (U.S.)
Wis.L.N.	Wisconsin Legal News		
Wis.L.Rev.	Wisconsin Law Review		
Wisc.Stud. B.J.	Wisconsin Student Bar Journal	Wood. & M.	Same
Wis.Tax. App.C.	Wisconsin Tax Appeals Commission Reports	Woodb. & M.	Same
Withrow	Withrow (Iowa)	Woods	Woods Circuit Court (U.S.)
Wkly.Dig.	Weekly Digest (N.Y.)		
Wkly.L.Bul.	Weekly Law Bulletin (Ohio)	Woodw.	Woodward's Decisions (Pa.)
Wkly.L.Gaz.	Weekly Law Gazette (Ohio)	Woolw.	Woolworth (Neb.)
			Woolworth Circuit Court (U.S.)
Wkly.Law Bull.	Weekly Law Bulletin (Ohio)	Workmen's Comp.L.Rev.	Workmen's Compensation Law Review
Wkly.N.C.	Weekly Notes of Cases (Pa.)	World Jurist	World Jurist
		World Pol.	World Polity
		Wright	Wright (Ohio) (Pa.)
Wkly.Rep.	Weekly Reporter (Eng.)	Wy. & W.	Wyatt & Webb (Vict.)
		Wy., W. & A'Beck.	Wyatt, Webb & A'Beckett (Vict.)
Wm. & Mary L.Rev.	William & Mary Law Review	Wyo.	Wyoming
Wm. & Mary Rev.Va.L.	William and Mary Review of Virginia Law	Wyo.L.J.	Wyoming Law Journal
		Wythe	Wythe's Chancery (Va.)

Y

Y.	Yeates' (Pa.)	Y.B.A.A.A.	Yearbook of the Association of Attenders and Alumni of the Hague Academy of International Law
Y. & C.	Younge & Collyer's Chancery (Eng.)		
Y. & C.C.C.	Same		
Y. & J.	Younge & Jervis' Exchequer (Eng.)	Y.B.A.S.L.	Yearbook of Air and Space Law
Y.A.D.	Young's Admiralty Decisions (Nova Scotia)	Y.B.Ed. I	Year Books, Edward I
		Y.B.Eur. Conv. on Human Rights	Yearbook of the European Convention on Human Rights
Y.B.	Year Book, King's Bench, etc. (Eng.)		
Y.B. (Rolls Series)	Year Books Rolls Series (Eng.)	Y.B.Human Rights	Yearbook on Human Rights
Y.B. (Sel. Soc.)	Year Books (Selden Society) (Eng.)	Y.B.Int'l Org.	Yearbook of International Organizations

Y.B.Int'l L. Comm'n	Yearbook of the International Law Commission
Y.B.League	Yearbook of the League of Nations
Y.B.P. 1, Edw. II	Year Books, Part 1, Edward II
Y.B.S.C.	Year Books, Selected Cases
Y.B.U.N.	Yearbook of the United Nations
Y.B.World Pol.	Yearbook of World Polity
Yale L.J.	Yale Law Journal
Yale Rev.Law & Soc.Act'n	Yale Review of Law and Social Action
Yale Stud. World Pub. Order	Yale Studies in World Public Order
Yates Sel.Cas.	Yates' Select Cases (N.Y.)
Yea.	Yeates (Pa.)
Yearb.	Year Book, King's Bench (Eng.)
Yearb.P.7, Hen.VI	Year Books, Part 7, Henry VI
Yeates	Yeates (Pa.)
Yel.	Yelverton, King's Bench (Eng.)
Yelv.	Same
Yerg.	Yerger (Tenn.)
York Leg.Rec.	York Legal Record (Pa.)
Yorke Ass.	Yorke Assizes (Clayton)

You.	Younge's Exchequer (Eng.)
You. & Coll. Ch.	Younge & Collyer's Exchequer (Eng.)
You. & Coll. Ex.	Same
You. & Jerv.	Younge & Jervis Exchequer (Eng.)
Young	Young (Minn.)
Young Adm.	Young Admiralty (N.S.)
Young Adm. Dec.	Same
Young Naut. Dict.	Young's Nautical Dictionary
Younge	Younge's Exchequer (Eng.)
Younge & C.Ch. Cas.	Younge & Collyer's Chancery or Exchequer Equity (Eng.)
Younge & C. Exch.	Younge & Collyer's Exchequer Equity (Eng.)
Younge & Coll. Ex.	Same
Younge & J.	Younge & Jervis Exchequer (Eng.)
Younge & Je.	Same
Younge Exch.	Younge Exchequer (Eng.)
Younge M.L. Cas.	Younge Maritime Law Cases (Eng.)
Yugo.L.	Yugoslav Law

Z

Zab.	Zabriskie (N.J.)
Zambia L.J.	Zambia Law Journal
Zane	Zane (Utah)

*

INDEX

References are to Pages

Italic type indicates Titles of Publications

PROFESSIONAL RESPONSIBILITY.
Code of Professional Responsibility, 376.
Importance of in legal research, 6.
Opinions on, 377.
Standards of, 376–377.

RATIO DECIDENDI, 22.

RECEPTION STATUTES, 4.

RECORDS AND BRIEFS.
See Briefs and Records.

REGIONAL DIGESTS, 74.
Summary of, 95.

REGNAL YEARS, 534.

REORGANIZATION PLANS, 226.

RESTATEMENTS OF THE LAW, 342–351.
Citation form. 526.
Citators for, 344.
Description of, 342–343.
Features of, 343–344.
Illustrations of, 346–351.
Indexes to, 344.
Research in, 365.
Restatements in the Courts, 344.
Shepard's Citations for, 344–345.
State annotations to, 345.
Summary of, 366–367.

REVISED STATUTES.
See United States Revised Statutes.

ROMAN LAW, 5.

SECONDARY LAW, 3.
Citation form, 522.
Defined, 6.
Types of, 9.
Use of in determining facts, 11.

SERIAL SET, 170.
In microform, 483.

SESSION LAWS, 188.
Citation form, 512–514.
Illustrations of, 194–195.
In microform, 480.

SHEPARD'S CITATIONS, 261–277.
Abbreviations used, 263, 273.
As a research aid, 266.
Case citators, 261–277.
Federal Law Citations in Select Law Reviews, 321.
For charters, 275.
For court rules, 275–276.
For federal reports, 265.
For *National Reporter System,* 263–264.
For ordinances, 275.

SHEPARD'S CITATIONS—Cont'd
For regional reporters, 264.
For states, 264.
For statutes. 273.
For the *Restatements of the Law,* 344–345.
History of a case, 261–266.
Illustrations, use of,
    Cases, 267–272.
        Court rules, 280.
            Statutes. 277–279.
Keeping current, 287.
Law Review Citations, 321.
Legal periodicals cited in, 265–266.
Other units of,
    Illustrations, 285–286.
Others uses of, 266–267.
Parallel citations in, 266.
Purpose of, 261–262.
Summary of, 287–289.

SHEPARD'S ORDINANCE LAW ANNOTATIONS, 192.

SLIP LAWS.
Federal. 137, 144.
State. 188.

SLIP OPINIONS.
State reports, 55.
U. S. Supreme Court, 36.

SOURCES OF THE LAW, 2–3.
Defined, 3.
Primary, 3.
Reception statutes, 4.
Secondary, 3.
States, 4.
Summary of, 8–9.
United States, 4.

STAR PAGINATION, 50.

STARE DECISIS.
Definition, 1–2.
In civil law, 5.

STATE ADMINISTRATIVE LAW.
See Administrative Law, States.

STATE CONSTITUTIONS.
See Constitutions, State.

STATE COURT REPORTS.
See Court Reports, State.

STATE DIGESTS.
See Digests, State.

STATE STATUTES.
See Legislation, State.

End of Volume